ECONOMIC
REPORT

OF THE

PRESIDENT

TRANSMITTED TO THE CONGRESS

FEBRUARY 2016

TOGETHER WITH

THE ANNUAL REPORT

OF THE

COUNCIL OF ECONOMIC ADVISERS

CONTENTS

---

*For a detailed table of contents of the Council's Report, see page 11.

ECONOMIC REPORT
OF THE
PRESIDENT

ECONOMIC REPORT OF THE PRESIDENT

When I took office, our Nation was in the midst of the worst recession since the Great Depression. The economy was shedding 800,000 jobs a month. The auto industry was on the brink of collapse, and our manufacturing sector was in decline. Many families were struggling to pay their bills and make ends meet. Millions more saw their savings evaporate, even as retirement neared.

Seven years later, thanks to the grit and determination of the American people, the United States of America has rebuilt, reformed, and emerged as the strongest, most durable economy in the world.

We are in the middle of the longest streak of private-sector job creation in history: 14 million new jobs; the strongest two years of job growth since the '90s; an unemployment rate cut in half. Manufacturing has added 900,000 jobs in the past six years, and our auto industry just had its best year of sales ever. We are less reliant on foreign oil than at any point in the previous four decades. Nearly 18 million people have gained health coverage under the Affordable Care Act, cutting the uninsured rate to a record low. And we've done all this while dramatically cutting our budget deficit.

In 2015, we continued to take steps forward, with strong job growth and wages rising at their fastest rate in the recovery. Here in Washington, Congress came together to pass a budget, secure long-term transportation funding, reform education laws, and make tax cuts for working families permanent.

So claims that America's economy is in decline or that we haven't made progress are simply not true. What is true—and the reason that a lot of Americans feel anxious—is that the economy has been changing in profound ways, starting long before the Great Recession. Today, technology doesn't just replace jobs on the assembly line, but rather affects any job where work can be automated. Companies in a global economy face tougher competition from abroad, and they can locate anywhere. As a result, workers have less leverage for a raise. And more and more wealth and income is concentrated at the very top.

All these trends have squeezed workers, making it difficult for middle-class families to feel secure, even when they have jobs and the economy is growing. For the past seven years, our goal has been not just strengthening economic growth but also creating an economy where everyone who works hard gets a fair shot. We've made progress. But we need to make more. And we must choose policies that not only make us stronger today, but also reflect the kind of country we aspire to be in the coming decades.

Real opportunity requires every American to get the education and training they need to land a good-paying job. Together, we've increased access to early childhood education, lifted high school graduation rates to new highs, and boosted graduates in fields like engineering. In the coming years, we should build on that progress, by providing pre-school for all, offering every student the hands-on computer science and math classes that make them job-ready on day one, and recruiting and supporting more great teachers for our kids. And we have to make college affordable for every American. Because no hardworking student should be saddled with unmanageable debt. We've already doubled investments in college scholarships and tax credits and capped student loan payments to 10 percent of a borrower's income. Now, we need colleges to find innovative ways to cut costs and help more students finish their degrees.

Of course, a great education isn't all we need in this new economy. We also need benefits and protections that provide a basic measure of security. Social Security and Medicare are more important than ever, and we shouldn't weaken them; we should strengthen them. For Americans short of retirement, basic benefits should be just as mobile as everything else is today. That's part of what the Affordable Care Act is all about. It helps fill the gaps in employer-based care so that when we lose a job, or go back to school, or start that new business, we'll still have coverage.

We can build on this progress by further strengthening our social safety net and modernizing it for the changing economy. For example, when a hardworking American loses his job—we shouldn't just make sure he can get unemployment insurance; we should make sure that program encourages him to retrain for a business that's ready to hire him. If that new job doesn't pay as much, there should be a system of wage insurance in place so that he can still pay his bills. And even if he's going from job to job, it shouldn't be difficult for him to save for retirement and take his savings with him. That's the way we make the economy work better for everyone.

But there are broader choices to make about what role the government should play in making sure the system's not rigged in favor of the wealthiest and biggest corporations. A thriving private sector is the lifeblood of our economy, and we can all agree that there are outdated regulations that need to be changed, and red tape that needs to be cut. But after years of record corporate profits, working families won't have more opportunities or see faster wage growth by letting the biggest companies make their own rules at the expense of everyone else; or by allowing attacks on collective bargaining to go unanswered.

In this new economy, workers and start-ups and small businesses need more of a voice, not less. The rules should work for them. And this year I plan to lift up the many businesses that have figured out that doing right by their workers ends up being good for their shareholders, their customers, and their communities, so that we can spread those best practices across America.

In fact, many of our best corporate citizens are also our most creative, and that spirit of innovation is essential to helping us meet our biggest challenges. Over the past seven years, we have nurtured that spirit by protecting an open Internet, creating online tools to help entrepreneurs start their businesses in a single day, and taking bold new steps to get more students and low-income Americans online. But we can do so much more, especially for medical research and clean energy sources. With 2015 marking the warmest year on record, we need to build on our existing investments in clean energy and accelerate the transition away from fossil fuels.

At the same time, I'll keep pushing forward on work that still needs to be done, like fixing our broken immigration system, raising the minimum wage, providing two years of free community college to responsible students, ensuring equal pay for equal work, opening U.S. exports to new markets, and expanding tax cuts for low-income workers without kids. All these things still matter to hardworking families; they are still the right thing to do, and I will not let up until they get done.

I have never been more optimistic about America's future than I am today. Over the past seven years, I have seen the strength, resilience, and commitment of the American people. I know that when we are united in the face of challenges, our Nation emerges stronger and better than before. And when we work together, there are no limits to what we can achieve.

THE WHITE HOUSE
FEBRUARY 2016

THE ANNUAL REPORT
OF THE
COUNCIL OF ECONOMIC ADVISERS

LETTER OF TRANSMITTAL

COUNCIL OF ECONOMIC ADVISERS
Washington, D.C., February 22, 2016

MR. PRESIDENT:

The Council of Economic Advisers herewith submits its 2016 Annual Report in accordance of the Employment Act of 1946 as amended by the Full Employment and Balanced Growth Act of 1978.

Sincerely yours,

Jason Furman
Chairman

Sandra E. Black
Member

Jay C. Shambaugh
Member

C O N T E N T S

APPENDIXES

FIGURES

TABLES

BOXES

CHAPTER 1

INCLUSIVE GROWTH IN
THE UNITED STATES

The U.S. economic recovery entered its seventh year in 2015. Our businesses created 2.6 million jobs in 2015 and the unemployment rate fell to 5.0 percent, half its level in fall 2009, far faster than forecasters expected. Private domestic final purchases—the most stable and persistent components of economic output—rose 2.7 percent over the four quarters of the year, bolstered by solid personal consumption, strong residential investment, and record-setting investment in research and development. Health care price growth remained at low levels not seen in nearly five decades as the Nation's uninsured rate fell below 10 percent for the first time ever. Overall, consumers were more confident about the economy than in any year since 2004. Nominal wage growth remained too low, but still grew faster in 2015 than at any time since the recovery began. While more work remains to be done on each of these fronts—especially in terms of wage growth—the U.S. economy exhibited substantial strength throughout the year.

At the same time, slowing foreign demand has weighed on exports and impacted the manufacturing sector, low oil prices—while boosting household balance sheets—have constrained investment and job growth in the drilling industry, and financial market volatility is also impacting the economy. The divergence between strong domestic demand and these global factors will remain an important macroeconomic dynamic in 2016.

But we must not lose sight of the longer-term challenges that the U.S. economy has faced for decades, most notably the insufficient growth of middle-class incomes. Last year's *Economic Report of the President* focused on the three factors that drive middle-class incomes: productivity growth, inequality, and participation in our economy. This year's *Report* examines the economics and policies that can strengthen productivity without exacerbating inequality, promoting robust and inclusive growth that can be shared by a broad group of households. Many of these policies increase economic efficiency as well as equity, unleashing productivity growth that benefits families across the income distribution.

Despite progress during the recovery and promising economic trends, inequality remains a defining challenge of the 21st century economy. This is a global issue, but one that is particularly salient in the United States. While rising income and wealth inequality tend to attract the most attention, the last few decades have seen an especially unequal distribution of something more fundamental—the *opportunity* to succeed in our economy. Too many Americans' ability to innovate and participate in the labor force is constrained by their circumstances. For example, children of low-income families face broad disadvantages that limit their ability to get ahead in school and later in life; our criminal justice system fosters inequities and inefficiencies that limit opportunity; and persistent biases against women and minorities limit their full economic participation. Unequal outcomes often reward hard work and innovation, and may promote the efficient use of our resources and raise overall living standards. But unequal outcomes that arise from unequal *opportunities*—barriers that keep some individuals from realizing their full potential—are a detriment to growth and fairness. The President supports a wide range of policies to promote equality of opportunity for all Americans, detailed extensively later in this chapter.

The overall increase in income inequality in recent decades is large enough to accommodate many partial explanations. The traditional view is that inequality arises from competitive markets, paying workers, investors, and innovators according to their productivity—with divergences in productivity stemming from changes in technology, globalization, and education. Such a mechanism promotes productivity growth by encouraging productive labor, wise investments, and innovation.

But many economists have recently emphasized another contributor to rising income inequality: "economic rents." Rents are unproductive income paid to labor or capital above what is necessary to keep that labor at work or that capital invested. Rents arise when markets are not perfectly competitive, such as when uncompetitive markets yield monopoly profits or preferential regulation protects entities from competition. For example, a firm might be willing to sell a piece of software for $20 based on costs and a reasonable return to capital. But if the firm has no competition, it may be able to sell the same product for $50—the $30 difference reflects an economic rent. Rents can serve a productive purpose in encouraging innovation. Some rents are inevitable, but the critical question is how they are divided—for example, between profits and wages. And in many cases the evidence suggests that the pursuit of such rents ("rent-seeking behavior") exacerbates inequality and can actually impair growth.

To promote inclusive growth, both channels of inequality—competitive markets and economic rents—must be addressed from a pro-growth perspective. Since the competitive channel most effectively promotes growth when competition is open to the widest set of economic actors, promoting equality of opportunity helps the competitive channel work better. And because the abuse of market power in pursuit of economic rents results in inherently unproductive inequality, strategies to reduce such unfair advantages can promote equality and opportunity. Both of these broad goals would reduce inequality while unleashing productivity growth, raising living standards across the income distribution.

Forms of Economic Inequality: Income, Wealth, and Opportunity

Unequal outcomes may provide incentives for individual effort and therefore play a productive role in the economy. Large rewards can motivate innovators, entrepreneurs, and workers and compensate them for taking large personal risks—choices that, in some cases, can benefit households more broadly across the economy. Hard work and personal capital developed the first personal computer; its developer reaped great rewards, but so too did aggregate productivity. Inequality can also simply reflect the choices of two otherwise identical people who make different decisions about how to balance work versus leisure, or an undesirable job versus a desirable job. But excessive inequality may also reflect substantially more than "just deserts," ranging from pure luck to economic rents. Moreover, while inequality can play an important role in economic growth, excessive inequality is not necessarily essential to growth and may even impede growth. This is especially true to the degree that inequality derives from interfering with the competitive market or protecting high returns to capital or labor with barriers, natural or otherwise.

To understand how to promote widely shared growth, it is critical to distinguish among various forms of economic inequality to better understand their sources. This *Report* considers three broad forms: inequality of income, inequality of wealth, and inequality of opportunity. All are closely related and can influence one another.

Income Inequality

Although a global issue, income inequality is particularly important in the United States in terms of both its level and in recent changes. Large advanced economies have seen a persistent trend of rising inequality for decades, as the very highest earners capture a larger share of aggregate income. Until the 1980s, the United States experience was similar to other countries; as recently as 1975, the top 1 percent garnered a similar share of the income in the United States as in other G-7 countries, as shown in Figure 1-1. But since 1987 the share of income going to the top 1 percent in the United States has exceeded every other G-7 country in each year that data are available. Moreover, the United States has continued to diverge further from other advanced economies, with the top 1 percent's income share rising 0.2 percentage point a year on average in the United States from 1990 to 2010, well above the 0.1 percentage point average increase in the United Kingdom. While comparable international data are scarce after 2010, the gains of the top 1 percent have continued in the United States. In 2014, the top 1 percent captured 18 percent of income, up from 8 percent in 1975 (World Top Incomes Database 2015).

In contrast to rising inequality within countries, inequality across the globe as a whole has been largely stable and possibly even decreasing. Fast growth in many poorer and emerging countries has lifted hundreds of millions of people out of poverty in recent decades, moderating the trends observed in the advanced world. In fact, when measured at a global level, the biggest income gains from 1988 to 2008 went to households between the 15th percentile and the 65th percentile of global income (Milanovic 2012).

The dynamics of income inequality across many countries have gained considerable attention in recent years, perhaps most notably in Thomas Piketty's 2014 work *Capital in the Twenty-First Century.* Following Piketty, previous Council of Economic Advisers (CEA) analysis has decomposed inequality into three components:

- Inequality within labor income (wages, salaries, and benefits);
- Inequality within capital income (capital gains, dividends, and interest); and
- The division of aggregate income between labor and capital.

All three of these have different causes, dynamics, and policy implications.

CEA has decomposed the changes in inequality in the United States into the three sources using a combination of data from Piketty and his colleague Emmanuel Saez, the U.S. Congressional Budget Office (CBO), and the U.S. National Income and Product Accounts (NIPA). Figures 1-2a and 1-2b shows the top 1 percent shares of labor and capital income according to various datasets.

The data present several issues with volatility, systematic measurement error that results from using administrative tax data in an environment of changing tax policies, and definitional nuances around what should be

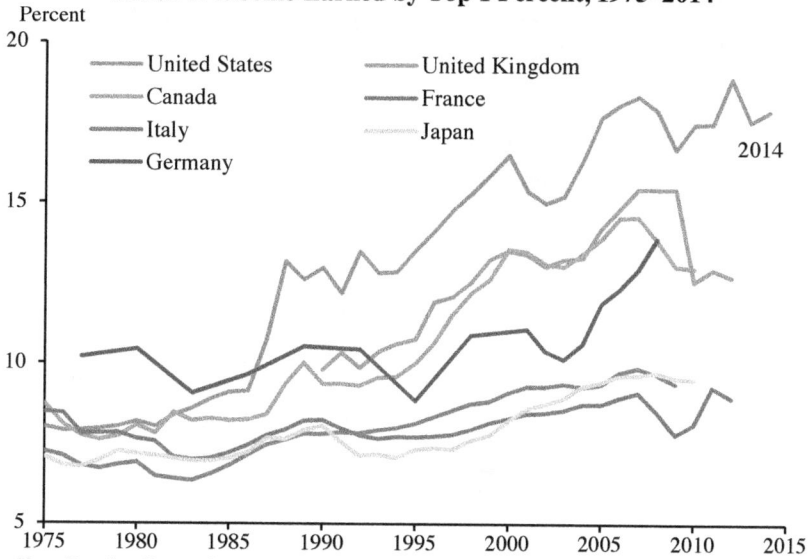

Figure 1-1
Share of Income Earned by Top 1 Percent, 1975–2014

Note: Data for all countries exclude capital gains.
Source: World Top Incomes Database (Alvaredo et al. 2015).

classified as labor or capital income. Nonetheless, this decomposition exercise illustrates a few broad points.

In the United States, the top 1 percent's share of total income rose from 8 percent in 1970 to 17 percent in 2010, according to the Piketty-Saez data. Throughout this period, the top 1 percent's share of labor income rose steadily while its share of capital income only began a sustained rise around 1990, as shown in Figure 1-2a. Overall, the 9-percentage-point increase in the share of income that Piketty and Saez find going to the top 1 percent from 1970 to 2010 is attributable to the three factors discussed above in the following dimensions: 68 percent due to increased inequality within labor income; 32 percent due to increased inequality within capital income; and 0 percent due to a shift in income from labor to capital. This finding is broadly consistent with the recent emphasis on labor income inequality, though it tells us that capital income is also a reasonably important driver of income inequality. Other data discussed below show a bigger share for the shift from labor to capital income.

However, when looking at the extreme upper end of the income distribution in more recent periods, capital income becomes much more important. Table 1-1 shows the relative importance of the distribution of income within labor in explaining the increased share of income going to the top in different data sets and different periods.

Figure 1-2a

Share of Total, Labor, Capital Income Accruing to Top 1 Percent Based on Piketty-Saez Data

Index, 1970 = 100

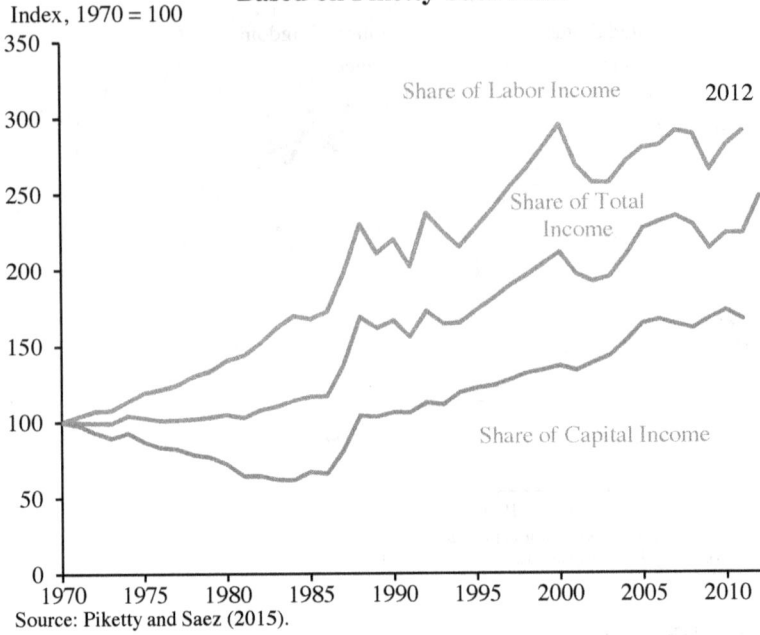

Share of Labor Income

2012

Share of Total Income

Share of Capital Income

350

300

250

200

150

100

50

0

1970   1975   1980   1985   1990   1995   2000   2005   2010

Source: Piketty and Saez (2015).

Figure 1-2b

Share of Total, Labor, Capital Income Accruing to Top 1 Percent Based on Congressional Budget Office Data

Index, 1979 = 100

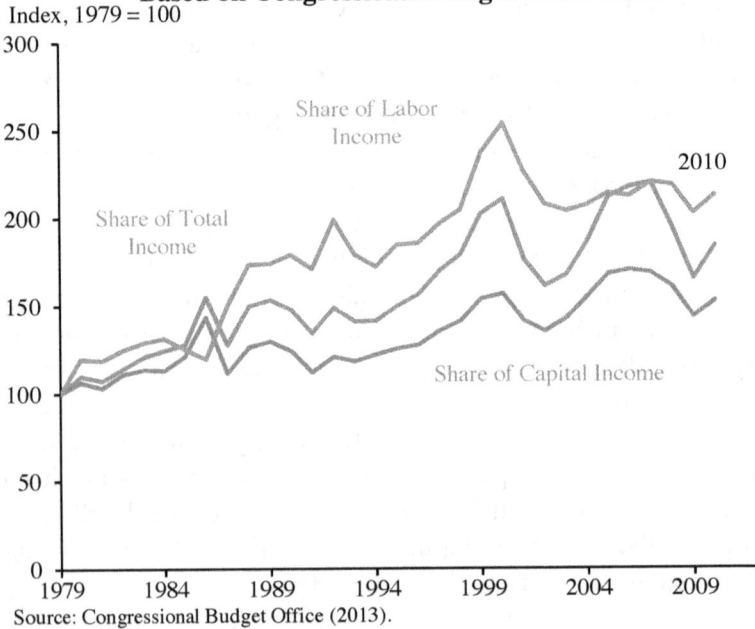

Share of Labor Income

2010

Share of Total Income

Share of Capital Income

300

250

200

150

100

50

0

1979   1984   1989   1994   1999   2004   2009

Source: Congressional Budget Office (2013).

Table 1-1
**Increase in Income Share Accounted for by
Inequality Within Labor Income**

	Top 10%	Top 1%	Top 0.1%
Income Excluding Capital Gains			
1970-2010 (Piketty-Saez)	83%	68%	53%
1980-2010 (Piketty-Saez)	71%	54%	59%
1990-2010 (Piketty-Saez)	64%	51%	53%
Income Including Capital Gains			
1970-2010 (Piketty-Saez)	80%	63%	47%
1980-2010 (Piketty-Saez)	67%	50%	52%
1990-2010 (Piketty-Saez)	61%	45%	44%

Note: Values for any given year calculated as a centered three-year moving average.
Source: CEA calculations based on Piketty-Saez (2015) and Congressional Budget Office (2013).

The higher up the income scale, the less important inequality within labor income is in explaining the overall increase in inequality, and the commensurately more important the degree of inequality within capital income. There is a strong temporal pattern as well, with inequality within capital income becoming increasingly important over time. The relevant CBO data only go back to 1979 and do not show any finer measurements than the top 1 percent, but they tell a similar story both in terms of the overall magnitudes and in terms of within-capital inequality being more important higher up the income scale.

Inequality within Labor Income

The topic of inequality within labor income has been studied extensively. As a factual matter, those at the very top of the income distribution (top 0.1 percent) are about 40 percent managers in non-financial industries and about 20 percent financial professionals, with the remaining 40 percent spread across law, medicine, real estate, entrepreneurship, arts, media, sports, and other occupations (Bakija, Cole, and Heim 2010). A variety of explanations have been put forward for the overall rise in labor income inequality, including the increased return to skills, especially given technological change, the increased national and global reach of corporations, the slowdown in increases in educational attainment (weakening the skill base and earning power of the lower part of the income distribution), and changes in norms and corporate governance (such that a wider gap between CEO and worker pay is now acceptable). The rising importance of unproductive economic rents is likely also contributing to the broad increase in inequality. Workers and managers at firms earning supernormal return—likely reflecting increased aggregate rents—are paid progressively more than their counterparts at other firms. Moreover, as union membership declines, inequality can rise further as workers at the bottom of the income distribution lose market power.

Inequality within Capital Income

A second source of increased inequality is the distribution of capital income. As the distribution of wealth becomes increasingly unequal, the returns to that wealth—like interest, dividends, and capital gains—will generate more inequality. In addition, the fact that those at higher wealth levels seem to receive higher returns to capital, when coupled with reductions in tax rates on capital income in recent decades, has increased the contribution of capital income to overall inequality. Further, if some firms earn monopoly profits, owners of those firms may benefit more than others. These issues have been studied much less than labor income inequality, though they clearly merit much more attention given their increasing importance over time.

Division of Income between Labor and Capital

Wealth is much more unequally distributed than labor income. As a result, the extent to which aggregate income is divided between returns to labor and returns to wealth (capital income) matters for aggregate inequality. When the labor share of income falls, the offsetting increase in capital income (returns to wealth) is distributed especially unequally, increasing overall inequality. In Europe, the share of income going to labor has been falling since about 1970. In contrast, a marked decline in the labor share of income occurred only after 2000 in the United States, though there is some volatility in the data. The relative importance of this factor in the overall increase in inequality is harder to consistently quantify, although the importance of labor and capital income inequality in recent decades suggests that it plays only a supporting role.

Wealth Inequality

When unequally distributed income is saved, it results in unequally distributed wealth. Growing wealth inequality in the United States reflects many of the trends and many of the same causes as rising income inequality. Wealth inequality is particularly difficult to measure accurately because we do not track wealth in the way we do income and trends in wealth inequality are concentrated among a small number of households. One perspective on wealth inequality comes from the Federal Reserve's Survey of Consumer Finances (SCF) which, as shown in Figure 1-3, shows that the top 3 percent

Figure 1-3
Distribution of Household Wealth (Survey of Consumer Finances),
1989-2013

Percent of Total Household Wealth

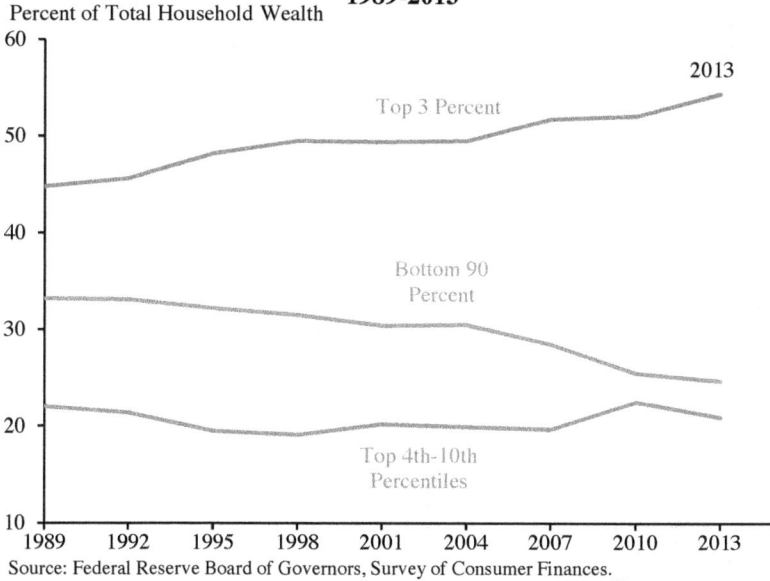

Source: Federal Reserve Board of Governors, Survey of Consumer Finances.

of households have held more than 50 percent of aggregate wealth since 2007 (Bricker et al., 2014). This share has been on a consistent uptrend since the late 1980s. The next 7 percent of households in the wealth distribution hold roughly 25 percent of aggregate wealth, a share that been fairly stable time during this period. Notably, the loss in wealth share experienced by the bottom 90 percent of households, which in 2013 held only 25 percent of all wealth is accounted for by the rise in share captured by the top 3 percent. This is not a uniform spreading of the wealth distribution; it is a rising concentration of wealth at the very top.

An alternative analysis by Emmanuel Saez and Gabriel Zucman finds that the rise in wealth inequality is due to the very top of the wealth distribution. Using capital income reported on tax returns, they estimate that the share of wealth held by the top 0.1 percent of households has more than tripled, from 7 percent of total household wealth in 1979 to 22 percent in 2012—reversing a decline over the prior decades.[1] As shown in Figure 1-4, the wealth share of these households (approximately 160,000 families with average net wealth per family above $20.6 million) is now nearly as large as it was in 1929 (Saez and Zucman 2015).

---

[1] Any method to measure wealth is imperfect and unlike income, individuals are not required to report the value of their wealth each year, so there is no administrative data to use as a benchmark for the distribution, the two methods discussed here each have their advantages and disadvantages. (Bricker et al 2015, Saez and Zucman 2015).

Figure 1-4

Distribution of Household Wealth (Saez-Zucman), 1913–2012

Percent of Total Household Wealth

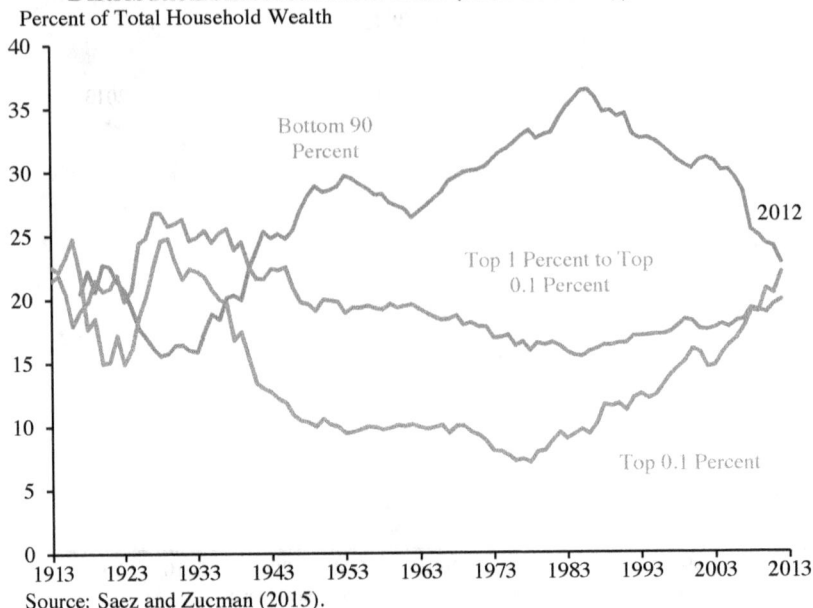

Source: Saez and Zucman (2015).

Saez and Zucman argue that this increase in wealth concentration is compounded by an increase in differences in saving rates across wealth classes (for instance, wealthier individuals save a larger percentage of their income). More generally, they hypothesize that income inequality has a "snowballing effect" on the wealth distribution: a larger share of income is earned by top wealth holders, who then save at higher rates, which pushes wealth concentration up; this dynamic leads to rising capital-income concentration and contributes to even greater top income and wealth shares.

Rising wealth inequality is perhaps best understood as the ultimate outcome of economic growth that leaves the middle class behind. But it is also an important cause of income inequality. In part, it directly reinforces itself because concentrated wealth leads to concentrated capital income. But more importantly, it helps entrench a broader inequality of opportunity that blocks the path to full economic participation for wide swaths of the potential U.S. labor force and innovation force.

Inequality of Opportunity

The traditional argument that inequality results from normal economic competition rests on the notion that competition for unequally distributed rewards encourages production. But when inequality has become so entrenched that it passes across generations and limits opportunity, it narrows the pool of human capital that can compete. Such throttling of opportunity is unambiguously bad for growth, preventing potential innovators from full economic participation and weighing on productivity growth. Further, if entrenched interests are able to limit future competition either by influencing the policymaking process or by abusing their market power, dynamism in labor markets or firm entry can decrease. While some level of income and wealth inequality can play a constructive role, the implications of unevenly distributed opportunity are simpler—working the wrong way for both equity and efficiency.

While inequality of opportunity is an international phenomenon, it is especially important in the United States. Mishel et al. (2012), based on data from Corak (2011), assembles a set of intergenerational earnings elasticities across large advanced economies with similar incomes to the United States. The intergenerational earnings elasticity reflects the extent to which the earnings of parents and children are correlated—the higher the elasticity, the less mobile the society. Such mobility can be understood as a measure of the inequality of opportunity. If children at all income levels faced the same set of opportunities, one might expect a lower elasticity. Among the 17 peer countries identified by Mishel, the United States ranks in the top half, as shown in Figure 1-5. Other measures of mobility support the observation: Raj Chetty has found that a child born in the 1980s to parents in the bottom 20 percent of the income distribution has only a 7.5 percent chance of moving to the top 20 percent. A similar child has a 12 percent chance in Denmark and a 13 percent chance in Canada (Chetty 2014).

It is important to understand the forms that this inequality of opportunity takes and to explore the institutional structures that entrench the pattern. Three particular examples that the Council of Economic Advisers has recently explored in a series of reports include the experience of children in low-income families, inequities in the criminal justice system, and the systemic challenges faced by women in the U.S. economy. The President has a robust agenda to promote equality of opportunity for all Americans, detailed extensively later in this chapter.

Children in Low-Income Families

Barriers to opportunity take many forms, but those that appear early in life for children and youth are particularly costly to society, as their impacts accumulate over many years, shaping adolescents and young adults during their critical transition to adulthood beyond. Moreover, there is evidence that in recent decades, family income has become more important in shaping children's outcomes. Chapter 4 of this *Report* focuses on

Figure 1-5
Intergenerational Earnings Mobility

Elasticity Between Earnings of Fathers and Sons

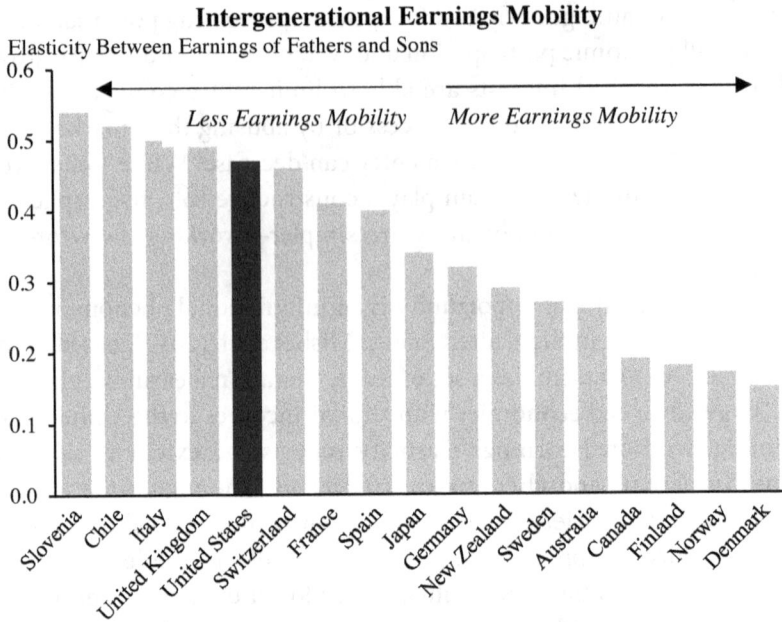

Source: Mishel et al. (2012); Corak (2011).

the particular challenges facing children and the policies that can improve outcomes for them.

Parents' socioeconomic status can produce an inequality of opportunity via a number of channels. Financial expenditure is one obvious pathway. As income inequality has grown, so has inequality in child-related expenditures. Parents in the top income quintile now spend seven times more on children's materials and enrichment activities—such as books, computers, summer camps, and music lessons—than families in the bottom income quintile, and other research suggests that this inequality in expenditure has grown over time (Duncan and Murnane 2011). A family's socioeconomic status can also impact a child's chances through housing stability and neighborhood conditions, food security, and access to medical care, as well as in the types of activities that parents participate in with their children. Sustained exposure to the toxic stresses of poverty during childhood can prevent children from achieving their potential, exacerbating later-life income inequality and limiting national economic growth.

Criminal Justice

The criminal justice system is plagued with inequalities of opportunity, both along racial lines, and along income lines in the form of monetary payments such as fines, fees, and bail. The dramatic rise in incarceration over the past several decades has been distributed unequally, disproportionately impacting low-income households and minorities. In 1984, the majority of State and Federal prisoners were White; but by 2014, over 65 percent of sentenced prisoners were minorities (Minor-Harper 1986; Carson 2015). Even when there is little difference in the likelihood of committing a crime, individuals of color are much more likely to be arrested. For example, an African-American individual is nearly four times as likely as a White individual to be arrested for marijuana possession, even though individuals of both races reported using marijuana at similar rates in 2010 (ACLU 2013). Different rates of interaction with the criminal justice system by income and race can create substantial barriers to economic success, limiting opportunity for many.

The expanding use of monetary penalties—fines, fees, and bails—also disproportionately impact poor defendants and offenders who have fewer resources available to manage criminal justice debt. Financial penalties also serve as a regressive form of punishment as the same level of debt presents an increasingly larger burden as one moves down the income scale. Such systemic challenges limit the opportunities available to low-income families, preventing them from full participation in our economy (CEA 2015a).

Women in the Economy

Over the last five decades, women have made enormous strides in the U.S. labor market. Our economy is $2.0 trillion, or 13.5 percent, larger than it would have been without women's increased participation in the labor force and hours worked since 1970 (CEA 2014).

Although the United States was initially a leader in bringing women into the labor force, our progress has stalled somewhat over the past 20 or 30 years. In 1990, the United States ranked seventh in female prime-age (25-54) labor force participation out of 24 advanced economies for which data is available—but in 2014, the United States fell to 20th place (OECD 2015). Part of the explanation may be that the United States lags behind many of its peer countries in terms of pro-family policies like paid leave requirements that ease the burden on working families.

Moreover, women in the labor force face a persistent wage gap. The typical woman working full-time full-year earns 21 percent less than the typical man. In addition, while the pay gap closed by 17 percentage points between 1981 and 2001, it has remained flat since 2001. In the past two years, some modest progress has been made, with the gap closing by 1.8 percentage point from 2012 to 2013 and by an additional percentage point between 2013 and 2014. The wage gap has many causes and contributors, including gender gaps in education and experience; differences in choices of occupation and industry; decisions about family responsibilities; and discrimination.

The Interplay of the Forms of Inequality

These three forms of inequality discussed above are not conceptually distinct phenomena—they closely affect one another. Wealth inequality is, in some respects, an outcome of income inequality, as the saving of unequally distributed income produces unequally distributed wealth. But inequality of opportunity is in many ways both a cause and a result of income and wealth inequality. Therefore, unequally distributed opportunities entrench an unequal income distribution, and an unequal income distribution leads to many of the inequities faced by low-income and low-wealth children.

The "Great Gatsby" curve, a term introduced by former CEA Chair Alan Krueger, illustrates the relationship between income inequality and inequality of opportunity. When plotted across counties or across countries, Figures 1-6a and 1-6b shows that areas with more income inequality also tend to have less mobility for children from low-income families. This relationship also holds across large advanced economies.

The Great Gatsby curve shows that inequality is correlated with lower mobility, and one important transmission mechanism is the distribution of opportunity. When disparities in education, training, social connection, and the criminal justice system are distributed as unequally as overall wealth, poorer families have a much harder time succeeding in the economy.

SOURCES OF INEQUALITY:
COMPETITIVE MARKETS AND ECONOMIC RENTS

Classical economics suggests that income inequality is a product of competitive markets, with income differences reflecting pure productivity differences. Under this view, inequality encourages growth by rewarding the most productive labor and the highest-returning capital. But recently, economists and commentators have suggested that much of the rise in inequality can be explained by the rising importance of economic rents. Recent work by the Council of Economic Advisers has focused on the influence of economic rents or their division in the labor market (CEA 2015c), in the housing sector (Furman 2015a), in occupational licensing (Furman 2015b), and in the broader capital markets (Furman and Orszag 2015).

The long-term trend of rising inequality is sufficiently large that multiple forces are likely playing a part. While there is truth to the "competitive markets" view that an unequal distribution of income compensation for

Figure 1-6a
The "Great Gatsby Curve" Within the United States

Upward Mobility

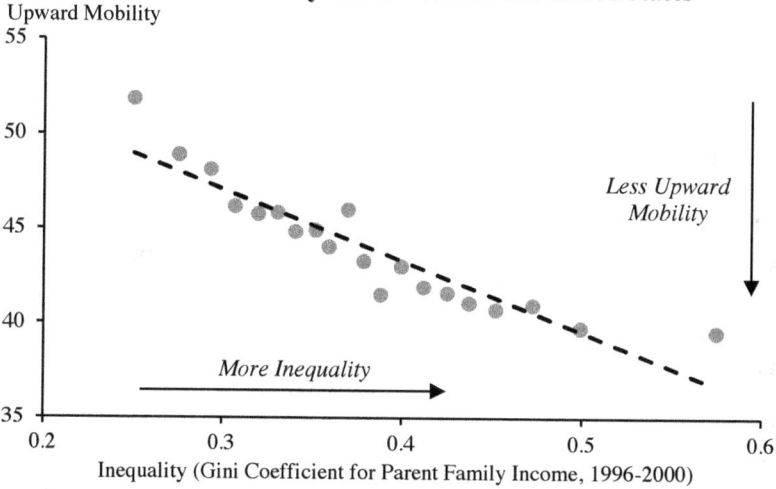

Inequality (Gini Coefficient for Parent Family Income, 1996-2000)

Note: U.S. commuting zones were ordered by Gini coefficient and divided into 20 equally sized bins. Each blue dot represents a single bin. Upward mobility reflects the mean percentile in the 2011-2012 national income distribution for those individuals in each bin whose parents were at the 25th percentile of the national income distribution between 1996 and 2000.
Source: CEA calculations based on Chetty (2014).

Figure 1-6b
The "Great Gatsby Curve" Across Countries

Upward Mobility (Inverted Intergenerational Earnings Elasticity)

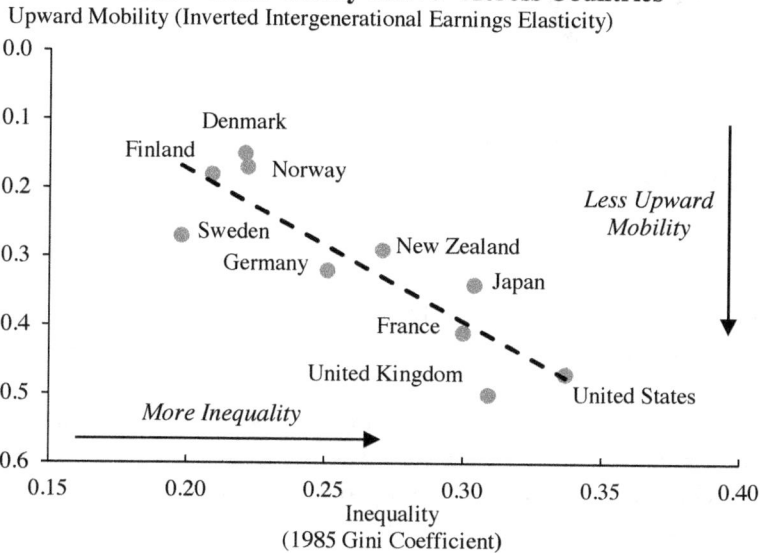

Inequality
(1985 Gini Coefficient)

Note: Intergenerational earnings elasticity is measured as the elasticity between a father's earnings and their son's adult earnings. The children studied were born during the early to mid 1960s and their adult income was measured in the mid to late 1990s.
Source: Corak (2011); OECD.

differences in productivity, there is also evidence of rents complicating the income-productivity link. This *Report* considers each channel in turn.

The Competitive Channel

The traditional economic explanation of inequality is grounded in competitive markets, wherein workers receive wages commensurate with their productivity. According to this explanation, a combination of skill-biased technological change, a slowdown in the increase in educational attainment, and globalization have increased the demand for highly skilled workers at the same time that their relative supply has not kept pace—resulting in higher wages for these high-productivity workers and greater inequality.

Skill-Biased Technological Change

Many economists have pointed to the role of technology in increasing inequality (Autor 2010). This argument asserts that technology can most readily replace labor in tasks that are easily automated, which tend to involve routine tasks that place them in the middle of the skill and wage distributions. Over time, employment moves to both the lower and higher ends of the occupational skill ranking, as shown in Figure 1-7, where occupations are ranked by average wage as a proxy for skill. While technology is a better replacement for tasks that are easy to routinize, it complements the abilities of highly skilled workers and improves their productivity, thereby increasing their earnings and employment opportunities. Lower-skilled workers are not necessarily made more productive, but neither are they easily replaced, as their jobs often include interpersonal interactions and variable situations that are difficult to automate. Taken together, this view of the role of technology points to both rising inequality and rising job polarization.

Educational Attainment

The increase in skill-biased technological change has been compounded by a slowdown in the rate of increase in educational attainment. Schooling attainment rose for much of the 20th century, in part due to measures like the G.I. Bill, the expansion of high schools and community colleges, and greater educational attainment by women. However, growth in years of schooling slowed substantially around 1980. The rate of growth in the college-educated population fell by almost 60 percent, from 3.9 percent a year between 1960 and 1980 to 2.3 percent per year between 1980 and 2005, according to estimates by Lawrence Katz and Claudia Goldin. While the pool of skilled workers is still growing, in recent decades it has

Figure 1-7
Change in Employment by Detailed Occupation, 1989–2015

Change in Total Employment, Millions

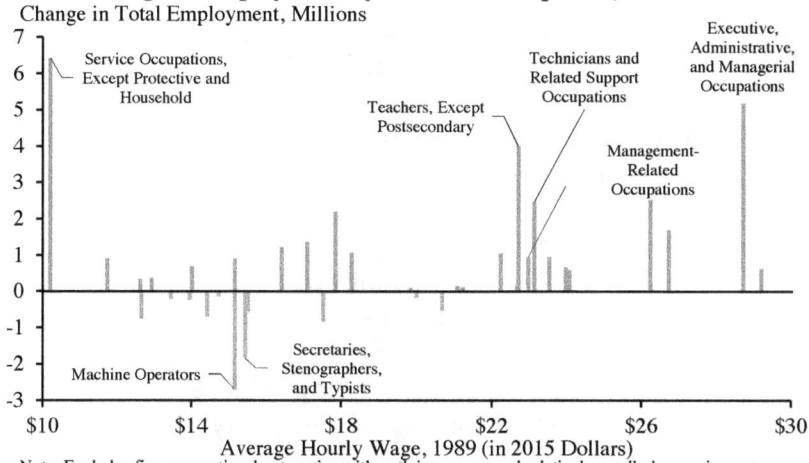

Note: Excludes five occupational categories with outlying wages and relatively small changes in employment (Farm Occupations, Except Managerial; Private Household Occupations; Engineers, Architects, and Surveyors; Lawyers and Judges; and Health Diagnosing Occupations). Average wages exclude individuals who are self-employed, who have real wages below $0.50 or greater than $100 (in 1989 dollars), or whose wages are imputed. Top-coded earnings are adjusted following Lemieux (2006), and all wages are adjusted for inflation using the CPI-U-RS.
Source: Bureau of Labor Statistics, Current Population Survey; CEA calculations.

grown at a slower rate than has the demand for these workers, increasing the wage premium that more educated workers command and thus raising inequality.

Globalization

Other economists have pointed to the rapid rise in globalization that has occurred since the 1980s as a potential explanation for growing inequality within the United States, especially the expansion of trade with China since 2000. (Greater globalization also coincided with a shift in national income shares from labor to capital, a worldwide phenomenon.) Economic theory predicts that such trade may have some effect on wages for low-skilled workers in the United States who now face more competition from low-skilled Chinese workers, while reducing wages for high-skilled workers in China who now face more competition from high-skilled American workers. But some evidence militates in the other direction. For example, the returns to education have increased in a wide range of countries over the last several decades, including many relatively poor countries. This suggests either that some other more-subtle globalization explanation is operative or, alternatively, that the technology/education explanations are even more important than the globalization explanation.

To some extent, some of these forces—like skill-biased technological change and globalization—reflect the type of desirable economic progress that promotes productivity growth. But that competitive channel works best when the competition is open to the broadest pool of potential labor and investable capital. Public policy is therefore critical to ensuring that the competitive channel works well, in part by providing a cushion for those disadvantaged by the system—such as providing job retraining, unemployment insurance, robust Social Security, access to health care, and other policies for which the President has advocated. But government also has an important role in reducing the inequality of opportunity that creates barriers to success for some groups and thus limits the pool of workers who can successfully compete in the labor market.

As important as these forces are, the competitive channel does not appear to explain the full rise in income inequality in recent decades. Indeed, as mentioned earlier, there is evidence that an especially unproductive element is at work—the rising influence of economic rents and their distribution.

The Rents Channel

Many economists have recently advanced an explanation of inequality grounded in the importance of economic rents—the notion that investors or highly compensated workers are receiving more income than they would require to undertake their production or work. Classic examples of such rents include monopoly profits and the unearned benefits of preferential government regulation. Rents can result from abuses of market power and tend to encourage "rent-seeking behavior," the unproductive use of resources to capture such rewards.

According to this view, the unequal distribution of these rents—rather than the conventional explanation that inequality reflects only actual differences in worker productivity or the allocation of capital—is an important cause of rising income inequality. To the degree that this interpretation is correct, it suggests that it is possible to reduce inequality without hurting efficiency by changing how the rents are divided or even while increasing efficiency by acting to reduce these rents. There is relatively little academic literature on this question and data are scarce since rents cannot be directly observed, but considerable evidence appears to support the notion that rents are exacerbating inequality.

It is important to note that not all economic rents are undesirable. For example, in a perfectly competitive market, the price settles at a level below that which some buyers would be willing to pay and above that which some sellers would be willing to accept. The rents collected by these buyers and sellers—consumer and producer surplus—are widely considered one of the chief benefits of market competition. In addition, temporary monopoly power that guarantees rents for a firm can be an incentive for additional innovation—one of the goals of our patent system. Nevertheless, growing rents, the increasingly unequal division of rents between workers and firms, and rent-seeking behavior are often highly problematic and appear to have become more so in recent decades (Furman and Orszag 2015).

The Division of Rents in Wage Negotiations: Declining Unionization and the Minimum Wage

Whenever a firm hires a worker, the difference between the highest wage the firm would pay and the lowest wage the worker would accept is the surplus created by the job match—an economic rent. The division of that rent between firm and work depends on their relative bargaining power. As markets grow concentrated and certain forms of labor are commoditized, the balance of bargaining power leans toward the firm. Unionization and collective bargaining—along with policies like the minimum wage—help level the playing field, concentrating labor and encouraging the firm to share those rents with labor. This process traditionally helped bolster the wages of lower- and middle-wage workers, thereby reducing inequality.

But union membership has declined consistently since the 1970s, as shown in Figure 1-8. Approximately a quarter of all U.S. workers belonged to a union in 1955 but, by 2014, union membership had dropped to just below 10 percent of total employment, roughly the same level as the mid-1930s. In some states, just 3 percent of workers belong to unions (CEA 2015c).

Research suggests that declining unionization accounts for between a fifth and a third of the increase in inequality since the 1970s (Western and Rosenfeld 2011). Other research shows that union workers have higher wages than their nonunion counterparts, with unions raising wages by up to 25 percent for their workers compared with similar nonunion workers (Boskin 1972). Unions also increase the likelihood workers have access to benefits and work under safe conditions.

Of course, other specific policies can help promote wage growth by affecting the division of economic rents. The minimum wage is one such policy, geared to those workers with the very-least bargaining power. A minimum wage protects some workers from having their lack of bargaining power exploited by firms in the wage negotiation, helping direct some of the rents from their job match to the workers themselves. But the real value of the minimum wage has declined [20] percent over the past three decades, losing its ability to protect workers in parallel with declining unionization.

Figure 1-8

U.S. Union Membership & Top 10 Percent Income Share, 1917–2015

Percent

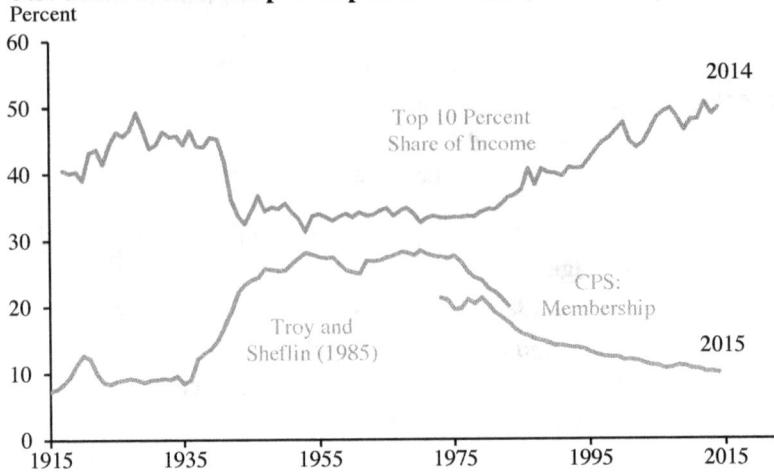

Note: Union membersahip is expressed as a percent of total employment. Total employment from 1901 to 1947 is derived from estimates in Weir (1992). For 1948 to 2014, employment data are annual averages from the monthly Current Population Survey.
Source: Troy and Sheflin (1985); Bureau of Labor Statistics, Current Population Survey; Weir (1992); World Wealth and Income Database; CEA calculations.

Greater support for collective bargaining and the minimum wage are both policies that can help address the increasingly unequal division of economic rents, promoting stronger wage growth and reduced inequality—and to the degree that such policies are about changing the divisions of rents, they need not reduce efficiency. In some respects, like improving worker's voice and motivation, such policies can actually boost efficiency.

Some Evidence for the Growth of Aggregate Rents

The challenge is not just that the division of rents is changing based on comparative bargaining power. Moreover, the economic structure appears to be generating greater rents and tilting these toward profits and profitable firms.

Corporate Profits and Interest Rates

One important piece of evidence that rents are on the rise is the divergence of rising corporate profits and declining real interest rates. In the absence of economic rents, corporate profits should generally follow the path of interest rates, which reflect the prevailing return to capital in the economy. But over the past three decades, corporate profits have risen as interest rates have fallen, as shown in Figure 1-9. This suggests that some corporate profits could reflect an increase in the economic rents collected by corporations, not a "pure" return to capital. Of course, this divergence can

Figure 1-9
Corporate Profits and Real Interest Rates, 1985–2015

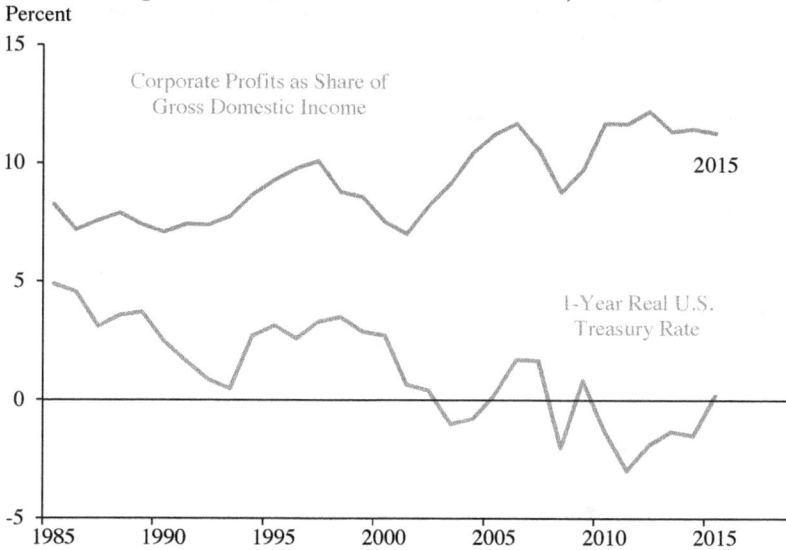

Percent

Corporate Profits as Share of
Gross Domestic Income

2015

1-Year Real U.S.
Treasury Rate

1985   1990   1995   2000   2005   2010   2015

Note: Corporate profits for 2015 are an average of the first three quarters of the year. The
real U.S. Treasury rate is defined as the nominal constant-maturity rate estimated by the
Federal Reserve, less realized inflation defined by the Consumer Price Index.
Source: Bureau of Economic Analysis; Bureau of Labor Statistics; Federal Reserve.

Figure 1-10
Return on Invested Capital Excluding Goodwill,
U.S. Publicly-Traded Nonfinancial Firms, 1965–2014

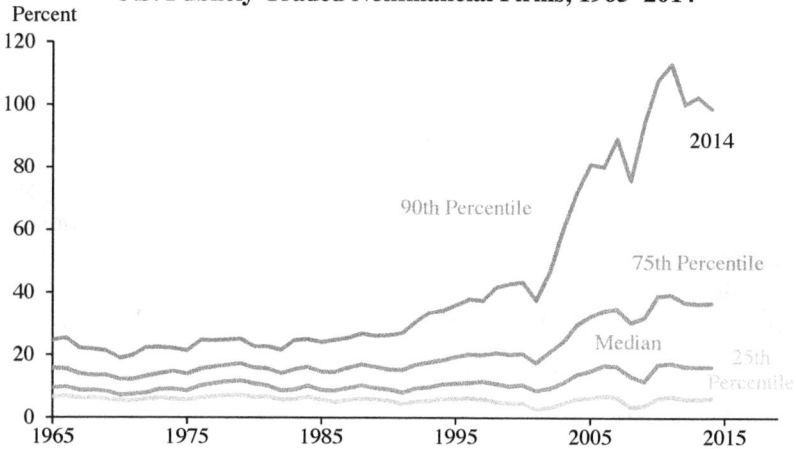

Percent

2014

90th Percentile

75th Percentile

Median
25th
Percentile

1965   1975   1985   1995   2005   2015

Note: The return on invested capital definition is based on Koller et al (2015), and the data
presented here are updated and augmented versions of the figures presented in Chapter 6 of that
volume. The McKinsey data includes McKinsey analysis of Standard & Poor's data and exclude
financial firms from the analysis because of the practical complexities of computing returns on
invested capital for such firms.
Source: Koller et al. (2015); McKinsey & Company; Furman and Orszag (2015).

Table 1-2

Change in Market Concentration by Sector, 1997-2007

Industry	Percentage Point Change in Revenue Share Earned by 50 Largest Firms, 1997-2007
Transportation and Warehousing	12.0
Retail Trade	7.6
Finance and Insurance	7.4
Real Estate Rental and Leasing	6.6
Utilities	5.6
Wholesale Trade	4.6
Educational Services	2.7
Accommodation and Food Services	2.6
Professional, Scientific and Technical Services	2.1
Administrative/ Support	0.9
Other Services, Non-Public Admin	-1.5
Arts, Entertainment and Recreation	-2.3
Health Care and Assistance	-3.7

Note: Concentration ratio data is displayed for all North American Industry Classification System (NAICS) sectors for which data is available from 1997 to 2007.
Source: Census Bureau.

be affected by other factors such as credit risk, but such factors are unlikely to explain the full gap.

Market Concentration and the Distribution of Profits

Another piece of evidence for the rising importance of rents is increased market concentration across a number of industries. Table 1-2 shows that the share of revenue earned by the largest firms increased across most industries between 1997 and 2007. This observation complements a range of studies that find increasing concentration in air travel, telecommunications, banking, food-processing, and other sectors of the economy.

Increased concentration may play a role in the strikingly large and growing disparity in return to invested capital across major corporations (Furman and Orszag 2015). As shown in Figure 1-10, the returns earned by firms at the 90th percentile are now more than six times larger than those of the median firm, up from less than three times larger in 1990.

Occupational Licensing

There is also evidence of increased rent-seeking in the requirement of a government-issued license to be employed in certain professions ("occupational licensing"). As documented in Kleiner and Krueger (2013), the share of the U.S. workforce covered by state licensing laws grew five-fold in the

Figure 1-11
Share of Workers with a State Occupational License

Percent

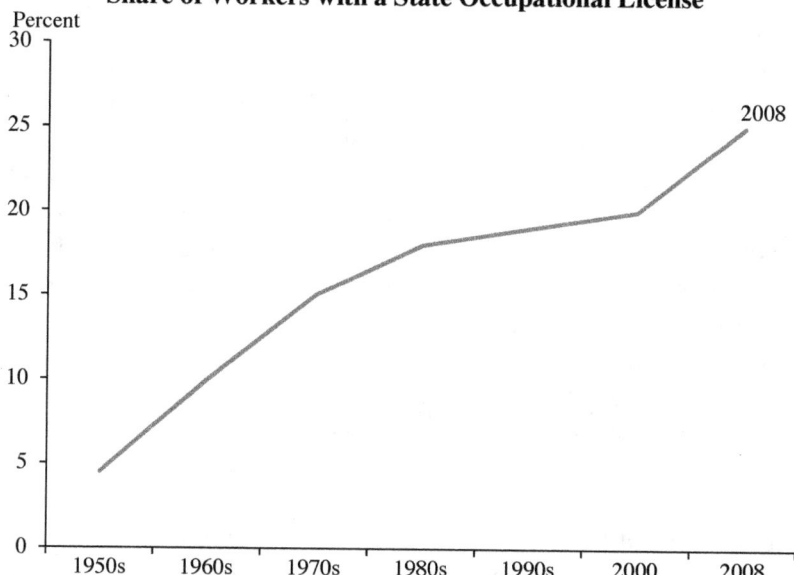

Source: Council of State Governments (1952); Greene (1969); Kleiner (1990); Kleiner (2006); and Kleiner and Krueger (2013), Westat data; CEA calculations.

second half of the 20th century, from less than 5 percent in the early 1950s to 25 percent by 2008, as shown in Figure 1-11. Although state licenses account for the bulk of licensing, the addition of locally and Federally licensed occupations further raises the share of the workforce that is licensed to 29 percent.

While licensing can play an important role in protecting consumer health and safety, there is evidence that some licensing requirements create economic rents for licensed practitioners at the expense of excluded workers and consumers—increasing inefficiency and potentially also increasing inequality. First, the employment barriers created by licensing raise wages for those who are successful in gaining entry to a licensed occupation by restricting employment in the licensed profession and lowering wages for excluded workers. Estimates find that unlicensed workers earn 10- to 15-percent lower wages than licensed workers with similar levels of education, training, and experience (Kleiner and Krueger 2010). Second, research finds that more restrictive licensing laws lead to higher prices for goods and services, in many cases for lower-income households, while the quality, health and safety benefits do not always materialize (Kleiner 2015). Finally, some state-specific licensing requirements create unnecessary barriers to entry for out-of-state licensed practitioners, reducing mobility across state lines (Johnson and Kleiner 2014).

Housing and Land-Use Restrictions

There is evidence that land-use regulation may also play a role in the presence of increased economic rents. Such regulation in the housing market can serve legitimate, welfare-enhancing purposes, such as restrictions that prohibit industrial activities from occurring alongside or within residential neighborhoods or limitations on the size of a dwelling due to a fragile local water supply. But when excessive and primarily geared toward protecting the interests of current landowners—including their property values—land-use regulations decrease housing affordability and reduce nationwide productivity and growth. These are impacts detailed in Chapters 2 and 6 of this *Report*, respectively. The presence of rents in the housing market, moreover, may also restrict labor mobility and exacerbate inequality.

One main indication that land-use regulation gives rise to economic rents is that, in the aggregate, real house prices are higher than real construction costs, and this differential has increased since at least the early 1980s, as shown in Figure 1-12. In fact, Glaeser, Gyourko, and Saks (2005) find that more stringent land-use regulations have driven house price appreciation in excess of construction costs since 1970, before which time quality improvements actually drove much of the price increases. Further, in a large and growing set of U.S. cities—including major population centers such as New York and Los Angeles and high-productivity cities like San Francisco—home prices are usually at least 40 percent above construction costs. (Glaeser and Gyourko 2003). In addition, rental payments in the housing market in these areas often rise faster than wages.

THE INTERPLAY OF INEQUALITY AND GROWTH

The relationship between inequality and growth continues to be the subject of much debate in the economics literature. The traditional finding for canonical policy responses to inequality, like progressive taxation and income support for low-income households, is that there is a tradeoff between equity and efficiency, the famous "leaky bucket" coined by Arthur Okun (1975). There has also been a long-standing macroeconomic debate about the consequences of inequality, with one traditional view being that more inequality leads to more savings by high-income households and thus a higher level of output (Duesenberry 1949).

The current theory and evidence at both a micro and macro level is considerably more ambiguous than these traditional views and suggests a number of mechanisms by which inequality can be harmful to growth. As discussed above, one clear-cut example is that to the degree that inequality is

Figure 1-12
Real Construction Costs and House Prices, 1980–2013

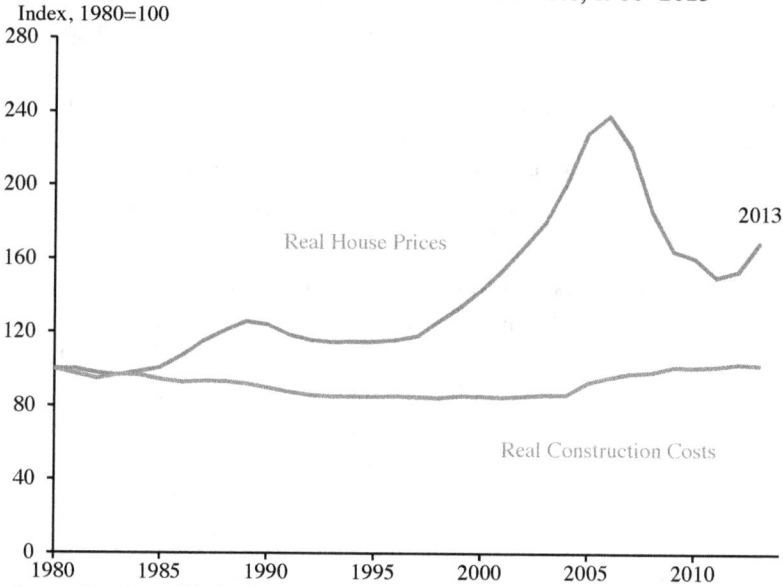

Index, 1980=100

Source: Gyourko and Molloy (2015).

generated by anti-competitive rents, then fostering greater competition has the potential to improve both equity and efficiency simultaneously.

But even with respect to inequality that stems from competitive markets, the relationship between such inequality and output is unclear. While there are no doubt respects in which such inequality can help motivate additional innovation and growth, a range of new research has also emphasized that there are a number of ways through which inequality may in fact constrain economic growth. This literature starts from the observation that the traditional emphasis on the quantity of capital, even if true, is dwarfed by the importance of the quality of capital, technology, and entrepreneurship. In particular, this approach emphasizes a number of ways by which inequality could harm growth: (1) by reducing access to the education necessary for the full population to reach its full potential; (2) by reducing entrepreneurship and risk-taking; (3) by undermining the trust necessary for a decentralized market economy and by increasing monitoring costs; and (4) by leading to increased political instability, growth-reducing policies, and uncertainty (Ostry, Berg, and Tsangarides 2014).

In keeping with this, much recent microeconomic evidence finds important exceptions to the "leaky bucket." For example, as discussed in Chapter 4, a number of anti-poverty programs focused on children have been shown to increase incomes in later life, illustrating the importance of the educational channel between inequality and growth.

It is impossible to have the same degree of confidence about causation at the macroeconomic level as at the microeconomic level. There are no comparable natural experiments and the causality between inequality and growth clearly runs in both directions. Nevertheless, the fact that several recent papers have found that inequality is harmful to growth suggests—at a minimum—that it is unlikely that there is a substantial tradeoff between equality and growth.

For example, cross-country analysis from Jonathan Ostry, Andrew Berg and Charalambos Tsangarides at the International Monetary Fund (IMF) provides better evidence of the harm done by inequality and the lack of harm done by progressive policies. The IMF study finds that inequality decreases both the magnitude and sustainability of growth and that progressive redistributive policies alone are neutral for the magnitude and sustainability of growth (with a small caveat that very large amounts of redistribution—those policies that redistribute above the 75th percentile of income—could have a small negative effect on growth).

The Organisation for Economic Co-operation and Development (OECD) also found associations between higher inequality and reduced growth across OECD member countries (Cingano 2014). The OECD focused on inequality of opportunity, particularly disparities in education, as the chief transmission mechanism of inequality's restraint on growth.

Ultimately, the link between growth and inequality at an aggregate level is ambiguous, not admitting a single direction for all countries at all times and all types of inequality. Rather, the most important question is the one that policymakers face when they have the opportunity to address these trends on the margins: What are the policies that address inequality in a relatively efficient manner?

POLICIES TO PROMOTE INCLUSIVE GROWTH

As economists' understanding of the relationship between growth and inequality evolves, it is critical to choose economic policies that can unleash growth in an inclusive manner along with those policies that can reduce inequality in an efficient manner. Analysis of the various forms and sources of inequality in the United States can help to elucidate the mechanisms by which certain pro-growth policies can reduce inequality through either the competitive channel or the rents channel. Policies that promote inclusive growth can be grouped in four categories: those that strengthen aggregate demand in general; those that make the competitive channel work better by promoting equality of opportunity; those that reduce unproductive inequality by reducing inefficient rents and rent-seeking behavior; and those that help better protect workers and their families from the consequences of inequality—while in many cases also serving as a springboard for upward mobility. The President's agenda for middle-class economics includes a range of policies along each of these dimensions.

Strengthening Aggregate Demand

When an economy operates below its full potential, pro-growth policies that help to close the output gap naturally combat inequality. Indeed, unemployment or sub-optimal employment is a form of inequality itself, resulting in zero or insufficient labor earnings for a subset of workers. The same macroeconomic policies usually employed to boost growth and return the economy to full employment can unambiguously reduce this cyclical form of income inequality.

Aggressive demand management strategies implemented by the United States can, in this context, also be seen as distributional policies. Part of the U.S. response to the global financial crisis involved massive support to low-income households via the fiscal expansion in the American Recovery and Reinvestment Act of 2009 and extended unemployment insurance, among other programs. While fiscal expansion and accommodative monetary policy worked to boost aggregate incomes, their principal goal was the restoration of income to those who found themselves out of work during the crisis.

Additionally, a lower unemployment rate—one important effect of boosting aggregate demand—can help increase wages and draw marginalized workers back into the labor force. Rising labor demand and higher wages can also encourage workers to upgrade their skills and education. Therefore, a tight labor market can have substantial advantages for workers—particularly those at the bottom of the economic ladder—making a strong economy an important tool for fighting inequality.

Moreover, weak aggregate demand can have long-lasting effects. Many unemployed workers receive lower incomes for years to come, even after finding a job; the other side of these potentially long-lasting reductions in earnings is the possibility of long-run scarring in the economy and persistently lower output in the years after a recession ends. That is why continuing to support stronger growth, a low unemployment rate, and expanded labor force participation remains a critical goal of Administration policy.

The need for such policies was closely aligned across countries in the immediate wake of the recent crisis. Today, many advanced economies find themselves at different stages of the business cycle. However, as sub-par wage growth manifests itself as a global phenomenon, it is clear that most of the industrialized world remains below full employment, underscoring the continued need for appropriate demand-management strategies.

Promoting Equality of Opportunity

The competitive channel of inequality works best when that competition is open to the largest pool of potential labor and investable capital—so it depends upon equality of opportunity that allows all Americans to participate in the economy to their full potential. Education and training are critical in this respect. To that end, the President put forward a plan to increase access to child care for working families while investing billions of dollars in quality early learning and preschool programs to help our youngest learners succeed—especially those from low-income families. The Administration has provided unprecedented resources and worked with business leaders, state and local governments, and others to align job training programs with labor market demand—and the President signed the bipartisan Workforce Innovation and Opportunity Act (WIOA), the first legislative reform of Federal job training programs in nearly 15 years, which will improve business engagement, accountability, access, and alignment across job training, employment service, and adult education programs. Moreover, the President continues to lead a movement to make community college free for responsible students. All of these steps help increase the supply of skilled workers, allowing more people to take advantage of the returns to skills while also increasing the relative demand for unskilled workers, driving up their wages and reducing the dispersion of incomes.

In addition, an important element of opportunity is giving everyone the opportunity to participate in the workforce if they choose to and it makes sense given their family situation. The President supports a range of policies to boost labor force participation, including promoting access to paid leave and paid sick days to help encourage Americans to join the labor force; promoting greater access to high-quality child care; reforming taxes to make work more attractive for secondary earners; and helping provide training programs and other assistance finding jobs.

Reducing Market Power Concentration and Rent-Seeking Behavior

To the degree that rising aggregate rents stemming from growing market power are contributing to increased inequality, then changing the balance of that power or fostering more competitive markets will increase efficiency while reducing inequality. Policies like a minimum wage and greater support for collective bargaining can help level the playing field for workers in negotiations with employers. Because such policies only change the division of rents, they can reduce inequality without necessarily reducing overall welfare. In fact, when appropriately tailored, they can foster the previously discussed growth benefits of a better-paid workforce like greater access to education and increased entrepreneurship.

Heightened antitrust enforcement, rationalizing licensing requirements for employment, reducing zoning and other land use restrictions, and appropriately balancing intellectual property regimes, all can help reduce excessive rents. Firms with extensive market power can take many anti-competitive actions that generate inefficient rents. Often, there are existing regulations prohibiting such behavior. A robust enforcement regime for the regulations that fight rent-seeking can therefore improve efficiency and inequality at the same time.

Finally, to the degree that rent-seeking warps regulations, policymakers should reduce the ability of people or corporations to seek rents successfully through political reforms and other steps to reduce the influence of regulatory lobbying. Much like the first two channels, policies that reduce these rents can also increase efficiency while reducing inequality.

Protecting Families Against the Consequences of Inequality While Fostering Mobility

A progressive tax system combined with important benefits that exist today—like unemployment insurance and the Affordable Care Act—and new proposals the President has made, like wage insurance, can help both reduce inequality and protect the people who get an unlucky draw in a given year or over time. In many cases, such policies do not just affect after-tax incomes, but also help increase before-tax incomes over time. The Earned Income Tax Credit (EITC), for example, has been shown to increase labor force participation by single mothers, raising their earnings and their after-tax income (Liebman 1998).

Moreover, a growing body of economic research has helped confirm that programs to support low-income families can not only strengthen the position of the families themselves, but also have important benefits for long-term productivity (Brown, Kowalski, and Lurie, 2015; Hoynes, Schanzenbach, and Almond, 2012; Chetty, Friedman, and Rockoff, 2011). Indeed, the link between growth and equality is especially apparent at the lower end of the income distribution where the unequal distribution of opportunity is most important.

Economists have evaluated the long-term benefits of historical government programs targeted toward low-income families in the United States. Compared with similar children who received no support, children from families who received temporary income support at the start of the

20th century saw higher wages, more education, and lower mortality—with benefits from a few years of income support lasting for 80 years or more (Aizer, Eli, and Ferrie, 2014). The U.S. Supplemental Nutrition Assistance Program—formerly known as the Food Stamp Program; the EITC, one of the government's largest tools to reduce child poverty; and Medicaid, the health program for low-income Americans, have all been shown to have similar benefits (CEA 2015b).

Greater education, lower mortality, and lower crime rates do not just benefit the affected individual, but also support productivity and potential growth in the aggregate. Many of these policies would also strengthen labor force participation. When the public sector makes important investments in supporting the most disadvantaged families, there are clear benefits to aggregate growth.

Conclusion:
The 2016 *Economic Report of the President*

Middle-class incomes are driven by productivity growth, labor force participation, and the equality of outcomes. As the U.S. economy moves beyond the recovery from the financial crisis, our policy stance should focus on promoting each of those factors to foster inclusive growth. This year's *Economic Report of the President* considers several elements of the inclusive growth agenda. Chapter 2 begins by reviewing the United States' macroeconomic progress in 2015 and considering the outlook for the years to come, and Chapter 3 focuses on the United States' progress in a global context. Chapter 4 focuses on one especially important element of the inequality of opportunity discussed in this chapter—the particular economic challenges low-income children face. Chapters 5 and 6 consider two key elements of productivity growth on which American businesses and policymakers should focus even more closely: technological innovation and infrastructure investment. Finally, Chapter 7 concludes with a retrospective look at the institutional structure and history of the President's Council of Economic Advisers on its 70th anniversary.

C H A P T E R   2

THE YEAR IN REVIEW AND THE YEARS AHEAD

The U.S. economy continued to grow in 2015, as the recovery extended into its seventh year with widespread growth in domestic demand, strong gains in labor markets and real wages, and low inflation. Real gross domestic product (GDP) increased 1.8 percent during the four quarters of the year, down from 2.5-percent growth during 2013 and 2014. In 2015, residential investment led the growth in demand, while consumer spending again rose solidly. Business fixed investment growth slowed from earlier in the recovery and increased at about the same pace as real GDP. Weak growth among our foreign trading partners restrained exports, and government purchases increased modestly after falling for most of the preceding five years.

Over the course of 2015, the economy added 2.7 million jobs, completing the strongest two years of job growth since 1999. In December, private-sector employment had grown for 70 consecutive months, the longest stretch of uninterrupted job gains on record, with a total of 13.8 million jobs added. During 2015, nonfarm job growth averaged 228,000 a month, a somewhat more moderate pace than during 2014, but similar to the strong pace of the three preceding years. The unemployment rate fell 0.6 percentage point during the 12 months through December, after falling a percentage point a year, on average, during the three preceding years (Figure 2-1).

Inflation remained low with consumer price inflation (CPI) at only 0.7 percent during the 12 months of 2015, reflecting a sharp decline in oil prices. Core CPI, which excludes food and energy, increased 2.1 percent, above the year-earlier rate of 1.6 percent. Real average hourly earnings of production and nonsupervisory workers rose 2.3 percent over the 12 months of 2015, as nominal wage growth exceeded price inflation.

Challenges remain for 2016, including uncertain prospects for global growth, constraints posed by slowing trend growth in the labor force due to demographic shifts, and the yet incomplete labor market recovery. Turmoil

Figure 2-1
Unemployment Rate, 1975–2015

Percent

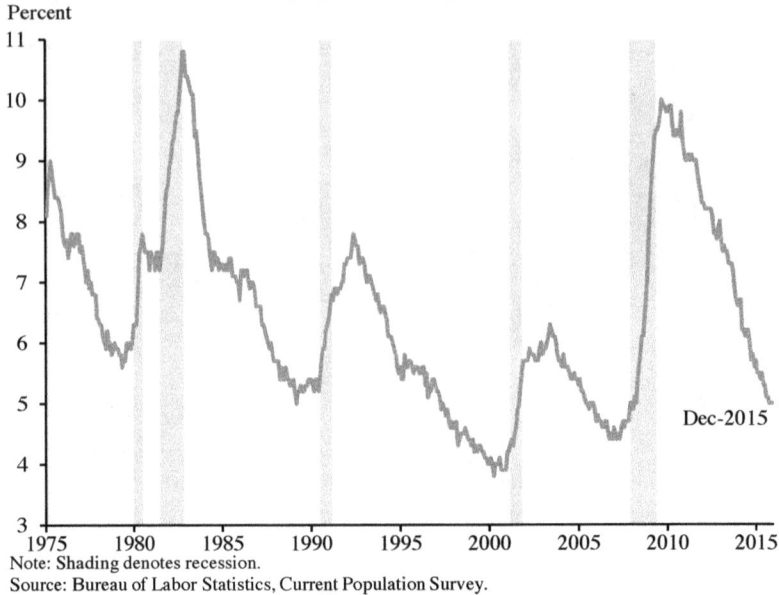

Note: Shading denotes recession.
Source: Bureau of Labor Statistics, Current Population Survey.

in stock markets around the world, and further sharp declines in oil prices in early 2016, underscore the risks facing the U.S. economy; in particular, in the energy-producing and export-intensive sectors. And yet, the labor market continues to recover with the unemployment rate declining to 4.9 percent in January 2016, its lowest level since February 2008.

The economic recovery in recent years has differed across labor and output measures. The labor market continued to strengthen and, by the end of 2015, the unemployment rate had fallen to half its recessionary peak, but real output growth, at 1.8 percent during the four quarters of 2015, was slower than its pace in recent years. As a consequence, labor productivity—measured as real output-per-hour—in the nonfarm sector has grown more slowly than its long-term trend thus far during this business cycle. The labor force participation rate has fallen largely due to the baby-boom cohorts moving into retirement, but some of the decline represents the continuation of the decades-long downward trend in the participation of prime-age males as well as the decline in participation of prime-age females since 2000.

While real GDP grew moderately during 2015, the quarterly pace of economic growth was uneven. First-quarter growth (0.6-percent annual rate) was held down by a labor dispute at the West coast ports and unusually cold weather.[1] The economy rebounded in the second quarter, growing at a 3.9-percent annual rate followed by more steady growth of 2.0 percent in the third quarter. Growth slowed again in the fourth quarter to 0.7 percent at an annual rate, weighed down by declines in inventory investment and exports.

The price of oil, as measured by the spot price of European light crude oil from the North Sea (known as Brent), fell to $37 per barrel at the end of December 2015, about a third of its level in June 2014 (Figure 2-2).

The oil-price decline from mid-2014 to the end of 2015 reflected both increased global supply of oil, including rising production in the United States, Saudi Arabia, and Iraq, and slower global economic growth. It is difficult to precisely separate the role of supply and demand, but the comparison to non-energy commodity prices highlights the mix of factors affecting oil prices. Non-energy commodity prices also declined over this period—a sign of weakening global demand. But the non-energy commodity price decline of about 25 percent was considerably less than the about 65-percent decline in oil prices, pointing to the role of oil supply in lowering prices. Lower oil prices affect the U.S. economy through numerous channels (CEA 2014). On balance, CEA estimates that lower oil prices directly boosted real GDP growth by 0.2 percentage point during 2015, despite the adverse impacts on domestic energy producers and manufacturers that sell to the energy sector (see Box 2-1). Relatedly, the decline in oil prices noticeably held down price inflation and supported real income growth in 2015. Oil and commodity prices continued to fall sharply in early 2016 and are likely to continue to affect consumers and energy producers.

Foreign growth slowed markedly in 2015, particularly in China and other emerging-market economies, with the International Monetary Fund's (IMF) October 2015 report estimating that world year-over-year growth was 3.1 percent in 2015, the slowest rate of global growth since 2009 (see Chapter 3 for more discussion). Spillovers from the slowing pace of China's growth affected many commodity-exporting countries. Slowing foreign growth sharply reduced U.S. exports, as the growth rate of our trade partners was 0.4 percentage points lower during the four quarters ending in 2015:Q3 (the latest available data) than during the year earlier period.

---

[1] Three snowstorms occurred during 2015:Q1 that were so severe that the National Climate Data Center rated them in the Northeast Snowfall Impact Scale (NESIS). NESIS scores are a function of the area affected by the snowstorm, the amount of snow, and the number of people living in the path of the storm (Kocin and Uccellini 2004). During the 59 years on record, 2015:Q1 was only the fourth time that a quarter was impacted by three or more NESIS-rated storms.

Figure 2-2
Oil and Commodity Prices, 2014–2015

Index (Jun-2014=100)

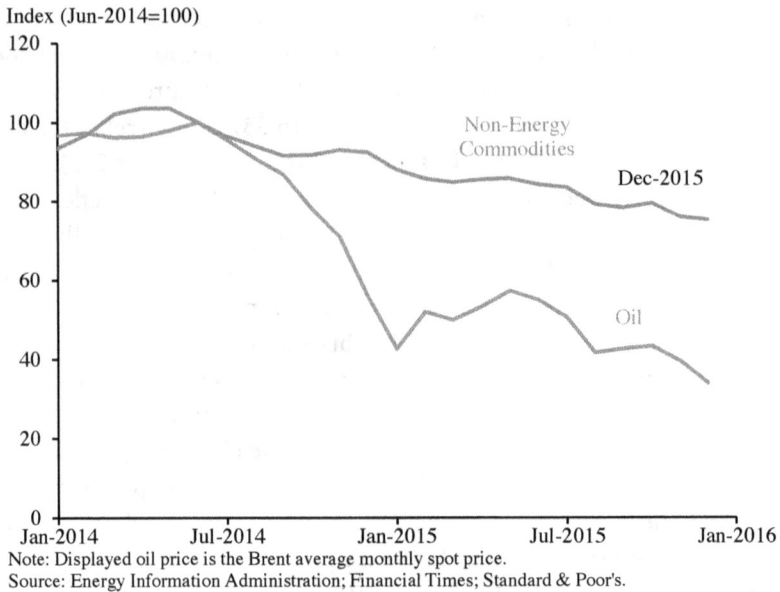

Note: Displayed oil price is the Brent average monthly spot price.
Source: Energy Information Administration; Financial Times; Standard & Poor's.

POLICY DEVELOPMENTS

Fiscal Policy

Fiscal restraint in the United States continued in fiscal year (FY) 2015 with the Federal budget deficit falling 0.3 percentage point to 2.5 percent of GDP, the lowest level since 2007 and below the average over the last 40 years. The deficit as a share of GDP has fallen by about three-fourths since 2009, the most rapid six-year deficit reduction since the demobilization after World War II (Figure 2-3). The additional deficit reduction in 2015 was through automatic stabilizers, such as the increase in tax collections as income rises, and was much less severe than the 1.9 percentage point a year decline in the deficit-to-GDP ratio during the three preceding years when changes in tax or spending policy were the primary driver.

The two-year Bipartisan Budget Act of 2013, passed in December 2013, helped provide fiscal-policy stability during FY 2014 and FY 2015. Since that time, a series of agreements—most recently the Bipartisan Budget Act of 2015—have avoided a Federal shutdown, partly relieved automatic Federal spending cuts known as sequestration, and relaxed the Federal debt limit. Government purchases, including consumption and gross investment, at the Federal as well as State and local levels, added modestly to overall

Box 2-1: Impact of Oil Price Declines on Spending and Production

The United States is a net importer of oil, so a decline in oil prices is generally expected to boost domestic real income and lower incomes in countries that are net exporters of oil, such as Saudi Arabia and Russia. Yet, U.S. net oil imports have fallen 63 percent in the last ten years due to both greater domestic production and lower consumption, so the U.S. economy is less sensitive to oil price movements today than in the past. Moreover, the direct impact of oil price changes on energy consumers and energy producers moves in opposite directions. The overall impact of oil price changes also depends on the sources of those price changes.[1] For example, if oil prices fall due to lower demand in a weakening global economy, this is likely to also coincide with a reduction in U.S. GDP growth, but it would be incorrect to infer that the oil price decline itself hurt U.S. GDP growth. In contrast, if the price of oil falls due to an increase in oil supply, such as from technological advances in oil extraction or improving geopolitical conditions in oil producing countries, lower oil prices would tend to increase U.S. GDP. This box analyzes the direct impact of the fall in the price of oil from mid-2014 to late 2015 on the U.S. economy, an exercise that is most informative when the oil price declines are driven primarily by an increase in oil supply.

Overall, CEA estimates, as shown in Table 2-i, that the decline in oil prices had the direct impact of boosting real GDP growth by 0.1 percentage point during 2014 and 0.2 percentage point during 2015. Considerable uncertainty surrounds these estimates of the direct effects of the oil price decline, and moreover, these estimates exclude indirect effects.

The boost to output and consumption from lower oil prices is largely due to the lower cost of imported oil. U.S. net imports of petro-

Table 2-i

Estimated Impact of Oil Price Declines on Output, 2014–2015

	Growth (Q4-to-Q4)		
	2014	2015	Cumulative Level
Total Impact	**0.1**	**0.2**	0.3
Contribution from:			
Consumption (via imported-oil savings)	0.1	0.5	0.6
Drilling and mining investment	0.0	-0.3	-0.3

Source: CEA calculations; Bureau of Economic Analysis; Energy Information Administration.

---

[1] See also Hamilton (2003) and Kilian (2014) for differing empirical assessments of the source of oil price shocks since the mid-1970s and how oil price shocks have affected the economy.

leum and products averaged 1.8 billion barrels per year in 2014 and 2015, so each $10 per barrel decline in the price of imports saved the U.S. economy about $18 billion per year, or about 0.1 percent of nominal GDP. In 2015 as a whole, the United States spent about $100 billion less on net imported oil than if prices had stayed at their mid-2014 level. In total, the net transfer of income to the United States depends on how much oil prices decline and how long those low prices persist. These savings are spread across all oil-using sectors, especially consumers for whom lower gasoline prices freed up income for other purchases. It may take time for consumers to make those additional purchases, so the timing of the additional spending may lag the declines in oil prices. In fact, the personal saving rate moved up around the start of 2015 when oil prices declined rapidly, but then consumer spending grew strongly in the middle of the year. As oil prices declined sharply in late 2015, the personal saving rate moved up back up in the fourth quarter, suggesting some delay again in the consumption response. CEA estimates that assuming all the savings on imported oil were spent within the year then they would add 0.5 percentage point to GDP growth in 2015 (shown in the "Consumption" line in Table 2-i). This direct estimate does not include additional effects like the multiplier associated with additional economic activity, the boost to consumer confidence, and the potential benefits of lower inflation for monetary policy management.

Figure 2-i
North American Oil Rig Count and Oil Price, 2000–2015

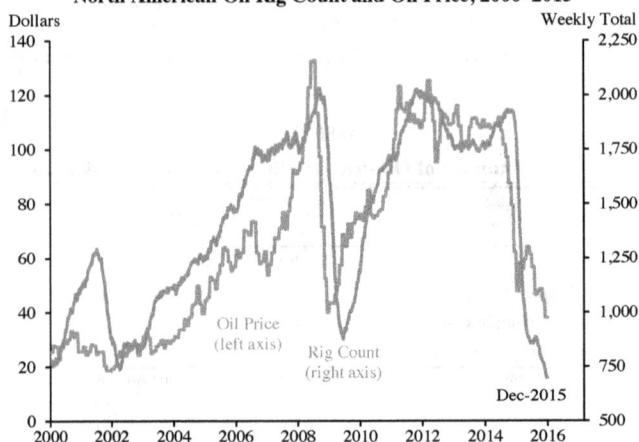

Note: Displayed oil price is the Brent average monthly spot price.
Source: Energy Information Administration; Baker Hughes Inc.

Roughly speaking, the decline in the price of domestically-produced oil sold to U.S. consumers has largely offsetting effects for American oil producers and consumers—although differences in how consumers and producers adjust to lower oil prices may differ enough for aggregate impacts from this channel to appear over shorter horizons. Thus, the primary boost to overall output comes from imported oil. However, the share of imported oil has declined as domestic production increased and domestic oil use fell, so the overall boost to the U.S. economy from this oil price decline is smaller than would have been the case historically.

Changes in oil prices also affect the amount of investment done by oil firms. Oil drilling and exploration dropped sharply in 2015 as shown in Figure 2-i, and these declines weighed down U.S. investment (and GDP) and are not reflected in the net-import savings discussed above. Oil drilling and exploration, as measured by the number of oil rigs in operation, peaked in September 2014 and dropped 62 percent by December 2015. In addition, investment in oil and mining equipment fell 40 percent during 2015. As shown in the "Drilling" line in Table 2-i, the cutback in this investment reduced real GDP growth by 0.3 percentage point in 2015, assuming that investment growth in the drilling sector would have been unchanged if the price had not fallen. In addition, this direct estimate excludes potential additional economic costs, including the multiplier effect and also spillovers from the stresses in credit markets associated with increased default risks of oil companies. On the

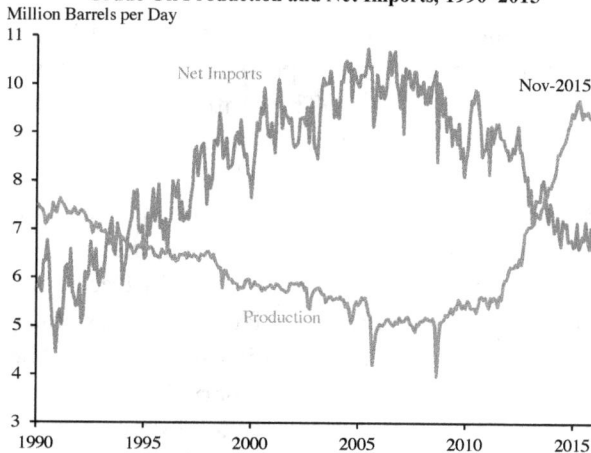

Figure 2-ii
Crude Oil Production and Net Imports, 1990–2015
Million Barrels per Day

Note: Data are not seasonally adjusted.
Source: Energy Information Administration, Petroleum Supply Monthly.

other hand, oil-using industries benefit from lower oil prices and might increase investment, an effect that is also not captured here.

The current direct estimate of a 0.2 percentage point increase in GDP growth in 2015 is well below the 1 percentage point boost implied by the econometric model used in earlier CEA analysis (CEA 2014).[2] One explanation for the difference is that the econometric models, which are estimated off past oil price changes, also pick up the indirect effects on demand described above. Moreover, any model which assumes a linear relationship between oil prices and output may be less applicable when oil prices fall below production costs. Price declines large enough to cause bankruptcies or large equity price declines in the energy sector could have additional negative impacts. Thinking more broadly about previous historical episodes, another explanation for the smaller boost to GDP from this oil price decline is that the United States now consumes less oil than it did in 1997 (CEA 2015c for an extensive discussion) and produces 4 million barrels a day more than in 2005, so that net oil imports are down (see Figure 2-ii). As a result, the boost to consumption from cheaper imported oil is smaller than in the past, and the impact on oil-sector investment is larger. Moreover, new technologies, such as hydraulic fracturing (fracking), may make investment even more sensitive to oil price changes. By this same logic the U.S. economy will be more resilient to possible future increases in the price of oil.

---

[2] The vector auto-regression in the earlier CEA report showed a range of GDP impacts from a 10-percent oil price change depending on the import share of oil. The lower end of the range, cited here, is consistent with the current import share.

output growth in calendar year 2015 (0.2 percentage point), shown in Figure 2-4, after subtracting an average of 0.4 percentage point a year from growth during the four years through 2014. The contribution of Federal purchases to real GDP growth is expected to increase further in 2016, a positive change reinforced by the recent Federal budget deal.

Federal. Having contracted substantially in recent years, Federal fiscal policy was less restrictive in FY 2015. The Consolidated and Further Continuing Appropriations Act, signed into law in December 2014, made the fiscal environment through the end of FY 2015 more stable (that is, compared with a string of short-term continuing resolutions). The Temporary Debt Limit Extension Act, signed in February 2014, suspended the debt ceiling through March 2015. When the Federal debt reached its limit on March 16, 2015, the U.S. Treasury resorted to "extraordinary measures" to function through October without exceeding the debt limit. As the new fiscal year approached on October 1 and budget negotiations began in Congress,

Figure 2-3
Federal Budget Deficit, 1950–2015

Percent of GDP

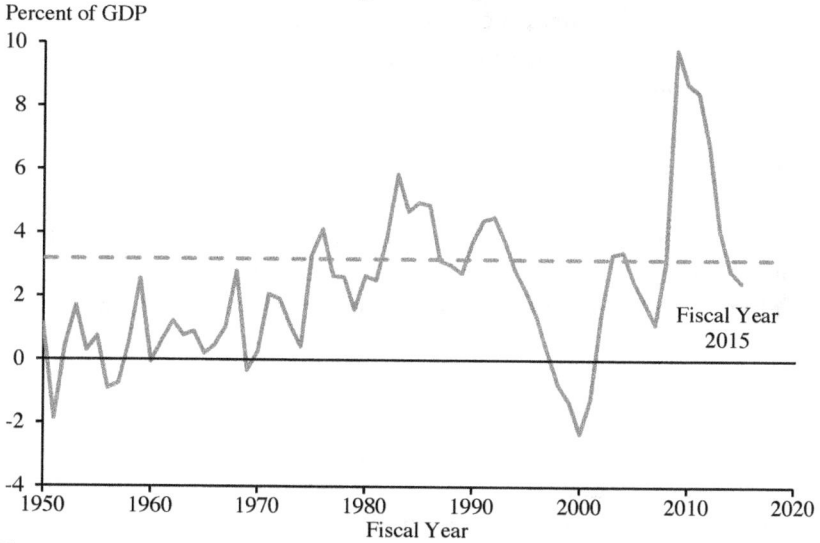

Fiscal Year

Note: Dashed line represents average over 1975–2014.
Source: Office of Management and Budget; Bureau of Economic Analysis, National Income and Product Accounts.

Figure 2-4
**Contribution of Government Purchases to
Real GDP Growth, 2011–2015**

Percentage Point, Annual Rate

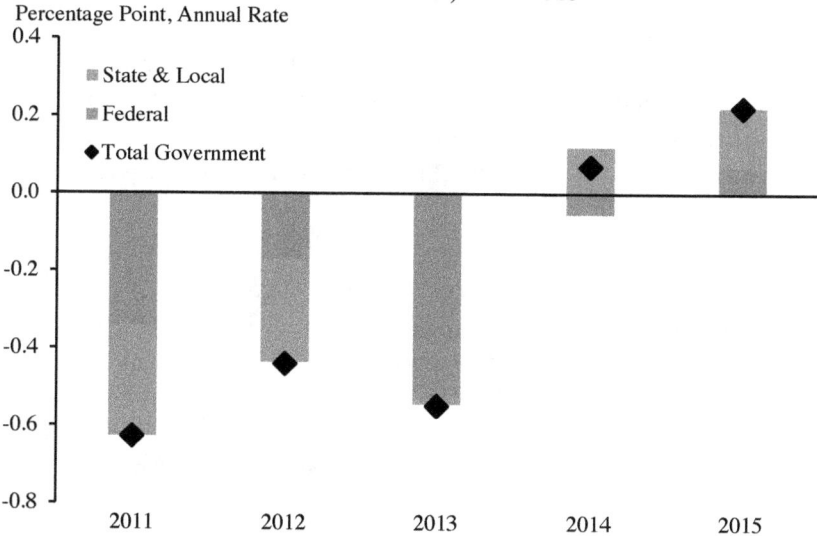

■ State & Local
■ Federal
◆ Total Government

Note: Contributions are computed using Q4-to-Q4 changes.
Source: Bureau of Economic Analysis; Haver Analytics.

there was some risk of a government shutdown, but a continuing resolution extended spending (at static levels) through December 11. Negotiations continued during the period covered by the continuing resolution, eventually resulting in the Bipartisan Budget Act of 2015 signed on November 2. That agreement suspended the debt ceiling again through March 15, 2017 and lifted sequester spending caps by $50 billion in FY 2016 and by $30 billion in FY 2017 (about 0.3 and 0.2 percent of GDP, respectively) split equally between defense and nondefense spending. The passage of the Consolidated Appropriations Act of 2016 in December 2015 set programmatic spending levels consistent with the new caps established by the budget agreement, including increases in investment in research and development, early education, and infrastructure. December legislation also made permanent a number of expiring tax provisions, including credits for research and development, small businesses, and low-income households. Absent any further changes in policy, the debt-to-GDP ratio is expected to rise steadily over the 10-year budget window, increasing from 76.5 percent of GDP at the end of FY 2016 to 87.6 percent at the end of FY 2026. The policies proposed in the President's Budget would stabilize the debt and put it on a declining path through 2025 when it reaches 75.2 percent of GDP.

State and Local. State and local government purchases (consumption plus gross investment) contributed positively, but weakly, to real GDP growth in 2015 for the second consecutive year following four years of negative contributions. The State and local share of nominal GDP fell from its historical peak of 13.0 percent in 2009 to 10.9 percent in 2015, a level not seen since the late 1980s as State and local governments cut their purchases in the face of budget pressures (Box 2-2).

In 2015, State and local government purchases were about 60-percent larger than Federal purchases and four times larger than Federal nondefense purchases (Figure 2-5). In a broad view of fiscal policy, changes in State and local purchases can be as important as changes in Federal purchases.

Monetary Policy

In December 2015, the Federal Open Market Committee (FOMC) increased the target range for the federal funds rate by 0.25 percentage point, ending seven years at its effective lower bound, and maintained that range in January of this year. The FOMC's decision to tighten monetary policy was based on its judgment that labor markets had improved considerably and that it was reasonably confident that inflation would move up over the medium term to its 2-percent objective. When it raised the federal funds rate—an event widely referred to as "lift off"—the FOMC stated that it "expects that economic conditions will evolve in a manner that will warrant

Figure 2-5
Government Purchases as Share of Nominal GDP, 1948–2015

Percent

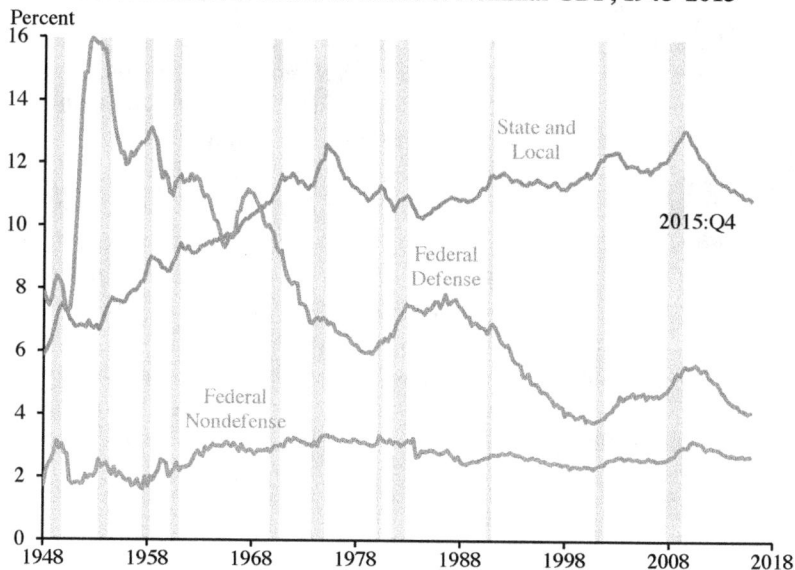

State and
Local

2015:Q4

Federal
Defense

Federal
Nondefense

Source: Bureau of Economic Analysis; Haver Analytics.

Figure 2-6
Forecast of Federal Funds Rate at Year End 2015

Percent

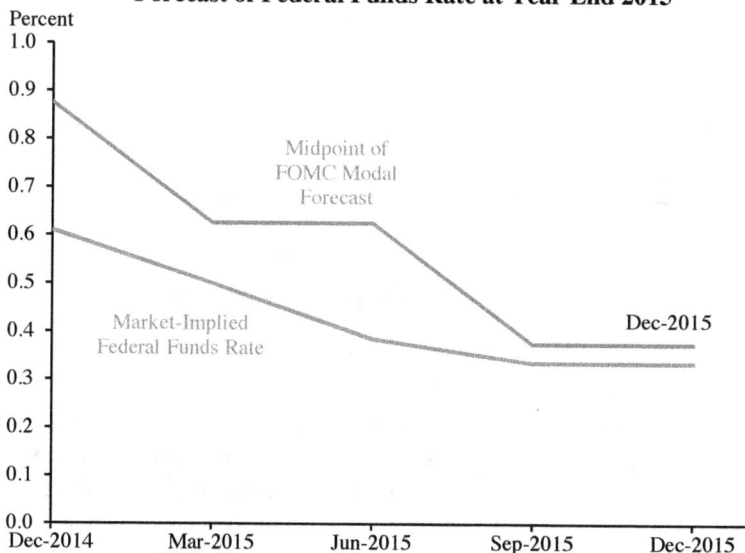

Midpoint of
FOMC Modal
Forecast

Dec-2015

Market-Implied
Federal Funds Rate

Note: Market-implied rate is computed using federal funds rate futures contracts.
Source: Bloomberg Professional Service; CEA calculations.

Box 2-2: Challenges in the State and Local Sector

During the current expansion, growth in State and local purchases has been the weakest of any business-cycle recovery in the post-World War II period (Figure 2-iii). During the four quarters of 2010, State and local purchases subtracted 0.5 percentage point from GDP growth, and then subtracted about another 0.3 percentage point in both 2011 and 2012. Spending in this sector stabilized in 2013 and added modestly to GDP growth in 2014 and 2015. State and local governments also cut jobs early in the recovery. Beginning in 2013, though, this trend began to shift. State and local governments have added 210,000 jobs since January 2013. Even so, employment in this sector remains 528,000 below its previous high in 2008, with about 40 percent of this net job loss in educational services. The 1.4-percent decline in education employment exceeded the 0.9-percent decline in the school-age population (ages 5 to 19) over the 2008-14 period. This mismatch implies a rising student-teacher ratio.

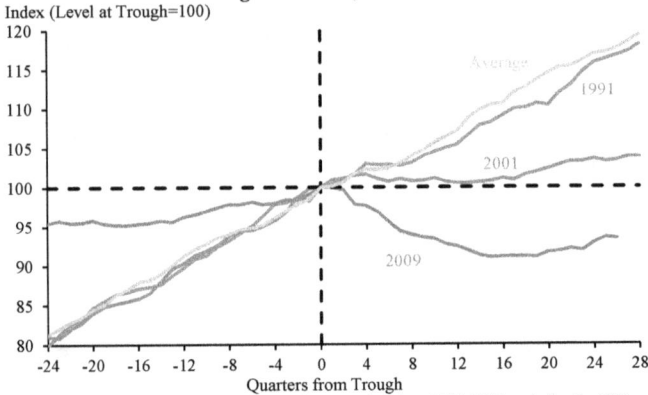

Figure 2-iii
Real State and Local Government Purchases During Recoveries, 1960–2015

Index (Level at Trough=100)

Note: "Average" indicates average across recessionary periods from 1960–2007, excluding the 1980 recession due to overlap with the 1981–1982 recession.
Source: Bureau of Economic Analysis, National Income and Product Accounts; National Bureau of Economic Research; CEA calculations.

Despite some recovery in 2015, there are still factors likely to restrain State and local spending growth. State and local governments continue to spend more than they collect in revenues and their aggregate deficit during the first three quarters of 2015 amounted to nearly 1 percent of nominal GDP. This deficit has shrunk, however, during the recovery (Figure 2-iv). During 2015, State and local expenditures (including transfers and interest payments, as well as purchases) were roughly flat at about 14 percent of GDP, and revenues held at about

13 percent of GDP. Until 1990, State and local governments only ran deficits during recessions.[1] Since then, State and local governments have frequently run deficits.

Unfunded pension obligations place a heavy burden on State and local government finances. The size of these unfunded pension liabilities relative to State and local receipts ballooned immediately after the recession and remains elevated at a level that was about 65 percent of a year's revenue in the first three quarters of 2015 (Figure 2-v).

Figure 2-iv
State and Local Government Surplus as
Percent of Nominal GDP, 1947–2015

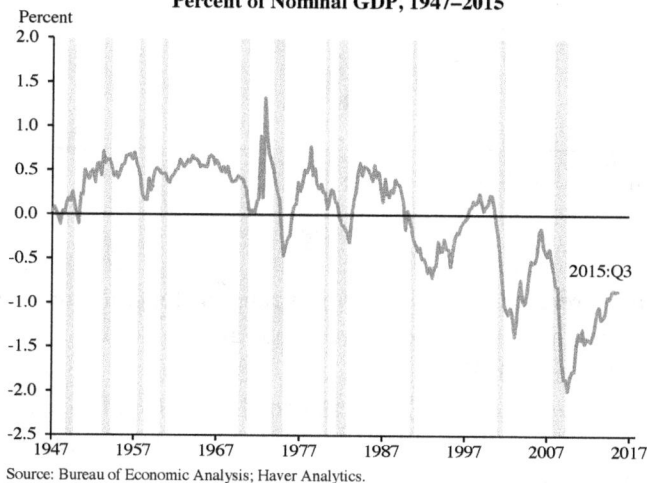

Percent

Source: Bureau of Economic Analysis; Haver Analytics.

---

[1] 49 out of 50 states have constitutions or statutes mandating a balanced budget and many local governments have similar provisions. This does not prevent them from running deficits. Many of those balanced budget statutes apply only to the operating budget, while deficits may be allowed on their capital accounts. Also, spending from rainy day funds" appears as a deficit on the government balance sheet in the national income and product accounts.

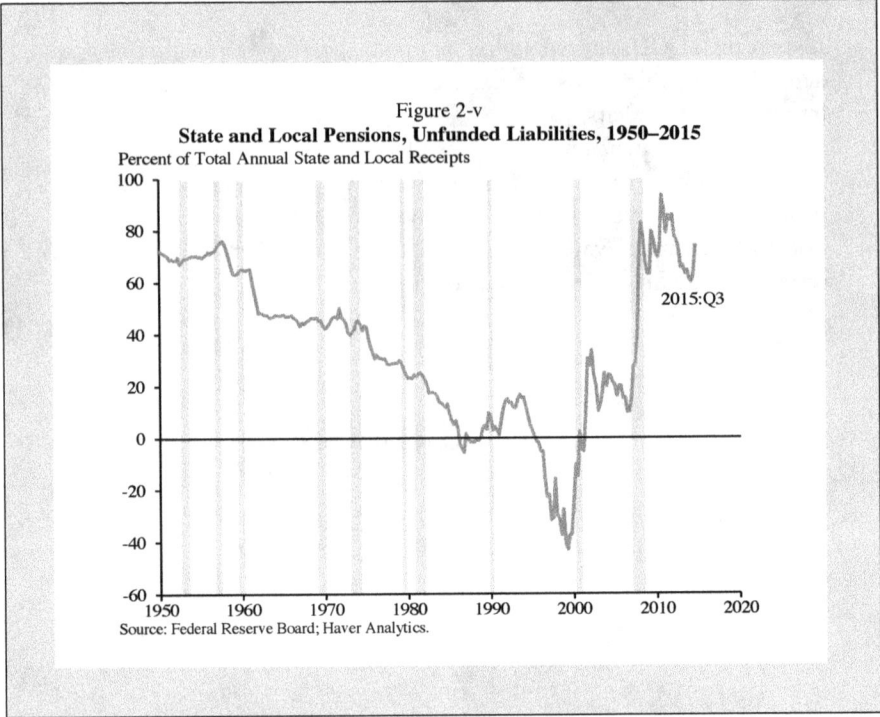

Figure 2-v
State and Local Pensions, Unfunded Liabilities, 1950–2015
Percent of Total Annual State and Local Receipts

2015:Q3

Source: Federal Reserve Board; Haver Analytics.

only gradual increases in the federal funds rate; the federal funds rate is likely to remain, for some time, below levels that are expected to prevail in the longer run" (FOMC 2015).

Over the course of 2015, forecasts for the year-end federal funds rate from both monetary policymakers and financial markets were revised down, as shown in Figure 2-6, implying a later date of "lift off" and fewer rate increases in 2015. By the time the FOMC voted to raise rates in December, financial markets had largely anticipated the increase. Moreover, "lift off" had already largely been incorporated in many investors' expectations about longer-term interest rates, stock prices, and the dollar. Accordingly, changes in yields on 10-year Treasury notes (Figure 2-37) and 30-year mortgage rates were small in the immediate wake of "lift off."

The size of the Federal Reserve's balance sheet at the end of 2015 was $4.4 trillion—more than five times its size in 2007, reflecting several large-scale asset purchase programs (quantitative easing) from 2008 to 2014, which are estimated to have lowered long-term interest rates by about a percentage point (Engen et al. 2015 and the references therein). Moreover, the Federal Reserve believes the larger stock of Federal Reserve asset holdings has continued to influence long-term interest rates even after the end of new purchases.[2] The increase in the Federal Reserve assets has coincided with a large increase in reserves held by banks. In an environment of super-abundant reserves, the Federal Reserve has had to change the way in which it raises the federal funds rate. In its communications over the course of 2014 and 2015, the FOMC indicated that the tools that the Federal Reserve intended to use during policy normalization would include interest paid on reserves and overnight reverse repurchase agreements.[3]

In recent years, FOMC participants have tended to lower their forecasts for the longer-run level for the federal funds rate. The revisions have been consistent with downward trends in long-term interest rates in U.S. and global financial markets.

Labor Market

The labor market continued to improve rapidly in 2015, with many measures of labor-market performance now recovered to or near their pre-recession levels. Over the course of the year, the economy added 2.7 million jobs, completing the strongest two years of job growth since 1999. American businesses have now added 13.8 million jobs over 70 straight months through December, extending the longest streak on record. The unemployment rate had fallen by half from its peak during the recession to 5.0 percent in December, its lowest level since April 2008. The robust pace of job growth has translated into broad-based gains, but some slack remains in the labor market, including a somewhat elevated level of part-time employment and a depressed level of labor force participation. Moreover, the pace of nominal wage growth picked up only modestly during 2015.

Private employment increased by 2.6 million jobs during the 12 months of 2015, after rising by 2.8 million jobs in 2014 (Figure 2-7). About half of the jobs in 2015 came from professional and business services as well as education and health services, both of which have been major drivers of job growth in this recovery. These sectors account for a large part of growth despite the fact that they make up only about 35 percent of private-sector jobs in the economy. Education and health services added 692,000 jobs in

---

[2] Federal Reserve Chair Yellen (2011) has stated that "the underlying theory, in which asset prices are directly linked to the outstanding quantity of assets, dates back to the early 1950s … Consequently, the term structure of interest rates can be influenced by exogenous shocks in supply and demand at specific maturities. Purchases of longer-term securities by the central bank can be viewed as a shift in supply that tends to push up the prices and drive down the yields on those securities."

[3] See Ihrig et al. (2015) for a discussion of how interest rates paid on excess reserves and overnight reverse repurchase agreements have replaced open market operations—the buying and selling of Treasury securities—as the way in which the Federal Reserve achieves its target policy rate.

Figure 2-7
12-Month Change in Nonfarm Payroll Employment, 2007–2015

Millions, Not Seasonally Adjusted

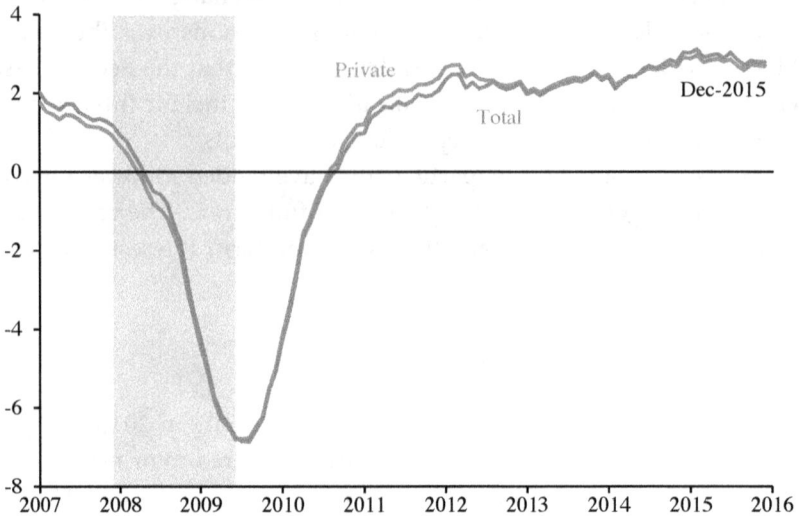

Note: Total excludes temporary decennial Census workers. Shading denotes recession.
Source: Bureau of Labor Statistics, Current Employment Statistics.

2015—its largest one-year increase on record—and professional and business services added 621,000 jobs, consistent with its growth over the course of this recovery.

Despite overall strength, particularly in the services sector, some industries faced specific headwinds that held down growth in 2015. Slower job growth in the oil-sensitive mining and logging sector and the export-sensitive manufacturing sector can more than account for the modest slowdown in job growth during 2015. Mining and logging lost 133,000 jobs in 2015, largely due to industry cutbacks in the face of the sharp fall in oil prices and has reverted to its 2011 level of employment. Manufacturing also experienced a weak year of job growth, adding only 33,000 jobs, likely reflecting the global economic slowdown dampening demand for U.S. exports. Given that exports are comprised disproportionately of goods and manufactured products, a slowdown in exports affects goods-producing jobs more than the service sector.

The labor market's improvement was also apparent in the continued rapid decline of the unemployment rate. By December 2015, the unemployment rate had fallen to 5.0 percent, falling an average of 0.8 percentage point a year from 2010 to 2015, below its pre-recession average of 5.3 percent.[4]

---

[4] Throughout this section, pre-recession average refers to the average from December 2001 to December 2007.

Figure 2-8
Actual and Consensus Forecast Unemployment Rate, 2008–2020

Percent of Labor Force

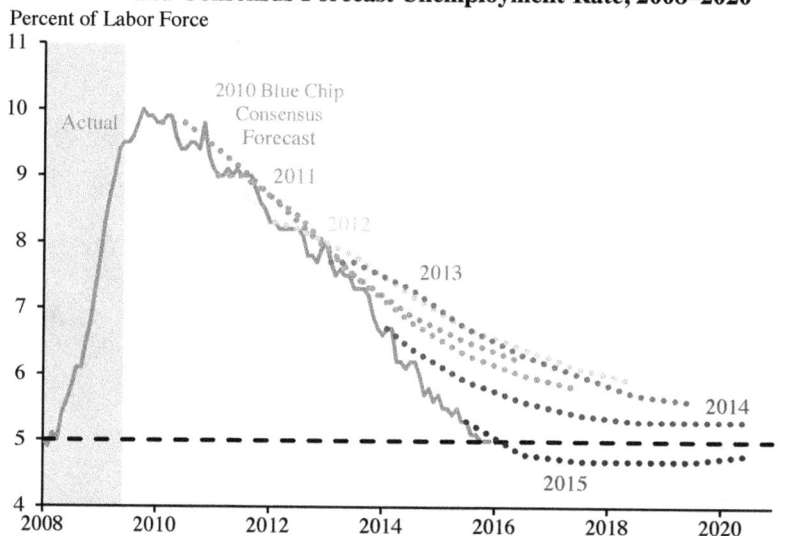

Note: Annual forecasts are current as of March of the stated year. Black dashed line represents December 2015 value (5.0 percent). Shading denotes recession.
Source: Bureau of Labor Statistics, Current Population Survey; Blue Chip Economic Indicators.

The unemployment rate reached this level before most forecasters expected. As of March 2014, economists generally expected the unemployment rate to remain above 5.0 percent at least until 2020 (Figure 2-8). The unexpectedly low level of the unemployment rate, along with little pickup in inflation, also led many economists to revise down the "natural" rate of unemployment. Still it appears that the unemployment rate is almost back to normal levels and the pace of decline is expected to moderate next year.

Although the overall unemployment rate is now below its pre-recession average and mirrors other indicators of labor market strength, some broader indicators of labor market slack remained above their pre-recession levels. For example, the long-term unemployment rate was 1.3 percent in December, the lowest it has been since 2008 but above its pre-recession average of 1.0 percent (Figure 2-9). Despite this continued elevation, the number of long-term unemployed fell faster in 2015 than the number of short-term unemployed. In 2015, the long-term unemployment rate fell by 0.5 percentage point, accounting for over 85 percent of the decline in the overall unemployment rate, though the long-term unemployed make up about one-quarter of the unemployed. If the number of long-term unemployed continues to fall at the same rate as it has over the past year, it will reach its pre-recession average in 2016.

Figure 2-9
Unemployment Rate by Duration, 1990–2015

Percent of Labor Force

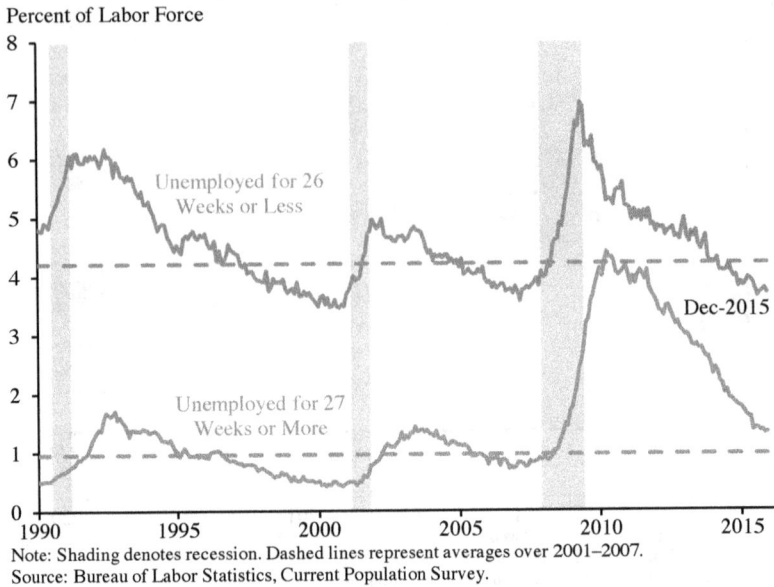

Note: Shading denotes recession. Dashed lines represent averages over 2001–2007.
Source: Bureau of Labor Statistics, Current Population Survey.

Similarly, the share of the labor force working part-time for economic reasons, while falling steadily, remains above its pre-recession average and could indicate continued underutilization of labor. Between December 2007 and December 2009, the share of the labor force usually working part-time rose from 16.1 to 17.9 percent, driven by a large rise in the share of people working part-time for economic reasons. As the recovery progressed, the share of the labor force working part-time began to recede (Figure 2-10).[5] In 2015, the share of the labor force working part-time for economic reasons continued to fall, declining 0.5 percentage point. As of December, the rate stood at 3.8 percent, 2.2 percentage points below its peak in 2010, but still above its pre-recession average of 3.0 percent.

The persistence in the rate of part-time work for economic reasons, especially relative to other measures of slack, is largely responsible for the continued elevation of the U-6 "underemployment" rate. The

---

[5] Care must be taken when comparing the share of workers who are part-time for economic reasons before and after the 1994 redesign of the Current Population Survey. CEA used the multiplicative adjustment factors reported by Polivka and Miller (1998) in order to place the pre-1994 estimates of the part-time for economic reasons rate on a comparable basis with post-redesign estimates. For the part-time series for which Polivka and Miller do not report suitable adjustment factors, the pre- and post-redesign series were spliced by multiplying the pre-1994 estimates by the ratio of the January 1994 rate to the December 1993 rate. This procedure generates similar results to the Polivka and Miller factors for series for which multiplicative factors are available.

Figure 2-10
Rates of Part-Time Work, 1960–2015

Percent of Labor Force

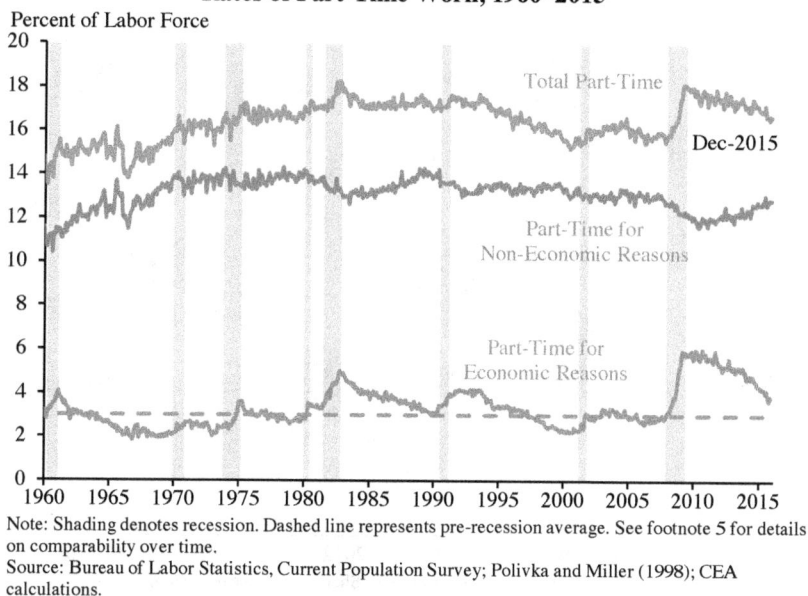

Note: Shading denotes recession. Dashed line represents pre-recession average. See footnote 5 for details on comparability over time.
Source: Bureau of Labor Statistics, Current Population Survey; Polivka and Miller (1998); CEA calculations.

underemployment rate uses a broader concept of labor market slack than the unemployment rate, including discouraged workers who have given up on looking for a job, those marginally attached to the labor force, and those employed part-time for economic reasons. Although it has recovered 90 percent from its peak during the recession, as of December 2015, it stood at 9.9 percent. During the 12 months of 2015, the U-6 rate declined 1.5 percentage point (Figure 2-11).

The labor force participation rate (LFPR) edged down over the year, by 0.1 percentage point, roughly in line with what one would have expected based on shifting demographics. Throughout the recovery and following the longer-term trend of population aging, the decline in the working-age share of the population has pushed down the LFPR. Between the first quarter of 2009 and the fourth quarter of 2015, the LFPR fell 3.2 percentage points. CEA estimates that more than half of this decline was due to the aging of the baby-boom generation into retirement (Figure 2-12). These demographic-related declines will become steeper in the near term, as the peak of the baby-boom generation retires. Between the first quarter of 2009 and the fourth quarter of 2013, about a sixth of the participation-rate decline was due to cyclical factors indicated by the high unemployment rates that caused potential job-seekers to delay entry into the labor force or become discouraged. The cyclical contribution to the participation decline has eased in recent years to

Figure 2-11
Alternative Measures of Labor Force Underutilization, 2007–2015

Percent of Labor Force

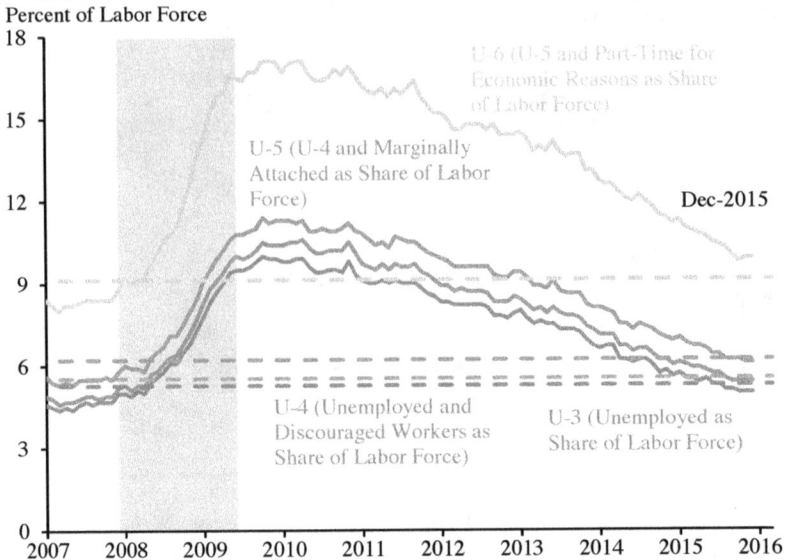

Note: Dashed lines represent pre-recession averages. Shading denotes recession.
Source: Bureau of Labor Statistics, Current Population Survey.

Figure 2-12
Labor Force Participation Decomposition, 2009–2015

Percent of Civilian Non-Institutional Population Aged 16+

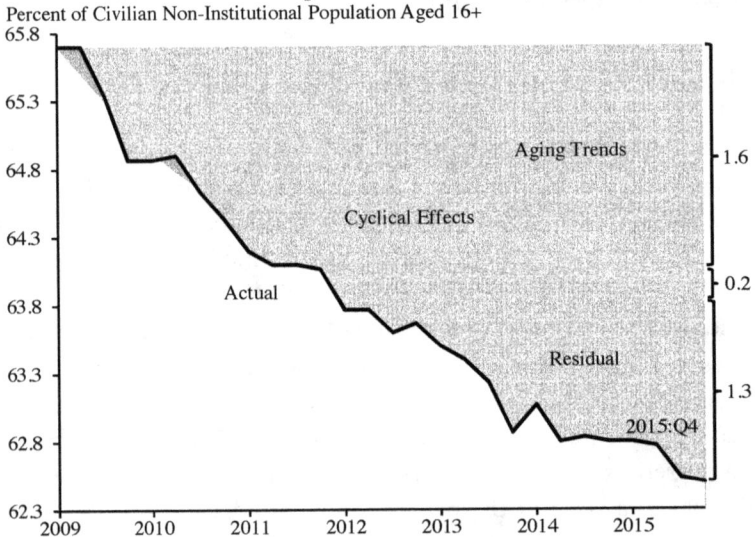

Source: Haver Analytics; Social Security Administration; Bureau of Labor Statistics; CEA calculations.

less than a tenth of the overall decline in participation as the economy has recovered, and is likely to ease further as the unemployment rate continues to decline. The remaining 40 percent of the decline in the participation rate since 2009 is unrelated to population aging or changes in the unemployment rate. This "residual" likely reflects structural factors like the longstanding downward trend in participation among prime-age workers and other cyclical factors, such as the high levels of long-term unemployment in the Great Recession, that are not fully captured in the unemployment rate. In 2015 the additional drag from unexplained factors largely offset the boost to participation from the cyclical recovery. In light of ongoing demographic shifts and longer-term trends, the participation rate is expected to decline modestly in 2016, even as cyclical factors recede further. The Administration has proposed policies to support labor force participation through more flexible workplaces and paid leave, expanded high-quality pre-school, increased subsidies for child care, and a wage insurance system that would encourage reentry into work (Box 2-8).

As the recovery in the labor market progresses, the pace of job growth consistent with a strong overall labor market is likely to fall as the unemployment rate begins to plateau, particularly in light of demographic patterns (Box 2-3).

OUTPUT

Real GDP grew 1.8 percent over the four quarters of 2015, somewhat below its pace in recent years. GDP grew at a similar pace as gross domestic output (GDO)—a more accurate measure of output than GDP—during the four quarters through 2015:Q3, which is the most recent quarter of GDO data, (Figure 2-13). Gross domestic output, discussed more in Box 2-4, is a newly published aggregate calculated as the "average of real GDP and real gross domestic income."

The overall composition of demand during 2015 shows that most of the growth was accounted for by the household spending sectors: consumer spending and residential investment, while contributions from the other sectors were small and generally offsetting. Residential investment was the fastest-growing major component of demand increasing 9.0 percent during the four quarters of the year, and contributing 0.3 percentage point to the four-quarter growth of GDP. Consumer spending, which comprises about two-thirds of GDP, increased 2.6 percent and can account for all the year's output growth. In addition, sales of new cars and light trucks hit 17.4 million in 2015, the highest level on record.

Box 2-3: Expectations for Future Job Growth

Given the progress of the labor market recovery as well as ongoing population aging, "steady state" job growth—the level consistent with a stable, low unemployment rate—is lower than the robust growth seen over the past several years. As the unemployment rate reaches a low level, it is unlikely to continue declining at the same pace as earlier in the recovery and could begin to plateau. Thus, the economy would not need to add as many jobs to maintain a strong overall labor market. In fact, CEA estimates that only 78,000 jobs a month would be needed in 2016 to keep the unemployment rate unchanged at 5.0 percent (top middle cell in Table 2-ii) if labor force participation declined in line with demographics. In contrast, if job gains were 141,000 a month in 2016—still well below the pace in 2015—and participation declined with its aging trend, the unemployment rate would be expected to fall another 0.5 percentage point by 2016:Q4. In reality, the relationship between jobs and the unemployment rate could differ for a variety of reasons, including that the two series are drawn from different surveys that are subject to different measurement errors.

Both male and female labor force participation have been falling on an age-adjusted basis (For men, this has been happening since the 1950s; for women, since 2000). In the business cycle from 2000 to 2007, the labor force participation rate fell 0.15 percentage point a year, during a period when the demographics of aging exerted little downward force on the aggregate participation rate. If this were to continue, then only 51,000 jobs a month would be needed to stabilize the unemployment rate.

If instead, there were enough cyclical improvement to keep the labor force participation rate constant in 2016, offsetting any aging and other trends, then more job growth would be needed for each level of the unemployment rate. Even if the unemployment rate falls to 4.5 percent and there is a cyclical rebound in labor force participation, the economy would only need to add 190,000 jobs a month, a slower pace than during the past two years. Thus, a slower pace of job growth in 2016 would be consistent with a normalizing and strong labor market.

Table 2-ii

Job Growth Consistent with Unemployment and Participation Paths

(Thousands, Monthly Average in 2016)

	Labor Force Participation Rate		
Unemployment Rate	Flat	Falls with Aging	Aging & Secular Declines
Flat	127	78	51
Falls 0.5 percentage point	190	141	114

Source: Bureau of Labor Statistics; Social Security Administration; CEA calculations.

Business fixed investment grew 3.1 percent, with strong growth in intellectual property, but slow growth in equipment and structures, which was held back by investment in the drilling sector amid low oil prices. Inventory investment added almost a percentage point to growth at an annual rate in the first quarter of 2015, but subtracted almost as much during the second half of the year. Manufacturing production continued to expand, but at a slower pace than in 2014. Domestic motor vehicle assemblies grew 2.5 percent during the four quarters averaging 12.1 million units in 2015, their highest level since 2003.

Growth in domestic demand was resilient in 2015, though weaker foreign growth was a headwind. The aggregate of consumption and fixed investment, known as private domestic final purchases (PDFP), also rose faster than overall output at 2.7 percent in 2015 (Figure 2-13). The solid pace of PDFP growth in 2015, which is typically a better predictor of the next quarter's future output growth than current output growth, suggests that near-term U.S. growth prospects are positive. Nevertheless, CEA expects that the components of real GDP that are not in PDFP, such as net exports, will hold back overall real GDP growth next year. In particular, weaker foreign growth likely will continue to weigh on net exports. Real exports decreased 0.8 percent in 2015, compared with 2.4-percent growth in 2014 and 5.2-percent growth in 2013.

Figure 2-13
Real Growth in GDP, Private Domestic Final Purchases (PDFP), and Gross Domestic Output (GDO), 2007–2015

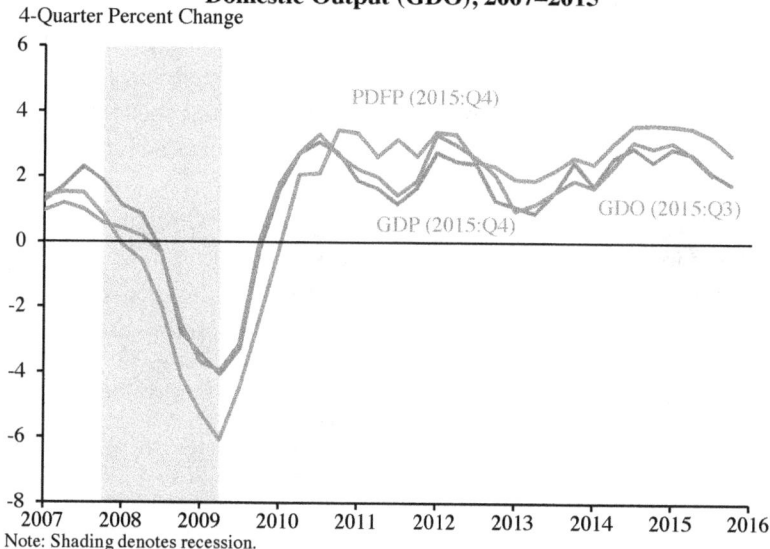

4-Quarter Percent Change

Note: Shading denotes recession.
Source: Bureau of Economic Analysis.

Consumer Spending

Real consumer spending increased 2.6 percent during the four quarters of 2015, somewhat below the 3.2-percent growth last year. Moderate spending growth was accompanied by stronger growth in real disposable income, due in part to the direct impact of lower oil prices (see Box 2-1), as well as by upbeat consumer sentiment and earlier gains in household wealth. Low interest rates and improving access to credit, particularly auto loans, also supported consumer spending. Overall, the personal saving rate has largely been fairly stable at around 5 percent of disposable personal income since the beginning of 2013, implying that consumer spending growth has largely tracked real income growth (Figure 2-14).

Growth was strong for real household purchases of durable goods (5.2 percent). Growth was moderate for nondurables (2.6 percent) and services (2.2 percent). As discussed above in Box 2-1, CEA estimates that the direct impact of the decline in oil prices via its reduction in net imported oil costs since mid-2014 boosted consumer spending growth by 0.7 percentage point in 2015 following about 0.1 percentage point in 2014.[6]

Light motor vehicle sales rose to 17.4 million units in 2015, the highest level on record and the sixth consecutive yearly increase. Sales trended up during the year, near 18 million units at an annual rate in the fourth quarter. Motor vehicle assemblies also increased from the first to the second half of the year and, at year end, inventory-to-sales ratios were near their long-term averages. Between 2007 and 2014, the average age of the fleet of private light motor vehicles rose from 10.0 to 11.4 years, likely reflecting an increase in vehicle quality as well as some delay in new purchases during the recession. If so, replacement demand—in addition to ongoing recovery in labor markets and income growth—should support new vehicle sales during 2016.

Consumer sentiment improved noticeably around the start of 2015 as gasoline prices declined sharply, and remained more optimistic in 2015 than at any point in the recovery.

In 2015, the University of Michigan's Index of Consumer Sentiment moved back in line with its levels before the recession and the Conference Board Index, while still somewhat lower than before the recession, was also at its highest level in the recovery (Figure 2-15). Relatedly, the recovery in

---

[6]Note that the estimated boost to spending in Box 2-1 is somewhat smaller since those are contributions to GDP growth and PCE is only 68 percent of GDP. Some of the boost to consumer spending growth from lower oil prices may be missing in the official data, since BEA is unable to remove gasoline sales at non-gasoline establishments, such as Big Box retailers, in its translation of the retail sales data. Sharp declines in gasoline prices make the real outlays at these establishments, which are all treated as non-gasoline spending, look weaker than they actually are. CEA estimates that this measurement error is understating real PCE growth by about 0.1 percentage point during 2015.

Figure 2-14
Personal Saving Rate, 2000–2015

Percent

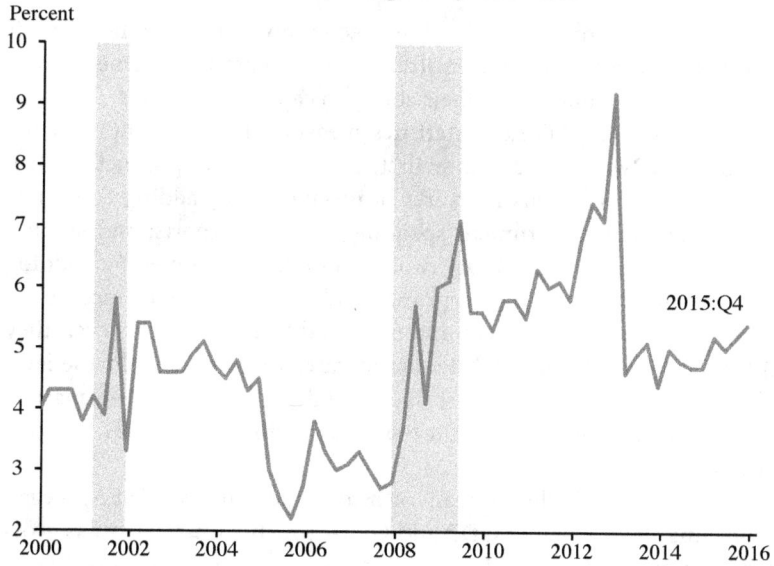

Source: Bureau of Economic Analysis; Haver Analytics.

Figure 2-15
Consumer Sentiment, 2006–2015

Diffusion Index

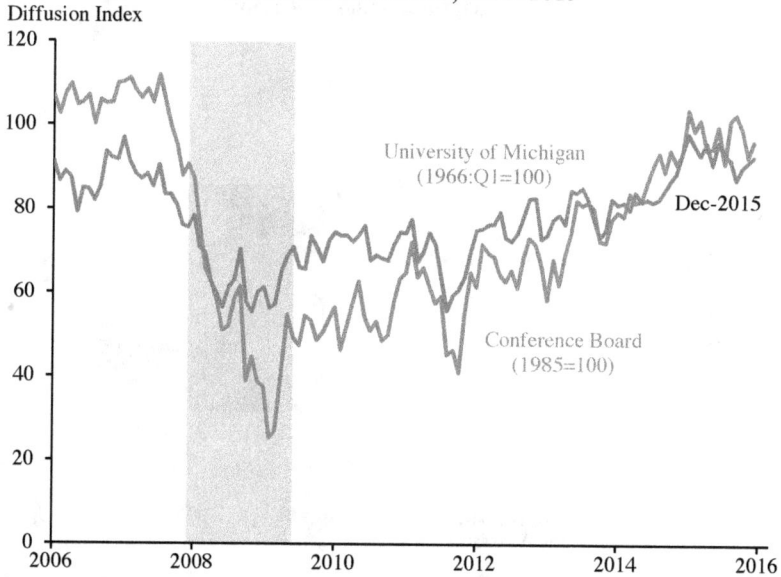

Source: The Conference Board; University of Michigan; Haver Analytics.

Box 2-4: A Better Measure of Output: Gross Domestic Output (GDO)

Measuring the strength of the economy can be difficult as it depends on surveys and administrative source data that are necessarily imperfect and incomplete in their ability to capture a complex, dynamic, and large economy. Official statistics measure the total output of the economy in two distinct ways: first, gross domestic product (GDP), which cumulates various measures of production by adding consumption, investment, government spending, and net exports; and second, gross domestic income (GDI), which cumulates incomes by adding labor compensation, business profits, and other sources of income. In theory, these two measures of output should be identical; however, they differ in practice because of measurement error. For example, the level of GDP was about 1-percent less than GDI during the first three quarters of 2015, though over longer time periods neither measure is typically stronger or weaker.[1]

In July 2015, the Bureau of Economic Analysis (BEA) began publishing the average of GDP and GDI—which CEA refers to as gross domestic output (GDO). Real GDO growth is often close to real GDP growth, but differences can be important. For example, GDO slowed more in 2007 than GDP and gave an earlier signal of the impending severe recession.

Figure 2-vi
Average GDP Revision, 1994–2013

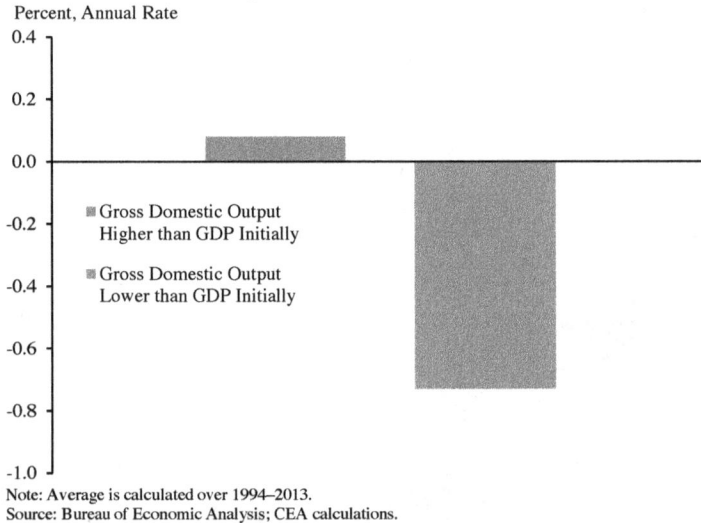

Percent, Annual Rate

- Gross Domestic Output Higher than GDP Initially
- Gross Domestic Output Lower than GDP Initially

Note: Average is calculated over 1994–2013.
Source: Bureau of Economic Analysis; CEA calculations.

---

[1] The fourth-quarter estimate of GDI was not published when this *Report* went to press.

BEA revises the official statistics on output several times because the first estimates within months of a quarter's end use incomplete and preliminary data—an unavoidable tradeoff for getting a quick read on economic activity. Research has shown that GDO can be especially helpful in predicting future revisions to GDP, and thus may improve CEA's ability to assess current economic conditions (CEA 2015a). In fact, when GDO growth is initially estimated to be faster than GDP growth, GDP growth tends to revise up and vice versa (Figure 2-vi).[2] Through the third quarter of 2015, GDP and GDO grew 2.2 percent and 2.0 percent, respectively, from a year earlier.

GDO also sheds light on recent economic anomalies, such as the weakness in first-quarter GDP growth in recent years. When initial estimates showed a decline in real GDP in 2015:Q1, some analysts argued first-quarter growth was being systematically understated because of incomplete adjustment for seasonal changes (referred to as "residual seasonality"). One sign of a measurement problem for the 2005-10 interval was that estimates of first-quarter GDI (and thus GDO) growth at the time were less depressed than was first-quarter GDP growth (Figure 2-vii). In 2015, the initial estimate of first-quarter GDO growth was again

Figure 2-vii
Average Output Growth by Calendar Quarter, 2005–2014
Estimates 3 Months After Quarter's End

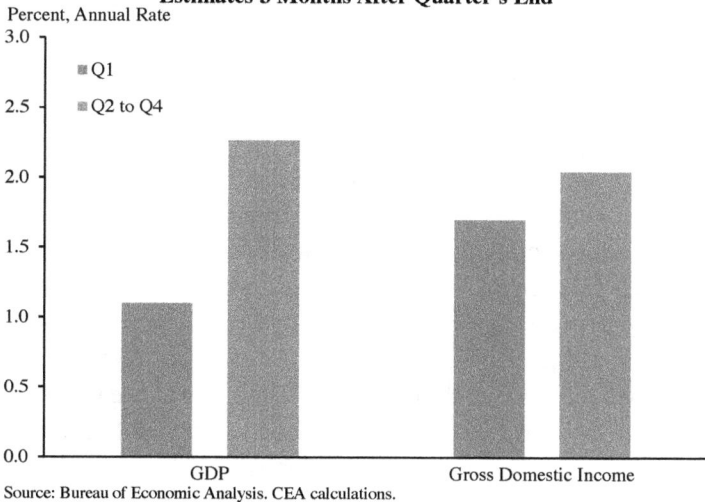

Source: Bureau of Economic Analysis. CEA calculations.

---

[2] The analysis in Figure 2-vi and Figure 2-vii uses the BEA's third estimate of GDP, which is published three months after a quarter's end. This data release also includes either the first (in the fourth quarter) or second estimate of GDI.

above GDP growth. In fact, at the annual revision in July, BEA revisited its seasonal adjustment and incorporated revised source data, which led to an upward revision in 2015:Q1 GDP growth.

It has long been the practice in many economic analyses, including those at CEA, to combine product- and income-side measures of output as a way to reduce measurement error and gain a more accurate picture of the economy. In fact, CEA began using an average of GDP and GDI with the 1997 *Economic Report to the President*. No single measure of the economy is perfect. Measures are subject to measurement error, transitory shocks, and conceptual challenges. As a result, it is important to look at multiple measures of economic conditions and over longer periods of time to discern trends. Widening the focus from GDP to other measures of output like GDO provides a more accurate and forward-looking picture of the state of the economy.

income expectations was particularly welcome and likely supported spending growth in 2015. Expected real income growth, as measured in the Michigan Survey, fell sharply during the recession and remained depressed even after actual real income growth had begun to recover. This heightened pessimism contrasted with the past several decades—when income expectations and actual income growth tended move together reasonably well (Figure 2-16; Sahm 2013). Unusual caution about income prospects may have weighed on consumer borrowing and spending growth. The rebound in income expectations in 2015 was a sign that the extra pessimism may have begun to wane.

Meanwhile, the debt of U.S. households relative to their disposable income continued to fall (Figure 2-17). Before the financial crisis, household debt relative to income rose dramatically, largely due to net mortgage originations, and then declined sharply after the crisis, a pattern known as "deleveraging." Charge offs of delinquent mortgage debt played an important role in lowering household debt, but the decline in new mortgage originations played a role as well (Vidangos 2015). By the end of 2015:Q2, the debt-to-income ratio was at its lowest level since 2002. The level of mortgage debt relative to income continued to decline in 2015, while consumer credit (including credit card, auto, and student loans) relative to income increased slightly.

Moreover, with historically low interest rates, the amount of income required to service these debts has fallen dramatically. Estimates based on aggregate data, could mask higher debt burdens for some families; that is, the health of personal finances varies substantially across households.

Figure 2-16
Real Income Growth Over Next Year, 1978–2015

Index*   1-Year-Ahead Percent Change

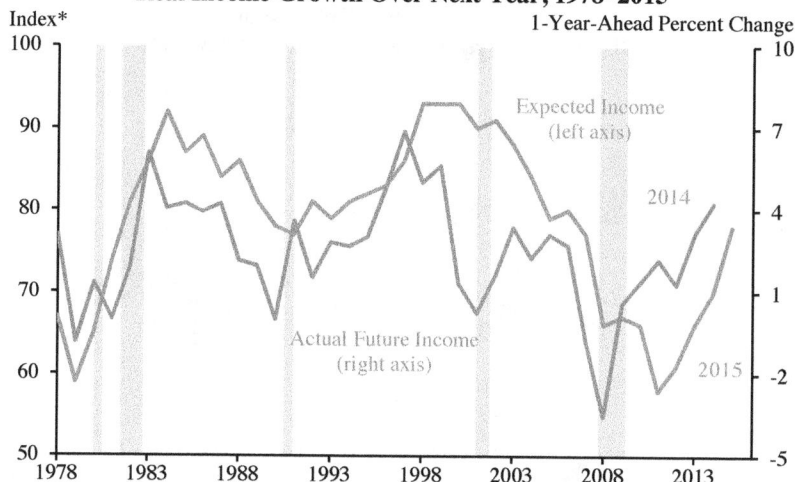

* Index is 100 when the share of the population expecting an increase in income exactly balances the share of the population expecting a decrease in income. An index above 100 means a larger share expects an increase in income.
Note: Shading denotes recession.
Source: University of Michigan; Bureau of Economic Analysis; CEA calculations.

Nonetheless, according to the 2013 Survey of Consumer Finances, the fraction of families with payment-to-income ratios greater than 40 percent declined below the level seen in 2001 (Bricker et al. 2014).

Earlier gains in household net worth (that is, assets less debts, also referred to as household wealth) also supported consumer spending growth in 2015, but to a lesser extent than in 2014 (Figure 2-18). Yet, declines in equity wealth since the second quarter of 2015 have likely weighed some on spending. The wealth-to-income ratio remained elevated in 2015, following its marked increase during 2013. Changes in net worth have been spread unevenly across households, though, and these disparities may have implications for families and macroeconomic activity. For example, wealth has become increasingly concentrated, such that the share of wealth held by the bottom 90 percent of households fell from 33.2 percent in 1989 to 24.7 percent in 2013 (Bricker et al. 2014).

Housing Markets

The housing market recovery picked up steam in 2015, undergoing what was by some measures the largest improvement since 2007. Single-family home sales, bolstered by stronger labor market conditions and low mortgage interest rates, increased substantially to their highest level since 2007. Real residential investment increased 9.0 percent during the four

Figure 2-17
**Household Debt Relative to
Disposable Personal Income (DPI), 1995–2015**

Ratio to Annual DPI

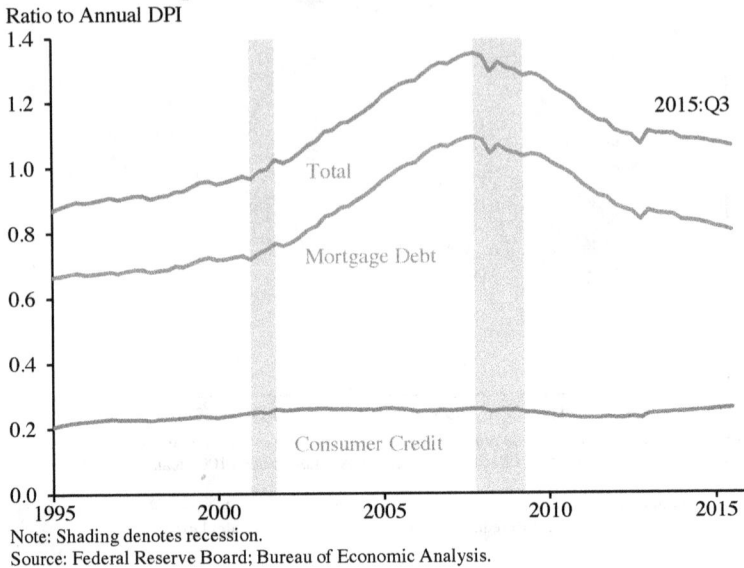

2015:Q3

Total

Mortgage Debt

Consumer Credit

1995   2000   2005   2010   2015

Note: Shading denotes recession.
Source: Federal Reserve Board; Bureau of Economic Analysis.

Figure 2-18
**Consumption and Wealth Relative to Disposable
Personal Income (DPI), 1950–2015**

Ratio to Annual DPI   Years of DPI

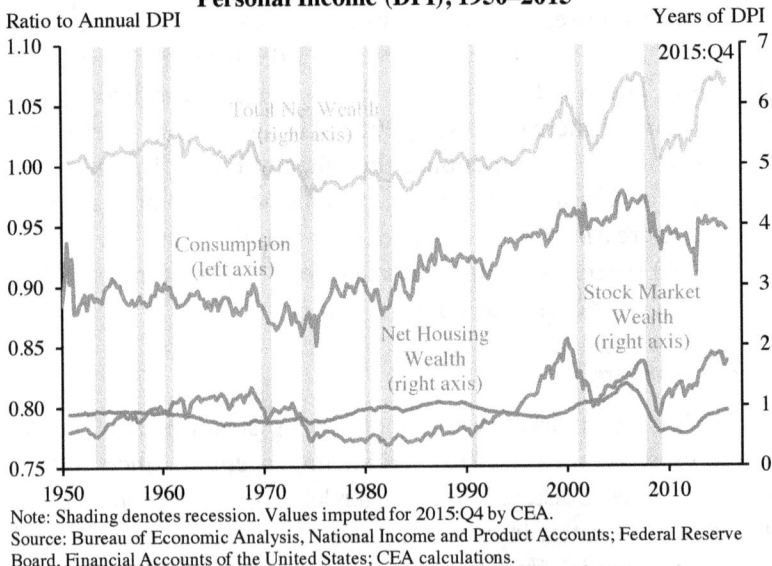

2015:Q4

Total Net Wealth
(right axis)

Consumption
(left axis)

Stock Market
Wealth
(right axis)

Net Housing
Wealth
(right axis)

1950   1960   1970   1980   1990   2000   2010

Note: Shading denotes recession. Values imputed for 2015:Q4 by CEA.
Source: Bureau of Economic Analysis, National Income and Product Accounts; Federal Reserve
Board, Financial Accounts of the United States; CEA calculations.

Box 2-5: Are Official Estimates of GDP Missing More Growth?

While GDP growth rebounded after its sharp drop in the recession, it has held above 2 percent, on average, since 2013, despite marked improvement in the labor market. The unemployment rate is one of the most informative statistics on business-cycle changes in economic activity, and generally seen as less prone to mis-measurement than real GDP. Thus, when the unemployment rate sends a more positive signal than GDP growth, it is natural to question, among other things, whether measurement error in GDP has gotten worse.[1] If true, this would change one's understanding of the economy and recovery.

Official GDP estimates from the Bureau of Economic Analysis use high-quality data from various sources and follow international standards for national accounting. Even with diligent efforts and improving methods, accurately measuring the U.S. economy is a formidable challenge given its size and complexity. The potential understatement of growth in the official GDP estimates could come from incomplete coverage of new goods and services, as well as prices that do not fully reflect quality improvements. This is a long-standing and well-known issue and has motivated a series of methodological improvements since the first estimate of national income was published in 1934.

The substantial declines in the unemployment rate and robust job gains in recent years would historically have tended to coincide with a pickup in real GDP growth relative to its trend. Yet, as Figure 2-viii shows, the official estimate of real GDP growth (the blue line) has held slightly above 2 percent in recent years, as opposed to picking up. One way to roughly quantify the amount of "missing" GDP growth vis-à-vis labor market recovery, is with an empirical regularity known as "Okun's Law." Official GDP growth has been about 1-percent point below the output growth predicted from the labor market (the orange line) since 2005 and about 2 percentage points below since 2010.[2] The persistent discrepancy between recovery in the product market and labor market

---

[1] For example, Hatzius and Dawsey (2015) calculated that measurement problems, including an underestimate of the high-tech price declines and free online media, have led to official statistics to miss 0.7 percentage point of annual growth this decade, up from 0.2 percentage point of missing growth in the 1996-2001 period.

[2] The labor-market prediction of output growth using "Okun's Law" relies on several assumptions and is intended as an illustration. On its own, this gap is not evidence of measurement error in GDP. According to "Okun's Law," a 1 percentage point decline in the unemployment typically coincides with a 2 percentage point pickup in real output growth above its trend. . The trend here counterfactually assumes annual labor productivity growth at its historical average, changes in the labor force participation rate only due to demographics, and a constant unemployment rate of 4.9 percent.

might be a sign of a growing measurement problem or it may signal a slowdown in trend productivity.

Goods and services without a direct market exchange have long posed a challenge in GDP statistics, but the proliferation of free online media and open-source software have led to claims that digital "dark matter" is increasingly a source of missing GDP growth. Researchers have used various methods to value the real output in this sector, despite the fact that in some cases the inputs as well as the outputs do not have a market price. The quantitative impact on real GDP growth in each case is fairly modest. In many cases, the impact on consumer surplus, which is related to how much more consumers or firms would be willing to pay for these free goods and services, is large, but that is a measure of overall welfare, not simply output. Taken together, however, missing GDP from digital dark matter could be substantial; the question is whether we are missing more GDP growth than in the past. As one example, online videos may have largely substituted for television shows, neither of which are fully reflected in real GDP growth.

Alternate methods have led to widely different estimates of the value of online media to consumers. One method relies on the market-value of consumers' time, either to value the time they spend watching online media, as in Brynjolfsson and Oh (2012), or to value the time saved with online search tools, as in Varian (2011). The estimates from this method tend to be considerable, though they are framed in terms

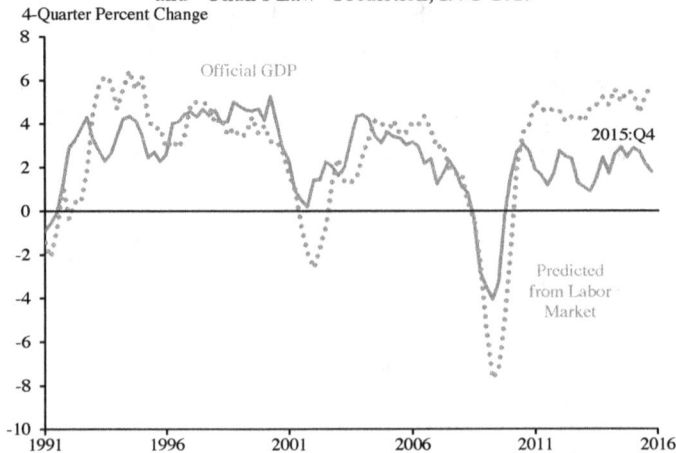

Figure 2-viii
GDP Growth: Official Statistics
and "Okun's Law" Prediction, 1991–2015

4-Quarter Percent Change

Source: Bureau of Economic Analysis; Bureau of Labor Statistics; Haver Analytics; CEA calculations.

of consumer surplus, which should, in general, be much larger than the contribution to GDP. There are many goods and services, such as electricity or indoor plumbing, which consumers value more than their market price suggests, but GDP focuses on market prices not subjective willingness to pay. Taken together,　research estimates roughly 0.4 percentage point of missing GDP growth a year from free online media accounts since 2007 (Hatzius and Dawsey 2015).

One way to value the output from online media is by its cost of production plus the cost of advertising that supports the content. The media is not "free" because consumers exchange exposure to ads for access to the media. Currently, advertising is not included in GDP, because it is treated as an intermediate good, yet this new method follows the national accounting framework for nonmarket goods. This method estimates much less missing GDP growth, only a few basis points of growth a year (Nakamura and Soloveichik 2014). The main reason for the modest overall effect is that advertising-supported media existed in the past, and so this method weighs the substitution from advertising-paid print media to online media. The Internet's contribution to total advertising growth has increased considerably, while the contribution of print advertising has declined (Figure 2-ix).

Relative to the recession, there has been a pickup in advertising growth, consistent with more missing GDP growth. Yet, this approach also highlights a drawback with the official statistics, because currently

Figure 2-ix
Contribution to Growth in Real Advertising, 1980–2013

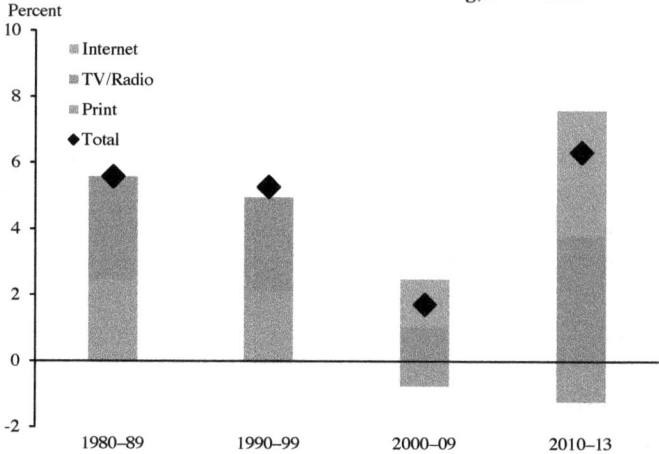

Note: Components may not sum to total due to rounding.
Source: Nakamura and Soloveichik (2014).

any shift from consumer-paid media to ad-supported media would show up as a decline in output.

Open-source software is an example of an even more daunting measurement challenge because, in many cases, it is both acquired and produced for free.[3] One way to estimate the real investment of firms in open-source software is to use the "near-market good" approach from Nordhaus (2006). It is less clear how much more GDP growth is missing in recent years due to open-source software, but the expansion of online platforms providing these goods suggests a growing measurement issue.

Taken together, it appears that the official statistics have always missed some GDP growth, and it is possible that the bias has worsened some in recent years, though not by nearly enough to explain the slowdown in productivity growth or the mismatch between labor and product market growth. Some of the measurement problems, particularly those related to quality-adjusted prices of high-tech goods, appear to have worsened lately. Still, the contributions to GDP and productivity growth from this mis-measurement are relatively modest, while mis-measurement in larger, hard-to-measure sectors like health care merit further in-depth study.

---

[3] BEA measures "own account" software based on an estimate of wages paid to computer programmers and system analysts (see NIPA Handbook p. 6-29). To the extent that employers are paying programmers to produce open-source software, it will be included in BEA's investment and GDP numbers. However, unlike traditional "prepackaged" software, open-source software does not generate investment from the sale of copies, so less investment is captured in GDP with the open-source approach than with traditional sales of prepackaged software.

quarters of 2015, above the 5.1-percent growth in 2014 and far faster than overall real GDP growth of 1.8 percent in 2015. While the cyclical recovery in the housing market is well underway, several structural challenges remain, including a constrained housing supply, low affordability in some areas of the country (see Box 2-6), and persistently muted household formation for 25-34 year-olds. These challenges may explain why some aspects of the housing market or areas of the country have yet to recover.

House prices continued to rise in 2015, similar to the pace in 2014 but below that of 2013. National home prices increased between 4 and 7 percent (depending on the index) during 2015, broadly in line with growth in 2014 but well below the rapid growth in 2013. Nominal house prices are between 19 and 36 percent above their recessionary trough and between 5 and 7 percent below their pre-recession peak (Figure 2-19). However, in real terms

Figure 2-19
National House Price Indexes, 2000–2015

Index, Jan-2012=100

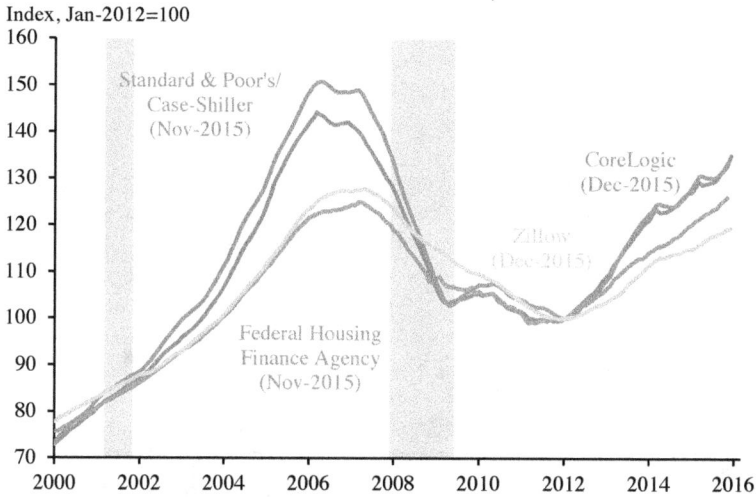

Note: Shading denotes recession. The Standard & Poor's/Case-Shiller, Federal Housing Finance Agency, and CoreLogic indexes all adjust for the quality of homes sold but only cover homes that are bought or sold, whereas Zillow reflects prices for all homes on the market.
Source: Zillow; CoreLogic; Federal Housing Finance Agency; Standard & Poor's/Case-Shiller.

(measured relative to the general rise in consumer prices), house prices still remain roughly 20 percent below their pre-recession peak.

Continued house price increases improved owners' equity relative to the debt they owe on their houses. Homeowners' equity as of December 2015 equaled slightly more than half of the total value of household real estate (57 percent), 20 percentage points higher than the recessionary trough and near the average of 60 percent in the two decades prior to the Great Recession. As of 2015:Q3, rising home prices since 2012:Q4 helped lift more than 7 million households out of a negative equity position (Gudell 2015). The overall share of single-family homeowners with an underwater mortgage (when mortgage debt exceeds the value of their house) was 13.4 percent in 2015:Q3, down from a high of 31.4 percent in 2012. In addition, the number of delinquent home mortgages (when the homeowner misses at least one monthly payment) has fallen to its lowest level since 2006, though the share of mortgages that are seriously delinquent (payment more than 90 days overdue with the bank considering the mortgages to be in danger of default) remains somewhat elevated. This improvement supports overall economic growth because homeowners with underwater or delinquent mortgages are less likely to spend or relocate in search of better-paying jobs.

Single-family homes remained more affordable in 2015 than the historical average, as rising incomes and low and steady mortgage rates partially

Figure 2-20
Housing Affordability Index, 1990–2015

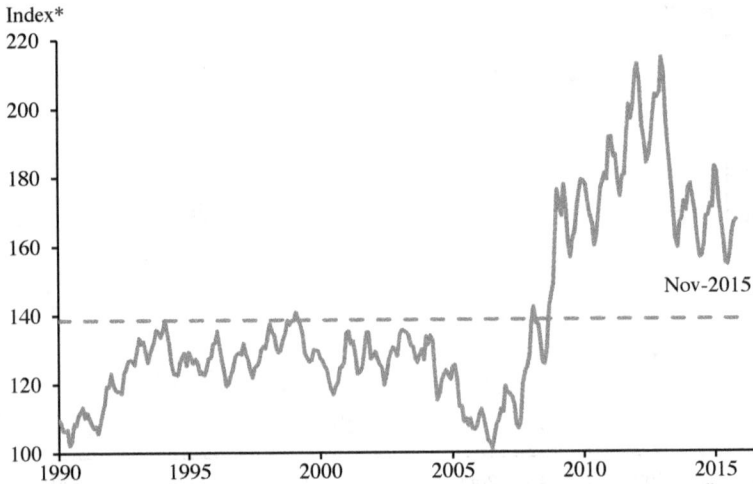

* Index is 100 when the median income family can exactly qualify for a mortgage on a median-priced home. An index over 100 means that the median income family has more than enough income to qualify for a mortgage on a median-priced home.
Note: Dashed line represents average over 1990–2015.
Source: National Association of Realtors.

offset the effect of rising house prices on the cost of homeownership (Figure 2-20). Nevertheless, affordability decreased somewhat in the past two years because median home prices grew faster than median family incomes. Box 2-6 covers an additional threat to affordability—housing supply constraints.

Despite the affordability of housing, national homeownership was 63.7 percent in the fourth quarter of 2015, much lower than the historical average due to a variety of trends in the housing market. The decline has been particularly concentrated among young households. The homeownership rate of those under the age of 35 was nearly 35 percent at the end of 2015, roughly 10-percentage points lower than its all-time high in 2004. A number of factors contributed to this decline. Most importantly, young adults are waiting longer to get married or form households. First-time home buyers are about three years older, on average, than the previous generation of homebuyers. Second, credit availability remains tight for borrowers with credit scores below 620. Third, it can be difficult for households, especially those living in urban areas, to save for a down payment. In response, the Administration has pursued policies to improve access to credit and expand homeownership. In January 2015, the President announced a reduction in the annual mortgage insurance premium on Federal Housing Administration (FHA) loans. The lower premium saved the typical new homeowner $900 in 2015, and existing homeowners who refinanced realized similar savings. In addition, FHA's new guidance for lenders of single-family loans took effect in

Box 2-6: Constraints on Housing Supply

Supply constraints provide a structural challenge in the housing market, particularly in high-mobility, economically vibrant cities. When housing supply is constrained, it has less room to expand when demand increases, leading to higher prices and lower affordability. Limits on new construction can, in turn, impede growth in local labor markets and restrain aggregate output growth. Some constraints on the supply of housing come from geography, while others are man-made. Constraints due to land-use regulations, such as minimum lot size requirements, height restrictions, and ordinances prohibiting multifamily housing, fall into the man-made category and thus could be amended to support more inclusive growth. While these regulations can sometimes serve legitimate purposes such as the protection of human health and safety and the prevention of environmental degradation, land-use regulations can also be used to protect vested interests in housing markets.

Gyourko and Molloy (2015) argue that supply constraints have worsened in recent decades, in large part due to more restrictive land-use regulations. House prices have risen faster than construction costs in real terms (Figure 2-x), providing indirect evidence that land-use regulations are pushing up the price of land.

According to Gyourko and Molloy (2015), between 2010 and 2013, real house prices were 55 percent above real construction costs, compared with an average gap of 39 percent during the 1990s. Several other

Figure 2-x
Real Construction Costs and House Prices, 1980–2013

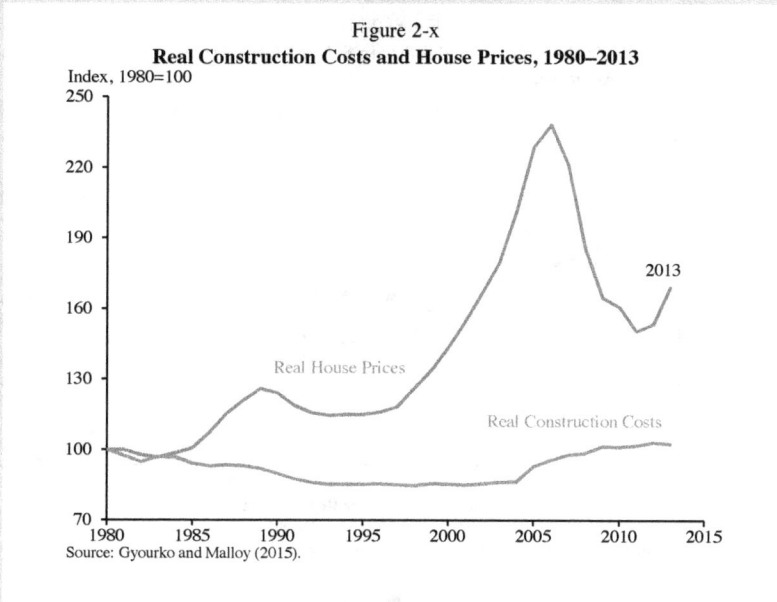

Source: Gyourko and Molloy (2015).

studies note that land-use regulations have been increasing since roughly 1970, driving much of the real house appreciation that has occurred over this time (Glaeser, Gyourko, and Saks 2005; Glaeser and Ward 2009; Been et al. 2014). This pattern is noteworthy because of the positive correlation between cities' housing affordability and the strictness of their land use regulations, as measured by the Wharton Residential Land Use Regulation Index (Figure 2-xi; Gyourko et al. 2008). Cities to the lower right of the figure which include Boston and San Francisco, have stringent land-use regulations and low affordability. Cities at the upper left, which include St. Louis and Cleveland, have low regulation and high affordability. Supply constraints by themselves do not make cities low in affordability. Rather, the less responsive housing supply that results from regulation prevents these cities, which often happen to be desirable migration destinations for workers looking for higher-paying jobs, from accommodating a rise in housing demand.

In addition to housing affordability, these regulations have a range of impacts on the economy, more broadly. Reduced housing affordability—whether as an ancillary result of regulation or by design—prevents individuals from moving to high productivity areas. Indeed, empirical evidence from Molloy, Smith, and Wozniak (2012) indicates that migration across all distances in the United States has been in decline since the middle of the 1980s. This decreased labor market mobility has important implications for intergenerational economic mobility (Chetty et al. 2014)

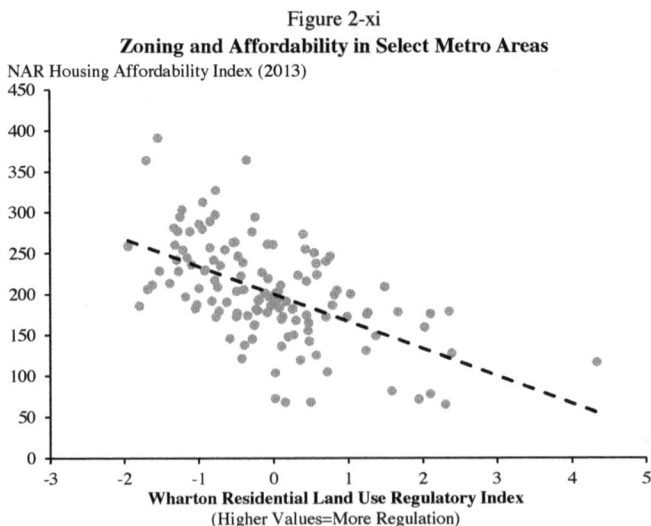

Figure 2-xi
Zoning and Affordability in Select Metro Areas
NAR Housing Affordability Index (2013)

Wharton Residential Land Use Regulatory Index
(Higher Values=More Regulation)

Source: National Associaltion of Realtors (NAR); Gyourko, Saiz, and Summers (2006).

and also was estimated in recent research to have held back current GDP by almost 10 percent (Hsieh and Moretti 2015).

Land-use regulations may also make it more difficult for the housing market to accommodate shifts in preferences due to changing demographics, such as increased demand for modifications of existing structures due to aging and increased demand for multifamily housing due to higher levels of urbanization (Goodman et al. 2015). A number of Administration initiatives, ranging from the Multifamily Risk-Sharing Mortgage program to the Affirmatively Furthering Fair Housing rule, try to facilitate the ability of housing supply to respond to housing demand. Ensuring that zoning and other constraints do not prevent housing supply from growing in high productivity areas will be an important objective of Federal as well as State and local policymakers.

September 2015, while additional work is underway to further increase clarity and transparency to encourage more lending to creditworthy borrowers.

Another phenomenon holding back homeownership that has less to do with access to credit is that, in some areas, home prices and rents are rising more quickly than either per capita personal income or wages. And real median income for household heads aged 25-34 in 2014 remained modestly below pre-recession levels. While homes are more affordable at the national level, housing has become more expensive in many desirable cities like San Jose, San Francisco, Los Angeles, San Diego, and New York (see Box 2-6). Finally, inventories of existing homes available for sale have not recovered fully and, by the end of 2015, were 7 percent below their average over 1997-2007.

Household formation showed some tentative signs of picking up in recent years from the low pace prevailing since the recession. The number of households continued to increase in 2015, albeit at a slower pace than in 2014. Most of the new households formed were among those between the ages of 65 and 74 (Kolko 2015). This uptick contributed to a solid rise in housing starts. Housing starts, including multifamily starts, were about 1.1 million units in 2015 (Figure 2-21). Nevertheless, starts remained well below the 1.5-to-1.7 million rate that is consistent with long-term demographics and the replacement of existing housing stock.[7] Furthermore, because homebuilding has been below that pace since the recession, pent-up demand for housing may play a role in supporting further recovery in the housing

---

[7] Demographics and historical trends would have predicted 1.2 to 1.4 million new households formed each year requiring housing (Joint Center for Housing Studies 2015). Together with the assumption that about 0.25 percent of the existing homes deteriorate and need to be replaced a given year, this yields an underlying trend of 1.5 and 1.7 million housing starts per year.

Figure 2-21
Single-Family and Multifamily Housing Starts, 2000–2015

Thousands of Units, Annual Rate

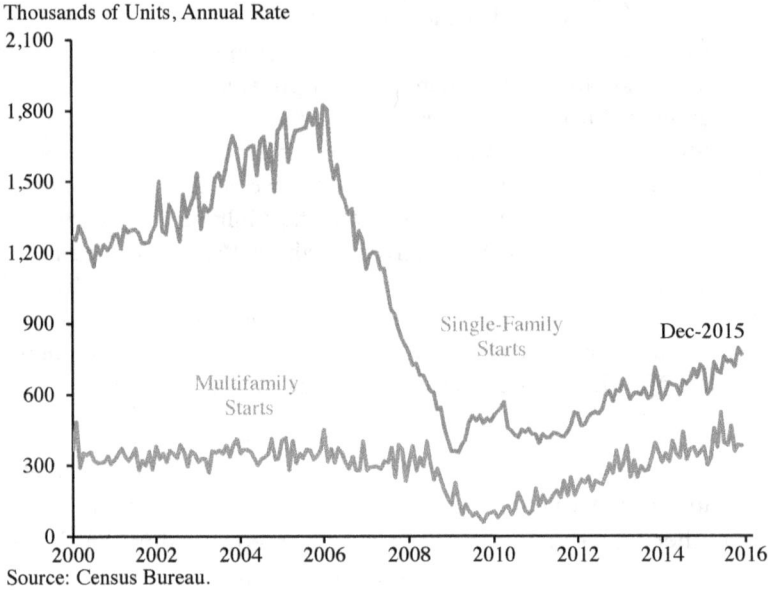

Source: Census Bureau.

Figure 2-22
**Average Annual Growth in Real
Business Fixed Investment (BFI), 2010–2015**

Percent, Annual Rate

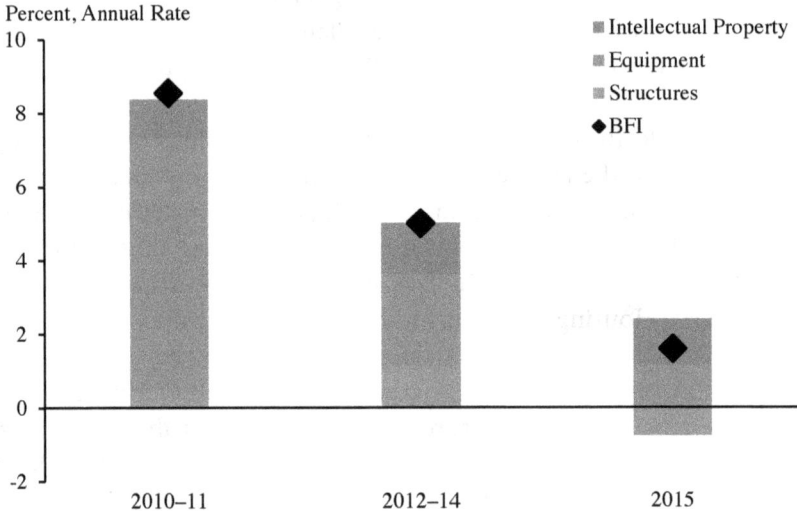

Note: Components may not sum to total due to rounding. Growth rate computed using Q4-to-Q4 changes.
Source: Bureau of Economic Analysis; Haver Analytics.

market. Nevertheless, the construction of multifamily units, mostly rental apartments, also picked up and now exceeds its pre-recession levels.

Investment

Business Fixed Investment. After being a bright spot early in the recovery, investment growth moderated in 2015. Real business fixed investment grew only 1.6 percent during the four quarters of 2015, slower than the 5-percent increase during 2012-14, and much slower that the 9-percent increase in 2010-11. In 2015, the rate of investment growth was largely maintained for intellectual property, but was offset by sharp declines in drilling and mining structures (see Box 2-1 for more details) and slower growth in equipment investment. The slowdown in investment growth is largely associated with the moderate pace of recovery in overall U.S. output and is not limited to the United States (Box 2-7).

Slower investment growth is a concern because it limits the productive capacity of the economy. Investment net of depreciation is required to increase the capital stock. In 2009, net investment as a share of the capital stock fell to its lowest level in the post-World War II era, and the nominal capital stock even declined. Although net investment has rebounded somewhat in the recovery, its level as a share of the capital stock remains well below the historical average (Figure 2-23).

The slowdown in investment has also contributed to the slowdown in productivity growth. Historically, capital deepening—capital per hour worked—has added nearly 1 percentage point to labor productivity growth, but since 2007, capital deepening has added only about a half percentage point. The recovery in output has not been matched by a level of investment sufficient to generate substantial growth in the capital-to-labor ratio. Changes in capital deepening tend to reverse themselves, yet the persistence of low productivity is likely tied to the persistence of the investment slowdown. The pessimistic view is that the recent investment slowdown reflects a trend toward less capital due to a shift toward production with lower capital intensity, slower trend labor force growth, or fewer start-ups. The optimistic view, which is in line with historical experience, is that having largely bounced back from the capital overhang following the Great Recession, investment will return toward its prior, stronger trend.

With the sharp fall in output in 2008-09, the amount of capital services relative to output rose considerably (see Figure 2-24). Even years into the recovery, businesses had access to more capital services than the level of output would typically have required. The excess of capital suppressed new investment and helped lower capital services growth. Capital services relative to output have now regressed back to trend, a factor supporting

Box 2-7: Slowdown in Investment Growth
across Advanced Economies

Across advanced economies, including the United States, business fixed investment is currently 20 percent below what would have been expected from pre-crisis trends (Figure 2-xii). The shortfalls have been in all categories of investment—not just business investment but also public investment and housing.

Weak investment in advanced economies may largely be explained by the steady, rather than increasing, pace of the recovery in output as opposed to other issues: such as confidence, regulatory factors or excessive share buybacks (IMF 2015). In the standard "accelerator" model, investment increases when output growth is expected to increase. With steady growth and some excess capacity left from the recession, it is not that surprising that firms' demand for investment goods has increased slowly. Other trends common across advanced economies may be suppressing investment, such as: a digital start-up requiring less capital investment (Summers 2015); or constraints on entry of new firms (Decker et al. 2014).

Figure 2-xii

Business Fixed Investment Across Advanced Economies, 1990–2014

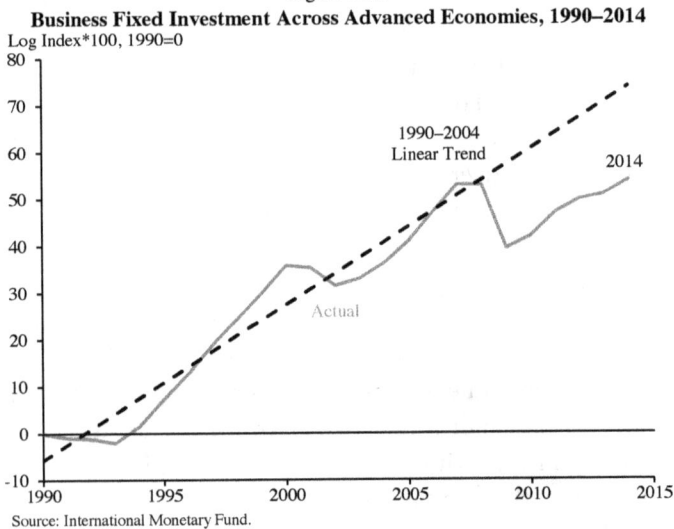

Source: International Monetary Fund.

future investment. This view is consistent with historically weaker periods of investment growth being, on average, followed by stronger periods. This historical pattern argues for faster growth in investment spending during 2016 than in the recent past.

Figure 2-23
Net Investment as a Share of the Capital Stock, 1940–2014

Percent

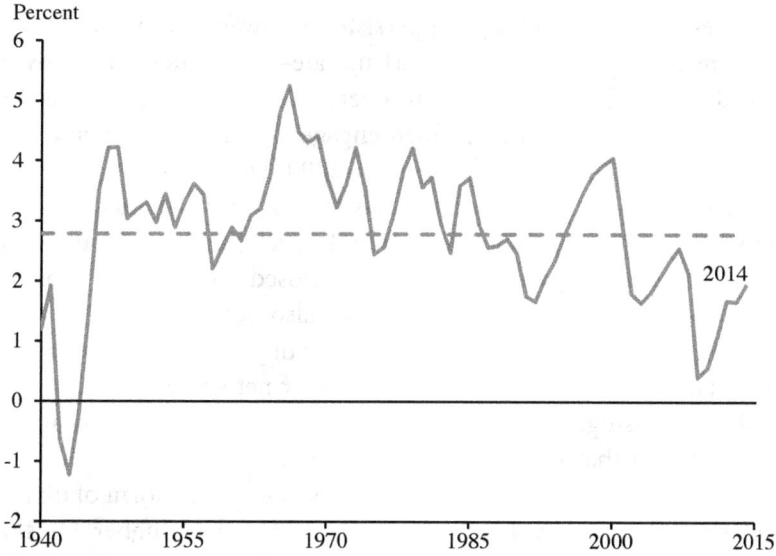

Note: Dashed line represents average over 1940–2014.
Source: Bureau of Economic Analysis.

Figure 2-24
Capital Services per Unit of Real Output,
Private Business Sector, 1948–2015

Index, 2009=100

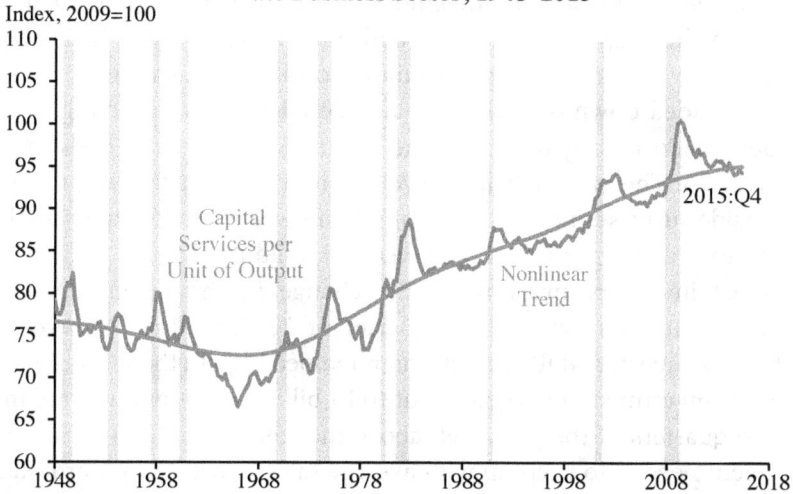

Note: Post-1964 data interpolated quarterly using Macroeconomic Advisers quarterly data. Pre-1965
data interpolated by moving average. Nonlinear trend is a bi-weight filter using a 60-quarter window.
Source: Bureau of Labor Statistics, Labor Productivity and Costs; Macroeconomic Advisers; CEA
calculations.

On the other hand, there are longer-running trends of less dynamism in the business sector, as discussed in Chapter 5 on innovation, pre-dating the last recession that could suggest persistently lower investment. The share of new firms among all firms—the start-up rate—has trended down over the past decades and fell further in this recovery. Moreover, research has shown that start-ups and young firms, which engage heavily in hiring and investment, are also failing at a higher rate since 2000 (Decker et al. forthcoming). The Administration has pursued policies to support investment, including additional funding for public research and development and public infrastructure. In addition, the President has proposed business tax reform that would directly spur private investment. (See also Box 2-8).

While investment has been low, the rate of payouts to shareholders by nonfinancial firms, in the form of dividends or net share buybacks (Figure 2-25) has been rising. Nonfinancial corporations are now returning nearly half of the funds that could be used for investment to stockholders. The share of funds being returned to stockholders, both in the form of dividends and net share buy backs, has been gradually trending higher for several decades and the current combined level was markedly exceeded only in the run-up to the last recession. The lower investment growth and higher share of funds returned to shareholders suggests firms had more cash than they thought they could profitably invest. The rise in payouts to shareholders may be related to the decline in the start-up rate as young firms are more likely to re-invest their cash flow than mature firms.

Inventory Investment. Inventories increased faster than final sales in 2015, pushing up manufacturing and trade inventories to 1.48 months' supply in November 2015. The inventory-to-sales ratio has risen this year, but has trended down over the past few decades, likely reflecting changes in supply-chain management and the diminishing share of goods in GDP (Figure 2-26). The unusually high level of oil inventories in 2015, related to both upside surprises in the supply of oil and weaker-than-expected global demand for oil, is a portion of the inventory buildup.

Real inventory investment—the change in the inventory stock—picked up noticeably in the first quarter of 2015, adding 0.9 percentage point to first-quarter GDP growth, and remained high in the second quarter. Inventory investment averaged about $113 billion at an annual rate in the first two quarters of the year, well above the $50 billion level of inventory investment needed to keep up with average sales growth. The third quarter saw a drop back down to $86 billion, subtracting 0.7 percentage point from GDP growth. Inventory investment declined further in the fourth quarter to $69 billion and subtracted 0.5 percentage point from GDP growth. As shown

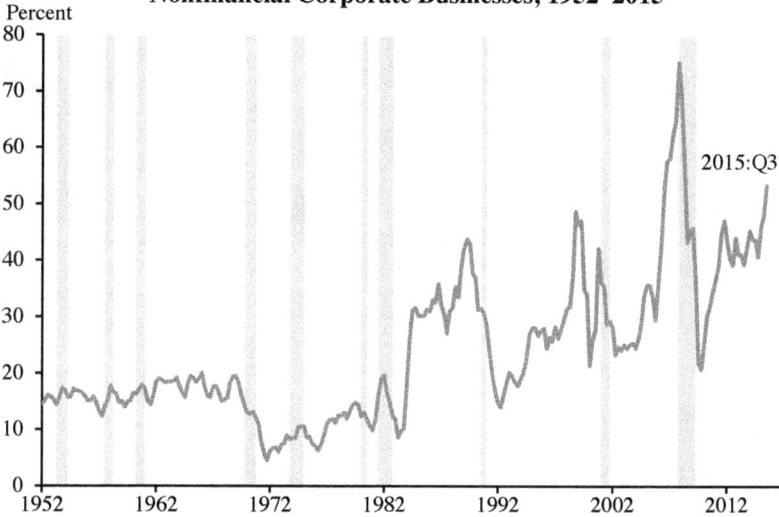

Figure 2-25
**Total Payouts to Shareholders,
Nonfinancial Corporate Businesses, 1952–2015**

Percent

2015:Q3

Note: Series shown is the four-quarter moving average of the ratio of dividends plus share buybacks relative to profits plus depreciation minus taxes.
Source: Federal Reserve Board; Haver Analytics; CEA calculations.

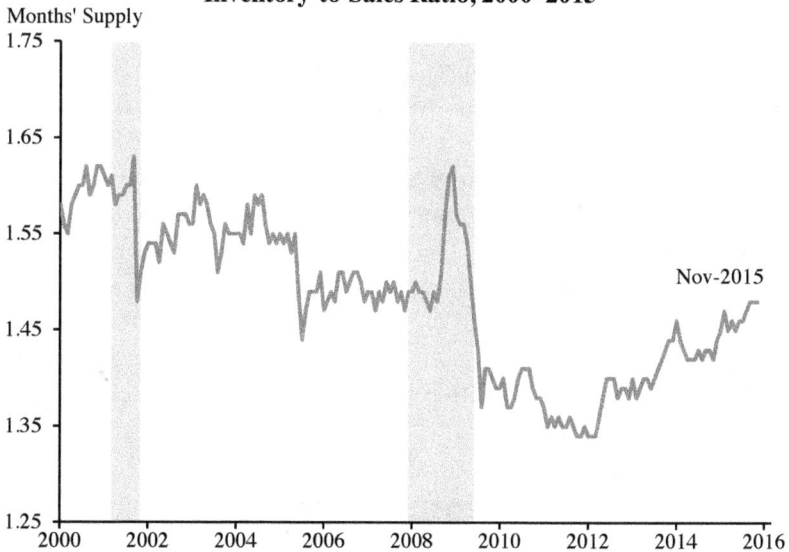

Figure 2-26
Inventory-to-Sales Ratio, 2000–2015

Months' Supply

Nov-2015

Note: Manufacturing and trade inventories at book value.
Source: Census Bureau, Manufacturing and Trade Inventories and Sales; Haver Analytics.

Figure 2-27
**Contribution of Inventory Investment
to Real GDP Growth, 2012–2015**

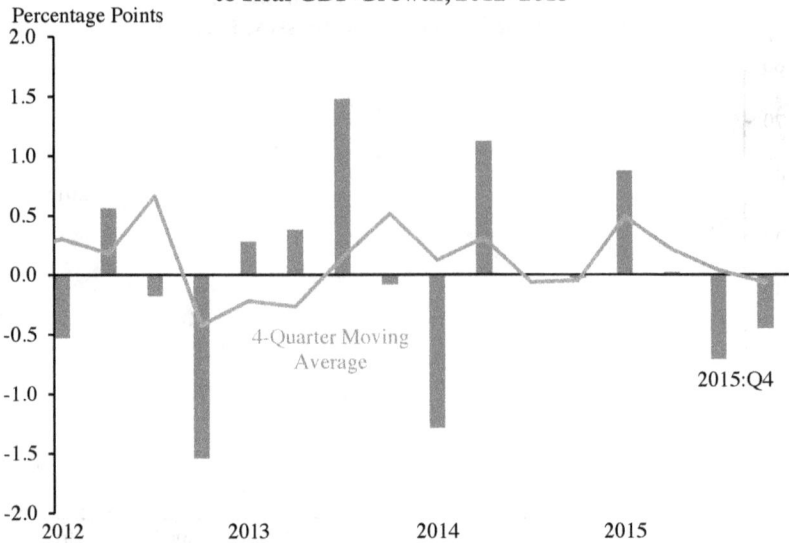

Source: Bureau of Economics Analysis; Haver Analytics.

in Figure 2-27, changes in inventory investment often affect the quarterly pattern of output growth, but have limited effect on annual growth.

Net Exports

Weak demand in much of the world outside the United States—as discussed more in Chapter 3—and the stronger dollar that has come with it has been a drag on U.S. exports, which declined 6.9 percent in nominal terms during 2015. Part of this was due to the drop in export prices, as lower oil and commodity prices have meant lower prices for U.S. exports of agricultural goods or oil-related products. Adjusting for prices, real exports declined 0.8 percent during the four quarters of 2015, shown in Figure 2-28.

At the same time, real U.S. imports increased 3.4 percent, reflecting both the relative strength of domestic demand and the lower price of imports. Taken together, Figure 2-29 shows net exports subtracted 0.6 percentage point from GDP growth during 2015, after subtracting a comparable amount to overall growth in 2014. The external sector is likely to be a drag on growth in 2016 as well.

PRODUCTIVITY

Although employment growth has been strong, the growth in output has been more moderate. Thus, recent growth of labor productivity (that

Figure 2-28
Foreign Real GDP and U.S. Export Growth, 2000–2015

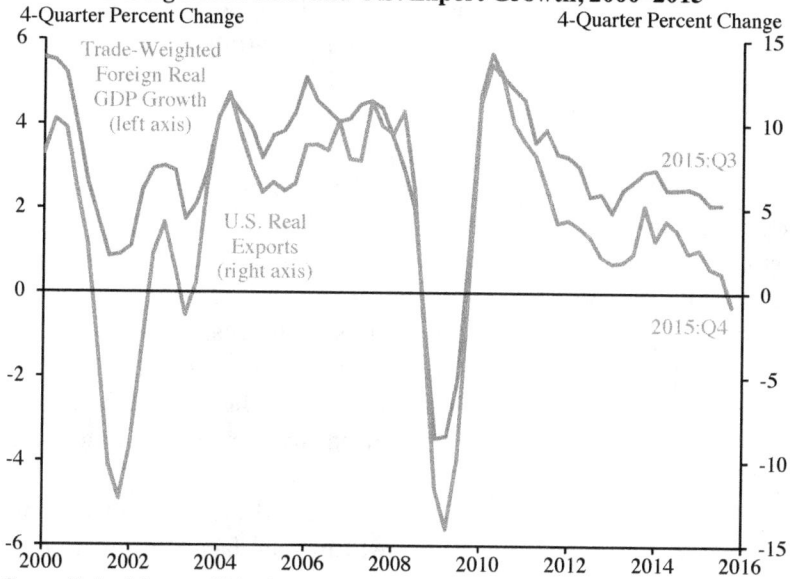

4-Quarter Percent Change   4-Quarter Percent Change

Trade-Weighted
Foreign Real
GDP Growth
(left axis)

U.S. Real
Exports
(right axis)

2015:Q3

2015:Q4

Source: National Sources; CEA calculations.

Figure 2-29
**Contribution of Net Exports to U.S.
Real GDP Growth, 2000–2015**

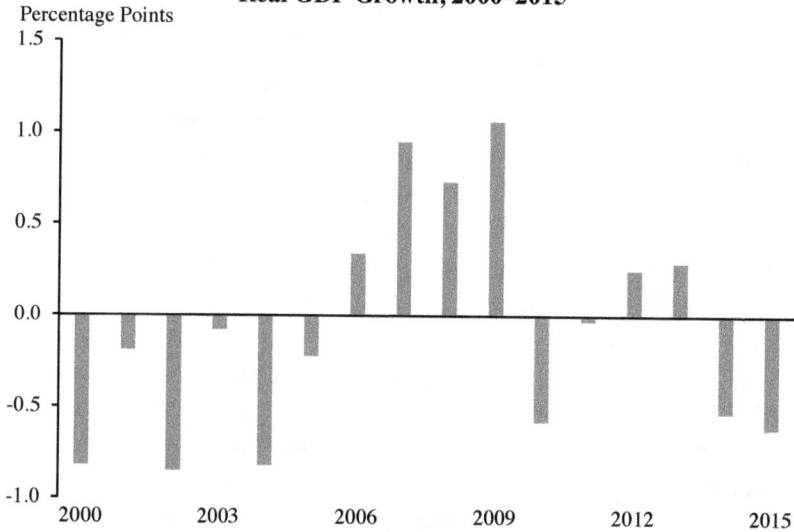

Percentage Points

Note: Contributions are computed using Q4-to-Q4 changes.
Source: Bureau of Economic Analysis; Haver Analytics.

is, output per hour) has been below its long-term average pace. Because productivity fluctuates with the business cycle, it should be measured over a long interval, or between comparable cyclical stages. When measured with product-side data from the national income and product accounts (the measure published by the Bureau of Labor Statistics and based on data from the Bureau of Economic Analysis), labor productivity has risen at a 1.2-percent annual rate during the almost eight years from the business cycle peak in 2007:Q4 to 2015:Q3. But when using the income-side measure, nonfarm productivity has risen at a 1.6-percent rate. The best measure of productivity growth is probably the average of these figures, similar to the average used for gross domestic output in Box 2-4, yielding an estimate of a 1.4-percent annual rate of growth in productivity thus far in this business cycle. This is a slower pace of growth than the 2.2-percent growth seen between business-cycle peaks in 1953 and 2007, partially due to the transitory after-effects of the severe recession, including reduced investment associated with the capital overhang.

The slowdown in labor productivity growth in the post-recessionary period can be attributed to lower growth in total factor productivity and a reduction in capital intensity, as shown in Figure 2-30. Historically, capital intensity, or changes in capital per hour, has added nearly 1 percentage point to labor productivity growth. But, since 2007, capital intensity has added about a half percentage point, as discussed previously in the investment section. Thus, reduced capital deepening can account for roughly a third of the below-average productivity growth since 2007. Moreover, the contribution from total factor productivity growth over the past few years has been half its historical average of 1.1 percentage points. Increasing public infrastructure investment, an issue discussed in Chapter 6, and raising educational levels, as discussed in Chapter 4, will support labor productivity growth.

Since 2010:Q4, productivity growth has been even lower, averaging only 0.7 percent per year (using information from the income and product sides of the accounts). It is difficult to interpret productivity growth over very short windows, in part because it is affected by changing business-cycle conditions and also because it is subject to sizeable measurement error. Nevertheless, the same pattern applies even more strongly to this shorter window, with the majority of the most recent slowdown in productivity growth accounted for by the reduction in the amount of capital services per worker. As shown in Figure 2-31, a decline in capital intensity has not occurred previously in the postwar period.

How should recent productivity growth color forecasts of future productivity? The degree that a slowdown in capital accumulation has played an important role in the recent slower productivity growth offers some

Figure 2-30
Sources of Productivity Growth, 1953–2007 vs. 2007–2014
Percentage Points, Average Annual Rate

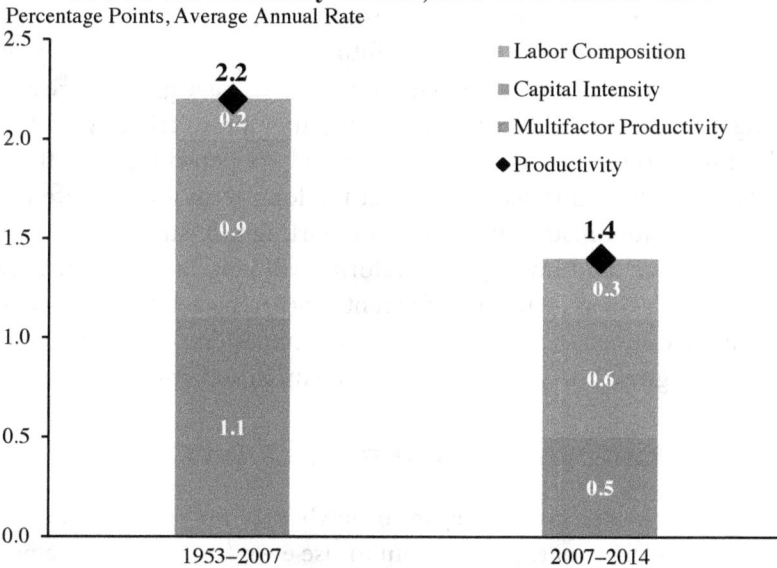

Labor Composition
Capital Intensity
Multifactor Productivity
◆ Productivity

2.2
0.2
0.9
1.1

1.4
0.3
0.6
0.5

1953–2007   2007–2014

Note: Contributions computed using annual data.
Source: Bureau of Labor Statistics; CEA calculations.

Figure 2-31
Labor Productivity and Major Components, 1950–2014
Percent Change, Annual Rate (5-Year Moving Average)

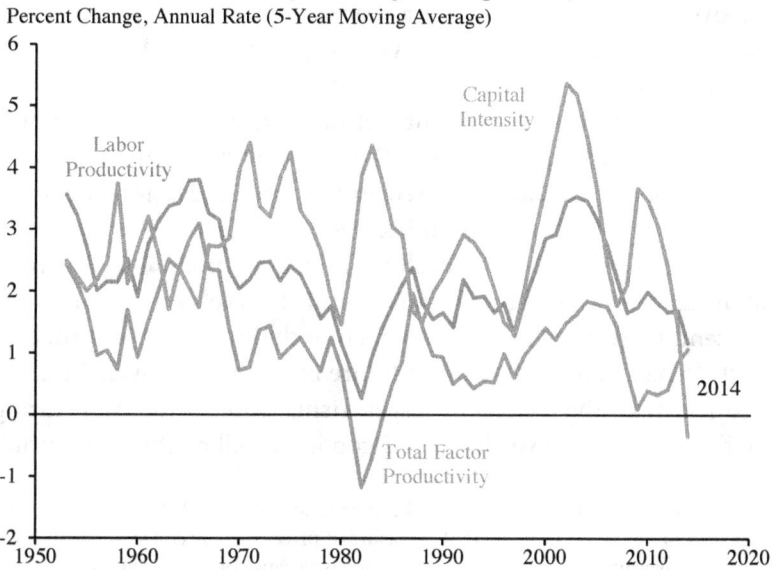

Capital
Intensity

Labor
Productivity

2014

Total Factor
Productivity

Source: Bureau of Labor Statistics; Haver Analytics.

grounds for optimism about the future. Historically, capital accumulation tends to pick up after a period of weakness. This could be even truer in the wake of the Great Recession, which is a rare enough event in its severity that it should not form a basis for future extrapolations about long-run trends. Moreover, historically longer time periods have given more accurate readings on future productivity growth. Labor productivity growth since the business-cycle peak in 1953 has averaged 2.1 percent a year, the figure that the Administration uses to project the long-term growth rate of labor productivity. Administration policies supporting infrastructure investment, education, trade, and immigration reform, will help facilitate the acceleration from the slow growth rate of recent years. However, in the near-term, the Administration's outlook foresees a continuation of relatively subdued productivity growth in 2016 but then a pickup in subsequent years.

WAGE GROWTH AND PRICE INFLATION

Nominal wage growth began to slowly pick up in 2015, but, with the strengthening labor market, has room to rise even further. Average nominal hourly earnings for all private employees increased 2.7 percent during the 12 months of 2015, compared with 1.8 percent on average in the two prior years. Hourly compensation, as measured in the Employment Cost Index, increased 1.9 percent in 2015, down from 2.3 percent a year earlier. In contrast, the more-volatile compensation per hour rose 3.1 percent during 2015, above its 2.8 percent growth a year earlier. Taken together, as shown in Figure 2-32, wage growth has moved up gradually as labor markets have tightened, but has not reached a pace that would signal a full recovery. An important question in the labor market this year will be whether nominal wages will continue to grow faster as the labor market tightens.

Consumer prices, as measured in the price index for personal consumption expenditures (PCE) and shown in Figure 2-33, were up only slightly over 2015 due to large declines in energy prices (see Figure 2-34). Overall inflation was well below the Federal Reserve's longer-run objective of 2 percent. Core PCE inflation—which excludes energy and food prices and tends to be a better predictor of future inflation than overall inflation— was also less than the 2-percent target, rising only 1.4 percent during the 12 months of 2015.[8] Lower imported goods as well as the pass through of

---

[8] The Federal Reserve's defines its inflation objective in terms of the PCE price index. The consumer price index (CPI) is an alternate measure of prices paid by consumers and is used to index some government transfers and taxes. Largely because of a different method of aggregating the individual components, PCE inflation has averaged about 0.3 percentage point a year less than the CPI inflation since 1979. During the 12 months of 2015, for example, core CPI prices increased 2.1 percent, more than the 1.4 percent increase in core PCE prices.

Figure 2-32
Nominal Wage Growth Over Past Year, 2003–2015

Percent Change

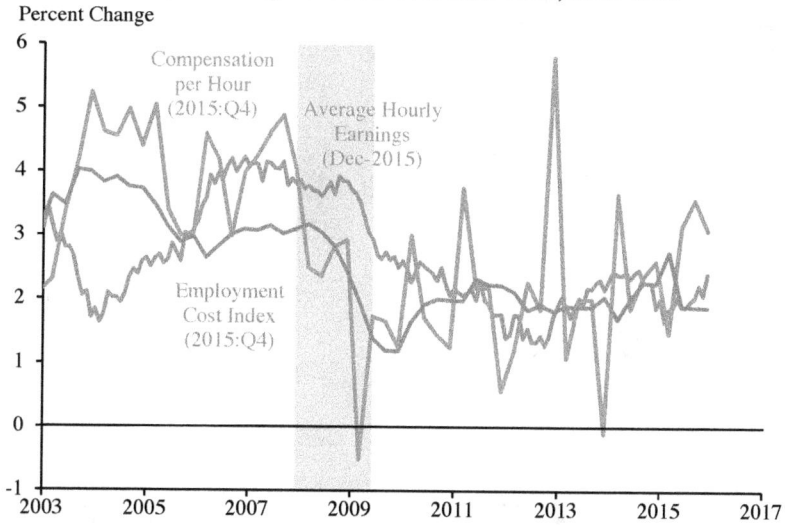

Note: Compensation per hour is for the business sector. Average hourly earnings are for production and nonsupervisory workers. The employment cost index is for the private sector.
Source: Bureau of Labor Statistics; Department of Labor; Haver Analytics.

Figure 2-33
Consumer Price Inflation, 2012–2015

12-Month Percent Change

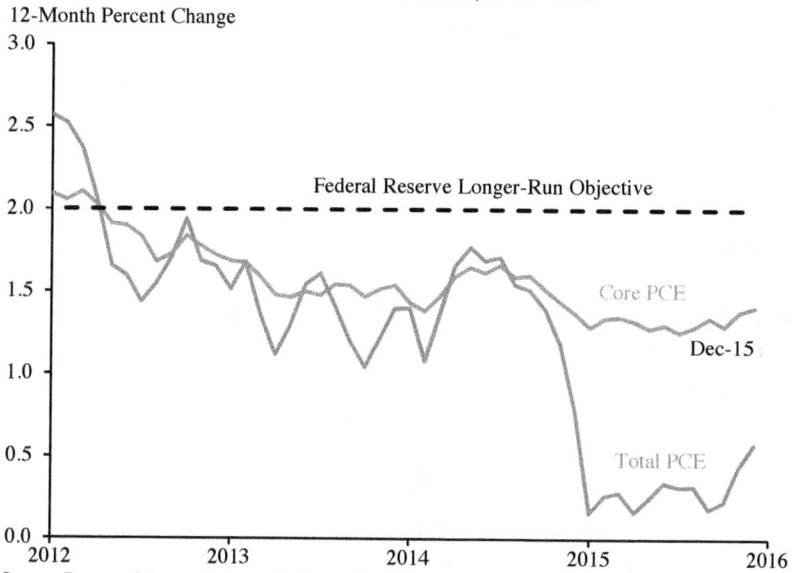

Source: Bureau of Economic Analysis; Haver Analytics.

Figure 2-34
Energy and Import Price Inflation, 2005–2015

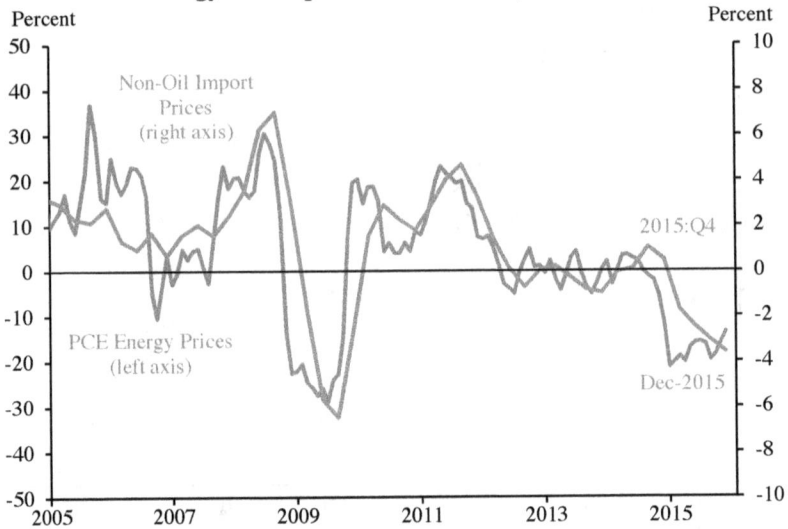

Note: The Personal Consumption Expenditures (PCE) energy price index is used to compute inflation.
Source: Bureau of Economic Analysis; Haver Analytics.

lower energy costs to non-energy goods likely weighed on core inflation this year. The speed and degree to which these factors wane are two keys to the inflationary pressures in the economy this year.

Changes in import prices can meaningfully affect domestic price inflation through various channels. If imports become less expensive, then domestic price inflation may be reduced as consumers switch to relatively cheaper goods from abroad. Competitive pressures from lower import prices may also lead domestic producers to lower their prices. Finally, the lower price inflation for imported inputs may be passed through to goods produced domestically. Prices for non-oil imports declined sharply in 2015, weighing on domestic core price inflation (Figure 2-33). Over the four quarters of 2015, the price of non-oil imports fell 3.6 percent, the largest four-quarter decline since 2009:Q3. The decline in non-oil import prices likely reflects a stronger dollar as well as falling non-energy commodity prices. The pass through of non-oil import prices to core inflation is expected to continue, albeit to a lesser extent, in 2016.

Survey-based measures of long-term expectations for inflation, have been generally well-anchored, both during the last recession and more recently. This steadiness suggests a view that the factors that pushed down inflation in 2015 will be temporary as well as confidence that the Federal Reserve will be able to address any inflationary pressures in the coming years. Nevertheless, market-based measures of inflation compensation

Figure 2-35

Long-Term Inflation Expectations, 2007–2015

4-Quarter Percent Change

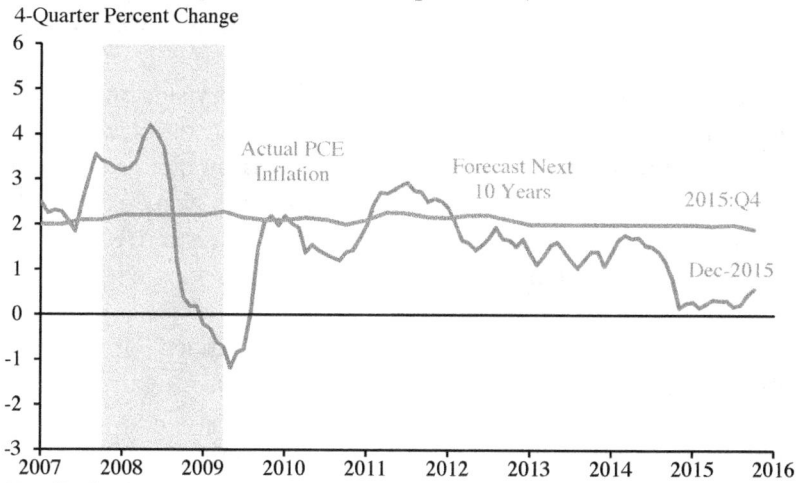

Note: Shading denotes recession. The Forecast Next 10 Years is the median forecast for CPI inflation from the Survey of Professional Forecasters. The Personal Consumption Expenditures (PCE) price index is used to compute inflation.
Source: Bureau of Labor Statistics; Federal Reserve Bank of Philadelphia, Survey of Professional Forecasters.

(estimated from the rates on Treasury inflation protected securities) have declined, raising some concerns about long-term inflation expectations.

FINANCIAL MARKETS

Over the course of the year, developments in U.S. financial markets largely reflected diminished prospects for global growth, particularly in China and other emerging markets, and expected tightening of monetary policy. At the same time, consensus forecasts of long-run U.S. interest rates have fallen, following the long downward trend that reflects a variety of factors ranging from demographics to changing term premiums. This section, like the rest of this chapter, focuses on developments through the end of 2015. In early 2016, U.S. and global equity indexes and commodity prices—especially oil—fell while spreads on high-yield bonds rose.

Since the early 1980s, long-term interest rates, as measured by the yields on 10-year Treasury notes, have trended downward, as shown in Figure 2-36. The evolution of U.S. interest rates over the past 20 years has coincided with interest-rate movements in advanced economies, including the United Kingdom and the euro area. The global trend in long-term rates is partly the result of lower inflation, lower foreign output growth, aging demographics, lower investment demand, and increased world saving, as evidenced by the reduction in rates beginning well before the financial crisis.[9] But these changes have been greatly exacerbated by some more transitory factors, including the effects of quantitative easing on the supply of long-term debt, lower term premiums, private-sector deleveraging, and flight-to-safety flows.

Longer-term interest rates, as measured by the yields on 10-year U.S. Treasury notes and shown in Figure 2-37, were relatively stable, on net, in 2015, ending the year at 2.3 percent, about the same rate as at the end of 2014, but noticeably down from year-end 2013. The yields on 3-month U.S. Treasury notes also remained low in 2015, only starting to rise meaningfully above zero in mid-November, reflecting expectations for the FOMC to raise its target rate.

Similarly, corporate borrowing costs rebounded almost 70 basis points over the 12 months of 2015 to 4.9 percent, roughly in line with its level at year-end 2013. Increased corporate bond yields coupled with roughly unchanged Treasury yields point to rising credit spreads.

Market estimates for long-term U.S. Treasury rates increased over the past year. The 10-year U.S. Treasury rate, 10 years forward, which measures the market's expectation of the 10-year interest rate a decade from today, was 3.2 percent in December 2015. The market-based forward rate was nearly 1 percentage point below the consensus forecast of 4.1-percent for 2022-26. Some of the gap may be explained by a lower term premium, global flight-to-safety flows, or divergent expectations about long-term productivity and output growth. Forward rates incorporate risk premiums, can be highly volatile, and their movements may reflect transitory developments as opposed to structural changes; as such, they may be poor predictors for future rates. For a more in-depth analysis into the 10-year U.S. Treasury rate, 10 years forward, and the overall shift to lower long-term rates, see the Council of Economic Advisers (2015) report, "Long-Term Interest Rates: A Survey."

Overall stock prices were little changed, on net, in 2015. The Standard and Poor's 500 (S&P) index edged down less than 1 percent for the year, following a 30 percent rise in 2013 (the best year since 1997) and another 11 percent rise in 2014. In the first half of 2015, the S&P index had increased; however, declines since August erased most of the year's gains. Nevertheless, at the end of December 2015, the S&P index was about 30 percent above its pre-recession peak in 2007.

---

[9] Recent aging of the baby-boom generation has led to a disproportionate share of the population being distributed into age cohorts with relatively high saving rates, which in turn, has held down interest rates. Continued aging of the baby-boom generation will likely exert upward pressure on interest rates as its members enter retirement and consume their savings.

Figure 2-36
Nominal 10-Year Treasury Yields, 1980–2015

Percent

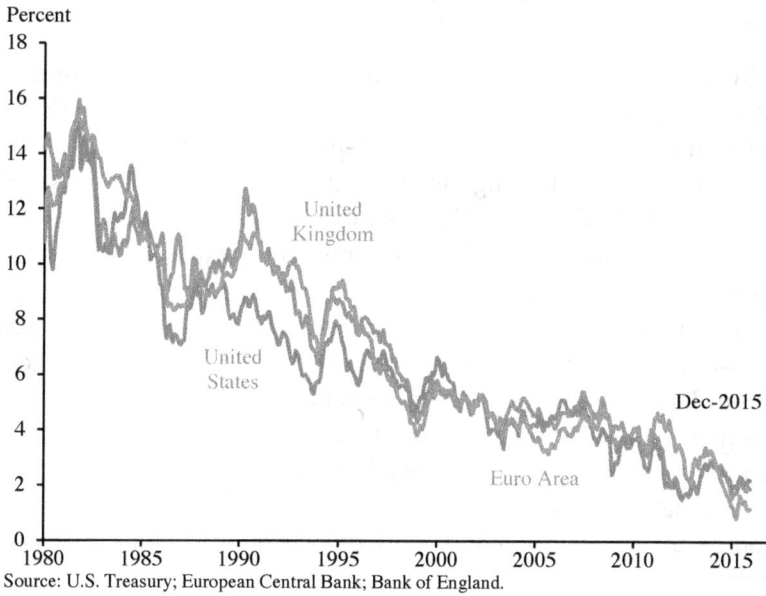

Source: U.S. Treasury; European Central Bank; Bank of England.

Figure 2-37
Nominal Long- and Short-Term Interest Rates, 2015

Percent

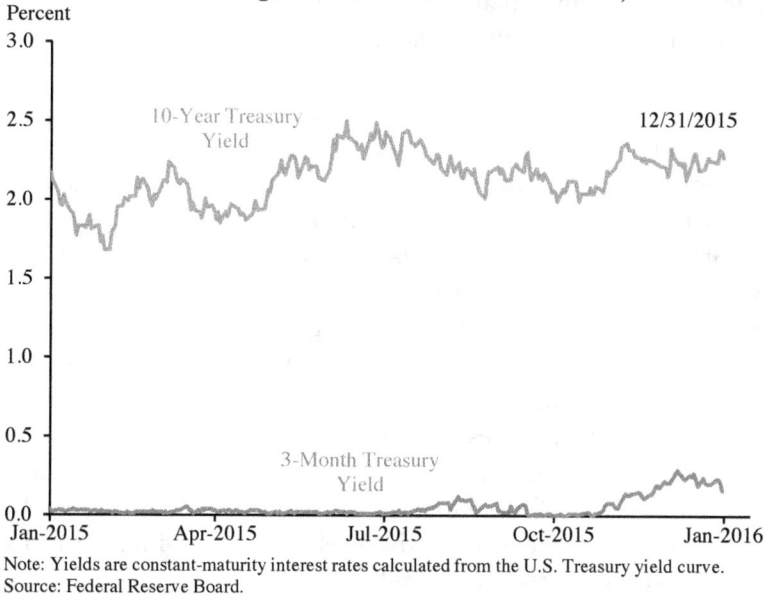

Note: Yields are constant-maturity interest rates calculated from the U.S. Treasury yield curve.
Source: Federal Reserve Board.

THE OUTLOOK

Forecast over the Next Three Years

Real GDP grew 2.2 percent on average during the three years through 2015, and the Administration forecast (finalized on November 17, 2015) projects an acceleration to 2.7-percent growth during 2016. The Administration forecast is slightly above the Blue-Chip consensus forecast of 2.6 percent and in line with the CBO forecast of 2.7 percent, two outside forecasts from January 2016. The Administration expects that investment will grow faster in 2016 than in the recent past, though weaker global demand likely will be partially offsetting. Federal fiscal policy will be simulative in 2016 and even more so than it might otherwise have been without the Bipartisan Budget Agreement. With a strengthening State and local sector, fiscal actions will likely be expansionary in 2016. Meanwhile, core inflation (excluding food and energy) remains low, partly due to declining import prices, and below average capacity utilization, so resource utilization does not appear to impose any constraints during the next four quarters. For consumers, a pickup in nominal and real wage gains in 2015—together with strong employment growth—will probably boost spending in 2016. These income gains—following a multiyear period of successful deleveraging— leave consumers in an improved financial position. Business investment also shows brighter prospects for growth in 2016 than in earlier years as the overhang of excess capital that suppressed investment earlier in this expansion has been reduced. As the economy continues to grow, businesses will need new facilities, equipment, and intellectual property to meet growing demand. The decline in oil prices over the last year and half are likely to add to GDP, on net, in 2016, as discussed in Box 2-1.

Although most domestic signals are positive, the United States faces headwinds from abroad. The available indicators suggest that the economies of Brazil, Canada, China, India, and our euro area trading partners are growing slowly. The trade-weighted average of foreign GDP growth in 2015 was slower than in 2014. Slow global growth is forecasted for 2016 as well. Weakness abroad not only reduces our exports, but also raises risks of adverse financial and other spillovers to the U.S. economy.

With broader measures of labor market slack somewhat elevated and the capacity utilization rate in manufacturing at about 76 percent, the economy still has a bit of room to grow faster than its potential rate. Even if the unemployment rate falls below the level consistent with long-run stable inflation, near-term inflation likely will be held down by the recent declines

Table 2-1

Selected Interest Rates, 2015

	Dec-2014	Dec-2015	Difference
Federal Funds Effective	0.06	0.20	0.14
3-Month U.S. Treasury Yield	0.04	0.16	0.12
2-Year U.S. Treasury Yield	0.67	1.06	0.39
5-Year U.S. Treasury Yield	1.65	1.76	0.11
10-Year U.S. Treasury Yield	2.17	2.27	0.10
10-Year BBB Corporate Bonds Yield	4.18	4.87	0.69
30-Year U.S. Treasury Yield	2.75	3.01	0.26
30-Year Fixed Mortgage Rate	3.83	4.01	0.18

Note: All interest rates are the final daily or weekly data in the given month. Treasury yields are constant-maturity yields estimated by the Federal Reserve Board. Corporate bond yields are option-adjusted yields estimated by Standard & Poor's Global Fixed Income Research. The mortgage rate is that reported in the Freddie Mac Primary Mortgage Survey.
Source: Federal Reserve Board; Standard & Poor's; Freddie Mac; CEA calculations.

in import prices. And even if inflation increases modestly, it may remain below the Federal Reserve's long-run target of 2-percent inflation.

The Administration's economic forecast, presented in Table 2-2, underpins the President's FY 2017 budget. When the Administration forecast was finalized in November 2015, real GDP growth during the four quarters of 2015 was projected at 2.2 percent. Data released after the forecast was finalized point to real GDP growth during 2015 that is below the Administration's forecast.

By long-standing convention, this forecast reflects the economic effects of the President's budgetary and other economic policy proposals in the FY 2017 budget. Together these act to increase the growth rate of GDP during the 10-year budget window (Box 2-8).

Real GDP is projected to grow 2.7, 2.5, and 2.4 percent during the four quarters of 2016, 2017, and 2018, respectively. These growth rates exceed the Administration's estimated rate of potential real GDP growth over the long run of 2.3 percent a year. As a consequence, the unemployment rate is likely to fall from its 5.0 percent level in 2015:Q4—eventually falling to 4.5 percent in 2016:Q4 and remaining at that level before ticking back up to 4.6 percent in 2017:Q4. These levels, below the Administration's estimate of 4.9 percent for the rate of unemployment consistent with stable inflation, can be expected to incrementally raise inflation. As discussed in (Box 2-9), the effect of unemployment on changing the rate of inflation appears to have diminished in recent decades and estimates derived over the past two decades suggest that if the unemployment rate were to remain 1 percentage point below the stable-inflation rate of unemployment for a full year,

Table 2-2

Administration Economic Forecast

	Nominal GDP	Real GDP (Chain-Type)	GDP Price Index (Chain-Type)	Consumer Price Index (CPI-U)	Unemploy-ment Rate (Percent)	Interest Rate, 91-Day Treasury Bills (Percent)	Interest Rate, 10-Year Treasury Notes (Percent)
	Percent Change, Q4-to-Q4				Level, Calendar Year		
2014 (Actual)	3.9	2.5	1.3	1.2	6.2	0.0	2.5
2015	3.3	2.2	1.1	0.5	5.3	0.0	2.1
2016	4.3	2.7	1.6	1.9	4.7	0.7	2.9
2017	4.4	2.5	1.8	2.1	4.5	1.8	3.5
2018	4.3	2.4	1.9	2.2	4.6	2.6	3.9
2019	4.3	2.3	2.0	2.3	4.6	3.1	4.1
2020	4.3	2.3	2.0	2.3	4.7	3.3	4.2
2021	4.4	2.3	2.0	2.3	4.7	3.4	4.2
2022	4.4	2.3	2.0	2.3	4.8	3.4	4.2
2023	4.3	2.3	2.0	2.3	4.9	3.3	4.2
2024	4.3	2.3	2.0	2.3	4.9	3.3	4.2
2025	4.3	2.3	2.0	2.3	4.9	3.2	4.2
2026	4.3	2.3	2.0	2.3	4.9	3.2	4.2

Note: Forecast was based on data available as of November 17, 2015, and were used for the FY 2017 Budget. The interest rate on 91-day T-bills is measured on a secondary-market discount basis.
Source: Forecast was done jointly with the Council of Economic Advisers, the Department of the Treasury, and the Office of Management and Budget.

then the rate of inflation would increase by 0.2 percentage point. In the Administration forecast, the economy will be below the stable-inflation level of unemployment by an average of 0.3 percentage point in 2016, 2017, and 2018, which can be expected to raise the rate of core inflation by less than 0.1 percentage point each year. With the rate of core PCE inflation during 2015 at 1.4 percent, the 0.2-percentage point inflation increase during the next three years would still leave the rate of inflation at the end of 2018 below the Federal Reserve's 2-percent target for this index.

Nominal interest rates are currently low because of a reduction in the long-run interest rate and that the economy has not fully healed from the last recession. Monetary policy has also kept rates low. Consistent with the Federal Reserve's forward policy guidance at the time of the Administration forecast, long-term interest rates are projected to rise, consistent with the rise in short-term rates. Eventually, real interest rates (that is, nominal rates less the projected rate of inflation) are predicted to move toward, but still remain well below, their historical average. These interest-rate paths are close to those projected by the consensus of professional economic forecasters. During the past several years, consensus forecasts for long-term interest rates and long-term economic growth have fallen, reflecting changes in views on productivity, the term premium, along with other global and domestic factors.

Forecast over the Long Term

As discussed earlier, the long-run growth rate of the economy is determined by the growth of its supply-side components, including those governed by demographics and technological change. The growth rate that characterizes the long-run trend in real U.S. output—or potential output—plays an important role in guiding the Administration's long-run forecast. The potential output projections are based on the assumption that the President's full set of policy proposals, which would boost long-run output, are enacted (Box 2-8) After three years of growth above potential through 2017, real output growth shifts down to its long-term trend rate of 2.3 percent. These growth rates are slower than historical averages due to the retirement of the baby-boom generation and slower growth of the working-age population.

Table 2-3 shows the Administration's forecast for the contribution of each supply-side factor to the growth in potential real output: the working-age population; the rate of labor force participation; the employed share of the labor force; the length of the workweek; labor productivity; and the difference between productivity growth for the economy as a whole and the nonfarm business sector. The two columns of Table 2-3 show the average annual growth rate for each factor during a long period of history and over the forecast horizon. The first column shows the long-run average growth rates between the business-cycle peak of 1953 and the latest quarter available when the forecast was finalized (2015:Q3). Many of these variables show substantial fluctuations within business cycles, so that long-period growth rates must be examined to uncover underlying trends. The second column shows average projected growth rates between 2015:Q3 and 2026:Q4; that is, the entire 11¼-year interval covered by the Administration forecast.

The population is projected to grow 1.0 percent a year, on average, over the projection period (line 1, column 2), following the latest projection from the Social Security Administration. Over this same period, the labor force participation rate is projected to decline 0.4 percent a year (line 2, column 2). This projected decline in the labor force participation rate primarily reflects a negative demographic trend from the retirement of the baby-boom generation. During the next couple of years, however, rising labor demand

Box 2-8: Policy Proposals to Raise Output over the Next-Ten Years

The Administration has a wide-ranging and robust economic agenda that, if enacted, would expand the labor force and boost productivity. In line with long-standing precedent, the Administration's economic forecast incorporates the impact of the President's policy proposals. CEA estimates that, in total, these proposals would add over 5 percent to the level of output in 2026. The Administration's economic forecast, however, only incorporates 3-percentage points of the total boost to the level of output from these proposals. This adds about 0.3 percentage point on average to annual growth over the next 10 years. The remaining 2 percentage points are not included in the forecast for reasons discussed below. As a result, the Administration's forecast for the level of output in 2026 is about 1 percent higher than the forecasts from both the Congressional Budget Office and the Blue Chip consensus panel, as well as about 4 percent higher than the median forecast from the Federal Open Market Committee.

Immigration reform. The policy proposal with the largest effect on output is immigration reform, as embodied in the bipartisan Border Security, Economic Opportunity, and Immigration Modernization Act that passed the U.S. Senate in June 2013. CBO (2013b) estimated that this legislation, if enacted, would raise the level of real GDP by 3.3 percent after 10 years. This effect is so large because immigration reform would benefit the economy by counteracting the effects of an aging native-born population, attracting highly skilled immigrants that engage in innovative or entrepreneurial activities, and enabling better job-matching for currently undocumented workers who are offered a path to citizenship. Much of the overall effect is due to an expanded workforce, a factor that is incorporated in the budget savings from immigration reform. Thus, to avoid double counting in the budget savings, the workforce effects of immigration reform are not incorporated in the economic forecast. However, 0.7 percentage point of the total effect from immigration reform is due to increased total factor productivity, and this is reflected in the Administration's economic forecast.

Policies to expand cross-border trade and investment. The other set of policies with a large effect on output are a number of international agreements that would boost cross-border trade and investment, including the Trans-Pacific Partnership (TPP), the Transatlantic Trade and Investment Partnership (TTIP), an expansion of the Information Technology Agreement (ITA), a Trade in Services Agreement (TISA), and a possible Bilateral Investment Treaty (BIT) with China. TPP negotiations have concluded, and the Administration is working with Congress to secure its passage. A new study supported by the Peterson Institute for

International Economics (Petri and Plummer 2016) finds that TPP could raise U.S. real income by 0.5 percent in 2030. The European Commission (2013) estimates a roughly similar effect of TTIP on the U.S. economy, an increase of 0.4 percent in GDP in 2027.

Investments in surface transportation infrastructure. The Administration recognizes that investments in infrastructure support economic growth by creating jobs, boosting productivity, and strengthening the manufacturing sector. In December 2015, the bipartisan Fixing America's Surface Transportation Act (H.R. 22), which authorizes a $17.8 billion increase in surface transportation investment over five years, was enacted into law. This funding is an important down payment, but the country must further transform our transportation system to achieve a cleaner, safer transportation future. The President's FY 2017 budget calls for $32 billion per year over 10 years to support innovative programs that make our communities more livable and sustainable. The IMF (2014) estimates that given the current underutilization of resources in many advanced economies, a 1 percent of GDP permanent increase in public infrastructure investment could help increase output by as much as 2.5 percent after 10 years. See Chapter 6 in this *Report* for more discussion.

Policies to boost labor force participation. The Administration has pursued policies that enable all workers to participate in the labor force to their full potential by making it easier for workers to balance career and family responsibilities. The Administration's FY 2017 budget calls to triple the maximum child care tax credit to $3,000 for children younger than 5, while enabling more middle-class families to receive the maximum credit. In addition, every year since 2013, the President has proposed a Federal-State partnership that would provide all 4-year olds from low- and moderate-income families with access to high-quality preschool. Finally, the budget calls to provide technical assistance to help States implement and develop paid parental leave programs. These policies would increase labor force participation and the level of output.

Policies to make college affordable. The Administration is committed to making college affordable. The budget includes $60.8 billion over 10 years to make the first two years of community college tuition free for responsible students through a Federal-State cost sharing partnership. This plan would increase America's human capital and productivity by enabling 2 million people who would not have enrolled in college to earn an associate's degree.

Business tax reform. President Obama's framework for business tax reform issued in 2012 sets out a series of changes that would strengthen the economy in three main ways. First, by lowering average tax rates, the President's plan would boost investment in the United

States. Second, by moving to a more neutral tax system, the proposals would result in a more efficient allocation of capital. And third, to the degree the new system better addresses externalities, for example with a more generous research and development credit, it would also increase total factor productivity and therefore growth. (See Chapter 5 of last year's *Report* for a discussion of the economic benefits of business tax reform.)

Deficit reduction. CBO's (2013a) analysis of the macroeconomic effects of alternative budgetary paths estimates that a hypothetical $2 trillion in primary deficit reduction over 10 years raises the long-term level of real GDP by 0.5 percent. This effect arises because lower Federal deficits translate into higher national saving, lower interest rates, and in turn, greater private investment. The Administration's FY 2017 budget proposal includes $2.5 trillion in primary deficit reduction relative to the Administration's plausible baseline. Using CBO's methodology this would raise the level of output in 2026 by 0.6 percent.

due to the continuing business-cycle recovery is expected to offset some of this downward trend.

The employed share of the labor force—which is equal to one minus the unemployment rate—is expected to rise less than 0.1 percent a year during the next 11 years because the long-run unemployment rate is only slightly below the rate in 2015:Q3. The workweek is projected to be roughly flat during the forecast period, following a long-term decline of 0.2 percent a year. The workweek is expected to stabilize because some of the demographic forces pushing it down are largely exhausted.

Labor productivity in the nonfarm business sector is projected to increase 2.1 percent a year over the entire forecast (line 6, column 2), the same as the average growth rate from 1953 to 2015 (line 6, column 1). Productivity tends to grow faster in the nonfarm business sector than for the economy as a whole, because productivity in the government and household sectors of the economy is presumed (by a national-income accounting convention) not to grow (that is, output in those two sectors grows only through the use of more production inputs). The difference in these growth rates is expected to subtract 0.3 percent a year during the projection, similar to the 0.2 percent a year decline historically (line 10, columns 1 and 2). This productivity differential is equal to the sum of two other growth rates in the table: the ratio of nonfarm business employment to household employment (line 4) and the ratio of real output to nonfarm business output (line 7).

Summing the growth rates of all of its components, real output is projected to rise at an average 2.4 percent a year over the projection (line

Table 2-3

Supply-Side Components of Actual
and Potential Real Output Growth, 1953–2026

	Component	Growth rate[a]	
		History	Forecast
		1953:Q2 to 2015:Q3[b]	2015:Q3 to 2026:Q4
1	Civilian noninstitutional population aged 16+	1.4	1.0
2	Labor force participation rate	0.1	-0.4
3	Employed share of the labor force	0.0	0.0
4	Ratio of nonfarm business employment to household employment	0.0	0.0
5	Average weekly hours (nonfarm business)	-0.2	0.0
6	Output per hour (productivity, nonfarm business)[c]	2.1	2.1
7	Ratio of real output to nonfarm business output[c]	-0.2	-0.4
8	Sum: Actual real output[c]	3.0	2.4
	Memo:		
9	Potential real output[d]	3.1	2.3
10	Output per worker differential: output vs nonfarm[e]	-0.2	-0.3

[a] All contributions are in percentage points at an annual rate, forecast finalized November 2015. Total may not add up due to rounding.

[b] 1953:Q2 was a business-cycle peak. 2015:Q3 is the latest quarter with available data.

[c] Real output and real nonfarm business output are measured as the average of income- and product-side measures.

[d] Computed as (line 8) - 2 * (line 3).

[e] Real output per household worker less nonfarm business output per nonfarm business worker. This can be shown to equal (line 7) - (line 4).

Note: Output is the average of GDP and GDI. Population, labor force, and household employment have been adjusted for discontinuities in the population series. Nonfarm business employment, and the workweek, come from the Labor Productivity and Costs database maintained by the Bureau of Labor Statistics.

Source: Bureau of Labor Statistics, Current Population Survey, Labor Productivity and Costs; Bureau of Economic Analysis, National Income and Product Accounts; Department of the Treasury; Office of Management and Budget; CEA calculations.

8, column 2), slightly faster than the 2.3 percent annual growth rate for potential real output (line 9, column 2). Actual output is expected to grow faster than potential output primarily because of the small projected rise in the employment rate (that is, the decline in the unemployment rate) as currently unemployed workers find jobs, and others reenter the labor force or shift from part-time to full-time jobs.

Real potential output (line 9, column 2) is projected to grow less than the long-term historical growth rate of 3.1 percent a year (line 9, column 1), primarily due to the lower projected growth rate of the working-age population and the retirement of the baby-boom cohort. If the effects of

Box 2-9: Stable Inflation Rate of Unemployment

Economic theory generally relates inflation rates and unemployment rates under the view that very low unemployment may signal tight labor markets that generate upward pressure on wages and high demand for goods and services that put upward pressure on prices. The accelerationist Phillips curve relates the increase in the rate of inflation to the rate of unemployment, or possibly some other measure of economic slack. It can also be used in conjunction with other inflation-sector equations to derive estimates for the rate of unemployment that keeps inflation stable (NAIRU), an essential notion for maximizing growth without ever increasing inflation rates. According to the Phillips curve, an unemployment rate below the one that would keep inflation stable will result in upward pressure on price inflation. Many have noted that the fit of the Phillips curve has deteriorated (for instance, Ball and Mazumder 2011). They observed that the Phillips curve would have predicted inflation to fall much more during the Great Recession than it did.

The deterioration in the ability of a simple Phillips curve model to fit the data is shown in Figure 2-x. As shown by the equation embedded in Figure 2-x, the change in the rate of inflation from its expectation (on the left hand side) is regressed against a demographically adjusted unemployment rate and a constant term. (From this regression, one can estimate the NAIRU as the ratio of the coefficient on the unemployment rate to the constant.) The measure of inflation expectations is lagged

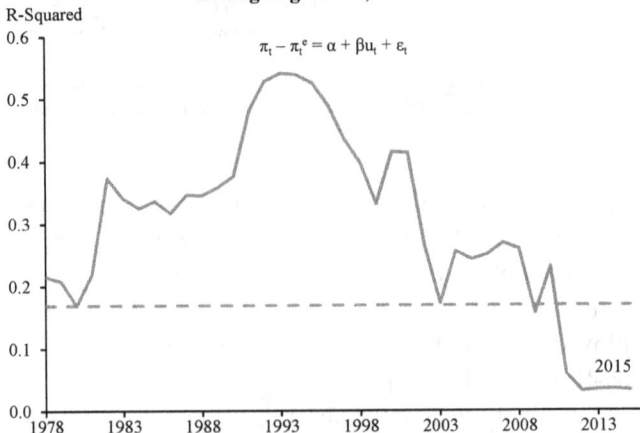

Figure 2-xiii
R-Squared from Trailing 20-Year Price-Price Phillips Curve Rolling Regression, 1978–2015

$$\pi_t - \pi_t^e = \alpha + \beta u_t + \varepsilon_t$$

Note: Dashed line represents result from regression over entire sample period.
Source: Bureau of Labor Statistics; Federal Reserve Board, Haver Analytics; CEA calculations.

inflation up to 2007 and then expectations from the Federal Open Market Committee onward. Measuring inflation by the core CPI (that is, excluding food and energy), Figure 2-x depicts the goodness-of-fit (known as R^2) over rolling 20-year periods. During the 1990s, this relationship was robust, averaging an R^2 of 0.46 (meaning that movements in the unemployment rate accounted for 46 percent of the variation in inflation). Over an estimation period that includes the past 20 years, however, the R^2 is only slightly above zero (meaning that this model explains almost none of the recent variation in inflation).

The deterioration in fit in this Phillips curve relationship results in dramatically less precise estimates for the NAIRU, as shown in Figure 2-xi, which shows the band associated with a 50-percent probability that the true estimate lies within.[1] An increased goodness-of-fit corresponds to a thinner confidence band, implying less uncertainty over the true value of the NAIRU. Since 2011 though, uncertainty surrounding the true NAIRU has risen: A mere 50-percent confidence band in 2014 ranges from -4.3 to 6.1, providing little certainty over the current rate of unemployment that will keep inflation stable. Moreover this is only one model of the NAIRU, other models show similar increases in uncertainty over time and the total uncertainty is even larger than shown by any

Figure 2-xiv
NAIRU from Trailing 20-Year Price-Price Phillips Curve Rolling Regression, 1978–2015

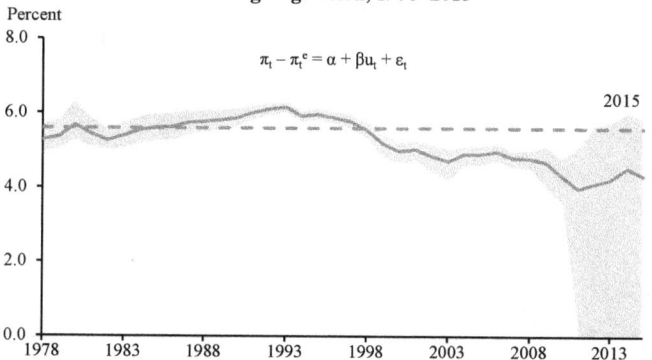

Note: NAIRU is the unemployment rate that keeps inflation stable. It is calculated as α/β. Dashed line represents result from regression over entire sample period. Shaded area indicates a 50 percent confidence band around the point estimate, calculated using a method discussed in Staiger, Stock, and Watson (1997) for analyzing the ratio of the means of two dependent normal random variables. Confidence bands since 2012 include implausible negative values.
Source: Bureau of Labor Statistics; Federal Reserve Board, Haver Analytics; CEA calculations.

[1] Confidence band calculated using a method discussed in Staiger, Stock, and Watson (1997), which extends upon a technique introduced in Fieller (1954). A 50 percent band is used—as opposed to a one-sigma band—because increasingly higher levels of confidence produce confidence bands that approach unboundedness starting after 2010.

individual model because of uncertainty over the true process driving inflation.

Similarly, the coefficient on the unemployment gap has changed noticeably, evolving toward zero as shown in Figure 2-xii. Over the entire estimation period, this coefficient has been about –0.4 (meaning that every point-year of low unemployment raises the rate of inflation by four-tenths of a percentage point). In contrast, from 2002 to 2010, this coefficient averaged about –0.25, implying that for each point-year of unemployment rate below the NAIRU, inflation would rise by a quarter of a percentage point. And the most recent estimate suggests that each point-year of an unemployment rate below the NAIRU would result in a 0.03-percentage point increase in the inflation rate.

Although uncertainty surrounding the NAIRU has risen drastically over the past few years, a small coefficient on the unemployment rate reduces the economic importance of a precise estimate for the NAIRU. With an unemployment coefficient of -0.25 or less, an estimated NAIRU that differs by half of a percentage point from its true value will only move core CPI inflation slightly.

Figure 2-xv

Unemployment Rate Coefficient from Trailing 20-Year Price-Price Phillips Curve Rolling Regression, 1978–2015

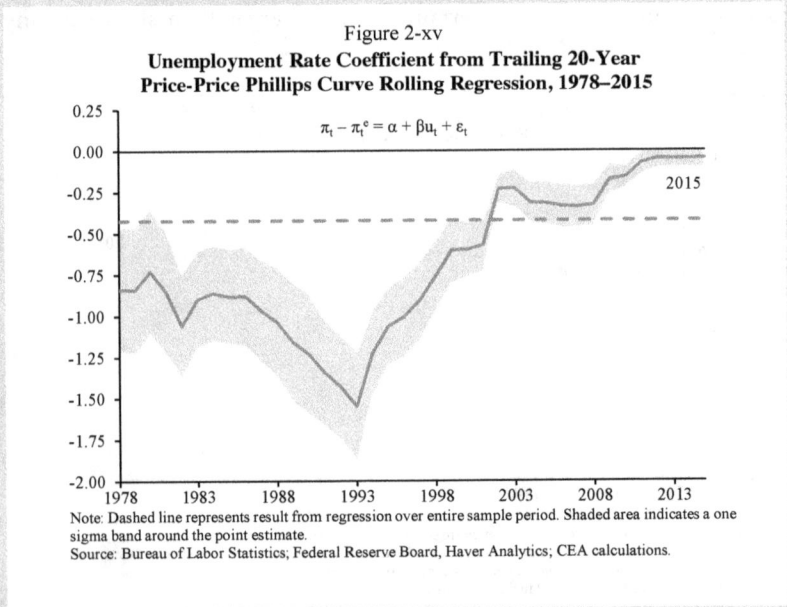

$$\pi_t - \pi_t^e = \alpha + \beta u_t + \varepsilon_t$$

Note: Dashed line represents result from regression over entire sample period. Shaded area indicates a one sigma band around the point estimate.
Source: Bureau of Labor Statistics; Federal Reserve Board, Haver Analytics; CEA calculations.

immigration reform on labor-force size were incorporated into this forecast, then potential real output growth would exceed the 2.3-percent rate shown in the table.

Upside and Downside Forecast Risks. Like any forecast, the Administration's economic forecast is uncertain, and several risks are worth enumerating here. One upside risk is from the homebuilding sector which has some upside potential given the current low level of household formation and its potential for increase. Another upside risk would be that more workers are drawn back into the labor force than expected. On the downside, it appears that growth in China and many other emerging-market countries is slowing, which may reduce U.S. exports. In addition, financial market developments—either reflecting spillovers from abroad or U.S.-specific issues—are another downside risk. Over the longer-run, there are some downside risks to the estimate of potential growth insofar as more recent lower productivity growth rates continue. Yet, as Box 2-5, discusses, some of the recent slowdown in productivity growth may be an artifact of the measurement issues in the official statistics and not entirely a reflection of the economy.

CONCLUSION

The economy continued to strengthen during 2015, especially in the labor market with robust employment gains and continued declines in unemployment. Job growth continued to exceed 200,000 a month for the year as a whole, extending the longest streak of uninterrupted private-sector job growth on record and contributing to an American recovery that has outpaced most other advanced economies. Demand is strong is the United States, especially in the household sector, and will continue to support solid growth in 2016.At the same time, we face challenges associated with the slowing global economy that are discussed in the next Chapter.

Looking ahead, some of the most important decisions that we make as a Nation are the structural policies that influence long-term growth. The President's budget sets forth a number of policies that can be expected to increase the level or long-term growth rate of potential output.

Such policies also aim to boost aggregate demand in the near term and to improve our long-term competitiveness, while promising fiscal restraint over the long run. They are an essential complement to policies that make sure this growth is shared by the middle class and those working to get into the middle class.

CHAPTER 3

THE GLOBAL MACROECONOMIC SITUATION

Although the United States experienced continued growth and robust job creation, the global economy in 2015 had unexpectedly low growth across many regions relative to expectations and even relative to the more-subdued growth seen in recent years. The downward shift in growth has both a broader, longer-term aspect, as it has applied to both many advanced economies and emerging markets continuously over the last five years, and a more acute presentation over the last year and into the beginning of 2016 arising in large part from developments in emerging markets. The broader downward revisions to growth forecasts have involved an overall environment of weak global demand, disappointing global productivity, and shifting demographics. While both advanced and emerging economies have missed growth expectations, over the last year a number of advanced economies have roughly met or exceeded expectations, while the biggest downward revisions in forecasts have been among large emerging market countries.

To illustrate the unexpected nature of the developments, the International Monetary Fund (IMF) in January 2016 estimated global real gross domestic product (GDP) growth of 3.1 percent in 2015 and predicted that it would rise to 3.4 percent in 2016 (IMF 2016). The Organisation for Economic Co-operation and Development (OECD), in a separate analysis in November 2015, forecast global growth of 2.9 percent in 2015 and 3.3 percent in 2016 (OECD 2015). Both of these growth estimates for 2015 were well below those forecasted just over a year earlier of 3.8 percent and 3.7 percent, respectively. The deteriorating estimates underscore that weaker global growth, particularly among U.S. trading partners, was a headwind to U.S. economic growth in 2015.

The IMF's estimated 3.1-percent growth rate of global real GDP in 2015 was slightly lower than the growth rate over the last three years, and well below both the growth rate earlier in the recovery and the pre-crisis average of between 4 and 5 percent. This slowdown was not anticipated in earlier forecasts. Figure 3-1 shows the IMF's forecast for global growth at different points in time. The solid line represents the actual growth outcomes while the dotted lines show the forecast. At first, as growth slowed, the IMF—along with most other forecasters—expected a near-term pickup in growth to over 4 percent. Growth has fallen short of expectations in many regions, including both advanced and emerging-market economies.

The global slowdown and the contrast in U.S. growth expectations compared with the world have contributed to a major appreciation of the U.S. dollar. The real trade-weighted dollar as measured by the Federal Reserve's broad index began appreciating sharply in mid-2014 and strengthened 17 percent between July 2014 and December 2015 (see Figure 3-2). This is a historically large appreciation. Since the collapse of the Bretton Woods system in the early 1980s, the dollar has appreciated that quickly only two other times: first during the sharp monetary tightening in the early 1980s and again after the onset of the East Asian Crisis in 1997-98. Among the drivers of the recent appreciation is the strong performance of the U.S. economy against a backdrop of relatively weak growth in the rest of the world. As a result, U.S. Federal Reserve policy is at a different juncture than monetary policy in most foreign countries. While markets expect the Federal Reserve to reduce monetary policy accommodation throughout 2016, the European Central Bank (ECB) and the Bank of Japan (BOJ) are in the midst of maintaining or expanding monetary stimulus with the aim of raising inflation from low levels toward 2 percent.

As discussed in Chapter 2, the slowdown in global growth is a headwind for the U.S. economy—contributing to slower growth of exports. Real net exports subtracted more than half a point from U.S. real GDP growth over the four quarters of 2015 on a growth accounting basis. In addition, if the global situation deteriorated, it would present a more substantial risk to the U.S. economy—as well as to economies worldwide. That is why it is critical for economies around the world to focus on growth, undertaking the necessary steps to expand demand, reform supply, encourage trade, and manage economic and financial developments as appropriate in different contexts.

SOURCES OF THE BROADER SLOWDOWN

The slower growth in the world economy relative to the pre-crisis era stems largely from slowdowns relative to expectations in emerging-market economies, including large economies like India and China, as well as disappointing growth in Europe. Figure 3-3 compares the growth of GDP per working-age person from 2011 to 2014 relative to 2002 to 2007, with points

Figure 3-1
IMF World Real GDP Growth Forecast, 2010–2020
Percent Change, Year-over-Year

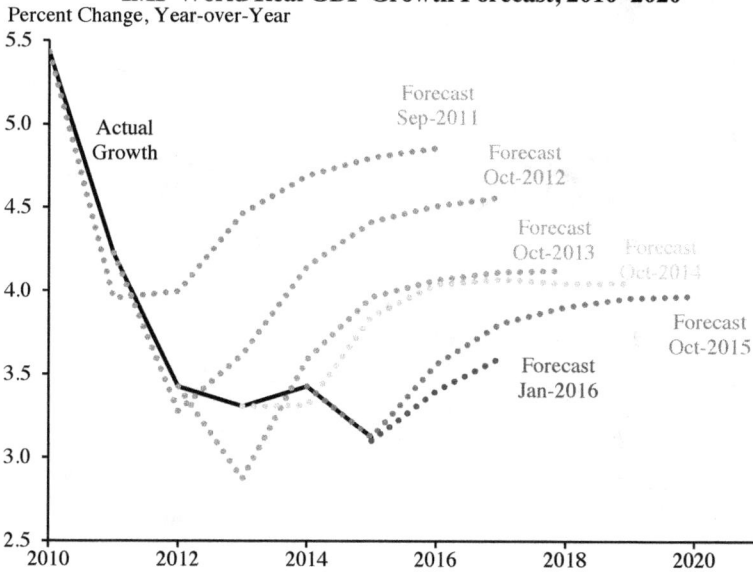

Source: International Monetary Fund (IMF).

Figure 3-2
Real Broad Trade-Weighted Dollar, 1973–2015
Index (Mar-1973=100)

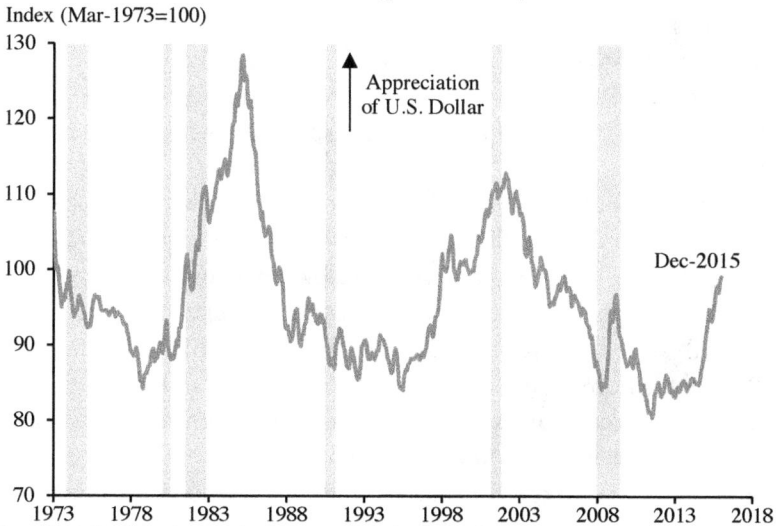

Note: The index above is a weighted average of the foreign exchange values of the U.S. dollar against major U.S. trading partners.
Source: Federal Reserve Board; Haver Analytics.

Figure 3-3

Real GDP per Working Age Population (WAP), Pre- vs. Post-Crisis
(Average Annual Percent Change)

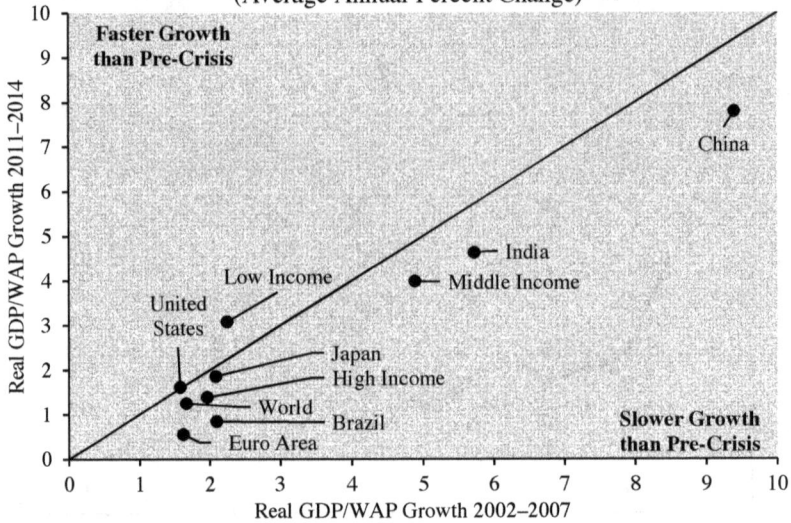

Note: Working age population is aged 15-64.
Source: World Bank; CEA calculations.

on the 45-degree line representing unchanged growth rates between these two periods. In general, while they may still have some demand-related slack to make up following the crisis, the United States and Japan are growing at similar rates compared with their growth before the financial crisis after adjusting for changes to working-age population. Low-income countries have, on average, seen an increase in growth. The euro area has slowed relative to pre-crisis rates of growth, with some large emerging markets also slowing.

A similar pattern emerges in downgrades to the IMF forecasts over the past five years. Overall, the level of output among G-20 countries is 6-percent smaller in 2015 than what the IMF had predicted in 2010, after the full extent of the recessions caused by the financial crisis became apparent. Growth over the last five years has fallen short of expectation in 18 of the 20 G-20 economies, as shown in Figure 3-4, with only Saudi Arabia and Turkey slightly exceeding expectations, compared with substantial shortfalls across some other nations. In total, China and India account for about half of the 6-percent underperformance of the G-20 economy relative to the 2010 projections—with shortfalls in the United States and the European Union accounting for another one-quarter. The United States accounts for a sizeable part of the aggregate slowdown despite good growth in GDP per working-age person and having a relatively small cumulative growth short-fall (just 3.2 percent over the period) because it is such a large share of the

Figure 3-4
Percent Gap Between Actual and Projected (Oct-2010) Cumulative Real GDP Growth between 2010 and 2015

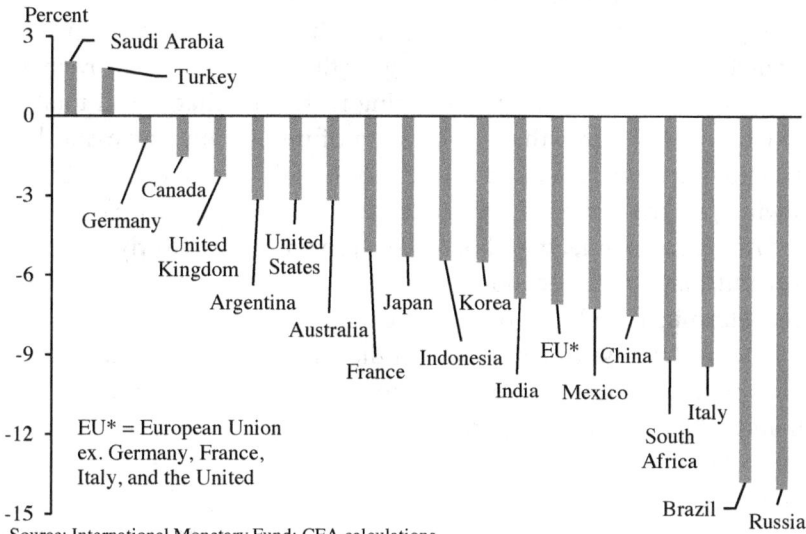

Percent

3
— Saudi Arabia

— Turkey

0

-3
Canada
Germany
United
Kingdom
United
States

-6
Argentina
Australia
Japan
Korea

France
Indonesia
India
EU*
Mexico
China

-9

-12
EU* = European Union
ex. Germany, France,
Italy, and the United
Italy
South
Africa

-15
Brazil
Russia

Source: International Monetary Fund; CEA calculations.

world economy. Likewise, China and India did not underperform as much as Russia or Brazil, but they make up a larger part of the shortfall because they are a much more significant part of the world economy.

The persistently disappointing world growth over the last half-decade has root causes both in longer-term demand and supply. On the supply side, there has been disappointing labor productivity growth, or the ability to produce more output from the same labor inputs, across a range of countries since the crisis. While variable from year to year, G-7 countries had average labor productivity growth rates near or above 2 percent a year throughout the latter half of the 20th century. Those rates have all dropped; in some cases, to near zero. Labor productivity growth for Japan is projected to be a sixth of its annual rate from 1999 to 2006 and, for the euro area, a third of its average preceding the financial crisis. Similarly, for most other advanced economies, labor productivity is projected to be much lower in 2015 than it was prior to the financial crisis (Conference Board 2015). Productivity growth in the United States has broadly outperformed other countries with both a smaller decline from the 1950-2007 period and one of the higher growth rates in the G-7 at present. Some of the slowdown may simply reflect a slow global recovery. An important factor in lower productivity growth has been the decline in the pace of investment per worker—referred to as capital deepening. To the extent that this represents a cyclical shortfall in demand, economists would expect capital deepening and productivity growth to pick up in the coming years.

Sharp and persistent productivity slowdowns are not unprecedented (Eichengreen, Park, and Shin 2015), but, if sustained, slower productivity growth will mean slower output growth and slower improvements in living standards. Particularly concerning is the fact that global total factor productivity (TFP) growth, an indication of innovation above-and-beyond just deploying more capital, has slowed to roughly zero in the last three years following pre-crisis rates of 1 percent (Conference Board 2015).

At the same time, the labor force is growing more slowly in the United States and many other economies around the world. The size of the labor force, determined both by population changes and movements in the rate at which people choose to participate in the labor market, provides the other key supply-side input for overall economic growth. With an aging population and falling labor force participation rates across demographic groups, the size of the labor force has presented a headwind to U.S. growth, mirrored to varying degrees across other economies globally (See Box 3-1).

In addition, as noted in Chapter 2, investment has been disappointing in all of the major advanced economies since the financial crisis. This is worrying from a supply perspective, as there will be a lower capital stock and possibly lower productivity growth in the future due to reduced investment today; but it also represents a lack of demand in the world economy. Lower investment can generally be explained by the slower pace of global recovery, as faster growth generates more investment demand by firms, but lower investment also represents lower demand for goods and services itself.

Persistent demand weakness has been visible in many countries. The unemployment rate has stayed well above pre-crisis averages in many countries and weak price growth has been a signal of a lack of demand pressure in the economy. Beyond weak investment demand, aggregate demand may have been persistently weak for reasons related to debt overhang and wealth loss remaining from the financial crisis. Families, firms, and, in some countries, governments saw a significant run-up in debt prior to the financial crisis, as well as a loss of wealth from falling asset and home prices and high levels of insolvency during the crisis itself. Even several years later, they may hold back on spending and investment as they try to deleverage and rebuild their balance sheets.

"Secular stagnation," where chronically insufficient aggregate demand cannot be remedied by conventional monetary policy, could also play a role in weak growth in certain economies. Stagnation occurs when even a real interest rate of zero does not generate enough investment growth to fully utilize the economy's resources. A number of features of the economy could

Box 3-1: Changing Demographic Trends and Global Growth

Demographics play a large role in the long-run trend of economic growth by affecting labor supply, capital formation, and productivity (IMF 2004). A major part of any country's real GDP growth is simply its population growth, as growing populations provide more workers as well as rising demand for products, new homes, and services. Beyond that, increases in the relative size of the working-age population (people aged 15 to 64) can also have a major impact on output per capita by directly changing the labor supply. Demographic changes also indirectly affect the amount of resources per capita through changes in household savings behavior across their life cycles. Lower dependency ratios (the ratio of people younger than 15 or older than 64 to the working-age population) can raise savings, which helps finance more investments and increases output. Finally, demographics indirectly affect productivity growth through changes in the quality of human capital formation and innovation. Nevertheless, the reverse is also true. Demographic changes can act as a drag on economic growth (Kohshaka 2013).

Global demographic trends are at a turning point. Population growth is slowing and, after increasing for the previous five decades, the proportion of the population that is working-age peaked at 66 percent in 2012. This proportion is projected to decline steadily for the next century. This slower growth in the working-age population—or outright contraction—will continue to be a drain on global growth for the foreseeable future. Stark differences at the country level lie beneath this global trend. As seen in Figure 3-i, working-age populations are now shrinking in Europe and in East Asia broadly, not just as a share of the population, but in raw numbers. In North and Latin America, working-age populations are projected to flatten out over time, while Southern Asia and Africa will continue to see an increase. Collectively, these regional demographic trends signal additional risks to future global economic growth.

Over the next 30 years, half of the world's population will live in Africa and Southern Asia; global population growth will be driven by their high fertility and relatively young populations. As a result, the bulk of new workers in the global economy will be added in economies that have lower levels of education, technology, and capital, implying those workers will not be as productive, if current circumstances continue. By 2035, the number of people joining the working-age population from Sub-Saharan Africa and Southern Asia will exceed that from the rest of the world combined. This means both South Asia and Africa will be increasingly important to global growth. It will be necessary to build

Figure 3-i
Actual and Forecasted Working-Age Population by Region, 1950–2070
Millions of People Aged 15-64

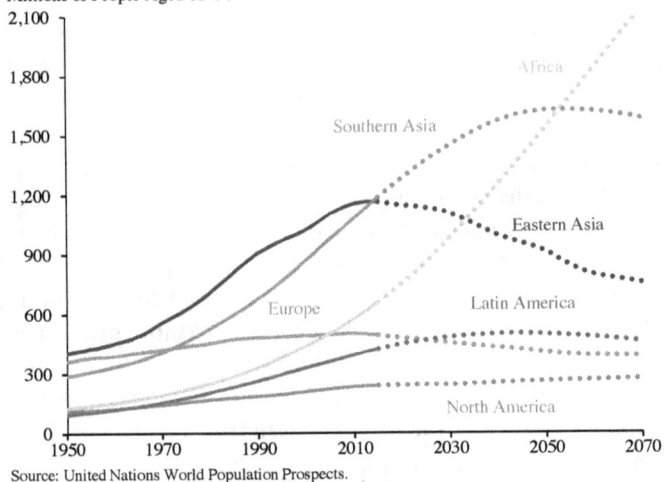

Source: United Nations World Population Prospects.

institutions and economies that can lead global growth in these places (IMF 2015c).

The other half of the world's population will experience slowdowns in population growth with rising shares of the elderly. Substantial aging is projected in Europe and East Asia (see Figure 3-ii). By 2050, the

Figure 3-ii
Actual and Forecasted Dependency Ratios by Region, 1950–2070
Number of Dependents per 100 People Aged 15-64

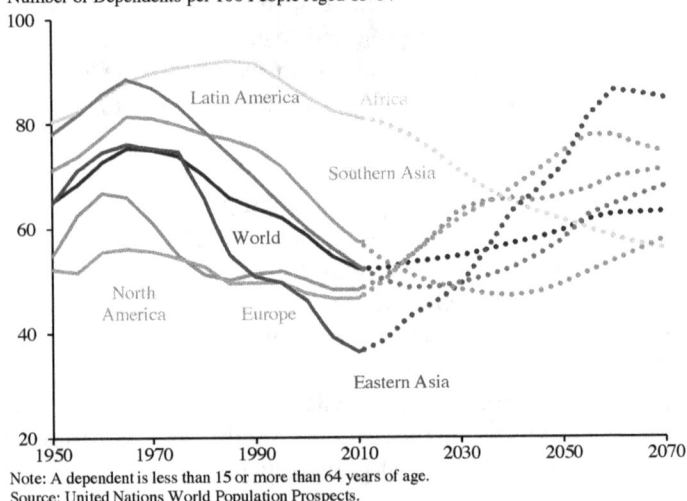

Note: A dependent is less than 15 or more than 64 years of age.
Source: United Nations World Population Prospects.

regions are forecasted to have 73 dependents (people younger than 15 or older than 64) for every 100 working-age persons.

Aging populations can put pressure on public budgets, with fewer workers supporting more pensions, and generally supporting slower growth. These dangers have materialized in Japan. Economic growth in Japan is stagnant (and forecasted to remain so) in large part because growth in the working-age population has lagged behind growth in the total population for the last 20 years (Mühlesisen and Faruqee 2001). The U.S. economy grew almost twice as fast as Japan's from 1989 to 2013. However, simply controlling for population by comparing growth of GDP per capita leads to much more similar growth rates (1.4 percent versus 1.1 percent). Even more striking is that when examining GDP per working-age person, Japan had slightly faster growth than the United States (Figure 3-iii). This highlights that even if a country is doing reasonably well conditional on its demographics—as Japan has—it still means slow growth over time if too few workers enter the labor force. And even if income per capita is rising, slow overall growth due to slow population growth can greatly increase the challenges associated with government debt and financing future government commitments (Karam, Muir, Pereira, and Tuladhar 2011). These issues are now coming to the forefront of the global economy.

Demographics is not just the exogenous result of developments outside of public policies, it also depends on those policies. In some countries, for example, pro-natal policies have raised birth rates and

Figure 3-iii
Real GDP Growth and Demographic Trends, 1989–2013

25-Year Average Annual Growth Rate

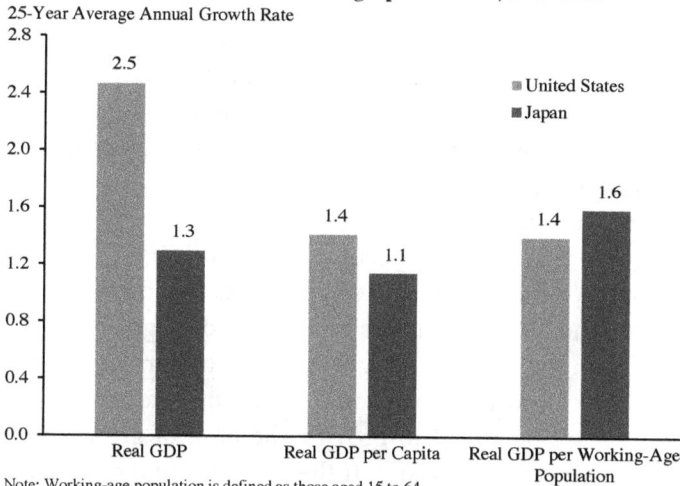

Note: Working-age population is defined as those aged 15 to 64.
Source: U.S. Bureau of Economic Analysis; Cabinet Office of Japan; OECD Data.

affected the demographic trajectory (Kalwij 2010; Wong, Tang, and Ye 2011). In the United States, immigration reform would expand the working-age population and reduce the ratio of children and elderly relative to prime-age workers. In addition, even for a given demographic structure, steps that facilitate work and raise the labor force participation rate will increase economic growth.

lead to this result, ranging from falling population growth that provides fewer consumers and shifts investment demand to rising inequality that concentrates spending power in the hands of people who have higher propensity to save. Secular stagnation is likely not an appropriate way to describe the overall world economy—or the United States—today, but it may be a useful way to think about some pockets of weakness or risks that could be faced if the zero lower bound becomes more constraining in dealing with future recessions. In some countries, like Japan and possibly the euro area, the combination of a low equilibrium real interest rate, low inflation expectations emanating from weak demand, and unfavorable demographics makes it very hard for monetary policy alone to stimulate the economy.

The current account balance provides another way to examine relative strengths and weaknesses in demand in the global economy. Countries that produce more than they consume and invest (net exporters) may have weaker aggregate demand—more demand-related "slack"—than those whose demand exceeds production (net importers). Despite substantial progress in reducing the current account deficit to a 14-year low in 2014, the United States still runs a larger current account deficit than its sustainability target as estimated by the IMF (see Figure 3-5); in part, reflecting the relative strength of U.S. demand compared with the rest of the world. China, Japan, and the euro area—especially Germany—all have larger current account surpluses than either their most recent IMF sustainability targets, current account norms, or both.

In short, various parts of the world economy are growing slowly, and likely too slowly. U.S. economic performance has clearly been stronger than the rest of the world and has left it with less demand-related slack in the economy. Still, the U.S. economy is not a large enough share of the world economy, nor can it grow fast enough, to solely support world growth. Even with relatively pessimistic projections for China and emerging markets, those countries are projected to provide the bulk of growth in the world economy over the coming decades. If they slow more than expected, global growth could fall further. 2015, though, has been a difficult year for many emerging markets (IMF 2014 and 2015d).

Figure 3-5

Current Account Balance as a Share of GDP, 2015

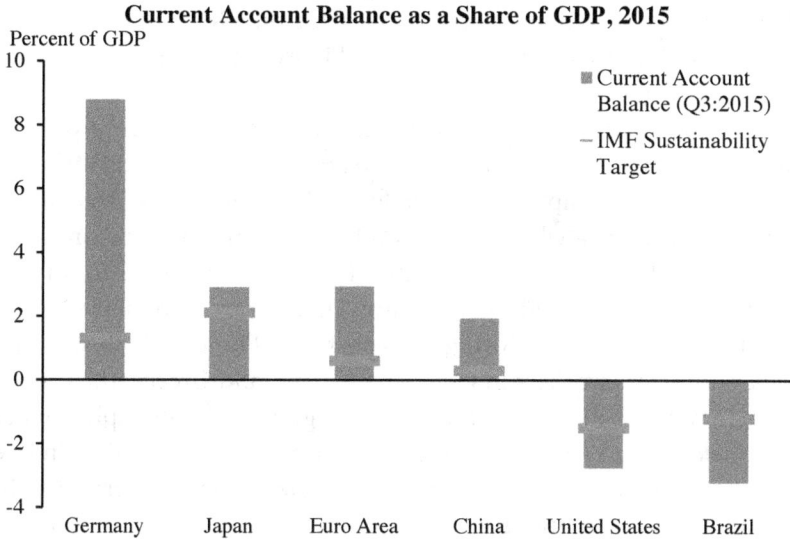

Note: The IMF Sustainability Target is the current account balance necessary to stabilize the nonfinancial account; targets as of 2015.
Source: International Monetary Fund (IMF); National Sources via Haver Analytics.

DEVELOPMENTS IN 2015

In contrast to the broader lack of demand affecting the global economy, 2015 brought a more acute set of challenges for some emerging markets. Over the past year, countries experiencing the biggest downward revisions in IMF forecasts were emerging markets and commodity producers; Argentina and India had the only upward revisions among emerging markets in the G-20. Advanced economies have fared slightly better relative to forecasts, in part because expectations have not been high. The European Union and Japan were not expected to grow rapidly and had only small revisions (IMF 2014 and 2015d).

Euro area

Recovery from the financial and sovereign debt crises in the euro area remained uneven, but gained some momentum in 2015. The euro area manufacturing sector rebounded in 2015, expanding in December at its fastest pace in 20 months. In addition, all major euro-area nations experienced positive growth in output and job creation in December for the first time since April 2014. Domestic demand in the euro area remains below its pre-crisis peak, driven by weak investment, but growth in real GDP across Greece, Ireland, Italy, Portugal, and Spain (GIIPS) as a group increased (see Figure 3-6), although Greece contracted by 0.8 percent at an annual rate over the first three quarters of 2015. Nonetheless, the level of output relative to before the crisis remained much lower for the GIIPS than in the rest of the euro area—especially Germany. (See Figure 3-6 and Box 2-7 on growth across advanced economies.)

Unemployment rates tell a similar story: they have improved in the past year, but many countries in the euro area are still suffering high levels of joblessness. The unemployment rate fell to 10.4 percent by December 2015 for the euro area as a whole, a full point lower than a year before. The rate either declined to, or remained within, the low range of 4.5 to 6.1 percent in Germany, Austria, and Luxembourg. In contrast, it remained above 10 percent in Slovakia; Italy; Portugal; Cyprus; and France, which saw a record number of jobless workers in October. In Spain and Greece, the unemployment rate was still above 20 percent. This huge range in unemployment rates across the euro area (from 4.5 percent in Germany to 24.5 percent in Greece) stands in contrast to the range across U.S. states (from 2.7 percent in North Dakota to 6.7 percent in New Mexico).

While output expanded in nearly all euro-area countries, weak domestic investment and demand abroad has weighed down growth in the euro area. Investment remains subdued in both the GIIPS (as a group) and Germany as a fraction of GDP relative to other euro-area countries in 2015. Euro area real GDP growth slowed to 1.2 percent at an annual rate in the third quarter of 2015, primarily due to a slowdown in export growth.

To some degree, the euro-area economy is still struggling with the vestiges of the euro crisis. Uncertainty over global and regional conditions—for instance, the path of monetary policy, regional political issues, or foreign demand conditions—may be one cause of the subdued level of investment. The Greek situation is one example of such uncertainty. Greece experienced a sharp upswing in sovereign borrowing rates in the first half of the year (from around 9 percent in January to a peak of over 18 percent in July) as failure to implement reforms required by lenders resulted in a lending freeze, raising tensions that peaked in a referendum in July, where voters rejected the conditions of international lenders. Fears arose that Greece would have to exit from the euro area's currency union when partner countries cut off credit to banks through the euro system, with Greece imposing strict currency controls and rationing cash withdrawals from banks. However, in late summer, Greece reached an agreement with euro-area partner countries to receive additional financing from the European Union. The Syriza government in Greece, under the leadership of Prime Minister Alexis Tsipras, followed the agreement with domestic votes on economic and fiscal reforms. The measures calmed investor fears of a Greek exit from the euro area (see Figure 3-7). Greece's manufacturing sector remained in a severe downturn

Figure 3-6
Real GDP, 2008–2015

Index (2008:Q1=100)

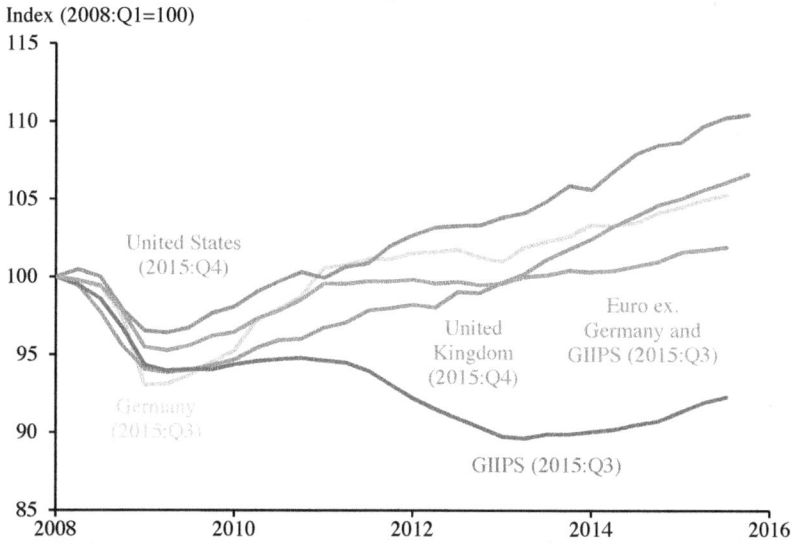

Note: GIIPS includes Greece, Ireland, Italy, Portugal, and Spain.
Source: National Sources via Haver Analytics.

throughout 2015, though its rate of contraction eased late in the year follow-ing the resolution of the acute problems in July with financial support from the European Union, other euro-area members, and accommodations from the European Central Bank (ECB) coinciding with progress on reforms.

Euro-area inflation was low in 2015, despite the labor market recov-ery in some countries, further evidence that domestic demand remains weak. Figure 3-8 shows that euro-area inflation remains well below the ECB's goal for the inflation rate of close to but not exceeding 2-percent. As inflation continued to slow, the ECB increased its monetary stimulus in 2015, purchasing 60 billion euro in sovereign bonds each month (quantita-tive easing) and lowering a key policy rate of interest to minus 0.3 percent. Despite the ECB's additional stimulus, a key challenge remained that interest rates were highest in countries where unemployment was highest. The inability to target monetary stimulus limits the ECB's ability to help countries with the greatest economic slack and may prevent convergence across regions. Thus, monetary policy alone is not sufficient to address the challenge of weak demand.

One reason that the United States has recovered more quickly than other advanced economies is its combination of accommodative monetary policy, quick action to recapitalize the financial sector, and aggressive demand management through countercyclical fiscal policy. In contrast,

Figure 3-7
Euro Area Sovereign Interest Rate Spreads
Over Germany, 2007–2015

Percentage Points

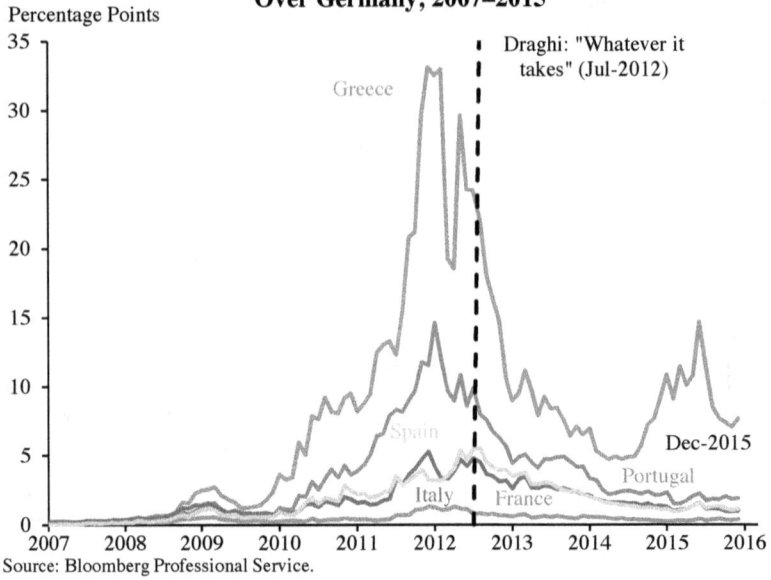

Draghi: "Whatever it takes" (Jul-2012)

Greece

Dec-2015

Spain

Portugal

Italy   France

Source: Bloomberg Professional Service.

Figure 3-8
Core and Overall Inflation in the Euro Area, 2007–2015

12-Month Percent Change

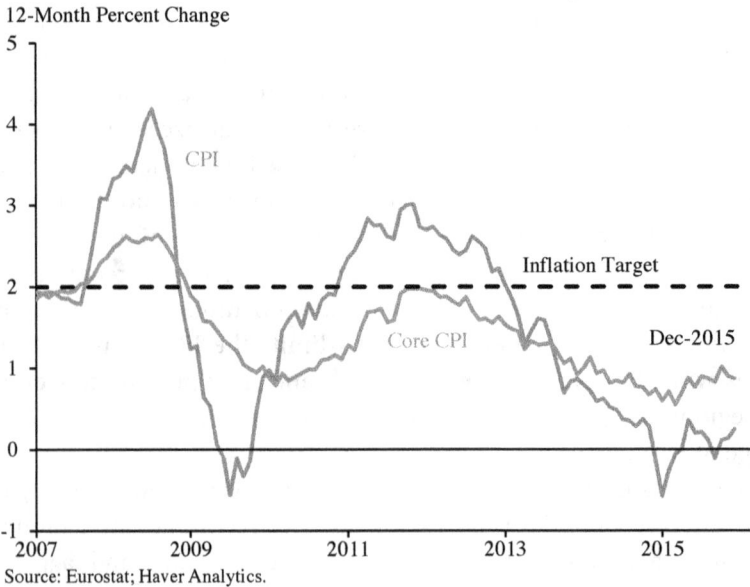

CPI

Inflation Target

Core CPI

Dec-2015

Source: Eurostat; Haver Analytics.

some euro-area countries are constrained by fiscal rules and were unable or unwilling to pursue stronger countercyclical measures. The Federal Reserve pursued several large-scale asset purchase programs from 2008 to 2014, dramatically expanding its balance sheet. In contrast, the ECB's balance sheet (as measured by the asset side) grew more slowly in the crisis and, after a brief surge in late 2011 and early 2012, was allowed to contract between mid-2012 and mid-2014, as euro-area banks repaid the ECB long-term loans taken out during the crisis. The ECB reversed course and began large-scale asset purchases in January 2015. Although the ECB voted in December 2015 to extend quantitative easing until at least March 2017 and to augment it with other measures, markets appeared to have expected more forceful monetary stimulus: the euro jumped 3.1 percent, producing the largest one-day appreciation of the euro since March 2009.

United Kingdom

Real GDP growth in the United Kingdom has oscillated somewhat since mid-2014. Real GDP grew 2.2 percent at an annual rate in 2015, down from 2.9 percent in 2014, which was the highest rate since 2005. U.K. real GDP in the fourth quarter of 2015 was 14 percent above its trough in the second quarter of 2009. The labor market recovered further in 2015, with unemployment falling to 5.1 percent in the three months to November, the lowest rate in at least 7 years. The slowdown in U.K. GDP growth in the third quarter was largely accounted for by a large decline in net exports, with exports declining amidst growth in imports. While the annual rate of core (excluding energy and unprocessed food) CPI inflation averaged 0.8 percent below its inflation target, the Bank of England held the policy rate steady throughout 2015.

Japan

Japan continued to face longstanding economic challenges in 2015, but experienced some signs of renewal. Japan's economy contracted in the second quarter of 2015, but rebounded in the third quarter and the economy is showing more fundamental signs of longer-term recovery. Periodic recessions have plagued Japan since a financial crisis in 1992 and may, in part, be a byproduct of the country's declining population, which weighs on both potential GDP growth and aggregate demand. When looking at real GDP per working-age population rather than real GDP, for example, Japan has recovered from the global financial crisis almost as robustly as the United States. Japanese real private domestic final purchases (PDFP), which excludes volatile components of GDP—like net exports, inventories, and government spending—has been growing (see Box 2-1 in the 2015 Economic Report of the President for a discussion of the merits of PDFP as a predictive measure of real activity in the United States). The spring *shunto* labor negotiations gave the biggest wage increases since 1998; as a result, real wages have grown this year. The Japanese economy has grown at an average annual rate of 1.6 percent over the first three quarters of 2015—faster than the average annual pace of approximately 1 percent experienced over the last five years.

Prime Minister Shinzo Abe has pursued a package of structural reforms aimed at jumpstarting growth in the Japanese economy, in addition to campaigning for monetary stimulus and advocating for "flexible" fiscal policy. To address the economic burdens of a population that is both aging rapidly and shrinking, the Abe administration has pursued new policies that have led to an increase in the female labor force participation rate and the overall share of working-age adults who are employed. Nonetheless, the aging population presents fiscal challenges and weighs on workforce participation, weakening domestic demand. To provide further support for domestic demand, the Bank of Japan (BOJ) expanded its monetary stimulus, voting various times over the course of 2015 to continue targeting growth in the money supply at an annual pace of 80 trillion yen (about $660 billion). Despite these efforts, inflation has fallen precipitously since late 2014, mostly on declining energy prices, hitting zero in the second half of 2015. While this raises concerns that the struggle with deflation is not yet over, measures of inflation that exclude energy are trending upward: the BOJ's recently emphasized "alternative core core" inflation metric, which strips out fresh food and energy, increased from 0.4 percent year-on-year in January to 1.2 percent year-on-year in September, October, and November 2015, closer to the BOJ's 2-percent target.

Emerging markets

Buffeted by both global and country-specific factors, many emerging markets have experienced slowdowns in growth this past year. Emerging markets generally led world growth coming out of the crisis. They generated 67 percent of world growth from 2010-2014, but just 57 percent of world growth in 2015, based on IMF estimates. To highlight their importance to global growth, the World Bank estimates that a 1 percentage-point slowdown of growth in Brazil, Russia, India, China, and South Africa slows growth in other emerging-market countries by 0.8 percentage point, in newer frontier markets by 1.5 percentage points, and global growth by nearly half a percentage point (World Bank 2016). In addition, though, changes in expectations of growth or financial stability have spilled over into global markets (see Box 3-2 for more discussion of financial spillovers). Often, direct trade linkages may understate the transmission of shocks if sharp nonlinear contagion takes place in financial markets. At various points in 2015 and early 2016, financial volatility in China seemed to spill into many markets around the world.

Real GDP in Brazil and Russia contracted over the first three quarters of 2015. Others, including Indonesia and Malaysia, grew more slowly between the first and third quarters of 2015 than during the same period in 2014. In South Korea, growth ticked up slightly, but remained below the average annual growth of real GDP from 2010 through 2014. Many emerging markets experienced both currency depreciation and declining official reserves during 2015, especially Malaysia, Turkey, Indonesia, South Africa, and Russia.

China is in the midst of rebalancing from an investment- and export-driven economy to an economy driven more by household consumption. Total (public plus private) investment accounted for 46 percent of GDP by the end of 2014. This is in contrast to advanced industrialized economies where total investment accounts for roughly 20 percent of GDP or other major emerging markets, like Brazil, India, Mexico, South Korea, and South Africa, where it tends to range between 20 and 30 percent of GDP. Between 2010 and 2014, China's private consumption share of GDP rose 2.0 percentage points while its investment share of GDP fell 1.4 percentage points, reflecting a slow shift in the composition of the economy. Rebalancing has become more a necessity than a choice as a large economy cannot both grow much faster than the world and be export-led. If it did, it would begin to crowd out the entire world market. For China to maintain strong growth and a constant export share of GDP, exports would have to rise from roughly 10 percent of total world exports to as much as half of world exports over the next 20 years, an unlikely occurrence. Even at a more moderate growth rate, keeping the same export contribution to growth would require China to take a very large share of world exports.

Thus, reforms that rebalance growth will be crucial to sustained and balanced growth in China and the rest of the world. China's economy is slowing from double-digit growth rates over the past decade (10 percent, on average, from 2005 to 2014) to still-rapid but more moderate rates between 6 and 7 percent. According to statistics based on official data, Chinese real GDP grew 6.9 percent in 2015, down from 7.3 percent in 2014 but close to the government's target of 7.0 percent. The extent of slowing in 2015 was unevenly felt in the economy. While service sector growth has picked up, consistent with a shift toward more consumption, Figure 3-9 shows various measures demonstrating slowing across industrial sectors, especially those related to construction.

Box 3-2: Market Volatility in the Second Half of 2015

Markdowns in expectations for global growth and commodities prices have at times in 2015 generated substantial swings in global financial markets. Beyond any direct effects from slower global growth, some of the potential acute risks for the U.S. economy come through spillovers from global financial markets. It can be possible for a large event or change in perceptions—such as an actual shift in policy or an abrupt rethinking of the growth prospects in a major economy—to shift investors' risk sensitivities in a dramatic way. Equity prices across major markets moved in a highly correlated fashion, on average, in the fall of 2015 and the early weeks of 2016, which could signal that changes in risk sentiment are moving rapidly from one country to another.

The summer and early fall 2015 were marked by gyrations in global asset markets. The degree and potential impact of the slowing of China's growth rate, uncertainty over changes in advanced-country monetary policies, the future of Greece's membership in the euro area, and the implications of declining commodity prices for commodity-producing countries and firms contributed to unease among investors, accompanied by market volatility. The VIX, a common measure of investor uncertainty, spiked in August and September (see Figure 3-iv) and correlations in equity prices across markets rose.

The period did see a considerable dive in equity prices as investors reacted strongly to even small changes in emerging data, like U.S. jobs

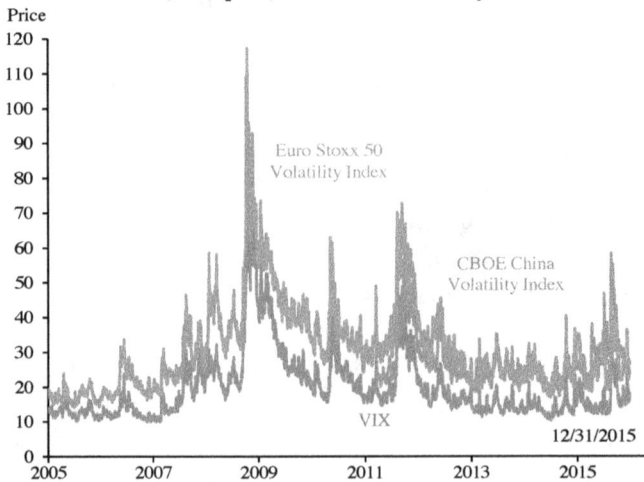

Figure 3-iv
U.S., European, and Chinese Volatility Indices

Source: Bloomberg Professional Service.

numbers or Chinese real GDP growth. Although markets in a number of countries did finish down for the year, the stock market in the U.S. finished roughly even, and in Germany and Shanghai finished up on the year despite the dramatic fluctuations in the summer.

Finance theory suggests that correlation in investor behavior can occur if investors are focusing on the same economic fundamentals to decide on trades, or when investors are just more uncertain about what will happen to economic fundamentals (Scharfstein and Stein 1990; Brunnermeier 2001; Veldkamp 2006 and 2011; Bacchetta and van Wincoop 2015). Some financial markets exhibited heightened correlation during this period of volatility. This heightened comovement has occurred again in the early weeks of 2016. It is important to note that markets are not always correlated and not every shock from abroad affects U.S. markets. During the substantial run-up of the Chinese equity market in the spring and then crash in the early summer of 2015, U.S. equity markets barely moved at all. But, in both late August 2015 and early January 2016, Chinese, European, and U.S. markets all moved together (see Figure 3-v). The elevated correlations could have been due to shocks that have a global reach (exchange rate policy changes in China, for example), or common shifts in perception (changing views of global demand or commodity market prospects), but it can also represent spillovers from one market to the next as investors act in a herd-like manner or losses in one market force asset sales in another. This suggests the

Figure 3-v
U.S., European, and Chinese Stock Markets, 2015

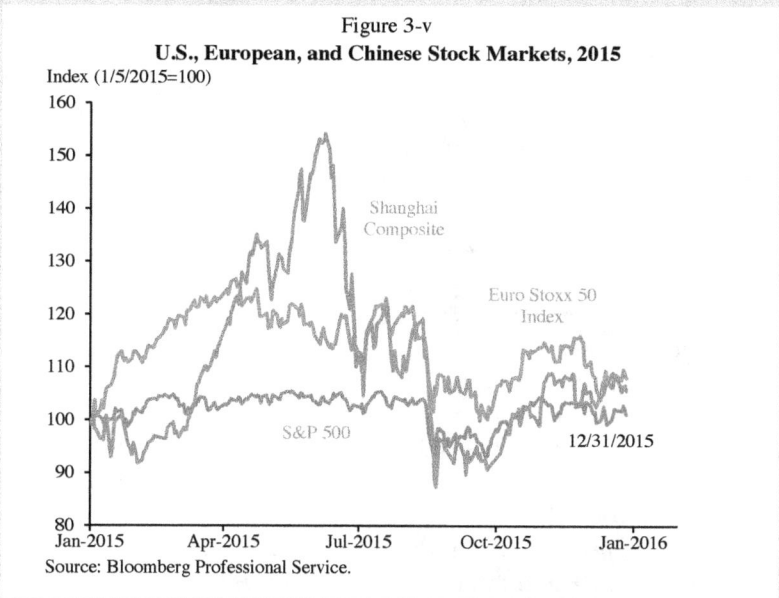

Index (1/5/2015=100)

Source: Bloomberg Professional Service.

potential for rapid spillovers between even apparently unrelated markets should investors shift their views more than usual due to an unexpected piece of news. Swings in global finance and investor attitudes can have important impacts on the world economy (Borio 2012).

This box surveys recent trends in leverage, commodity prices, and policy that may relate to the way movements in global growth expectations can feed through into financial markets.

Leverage. Rising leverage—especially in some emerging markets—may have made financial markets fragile right now. Credit growth enables output growth as it allows consumers, corporations and the government to borrow against the future GDP, but large expansions of leverage across many emerging markets leaves them vulnerable to not just the slower growth that a debt overhang sometimes prompts, but also to a sharper crash. Surveys of history have found that large credit booms result in a financial crisis about one-third of the time, and often are followed by a growth slowdown even if there is no crisis (Jorda, Schularick, and Taylor 2011 and 2013).

An example of how these risks come together is the current degree of corporate debt in some emerging markets – especially the debt in foreign currency. The IMF recently labeled it a principal risk in its latest Global Financial Stability Report. Based on IMF data, emerging market corporate debt has grown from under 50 percent of GDP prior to the crisis to nearly 75 percent today. Even in countries with lower overall leverage, this can be problematic, as particular firms may be overly indebted, leading to defaults. Even if debt levels are manageable, if their home currency depreciates against the U.S. dollar (the principal foreign currency in which there has been borrowing), then the real burden of that debt rises for these firms, again, pushing them towards bankruptcy and default. 2015 saw a rise of emerging market corporate defaults and some key downgrades in sovereign debt ratings.

Still, foreign currency borrowing in emerging markets may not be as problematic as two decades ago. First, many of the firms that are borrowing have U.S. dollar revenues because they are exporters. In that sense, even if their home currency depreciates, they are still earning revenues in dollars and as such can pay their debt. To the extent that these firms are commodity exporters, they may face problems from reduced earnings, but the foreign currency borrowing itself may not be the key risk. In addition, countries overall have much stronger currency balance sheets than they did two decades ago (Benetrix, Lane, and Shambaugh 2015). Many countries expanded their foreign currency reserves, saw an increase in private foreign assets, and took more liabilities in local currency debt, FDI, and equity. These developments may insulate some countries from downside risks in turbulent financial times. This has helped some emerging markets weather swings in exchange rates that previously would have involved substantial valuation losses. The IMF recommended in its January 2016 WEO update that emerging markets, in particular, continue to build resilience to volatile capital markets.

Commodity Prices and Nonlinear Effects. Many models assume a supply generated shock to world oil prices is a net positive for the world economy. Many oil producers, most notably Saudi Arabia, have substantial wealth buffers that smooth their spending across oil price changes, while oil consumer countries are often more liquidity constrained. But price declines that are deep enough can cause substantial changes in global capital expenditures on oil investment, and even deeper price changes can threaten corporate or sovereign borrowers. In the United States, eleven oil and natural gas producers with over $500 million in liabilities filed for bankruptcy in 2015, defaulting on a combined $21.2 billion of debt. This compares to 2014, when only one bankruptcy involving a firm with more than $500 million in liabilities occurred. Market expectations of default (measured by CDS spreads) also show a sharp increase for energy firms, especially those in the United States.

In both August and in December of 2015, oil prices and major equity markets appeared to take cues from one another. The comovement of oil prices and equity returns may have reflected a common response to changing expectations of future global growth. However, an ongoing concern is that oil prices could potentially decline below some threshold that would result in substantial increased number of bankruptcies by oil producers. Although increased oil-sector bankruptcies would have some modest negative effects on the economy, the chief risk is that the resulting oil-sector bond defaults could raise bond investors' concerns about credit markets more broadly, which in turn would depress aggregate economic activity. This is an example of nonlinear effects in asset markets where movements of a price or economic data may be harmless or even positive for the economy within a certain bound, but outside that bound, if there are highly leveraged players in the market, it can have negative effects on financial markets.

Policy. A crucial caveat to the potential financial risks is the extent to which financial systems are more robust than during financial crises over the past 20 years. First, U.S. investors do not have large exposure to emerging market corporate assets. Even with respect to broader volatility, regulations adopted under the Dodd-Frank Act have significantly reduced the exposure of large financial institutions in the United States to risk associated with recent bouts of instability in equity and other asset markets. Financial institutions' stock of capital serves as a cushion to absorb unexpectedly high losses. Increased capital requirements under Dodd-Frank increase the size of this cushion. Measures from the New York University Volatility Institute suggest banks are better armed to weather market turbulence than they were even just a few years ago. In addition, some rules have made it more costly for banks to engage in speculative trading: the "Volcker Rule" implemented in July also limits the kinds of risks that banks can take when they invest their stock of capital before raising alarms with regulators. Finally, some financial institutions that were previously able to exploit regulatory loopholes have been brought under the regulatory umbrella.

The rules that have helped push the industry in this direction are not unique to the United States, but have been part of a broader push in the Basel III agreement and discussions within the euro area. The designation of crucial global institutions as "globally systematically important financial institutions" has placed extra capital requirements and rules on some firms and established resolution authority for these institutions, making the likelihood that a major failure generates a "Lehman shock" smaller. It requires great hubris to assume that the financial markets are bulletproof, but they may now be able to better withstand shocks than a decade ago.

China's demand for imports from many trading partners also has slowed considerably since 2014, such that weakening demand is also being felt in some global commodity markets where China is an important consumer (see Box 3-3). For instance, according to the World Steel Association, China accounts for nearly 45 percent of the world's apparent steel consumption. Estimates based on available data suggest that China's demand for steel may have fallen by as much as 30 million tons or more in 2015, an amount close to 10 percent of total steel exports by the top 10 steel exporters. This reduced demand for a variety of commodities has had a significant impact on world markets, as China is a leading export destination for numerous countries.

China's currency policies also underwent noteworthy changes in 2015. China maintains a narrow trading band with respect to the U.S dollar. Market pressure forced the renminbi (RMB) toward the weak edge of its trading band during much of 2014 and the first half of 2015 (see Figure 3-10). On August 11, the People's Bank of China decided to adopt a new scheme in determining its reference rate, basing it on the RMB's previous closing and allowing a plus or minus a 2 percent trading band, accompanied by a depreciation of the RMB. This shift came amidst, and may have contributed to, global market volatility in August. Between August 10 and the end of

Figure 3-9
Measures of Industrial Activity in China, 2011–2015
4-Quarter Percent Change

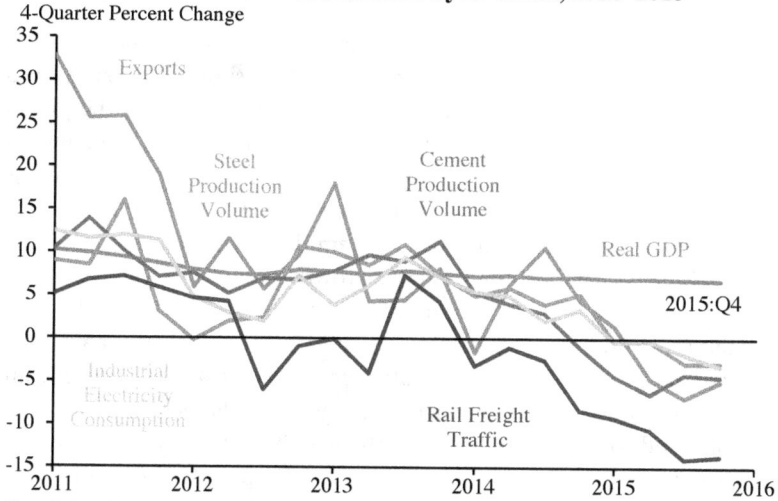

Note: Industrial electricity consumption is "secondary industry" consumption. Real GDP is year-to-year percent change.
Source: China National Bureau of Statistics; State Administration of Foreign Exchange; China Electricity Council; Haver Analytics.

Figure 3-10
China's Foreign Exchange Rate and Trading Band, 2011–2015
Renminbi per U.S. Dollar

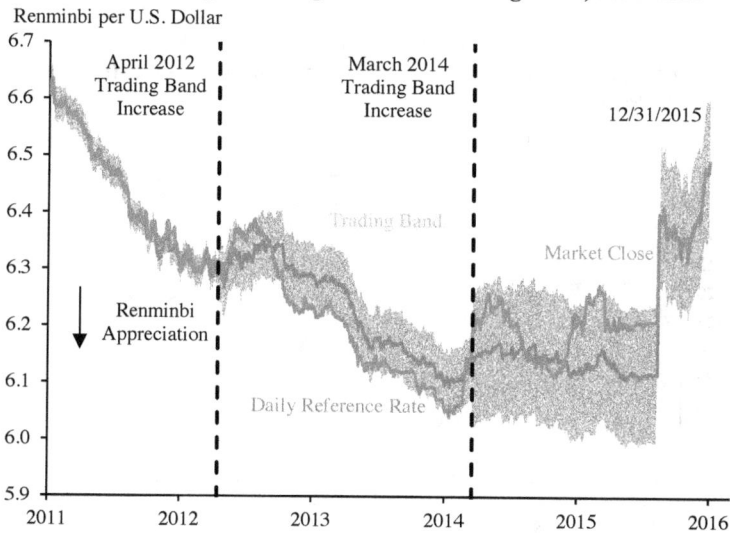

Source: Bloomberg Professional Service.

Box 3-3: Commodity Prices and Inflation in the Global Economy

The drop in commodity prices seen in Figure 3-vi resulted in part from weakness in the world economy, including slowing demand from China, which is a large consumer of many commodities in the global marketplace. The slowdown in the Chinese construction and manufacturing sectors contributed to a drop in demand for commodities that has been felt worldwide, and some of the most precipitous drops in commodity prices hit during the summer, amid growing market concerns about China's economy. Slower global growth has implied lower demand for various commodities; for example, Figure 3-vii shows that the rise and fall in world industrial production growth in recent years coincided with sharp movements in commodity prices. The most-recent significant drop in commodity prices occurred alongside a relatively small decline in global industrial production, which suggests that, to some degree, it is driven by weak demand. Still, the commodity price drop seen in 2015 was much steeper than the fall in industrial production, likely reflecting shifts in supply or re-evaluations of long-term demand prompted by the summer's financial market turbulence. Whatever the underlying reason, the drop in commodity prices has caused economic turbulence in a number of commodity-exporters, especially in emerging markets.

The decline also may be contributing to an interesting contrast in countries' experiences with inflation. Global inflation in 2015 is on pace to be at its lowest rate since 2009, and barring 2009, its lowest rate

Figure 3-vi
Change in Commodity Futures Prices, June to December 2015

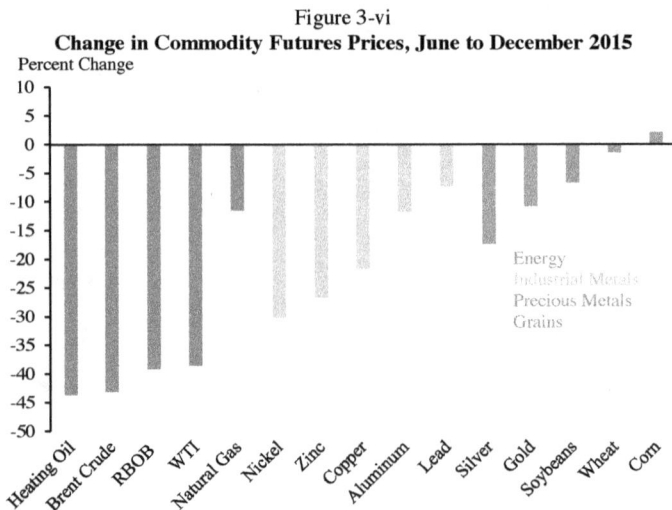

Note: RBOB is reformulated blendstock for oxygenate blending. WTI is West Texas Intermediate.
Source: Bloomberg Professional Service.

Figure 3-vii
World Industrial Production and Commodity Prices, 2006–2015

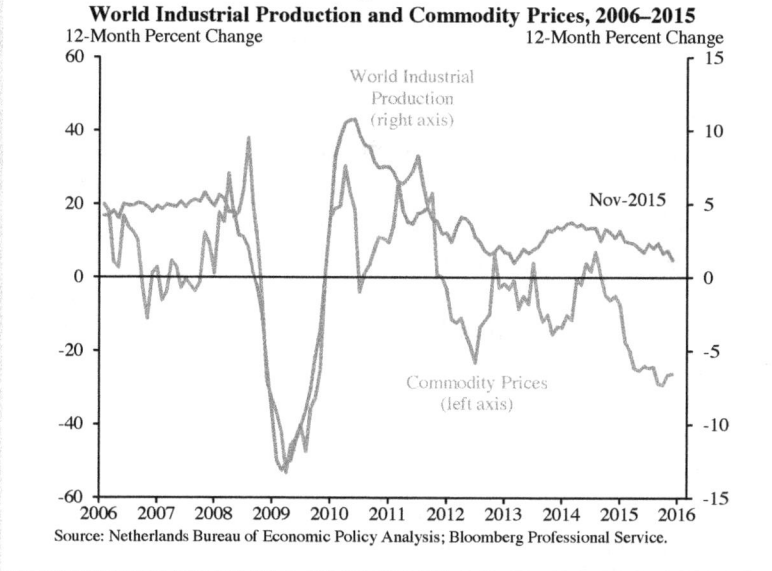

Source: Netherlands Bureau of Economic Policy Analysis; Bloomberg Professional Service.

since at least 1980. Out of the 20 G-20 economies, 8 (including 6 of the 7 G-7 countries) had four-quarter inflation rates below 1 percent in the third quarter of 2015, and three of them with rates below zero. All of the world's major advanced economies had rates below their target. While advanced economies are confronting the challenge of very low, or even negative, inflation, some major commodity exporters, like Brazil and Russia, have faced rapid currency depreciation and high inflation rates; in part, because currency depreciation makes imported goods more expensive to domestic consumers. Other emerging markets, like Mexico and South Africa, where commodity exports are 6 and 11 percent of GDP, respectively, have also experienced currency depreciation but lower inflation rates, ranging between 2 and 6 percent, still above those of a number of European countries, Japan, and the United States.

2015, the cumulative depreciation in the spot rate was 4.6 percent against the dollar. Since August, the authorities have sold foreign exchange to support the RMB, as the market was surprised by the sudden depreciation, exchange rate expectations reset, and private capital outflows continued. The end of 2015 and start of 2016 has also seen renewed discussion of the value of the RMB versus a basket of currencies—not just the U.S. dollar—as well as greater volatility in the exchange rate. Clear communication by China of its policies and actions to the market as it makes an orderly transition to a market-determined exchange rate will help guide market expectations.

In November 2015, the IMF voted to include the RMB as the fifth currency used to underpin the IMF Standard Drawing Right (effective October 1, 2016), which globally serves as an important unit of account. Despite many steps toward financial liberalization and openness, continuing controls on cross-border flows of capital and RMB trading pose many questions regarding the future path of its integration into the global economy.

Brazil is one of the countries hit hardest by the recent collapse in commodity prices, in combination with other domestic challenges, with GDP contracting more than 5 percent at an annual rate over the first three quarters of 2015. The currency lost roughly a third of its value against the dollar in the year after December 2014. Although it has fueled domestic inflation, currency depreciation has generated a rebound in exports (both in real, local-currency-denominated terms and as a fraction of GDP) and in the current account in 2015, which narrowed considerably from a deficit of 5 percent to about 3 percent of GDP (see Figure 3-11). The IMF has espoused flexible exchange-rate regimes like Brazil's for weathering commodity-price downturns under fiscal constraints.

As a group, the low-income economies (LICs)—defined as economies with gross national income (GNI) per capita of $1,045 or less by the World Bank, or a group of 60 countries identified as "low-income" by the IMF—were a bright spot in global economic growth in recent years. Real GDP growth in low-income economies had risen from just over 5 percent on average in the 2001-07 period, to about 6 percent in 2014. However, both the 2016 World Bank Global Economic Prospects and the IMF report that GDP growth in LICs fell to between 4.8 and 5.1 percent in 2015. Depending on how one defines the category, between a half and two-thirds of LICs are commodity exporters. The commodity price decline is taking a toll on public finances, current account balances, and economic growth in these countries, making them more vulnerable to both domestic challenges and external shocks such as global financial turbulence.

Not every emerging market has seen disappointing growth. India, for example, experienced strong GDP growth in 2015 with estimates for growth continuing at roughly 7 percent in 2014, 2015, and 2016 (projected). India, along with Argentina, were the only G-20 countries estimated to have grown faster in 2015 than the IMF had predicted a year earlier. Its status as an important player in service industries, as opposed to commodity or manufacturing exports, has likely helped its continued growth, and a pickup in investment may come as a result of recent policy reforms.

Still, the slower growth around the globe has had spillovers to the U.S. economy. Weaker growth abroad than in the United States tends to put

Figure 3-11
Brazil's Current Account Balance, 2005–2015

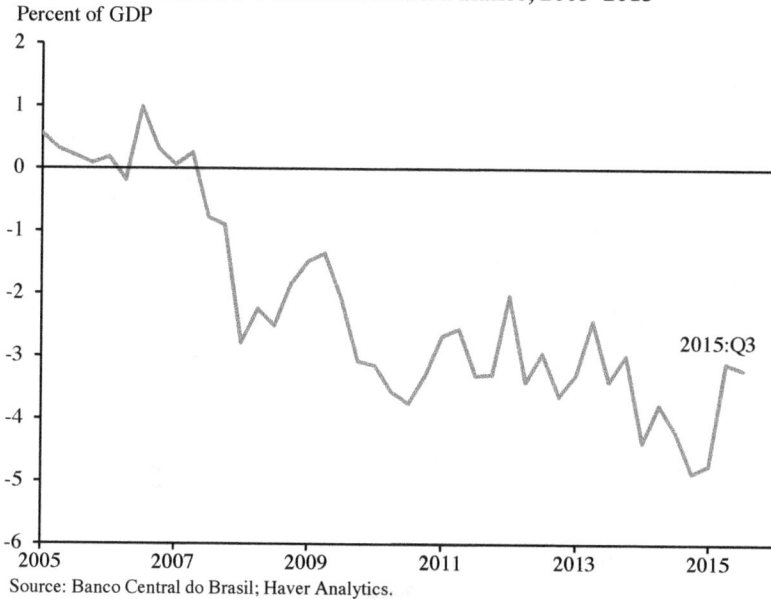

Percent of GDP

2015:Q3

Source: Banco Central do Brasil; Haver Analytics.

upward pressure on the U.S. dollar and downward pressure on exports, both of which were observed in 2015.

U.S. TRADE

The U.S. nominal trade deficit in goods and services narrowed slightly from 3.1 to 3.0 percent of GDP in 2015, as measured in the national income and product accounts. The trade deficit in levels widened slightly from $508.3 billion in 2014 to $531.5 billion in 2015 as goods exports fell faster than goods imports and trade in services remained almost stable, reflecting the global headwinds discussed above. The trade balance shrank as a share of GDP as output grew faster, reflecting the strength of the domestic economy relative to the rest of the world. Figures 3-12 and 3-13 show these balances calculated according to the balance of payments method. U.S. services exports continue to grow relative to U.S. goods exports, as they have since the start of the digital revolution in the 1990s.

Services make up 32 percent of our exports, but only 18 percent of our imports (see Figures 3-14 and 3-15). Four out of every five American jobs are in the service sector. The Department of Commerce estimates that services exports supported 4.6 million U.S. jobs in 2014.

Figure 3-12
U.S. Trade in Goods, 1992–2015

Billions of U.S. Dollars

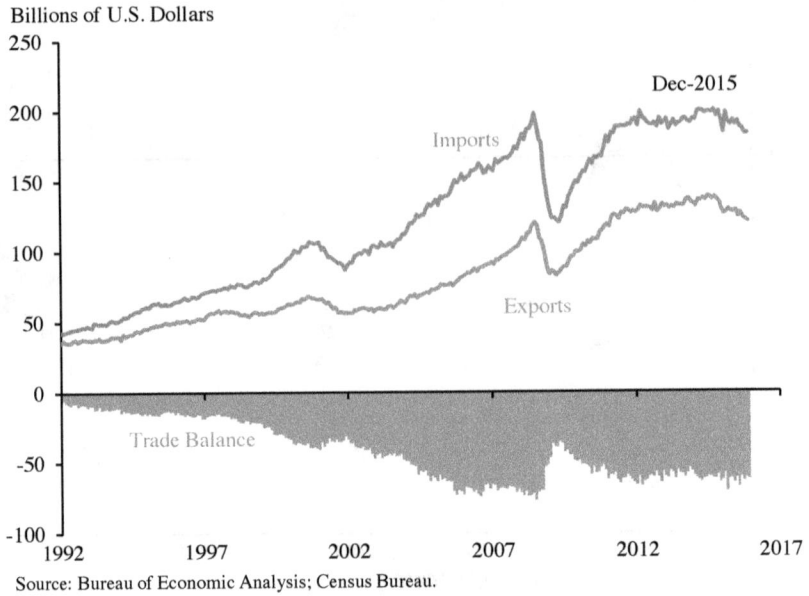

Source: Bureau of Economic Analysis; Census Bureau.

Figure 3-13
U.S. Trade in Services, 1992–2015

Billions of U.S Dollars

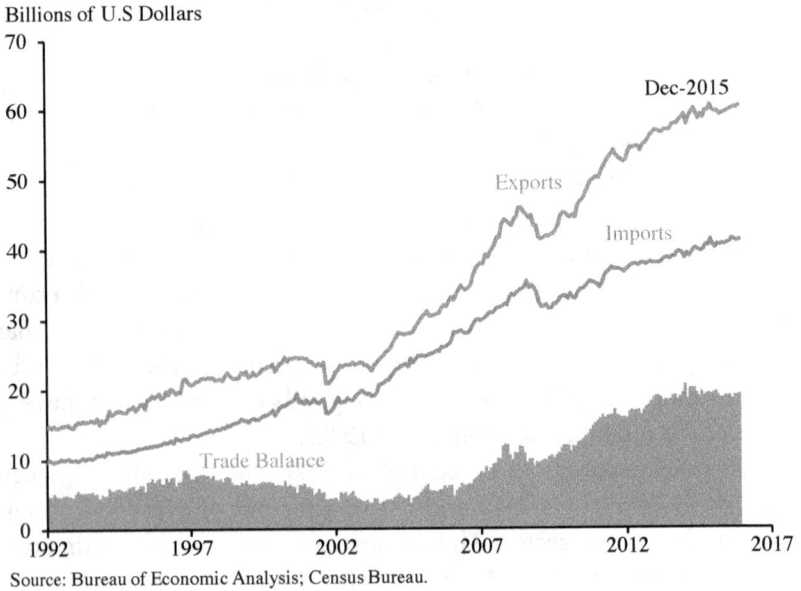

Source: Bureau of Economic Analysis; Census Bureau.

Figure 3-14
Composition of U.S. Exports, 2015

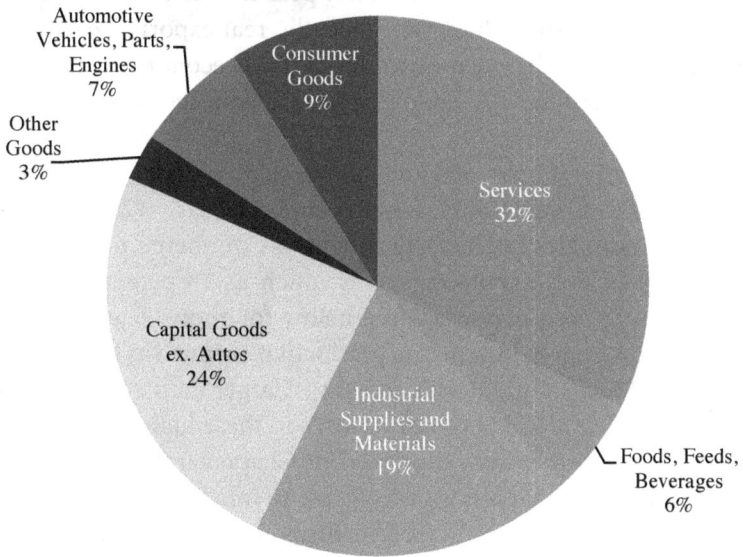

Source: Bureau of Economic Analysis; Census Bureau.

Figure 3-15
Composition of U.S. Imports, 2015

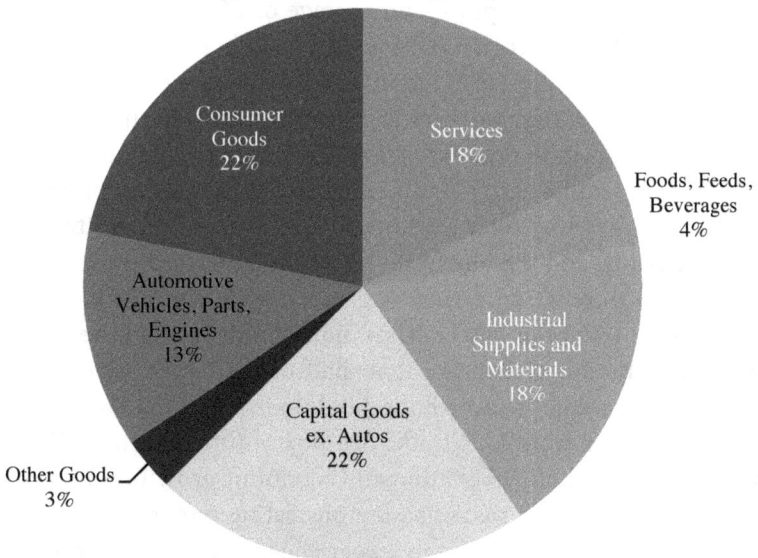

Source: Bureau of Economic Analysis; Census Bureau.

U.S. exports are 12.5 percent of the size of U.S. GDP, much higher than 10 years ago (see Figure 3-16). They peaked at nearly 14 percent of U.S. GDP in 2011 and 2013. Until very recently, real exports were consistently increasing, so the decline demonstrates that our economy is growing faster than global demand for U.S. goods, another manifestation of the headwinds discussed above.

Beyond the simple demand component of GDP, exports provide many benefits to the economy. Exports support nearly 12 million U.S. jobs according to estimates by the Department of Commerce, a fact that is more important given that exporters pay as much as 18 percent higher wages, on average, than non-exporters (see below for more detailed discussion). Growing exports can help generate productivity growth as higher productivity sectors and firms expand with access to a larger market. This allows them to employ a higher share of the labor force in these high-productivity firms. In addition, a rich literature discussed in Chapter 5 documents incentives that access to global markets give for firms to innovate.

Trade is important both for U.S. firms and for supporting high-paying jobs. Between mid-2009 and the end of 2015, exports of goods and services accounted for more than a quarter of U.S. economic growth. As of 2014 (the most recent data available), more than 300,000 U.S. companies were engaged in exporting, the vast majority of them small and medium-sized businesses. Research published by the U.S. Census Bureau illustrates the strikingly high-quality jobs these companies support. Non-exporting firms employed an average of 13 workers apiece at payrolls averaging $34,814 per worker while exporting firms employed an average of 243 workers each at payrolls averaging $51,302 per worker (Census 2012). Other research by Riker (2010) and Riker and Thurner (2011) confirms the existence of an exporter wage premium, showing that workers at exporting firms earn up to 18 percent more, on average, than non-exporting firms. Riker (2015) provides updated estimates in a similar range, with exporting firms paying premiums of up to 19 percent for blue collar workers, and 12 percent for white collar workers. Fajgelbaum and Khandelwal (2014) estimate that trade openness has increased the purchasing power of American consumers in a progressive way. According to their calculations, households in the lowest third of the income distribution gain more than half of their purchasing power from U.S trade and middle-income households gain more than a quarter of their purchasing power from U.S. trade. See Box 5-4 for a further discussion on how trade can promote innovation and economic growth. About half of U.S. exports go to emerging markets, demonstrating our interdependence with economies that have increasingly experienced challenges to growth during 2015 (see Figure 3-17).

Figure 3-16
Exports as a Share of GDP, 2005–2015

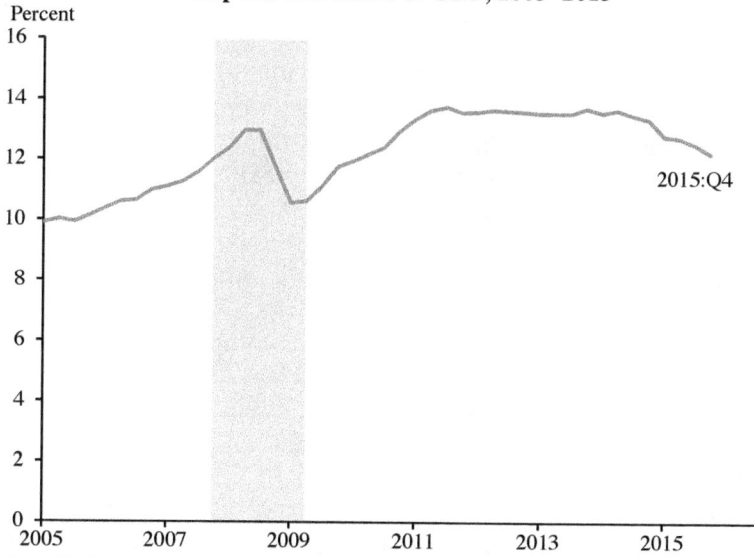

Note: Shading denotes recession.
Source: Bureau of Economic Analysis.

Figure 3-17
Destinations of U.S. Goods Exports, 2015

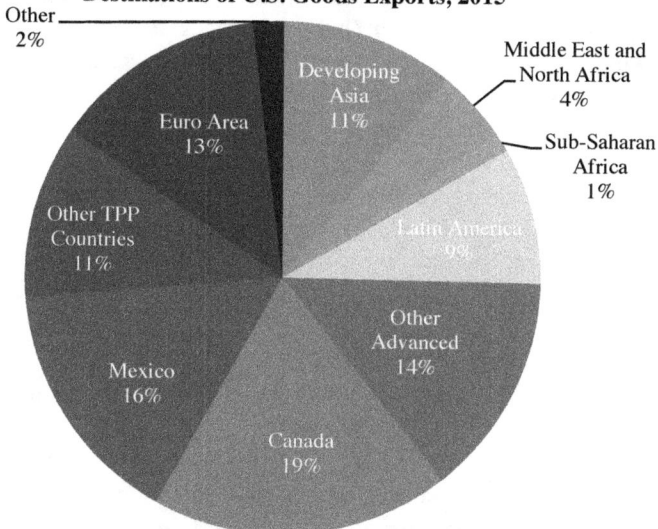

Note: Reflects data through September. TPP denotes the Trans-Pacific Partnership trade agreement.
Source: International Monetary Fund.

Box 3-4: The Importance of the Trans-Pacific Partnership (TPP) for the U.S. Economy

The complicated global economic environment underscores the importance of the President's trade agenda in opening new markets and ensuring a level playing field for U.S. firms. The centerpiece of that agenda is the Trans-Pacific Partnership (TPP), a comprehensive and high-standard trade agreement with 11 other countries—including 3 of the United States' 5 largest trading partners—in one of the most dynamic, fastest-growing regions of the world. With 45 percent of the $726.5 billion in U.S. exports of goods and 25 percent of the $178.3 billion in U.S. exports of services going to TPP countries in 2014, no previous free trade agreement has covered such a large share of U.S. trade. U.S. exports to TPP countries supported an estimated 4.2 million U.S. jobs in 2014, more than a third of the 11.7 million U.S. jobs supported by exports to the world.

The TPP will make it much easier to sell American goods and services to this rapidly growing market. It will eliminate over 18,000 tariffs on U.S. goods exports. It locks in zero-tariffs on 98 percent of goods traded, not just eliminating tariffs but ridding businesses of the uncertainty that tariffs might suddenly rise in a market they serve. For example, tariffs up to 59 percent on machinery and up to 32 percent on fresh fruit, industries where it can take time between investing in expanded capacity and when producers start earning revenues, would be phased out or eliminated, enabling producers to invest upfront without worrying that tariffs might later arbitrarily be revived. It promotes expanded digital and services trade with safeguards for privacy and security. It makes important strides to help small- and medium-sized businesses, including streamlining trade barriers like complicated standards and technical regulations, which make it hard for small businesses to access new markets, providing only one set of rules to export their goods rather than separate standards for each of the 11 countries. It reduces a slew of customs frictions, allowing e-filing of customs forms and advance valuation and ensuring that goods can pass through ports expediently, with special provisions for the express deliveries so important to many smaller firms.

Under the TPP, the United States will help set the standards for free and fair trade in the Pacific Basin. The TPP is part of a new generation of agreements, going further than any prior agreement to advance the wellbeing of workers and firms in the United States and the region as a whole. Under TPP, partners have agreed to adhere to labor standards of the International Labor Organization, including the right to unionize and commitments to enforce prohibitions on child and forced labor. For instance, Vietnam's and Malaysia's workers will for the first time gain the freedom to form independent unions, lifting decades-old restrictions. TPP will also require Malaysia to fully implement recently passed amendments to the country's Anti-Trafficking law, taking an important step to address human trafficking issues. The TPP has enforceable provisions to prevent illegal wildlife trafficking, discourage subsidy programs that increase pressure on fisheries stocks, and help prevent illegal logging. The labor and environmental standards will be enforceable with dispute settlement and trade sanctions, if necessary, helping improve quality of life in the region and avoid unfair competition. In dispute settlement, it offers improved transparency, includes opportunities for public comment in dispute settlement, and reaffirms each country's right to regulate in the public interest for national security, health, safety, financial stability, and environmental reasons. It levels the playing field with strong rules to help make sure that governments cannot give unfair advantages to their state-owned enterprises and companies cannot gain a competitive advantage by undermining worker protections and environmental regulations, which is a high risk if trade integration continues in the region without U.S. involvement.

Research suggests substantial positive impacts on both U.S. exports and incomes if TPP is put into force. One prominent study by Petri and Plummer (2016) from the Peterson Institute predicts a significant gain for the United States—an additional 0.5 percent in real annual income, with the majority of the benefit going to labor in the form of higher wages—including an expansion of U.S exports by more than 9 percent relative to a world without the agreement. It also predicts large gains for even the poorest among the TPP countries. Although the authors note that tariff reductions were more ambitious than many anticipated, roughly half of the economic benefits arise from reductions in non-tariff barriers. Another study released recently by the World Bank concurs that TPP would deliver significant benefits to the U.S. economy, boosting income and exports by tens of billions relative to a world without TPP.

Delay or failure to implement TPP risks substantial costs. Exporters may watch new opportunities to expand delayed or missed, a cost which Petri and Plummer (2016) estimate to be $94 billion if implementation is delayed by even just one year. At the same time, China, the European Union, Japan, and other economies are negotiating preferential agreements whose effect in the absence of TPP would be to create or exacerbate tariff differentials that put U.S. exports at risk and may reduce incentives for goods-producing industries to invest in the United States.

The challenging environment for U.S. exports is an important motivation for the President's trade agenda, including the Trans-Pacific Partnership agreement, which was closed in October and submitted to Congress soon afterward (discussed in Box 3-4, as well as in Chapters 1 and 5), and the Trans-Atlantic Trade and Investment Partnership negotiations currently in progress, as well as a number of other initiatives.

CONCLUSION

Slower global growth in 2015 was both a product of longer-term supply—slower productivity growth and slowing labor force growth—and demand factors—weak investment growth and longer-term demand slow-downs. In addition, though, continued cyclical weakness in many areas of the world combined with a sharp emerging-market slowdown produced the slowest global growth rate since the recovery from the global financial crisis began. The United States has been a relative bright spot in the world economy, gradually approaching full employment levels of output and generating substantial portions of global demand. It will be crucial that the world economy not return to a model prevailing prior to the crisis where too much of the global economy relied on the U.S. consumer. Still, forecasts are for these global headwinds to continue to weigh on U.S. growth in the near future—which is why both strengthening the U.S. economy to ensure it is more resilient while working with partners abroad on their growth is a key priority for the President.

CHAPTER 4

INEQUALITY IN EARLY CHILDHOOD AND EFFECTIVE PUBLIC POLICY INTERVENTIONS

INTRODUCTION

Economic research has established that investments in children's health, education, nutrition, and income support have large benefits both for individuals and for society as a whole. For example, public provision of K-12 education has long been viewed as essential for promoting equality of opportunity and for fostering a productive workforce. More recently, however, research has shown the critical importance of investments made in the years before children enter school.

Many measures of abilities and skills that contribute to future productivity—referred to by economists as "human capital"—were once considered by many to be hereditary. Yet a growing body of research at the intersection of economics, neuroscience, and developmental psychology has shown that early indicators of a child's potential are often highly responsive to changes in environment and to the actions of parents and caregivers. In turn, improvements or deficits in early investments can perpetuate themselves, in part by enhancing or reducing the efficacy of later childhood investments. Indeed, at the time of school entry, the characteristics of a child and his or her family explain much of the variation in later educational achievement, and even in subsequent earnings and employment. Further, gaps that exist at school entry tend to remain stable or even widen as children progress through school.

The persistence of these early childhood disparities has profound consequences for the life chances of those born into poverty and disadvantage. Comparisons of early health and human capital measures across different groups in society reveal large gaps by household income and by race/ethnicity, geography, and family structure. These gaps are mirrored by gaps in a variety of parental characteristics and inputs, as well as by differences in the child's environment. Despite the high potential returns, many families lack the resources, time, and opportunities to make essential early investments in their children.

Opportunity gaps among young children have important implications for public policy. Researchers have studied a broad set of policies that provide investment in early childhood and found significant and wide-ranging benefits for parents and children.[1] Public investment that improves the inputs in a child's early years can help to close critical achievement, health, and development gaps, and can lead to benefits such as higher earnings that accumulate over a lifetime. In fact, some researchers argue that closing the gaps in early childhood is the easiest and most cost-effective way to reduce inequality in later-life outcomes.[2] Closing these gaps is not just about education, but also about more broadly alleviating the budget constraints facing families of younger children.

Importantly, the benefits of early investment accrue not only to individual children and their families, but also to society. The public benefits include: higher tax revenue from a more productive workforce; lower rates of criminal activity; reduced inequality; and reductions in public spending on medical care, remedial education,[3] incarceration, and transfer programs.

This chapter surveys the research on the benefits of early childhood investment, with an emphasis on the role of public policy. The first part of the chapter begins with an overview of the main theories explaining why early investments may have especially high returns. It then presents evidence on the early appearance of large gaps by socioeconomic status (SES)—including gaps in measures of early health and human capital, in a variety of parental characteristics and inputs, and in other environmental factors. The first part concludes by presenting the main economic arguments on why government policy is crucial to ensuring an optimal level of investment in early childhood, especially for children from disadvantaged households.

In the second part, the chapter surveys existing Federal policies and programs that invest in early childhood health, development, and education and reviews the most rigorous research on the impacts of these policies on children's short- and long-run outcomes. The broad range of policies and programs considered here operate through multiple mechanisms. These include: direct investments in early education such as high-quality child care

---

[1] Chapter Four of the 2015 *Economic Report of the President*, "The Economics of Family-Friendly Workplace Policies," and CEA's January 2015 report "The Economics of Early Childhood Investment" discuss the benefits that early childhood education can have for parents. This chapter focuses on the benefits for children.

[2] See, for example, Cunha et al. (2006).

[3] Encompasses both special education and additional education required by students that are held back.

and preschool; direct investments in health such as children's health insurance and home visitation to help new parents keep infants healthy; nutrition programs that supplement families' food budgets; and income transfers and other near-cash transfer programs that offer more flexible assistance to low-income families. This overview analyzes the benefits to the individual and to the public and assesses the role of policy in promoting economic opportunity for all children.

THE ECONOMICS OF INVESTING EARLY AND THE CONSEQUENCES OF EARLY LIFE DISADVANTAGE

Pathways for Returns to Early Investments

Researchers have outlined several theories that help explain why early childhood is a particularly important time to invest in children. First, investments made when children are very young will generate returns that accrue over a child's entire life. Since the benefits are realized over a longer time horizon, the earlier in life they are made, the more likely early childhood interventions are to generate substantial benefits—both to the child and to his or her community.[4]

A second reason that early childhood investments benefit children's development may be that the flexibility and capacity for change in cognitive functioning and brain development is the greatest for young children, and these changes can have lasting effects on behavior throughout life (Knudsen et al. 2006). Research shows that characteristics that are often assumed to be innate, like cognitive skills, can be influenced by environmental factors in early childhood (Jensen 1980; National Scientific Council on the Developing Child 2007). Under this model, not only do earlier investments generate benefits over a longer time period, but also each dollar invested produces greater impacts since children's brains are developing most rapidly when they are young.

Related developmental theories imply that a child's environment *in utero* has a large impact on the health of the child and indicate that even investments made before birth can have long-lasting consequences. The "fetal origins hypothesis" posits that adverse conditions in the womb can strongly influence whether a child develops metabolic issues such as diabetes and heart disease throughout their lives (Currie and Rossin-Slater 2015) and can even translate beyond physical health to mental health (Persson

---

[4] This is a central tenet of the human capital model in economics; see Becker (1962) and Ben-Porath (1967).

and Rossin-Slater 2015).[5] These adverse conditions can also affect cognitive and economic outcomes, including test scores, educational attainment, and income (Almond and Currie 2011; Lavy, Schlosser, and Shany 2016). The academic literature on the long-term health impacts of stress and nutrition *in utero* provides support for this theory, and support for intervening even before birth.

Third, early investments can have large impacts if early skills serve as a multiplier, or prerequisite, for later skills (Cunha et al. 2006; Cunha and Heckman 2007). For example, it may be that the extent of skill acquisition in early elementary school depends on the degree of skills attained before entering kindergarten, and skills learned in adolescence depend on mastery of these elementary skills. Under this "skill-begets-skill" model, early investments in child development can enhance the productivity of future investments in human capital. Since early education may serve as a complement for later skills gained in high-quality elementary and later education, it is important to reinforce children's learning throughout their schooling years to maximize the benefits of early education. A continuum of high-quality education ensures that early investments can be strengthened and built upon in later years (Currie and Thomas 2000).

These mechanisms are not mutually exclusive, as there is evidence to support each, and they may work together to produce the large benefits of early investments.

Inequality in Early Health and Human Capital Investments

Comparisons of early health and human capital measures across different groups in American society reveal large gaps by household income and by race/ethnicity and family structure. On nearly every measure of school readiness, children born into low-income households enter school at a substantial disadvantage relative to their higher-income peers. For example, Figure 4-1 shows that income-based gaps in math skills, attention, and social skills are well-established by kindergarten and that these achievement gaps persist (and, if anything, tend to widen) through fifth grade.

The barriers faced by young people who grow up in disadvantaged settings are compounded over time and may be exacerbated by unequal treatment in the educational and disciplinary systems later in childhood. By the time youth who have experienced these challenges reach adulthood,

---

[5] See also the large epidemiological literature connecting *in utero* exposure to famine and the onset of mental illness (Susserr and Lin 1992; Susser et al. 1996; Neugebauer et al. 1999; McClellan et al. 2006), and evidence that mental illness can be traced to brain abnormalities that may be related to fetal environment (Berquin et al. 1998; Stoner et al. 2014; Liu et al. 2012).

Figure 4-1
**Cognitive and Non-Cognitive Skills SES Gaps are
Mostly Established by Kindergarten**

Gap in Standard Deviation Units

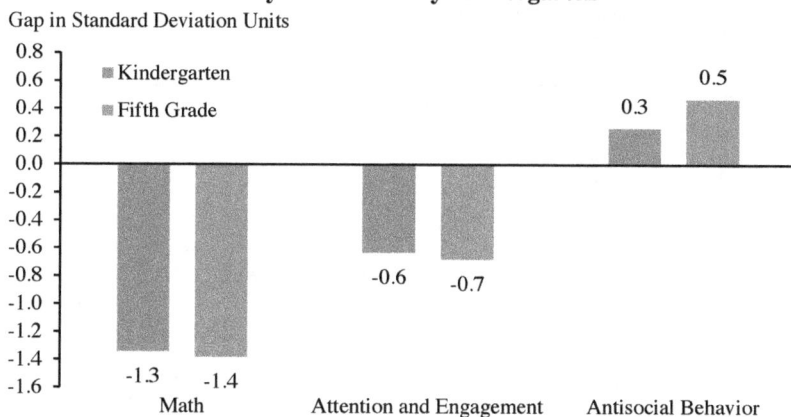

Note: SES refers to socioeconomic status. Calculations by Duncan and Magnuson (2011) based on data from the Early Childhood Longitudinal Study - Kindergarten Cohort. Kindergarten test scores were measured in 1998–1999; fifth grade test scores for the same students were measured in 2004. Source: Duncan and Magnuson (2011).

they are less likely to have the educational attainment and labor market skills critical to success in today's economy. As a result, they tend to participate less often in the labor force, experience higher rates of unemployment when they do participate, and earn less when they find work.

Recent research on the intergenerational transmission of wealth suggests that the close connection between family resources and children's adult outcomes is in large part due to differences in environment rather than genetics (Black et al. 2015). Research also points to specific pathways through which poverty can be detrimental for young children's immediate and long-run outcomes, including inequality in resources directed toward building human capital. Growing up with a lack of familial resources means there are simply fewer resources available to support health and education. In addition to restricted monetary investment due simply to a lack of resources, several other factors associated with poverty—such as low parental health and human capital, food insecurity, stress, and neighborhood factors like school quality—can have negative impacts on children's physical and mental health, cognition, and socio-emotional and behavioral skills.

This section examines the evidence on gaps in early childhood health, as measured by birth weight and other physical health indicators, and in early human capital measures, including both "cognitive skills," as measured by school achievement, and "non-cognitive skills," as measured by socio-emotional and behavioral skills. Research has demonstrated that these

Figure 4-2
**Official Poverty Rate for Households
with Children by Householder Characteristic, 2014**
Percent Below Federal Poverty Level

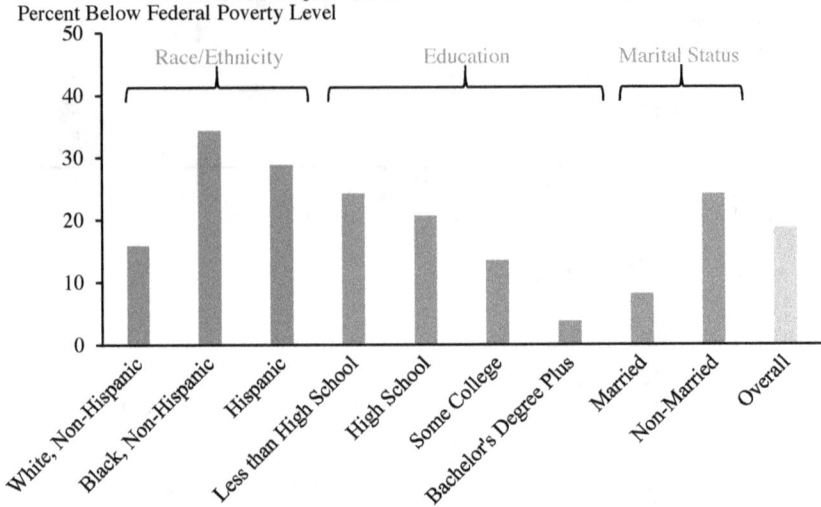

Source: CPS ASEC (2015); CEA calculations.

measures are both mutable and strong predictors of long-run outcomes. Evidence is also presented on the parallel gaps in a variety of parental characteristics and inputs as well as other characteristics of children's environments that likely contribute to the gaps in early outcomes.

Here and throughout this chapter, the focus is on income-based gaps and disadvantages associated with poverty. While poverty is strictly defined in terms of income, it is important to note that poverty can also serve as a proxy for many other forms of disadvantage that may also stifle investment in early childhood. Poverty is unevenly distributed by race/ethnicity and family structure. In 2014, 15.5 million children lived in poverty in the United States—an overall child poverty rate of 21 percent. But youth of color were disproportionately impoverished, including 37 percent of African-American youth and 32 percent of Hispanic youth. Young children of single mothers were also disproportionately impoverished, with over one-half of all related children under age 6 in households headed by a female in poverty (Census Bureau 2015).

Finally, as Figure 4-2 shows, children whose households are headed by individuals who are non-White, less-educated, and/or single are especially likely to experience poverty; as a result, they are more likely to experience deficits in early health and human capital inputs and in later-life outcomes.

Disparities in Early Health

Prenatal, neonatal, and post-neonatal health (through the first year of life) are crucial early determinants of later-in-life health and academic success. Good health and nutritional baselines are directly linked to better health in childhood. Early health outcomes carry over into adult health outcomes and even connect to non-health outcomes such as cognition, which can continue into adulthood. Even before birth, children born into lower socioeconomic status households face disadvantages in the area of health.

Individuals of lower socioeconomic status experience higher levels of stress than more advantaged individuals. As such, the link between maternal stress and child physical and mental health outcomes puts children born into poorer households at higher risk of adverse health outcomes (Persson and Rossin-Slater 2015; Thompson 2014; Kunz-Ebrecht et al. 2004; Cohen et al. 2006; Aizer, Stroud, and Buka 2012). Health disadvantages continue throughout children's earliest years in the form of food insecurity, stress, and cognitive overload (an accumulation of concerns to the point that the stress becomes overwhelming and impairs cognitive functioning). The stress and concerns associated with living in poverty can affect cognition and health into adulthood. Children born to lower-income mothers are also less likely to receive early and adequate prenatal care. Rates of first trimester prenatal care increase with educational attainment, from only 58 percent of mothers with less than a high school diploma to 86 percent of mothers with a bachelor's degree or higher (Health Resources and Services Administration 2013).

As a result of exposure to these adverse early childhood health conditions, children growing up in poverty may experience more physical and mental health problems throughout their lives. Researchers have shown that maternal stress during pregnancy depresses birth weight (Persson and Rossin-Slater 2015; Black, Devereux, and Salvanes 2016) and can increase the risk of hospitalizations in the first five years of life (Persson and Rossin-Slater 2015). The impacts of maternal stress during pregnancy can even be traced to educational attainment (Aizer, Stroud, and Buka 2012) and adult mental health (Persson and Rossin-Slater 2015).

Children growing up in poverty tend to do worse across a spectrum of important early health outcomes. They are nearly twice as likely to be born at a low or very low birth weight and are four times more likely to have poor overall physical health (Figure 4-3). Birth weight is one early indicator of health that can be highly predictive of later-life success. Studies of birth weight find that it is not only a good predictor of short-term health and mortality, but also of longer-term health and human capital variables,

Figure 4-3
Likelihood of Scoring Very Low on Early Health Measures
Percent Scoring Very Low

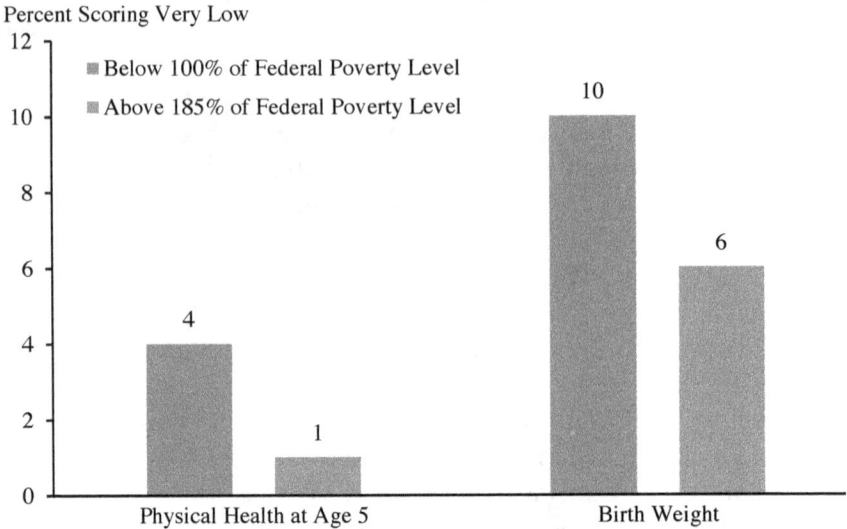

Note: Data are from the Early Childhood Longitudinal Study - Birth Cohort and for children born in 2001. Very low physical health defined as at least one standard deviation below the average. Very low birth weight defined as below 5.5 pounds.
Source: Isaacs (2012).

including school achievement and earnings (Black, Devereux, and Salvanes 2007; Figlio et al. 2014).

Poor children are also much more likely to experience food insecurity, or the lack of resources necessary for consistent and dependable access to food, which can compromise early nutrition and lead to worse short- and long-term outcomes. Overall, about 19 percent of households with children, including 15 million children, experienced food insecurity in 2014 (Coleman-Jensen et al. 2015). Rates of food insecurity are much higher among certain vulnerable populations, including poor households and households headed by single women and minorities (Figure 4-4). Food security and access to good nutrition are critical *in utero* and in the early years of life, setting up a child for physical and mental health throughout their lives. For example, the type of nutrition young children receive can shape the architecture of the brain and central nervous system in a variety of ways (Georgieff 2007; Rosales, Reznick, and Ziesel 2009). Maternal malnutrition can impair fetal development, with effects that carry into childhood and adulthood physical and mental health (Almond and Mazumder 2011; Adhvaryu et al. 2014).[6]

Parental and child stress can also be contributors to inferior mental and physical health outcomes for poor children. Parents living in poverty are more likely to experience cognitive overload, meaning that the stress

[6] See also Persson and Rossin-Slater (2015) for a review of this literature.

Figure 4-4
Household Food Insecurity Rates, 2014
Percent Food Insecure

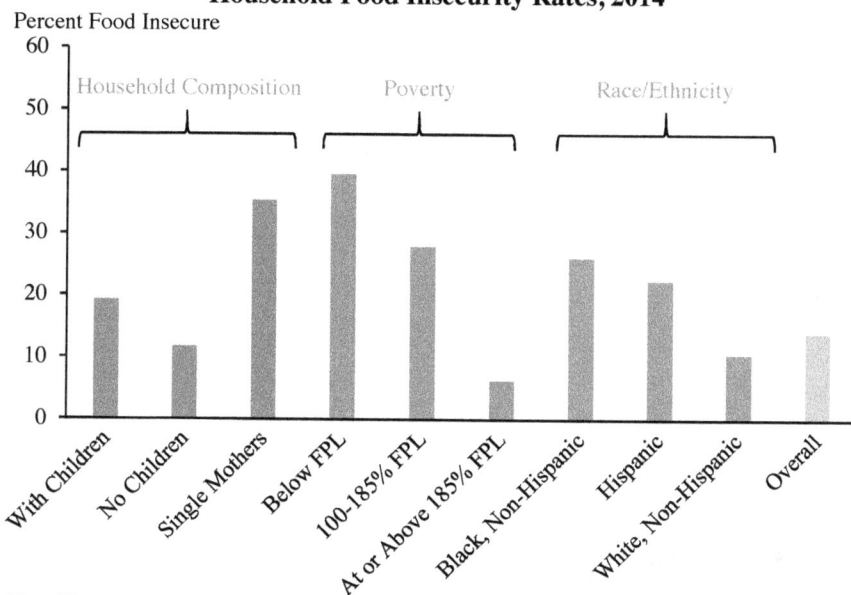

Note: FPL refers to the federal poverty level.
Source: Coleman-Jensen et al. (2015).

and concerns associated with living in poverty can become overwhelming to the point that it affects cognitive functioning, which can further perpetuate poverty (Mani et al 2013). Mothers living in poverty are also more likely to be depressed and in poor health, and to smoke during pregnancy (Figure 4-5). When children live in poverty, they may also experience chronic stress and cognitive overload, which can harm cognition in adulthood (Evans and Schamberg 2009). Children in poor households are disproportionately likely to be exposed to adverse childhood experiences, including neglect and abuse, which can lead to poorer health and human capital outcomes later in life (Hillis et al. 2004; Felitti et al. 1998; Campbell, Walker, and Egede 2015; Flaherty et al. 2013). All of these differential inputs and experiences contribute to gaps in early physical and mental health.

Disparities in Early Human Capital

Insufficient family financial and non-financial resources mean that children from low-income families are less likely to have access to activities and materials that promote learning and wellness, such as high-quality early education and enriching home environments. These factors, and others associated with poverty (such as higher health risks, food insecurity, and increased stress) contribute to the disparities between these children and their higher-income peers in school readiness. In turn, the disadvantage

Figure 4-5
Disparities in Underlying Factors Behind Outcome Gaps

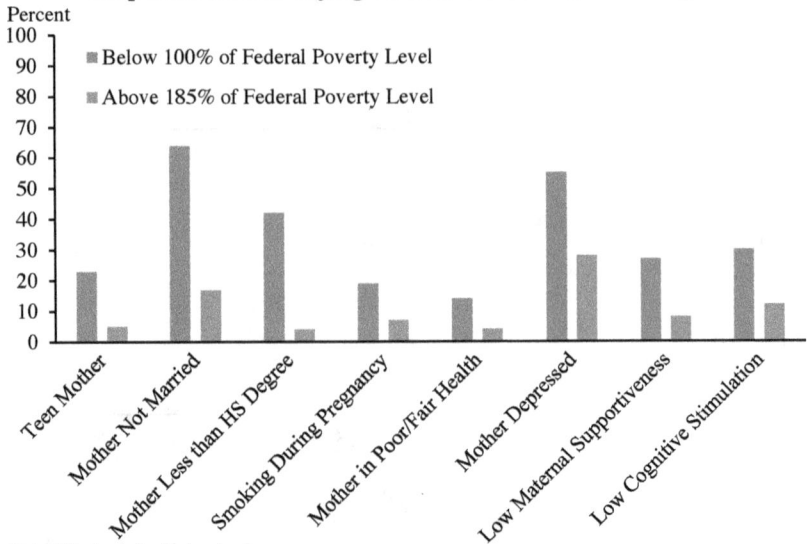

Note: HS stands for high school.
Source: Isaacs (2012).

these children face upon school entry has long-lasting consequences for academic achievement and behavior throughout their schooling years (Duncan, Magnuson, and Votruba-Drzal 2014; Duncan, Ziol-Guest, and Kalil 2010).

A child's early years, beginning in infancy, are a period of profound advances in reasoning, language acquisition, and problem solving. Importantly, a child's environment can dramatically influence the degree and pace of these advances. By supporting development when children are very young, early childhood development and education programs can complement parental investments. Children who enter school at higher levels of readiness have higher earnings throughout their lives. They are also healthier and less likely to become involved with the criminal justice system.

Early Gaps in Cognitive and Non-Cognitive Outcomes

Socioeconomic disparities in cognitive, social, behavioral, and health outcomes are evident in children as young as 9 months of age and these gaps tend to widen as children grow older. At just 9 months, infants and toddlers from low-income families score lower on cognitive assessments, are less likely to be in excellent or good health, and are less likely to receive positive behavior ratings than their counterparts from higher-income families; by 24 months, the cognitive and behavioral gaps have at least doubled (Halle et al. 2009). By the time children enter school around age 5, children in poor households are nearly 4 times more likely to score "very low" on assessments

Figure 4-6

**Likelihood of Scoring Very Low
on Measures of Cognition at Age 5, 2006**

Percent Scoring Very Low

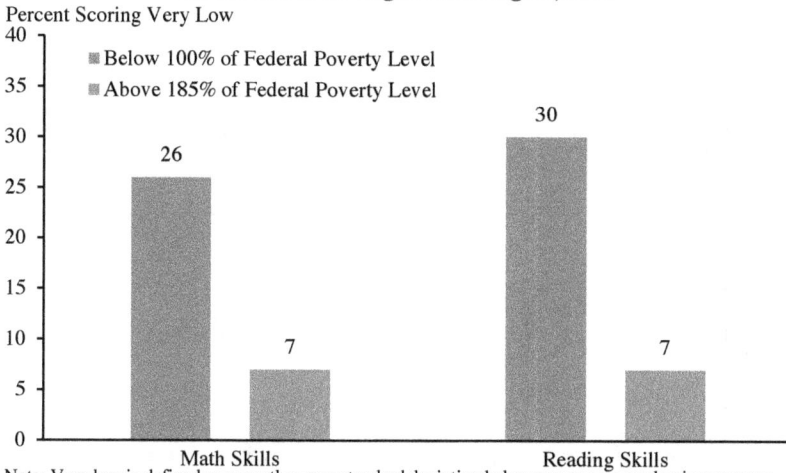

Note: Very low is defined as more than one standard deviation below average on academic measures.
Data are from the Early Childhood Longitudinal Study - Birth Cohort. Test scores were measured in
fall of 2006 or 2007.
Source: Isaacs (2012).

of math skills and over 4 times more likely to score "very low"' on reading skills than children in more well-off households (Figure 4-6).

These gaps tend to follow children throughout their school careers, putting impoverished children at a substantial academic disadvantage that can be hard to overcome. As shown in Figure 4-7, most of the income achievement gap emerges before age 5, and it remains relatively constant through the beginning of high school—suggesting that achievement gaps in later years are established in the earliest years of childhood. Some researchers argue that these gaps have grown over the past 50 years as overall income inequality has grown, and as the relationship between income and achievement has become stronger (Reardon 2011).[7] Family income is an increasingly important determinant of children's future earnings, suggesting that parental income inequality can have a long-run impact on educational and labor market inequality as their children age (Duncan, Kalil, and Ziol-Guest 2015).

Children experiencing poverty are also more likely to exhibit behavioral problems and to perform worse on non-cognitive skills tests. As shown in Figure 4-8, at age 5, children in poor households are nearly 80 percent

---

[7] There is some disagreement on the comparability of achievement gaps across studies over time. While some studies suggest gaps in test scores across socioeconomic groups stabilize from primary school (Reardon 2011; Heckman 2006), others argue that differences in academic achievement based on standardized test scores are not comparable over time (Nielsen 2015).

Figure 4-7
Achievement Gap is Largely Set by Age 5

Test Scores in Standard Deviations

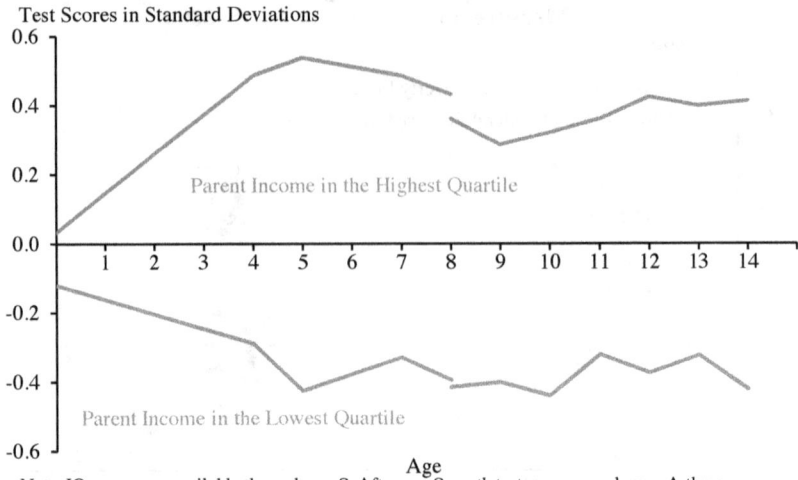

Note: IQ scores are available through age 8. After age 8, math test scores are shown. A three
year moving average is used for math scores.
Source: U.S. Collaborative Perinatal Project from Fryer and Levitt (2013) (through age 8);
NLSY79 Child and Young Adult Supplement from Cunha et al. (2006) (after age 8);
CEA calculations.

more likely to exhibit learning-related behavioral issues, such as not paying
attention in class, and more than 50 percent more likely to exhibit external-
izing behavioral problems. These findings are likely attributable to a host
of stressors that these children face, including less-safe neighborhoods,
increased exposure to trauma, insufficient resources to address their physical and mental health needs, and having parents with unmet physical or
mental health needs.

In addition to cognitive skills, non-cognitive skills, or socio-emotional
and behavioral skills, are also strong predictors of educational attainment,
and therefore of longer-term human capital accumulation, employment,
and wages. For example, teacher-rated social adjustment is a strong predictor of educational attainment and employment (Carneiro, Crawford,
and Goodman 2007). Social and behavioral skills in childhood have also
been shown to be strong predictors of physical health and engagement
in risky behaviors later in life. Indeed, non-cognitive factors can be even
stronger predictors than cognitive factors of risky behaviors and their
consequences—including smoking, participation in illegal activity, and
incarceration (Heckman, Stixrud, and Urzua 2006). This means that children from disadvantaged backgrounds who have had less support in their
socio-emotional and behavioral development from their earliest years are at
a higher risk of engaging in unhealthy and harmful behavior.

Figure 4-8
**Likelihood of Scoring Very Low
on Behavioral Indexes at Age 5, 2006**

Percent Scoring Very Low

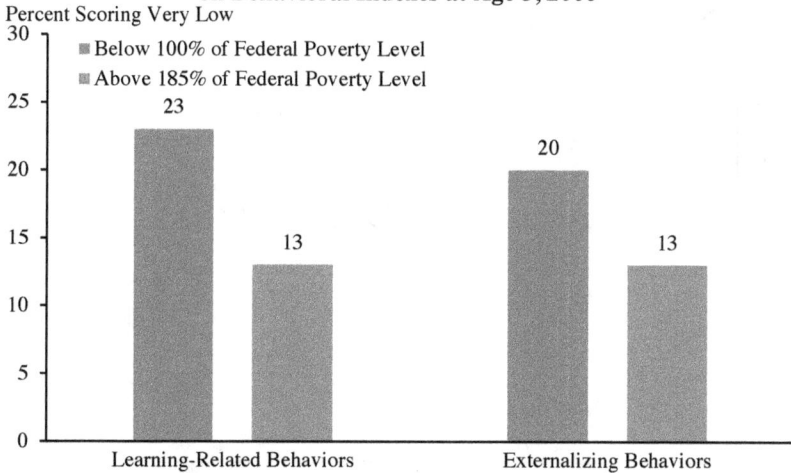

Note: Very low is defined as more than one standard deviation below average on behavioral measures.
Data are from the Early Childhood Longitudinal Program Birth Cohort. Test scores were measured in
the fall of 2006.
Source: Isaacs (2012).

Gaps in Resource and Time Investment

As discussed above, these large gaps in cognitive and non-cognitive skills may be due in part to large differences in inputs, including both parental inputs and formal, high-quality early learning opportunities. Today, inequalities in parental inputs such as time, resources, earnings, and education are higher than in the past. Parents in the top fifth of income earners now spend seven times more on enrichment activities and materials for their children—such as books, computers, summer camps, and music lessons—than families in the bottom fifth (Duncan and Murnane 2011). Moreover, as income inequality has grown, so has inequality in child-related expenditures.

Higher-income parents generally have more time to spend with their children, and the amount of time they spend has been increasing at a faster rate than among lower-income parents (Figure 4-9).[8] This may reflect, in part, that higher-income workers are much more likely to have access to paid time off and workplace flexibility, which they can use to spend quality time with young children (CEA 2015b). This additional time, particularly time spent playing and engaging in a child's development, is important for early cognitive and socio-emotional development. For example, research demonstrates that reading to children is crucial for early language acquisi-

---

[8] See Ramey and Ramey (2010) and Bianchi (2010) for further details.

Figure 4-9
**Mother's Time Spent on Child Care
by Educational Attainment, 1965—2008**

Hours per Week

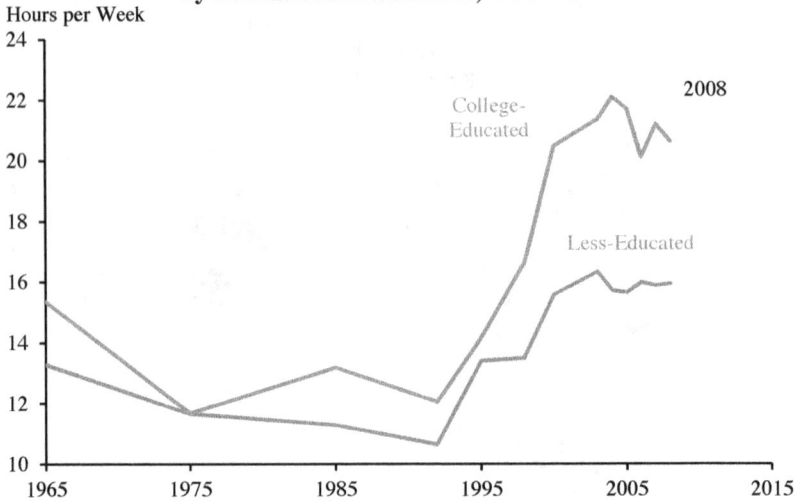

Note: Estimates are for mothers aged 25-34.
Source: Ramey and Ramey (2010).

tion and communication skills (National Research Council and Institute of Medicine 2000; Tamis-LeMonda et al. 2004). This inequality during early childhood creates an income-based advantage in educational outcomes early in life and leads to inequality in adult outcomes, one reason suggested for the persistence of income levels across generations (Solon 1992). For instance, when mothers obtain more education, it improves birth outcomes for their children (Currie and Moretti 2003). This may be due to the increases in marriage, use of prenatal care, lower fertility, reduction in smoking, or other factors that are correlated with higher levels of maternal education.

The gap is also reflected in the total time spent with children and in activities that engage children. In particular, high-income parents spend more time on educational activities with their children (Figure 4-10), creating an income-based advantage in educational outcomes in the first few years of life.

Highly educated parents are also spending more time on child-care activities, such as playing with young children and helping with children's activities (Ramey and Ramey 2010). For example, highly educated parents spend more time on developing their children's reading and problem-solving skills in preschool, and on extra-curricular activities for older children (Kalil 2014). In contrast, less-educated parents are less likely to adapt their time-use patterns with children to developmental stages (Kalil, Ryan, and Corey 2012). Gaps in children's vocabulary can reflect these differences in

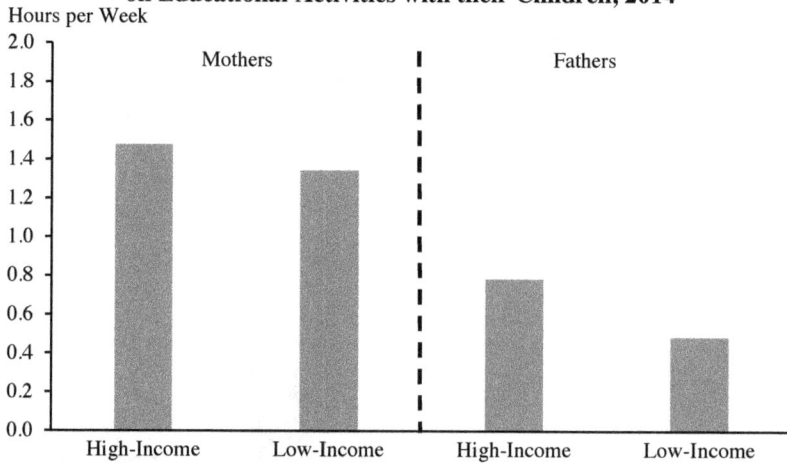

Figure 4-10
**High-Income Parents Spend More Time
on Educational Activities with their Children, 2014**

Note: High-income refers to top quartile while low-income refers to bottom quartile. Includes time spent helping with homework, attending school meetings, reading to or with children, and other activities assosciated with children's education.
Source: American Time Use Survey (2014).

time use by parents' educational attainment: highly educated mothers tend to engage in more complex talk with their children and spend more time reading and, at 3 years old, their children have more expansive vocabularies than children with less exposure to books and language (Vernon-Feagans et al. 2015).

These disparities in early childhood development can be exacerbated by later gaps in formal early schooling opportunities, as demonstrated by an extensive literature on the positive impacts of preschool on cognitive and non-cognitive outcomes. Children's enrollment in formal learning environments is especially affected by socioeconomic status. About 60 percent of 3- and 4-year olds whose mothers have a college degree are enrolled in preschool, compared to about 40 percent of children whose mothers did not complete high school (Figure 4-11). Although preschool attendance has increased for all maternal education groups since the 1970s, children of less-educated mothers are still less likely to attend preschool, in part due to the significant cost burden of high-quality early childhood care. Lower-income families are less likely to be able to afford care: among families with child-care expenses and working mothers, families below the Federal Poverty Level pay an average of 30 percent of their income in child-care costs, compared with 8 percent among non-poor families (Laughlin 2013).

Since formal early childhood education is less affordable for children who grow up in disadvantaged settings, inequalities in achievement

Figure 4-11
Preschool Enrollment by Mother's Education, 2014

Percent

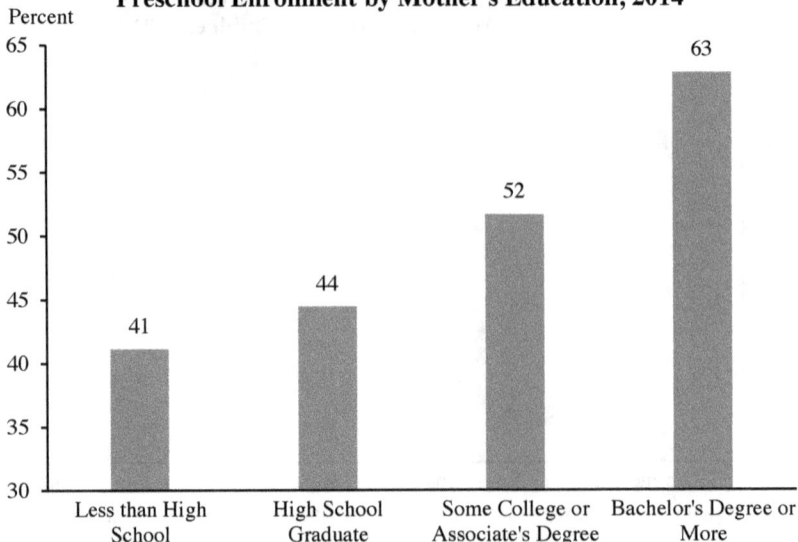

Note: Excludes children in kindergarten.
Source: Current Population Survey October Supplement (2014); Census Bureau calculations; CEA calculations.

that appear within the first few years of life continue to grow as children from disadvantaged families fall behind. Federal, State, and local programs help fill the socioeconomic status gap in the availability of early childhood education. For example, Head Start and Early Head Start provide formal high-quality learning environments for children from low-income families.

Gaps in Quality of Environmental & Neighborhood Factors

Around 4 million poor children grow up in high-poverty neighborhoods (Rawlings 2015). The health and human capital inputs that are available to poor children because of where they live are considerably worse than those available to children in more advantaged neighborhoods. A large body of literature confirms that neighborhood characteristics, such as accessibility and quality of learning, social and recreational activities, support networks, and the presence of physical risk (such as violence, victimization, and harmful substances), affect later-life outcomes (Leventhal and Brooks-Gunn 2000).

For example, school quality varies enormously with the level of poverty in a neighborhood. Access to high-quality schools with good teachers has been proven to improve later-life outcomes, such as earnings potential (Chetty, Rockoff, and Friedman 2014). However, because most public schools serve students within attendance district boundaries, children from low-income neighborhoods often lack access to high-quality schooling.

Black (1999) shows that school quality is capitalized in housing prices, meaning that houses in neighborhoods assigned to high-quality schools may be too expensive for low-income families to afford. Moreover, students in high-poverty school districts too often receive less investment than their peers in low-poverty districts, since local revenues account for a large fraction of school revenue (45 percent in 2011-2012) (National Center for Education Statistics 2015). In 23 States, districts serving the highest percentage of students from low-income families are spending fewer State and local dollars per pupil than districts that have fewer students in poverty (U.S. Department of Education 2015).

In addition to inadequate resources and support and the voluntary nature of the early childhood system, differential expulsion and suspension can also reduce disadvantaged students' access to early learning. Children from disadvantaged backgrounds may face biases that create barriers to their education, especially since children of color are overrepresented in low-income populations. For example, children of color, particularly boys are much more likely to be suspended or expelled from early learning settings (see Box 4-1 for further discussion of differential outcomes by gender in early childhood). In 2011-12, African-American students represented 18 percent of preschool enrollment but 48 percent of preschoolers suspended more than once (Office for Civil Rights 2014). This type of discipline can detract from learning, especially when children are removed from school and temporarily denied a formal learning environment.

Although traditional neighborhood school quality can be lacking in disadvantaged areas, there may be opportunities for government intervention to address barriers to quality schooling in these neighborhoods. Research shows that policies to expand disadvantaged students' access to quality schooling, like busing or charter schools, can improve educational attainment and close achievement gaps (Billings, Deming, and Rockoff 2014; Dobbie and Fryer 2011). Additionally, traditional public schools see marked improvement when they adopt best practices identified in alternative schooling policies. A study by Fryer (2014) shows that public schools in Houston experienced sizeable increases in student math achievement of 0.15 to 0.18 standard deviations per year when they adopted five best practices from charter schools.

Other characteristics of low-income neighborhoods can also inhibit healthy child development. The Centers for Disease Control and Prevention (CDC) reports that children living at or below the poverty line who inhabit older housing are at greatest risk for lead poisoning, which impairs brain development. Although much progress has been made in reducing rates of poisoning (CDC 2015), the effects of lead persist through a child's life.

Box 4-1: Gender Differences in Early Outcomes and Responses to Investment

Early investments are critical for both boys and girls, but parental and environmental inputs can differ for children of different genders, leading to disparate outcomes. Boys in low-income households tend to do worse on a myriad of health and human capital outcomes than similarly situated girls, ranging from educational attainment to test scores to crime involvement (Autor et al. 2015). A new working paper by Chetty et al. (2016) shows that these gender gaps in the impact of childhood disadvantage may be sustained through adulthood. Men who grew up in high-poverty, high-minority areas work significantly less than women from similar backgrounds, with the worst outcomes concentrated among men who grew up in low-income, single-parent households.

Researchers have found that environmental, rather than biological, factors drive this relationship. Autor et al. (2015) show that, though children born into families of low socioeconomic status (SES) have worse health than higher-SES newborns, birth outcomes are similar between low-SES siblings of different genders. The authors suggest that the gaps that emerge between low-SES male and female siblings later in childhood are due to differences in their environment after birth, or differential response to that environment.

Influences from both inside and outside of the home environment may lead both genders to be more sensitive to certain aspects of disadvantaged upbringing. Autor et al. (2015) suggest that gender gaps in outcomes between low-SES siblings, where boys tend to do worse, are related to home environment, partially through a lack of same-sex role models (fathers are more likely to be absent than mothers) and relatively smaller parental time investments as a result. They also posit that factors outside of the home but that are associated with low-SES status, including worse schools and neighborhoods, can have disproportionately negative impacts on boys. For example, a new working paper by the same authors shows that males on average benefit more from cumulative exposure to high-quality schools than their female siblings (Autor et al. 2016). Additionally, the stress associated with poverty appears to have more serious effects on males than on females (Bertrand and Pan 2013). This may be in part because boys' coping strategies tend to involve more aggressive behavior and less interaction with prosocial adults (Coleman and Hendry 1999). These differences in coping strategy may lead to different outcomes for the genders in different types of early intervention.

As a consequence, the effects of policies that support investment in children may vary for girls and boys. The policy section of this chapter examines how and why program impacts may differ by gender.

Differences in early life investments and adaptation behaviors between genders can affect the efficacy of childhood policy interventions. These disparities not only highlight the complexities in childhood development, but also the need to invest early. The earlier an intervention occurs, the fewer baseline gaps and maladaptive behaviors there are to overcome.

Besides diminished cognitive function, lead poisoning can manifest in behavioral problems as a child, pregnancy and aggression as a teen, and criminal behavior as a young adult (Reyes 2015a,b). Children from low-socioeconomic-status families are also more likely to be exposed to higher levels of pollution in their neighborhoods, making them more likely to be hospitalized with asthma complications (Neidell 2004). Exposure to pollution in a child's first year of life can also have negative long-term impacts on labor market outcomes, such as hours worked and earnings (Isen, Rossin-Slater, and Walker forthcoming).

Recent studies document large differences across counties in inter-generational economic mobility (Chetty et al. 2014) and find that these differences directly affect children's future outcomes (Chetty and Hendren 2015). About 60 percent of U.S. counties are positive contributors to inter-generational economic mobility, meaning that living in those counties during youth positively impacts the future income of children in low-income households.[9] Importantly, the duration of exposure to a better environment also matters—suggesting that the future benefits are greater when a child moves at an earlier age. For a child with parents at the 25th percentile of the income distribution, each year a child spends in DuPage, Illinois (which has the highest mobility of the 100 largest counties in the United States) raises that child's future earnings by 0.8 percent (Chetty and Hendren 2015). In contrast, every year of childhood spent in Baltimore City, Maryland (the worst of the 100 largest counties) reduces their future earnings by 0.7 percent.

Place also matters because segregation—both by race and by income—has negative implications for those who grow up in these neighborhoods. Living in a high-poverty neighborhood reduces access to jobs and career networks (Spaulding et al. 2015). Racial segregation has also been shown to have adverse effects on educational achievement and attainment, employment, earnings, single parenthood, and health (Cutler and Glaeser 1997;

---

[9] Causal effects on mobility based on Chetty and Hendren (2015) Online Data Table 2: Preferred Estimates of Causal Place Effects by County. http://www.equality-of-opportunity.org/index.php/data.

Card and Rothstein 2007; Dickerson 2007; Subramanian et al. 2005; Acevedo-Garcia and Lochner 2003).

The Role of Public Investment in Early Childhood

Early childhood investments can result in significant benefits for children, parents, and society. However, children from disadvantaged households often do not receive the investment they need to ensure their healthy development and success in school because optimal investments are resource-intensive and must happen early, while the benefits are realized over a long time horizon. Indeed, the challenges inherent in investing in children may be experienced by all parents; however, these obstacles can be especially daunting for parents with limited resources.

First, the need to invest early presents a challenge. Because many of the benefits—which include future earnings, health, and life satisfaction—are delayed and accrue to children in adulthood, children rely on parents and others to recognize these future returns on investment and to invest on their behalf.

Second, the gains these investments produce require significant up-front costs. This can be difficult for families to afford on their own, particularly for low-income households, since they lack sufficient time and financial resources or access to affordable credit to make these early investments.

Third, among factors that determine the quality of investment in young children, neighborhood quality and other environmental factors can be as important as family income. Many aspects of a child's environment can be difficult for parents to change on their own. Children from disadvantaged households face additional risks as a result of their environment, and public investments can improve these environmental inputs and supplement existing investments made by the family and community.

Finally, because many of the benefits accrue to society over a long time period, individuals lack the incentive to invest at the level that would achieve the highest social return. Indeed, the research surveyed later in this chapter suggests that the societal benefits are potentially large and wide ranging, and that these societal benefits often exceed the benefits received by the children themselves. These benefits include: reductions in crime; lower expenditures on health care, remedial education, and incarceration; and increased tax revenue and lowered public assistance expenditure due to higher earnings.

In light of these challenges, well-designed public investments can play a crucial role in closing income- and opportunity-related gaps that affect short- and long-run outcomes of children (see Box 4-2 for a discussion of the design of public investment). Public policy can also be key to ensuring that

Box 4-2: Types of Public Investment

Policies to improve investment in early health and human capital can take several forms. Income and in-kind transfers to families, direct investments in the health and human capital of young children, and investments that improve parental inputs can all help to compensate for underinvestment in their learning and development that stems from poverty. These various policies operate through different mechanisms but all support children's well-being in their formative years when it is easier to close gaps and influence children's lives.

1. <u>Direct investments in early childhood health and human capital services</u>: These investments provide direct access to early learning and care to promote healthy child development and prepare children for school. These programs include Head Start, child-care services, and State-funded preschool, among others. Access to these services can improve children's short- and long-term health and human capital outcomes and can have huge positive spillover effects for society as a whole.

2. <u>Indirect investments through improved parental and home inputs</u>: Many of the programs reviewed later in this chapter, such as the Nurse-Family Partnership Home Visiting Program and Head Start, involve parental engagement. Some programs, such as the READY4K! texting literacy intervention, are aimed entirely at improving children's home environments through parental behavior modifications. The goal of these investments, whether standalone or embedded in other initiatives, is to improve the quantity and quality of parental time with children.

3. <u>In-kind transfers</u>: Transfers in the form of health insurance or food help families to meet basic medical and nutritional needs while at the same time freeing up money for other types of consumption or investment. Examples include Medicaid, which helps parents afford health care for themselves and their children, and nutrition programs like the Special Supplemental Nutrition Program for Women, Infants, and Children (WIC) and the Supplemental Nutrition Assistance Program (SNAP), which provide food and nutritional guidance.

4. <u>Income transfers</u>: Transfers in the form of cash provide flexible support to low-income families and can help parents invest in their children by alleviating resource and credit constraints. Examples include Temporary Assistance to Needy Families (TANF), which provides a temporary cash benefit to the poorest families, and two others only available to those with earned income—the Earned Income Tax Credit (EITC) and the low-income portion of the Child Tax Credit (CTC). With regard to children's outcomes, the impact of these programs (as well as other programs that effectively increase disposable income) may

depend on how parents choose to invest the extra income. Further, these programs may have additional impacts on children through the work incentives (or disincentives) that they create for parents.

investments made now are large enough to pay off in the future and realize the gains shown by research—including numerous public benefits.

Underinvestment in children's health and human capital in their earliest years can become more costly for society later in children's lives. Societal efforts that attempt to intervene later in life, for example through remedial education or the juvenile justice system, tend to be less cost-effective than interventions that help children get, and stay, on the right track in the first place. For example, the cost of incarceration is substantially higher than investing in education or other programs to increase opportunity, even before one takes the returns to the investments into account. The annual cost of incarceration for a single juvenile is over $100,000— more than three times the average tuition and fees at a four-year, non-profit private university, and more than 10 times as expensive as an average year of Head Start (Figure 4-12).

Evidence suggests that investments in early childhood education may reduce involvement with the criminal justice system. Lower crime translates into benefits to society in the form of lowered costs of the criminal justice system and incarceration, as well as reductions in the costs of crime to victims (Heckman et al. 2010; Currie 2001; Reynolds et al. 2001). Likewise, these improvements in children's development may also reduce the need for special education placements and remedial education.[10] For example, studies of preschool programs for low-income children have found benefit-cost ratios of $7 to $12 for every $1 spent in the form of higher participant earnings, lower remedial education costs, reduced transfer payments, and reduced crime (Heckman et al. 2010).

Some early childhood investments, such as Early Head Start, Head Start, and home visitation programs, which offer access to immunizations, health services, and/or parenting education, have improved not only social-emotional and cognitive outcomes but also the health of program participants (Dodge et al. 2013; Kilburn 2014). These health improvements result in lower societal expenditures on emergency care and health care.

Finally, public investments in young children, such as preschool, public health care, and income transfers, have been shown to improve children's

---

[10] Anderson (2008); Reynolds et al. (2001, 2002); Belfield et al. (2006); Heckman et al. (2010); Carneiro and Ginja (2014).

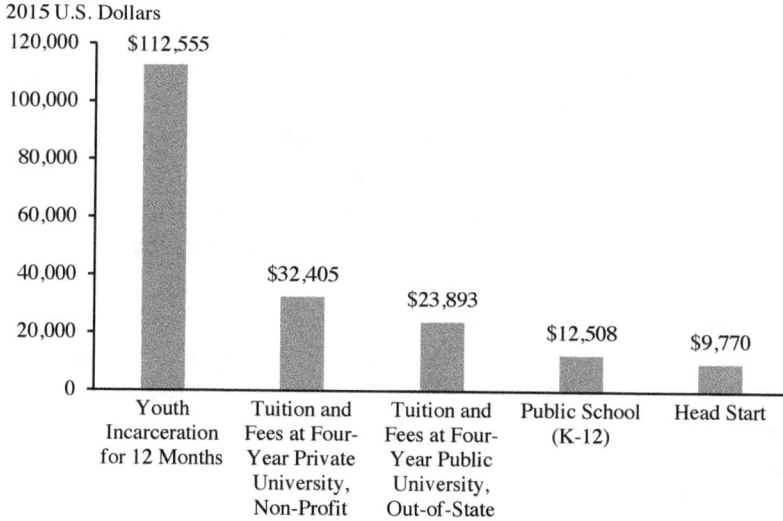

Figure 4-12
Annual Cost of Juvenile Incarceration vs. Other Youth Investments

Source: American Correctional Assocation; College Board; National Center for Education Statistics; CEA calculations.

long-term earnings potential (Brown, Kowalski, and Lurie 2015; Chetty, Friedman, and Rockoff 2011; Barnett and Masse 2007). When the children who receive these investments grow up, they pay more in taxes and are less likely to receive public assistance. As a result, making these early investments would actually increase government revenue and reduce government expenditure over time.

POLICY INTERVENTIONS THAT IMPROVE CHILDREN'S OUTCOMES

The evidence surveyed thus far overwhelmingly shows that, compared with their higher-income peers, children born into lower-income households receive fewer investments in their early health and education. They enter school at a substantial disadvantage on multiple measures of health, cognition, and non-cognitive skills. Mounting theoretical and empirical research also suggests that early investments in children can have especially large economic returns. Yet despite these returns, parents with few resources face several challenges to investing in their children.

Public policy has an important role to play in ensuring that high-return investments in early childhood are realized, and in preventing and closing opportunity gaps. Nevertheless, the relationships between early childhood experiences and long-run outcomes are complex and mediated by many factors, which makes it difficult to isolate the impact of any given policy. Research that demonstrates and measures the causal links between interventions and outcomes is crucial for guiding effective policy.

This section reviews the most rigorous research on the impacts of specific policy interventions that improve investments in early childhood (see Box 4-3 for a list of major Federal early childhood policy interventions). Attention is limited to studies that plausibly identify and measure the causal impacts of these policies on outcomes rather than documenting correlations. The section first presents the evidence on policies that provide direct investments in early childhood health and education, programs that aim to improve parental inputs, and in-kind transfers such as health insurance and food assistance programs. It then turns to the research on programs that provide more flexible assistance to low-income families, such as income transfers and housing assistance. A wide range of outcomes is considered— including measures of short-run health and human capital (such as infant and child mortality, birth weight, nutrition, test scores, and behavior and emotional skills) as well as long-run outcomes such as adult health, employment, earnings, and involvement in the criminal justice system.

On the whole, the research evidence confirms that policy interventions ranging from preschool provision to income transfers have large and sustained impacts on children's health and human capital accumulation. The evidence shows that these policies not only help children from disadvantaged families stay on pace with children from better-off families; they also lead to large benefits for society as a whole.

Direct, Indirect and In-Kind Investments in Early Health and Human Capital

The evidence discussed earlier in this chapter documented the existence of large gaps in health outcomes between children based on their mother's socioeconomic status. However, even as many measures of inequality have been rising in the United States, key measures of infant health, such as low birth weight, show a steady decline in the socioeconomic gap in health over the past 20 years (Figure 4-13). Recent research suggests that a range of successful public policy interventions targeted at improving maternal and infant health have played a key role in this trend. This section discusses some of the most successful policies aimed at improving early health.

Figure 4-13
Low Birth Weight by Maternal Socioeconomic Status, 1989–2011

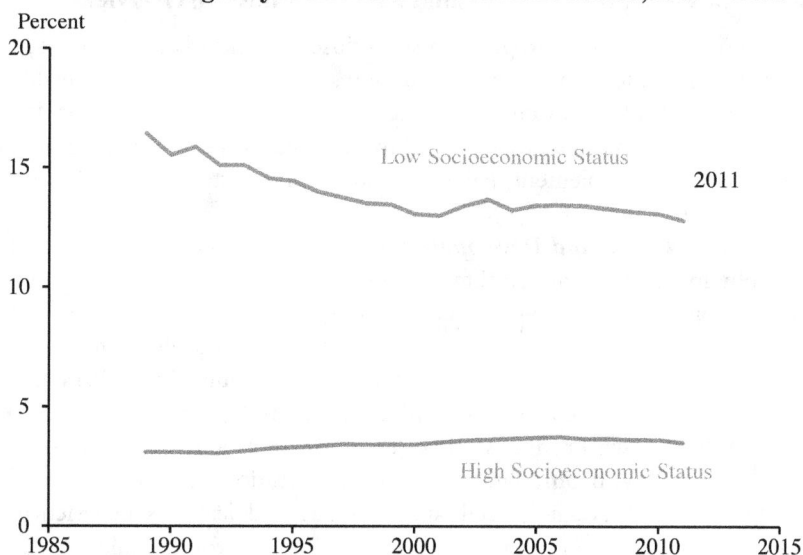

Percent

Low Socioeconomic Status

2011

High Socioeconomic Status

Note: Low socioeconomic status (SES) is defined as African-American, less than a high school degree, and unmarried. High SES is defined as White, college-educated, and married.
Source: Aizer and Currie (2014).

Policy Interventions in Early Health

Home Visitation

Several types of public investments target child development from before children are born and throughout early childhood. Home visitation programs, including those that are Federally funded by the Maternal, Infant, and Early Childhood Home Visiting program, rely on trained professionals, including nurses, teachers, or social workers, to visit families during pregnancy and shortly after a baby is born to provide a range of health, development, and parenting information. Depending on the model, this may include parental observations and instruction, nutrition and wellness education, and psychological consultations. The goal of home visitation programs is to ensure a healthy, safe, and supportive environment in the first years of a child's life. The programs tend to be targeted toward children who are most at risk of receiving insufficient prenatal and antenatal health care, including children of first-time, low-income, less-educated and/or unemployed mothers.

These programs—which were expanded through new grants to States under the Affordable Care Act of 2010 (ACA)—have shown promise in reducing mortality among infants between 4 weeks and 1 year of age born to mothers of low socioeconomic status. Poverty has been a major contributor

Box 4-3: Federal Early Childhood Programs: An Overview[1]

Various Federal programs help to close gaps in early investments in health and education, as well as family resources, and improve later-life outcomes. Millions of children benefit from this funding, often in the form of grants to States, each year. In many cases, Federal policies and investments complement, enhance, and expand State and local investments and policies.

Child Care and Development Fund: Assists low-income families in obtaining child care so they can work or attend training/education. The program, which is administered through block grants to States, also improves the quality of child care and promotes coordination among early childhood development and afterschool programs. In FY 2014, this $5 billion fund served about 1.4 million children each month.

Head Start: Promotes school readiness of 3- and 4-year-old children from low-income families through education, health, social and other services. Teachers facilitate individualized learning experiences to promote children's readiness for school and beyond. Children also receive health and development screenings, nutritious meals, oral health and mental health support. Additionally, parents and families are supported in achieving their own goals, such as housing stability, continued education, and financial security. Together with Early Head Start, this $9 billion program served approximately 1 million children and pregnant women in FY 2014 through grants to local entities.

Early Head Start: Provides early, continuous, intensive, and comprehensive child development and family support services to low-income infants and toddlers and their families, and pregnant women and their families. This program also includes the Early Head Start-Child Care Partnerships, which provide funding to States and local communities to increase the number of high-quality early learning opportunities for infants and toddlers across the country.

Preschool Development Grants: Supports States in building or enhancing a preschool program infrastructure that would enable the delivery of high-quality preschool services to children, and expanding high-quality preschool programs in targeted communities that would serve as models for expanding preschool to all 4-year-olds from low- and moderate-income families. This $250 million grant supported 18 States in FY 2015 and is funded at $250 million for FY 2016.

Individuals with Disabilities Education Act (IDEA): Serves infants and toddlers through age 2 and children ages 3-5 with developmental delays or high probabilities of developmental delays. These $791 million

---

[1] Figures for funding and number of beneficiaries are for the most recent year for which comprehensive data were available on February 1, 2016.

Federally funded programs, administered by States, provided approximately 1.1 million children with special education and related services in FY 2015.[2] Many of the children are able to enter kindergarten no longer needing special education services.

Maternal, Infant, and Early Childhood Home Visiting (MIECHV): Reaches pregnant women, expectant fathers, and parents and caregivers of children under the age of 5. In these voluntary, evidence-based programs, trained health care or social services professionals meet regularly with expectant parents or families with young children to: improve health and development; prevent child injuries, abuse, neglect, or maltreatment; improve school readiness and achievement; improve family economic self-sufficiency; and improve coordination with other community resources. Through State and Tribal grants, this $400 million program served approximately 115,500 parents and children in FY 2014.

Medicaid and Children's Health Insurance Program (CHIP): Provides health coverage to millions of Americans, including eligible low-income adults, children, pregnant women, elderly adults and people with disabilities. CHIP provides health coverage to eligible children through both Medicaid and separate CHIP programs. These programs receive both Federal and State dollars and are managed by States. Together, Medicaid and CHIP provided health coverage to nearly 44 million children in FY 2014, including one-half of all low-income children in the United States.

Special Supplemental Nutrition Program for Women, Infants, and Children (WIC): Serves to safeguard the health of low-income pregnant, postpartum, and breastfeeding women, infants, and children up to age 5 who are at nutritional risk by providing nutritious foods to supplement diets, information on healthy eating and breastfeeding, and referrals to health care services. In FY 2015, nearly $7 billion was provided to States through Federal grants, and, in FY 2014, approximately 8 million people received WIC services, including roughly 4 million children between 6 months and age 5, 2 million infants under 6 months, and 2 million mothers.

Supplemental Nutrition Assistance Program (SNAP): Provides nutrition assistance to millions of eligible, low-income individuals and families and provides economic benefits to communities. Formerly known as Food Stamps, recipients receive State-administered monthly benefits in the form of an Electronic Benefit Transfer (EBT) card, which can be used to purchase foods at authorized stores. This $76 billion

---

[2] U.S. Department of Education, EDFacts Data Warehouse (EDW): "IDEA Part B Child Count and Educational Environments Collection," 2014-15. Data extracted as of July 2, 2015 from file specifications 002 and 089; Department of Education calculations.

program served over 45 million Americans, including almost 7 million children under the age of 5, in FY 2014.

Earned Income Tax Credit (EITC): Reduces the amount of taxes qualified working people with low to moderate income owe and provides refunds to many of these individuals. According to the Internal Revenue Service (IRS), there were $68 billion in EITC claims from 28.8 million tax filers for tax year 2013.

Child Tax Credit (CTC): Allows taxpayers to claim a credit of up to $1000 per child under age 17, depending on the taxpayers' income, and is partially refundable, making it one of the largest tax-code provisions benefitting families with children. According to the IRS, there were $55 billion in CTC claims for tax year 2013. The Urban-Brookings Tax Policy Center (2013) estimates that roughly 40 million families claimed credits in that year.

Temporary Assistance to Needy Families (TANF): Provides temporary monthly cash assistance to needy families with dependent children, while also preparing program participants for independence through work. Replacing Aid to Families with Dependent Children (AFDC), TANF now provides block grants to States and Tribes, which States match with their own "maintenance of effort" funds to implement the program. In 2015, this $17 billion program supported roughly 3 million children—though this number is approximately one-third of the 1994 peak in AFDC (Falk 2015). As of FY 2013, over 40 percent of children receiving TANF were age 5 and under.

Housing and Neighborhood Programs: Increases affordable housing options for low-income families through a variety of Federal programs, including public housing, project-based rental assistance, and the Housing Choice Voucher Program. The Section 8 Housing Choice Vouchers Program—the largest Federal housing assistance program— allows very low-income families to lease or (in a small number of cases, purchase) safe, decent, and affordable privately owned rental housing, including housing in higher opportunity neighborhoods. The Promise Zone Initiative, announced in the 2013 State of the Union Address, is an innovative partnership with local communities and businesses, one of the major goals of which is to increase access to affordable housing and improve public safety.

to the United States' overall high infant mortality rate (Chen, Oster, and Williams 2015). Home visitation programs have also been shown to improve parenting behavior and children's cognitive outcomes, especially among families with low-birth-weight children (Sweet and Appelbaum 2004). By improving parental behavior and children's outcomes, these programs can benefit children and parents in the long run.

One well-established program, the Nurse Family Partnership, provides first-time, low-income mothers with home visits during pregnancy through their child's second birthday. A longitudinal evaluation of the program found that participants who were randomly assigned to receive home visitation services, compared with women who only received prenatal and well-child clinic care, waited longer after the birth of their first child before having a second child; had lower receipt of cash transfers; and exhibited lower rates of arrest, drugs and alcohol abuse, and child abuse (Olds et al. 1997). The children of mothers who received home visitation services were also less likely to be arrested, consumed less alcohol, had fewer behavioral problems, had fewer sexual partners, smoked fewer cigarettes, and were less likely to run away compared to children of mothers in the control group (Olds et al. 1998). These studies measured outcomes at age 15, indicating that the program impacts were sustained in the medium term.

A more recent analysis of the Nurse Family Partnership program examined its impacts on children's cognitive abilities and found improvement by age 6 among children whose mothers participated in the program. These early cognitive gains were attributable to improvements in the home environment and in parenting behavior, as well as to greater self-esteem and lower anxiety among mothers, and they translated into improved language and math abilities and fewer school absences at age 12 (Heckman et al. 2014).

Some home visitation programs are provided as part of the Federal Head Start preschool program (described further below). A recent study finds that Head Start programs that incorporated frequent home visitation were particularly effective at improving non-cognitive outcomes compared with other Head Start programs (Walters 2015). Other models of home visitation programs are also showing promising results, with 19 models meeting the Department of Health and Human Services' (HHS) criteria for evidence-based home visiting programs (Administration for Children and Families 2015). Ongoing data collection will allow for further rigorous evaluation and help expand the knowledge base of the most effective home visitation programs.

Based on the mounting evidence that home visiting programs have significant positive impacts on children's cognitive outcomes, Federal support for home visitation programs was introduced in 2008 and was further expanded under the Affordable Care Act two years later. This ACA expansion was extended with bipartisan support through March 2015, and the President proposed expanding and extending funding for another 10 years in his 2013 State of the Union address. The Medicare Access and CHIP

Reauthorization Act of 2015, signed into law by the President in April 2015, extends an annual $400 million in funding for the Maternal, Infant, and Early Childhood Home Visiting programs through September 30, 2017.

Health Insurance

Research has established that access to insurance coverage during childhood can have important benefits for educational and labor market outcomes much later in life—benefits that appear to be mediated, at least in part, through sustained improvements in health.

Medicaid and the Children's Health Insurance Program (CHIP) provide low-cost health coverage to millions of Americans, including nearly 44 million children and covering one-half of all low-income children (Centers for Medicare and Medicaid Services). The programs are funded jointly by States and the Federal Government and are administered by States. All children enrolled in Medicaid are entitled to the comprehensive set of health care services known as Early and Periodic Screening, Diagnosis, and Treatment (EPSDT). CHIP also ensures a comprehensive set of benefits for children. Most States have elected to provide Medicaid to children with family incomes above the minimum of 100 percent of the Federal Poverty Level, and all States have expanded coverage to children with higher incomes through CHIP.

A pair of recent studies have used the fact that States expanded access to health insurance for children through Medicaid and CHIP at different times and to different extents in recent decades to study how access to health insurance in childhood affects long-term educational and labor market outcomes. Using data that connect individuals' adult earnings and tax information to their residence and family income in childhood (ages 0-18), Brown, Kowalski, and Lurie (2015) find that female children with more years of Medicaid/CHIP eligibility in childhood (due to their State of residence and year of birth) had higher educational attainment and higher earnings in early adulthood. They also find evidence that both men and women with greater access to childhood coverage pay more in income and payroll taxes in their young adult years, potentially offsetting a substantial fraction of the cost of providing Medicaid/CHIP coverage to children. The authors estimate that a single additional year of Medicaid/CHIP eligibility in childhood increased cumulative tax payments through age 28 by $186 (Figure 4-14; Brown, Kowalski, and Lurie 2015). The more years a child is eligible, the larger the cumulative impact.

Related work by Cohodes et al. (2014) examines the impact of changes in Medicaid/CHIP eligibility rules affecting children (ages 0-18) on educational attainment. The authors also find improvements in educational attainment at age 22 to 29, with individuals who were eligible for Medicaid/

Figure 4-14
**Increase in Income and Payroll Taxes Paid Through Age 28 from an
Additional Year of Medicaid Eligibility in Childhood, 1996—2012**

2011 U.S. Dollars

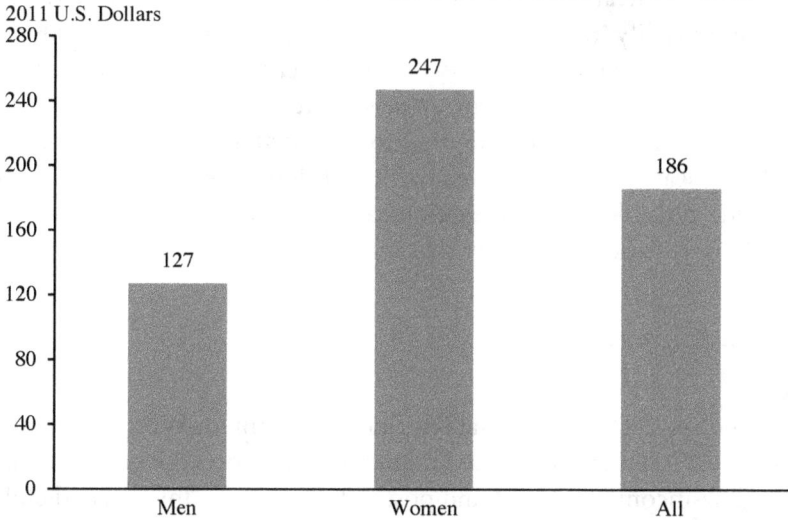

Note: Cumulative tax payments based on earnings through age 28.
Source: Brown, Kowalski, and Lurie (2015).

CHIP in childhood being more likely to complete high school and graduate from college. These attainment impacts were similar regardless of the age at which the child had Medicaid coverage.

New evidence from Miller and Wherry (2015) suggests that prenatal Medicaid receipt can also have large long-term effects on health and economic outcomes. Like some of the other studies discussed above, Miller and Wherry also examine variation in Medicaid and CHIP eligibility rules across States and over time, but focus on eligibility for pregnant women rather than children. Children whose mothers gained Medicaid coverage while pregnant had lower rates of obesity and fewer hospitalizations related to endocrine, nutritional, metabolic diseases, and immunity disorders between the ages of 19 and 32. The effects for children whose mothers gained Medicaid between birth and age 18 (as opposed to *in utero*) were generally insignificant, suggesting that receipt *in utero* is particularly important for these health outcomes. Health gains for children whose mothers received Medicaid while pregnant were also accompanied by improvements in educational and economic outcomes, including higher high school graduation rates, higher income, and lower SNAP receipt.

The literature on desegregation of health care facilities also demonstrates that access to health care during childhood can have large impacts on children's long-term outcomes. Almond, Chay, and Greenstone (2006) document that desegregation of hospitals during the 1960s resulted in increased hospital access for African-American families, dramatic improvements in infant health for these families, and large declines in the racial gap in infant mortality in the 1960s. Chay, Guryan, and Mazumder (2009) show that these improvements in access to health care at birth and health soon after birth led to large student achievement gains for African-American teenagers in the 1980s, contributing to a reduction in the racial test score gap. The researchers estimate that each additional early-life hospital admission made possible by desegregation raised test scores by between 0.7 and 1 standard deviation—an effect that implies a very large impact on lifetime earnings.

Nutrition Programs

WIC

The Special Supplemental Nutrition Program for Women, Infants and Children (WIC) is an assistance program that supports the health and nutrition of low-income pregnant and postpartum women, infants, and children under the age of 5. More than 8 million people received WIC services in FY 2014, including roughly 4 million children between 6 months and age 5, 2 million infants under 6 months, and 2 million mothers. WIC services include health care referrals, nutrition education, and the provision of nutritious foods to supplement the diets of both mothers and their children.

There is a robust literature on the impact that this comprehensive set of WIC services has on participants. Earlier studies comparing birth outcomes of women who participate in WIC to those of other low-income women with similar characteristics document that participants give birth to healthier babies as measured along several dimensions (Bitler and Currie 2005; Joyce, Gibson, and Colman 2005). More recent studies using rigorous methods confirm that WIC participation leads to improved birth outcomes. One such study focuses on the program's initial roll out, which was implemented in stages at the county level between 1972 and 1979. Hoynes, Page, and Stevens (2011) compare birth information from the Vital Statistics Natality Data among children who were born at similar times, but in different counties, and therefore had different *in utero* exposure to WIC. These results suggest that access to WIC increased birth weight among children born to mothers who participated in WIC from the third trimester by around 10 percent, and effects were largest among mothers with low levels of education.

Other work uses more recent data on local access to WIC. In some States, like Texas, clients must apply for WIC in person, and distance to a clinic can present a barrier to access. Rossin-Slater (2013) examines data from the Texas Department of State Health Services on WIC clinic openings,

Figure 4-15

Effects of WIC Participation on Birth Outcomes, 1994—2004

Percent Change

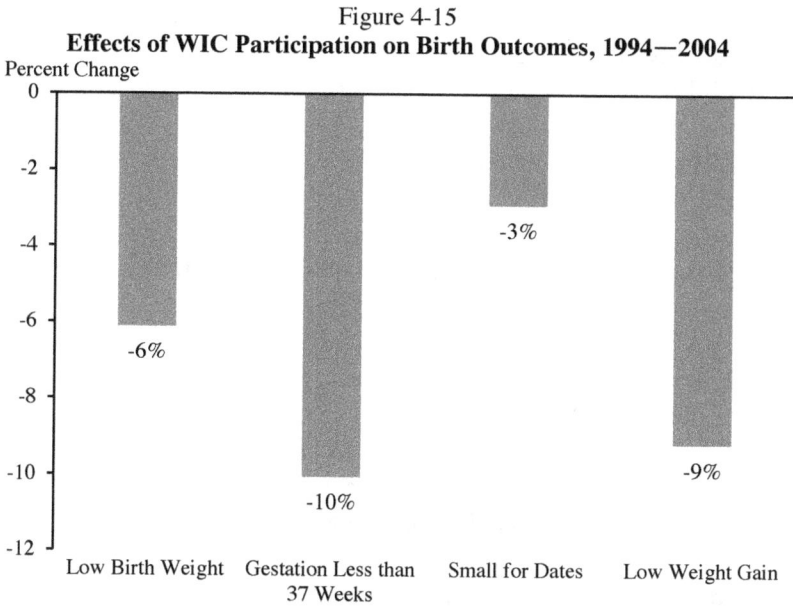

Source: Currie and Rajani (2015).

which include operating dates and ZIP codes for all clinics in the States, and birth records that include information on birth outcomes and maternal characteristics. The author compares birth outcomes between siblings, where one child was born when a clinic was open nearby, but one sibling was born without a clinic, to separate the effect of WIC access from genes and upbringing. This work shows that proximity to a WIC clinic increased weight gain during pregnancy, birth weights, and the likelihood of breastfeeding upon hospital discharge.

Another recent paper by Currie and Rajani (2015) uses birth records from New York City to look at birth outcomes, controlling for fixed and time-varying characteristics of mothers that might affect selection into the WIC program. The authors find that WIC reduced the probability that the mother gained too little weight during pregnancy, improved receipt of intensive medical services, and reduced the incidence of low birth weight, even among full-term infants (Figure 4-15). Overall, the literature shows that WIC has led to substantial gains in many of the most important indicators of early health, helping to close the gap in early health outcomes by socioeconomic status.

SNAP

The Supplemental Nutrition Assistance Program, or SNAP, is the cornerstone of the U.S. policy to address food insecurity—it is the largest and most universal of a set of Federal food and nutrition programs designed to alleviate hunger by supplementing the food budgets of low-income households. SNAP is broadly available to most low-income households, with eligibility based primarily on income and assets. Over 45 million Americans, including almost 7 million children under the age of 5, received SNAP in FY 2014, as well as the elderly, working families, and individuals with disabilities.

Eligible households generally must have a gross monthly income below 130 percent of the official poverty guideline for their family size and a net income that falls below the poverty line (USDA 2015). SNAP benefits are distributed to eligible households on a monthly basis in the form of an electronic benefit transfer (EBT) card, which can be used to purchase eligible foods at authorized retail stores. The level of SNAP benefits is intended to fill the gap between a household's cash resources that are available to spend on food and the amount needed to purchase a nutritious diet at minimal cost. The latter amount is calculated using a model-based market basket of foods known as the Thrifty Food Plan (TFP), which is adjusted for household size but not for other factors such as local prices. The benefit formula assumes that households can contribute 30 percent of their net income to purchase food. A household's SNAP allotment is thus equal to the TFP-based measure of need, which gives the maximum allotment for that household's size, less 30 percent of the household's net income.

SNAP plays an important role in reducing poverty in the United States and has been shown to be highly effective at reducing food insecurity. In 2014, SNAP benefits directly lifted at least 4.7 million Americans, including 2.1 million children, over the poverty line. Research has also shown that, among households who receive SNAP, food insecurity rates are up to 30 percent lower than they otherwise would be, with impacts for children that are at least this large (Council of Economic Advisers 2015c).

A growing body of high-quality research shows that SNAP and its functionally similar predecessor, the Food Stamp Program, have led to significant improvements in the health and wellbeing for those who receive food assistance as young children. Almond, Hoynes, and Schanzenbach (2011) study the impact of the early Food Stamp Program on birth outcomes by studying the initial rollout of the program across US counties between 1961 and 1975. Using county level variation in the timing of implementation, they find that a mother's access to Food Stamps during pregnancy led to increased birth weight, with the greatest gains at the lower end of the birth-weight distribution.

Related recent work uses similar cross-State variation and longitudinal data on children who received food stamps before birth and in the first few years of life, following them throughout their adolescence and into

Figure 4-16
Impact of Food Stamp Exposure on Metabolic Syndrome
by Age of First Exposure

Metabolic Syndrome Index (Exposure at Ages 10-11=0)

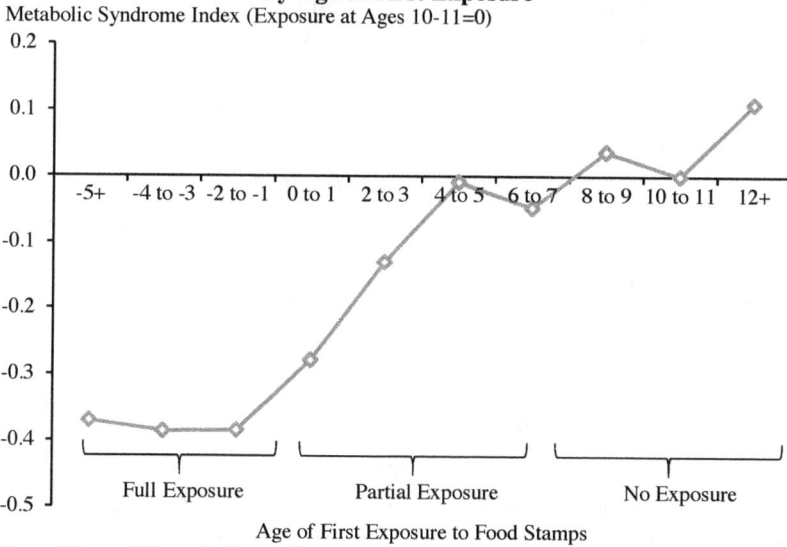

Age of First Exposure to Food Stamps

Source: Hoynes, Schanzenbach, and Almond (forthcoming).

Figure 4-17
Long-Term Impacts of Exposure to Food Stamps as a Child

Percentage Point Impact   Standard Deviation Impact

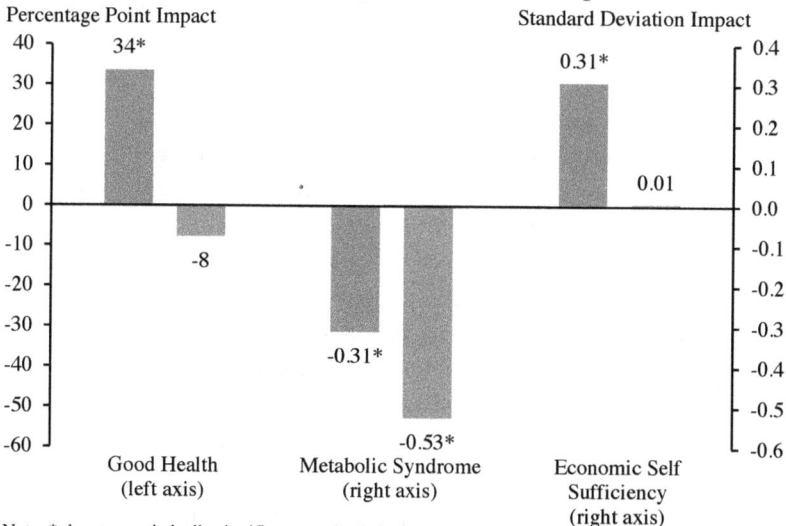

Note: * denotes statistically significant result. Estimates are for a high-impact sample where the head of houshold had less than a high school education.

Source: Hoynes, Schanzenbach, and Almond (forthcoming).

adulthood (Hoynes, Schanzenbach, and Almond forthcoming). They find that increased exposure to food stamps *in utero* and in early childhood led to a significant reduction in the incidence of "metabolic syndrome," including a 16 percentage-point drop in the likelihood of being obese as adults for the children of less-educated parents (Figure 4-16).[11]

Turning to the program's impact on economic success and self-sufficiency, the authors find that early access to food stamps led to an 18 per-centage-point increase in the likelihood of completing high school among disadvantaged adults. Finally, their results show even broader impacts for women, who benefitted through significant improvements in overall health and economic self-sufficiency—including increased educational attainment, increased earnings, and reduced participation in public assistance programs (Figure 4-17).

Policy Interventions in Early Education

Investments in early childhood education can take a number of forms and can benefit children through multiple channels. Policy interventions include preschool programs for children in the year before entering kindergarten; child-care programs that provide a stimulating environment for infants and toddlers; and programs that provide information and support services to parents and caregivers. Formal preschool and child-care programs typically aim to improve early human capital—including both cognitive and non-cognitive skills—through services provided directly to children. Yet these programs may also benefit children indirectly; for example, by helping parents to increase their labor force participation and raising household income. Other interventions affect children's outcomes indirectly by providing services to the parent or caregiver that improve the quality of their interactions with the children. Such caregiver interventions may be standalone or may be coupled with formal child-care and preschool programs (see Box 4-4 for examples of how technology can be used to supplement formal early learning settings).

The United States has, over the past half-century, made tremendous strides in expanding investment in formal early childhood education. Head Start, established as part of the War on Poverty in 1964, and Early Head Start, established in 1994, collectively provide comprehensive educational and health services—including formal schooling, health and development screenings, meals, and family support services—for approximately 1 mil-lion low-income children annually. States and localities are also making

---

[11] The study measures metabolic syndrome as an index that puts equal weight on five related components: high blood pressure, heart disease, heart attack, obesity, and diabetes. The results show that among these components, Food Stamp exposure had the largest impact on obesity, but all five components showed improvement.

Box 4-4: Technological Innovation that Stimulates Learning during Out-of-School Time

Sesame Street & Early Childhood Education

Massive open online courses (MOOCs) have the potential to enhance children's experiences in early education, by extending low-cost early education materials to large numbers of young children. One of the earliest examples of such innovation is the educational program Sesame Street.

A recent study on Sesame Street in its earliest years showed that preschool-aged children who lived in areas where Sesame Street was available were more likely to advance age-appropriately through school. The results were particularly pronounced for boys, for children in economically disadvantaged areas, and for students from disadvantaged backgrounds, including non-Hispanic African-American children. Although the long-term outcome results were inconclusive, the authors of the study suggest that the potential impacts of the program on advancing through school as appropriate, coupled with the very low cost for each student ($5 a child annually), and the enhanced impact for students from disadvantaged backgrounds, show promise for MOOCs to supplement early childhood education for low-income children (Kearney and Levine 2015). It is important to note that the National Research Council and the Institute of Medicine (2000) agree that children learn best through enriching, social interactions with adults and peers in their lives, including teachers and families. Sesame Street and other educational programs are not intended to replace formal high-quality early education, or high-quality adult-child interactions in the earliest years; rather they can serve as a supplement to the learning that happens in early learning settings and with families at home by providing an opportunity to spend out-of-school time learning.

This low-cost delivery of an effective curriculum continues to be important for disadvantaged children today, since the costs of early childhood care and educational activities have risen so rapidly in recent years, putting high-quality education out of reach of many low-income families. Low-cost supplements to early education, like Sesame Street, can help low-income children gain some of the out-of-school educational experience received by higher-income children.

Texting to Improve Parental Inputs

Text messaging is another promising delivery method that can improve parental behavior at low cost. Most American adults (88 percent) have cell phones and can receive texts (Zickuhr and Smith 2012), which have a 95-percent open rate (Mogreet 2013). READY4K!, an eight-month-long text messaging program designed to help parents of preschoolers support their child's literacy development outside of the classroom, significantly improved literacy during a pilot program in San Francisco. The text messages sent to parents suggested simple, concrete actions that could be taken at home to build on children's classroom learning, like suggesting specific ways to work on children's literacy skills during bath time. The intervention significantly increased positive parental behaviors and school involvement, and improved children's literacy scores by up to 0.34 standard deviation. There is some evidence that these impacts were larger for the children of African–American and Hispanic parents (York and Loeb 2014). More READY4K! pilots are underway across the country.

significant investments in early childhood education. Today, 40 States and the District of Columbia have in place State-funded preschool programs, serving more than one-quarter of all 4-year-olds in the 2012-13 school year.

To further increase opportunities for all children to begin kindergarten school-ready, the Obama Administration has proposed expanding high-quality preschool for all low- and middle-income 4-year-olds, expanding access to affordable high-quality child care for low- and moderate-income families, and making effective home visitation programs for new parents more widely available. Since President Obama put forth his Preschool for All proposal in the 2013 State of the Union Address, the Federal Government has invested $750 million in high-quality early childhood programs, through the Early Head Start-Child Care Partnerships for infants and toddlers, and Preschool Development Grants. In addition, the Every Student Succeeds Act, which President Obama signed into law in December 2015, includes a new version of the Preschool Development Grant program, building on the Administration's commitment to expanding and establishing State-supported high-quality preschool.

Child Care and Early Education Leading Up to Preschool

High-quality care for young children before they are eligible to attend preschool can provide direct and indirect benefits for both children and parents. Specifically, high-quality child care may benefit children by ensuring that they are in safe, stimulating, and nurturing learning environments while away from parents (Havnes and Mogstad 2011). By increasing the probability that parents are working, child-care access may also benefit children by supplementing family resources, thereby reducing financial hardship and possibly related stressors.

Parents are best able to work when they have access to stable, high-quality, affordable child-care arrangements, allowing them to better support their children through wages. Studies generally find that improving the affordability of child care increases employment for parents, particularly mothers. For instance, a universal subsidy that lowered the cost of child care to $5 a day in Quebec increased maternal labor force participation by about 8 percentage points (Baker et al. 2008; Lefebvre and Merrigan 2008). Similarly, an evaluation of a near-universal U.S. child-care program during the 1940s found that it substantially increased maternal employment (Herbst 2014). More recently, research showed that U.S. child-care subsidies that reduced the cost of child care by 10 percent increased employment among single women by 0.5 percent (Herbst 2010).

Evidence on the lifetime benefits of programs targeted to very young children comes from studies that have tracked participants in such programs into adulthood. One well-known program, the Abecedarian Project, provided poor children born in North Carolina between 1972 and 1977 with a full-time, high-quality educational intervention from infancy through age 5. The project, which was funded through both Federal and State grants, used a randomized design to allocate spots in the program and collected detailed longitudinal data on child and family outcomes. Although the program served a relatively small number of children (57), it is a landmark study for its rigorous design and for establishing credible, causal evidence that educational interventions at a very early age can affect participants over their lifetimes.

Children's gains from the Abecedarian Project persisted through adolescence and adulthood. Beginning at 18 months, program participants had higher scores on tests of various cognitive skills and scored higher on math and reading achievement tests, and these achievement gains persisted through ages 15 and 21 (Ramey and Campbell 1984; Campbell and Ramey 1995; Campbell et al. 2001). In addition, participants had higher high school graduation and college attendance rates, as well as more years of schooling. These achievement gains translated to large earnings gains as participants entered the labor force. At age 30, participants had income gains of over 60 percent relative to the control group (Campbell et al. 2012). The benefits of Abecedarian also accrued to parents, as the program increased maternal earnings by about $90,000 over the mother's career, approximately double the estimated earnings gains for participant children based on their higher levels of educational attainment (about $50,000) (Barnett and Masse 2007).[12]

Between 1985 and 1988, the Infant Health and Development Program (IHDP) expanded the Abecedarian model to eight U.S. cities, targeting a sample of low-birth-weight, premature infants. IHDP significantly improved cognitive outcomes among a diverse group of students during the

---

[12] Each of these figures is in 2015 dollars, with a 3 percent discount rate.

program and up to 15 years after completing the program (Brooks-Gunn et al. 1994; Gross et al. 1997; McCarton et al. 1997; McCormick et al. 2006). Low-income children benefited the most from the program, and projections suggest that either a universal or income-based program similar to IHDP would essentially eliminate income-based gaps in IQ at age 3 and would substantially reduce IQ gaps at ages 5 and 8 (Duncan and Sojourner 2014).

In 1994, the Head Start program, which was established in 1964 for preschool-aged children (mainly 3 or 4 years of age), expanded access to younger children through Early Head Start. Early Head Start provides services for at-risk pregnant women, new mothers, children ages zero to 3, and their families and focuses on positive parenting and home environments and children's developmental outcomes. Over 100,000 children ages 2 and younger were enrolled in Early Head Start in FY 2012 (Office of Head Start 2015).

The impacts of Early Head Start have been studied through the Early Head Start Research and Evaluation Project, which randomly assigned children to receive Early Head Start services and tracked children's performance through elementary school. Children who participated in Early Head Start showed less aggressive behavior, greater vocabulary and language development, and higher cognitive skills upon the program's completion. These gains were especially pronounced among African-American children. Parents who received Early Head Start services showed greater engagement during play and greater support for language and learning development at home (Love et al. 2005). Other studies of Early Head Start have found similar results for cognitive development and language acquisition (Vogel et al. 2013; Vallotton et al. 2012), as well as for home environments (Green et al. 2014; Love et al. 2002).

While most research on child care has focused on specific, targeted interventions like Abecedarian and Early Head Start, some studies have shown that government provision of child-care subsidies can also improve children's outcomes. Two studies from Norway demonstrate that child-care subsidies can improve children's academic performance (Black et al. 2012) and, later in life, increase educational attainment, decrease receipt of cash transfers, and increase labor-market participation (Havnes and Mogstad 2011). In the United States, evidence on the impact of child-care subsidies comes from a study of the Lanham Act of 1940, which funded the provision inexpensive and universal public child care through wartime stimulus grants between 1943 and 1946. A recent study examining outcomes of adults who were children during these years finds that growing up in a State that spent heavily on child care under the Lanham Act led to increased educational attainment and earnings capacity, making children more likely to graduate from high school, earn a college degree, and work full-time. For each $100 increase in spending on the program, participants' average annual earnings in adulthood rose by 1.8 percent. These benefits proved largest for the poorest children served (Herbst 2014).

To be sure, the quality of child care is important for children's outcomes, and higher-quality child care is associated with better social skills, cooperation, and language development. Important aspects of high-quality care may include the use of evidence-based curricula, longer program duration, high teacher effectiveness, and parental involvement, and productive and complementary use of out-of-school time (Council of Economic Advisers 2015a). Low-quality care may explain why some studies have found that universal $5 a day child care in Quebec adversely affected children's behaviors, and why some studies of U.S. child-care subsidies also find negative effects on child achievement and behavioral outcomes (Baker et al. 2008; Baker et al. 2015; Bernal and Keane 2011; Herbst and Tekin 2010, 2014). These disparate results underscore the importance of efforts to enhance not only the quantity, but also the quality of child-care programs.

Preschool

A large body of literature demonstrates that preschool can benefit children's school readiness and increase earnings and educational attainment later in life by improving both cognitive and non-cognitive skills. Preschool is one of the most studied early childhood human capital interventions, with an unusually deep research base beginning with randomized evaluations of well-known, but small, Federally supported programs like Abecedarian (described above) and Perry Preschool (described below) that began in the 1960s and whose participants' outcomes have been tracked well into adulthood. Much of what we know about the effects of larger-scale preschool programs comes from Head Start, the most widely available public preschool program for lower-income children. However, there is growing evidence from a number of new preschool programs, including State preschool programs in Georgia and Oklahoma and local initiatives in Chicago and Boston. Researchers have also collected results from numerous studies of smaller programs and used meta-analysis to discern general tendencies in impacts, thereby drawing more general conclusions from a large number of analyses.

The High/Scope Perry Preschool Program, which operated in Ypsilanti, Michigan during the 1960s, provided preschool education for low-income African-American children who were at high risk of failing in school. Perry is one of the most well-known preschool interventions in part because it was evaluated using a randomized trial yielding highly credible results and also because data on its participants were collected more routinely and over a longer period than is true of most other program evaluations of any kind (Schweinhart et al. 2005). Participants in Perry Preschool were randomly assigned to either a treatment group, who attended preschool at ages 3 and 4, or to a control group that received no preschool program. Researchers have examined how these two groups fared on a wide range of outcomes through the ages of 39 to 41.

Perry increased IQ scores at school entry, and other gains persisted through school and into adulthood (Schweinhart et al. 2005). Participants demonstrated higher motivation, placed a higher value on schooling, did more homework, and demonstrated higher achievement through age 15 (Schweinhart and Weikart 1981). The program group scored better on several cognitive and academic tests through age 27 (Barnett 1996; Schweinhart 2003). In addition to performing better on cognitive tests, educational attainment and labor market outcomes also improved among program participants. High-school graduation rates rose by about 19 percentage points, and when participants entered the workforce, they had earnings about 25 percent higher than their control group counterparts through age 40 (Heckman et al. 2010). Other observations of Perry participants later in life found similarly large increases in earnings ranging from 19 percent to nearly 60 percent (Bartik 2014; Karoly et al. 1998).[13]

While evidence from narrowly targeted programs like Perry provide valuable evidence that early interventions can have large and sustained benefits, an important policy question is whether larger-scale programs can provide similar benefits. One larger-scale early childhood education intervention for which research has found positive impacts in both the short term and long term is the Chicago Child-Parent Centers (CPC). Since 1967, the CPC have provided comprehensive early childhood education and family supports to low-income children and parents. At kindergarten entry, studies show that CPC preschoolers' cognitive readiness improved by about three months of learning and math and reading achievement gains persisted through sixth grade (Reynolds 1995). Later evaluations found that participation in the CPC preschool program led to higher high-school graduation and college attendance rates (Temple and Reynolds 2007), and that participants, in turn, saw increases in annual earnings in their late 20s of about 7 percent (Reynolds et al. 2011).[14]

Additional evidence on the effectiveness of large-scale and long-running preschool programs comes from modern evaluations of the Head Start

---

[13] CEA calculations based on the percent increase in earnings of students in the program relative to similar students who were not in the program.
[14] CEA calculations based on the percent increase in earnings of students in the program relative to similar students who were not in the program.

program. The Head Start Impact Study (HSIS) followed a nationally representative sample of nearly 5,000 children who were 3 or 4 years old in 2002 (Puma et al. 2012). One-half of these children were randomly assigned to a group that was allowed to enroll in a Head Start program, and the rest were assigned to a control group who did not receive access to Head Start but could enroll in another early childhood program. The study, which examined children's cognitive and non-cognitive outcomes through third grade, found positive impacts on children's language and literacy development during the first year of the program—especially for students whose scores were initially at the bottom of the distribution. These gains were generally attenuated over time, as measured by tests in elementary school, though the gains persisted through at least first grade for some Spanish speakers (Bitler, Hoynes, and Domina 2014).

Studies of Head Start have generally found positive, but somewhat smaller, impacts on test scores than the impacts found by studies of earlier programs like Perry. However, several factors are important for understanding these differences. One is that the early, narrowly targeted programs like Perry and Abecedarian were more intensive and more costly than Head Start and might therefore be expected to yield a higher return. A second issue, highlighted by a growing number of researchers, is that early education programs may have long-run benefits even when the program effect on test scores appears to "fade out" in elementary or middle school—and a study by Deming (2009) suggests that this is true for Head Start.[15] This study compares long-run outcomes of siblings who differed in their program participation and finds that, despite a fadeout of test score gains, children who participated in Head Start are more likely to graduate from high school. Looking at a summary index of young-adult outcomes, the study finds that Head Start participation closes one-third of the gap between children with median family income and those in bottom quarter of family income and is about 80 percent as large as model programs such as Perry. The finding of long-run benefits despite elementary school test score fadeout may also apply to other public preschool programs, such as Tennessee's Voluntary Pre-K program, where researchers found evidence of test-score fadeout, but where long-term outcomes cannot yet be measured (Lipsey, Farran, and Hofer 2015).

Yet another reason why modern program evaluations such as HSIS are likely to produce smaller measured effects than earlier studies of programs like Perry is simply that the outcomes of children in the "control group" of these studies, which provide a baseline for comparison, are likely

---

[15] Other studies, such as Heckman et al. (2010), also find evidence of long-term benefits despite short-term fadeout.

to be higher today than in the past. As highlighted in a new study by Kline and Walters (2015), children in earlier control groups typically received no formal education if they were not assigned to the program being studied, while children today—including those in the HSIS—are much more likely to attend an alternative preschool program. Kline and Walters (2015) also show that benefits of Head Start are larger for children who would not otherwise attend preschool, suggesting that further expansion of program access would yield significant gains.

In addition to the large positive impacts on cognitive skills and labor market outcomes, recent research also shows that the benefits of high-quality preschool programs like Perry, Abecedarian, and Head Start can extend to improvements in health and non-cognitive outcomes. Ludwig and Miller (2007), examining the effects of technical assistance provided to some counties to develop Head Start funding proposals that led to increased Head Start funding in the late 1960s and 1970s, find that access to Head Start at the age of 3 or 4 had significant implications for child mortality between the ages of 5 and 9. Their results indicate that, for children living in the 300 poorest U.S. counties, a 50 to 100 percent increase in Head Start funding reduced mortality rates from relevant causes enough to essentially close the gap between these counties and the national average. A new study examining the Perry Preschool and Abecedarian programs shows that these programs affected health and risky behavior over the long run, in part by reducing the likelihood of smoking as an adult for some participants (Conti, Heckman, and Pinto 2015). Similarly, Campbell et al. (2014) find that participation in the Abecedarian Project led to better adult health outcomes such as lower blood pressure.

Interestingly, the impacts of some early education initiatives appear to differ by gender, though the gender differences are not always consistent across studies and their underlying causes are not always well understood. Anderson (2008) finds larger impacts of three preschool programs on long-term outcomes for girls, possibly because girls respond differently to schooling interventions. Compared to boys, girls participating in the programs saw sharper increases in high-school graduation and college attendance rates, along with positive effects for economic outcomes, criminal behavior, drug use, and marriage. These results are consistent with Oden et al. (2000), who find that Head Start participation in Florida significantly raises high-school graduation rates and lowers arrest rates for girls but not boys. On the other hand, Conti, Heckman, and Pinto (2015) find that the long-run health benefits of Perry and Abecedarian are larger for boys.

In addition to the studies highlighted above, numerous other studies have rigorously evaluated the impact of preschool programs since the 1960s.

A meta-analysis by Duncan and Magnuson (2013) examines the distribution of impacts for more than 80 programs, including Head Start, Abecedarian, and Perry as well as dozens of other preschool programs. Overall, across all studies and time periods, early childhood education increases cognitive and achievement scores by 0.35 standard deviations on average, or more than one-quarter of the kindergarten math test score gap between the highest and lowest income quintiles (Duncan and Magnuson 2011). The estimated impacts in the studies considered in Duncan and Magnuson (2013) are illustrated in Figure 4-18, with bigger circles generally corresponding to studies that enrolled more children. Figure 4-18 shows that the vast majority of programs benefit children's cognitive development and achievement at the end of the program.

The downward slope of the line in Figure 4-18 suggests that the effect sizes of early childhood education programs have fallen somewhat over time. However, as discussed above, a new study by Kline and Walters (2015) suggests that this pattern does not reflect declining program quality, but may be driven in part by an improving counterfactual for students not enrolled in the program being studied.

One likely source of the improving academic outcomes for children who are not enrolled in Head Start or other more narrowly targeted programs is the recent expansion of large, State-run public preschool programs. Wong et al. (2008) examine five State-run preschool programs and find positive impacts on achievement test scores. Gormley et al. (2005) evaluate Oklahoma's preschool program in Tulsa and find that children's kindergarten achievement significantly improved. While it is too soon to directly estimate these programs' long-term effects since the oldest participants have not yet entered the labor force, Hill, Gormley and Adelstein (2015) find evidence of a persistent improvement in the Tulsa program's impacts through third grade for some students. Recent evaluations find positive cognitive outcomes at fourth grade of Georgia's State-run preschool program (Fitzpatrick 2008) and some persistent, though smaller, effects of Georgia and Tulsa's programs through eighth grade (Cascio and Schanzenbach 2013). These studies also show that, even when some participating children switch from private programs (a phenomenon often referred to as "crowd-out"), there can still be gains in achievement for these children who would have otherwise been in private programs, perhaps because families can use the savings from switching to a public program to make other positive investments in their children. A new working paper has also found evidence of the non-academic impacts of universal preschool on criminal activity. Oklahoma's universal preschool program lowered the likelihood that African-American

Figure 4-18
**Most Early Childhood Programs Have
Positive Cognitive and Achievement Impacts**

Average Effect Size in Standard Deviations

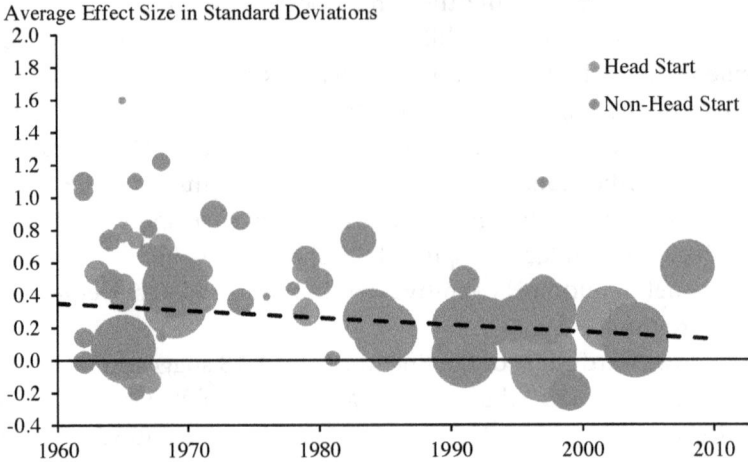

Note: Circle sizes reflect the inverse of the squared study-level standard error. 74 of 83 studies showed positive effects and CEA estimates that roughly 60 percent of estimates were statistically significant at the 10 percent level. The dashed line is a weighted trendline.
Source: Duncan and Magnuson (2013); Weiland and Yoshikawa (2013); CEA calculations.

participants were charged with a misdemeanor or felony in their late teen years (Smith 2015).

Students who attended State-run preschool, such as those in Georgia and Oklahoma, are not yet old enough to directly measure earnings; however, researchers have used achievement gains to estimate that adult earnings for these children will likely increase by 1.3 to 3.5 percent (Cascio and Schanzenbach 2013).[16] Other studies also project large positive effects on lifetime earnings (Bartik, Gormley, and Adelstein 2012; Duncan, Ludwig, and Magnuson 2010).

Although studies find that early childhood education yields a large return, the payoff may take time to materialize as benefits are realized through behavior or earnings changes over an individual's lifecycle. When a child attends an early education program, an upfront cost is incurred. Some benefits are realized immediately—for example, parents who choose to re-enter the labor force or increase their work hours are able to increase their earnings right away. However, the majority of benefits, from reduced crime to higher earnings for participants, accrue later in life. In the case of Perry Preschool, evidence on long-run outcomes, including increases in earnings and savings from education and social program utilization, suggests

---

[16] Studies generally use increases in test scores to predict the future increase in earnings using estimates from Chetty, Friedman, and Rockoff (2014) or Krueger (2003).

Figure 4-19
**Net Benefit Per Child of Perry Preschool Rises
Over the Lifecycle**

2015 U.S. Dollars

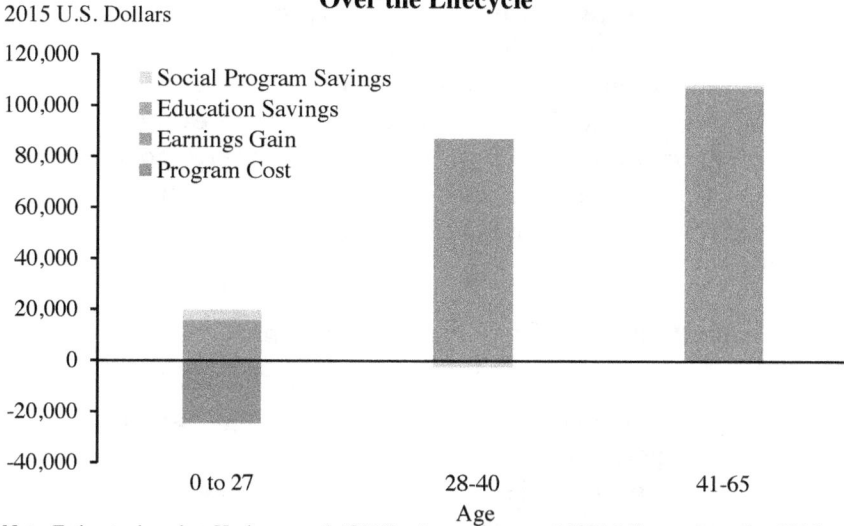

Note: Estimates based on Heckman et al. (2010) using undiscounted 2006 dollars converted to 2015 dollars using CPI-U-RS. Additional costs and benefits, such as education beyond age 27, vocational training, savings from crime reduction, health benefits, and maternal earnings, have not been quantified in this chart.
Source: Heckman et al. (2010); CEA calculations.

that benefits continue to rise throughout participants' lives (Figure 4-19; Heckman et al. 2010).

Although it took time for the benefits of Perry Preschool to appear, Heckman et al. (2010) estimate that the benefits quickly outweighed the initial cost and that the net benefit increased over the course of participants' lifetimes. The timing of benefits for modern universal programs will likely follow a similar lifecycle pattern. When the savings from crime reduction are also included, the estimated total discounted benefits of Perry are almost 80 percent higher.[17]

Estimates based on the substantial earnings gains alone indicate that investing in early childhood education would boost GDP in the long run. If all families enrolled their children in preschool at the same rate as high-income families, enrollment would increase by about 13 percentage points.[18] If the earnings gains per student were similar to the estimated gains from

---

[17] CEA calculation based on Heckman et al. (2010) discounted lifetime benefits from earnings, crime reduction, K-12 and other education up to age 27, and social program use, with a discount rate of 3 percent.
[18] In 2013, about 71.7 percent of four-year-olds from families with income of $100,000 or more were in preschool, but only 59.0 percent of the overall population was enrolled (Current Population Survey, October Supplement; CEA calculations). Thus about 12.7 percent of each cohort would be affected.

the preschool programs in Georgia and Oklahoma, the total gains resulting from the increase in enrollment would raise the level of GDP by 0.17 to 0.44 percent a year after 60 years, when higher levels of enrollment would be fully reflected in the labor force. This is equivalent to adding between approximately $30 and $80 billion a year based on 2015 GDP.[19] This estimate does not include the gains to GDP that would result from earnings gains for parents and the many non-earnings benefits of quality preschool education, including expanded economic activity due to reduced crime and possible spillovers to other workers who did not directly benefit from the program as children.

Income and Other Near-Cash Transfer Programs

In addition to providing direct investments or in-kind transfers to disadvantaged children and their families, public policy can also provide more flexible support to low-income families in the form of income transfers. Programs like the Earned Income Tax Credit, the Child Tax Credit, and Temporary Assistance for Needy Families are targeted mainly at families with children, and can benefit children by helping their families to invest more resources in their early development. Similarly, housing programs also provide flexible and multi-faceted support to low-income families and can produce especially large benefits for poor families with young children. Programs like the Housing Choice Voucher program not only free up a family's income so that more of it can be invested in their children, but can also improve children's living conditions in ways that can be highly beneficial to their development.

A large body of literature shows that a boost to income can vastly improve young children's health and human capital attainment. An influx of income in children's earliest years may provide a particularly large boost to short-term and long-term health and human capital outcomes (Duncan, Magnuson, and Vortuba-Drzal 2014). For programs that are not targeted solely at young children, the academic literature does not always distinguish between impacts in the first few years of life from impacts throughout childhood as a whole; where the evidence exists, this chapter presents evidence showing the impacts of income in children's earliest years (see Box 4-5 for discussion of sustaining these impacts in later childhood years).

---

[19] Cascio and Schanzenbach (2013) estimate that these programs increase earnings by 1.3 to 3.5 percent per year. After 60 years, the labor force would fully reflect the higher levels of enrollment; hence 12.7 percent of each cohort's earnings would increase by 1.3 to 3.5 percent per year, yielding an increase in aggregate earnings of 0.17 percent to 0.44 percent. Using 2015 GDP as of February 1, 2016 ($17.94 trillion), this yields an increase of $29.6 to $79.7 billion per year.

Box 4-5: Nutrition and Income Programs Help Sustain Human Capital Development throughout Childhood

While policies that address inequities in nutrition and family resources are critical for preventing and closing gaps in human capital before children enter school, these policies also help to sustain the gains from early childhood investments and to close gaps in children's cognitive and non-cognitive development once they enter school.

Two recent studies demonstrate a link between Supplemental Nutrition Assistance Program (SNAP) benefits and children's performance in school by showing how student outcomes vary with the timing of benefit receipt. SNAP benefits are distributed on a monthly basis and many low-income families see their food intake reduced over the course of each month as their budgets are depleted (Shapiro 2005; Hastings and Washington 2010; Todd 2014). Gassman-Pines and Bellows (2015) analyze test scores of students in grades 3 through 8 in North Carolina and find that for children in households receiving SNAP—but not for students from higher-income households—test scores fall at the end of the month when food budgets tend to be depleted. They find also that scores recover gradually after the next month's benefits are received—suggesting that a steady diet is a prerequisite for optimal learning and test performance. A related study of fifth through eighth graders in the City of Chicago School District suggests that disruptions in food budgets also lead to disciplinary problems in school. Gennetian et al. (2015) find that disciplinary incidents rise toward the end of the month, especially for students in SNAP households. This pair of findings suggests that food assistance programs like SNAP are important complements to educational investments. They also suggest that, for many families, additional support to help sustain food budgets throughout the month would lead to further improvements in children's academic performance and would help close achievement gaps.

Other studies have shown that children's performance in school responds to increases in their family's income due to policies such as the Earned Income Tax Credit (EITC) or the Child Tax Credit (CTC). Under both the EITC and the CTC, the transfer a family is eligible to receive depends on household income; both policies offer a flat subsidy in a certain range that is phased out at higher incomes, and the EITC also has a phase-in range at very low incomes. Chetty, Friedman, and Rockoff (2011) use these changes in the tax rates to identify the extent to which benefit receipt improves academic performance. Linking data from a large school district on children's test scores, teachers, and schools from grades 3 through 8 with administrative tax records on parental earnings, they find that a credit of $1,000 increases elementary- and middle-school test scores by 6 to 9 percent of a standard deviation. Similar effects are found in related work by Dahl and Lochner (2012), who examine the impact of EITC expansions in the late-1980s and mid-1990s on math and reading test scores using the National Longitudinal Survey of Youth. Their study finds that an additional $1,000 in family income raises children's test scores by about 6 percent of a standard deviation, with larger effects for children under 12 years of age.

Income Transfers: EITC, CTC, and AFDC/TANF

The Earned Income Tax Credit provides a refundable tax credit to lower-income working families. As of 2012, 97 percent of EITC dollars went to families with children (Falk and Crandall-Hollick 2014) and an earlier estimate suggests that approximately one-quarter of children receiving EITC benefits are under the age of 5 (Gothro and Trippe 2010). A family's credit amount is based on the number of dependent children and its earnings. A large and robust literature shows that the EITC increases labor force participation among single mothers (Eissa and Hoynes 2011; Eissa and Liebman 1996; Meyer and Rosenbaum 2001). The low-income portion of the Child Tax Credit, which is partially refundable, has a similar structure to the EITC and could therefore be expected to have proportionally similar positive impacts on low-income families. Together, the EITC and the refundable portion of the CTC directly lifted 5.2 million children over the poverty line in 2014 (Short 2015), and the additional work incentives and associated earnings may have amplified this effect. Empirical work on the EITC's impacts tends to compare families that became eligible for a larger credit with families with similar observable characteristics that were ineligible for a change in their credit.

The EITC has been expanded in every Administration since 1975 (Council of Economic Advisers 2014). Most recently, under the American Recovery and Reinvestment Act of 2009, the EITC was expanded for families with three or more children, the marriage penalty was reduced, and the refundable portion of the Child Tax Credit was expanded, all on a temporary basis. These changes were made permanent by Congress last December. Examining the 1986, 1990, and 1993 reforms, which expanded the amount for which some families were eligible, particularly families with multiple children, Hoynes, Miller, and Simon (2015) use Vital Statistics data covering all births from 1984 to 1998. These data provide information on birth weight and birth order, as well as some maternal demographic information. Since families with a first, second, or third and higher-order birth experience a different EITC schedule, the authors compare birth outcomes for single mothers across these groups and find that an additional $1,000 in EITC receipt lowers the prevalence of low birth weight by 2 to 3 percent (Hoynes, Miller, and Simon 2015). Using information on doctor visits during pregnancy and from birth certificate records on smoking and drinking during pregnancy, they speculate that one channel for health improvements is through better prenatal care and health.

Researchers also find impacts of Federal and State EITC receipt as a young child on educational attainment later in their school years. In these studies, the impacts are concentrated among students who received the EITC as young children, suggesting a particularly important role for income in early years. Michelmore (2013) finds that a $1,000 increase in the maximum EITC for which a child is eligible based on the State they live in is associated with a one percentage-point increase in the likelihood of college enrollment and a 0.3 percentage-point increase in the likelihood of receiving a bachelor's degree among 18-23 year olds. The attainment benefits of EITC receipt were almost entirely driven by children who were 12 or younger when their State implemented the EITC, with a 3 percentage-point impact on college enrollment. Using a similar method, Maxfield (2013) finds that an increase in the maximum EITC of $1,000 increases the probability of high school completion at age 19 by 2 percentage points and the probability of completing at least one year of college by age 19 by 1.4 percentage points. Like in the Michelmore (2013) paper, Maxfield (2013) finds that the magnitudes of these impacts decrease as the age at which children became eligible for the EITC increases. A $1,000 increase in the maximum EITC available to a preschooler increases high school completion by 3.6 percentage points, versus a 1.9 percentage-point increase for a middle schooler. Altogether, the studies show that EITC receipt as a young child can have profound impacts on educational and labor market outcomes later in life.

In a study of a similar kind of income transfer, but without a work requirement, Aizer et al. (forthcoming) examine the Mothers' Pension, a cash assistance program in effect from 1911 to 1935, and a precursor to AFDC and TANF. The authors use data from World War II enlistment records, the Social Security Death Master File through 2012, and 1940 Census records on 16,000 men to compare mortality of children of any age (0-18) who benefited from the program to similar children of the same age living in the same county whose mothers applied, but were denied benefits. They find that the program reduced mortality through age 87 among recipient children (Figure 4-20) and that the lowest-income children experienced the largest benefits. Census and enlistment records suggest that these improvements may be at least partly due to the improvements in nutritional status (measured by underweight status in adulthood), educational attainment, and income in

Figure 4-20

Increase in Probability of Survival Past Age 60-80 Among Mothers' Pension Recipients, 1965—2012

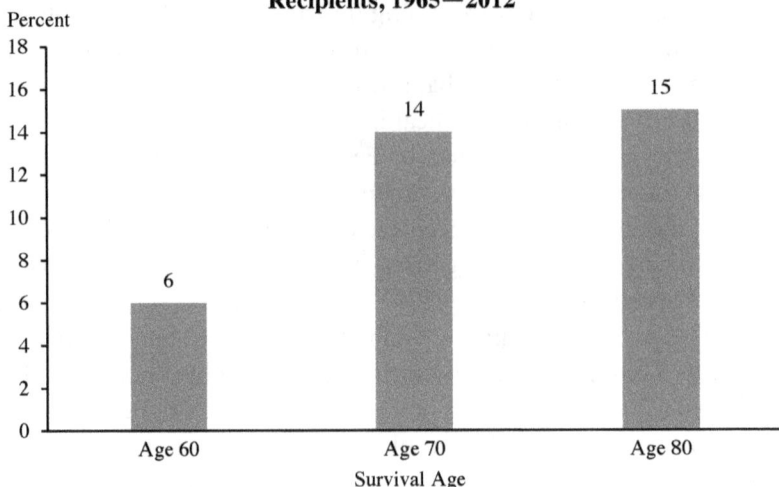

Note: Based on specification that includes individual controls and county and cohort fixed effects.
Increase in survival calculated as a percent of the average survival rate of rejected applicants.
Source: Aizer et al. (2014).

early- to mid-adulthood. Documenting that the most common reason for rejection was "insufficient need," the authors argue their results provide a lower-bound estimate of the program's effects.

The positive impacts associated with the EITC may operate through multiple channels. Most obvious is the increase in income that families experience. A less obvious channel for the positive impacts could be through increases in maternal labor supply that resulted from EITC expansions or via other policy changes that occurred at the same time as those expansions (Nichols and Rothstein 2015). It may be that at least some of the effects captured in the studies operate through the less obvious channels. Studies that use variation based on EITC expansions over time may be especially likely to capture some effects associated with other policy changes. For example, the 1991 EITC expansions coincide with an increase in the minimum wage, and the 1996 expansions coincide with welfare reform.

Some studies suggest that EITC impacts may differ somewhat by gender, since a lower baseline level of health and human capital among young boys may make income targeted toward these investments in them particularly impactful. For example, a study of Canadian child benefits finds that increases in benefits lead to larger improvements in education and physical health variables for boys (Milligan and Stabile 2011).

Figure 4-21
**Average Annual Earnings in Adulthood Among Children Younger than 13
When Their Family Participated in MTO, 2008—2012**

2012 U.S. Dollars

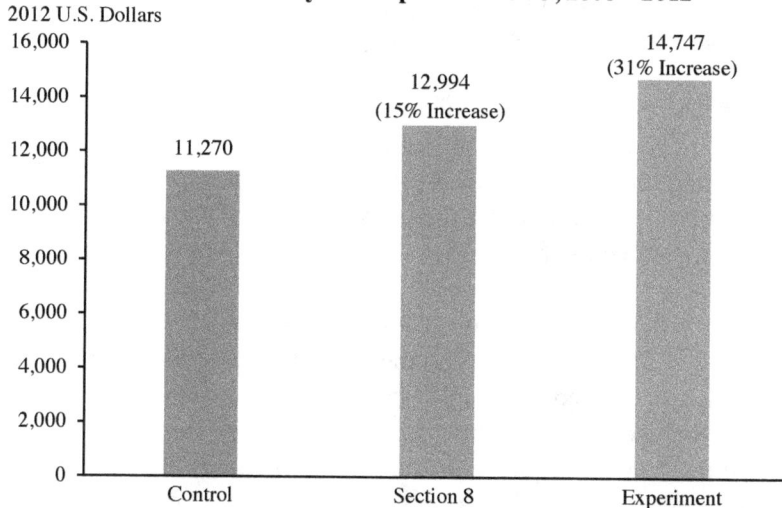

Note: MTO stands for the Moving to Opportunity experiment.
Source: Chetty, Hendren, and Katz (2015).

Housing and Neighborhoods

Moving to a lower-poverty neighborhood as a child can have a profound impact on multiple health and human capital outcomes, both in the
short term and long term. These impacts are driven in part by changes in
the availability of health and human capital inputs reviewed earlier in this
chapter, and in part due to related changes in peer effects, crime, safety, and
other environmental factors.

Compelling evidence that the opportunity to move to a better neighborhood can dramatically impact children's lives comes from a randomized controlled trial conducted in the mid-1990s known as the Moving to
Opportunity program (MTO). MTO allowed researchers to evaluate the
impact of both conventional Section 8 housing vouchers, which do not place
any geographic restrictions on where recipients can live, and experimental
vouchers that required families to move to lower-poverty neighborhoods for
at least one year.

A new study by Chetty, Hendren, and Katz (forthcoming), which
is the first to look at adult outcomes for children whose parents received
housing vouchers, finds remarkably large benefits—especially when voucher
receipt was contingent on moving to a low-poverty neighborhood. Among
children who were younger than 13 when their families moved, Section 8
vouchers increased adult earnings by 15 percent and experimental vouchers

Inequality in Early Childhood and Effective Public Policy Interventions | 205 increased earnings by 31 percent (Figure 4-21). Moreover, the earnings gains were largest when children's parents moved in their earlier years and fell with the age when children moved—suggesting that the cumulative impact of exposure to a better environment is highest when children move in early childhood.

The authors also find that children whose families received vouchers when they were young were ultimately 32 percent more likely to attend college and, among those who attended college, the voucher recipients went to higher-quality schools. While the program did not have a significant effect on birth rates, girls whose families received vouchers were more likely to be married between the ages of 24 and 30 and those whose families received experimental vouchers were more likely to have the father present when they did have children. Importantly, these positive outcomes were limited to individuals who moved at younger ages and did not accrue to those who moved past the age of 13—again suggesting that neighborhood quality is especially influential in a child's most formative years.

CONCLUSION

When we invest in young children, it is not just children and their families who benefit. The research highlighted here suggests that the investments we make in children today could benefit our economy in the long run by expanding our skilled workforce and increasing their earnings, as well as by improving health and wellness. This means society reaps the benefits of a better-educated, higher-earning, and healthier population in the future—including lower transfer payments, reduced involvement with the criminal justice system, lower health care costs, and a larger tax revenue base. Expanding access to high-quality programs that support children in their earliest years is a win-win opportunity for participating children, their parents, and society as a whole. It is time to build on demonstrated successes of programs that invest in young children and broaden their scope to boost opportunity for more American children.

CHAPTER 5

TECHNOLOGY AND INNOVATION

Productivity growth is critical to the well-being of the American economy, its workers, and its households. Growth in labor productivity means American workers generate more output for a given amount of work, which can lead to higher living standards via higher wages, lower prices, and a greater variety of products.[1] Labor productivity growth in the United States has come down from its highs in the middle of the 20th century (see Figure 5-1), though less dramatically than in other advanced economies that had experienced a surge in productivity in the immediate aftermath of the second World War. Between 1990 and 2000, U.S. labor productivity growth rebounded. However, over the last decade, even though the United States has led other advanced countries in labor productivity growth, achieving robust measured productivity growth has been a substantial challenge.[2]

Labor productivity growth—measured as output per hour—comes from three primary sources: increases in capital, improvements in the quality of labor, and "total factor productivity" (TFP, or what the U.S. Bureau of Labor Statistics formally refers to as multifactor productivity). The first source—the accumulation of physical capital—fuels productivity growth through investments in machines, tools, computers, factories, infrastructure, and other items that are used to produce new output. The second source, labor quality upgrades, comes from greater education and training of the workers who operate these machines, tools and computers, as well as manage factories and infrastructure, to produce output. Rapid increases in capital accumulation or educational attainment can increase the output per hour of an economy and potentially improve living standards. There are, however, generally limits to the extent of productivity gains that can result

---

[1] The 2010 Economic Report of the President, specifically Chapter 10, entitled "Fostering Productivity Growth through Innovation and Trade," covers this point in further detail.
[2] It is possible that some of the recent decline in productivity growth is due to measurement issues because official estimates do not count "free" online media and open-source software. Box 2-5 in Chapter 2 discusses these issues in more detail.

Figure 5-1
Labor Productivity Growth, 1955–2010
10-Year Centered Moving Average of Annual Percent Growth in Output per Hour

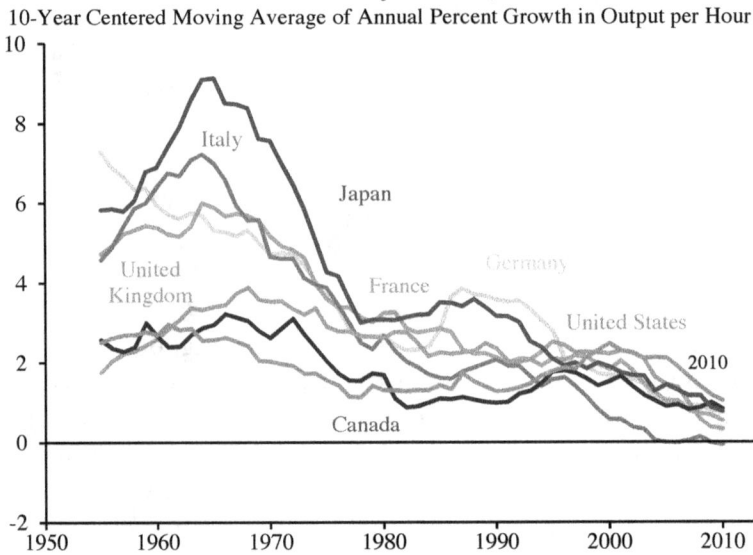

Source: Conference Board, Total Economy Database; CEA calculations.

from simply piling more resources (physical or human capital) into the production process.

The most important source of productivity growth overall is the third factor—total factor productivity. TFP can be thought of as the way that labor and capital come together to produce output. For example, imagine taking the same workers and the same equipment and changing the way that the workers use the equipment to get more output. Over one-half of the growth in productivity between 1948 and 2014 came from exactly such changes. Variations in TFP also explain most of the variations in productivity growth over longer periods, as the contributions of capital and labor quality have been roughly constant over time. More recently, however, the contribution from capital has decreased significantly.[3]

When TFP increases, a country experiences higher levels of output even when both the returns to, and the amount used of, capital and labor remain constant. Such TFP improvements happen when innovators, entrepreneurs, and managers create new products or make improvements to existing products, often in response to market incentives. This improvement might happen, for example, if a firm reorganizes the layout of its factory in a new way so that production lines run more smoothly. Or it might happen

---

[3] For more detail, see pages 7 to 9 of Chairman Jason Furman's July 9, 2015 speech entitled "Productivity Growth in the Advanced Economics: The Past, the Present, and Lessons for the Future."

if an inventor uncovers a new method for producing the same output at a lower cost. Either way, it should be noted that these types of innovations typically require significant effort and resources.

Sometimes these innovations can be relatively incremental, such as waste-reducing technology that improves soccer-ball production in Pakistan (Atkin et al. 2015), or management practices that improve quality and reduce inventory in Indian textile plants (Bloom et al. 2013). Even though each one is small, many such incremental innovations can lead to substantial aggregate TFP growth. A recent paper by Garcia-Macia, Hsieh, and Klenow (2015) estimates that much of the aggregate TFP growth in the U.S. manufacturing sector from 1992 to 2002 came from incremental innovations, such as product improvements, rather than the creation of entirely new products. Other times, innovations can have such profound effects on productivity growth, as was the case with steam and electricity, that their adoption becomes all but imperative for a firm. In such cases, the innovation approaches the status of a de facto industry standard. Whether incremental or transformative, technologies and innovations are critical to ensuring that the United States maintains and expands on its recent growth.

Competition from new and existing firms plays an important role in fostering this growth. Startups are a critical pathway for the commercialization of innovative new ideas and products. Startups, or the possibility of entry by a startup, also create incentives for established firms to innovate and reduce costs, which in turn drives growth. However, these productivity-enhancing channels may be weakening as the rate of new firm formation has been in persistent decline since the 1970s, as have various measures of worker mobility and job turnover. The share of patenting by new firms has also been in decline. At the same time, there are signs of increasing concentration across multiple industries. These trends point to the importance of removing barriers to entry for inventors and entrepreneurs.

This chapter describes the state of technology and innovation in the United States, including recent trends, challenges, and opportunities. The chapter begins by reviewing the recent trajectory of the rate of business dynamism and labor market dynamism. It then reviews trends in research and development (R&D) spending and patenting. Finally, it describes in detail two promising areas that can help the United States to boost TFP growth in the future—robotics and digital communications technology—as well as potential challenges posed by these innovations.

Competition and Dynamism Play a Critical Role

More than 50 years ago, the Nobel Prize-winning economist Kenneth Arrow (1962) argued that a monopolist may have relatively weak incentives to innovate since its innovations do not allow it to "steal" business from competitors. Competition pushes firms to invest in new technologies that help to lower costs and also to invest in innovations that can lead to quality improvements of existing products.[4] Competition can arise in multiple ways. An incumbent firm can face competition from other incumbents within the same market that have come up with a new way to produce a good or service or that have invented a new product that siphons off existing customers. Or, competition can come from firms new to the market, which include both startups and established firms. Entry can occur by established firms in a different product market in the same geography, as happened when "black cars" (that is, limousine and town car services) entered the taxi industry in many U.S. cities, or it could involve a firm in a similar product market but from a different geographic location (Rawley 2010). The latter case is often what happens with both domestic and international trade (see Box 5-1 on Trade).

The Role of Startups

Startups are vital to productivity growth in the United States. Startups are often the way in which a new product or service is first brought to market. A case in point is the small company that Bill Hewlett and Dave Packard founded in a garage in Palo Alto in 1939, which commercialized an early version of an electronic oscillator, a vital component in electronic devices. Hewlett and Packard's inventions, along with those of multiple other electronics inventors, helped spur the information technology-fueled productivity rebound in the mid-1990s, which saw average labor productivity growth jump more than a percentage point to 2.4 percent a year (Jorgenson and Stiroh 2000; Oliner and Sichel 2002).

Academic research finds that entrepreneurship can lead to long-run productivity growth (e.g., King and Levine 1993), much in the same way that Hewlett and Packard's entrepreneurial vision ultimately led to productivity gains decades after they founded their company. Notably, though personal computers were becoming widespread in the 1980s and 1990s, there was a lag until these innovations translated into a meaningful uptick in productivity

---

[4] As noted by many researchers, while some competition is better than none when it comes to stimulating innovation, there is evidence that too much competition can be detrimental. This so called inverted-U shape of the relationship between competition and innovation has been observed across multiple industries (Aghion et al. 2005).

Box 5-1: Trade

Domestic and international trade are of critical importance to the economy overall but also to innovation. Trade promotes innovation and associated productivity growth in two ways: 1) by increasing the efficiency of the innovation process, thus helping bring more innovations to market, faster and at lower prices; and 2) by increasing the rewards that an innovator realizes when his or her new idea succeeds.

Domestic trade—measured by commodity flows between geographies in the United States—is an important driver of U.S. gross domestic product (GDP) and productivity growth. Infrastructure is important to domestic trade because it provides the means by which a firm can efficiently ship its products from one location to another. Chapter 6 of this *Report* covers the preconditions for, and consequences of, improving the quality and quantity of U.S. transportation infrastructure in greater detail, as well as how the interstate highway, long-distance freight rail, and air transportation systems are particularly important to productivity. These infrastructure assets also facilitate international trade.

International trade is also an important driver of innovation and productivity growth. In the words of Nobel Prize-winning economist Robert Solow (2007), "[r]elatively free trade has the advantage that the possibility of increasing market share in world markets is a constant incentive for innovative activity." One recent review of the evidence calls the relationship between globalization and productivity growth a "robust finding" (De Loecker and Goldberg 2014).

International trade can drive productivity growth in several ways. When U.S. firms sell abroad, they can sell more products per firm, and this increase in scale may, in some cases, lead to lower costs and higher productivity. International trade allows companies to access a larger market, which results in greater revenues and potentially higher profits for a given level of innovation, and therefore raises the incentive to innovate. For example, recent economic research by Aw, Roberts, and Xu (2008) finds that firms with experience in foreign markets have a greater probability of R&D investment. Trade can also generate a positive effect on aggregate productivity through reallocation. When firms are able to grow and expand to meet demand from consumers in other countries, these firms become a larger part of the economy and employ a larger share of workers. Hence, the reallocation of labor and production toward more productive firms as they expand after trade liberalization generates higher aggregate productivity in the economy as a whole (Melitz 2003).

Moreover, trade can expose both exporters and importers to new ideas and novel tools, materials, or techniques that make them more productive. Some of this learning is simply copying, as when a firm adopts pre-existing technology or know-how. At the same time, since roughly one-half of all U.S. imports are inputs into the production process, imports can actually reduce firms' costs by making a greater variety of goods available at lower prices, and such growth can lead American businesses to expand production and employment, as highlighted in the academic literature. Romer (1994) shows that a country's gains from international trade are multiplied substantially when the benefits of cheaper, more varied imported inputs and commodities are taken into account. Halpern, Koren, and Szeidl (2015) also find that access to a wider variety of imported inputs following trade liberalization increases firm productivity. Amiti and Wei (2009) find that imports of service inputs had a significant positive effect on manufacturing productivity in the United States between 1992 and 2000. A recent paper by Boler, Moxnes, and Ulltveit-Moe (2015) demonstrates that improved access to imported inputs promotes R&D investment and thus technological innovation.

Finally, trade can also increase competition, which can spur innovation and productivity growth. Sutton (2012) argues that one of the pathways through which developed economies benefit from international trade is that entry by competitors at the low end of the productivity distribution induces innovation in firms at the high end of the productivity distribution. Aghion et al. (2004) studied U.K. firms from 1980 to 1993 and also found large gains in TFP for incumbent firms, in response to entry by foreign competitors.

The Trans-Pacific Partnership (TPP), the trade agreement between the United States and 11 other Pacific Rim countries, opens the world's fastest-growing markets to U.S. goods and services. The expanded opportunities for trade created by the TPP will help the most productive U.S. firms expand, make other U.S. firms more productive, and drive innovation and, ultimately, American productivity. Similarly, the Transatlantic Trade and Investment Partnership (T-TIP), a trade agreement currently under negotiation between the United States and European Union, will help further drive innovation and productivity.

growth. Research also tells us that institutions that protect property rights, that ensure the availability of affordable credit from healthy financial intermediaries, and that promote the rule of law have historically been important ingredients for fostering private-sector economic activity and entrepreneurial success (Acemoglu, Johnson, and Robinson 2005; North and Weingast 1989). Entrepreneurial success ultimately translates into improvements in quality of life and in productivity growth (King and Levine 1993).

In addition to commercializing new technologies, startups provide jobs. In 2013, startups accounted for over 2 million new jobs compared with established firms that accounted for over 8 million new jobs.[5] However, as discussed below, the birth rate of startups has been declining over time (see Figure 5-3). While many startups fail, those that remain in business tend to grow, creating demand for new jobs. Thus, a healthy environment for startups sets the stage for current and future job growth.

Most startups rely on a mix of debt and equity financing (Robb and Robinson 2014), meaning that a healthy, competitive financial system is vital to ensuring that startups can find the financing they need. Venture capital investments, both in number of deals and in dollars, provide two indicators of the health of financial markets for new firms. While such investments continue to lag historical highs from the dot-com boom, these indicators have improved greatly since the financial crisis in 2008 (see Figure 5-2). Average quarterly venture capital investment dollars (scaled by GDP) in 2015 were at a level not seen since 2001, indicating that access to capital for entrepreneurs and inventors is improving, though capital for innovative startups remains predominantly available in certain geographies, making high-growth business creation a challenge outside of a handful of metro hubs.

Not only do startups help to commercialize many innovative new ideas, but also startups—or even the threat of entry by a startup—help to motivate established businesses to innovate continuously to improve their existing products (Seamans 2012). This result suggests that an important function of startups is not only to innovate and commercialize new products, but also to push established firms to do so as well. In fact, there do not need to be many startups that actively enter into an industry before the incumbent firms in that industry undertake many changes to enhance productivity or improve consumer welfare. For example, Seamans (2012) shows that the mere possibility of entry by a city-owned cable system is enough to induce product upgrades by incumbent cable systems. Thus, this dual role of startups helps to improve consumer welfare and spur innovation and productivity growth.

Declining Business Dynamism

While startups are vital to the commercialization of new ideas and productivity growth, entry by startups has been declining in the United States since the late 1970s. With exit rates relatively constant, this trend means that the average age of U.S. firms is increasing, while the number of firms is declining. Business dynamism—the so-called churn or birth and death rates of firms—has been in persistent decline in the United States since

---

[5] These data come from the U.S. Census Bureau's Business Dynamics Statistics.

Figure 5-2

Quantity and Volume of Venture Capital Deals, 1995–2015

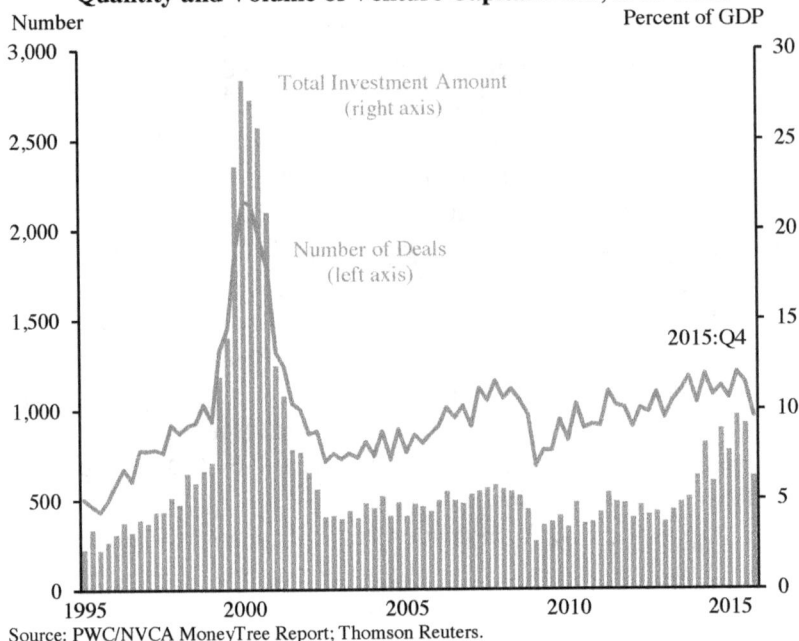

Source: PWC/NVCA MoneyTree Report; Thomson Reuters.

the 1970s (as shown in Figure 5-3). Moreover, whereas in the 1980s and 1990s declining dynamism was observed in selected sectors, notably retail, the decline was observed across all sectors in the 2000s, including the traditionally high-growth information technology sector (Decker et al. 2014).

This trend likely has some relationship to contemporaneous declines in productivity and innovation, though the direction of that relationship is not so clear. A decline in innovation and productivity may be leading to fewer entrants and successful challenges to incumbents, or some exogenous factor—for example, a business environment that limits competition or erects barriers to entry (see Box 5-2 on Occupational Licensing below)—may be driving lower rates of new firm formation that then result in lower levels of innovation. Lower rates of firm entry may be reducing the kind of competition among firms that usually leads them to innovate and improve their efficiency, thus weighing on total factor productivity growth.

The reasons for declining firm entry rates are not well understood, but the trend has been downward for nearly four decades. A partial explanation is that barriers to entry have increased in many industries. For some industries, these barriers could be in the form of occupational licenses (see Box 5-2 on Occupational Licensing). In other cases, these barriers could be in the form of Federal, State, or local licenses or permits. Oftentimes these

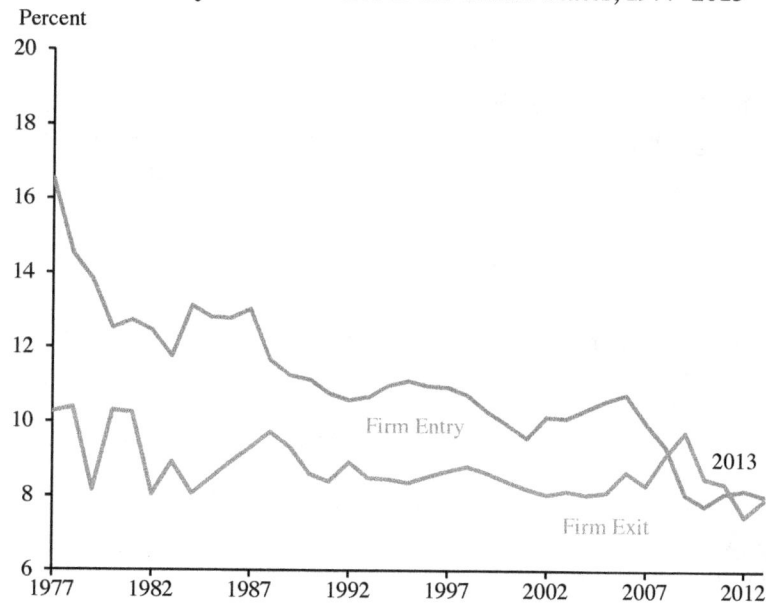

Figure 5-3
Firm Entry and Exit Rates in the United States, 1977–2013

Percent

Source: U.S. Census Bureau, Business Dynamics Statistics.

licenses and permits are designed to ensure that businesses comply with important consumer safety rules. For example, restaurants in New York City are required to have a manager who has passed a Food Protection Course.[6] Such regulations add fixed costs to an entrepreneur wanting to open a new business but oftentimes serve a valuable role in protecting public well-being.

In other cases, the barriers to entry may be related to various advantages that have accrued to incumbent firms over time. These could be political in nature; for example, existing firms could lobby for rules protecting them from new entrants, as have been seen in the case of the taxi and limousine industry, where Internet-based applications from new entrants have recently begun to disrupt the local ride-for-hire sector. The barriers could also be related to economies of scale, whereby the incumbent has become so large that it has effectively foreclosed on the viability of entry by another firm. Some industries, such as power transmission, water, and other utilities, have natural monopolies, which occur when the fixed costs are very high, and marginal costs are low and approaching zero. Some newer technology markets in which network effects are important, such as social media sites, may come to be dominated by one firm, because the network externalities in these markets tip to one provider of the network good.

[6] Requirements listed at: https://www1.nyc.gov/nycbusiness/description/food-service-establishment-permit/apply

Box 5-2: Occupational Licensing

One factor that may be contributing to the broad-based decline in the fluidity of the economy in the last several decades, including declining firm entry rates, less worker fluidity, and less job turnover, is the increasing prevalence of occupational licensing rules. This phenomenon can create barriers to entry for firms and workers in a market or geographic location, thus limiting competition and potentially generating other market distortions. Work by Kleiner and Krueger (2013) charting the historical growth in licensing from a number of different data sources shows that the share of the U.S. workforce covered by state licensing laws grew fivefold in the second half of the 20th century, from less than 5 percent in the early 1950s to 25 percent by 2008 (Figure 5-i below). Although state licenses account for the bulk of licensing, the addition of local- and Federal-licensed occupations further raises the share of the workforce that was licensed in 2008 to 29 percent.

While part of this increase in the percent of licensed workers is due to employment growth within certain heavily licensed fields such as health care and education, it is primarily due to an increase in the number of occupations that require a license. Analysis by the Council of Economic Advisers (CEA) finds that roughly two-thirds of the growth in the proportion of workers licensed at the State level from the 1960s to 2008 is attributable to growth in the number of licensed occupations,

Figure 5-i
Share of Workers with a State Occupational License, 1950–2008

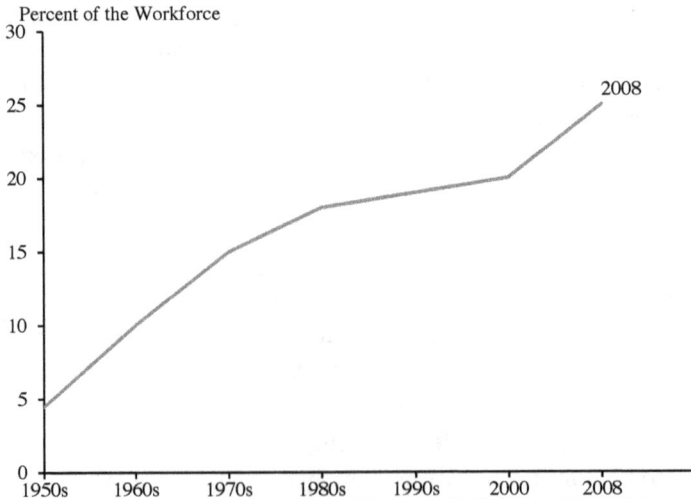

Sources: The Council of State Governments (1952); Greene (1969); Kleiner (1990); Kleiner (2006); and Kleiner and Krueger (2013); Westat data; CEA calculations.

while a little over one-third is due to changes in the occupational composition of the workforce (CEA et al. 2015).

When designed and implemented carefully, licensing can offer important health and safety protections to consumers and the public, as well as benefits to workers. However, some occupational licensing regimes can present a classic case of so-called rent-seeking behavior by incumbents, whereby these individuals and firms may successfully lobby government entities to erect entry barriers to would-be competitors that result in higher-than-normal returns to capital and labor. In addition, licensing requirements vary substantially by state—both in terms of which professions require licenses and the requirements for obtaining a license—making it more difficult for workers to move across state lines. Thus, it is possible that the steady increase in the number of licensed workers is contributing to the United States' decades-long decrease in interstate mobility, though it is unlikely that licensing is the main driver of this change (CEA et al. 2015).

Land use regulations and zoning can also make it more difficult for entrepreneurs to start new firms or for workers to move to more productive cities and firms. See Box 2-6 in Chapter 2 for discussion of the effects that result from overly restrictive land use regulations.

Whether a cause or consequence of declining firm entry rates, market concentration appears to have risen over the same time period. The U.S. Census Bureau's data on market consolidation, tabulated in a recent paper by Furman and Orszag (2015), shows a clear trend of consolidation in the nonfarm business sector. The data show that, in three-fourths of the broad sectors for which data are available, the 50 largest firms gained revenue share between 1997 and 2007. Their paper also highlights results from a number of independent studies that have documented increased market concentration across industries including agriculture, upstream agricultural supply, banking, hospitals, and wireless telecommunications.

To the extent that industries look more like oligopolies than perfectly competitive markets, meaning that some firms dominate the market and possess certain advantages, they will generate economic rents (Furman and Orszag 2015). Economic rents are returns to a factor of production, like capital or land, which exceed the level needed to bring that factor into production; in other words, returns in excess of the level expected based on economic fundamentals. Economic rents are split between firms and their workers, but firms with higher market power have greater leverage to retain rents, either by charging high prices or by paying their workers less. In the absence of some countervailing public purpose, such rents reflect a decrease in consumer welfare as they erode the surplus that would otherwise accrue to consumers and workers in a competitive market; for example, through lower prices for goods or higher wages from their employees. Moreover, absent entry or threat of entry by startups, incumbents in these concentrated industries have less incentive to innovate, leading to lower productivity growth in the long run.

Declining Labor Market Dynamism

Business dynamism is directly connected to labor market dynamism (or fluidity or churn), which refers to the frequency of changes in who is working for whom in the labor market—a topic that was covered in detail in Chapter 3 of the 2015 *Economic Report of the President*. From the worker's perspective, fluidity is measured by hires and separations; from the firm's perspective, it is measured by new positions (job creation) and eliminated positions (job destruction) (Council of Economic Advisers 2015a).

Figure 5-4 illustrates that both job creation and job destruction as a share of total employment have been in continuous decline since 1980 but that job creation has fallen faster in the last two decades. This trend can be explained in part by the decline in business dynamism. There are fewer young firms in the economy today than in the 1980s. Young firms that survive grow faster than older, established firms. Having fewer young firms thus delays recovery after recessions, accounting for part of the reason why job creation has fallen throughout this period. The rate of job destruction has fallen more slowly over the same timeframe in part because older firms are more resilient to macroeconomic shocks and other sudden, adverse events (Decker et al. 2014).

Lower rates of job creation and destruction may be contributing to reduced churn in the labor market and affecting the process by which workers find jobs best matched to their skills and vice versa, lowering overall productivity for all firms—young and old. Workers and firms alike benefit when there is a good match between the worker's skillset and the task required of him or her by the firm. This skillset-job match leads to cost savings, some of which may be passed on to consumers in the form of lower prices, some of which may be enjoyed by the worker in the form of higher wages, and some of which is retained by the firm via higher profits.

Thus, existing firms can increase their productivity by hiring workers with specific know-how or technological skills, or skills that better fit the jobs at a particular firm. The supply of such workers available to meet firms' demand, however, is limited in three ways. Know-how or skills may be acquired through schools and training programs, but it can take years to complete such educational programs, resulting in a lag between when

Figure 5-4

U.S. Job Creation and Destruction Rates, 1980–2012

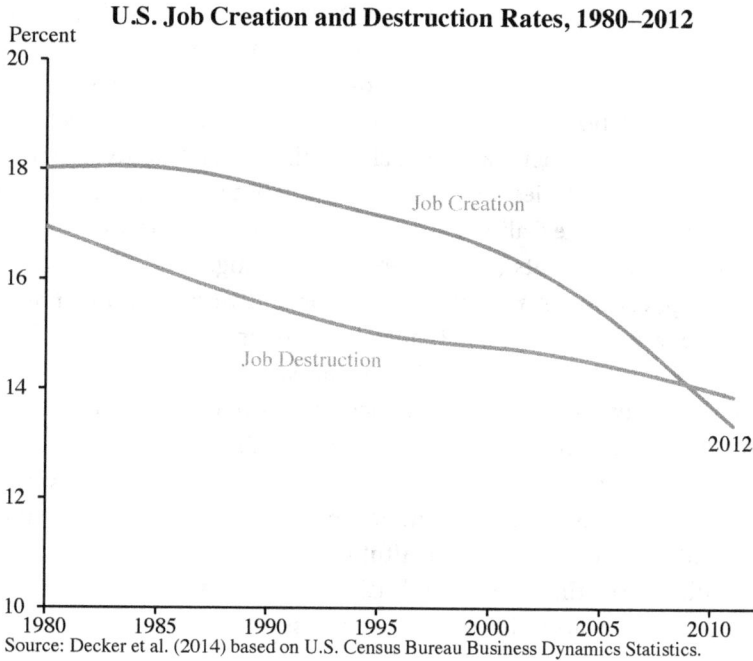

Source: Decker et al. (2014) based on U.S. Census Bureau Business Dynamics Statistics.

firms first signal demand to the labor market and when individuals who have made decisions to join educational programs are ready to enter the workforce.

Another way high-skill workers may enter the labor market is through immigration, the total volume of which is limited by the number of visas granted, which is capped by legislation. Recent evidence shows that the contribution of skilled migration to innovation has been substantial. For example, Peri, Shih, and Sparber (2014) find that inflows of foreign science, technology, engineering, and mathematics (STEM) workers explain between 30 and 50 percent of the aggregate productivity growth that took place in the United States between 1990 and 2010. There is also abundant anecdotal evidence that the contribution of immigrants to innovation, entrepreneurship and education is substantial in the United States. Immigrants accounted for about one-quarter of U.S.-based Nobel Prize recipients between 1990 and 2000. Immigrants were also among the key founders for one-quarter of all U.S. technology and engineering companies started between 1995 and 2005 with at least 1 million dollars in sales in 2006 and for over half of such companies in Silicon Valley (Wadhwa et al. 2007). These authors also report that 24 percent of all patents originating from the United States are authored by non-citizens.

Finally, some workers may acquire skills on the job that then may be useful in future employment. Many firms, however, require their employees to sign non-compete agreements, which provide another constraint on the mobility of highly skilled workers. Removing such restrictions should lead to higher levels of labor-market dynamism such that workers are better able to find jobs matched to their skills, which should in turn lead to higher labor productivity. Recent studies suggest that the high concentrations of entrepreneurship in states like California are due to these states' non-enforcement of non-compete agreements (Gilson 1999; Marx, Singh, and Fleming 2015).

The implications of reductions in labor and firm dynamism are less clear than the trends themselves. Reduced dynamism may be a sign of better matching in job markets to begin with or increased efforts by existing firms to reduce employee turnover. Yet, reduced flows may be the result of real reductions in innovation by new firms—which is discussed below—that are driving both reduced firm and labor market dynamism. Another source of both reductions may be an expansion of non-compete clauses, occupational licensing, and other labor market institutions that preclude employees from switching jobs or starting their own businesses. Increased concentration in many industries may also play a role, regardless of its cause.

Trends in R&D Spending and Patenting

Innovation is difficult to measure directly, but spending on research and development is a critical input into innovation, and one that can be closely tracked over time. Another indirect proxy that is often used by researchers is the number of patents granted annually. This section considers both of these measures.

The Growth of Private R&D and Decline of Public R&D

Basic research discoveries often have great social value because of their broad applicability. However, because it is difficult for a private firm to appropriate the gains from basic research, there tends to be underinvestment in basic research by private firms, in the absence of public investment. As a result, economic theory predicts that aggregate R&D investment (comprised not only of basic research but also of applied research and experimental development) is bound to fall short of what is socially optimal (Nelson 1959). Recent empirical analyses that attempt to measure spillover effects suggest that the socially optimal level of R&D investment—the amount that would produce the greatest rate of economic growth—is two to four times greater than actual spending (Jones and Williams 1998; Bloom, Schankerman, and

Van Reenen 2013), and that underinvestment is particularly acute in the area of basic research (Akcigit et al. 2012).

Investing in science and technology has been one of President Obama's priorities, and these investments have included major new research initiatives such as the Precision Medicine Initiative and BRAIN Initiative (see Box 5-3 on Major Research Initiatives). Since the President took office in 2009, private R&D spending has risen as a share of the economy, reaching its highest share on record, while public R&D has fallen as a share of the economy in part due to harmful budget cuts like the sequester, as shown in Figure 5-5. In total, R&D has grown from 2.37 percent of GDP in 2004 to an estimated 2.62 percent of GDP in 2015.[7] Under the Consolidated Appropriations Act of 2016, funding for Federal R&D in FY 2016 will rise by $11.2 billion (8.1 percent) above FY 2015 levels, according to analysis by the American Association for the Advancement of Science.

Private R&D investment growth has been faster during the current recovery (post 2008) than in the prior economic expansion (2001-07), and has been especially strong in the 2013-15 period. As indicated in Figure 5-6, private R&D investment has grown at an average annual rate of 3.5 percent during the current recovery, faster than the average annual pace of 3.0 percent during the previous expansion between 2001 and 2007. Since the beginning of 2013, R&D has grown 4.9 percent at an average annual rate. Based on data available as of this writing, 2015 was the best year for private R&D growth since 2008.

Private business accounts for virtually all of the recent growth in R&D. Nonprofit institutions like universities had a negligible impact on growth. The manufacturing sector is an important driver of R&D. In 2013 and 2014, manufacturing accounted for roughly 75 percent of R&D growth and non-manufacturing accounted for the other 25 percent (see Table 5-1). Two manufacturing sectors that have notably improved relative to the pre-crisis time period (2001–2007) are semiconductors and electronic components and motor vehicles and parts. In addition, manufacturing employs 60 percent of U.S. R&D employees and accounts for more than two thirds of total

---

[7] There is substantial variation in the measurement of R&D depending upon the source consulted. This chapter relies upon data from the Bureau of Economic Analysis (BEA), which have the advantage of being available for 2015 as of this writing. However, BEA data do not include private firms' outlays for software development. As a result, BEA data tend to underestimate R&D's share of GDP by roughly 0.1 percentage point as compared with data from the NSF, with the size of the underestimate growing in recent years. There is, however, a significant lag in the availability of NSF R&D funding data. The Battelle forecast attempts to update the latest available data from the National Science Foundation (2013) and the Census Bureau with forecasts based on more recent micro data from other sources. The most recent forecast from the Battelle Memorial Institute projects a U.S. R&D/GDP ratio of 2.8 percent in 2014, close to its all-time highs (Grueber and Studt 2013).

Box 5-3: Major Research Initiatives

The President's FY 2017 Budget builds on seven years' worth of the Administration's science and technology priorities in a variety of policy-critical domains. Specific attention in Federal R&D funding has been paid to those societal needs that are susceptible to the classic problem of private underinvestment in public goods. In other words, many of the areas that the Administration has identified for concerted Federal R&D investment efforts are those in which individual firms or investors have limited economic incentive to commit resources, even though the overall societal benefits of these investments would be substantial. Basic research comprises a large portion of efforts that are prone to this problem.

One major area of Federal focus is the effort to combat global climate change and promote clean energy technological development, as outlined in the President's Climate Action Plan, the U.S. Global Climate Change Research Program Strategic Plan, and the Department of Energy's Quadrennial Technology Review. Detailed in these documents is the Administration's emphasis on renewable energy and electric grid modernization, the potential for improved efficiency in buildings and industry, investments in smart, multi-modal and electrified transportation systems, and technology development that would reduce greenhouse gas emissions while also improving resilience. Also relevant in this domain is an emphasis on improving our understanding of ocean and Arctic issues.

Another area of attention centers on the life sciences. Agencies have been instructed to prioritize research that could lead to positive impacts on health, energy, and food security. Chief among such priorities are the BRAIN Initiative, efforts to combat antibiotic resistance, and initiatives to improve our bio-surveillance capabilities. Mental health-related research, especially that which assists our country's veterans, is also of high priority. A final area of commitment is the Administration's Precision Medicine Initiative, which seeks to tailor medical care to the needs of the individual patient. Accordingly, investments that improve a patient's usability and portability of his or her own electronic medical records are of particular interest, subject to robust privacy controls.

A final cluster of major research initiatives involves advanced technologies, including those that bolster the Nation's security, including cybersecurity, and those that support advanced manufacturing. Such efforts focus on nanotechnology, robotics, advanced materials, bio-engineering, and high-performance computing, as well as more specific national security research priorities in the domain of data analysis, hypersonics, and counter-proliferation. Many of these initiatives involve investing in the "industries of the future," as the development and application of these technologies may yield general purpose technologies with the potential to create entirely new industries, build jobs, and increase productivity.

Ultimately, investments in these research initiatives will both improve consumer welfare and drive productivity growth in the American economy. The resultant improvements in our capacity to combat climate change, the quality of the Nation's health care, and the effectiveness of our national security efforts will form the backbone of an innovation ecosystem that benefits workers and consumers.

R&D volume in the United States. Manufacturing is also responsible for the vast majority of U.S. patents issued (Sperling 2013).

Federal R&D spending can be decomposed into defense and non-defense R&D spending, as displayed in Figure 5-7. Compared to most of the last decade, both defense and non-defense R&D funding have dropped slightly as a percentage of GDP in this decade. As a result of the one-time boost from the American Recovery and Reinvestment Act (ARRA), Federal R&D funding approached 1.0 percent of GDP in fiscal years 2009-10; however, subsequent Congressional appropriations have failed to maintain these gains.

The decline in federally funded R&D is potentially consequential because Federal and industry R&D investments should be thought of as complements and not substitutes for each other. The Federal R&D portfolio is somewhat balanced between research and development, while industry R&D predominantly focuses on later-stage product development. Figure 5-8 shows that the Federal Government is the majority supporter of basic research—the so-called "seed corn" of future innovations and industries that generates the largest spillovers and thus is at risk of being the most underfunded in a private market—and, as such, the Administration's efforts have prioritized increasing Federal investments in basic research while also pushing for an overall increase in Federal R&D investment.

In absolute terms, the United States is the largest R&D investor in the world, with a share of about 30 percent of world R&D spending forecasted in 2014 (though second-place China is rapidly gaining share, it is only at 18 percent) (Grueber and Studt 2013). However, measured as a share of the economy, the United States ranks 10th in R&D among countries in the Organisation for Economic Co-operation and Development (see Figure 5-9). Unlike the United States, most of the other economies in the top 10

Figure 5-5
**Federal and Nonfederal Research and Development
as a Share of GDP, 1953–2015**

Percent of GDP

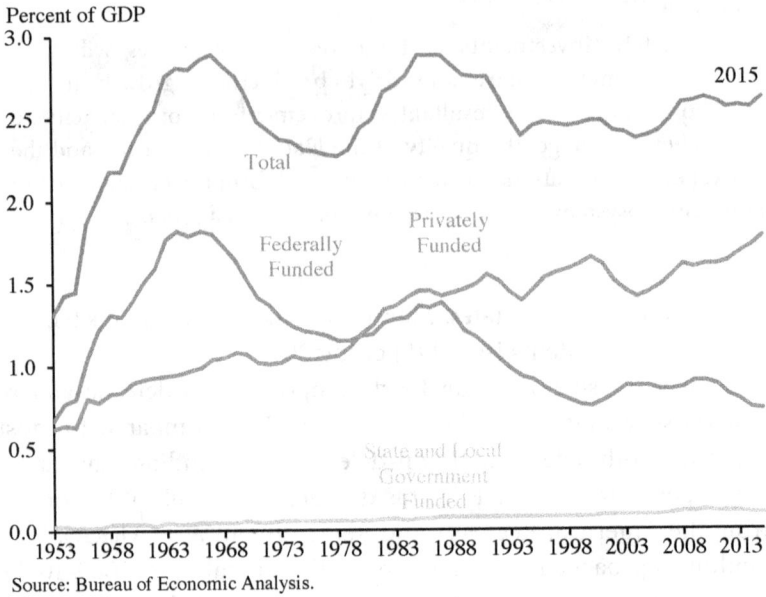

Source: Bureau of Economic Analysis.

Figure 5-6
**Real Private Research & Development (R&D)
Investment Growth, 2001–2015**

4-Quarter Percent Change

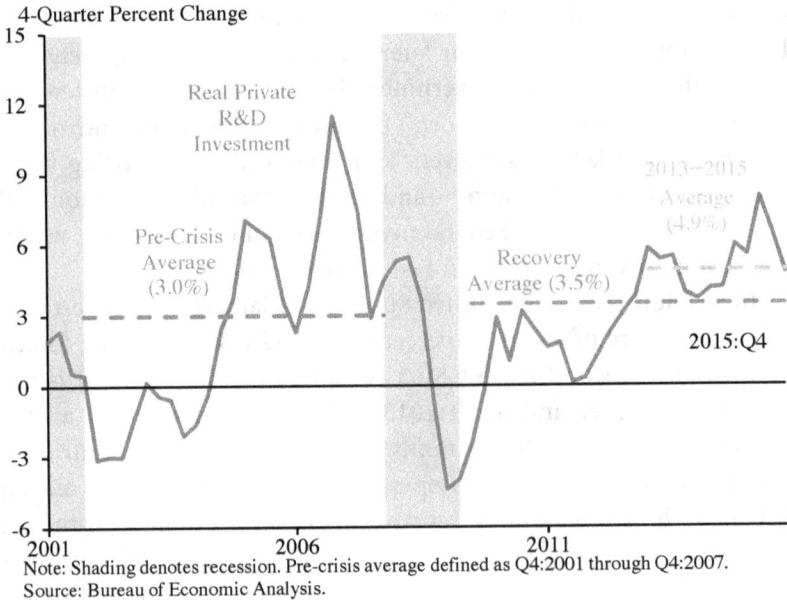

Note: Shading denotes recession. Pre-crisis average defined as Q4:2001 through Q4:2007.
Source: Bureau of Economic Analysis.

Table 5-1

Contribution to Average Annual Growth of R&D Investment

Sector	Percentage Points		
	2001-2007 Average	2013-2014 Average	Change
Total Business	2.3	4.8	2.5
Manufacturing	2.5	3.6	1.1
Pharmaceutical and Medicine	1.8	1.6	-0.2
Chemical ex Pharmaceutical	0.0	-0.1	-0.1
Semiconductors and Electronic Components	0.4	0.7	0.3
Other Computer and Electronic Products	-0.2	0.2	0.3
Motor Vehicles and Parts	-0.1	0.3	0.4
Aerospace Products and Parts	0.2	0.2	0.0
Other Manufacturing	0.4	0.7	0.3
Non-Manufacturing	-0.2	1.2	1.4
Scientific R&D Services	0.1	-0.3	-0.4
All Other Non-Manufacturing	-0.3	1.5	1.8
Total Non-Business	0.1	0.0	-0.1
Universities and Colleges	0.1	0.0	-0.1
Other Nonprofits	0.1	0.0	0.0
Headline R&D Growth	2.4	4.8	2.4

Source: Bureau of Economic Analysis; CEA Calculations

continue to expand their R&D investments from all sources—not just private ones—faster than their economic growth.[8]

Federal R&D is important not only for private firms' success, job creation, or aggregate measures of productivity. Federally funded research leads to innovations that improve consumer welfare as well, with a host of products and services being made possible by such investments—be they in the area of basic or applied research investigations. From Google Earth and global positioning systems to microwave ovens, and from vaccinations to photovoltaic cells, discoveries and products enabled by U.S. Federal investments in innovation have touched lives across the globe in ways that are likely to be understated in official growth and productivity statistics (see Chapter 2). Investments in R&D are therefore important to the health of the American economy as well as to general welfare. The innovations that these

---

[8] For comparison, Europe as a whole was forecast by Battelle to have an R&D/GDP ratio of 1.8 percent in 2014; China's R&D/GDP ratio was forecast at 2.0 percent but climbing rapidly. South Korea, Israel, Japan, Sweden, Finland, Denmark, Switzerland, Austria, and Germany are the 9 OECD economies ahead of the United States.

Figure 5-7
Federal Research and Development (R&D) Investment, 1980–2015

Percent of GDP

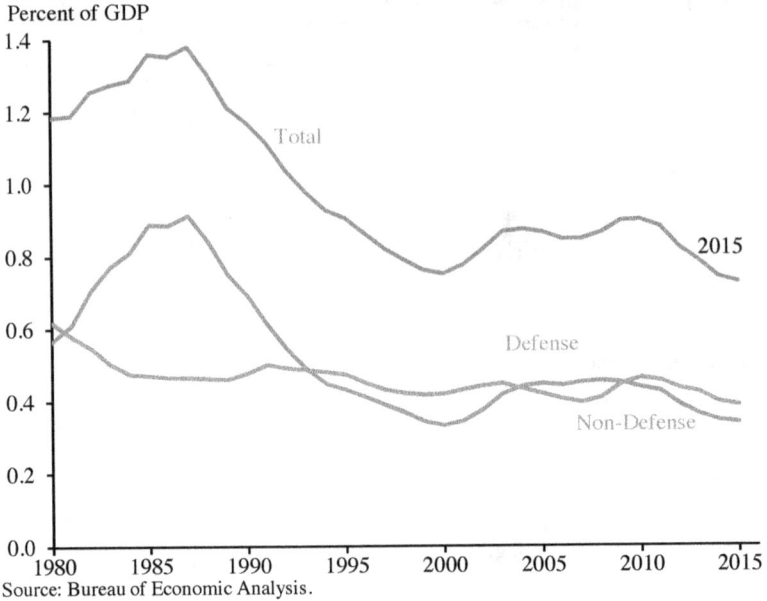

Source: Bureau of Economic Analysis.

Figure 5-8
Share of Research and Development (R&D) by Funding Source, 2011

Percent

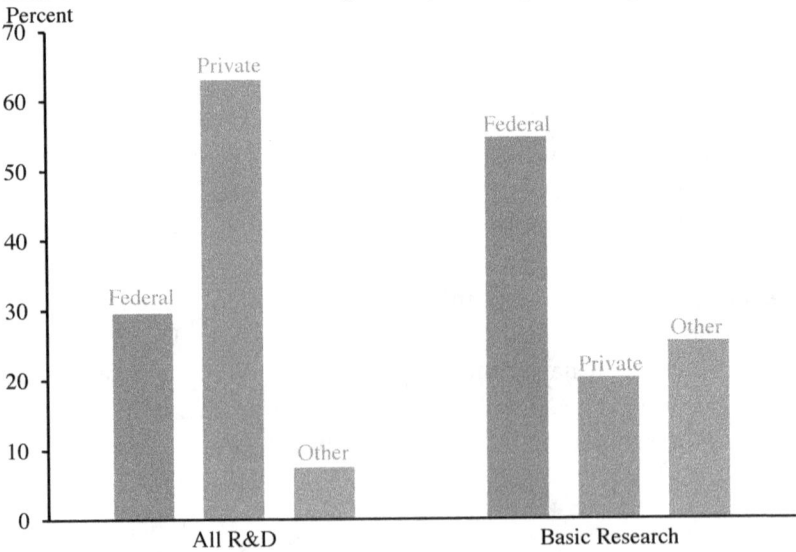

Source: National Science Foundation, Science and Engineering Indicators 2014, Table 4-3.

Figure 5-9
Gross Domestic Expenditure on Research and Development (R&D), 2013

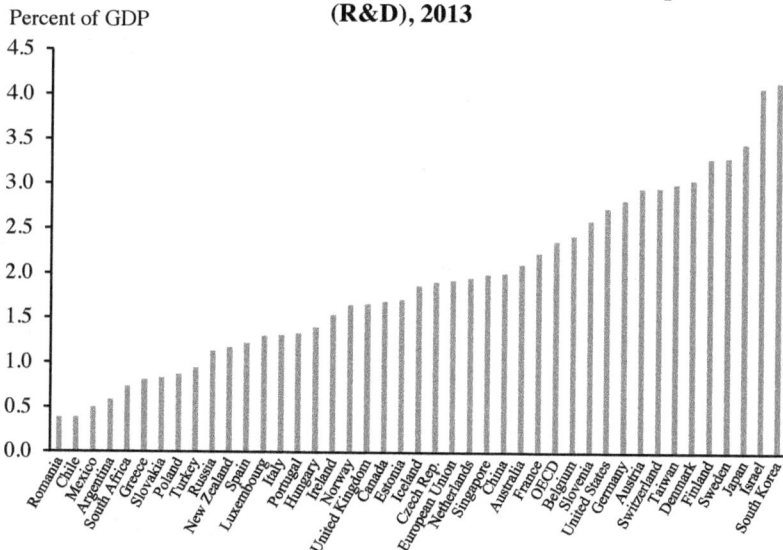

Note: Data for South Africa and Switzterland are not available for 2013 and so are instead displayed for the most recent available year.
Source: OECD Main Science and Technology Indicators (2015).

investments in R&D generate help lower costs and boost productivity, and the firms that these investments spawn compete with established firms, further driving innovation and productivity growth (Griliches 1986; Griliches 1992; Jones 2002; Jones and Williams 1998).

Recent Trends in Patenting

Although innovation is notoriously difficult to quantify, patents provide one measure of innovative activity. The link between patent grants and aggregate productivity growth is tenuous, because patenting can be driven by numerous factors, including the budget of the U.S. Patent and Trademark Office (Griliches 1989). Thus, while the number of new patents granted has increased over the past several decades (Figure 5-10, right axis), the extent to which this trend is indicative of current or future productivity growth is unclear.

Recent academic findings at the firm level, however, suggest that higher levels of patenting are associated with higher total factor productivity. For example, Balasubramanian and Sivadasan (2011) find evidence that a firm's productivity increases following its first patent. The U.S. Census Bureau and U.S. Patent and Trademark Office have started to link patent application data to administrative data on firms and workers. Initial research using this data indicates that most patenting firms are small, and that firms

Figure 5-10
Percent of Patent Applications by First Time
U.S. Patenters, 1976–2003

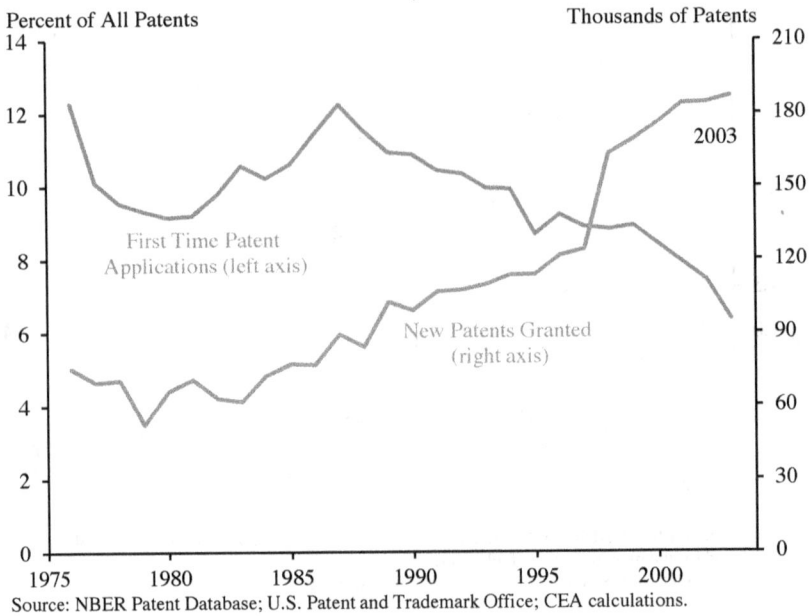

Percent of All Patents   Thousands of Patents

[Chart showing two lines: "First Time Patent Applications (left axis)" and "New Patents Granted (right axis)" from 1975 to 2000, with left axis from 0 to 14 and right axis from 0 to 210. A point labeled "2003" is marked near the upper right.]

Source: NBER Patent Database; U.S. Patent and Trademark Office; CEA calculations.

that patent are responsible for creating more jobs and shedding fewer jobs than non-patenting firms (Graham et al. 2015). Given evidence of slowing business dynamism and lower rates of entry by new firms discussed in the previous section, these new findings would then suggest that the share of patents by new firms is slowing over time. Figure 5-10 (left axis) graphs the percent of patents by first-time patent applicants (many of which are young or startup firms) from 1976 to 2003. While patenting has increased over time, the percent of patents by first-time applicants has been declining since the late 1980s, implying at the very least that the majority of the recent increase in the overall number of patents in the U.S. economy is likely not driven by first-timers.

The reasons behind the falling share of first-time patent applicants are not well understood. It may be that there are economies to scale in patenting, and so larger firms are patenting at a higher rate than startups. It may be that younger firms are starting to rely on trade secrets rather than patents; indeed, Png (2015) provides evidence that trade secrets may substitute for patents in some industries. It may be that costs associated with litigation disproportionately affect young firms (see Box 5-4 on Patent Litigation).

Strong institutions that protect property rights are an important ingredient for fostering economic activity and entrepreneurial success (Acemoglu, Johnson, and Robinson 2005; North and Weingast 1989). But

Box 5-4: Patent Legislation

While the number of annual patent grants have increased dramatically over the past several decades (Figure 5-10 above), so too has the amount of patent litigation (Figure 5-ii below, left axis). The rate of patent litigation, defined as the ratio of the number of patent litigation cases to the number of in-force patents, increased from the 1970s to mid-1990s, then fell from the mid-1990s to 2010, before increasing through 2014. (Figure 5-ii below, right axis). Some of the increase in patent litigation occurred after the America Invents Act (AIA) took effect in 2011. Part of the increase may have been due to the AIA's change in the "joinder rule" that previously allowed multiple cases involving a single infringed patent to be joined. Part of the increase may have also been due to a temporary increase in false marking cases (PWC 2013).

Patent litigation cases are brought by both non-practicing entities (NPEs) and practicing entities (PEs). NPEs are organizations that own patents on products or processes but do not make, use, or sell them. These include patent assertion entities (PAEs) that specialize in asserting patents, as well as individual inventors and universities who solely license patents to others (Lemley and Melamed 2013). PEs are organizations that own patents on products or processes that they make, use, or sell. According to research by RPX (2014; 2015), the percent of patent litigation cases brought by NPEs has grown over time, from below 30

Figure 5-ii
Trends in Patent Litigation, 1971–2014

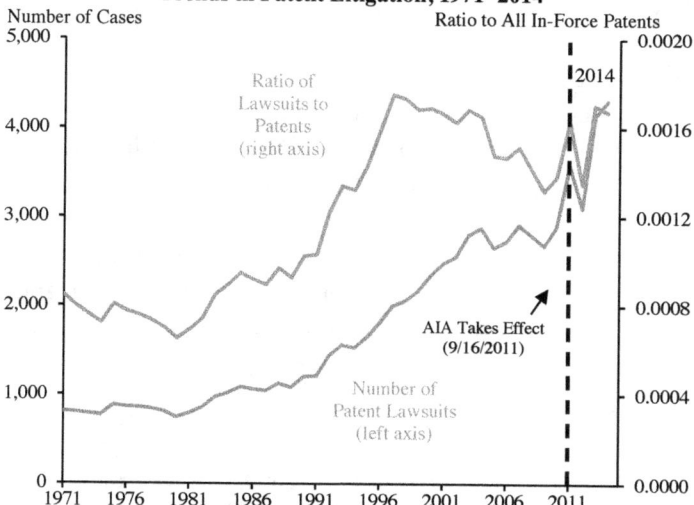

Note: AIA stands for the Leahy-Smith America Invents Act.
Source: USPTO; FJC; Lex Machina; CEA calculations.

percent of all cases in 2009 to over 60 percent in 2014. The majority of NPE cases are filed by PAEs, estimated to be 89 percent of all NPE cases by RPX (2015).

Patent litigation appears to negatively affect entrepreneurship and innovation. Chien (2015) reports that patent litigation disproportionately affects smaller companies. Kiebzak, Rafert, and Tucker (2016) conclude that venture capital investment, an indicator of levels of entrepreneurial activity, initially increases with the number of litigated patents, but that past a certain threshold, further increases in litigated patents are associated with decreased venture capital investment. The authors also find some evidence that a similar relationship exists between patent litigation and small firm entry. Scott Morton and Shapiro (2014) develop a theoretical model to assess how patent litigation affects innovation. When they fit the model with existing data, the results suggest that patent litigation hurts innovation. Feldman and Lemley (2015) find that very few patent license demands lead to new innovation but rather involve payment by the licensee to continue with its business. Galasso and Schankerman (2015) exploit the randomized assignment of judges to find that patent invalidation results in a 50 percent decrease in future patenting over a five-year window.

property rights protection regimes must balance addressing valid concerns with guarding against baseless or excessive complaints. This tradeoff is particularly important as the frequency of patent litigation has risen. With this goal in mind, the President has supported efforts to reform the U.S. patent system, including signing the America Invents Act (AIA) in September 2011. Among other changes called for in the AIA, there are now limits on the ability of patent holders to name (or "join") multiple defendants in a single patent infringement lawsuit. More work is needed to reform patent litigation and better align rewards provided to patent holders with their social contribution. By instituting reforms that better protect and incentivize innovators, motivate more entrepreneurial startups to enter and compete against established firms, and encourage workers to seek employment opportunities that are best matched to their skillset, the Administration aims to foster productivity growth.

NEW OPPORTUNITIES AND CHALLENGES

There are many opportunities for new technologies and business models to spur innovation and productivity growth. The range of technologies—from clean energy technology to biotechnology to 3-D printing technology—is broad. This section focuses on two new opportunities that have the potential for broad spillovers into different parts of the economy. One area is the rapidly growing field of robotics. The other area involves Internet communications technology. While these areas offer much promise, there are also a variety of challenges that result from their deployment and increasing role in American life. For example, it is important that the resultant gains from productivity growth from these technologies are shared widely.

More specifically, in the area of robotics, this section explores concerns that increased automation in the workplace threatens to displace elements of the conventional labor force. It is important to keep in mind that, while growing quickly, robotics are not poised to affect every area of the economy or replace human labor. Nonetheless, robotics still have the potential to be highly consequential for firms and, more broadly, for productivity.

This section also discusses two particular facets of Internet communications technology, namely the on-demand economy and the digital divide. The rise of the so-called on-demand economy—enabled by mobile Internet applications—also has the potential for productivity and welfare gains but could possibly lead to worker displacement, a prospect that is examined here as well. This section also emphasizes the need to narrow what is commonly called the digital divide—the gap between those who can access the Internet and those who cannot—so that all may share in its benefits, the existence of which is well-supported by empirical findings in the economics literature.

Robotics

One area of innovation that can help the United States to boost TFP growth in the future is robotics. The first U.S. robots were introduced into production by General Motors in 1961, and their prevalence has grown steadily over time, particularly in manufacturing and the auto industry (Gordon 2012). Recently, the deployment of robots has accelerated, leading them to contribute more to productivity, as described below. However, these changes potentially also create challenges in labor markets as concerns have arisen about the extent to which robots will displace workers from their jobs. An economy must carefully assess these developments to encourage innovation but also to provide adequate training and protections for workers.

The use of industrial robots can be thought of as a specific form of automation. As a characteristic of innovation for centuries, automation enhances production processes from flour to textiles to virtually every product in the market. Automation, including through the use of information technology, is widely believed to foster increased productivity growth

(Bloom, Sadun, and Van Reenen 2012). In many cases, mostly for higher-skilled work, automation has resulted in substantial increases in living standards and leisure time. The International Organization for Standardization (ISO) defines a robot to be an "actuated mechanism programmable in two or more axes with a degree of autonomy, moving within its environment, to perform intended tasks."[9] This degree of autonomy makes robotic automation somewhat different from historical examples of automation, such as the replacement of weavers with looms. Some of these machines can operate for extended periods of time without human control, presaging the rise of a potentially paradigm-shifting innovation in the productivity process.

Robots, like other types of automation, can be either complements to, or substitutes for, conventional labor. For example, at many of the country's biggest container shipping ports—the primary gateways to and from the United States for waterborne international shipments—automation has replaced longshoremen in a variety of activities, from computerized cargo management platforms that allow for visualization of the loading of a container ship in real time to software that allows for end-to-end management of individual containers throughout the unloading process (Feuer 2012). By contrast, there are a number of "smart warehouse" applications that involve varying amounts of automation to complement the work done by warehouse fulfillment workers. Examples include LED lights on shelves that light up when a worker reaches the appropriate location and mobile robots that bring inventory from the floor to a central place for packaging (Field 2015; Garfield 2016). The latter example realigns employees away from product-retrieval tasks and focuses them instead on the inventory-sorting phase of the process, for which humans have a comparative advantage over machinery.

Robotics have also played an important role in growth over the last two decades. A recent study estimates that robotics added an average of 0.37 percentage point to a country's annual GDP growth between 1993 and 2007, accounting for about one-tenth of GDP growth during this time period (Graetz and Michaels 2015). This same study also estimates that robotics added 0.36 percentage point to labor productivity growth, accounting for about 16 percent of labor productivity growth during this time period. This effect is of similar magnitude to the impact that the advent of steam engines had on labor productivity growth (Crafts 2004).

---

[9] Note that the requirement for a "degree of autonomy" can be fulfilled with anything from indirect interaction between human control inputs and the physical robot all the way up to full autonomy (ISO 8373, 2012, available at https://www.iso.org/obp/ui/#iso:std:iso:8373:ed-2:v1:en).

Figure 5-11
Estimated Worldwide Annual Supply of
Industrial Robots, 2004–2014

Thousands of Units

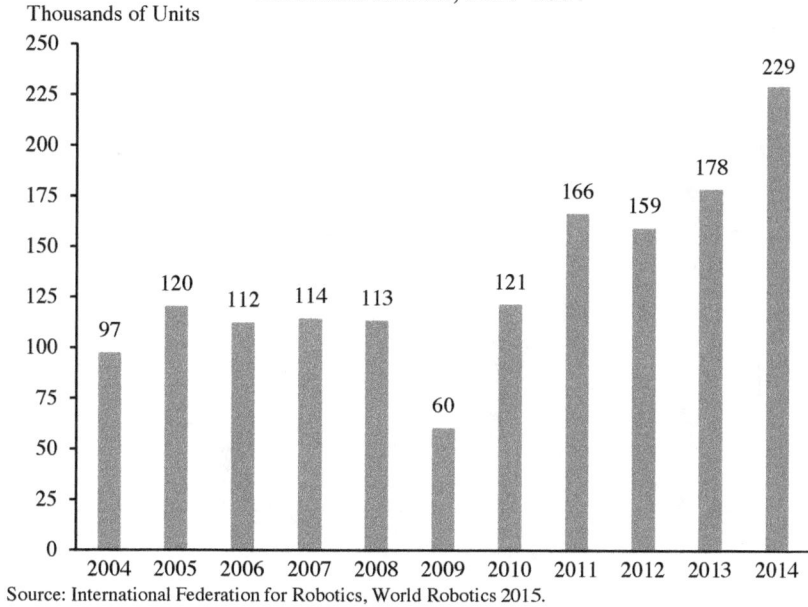

Source: International Federation for Robotics, World Robotics 2015.

Growth in robotics shipments has increased since 2007, suggesting that robotics may contribute even more to GDP and labor productivity growth in the future, though it is too early to tell. As indicated in Figure 5-11, from 2010 to 2014, worldwide shipments of industrial robotics have nearly doubled, according to the International Federation of Robotics (IFR). Research by the Boston Consulting Group also estimates that the dollar value of these industrial robotics shipments likely doubled during this time period (Sander and Wolfgang 2014). These estimates may even understate the pace of growth, since the IFR defines an industrial robot by ISO standard 8373: "An automatically controlled, reprogrammable, multipurpose manipulator programmable in three or more axes, which may be either fixed in place or mobile for use in industrial automation applications." In particular, the requirement that the device be reprogrammable to be considered an industrial robot may result in an undercount compared to other robotics definitions.

Industrial-services robots are primarily applied to manufacturing activities. The automotive sector accounts for approximately 40 percent of total robot shipments worldwide, and has seen rapid growth in shipments since 2010. Consumer electronics is the second-largest sector, comprising 20 percent of total shipments; other large sectors include chemical rubber and plastics, metal, and food processing, as indicated in Figure 5-12.

Figure 5-12
Estimated Annual Shipments of Industrial Robots
by Main Industries, 2010–2012

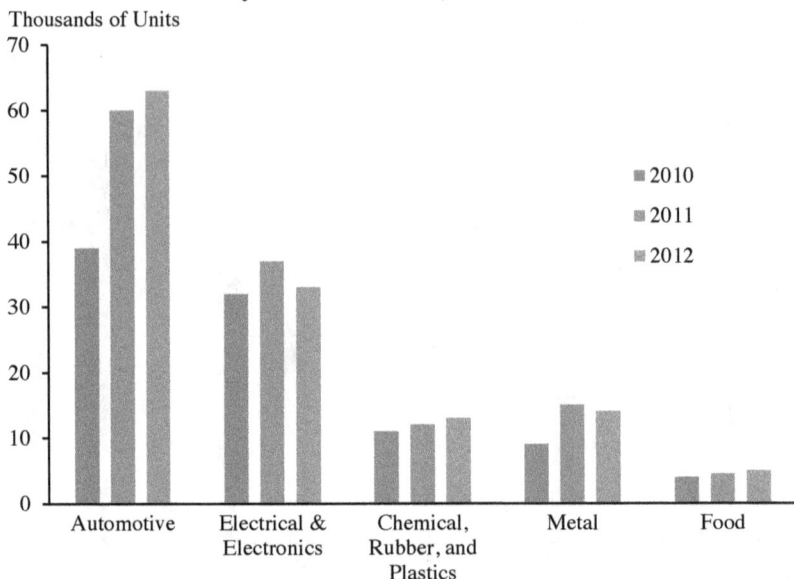

Source: International Federation for Robotics, World Robotics 2014.

Robotics are used in different ways across different industries. Figure 5-12 depicts changes over time within several industries and, in particular, highlights the rapid growth within the automotive industry. Another way to compare the intensity of robot use across industries is to normalize the number of robot units in the industry by the number of workers in the industry to create a "robot density." Figure 5-13 compares the robot density across industries and across countries. Again, the automotive industry appears to be the heaviest user of robots, both in terms of absolute number of robot units (shown in Figure 5-12) and in terms of density of robots per worker (illustrated by Figure 5-13). This trend may be because the skillset of robots lends itself well to the standardization and fixed nature of the automotive assembly process. The comparison also reveals that the United States lags Japan and Germany in the number of robots per worker, especially outside the automotive sector.

To examine the pace of innovation in robotics, CEA collected data directly from the U.S. Patent and Trademark Office on the total number of patents granted each year, as well as the number of robotics patents, from 2000 to 2014.[10] Figure 5-14 shows that the number of patents in this class

[10] Patents were counted as being "robotics patents" if they received the patent subclass number 901 (robots). For more information, see the USPTO's definition: http://www.uspto.gov/web/patents/classification/uspc901/defs901.htm.

Figure 5-13
Robot Density: Automotive vs. Non-Automotive, 2012
Number of Robots per 10,000 Workers

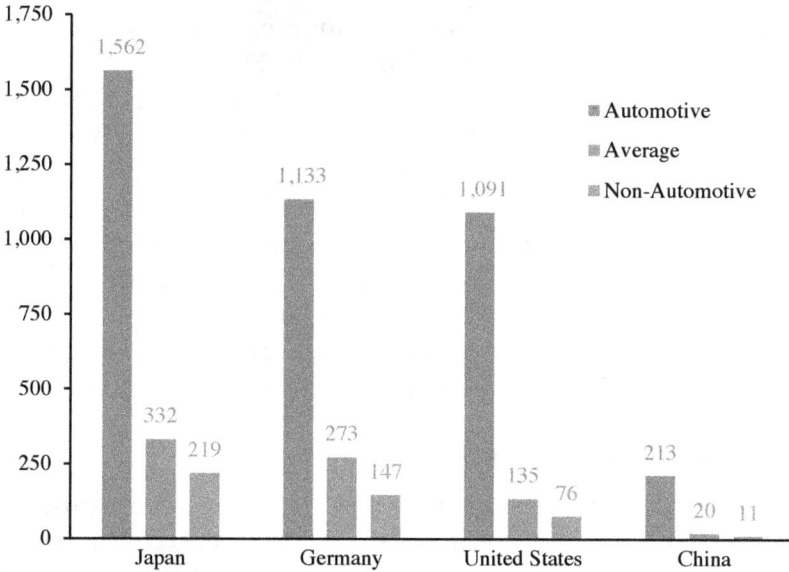

Source: Axium Solutions; International Federation for Robotics.

Figure 5-14
Patents with Robot Class, 2000–2014
Number of Patents   Percent of All Patents Granted

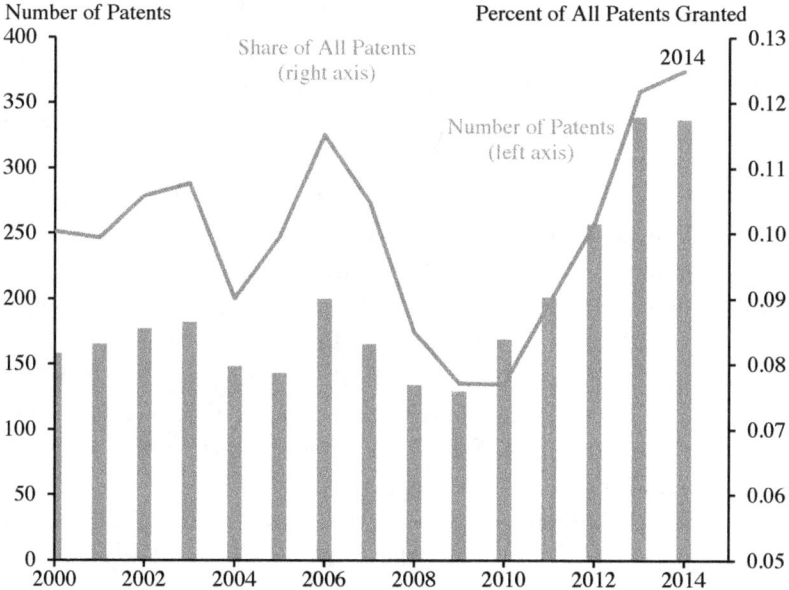

Source: United States Patent and Trademark Office.

was relatively flat through the 2000s, before starting to increase in 2012. There were close to 350 robotics patents granted in both 2013 and 2014, as compared to an average of about 150 in the 2000s. As also indicated in Figure 5-14, the share of patents that are for robotics decreased from 2006 to 2010 before starting to increase from 2011 to 2014.

CEA also conducted an analysis of patent ownership and found little evidence of concentrated ownership across industries. However, robotics are used differently across industries, and so it is unclear whether there is a concentration of patent ownership within different industries. Going forward, it will be important to be vigilant about intellectual property related to robotics. Low concentration in upstream markets implies healthy competition, which should lead to more innovation and lower prices. As a result, downstream firms should be able to acquire robot inputs at competitive prices, which should help to drive productivity growth even further.

Effect of Robotics on Workers

While industrial robots have the potential to drive productivity growth in the United States, it is less clear how this growth will affect workers. One view is that robots will take substantial numbers of jobs away from humans, leaving them technologically unemployed—either in blissful leisure or, in many popular accounts, suffering from the lack of a job. Most economists consider either scenario unlikely because several centuries of innovation have shown that, even as machines have been able to increasingly do tasks humans used to do, this leads humans to have higher incomes, consume more, and creates jobs for almost everyone who wants them. In other words, as workers have historically been displaced by technological innovations, they have moved into new jobs, often requiring more complex tasks or greater levels of independent judgment.

A critical question, however, is the pace at which this happens and the labor market institutions facilitate the shifting of people to new jobs. As an extreme example, if a new innovation rendered one-half of the jobs in the economy obsolete next year, then the economy might be at full employment in the "long run." But this long run could be decades away as workers are slowly retrained and as the current cohort of workers ages into retirement and is replaced by younger workers trained to find jobs amidst the new technological opportunities. If, however, these jobs were rendered obsolete over many decades then it is much less likely that it would result in large-scale, "transitional" unemployment. Nevertheless, labor market institutions are critical here too, and the fact that the percentage of men ages 25-54 employed in the United States slowly but steadily declined since the 1950s, as manufacturing has shifted to services, suggests that challenges may arise.

Over time, economists expect wages to adjust to clear the labor market and workers to respond to incentives to develop human capital. Inequality could increase; indeed, most economists believe technological change is partially responsible for rising inequality in recent decades. Whether or not robots will increase or decrease inequality depends in part on the extent to which robots are complements to, or substitutes for, labor. If substitution dominates, then the question becomes whether or not labor has enough bargaining power such that it can share in productivity gains. At present, this question cannot be answered fully, largely because of limited research on the economic impact of robots. One of the few studies in this area finds that higher levels of robot density within an industry lead to higher wages in that industry (Graetz and Michaels 2015), suggesting that robots are complements to labor. The higher wages, however, might be due in part to robots' replacing lower-skill workers in that industry, thus biasing wage estimates upwards.

The older literature on automation may give some clues about how robots will affect jobs in the future. This broader literature finds that, while there is some substitution of automation for human labor, complementary jobs are often created and new work roles emerge to develop and maintain the new technology (Autor 2015). One issue is whether these new jobs are created fast enough to replace the lost jobs. Keynes (1930) appears to have been concerned about the prospect for what he termed "technological unemployment," borne out of the notion that societies are able to improve labor efficiency more quickly than they are able to find new uses for labor.

There has been some debate about which types of workers are most affected by automation. That is, jobs are not necessarily destroyed by automation but instead are reallocated. Autor and Dorn (2013) argue that so-called middle-skill jobs are what get displaced by automation and robots. These jobs, which have historically included bookkeepers, clerks, and certain assembly-line workers, are relatively easy to routinize. This results in middle-skill workers who cannot easily acquire training for a higher-skilled job settling for a position that requires a lower-skill level, which may then translate into lower wages. In contrast, high-skill jobs that use problem-solving capabilities, intuition and creativity, and low-skill jobs that require situational adaptability and in-person interactions, are less easy to routinize. Autor, Levy, and Murnane (2003) point out that robots and computerization have historically not been able to replicate or automate these tasks, which has led to labor market polarization. While not specifically tied to automation, Goos, Manning, and Salomons (2014) find broad evidence of this labor market polarization across European countries.

In contrast, recent papers by Autor (2015) and Schmitt, Shierholz, and Mishel (2013) suggests that the labor market polarization seen in the 1980s and 1990s may be declining. Data from the 2000s suggests that lower- and middle-skill workers have experienced less employment and wage growth than higher-skilled workers. Frey and Osborne (2013) argue that big data and machine learning will make it possible to automate many tasks that were difficult to automate in the past. In a study specifically on robots and jobs, Graetz and Michaels (2015) find some evidence that higher levels of robot density within an industry lead to fewer hours worked by low-skilled workers in that industry.

While robotics is likely to affect industrial sectors of the economy differently, it also is likely to affect occupations within these sectors differently. Two recent studies have used data on occupational characteristics to study how automation might differentially affect wages across occupations (Frey and Osborne 2013; McKinsey Global Institute 2015). Both studies rely on the detailed occupational descriptions from O*NET, an occupational data source funded by the U.S. Department of Labor, to derive probabilities that an occupation will be automated into obsolescence. While the two studies have slightly different categorizations, they both find a negative relationship between wages and the threat of automation.

To better understand the relationship between automation and wages at the occupational level, CEA matched an occupation's median hourly wage to the occupational automation scores from Frey and Osborne (2013). The median probability of automation was then calculated for three ranges of hourly wage: less than 20 dollars; 20 to 40 dollars; and more than 40 dollars. The results, presented in Figure 5-15, suggest that occupations that are easier to automate have lower wages. Low probability of outright automation, however, would seem to make an occupation a better candidate for being complemented and improved by automation in the workplace (such as the role played by e-mail, statistical analysis, and computerized computation for a variety of office-based jobs) and so are not as prone to seeing an effect on wages from increased automation.

These data demonstrate the need for a robust training and education agenda, to ensure that displaced workers are able to quickly and smoothly move into new jobs. The bipartisan Workforce Innovation and Opportunity Act, which President Obama signed into law in July 2014, consolidates existing funding initiatives, helps retrain workers in skills that employers are looking for, and matches those workers to employers. In March 2015, the Administration launched the TechHire initiative, part of which aims to equip 17-29 year olds with skills necessary for jobs in information

Figure 5-15
Probability of Automation by an Occupation's Median Hourly Wage
Median Probability of Automation

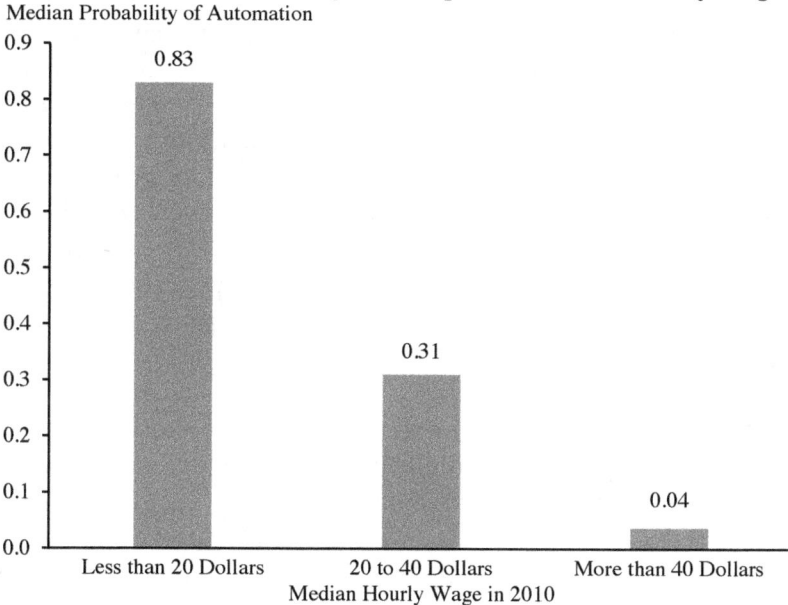

Median Hourly Wage in 2010

Source: Bureau of Labor Statistics; Frey and Osborne (2013); CEA calculations.

technology fields, including software development, network administration, and cybersecurity.

Internet and New Business Models

Digital communications technology is an area that has had a large impact on TFP growth. Such technologies are what some economists call General Purpose or "platform" technologies, meaning that improvements in communication technologies stimulate innovation across a wide variety of other sectors. This growth is expected to continue in the future as the Internet is used to connect employers to employees, to connect customers to suppliers, and to develop new businesses and business models that deliver products and services faster than in the past. Moreover, these new businesses compete with established firms, in many cases pushing existing businesses to innovate further, thereby providing customers with better products and services at lower prices. Competition can therefore lead to higher living standards, as customers can purchase a wider variety of products at lower prices.

The United States is among the world leaders in the development and deployment of cutting-edge broadband technology. Today, most Americans live in areas served by fixed-line Internet services, and the United States enjoys widespread availability of advanced wireless broadband Internet services, such as 4G LTE. At the same time, broadband access has become a nearly indispensable component of modern life. Numerous studies show that access to broadband contributes to local, regional, and national economic growth. A study of Organisation for Economic Co-operation and Development (OECD) countries finds that a 10 percentage-point increase in broadband penetration is associated with per capita income growth rates that are between 0.9 and 1.5 percentage points higher (Czernich, Falck, Kretschmer, and Woessmann 2011). Another cross-country analysis finds that a 1 percent increase in the size of a country's Internet-using population is associated with 8 to 15 dollars more in GDP per capita (Najarzadeh, Rahimzadeh, and Reed 2014). Kolko (2012), using panel data and instrumental variables approaches, finds that local broadband expansion leads to local employment growth.

These findings parallel a broad literature linking Internet and communications technology (ICT) to productivity. For example, Bartel, Ichniowski, and Shaw (2007) find that computerized numerically controlled machining centers can both lead to wider product variety and improve overall production efficiency. More generally, growth in the use of computers, as well as the changes in management and other organizational dynamics that ensued, partially explains the recovery in TFP growth during the 1990s from its historic lows in the 1970s and 1980s (Black and Lynch 2004). While the United States benefited from the integration of these technologies and management techniques, other countries that also invested in ICT did not see as large a pickup in productivity. Although the United States leads most other Western economies in both the share of ICT in value added (Figure 5-16) and TFP growth rates, some countries that lead the world in the former exhibit low levels of the latter.

Access to the Internet not only enables firms to increase productivity, but it also provides an opportunity for entrepreneurs to experiment with innovative product ideas and new business models, and scale these ideas and models up quickly and cheaply. For example, on-demand economy platforms would not be possible but for the widespread adoption of Internet and wireless devices (see Box 5-5 on On-Demand Economy). Not only do these new business models help lower costs for consumers, leading to greater consumer surplus, but also they may increase business productivity. For example, a survey of San Francisco transportation-network company (TNC) riders by University of California-Berkeley researchers found that TNC wait times were dramatically shorter and more consistent than taxis (Rayle et al. 2014). Shorter wait times mean that a worker is able to travel between meetings or work and home quicker than before, raising the amount of time a worker is able to spend being productive. As another example, entry

Figure 5-16
Share of Information and Communications Technology (ICT) in Value Added, 2011

Percent of Value Added

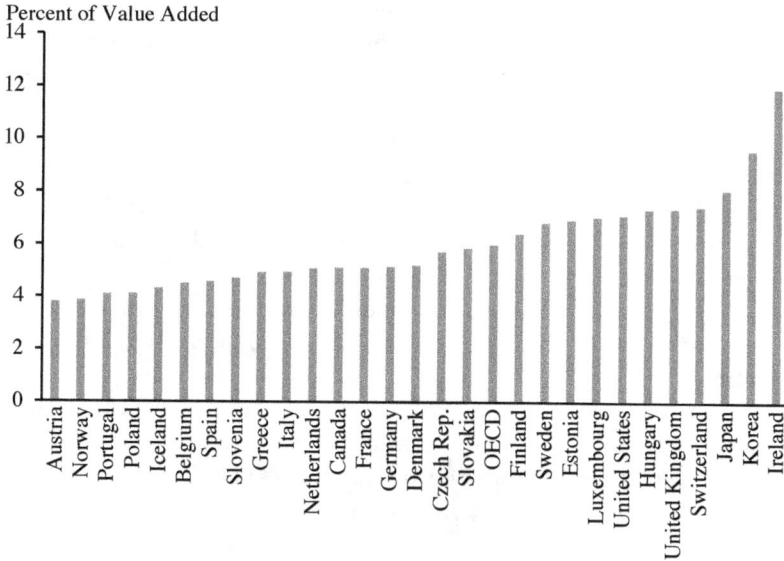

Source: OECD Factbook.

of online craft markets means that many craft artisans are able to increase exposure in multiple markets, leading to increased scale and ultimately productivity growth, much in the same way that higher exports from international trade leads to productivity growth. These business models also introduce new competitive dynamics into established industries.

The Digital Divide Challenge

Broadband access has become a nearly indispensable component of modern life, used for everything from engaging in personal communication, to searching for a job, and streaming online educational content to engaging in civic affairs (National Telecommunications and Information Administration and Economics and Statistics Administration 2013). Thus, access to the Internet has become an essential resource for many nascent entrepreneurs to reach potential customers. Customers who access the Internet can benefit from the array of new products and services offered by certain types of entrepreneurial new firms. However, a digital divide (for example, the fact that certain groups of individuals and businesses lack access to the Internet) means that some would-be entrepreneurs cannot compete, and some would-be customers cannot access these new products and services.

Box 5-5: The On-Demand Economy

"On-demand economy platforms" are online and mobile platforms that match consumers to providers for the purpose of purchasing goods or services on a "one-off" basis. This intentionally broad definition includes the following types of platforms:

- *Rental platforms* most commonly involve homeowners renting out their homes to business and vacation travelers. Other assets can also be rented through similar arrangements, such as car and bicycle rentals.
- *Craft platforms* allow individuals and small businesses who produce or collect craft-oriented goods to sell these goods to consumers.
- *Financing platforms* allow individuals and small firms to obtain financing from lenders, in exchange for fixed payments, equity, or rewards.
- *"Gig" platforms* allow individual providers to provide their labor services, which might be tied to a specialized physical asset, such as a car in the case of transportation-network companies (TNCs), or a specialized human asset, such as the ability to code, to individual consumers and small firms.

Because they are so nascent, relatively little economic research has been done on these models. Moreover, many of these activities cannot be isolated in official economic statistics and, in some cases, may in fact be omitted from these statistics. At present, this portion of the economy still appears relatively small—estimates suggest that it represents less than 1 percent of the working-age population and only accounts for a miniscule portion of the economy as a whole; PricewaterhouseCoopers estimated global revenues for the on-demand economy to be $15 billion in 2014 (PWC 2015). However, these business models are growing rapidly, and McKinsey Global Institute predicts these business models will increase global GDP by $2.7 trillion by 2025 (Manyika et al. 2015).

These platforms are already forcing incumbents to respond in several industries—notably the taxi industry in which TNCs have rapidly gained popularity and the lodging industry. For example, one independent study found that entry of an online housing rental platform led to lower hotel prices in Texas (Zervas, Proserpio, and Byers 2015). As noted above on the dual role of startups, there do not need to be many startups in an industry before the incumbents in that industry start to undertake changes to guard against business losses. These actions could take the form of innovative activity, which would boost both firm-level and overall economic productivity, or dropping prices, which would improve consumer welfare.

Medallion prices in New York City and Chicago have fallen substantially since the introduction of TNCs, which is indicative of increased competition in the taxi market.[1] Medallions in New York City and Chicago are treated as private assets, and the total number of medallions is limited by city government organizations—a practice that effectively caps the quantity of rides available. Demand for rides in these cities has previously exceeded the cap, so the medallion system works to sustain city-determined, artificially-high fares, resulting in rents for taxi medallion owners via this rationing process. Figure 5-iii below for New York City shows that the average price for a single taxi medallion, which had been increasing since 2010, started to fall in 2013. Similarly, the number of taxi medallion transfers has dropped during this time. Figure 5-iv below for Chicago reveals similar trends in that prices started to fall in 2013. By the end of 2015, the average transaction price for a medallion in Chicago had fallen to $230,000, less than two-thirds of its value of two years earlier. The number of medallions sold has also dropped during this time.

Consumers appear to benefit from the on-demand economy because of lower prices and a greater array of options, including pro-

Figure 5-iii
New York City Taxi Medallion Transactions, 2010–2015

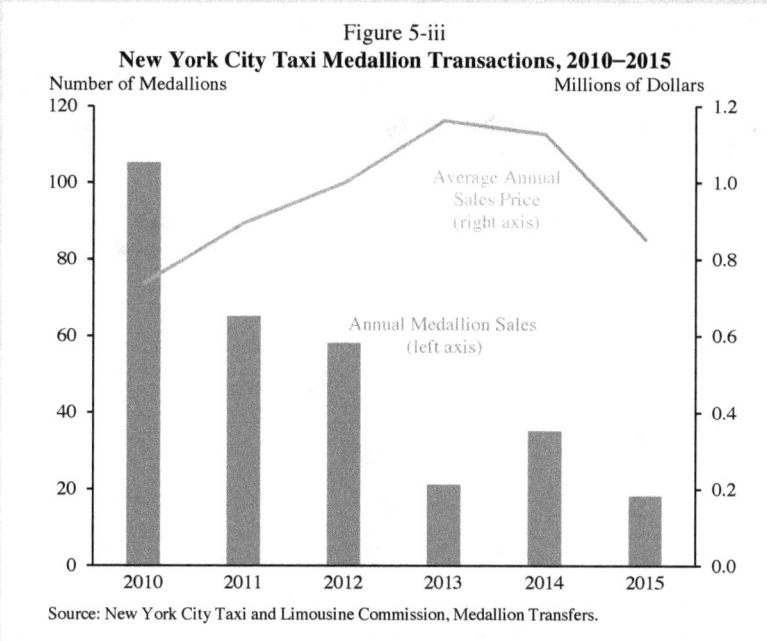

Source: New York City Taxi and Limousine Commission, Medallion Transfers.

---

[1] Data on New York City taxi medallion transfers can be found at: http://www.nyc.gov/ html/tlc/html/about/medallion_transfers.shtml. Data on Chicago taxi medallion transfers can be found at: https://www.cityofchicago.org/city/en/depts/bacp/supp_info/ medallion_owner_information.html. CEA aggregated the data by month and year to examine the number of medallion transfers and average value of transfer.

vision of services that may not have previously existed or now reach new geographic areas. While the evidence suggests that consumers benefit from competition between on-demand economy platforms and incumbent firms, the effect on wages and inequality is less certain. The optimistic view is that this sector will be a source of productivity growth that will increase consumer purchasing power across-the-board as well as set an example of technological innovations complementing low- and mid-skilled workers, thus putting downward pressure on income inequality. The pessimistic view is that, to the degree the on-demand economy prospers because of regulatory arbitrage, it will not increase productivity and could diminish social welfare. In this view, the firm that is able to circumvent regulations that correct for a negative externality in the marketplace (such as labor protection laws or safety regulations) will lead market transaction volume to a quantity that is higher and a quality that is lower than optimal. Moreover, dispersed employees will have a hard time organizing for higher wages, so low- and mid-skilled workers will be hurt, and certain features of the market could lead to high firm concentration. Regardless of which view prevails, or which aspects of both views, it remains important to balance innovative activities with appropriate protections for workers and consumers.

An important feature of on-demand economy platforms is the ratings and feedback mechanism that consumers use to rate providers,

Figure 5-iv
Chicago Taxi Medallion Transactions, 2011–2015

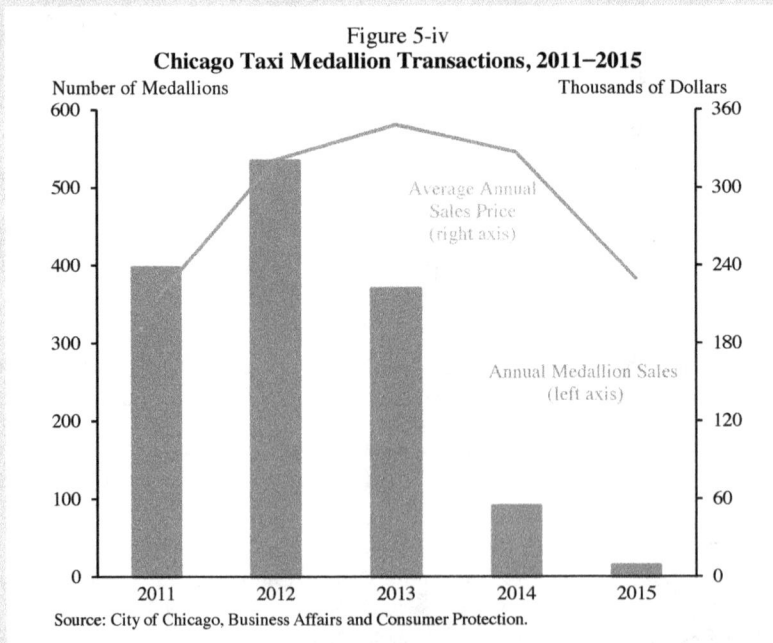

Source: City of Chicago, Business Affairs and Consumer Protection.

and that providers use to rate consumers. Without these feedback mechanisms, it would be very difficult for platform users to assess safety and propensity for fraud, which are often governed by regulations in traditional businesses that do not always extend to on-demand economy firms. Ratings and feedback mechanisms do very little, however, to promote basic labor standards for people performing the work, another important purpose of regulation. These ratings mechanisms and other user information collected by on-demand economy platforms also pose privacy concerns that are not yet fully understood.

As of 2014, slightly more than three-quarters of American households had adopted Internet in the home.[11] Non-adopters cite cost, availability in their communities, and perceived relevance as reasons to forego a broadband subscription.[12] There is substantial variation in broadband access across income groups. One way to visualize the digital divide is to consider the relationship between Internet use and household income across different areas of the entire United States. In Figure 5-17, each dot represents a single Public Use Microdata Area, or PUMA, all of which are constructed by the Census Bureau so that they contain roughly 100,000 residents.[13] The graph displays the share of residents in each PUMA who report using Internet in the home against median household income for that PUMA.[14]

Figure 5-17 shows a strong positive relationship between home Internet adoption and median income (Council of Economic Advisers 2015b). The wealthiest PUMAs tend to have home Internet adoption rates in excess of 80 percent, while the least well off PUMAs have adoption rates of 50 percent or below. Admittedly, higher income might lead to more Internet use, or vice versa, or there may be a third variable, such as education, that

[11] These data come from Census' 2014 American Community Survey. The relevant question is worded such that the respondent is not asked to differentiate between wireline as opposed to wireless access. Exact question text appears below in footnote 14.

[12] Data on the reasons for non-adoption are from the Current Population Survey, as tabulated by NTIA in its "Digital Nation" reports series.

[13] PUMAs are geographic areas defined for statistical use. PUMAs are built using census tracts and counties, nest within States, contain roughly 100,000 residents, and cover the entire United States. For more information on Figure 5-17, as well as other statistics on the digital divide, please see CEA's 2015 issue brief "Mapping the Digital Divide", available at: https://www. whitehouse.gov/sites/default/files/wh_digital_divide_issue_brief.pdf

[14] The specific question used to calculate the share of households using the Internet was the following, "At this house, apartment, or mobile home—do you or any member of this household access the Internet?" Thus, CEA does not include householders that only access the Internet at a public location, such as a school or library, in our measure of Internet adoption. Following the convention that Census uses in its public reports on computer and internet use, group quarters are excluded from these estimates, and a household is only counted as having internet access if it reports having a subscription.

Figure 5-17
Household Income and Home Internet Use, 2014
Percent of Households Using Internet by Public Use Microdata Area

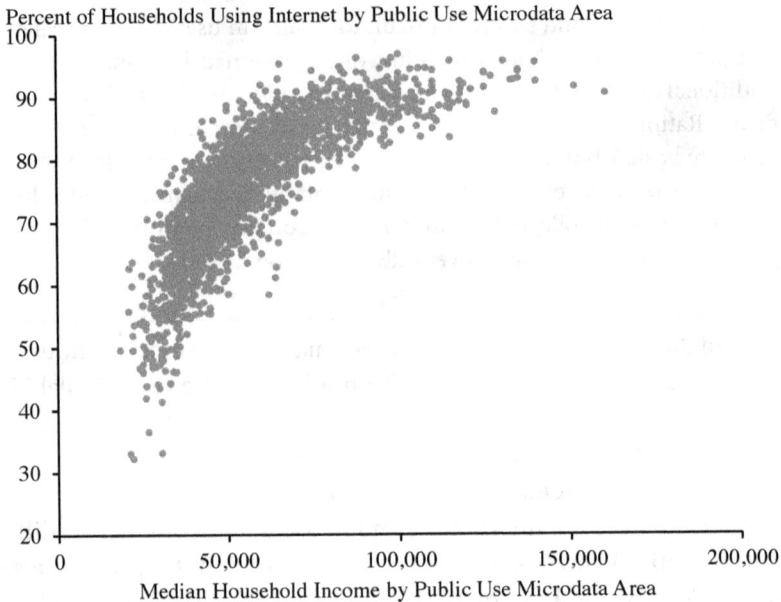

Median Household Income by Public Use Microdata Area
Source: Census Bureau, American Community Survey (2014); CEA calculations.

correlates with both outcomes. Keeping in mind these concerns about causal inference, a linear regression suggests that doubling a PUMA's median household income is associated with a 20.2 percentage-point increase in the expected rate of Internet adoption as of 2013 (Council of Economic Advisers 2015b).[15] Moreover, the fact that nearly all Americans live in communities where basic Internet service is available strongly suggests that income disparities play a dominant role in explaining this relationship. Thus, it does not appear to be the case that telecommunications firms are systematically choosing not to offer any form of Internet infrastructure in lower-income communities. It should be acknowledged, however, that the quality of Internet service available varies substantially, with more than one-half of the population lacking access to download speeds of 25 Mbps or greater as of 2013, often in rural or tribal areas (Council of Economic Advisers 2015b; Beede 2014).

Closing this digital divide will allow more Americans to access the opportunities afforded by the Internet, such as online job search and better educational opportunities (Stevenson 2008; Fairlie 2004). For example,

---

[15] If home computer use is examined rather than home Internet use, the overall pattern is very similar (although average computer adoption rates are higher (most so for the poorest 20 percent of households), and regression estimates suggest that doubling median household income is associated with a 19.3 percentage-point increase in the probability of having a computer at home.

Kuhn and Mansour (2014) find that unemployed workers who search online for work are re-employed 25 percent faster than comparable workers who do not go online. More recent innovations, such as the on-demand economy platforms, require workers to be connected to the Internet, either via mobile or wireline, so as to sell their goods via a platform such as Etsy or Ebay, or to sell their labor services via Taskrabbit, Lyft, or Uber. Thus, reducing the digital divide not only enables more Americans to take advantage of Internet for educational, health and other needs, it also enables more Americans to access jobs and other employment opportunities.

To address these issues, the Administration has undertaken multiple initiatives to make sure that all Americans can benefit from new technologies, a topic that was covered in detail in Chapter 5 of the 2014 *Economic Report of the President*, and that has gained momentum in 2015. Since 2009, the public and private sectors have together invested more than $260 billion into new broadband infrastructure. Investments from the Federal Government alone have led to the deployment or upgrading of over 110,000 miles of network infrastructure. At the same time, 45 million additional Americans have adopted broadband. In January 2015, the President announced concrete steps that the Administration would take to ensure fast and reliable broadband is available to more Americans at the lowest possible cost. Chief among these efforts is the promotion of community-based broadband, which includes a call for State and local governments to roll back short-sighted regulations that restrict competition. In March 2015, President Obama signed an Executive Memorandum creating the Broadband Opportunity Council, an interagency group comprised of 25 Federal agencies and departments. The Council was tasked with promoting broadband deployment, adoption, and competition. On September 21, 2015, the White House released a report from the Council outlining steps that agencies will take to make additional funds available for broadband deployment, eliminate barriers and promote broadband adoption. Also in 2015, the Department of Commerce's NTIA announced its Broadband USA initiative focused on empowering communities to expand their broadband capacity by providing technical assistance. And in July 2015, the U.S. Department of Housing and Urban Development unveiled Connect Home, a new initiative involving communities, the private sector, and the Federal Government, designed to expand high speed broadband to more families across the country. The pilot program launched in 27 cities and one tribal nation and will initially reach over 275,000 low-income households, including 200,000 children. Finally, the President's ConnectEd initiative is on track to connect 99 percent of American students to high-speed broadband in their classrooms and libraries by 2018. Data show that the connectivity gap has been cut by about half since ConnectED was launched in 2013, with 20 million more students and 1.4 million more teachers now having access to fast broadband.[16]

Reducing the digital divide is critical: it ensures that all Americans can benefit from new technologies and innovations; that more Americans find jobs for which their skills are a good match; and that more Americans are able to start new businesses and reach a larger customer base. Reducing the digital divide therefore may be one way to address the long-term downward trend in business dynamism and worker mobility. These new businesses in turn compete with established firms, driving the cycle of competition and innovation that is so vital to productivity growth.

CONCLUSION

Productivity growth is important for all Americans because it can lead to higher wages and a higher standard of living. Technology and innovation are key ingredients for productivity growth. New technologies and innovations help firms to produce products and services more efficiently, and also lead to new products and services that are valued by consumers.

For these reasons, this Administration has made, and will continue to make, increasing American productivity and innovation a top priority. These initiatives take on a variety of forms, including patent reform efforts to guarantee that the fruits of innovation go to their rightful recipients. Additionally, spectrum policies have played a key role in promoting innovation, including spectrum sharing, the dedication of spectrum to foster safety and mobility in next generation vehicles, incentive auctions, which re-allocate spectrum to its highest economic value use, and the Administration's pledge in 2010 to make available up to 500 MHz of Federal and non-Federal spectrum over 10 years in order to enable licensed and unlicensed wireless broadband technologies. Finally, international trade agreements like TPP and T-TIP also promote the flow of ideas, increase access to markets, promote competition, and increase specialization in R&D. The Administration's entrepreneurship initiatives—such as "Startup in a Day"[17] —are designed to lower the barriers to starting and scaling a new company for all Americans. Aspects of the Administration's proposals for business tax reform would reduce the effective tax on manufacturing to no more than 25 percent, at the same time encouraging R&D and use of clean technologies. Similarly, Chapter 6 in this *Report* covers in more detail how the Administration's

---

[16] These data are available through Education Superhighway's 2015 State of the States report, available at http://stateofthestates.educationsuperhighway.org/

[17] For more information about Startup in a Day, go to: https://www.whitehouse.gov/blog/2015/08/04/startup-day-four-things-you-should-know

infrastructure priorities would make sure that the supportive environment for innovation is as complete as possible.

The Administration's latest *Strategy for American Innovation*, released in October 2015, details three key areas of investment that the government can pursue to ensure that the United States retains its innovative edge in the decades to come by: 1) continuing to invest in Federal R&D and other building blocks for future private sector scientific and technological breakthroughs; 2) advancing Federal efforts in national priority areas like precision medicine and advanced manufacturing; and 3) improving the Federal Government's capacities for innovation.

Promoting productivity and innovation in the aggregate, however, is not enough. Beyond closing the digital divide and improving education in STEM, other policies such as the Affordable Care Act (ACA), Earned Income Tax Credit (EITC), and raising the minimum wage all have a role to play as well. The ACA has the potential to allow prospective entrepreneurs the flexibility to pursue creative ideas and found their own businesses, since their health care insurance is no longer tied to their employment. The EITC helps insure that low-wage workers are rewarded for their work, boosting incomes of millions of American families, and allowing for more Americans to share in rising prosperity. A higher minimum wage helps workers to increase their share of the productivity growth. These and other policies pursued by this Administration help insure that America will continue to enjoy high productivity growth and that all Americans will share in the gains from this growth.

CHAPTER 6

THE ECONOMIC BENEFITS OF INVESTING IN U.S. INFRASTRUCTURE

Transportation infrastructure has been a key ingredient of economic growth in this country. Ships and ports originally enabled the economic development of the U.S. colonies by fostering the export of natural resources and commodities and the import of manufactured products. Canals and systems of dams and locks on major waterways first opened up the interior of the country to global trade. Railways enabled the rapid expansion to the West, providing an efficient and reliable cross-country option for moving passengers and goods. Combined with the development of automobiles and freight trucks, roads and highways—particularly the Interstate Highway System—became the backbone of inter- and intra-state transportation, offering households and businesses easily accessible and affordable transportation. Airplanes, especially in this modern era of globalization, have fostered the expansion of international trade, the spread of new technology, and the exchange of information, accounting for about a third of the value of U.S. exports (U.S. Department of Transportation 2015a).

In each of these cases, investments in infrastructure not only contributed to increases in economic output, but also transformed the country. The geographic and modal distribution of infrastructure more broadly affects where people live and work, how we move goods from production to consumers, and how much carbon we emit. This chapter explores key aspects of our Nation's infrastructure: its current quality; the potential benefits of infrastructure investment; why now is an opportune time to increase it; the mechanisms through which transportation is typically funded; and the Federal, State, and local roles that make all this possible.

ECONOMIC PRINCIPLES FOR INFRASTRUCTURE POLICY

Infrastructure is defined as fixed capital assets that are consumed jointly in various production processes that facilitate and support economic activity, with "core" infrastructure referring to roads and other transportation facilities, power generation facilities and distribution networks, and water and sewer systems. The services provided by infrastructure are an indispensable input to the productive capacity of an economy, applied in tandem with other key inputs such as labor, human capital, land, and natural resources. Firms combine the use of infrastructure with these other inputs to produce goods and services, while households employ infrastructure services in both the production of output and the consumption of leisure activities. Deficiencies in infrastructure have the potential to adversely affect economic output, employment, and overall quality of life. At various points in time, the country has recognized the need to substantially upgrade its public infrastructure to foment economic development, and has subsequently invested in new and expanded infrastructure.

The crucial role of infrastructure is well recognized in economic theory. Macroeconomics emphasizes the importance of infrastructure capital in fostering economic growth, while microeconomics notes the private and social benefits that infrastructure services can provide for consumers, businesses, and entire communities. Economic theory also highlights how, to achieve optimal levels of investment, some forms of infrastructure may require government involvement in their provision and financing because they exhibit many characteristics of what economics defines as "public goods." Pure public goods have two unique characteristics: non-excludability in supply and non-rivalry in consumption. Non-excludability in supply means that consumers cannot be prohibited from enjoying the benefits of the public good; once the public good has been provided, the entity providing it cannot exclude members of the general public from utilizing its services (usually for technological reasons), and thus cannot charge anyone for its use. Non-rivalry in consumption means that any one consumer's decision to use a good does not reduce the amount available for others. One cannot keep a ship from seeing a lighthouse once it is lit (non-excludable), and one ship seeing the lighthouse does not prevent others from seeing it (non-rival).

Since the services they provide are both non-excludable and non-rival (for example, lighthouses and street lights), many types of transportation infrastructure are classic examples of pure public goods. In other cases, infrastructure may be excludable (a bridge with limited access) or rival (overcrowded roads or bridges). Furthermore, highway and transit infrastructure often have spillovers beyond their immediate users, providing benefits to a wide set of consumers and firms—thus making it difficult to identify who, and how much, to charge for those services. Other types of infrastructure also have positive spillovers that are difficult to monetize, such as public health benefits arising from improved clean water systems. As a result, individual entities, both public and private, may overlook projects that are not profitable for them, but nevertheless provide a net benefit for society as a whole. Moreover, some types of infrastructure may be characterized by economies of scale; as such, only one firm can profitably provide the service while competition with other firms would be inefficient. As a result, the private sector may lack the proper incentives to invest in such capital or may not provide the amount that is socially desirable, leading to market failure. These issues suggest that the government has a role to play in efficiently supplying and maintaining transportation infrastructure, especially when it spans across geographic borders.

Role of Government

The appropriate roles for different levels of government in planning and funding infrastructure investments may vary. Historically, Federal investments in infrastructure have been directed toward the formation of new capital while State and local investments have been geared toward the operation and maintenance of current infrastructure. There is a clear role for Federal funding and financing for projects that benefit the country as a whole. Still, many other arguments exist for a broader Federal role, including policy goals such as equity, safety, and enhanced access for all citizens, as well as safeguarding the environment. The Nation recently took a first step toward a sustained increase in Federal funding for infrastructure when the President signed into law the Fixing America's Surface Transportation (FAST) Act of 2015, the first law enacted in more than 10 years that provides guaranteed long-term funding for surface transportation. The FAST Act and its impact on public infrastructure spending are discussed in detail later in this chapter.

Private investment can also play an important role in the provision of infrastructure through, for example, the formation of public-private partnerships (PPPs), in which the government contracts out multiple stages in the development process for new infrastructure to single private actors. Through these partnerships, the private sector could be responsible for some, if not all, of the stages in the life cycle of an infrastructure asset: design, construction, financing, operation, and maintenance. Government involvement in PPPs and the potential benefits and drawbacks associated with these partnerships are discussed later in the chapter. In any case, the potential to attract private investment in specific circumstances does not diminish the importance of a strong Federal role in planning and funding critical public infrastructure.

The State of U.S. Infrastructure

Current Investment Levels

Over the past half-century, public spending on water and transportation infrastructure as a share of gross domestic product (GDP) has trended slightly downward, as shown in Figure 6-1. Federal, State, and local government spending on water and transportation infrastructure accounted for 2.42 percent of GDP in 2014, 0.6 percentage point below its peak share of GDP in 1959 and somewhat above the smallest annual share of GDP at 2.35 percent in 1998. Most of the public spending can be attributed to State and local governments, which have accounted for, on average, about 72 percent of public spending on water and transportation infrastructure since 1956.

The composition of public spending on water and transportation infrastructure is now measurably different than it was in the late-1950s. Mass transit and rail have acquired a markedly larger share of public infrastructure funds. On average, from 1956 to 1960, streets and highways accounted for just over 62 percent of public spending on water and transportation infrastructure, while mass transit and rail accounted for only about 5 percent. By the early 1980s, the former had fallen to just under 43 percent while the latter had risen to over 15 percent. Since then, the distribution of public funds on water and transportation infrastructure has been relatively unchanged: streets and highways (42 percent); water transportation, resources, and utilities (35 percent); mass transit and rail (14 percent); and aviation (9 percent).

In the United States, public gross investment in new capital formation as a share of GDP, which includes core infrastructure as well as other types of capital such as equipment, intellectual property products, and Federal defense spending, has been declining over the past half-century. Public gross fixed investment is emphasized, as opposed to a more narrowly defined, infrastructure-specific category, because it allows for a comprehensive comparison of public investment across most of the G-7 for the past 35 years. As shown in Figure 6-2, this downward trend in new capital investment is not unique to the United States. Other members of the G-7—including Japan, France, and Germany—have experienced similar declines in their respective shares of GDP accounted for by public investment in new capital in recent decades. From 2011 through 2015, U.S. public capital investment as a share of GDP averaged 3.7 percent, its lowest trailing five-year average since 1950.

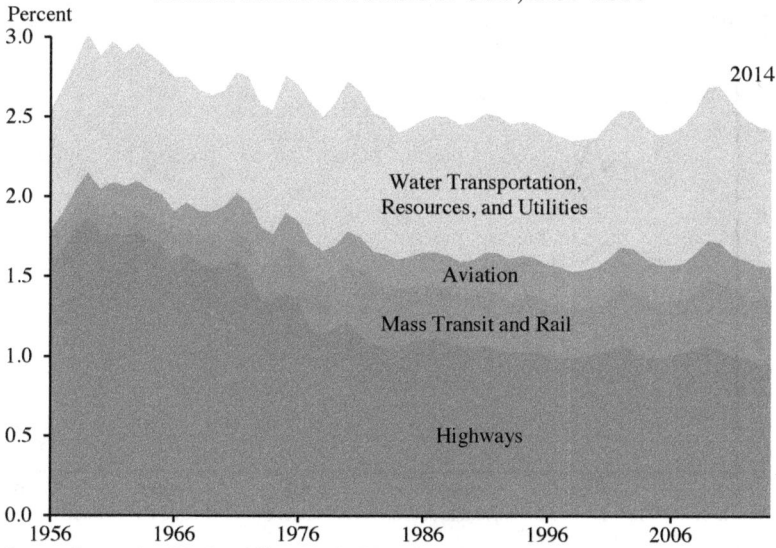

Figure 6-1
Composition of Public Spending on Water and Transportation Infrastructure as a Share of GDP, 1956–2014

Percent

2014

Water Transportation, Resources, and Utilities

Aviation

Mass Transit and Rail

Highways

Source: Congressional Budget Office (2015); CEA calculations.

Transportation Infrastructure Quality

The aging of U.S. transportation infrastructure has been widely recognized. The Urban Land Institute (2011) noted that road systems and water-treatment plants built with Federal grants over 40 to 50 years ago are now reaching the end of their life cycles. According to the Bureau of Economic Analysis (BEA), the average age of the net stock for different public core infrastructure assets has steadily increased over the past half-century, as shown in Figure 6-3.[1] In 2014, the average age of public streets and highways, water supply facilities, sewer systems, power facilities, and transportation assets reached historic highs. Though this result is not that surprising—given that in-place capital is constantly aging—what is striking is the rapidity with which their average ages have risen of late. From 2010 to 2014, the average age of streets and highways increased 3.2 years, the greatest four-year change on record and more than the 2.9-year increase over the two decades prior. Water supply facilities aged on average 1.2 years from 2010 to 2014, above the 0.7-year increase over the 20 years prior. Public sewer systems and power facilities aged slightly less from 2010 to 2014 than they

---

[1] The average age is calculated as the weighted average of the ages of all depreciated investment in the stock at the end of the year, with the weight for each age based on its value in the total net stock. Consequently, an asset with a net stock consisting of a high proportion of older investment will have a high average age. Average ages are based on current, or inflation-adjusted, asset costs.

Figure 6-2
**Public Gross Fixed Investment
as a Share of GDP for G-7 Countries, 1981–2015**

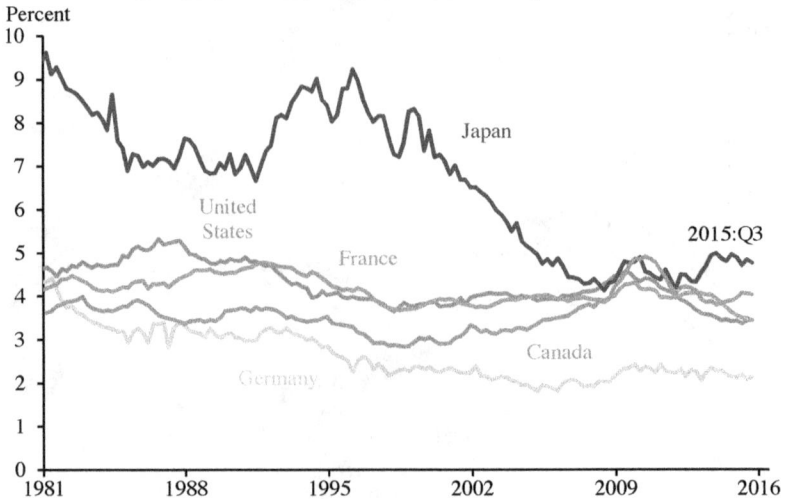

Note: Italy is excluded because comparable data are unavailable. United Kingdom is excluded because data are unavailable prior to 1997.
Source: National Sources via Haver Analytics.

did over the previous decade. And the average age of public transit assets increased nearly 20 percent over the decade ended 2014.

The declining quality of U.S. transportation infrastructure is also seen in global measures. The World Economic Forum releases annual ratings that gauge the quality of infrastructure throughout the world, and its ratings for the United States are displayed in Figure 6-4. These ratings are determined on a 1-7 scale, with a higher score indicating a better quality level. In 2015, the United States received a rating of 5.8 for its overall infrastructure, which was above the 5.4-average rating across the world's advanced economies, the 3.8-average across emerging and developing Asian nations, and the 4.1 global average. However, the overall U.S. rating for infrastructure in 2015 was noticeably below its level in the mid-2000s, falling nearly 8 percent since 2006. In comparison, the overall infrastructure rating for the world's advanced economies increased about 2 percent over the same period. Ratings for U.S. air transportation, ports, and roads are also lower today than they were in the mid-2000s. Ratings for railroads have been historically well below that of all U.S. infrastructure and of other transportation categories. Although some recent improvements have been observed, the quality of both U.S. infrastructure overall and various transportation subcategories remain either substandard or low relative to historical levels.

This trend of declining infrastructure quality is not uncommon among the G-7 countries, as seen in Table 6-1. The quality of overall

Figure 6-3
Average Age of Public Structures, 1956–2014

Age, Years

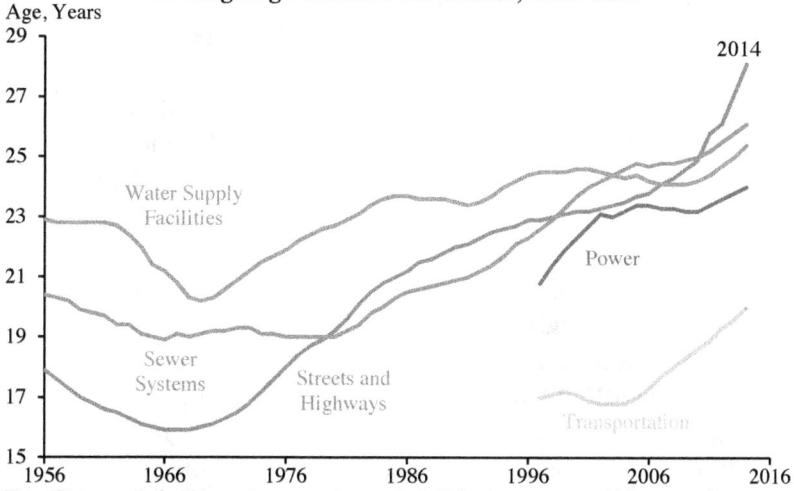

Note: Water supply facilities and sewer systems exclude Federal structures—which account for at most 6 percent of the value of their combined capital stock—because disaggregated Federal data are unavailable. Data for power and transportation fixed assets begin in 1997 because disaggregated data are unavailable for years prior to 1997.
Source: Bureau of Economic Analysis.

Figure 6-4
Quality of U.S. Infrastructure, 2006–2015

Rating

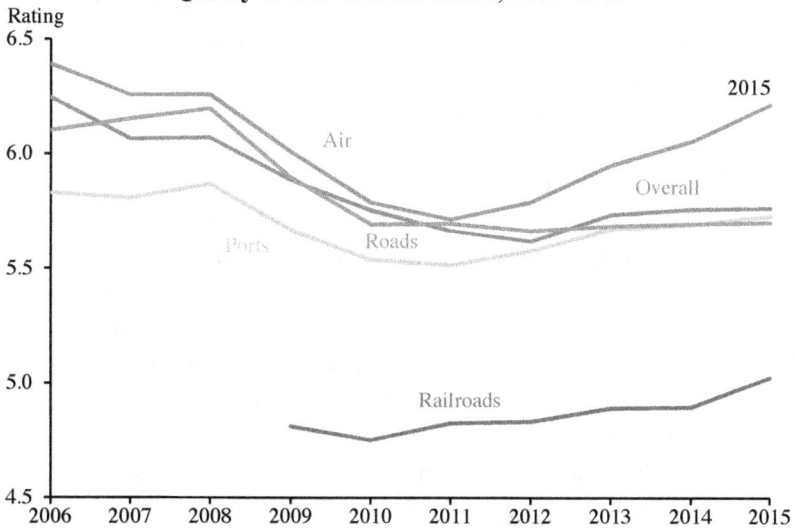

Note: Scale of 1-7, with a higher score indicating better infrastructure quality. Rating for railroads is first available in 2009.
Source: World Economic Forum, Global Competitiveness Report Survey.

infrastructure in 2015 for G-7 nations, with the exception of Japan and Italy, was lower than it was in the mid-2000s, declines comparable in magnitude to that observed in the United States. In regards to specific transportation infrastructure, the United States' performance in 2015 relative to the rest of the G-7 was mixed: The United States had the highest rating for air transportation and, along with the United Kingdom, ranked highest for ports, but ranked behind France and Japan for roads and was below the G-7 average for railroads.

Many U.S. roadways and bridges, in particular, are in poor condition. According to the International Roughness Index—a measure of the condition of road and highway surfaces—nearly 21 percent of U.S. roadways provided a substandard ride quality in 2013, the largest share from 1999 to 2013 (U.S. DOT 2015c).[2] In 2014, the number of bridges that were rated as structurally deficient was just above 61,000, while the number that were rated as functionally obsolete, or inadequate for performing the tasks for which the structures were originally designed, was slightly below 85,000 (DOT 2015d). The number of structurally deficient bridges has declined on average 2.7 percent a year since 2000, below the 4.2-percent average annual rate of decline throughout the 1990s. The number of functionally obsolete bridges has also declined steadily since 2000, falling on average about 0.5 percent a year. Combined, these two groups accounted for just below 24 percent of all bridges in 2014, the smallest annual percentage on record.

More investment is needed to resolve these deficiencies. The U.S. Federal Highway Administration estimates that noticeably improving roadway conditions and performance—rather than allowing congestion to increase further and pavement conditions to worsen—would require a capital investment in roads across all levels of government of $124 to $146 billion annually, with larger estimates corresponding to higher forecasts for the rate of growth in motor vehicle travel (DOT 2013). A growing population and economy will only serve to exacerbate these deficiencies. As the number of users who depend on transportation infrastructure increases, so too will the stress that is placed on these structures—leading to augmented congestion and necessary maintenance. Under higher expected growth rates for motor vehicle travel, roughly half (54 percent) of the aforementioned investment would be used for improving the physical conditions of current road infrastructure. The timeliness of such investment and the mechanisms through which it could occur are explored later in this chapter.

---

[2] A substandard quality of ride is defined as having an International Roughness Index value greater than 170. Data for 2010 and comparable data prior to 1999 are unavailable.

Table 6-1

Quality of Infrastructure in G-7 Member Countries

Type	CAN	FRA	DEU	ITA	JPN	GBR	USA	G-7 Average
2006								
Overall	6.0	6.5	6.6	3.7	6.1	5.6	6.2	5.8
2015								
Overall	5.4	5.9	5.9	4.1	6.2	5.3	5.8	5.5
Air	5.8	5.8	6.0	4.5	5.6	5.8	6.2	5.7
Ports	5.5	5.3	5.6	4.3	5.4	5.7	5.7	5.4
Roads	5.2	6.1	5.7	4.4	6.0	5.2	5.7	5.5
Railroads	4.7	5.8	5.6	4.0	6.7	4.8	5.0	5.2

Note: Scale of 1-7, with a higher score indicating better infrastructure quality.
Source: World Economic Forum, Global Competitiveness Report Survey.

Congestion

Individuals experience the costs of insufficient road and bridge infrastructure capacity partly through increased congestion, which will continue to rise as the number of cars driving on roads increases. Table 6-2 characterizes the evolution of U.S. roadway congestion over the past three decades. Commuter delays translate into economic costs through lost time that could be spent at work or consuming leisure activities, as well as through wasted fuel consumed by vehicles in congested traffic. In 1990, the average commuter was delayed a total of 26 hours over the course of the year, leading to an aggregate delay of 3 billion hours for all travelers collectively, a waste of 1.2 billion gallons of fuel, and an estimated total cost of $65 billion. Since then, a near 62-percent increase in the average commuter's annual delay, coupled with an estimated 42-percent rise in the total amount of commuters, has led to aggregate hours delayed, fuel wasted, and total cost more than doubling from their 1990 levels. Through the rest of the decade, these congestion measures are expected to continue increasing.

Higher levels of congestion also lead to increased carbon dioxide emissions: Congestion mitigation strategies that smooth traffic flows could reduce carbon dioxide emissions by about 7 to 12 percent based on typical conditions on Southern California freeways (Barth and Boriboonsomsin 2008). Clean energy transportation investments, discussed in Box 6-1, can lessen the impact congestion has on the environment. Increased congestion has also been associated with reduced employment growth: a 10-percent increase in congestion for a city with relatively high congestion levels could reduce long-run employment growth by as much as 4 percent (Hymel 2009). Investing in infrastructure will help alleviate congestion both in the short

Table 6-2
Measures of U.S. Traffic Congestion

Year	Delay per Commuter (Hours)	Total Delay (Billion Hours)	Fuel Wasted (Billion Gallons)	Total Cost (Billions of 2014 Dollars)
1982	18	1.8	0.5	42
1990	26	3.0	1.2	65
2000	37	5.2	2.1	114
2010	40	6.4	2.5	149
2014	42	6.9	3.1	160
2020[1]	47	8.3	3.8	192

[1] Forecast obtained from source assumes that pre-recession population growth and congestion trends will persist in the near-future.
Source: Schrank et al. (2015).

run, by providing increased road capacity and easing bottlenecks to allow more fluid transportation, as well as in the long run, by providing enhanced travel options that can help divert traffic away from frequently congested roadways and bridges.

More time spent commuting can also produce individual behavioral and socioeconomic costs. Transportation congestion induces more stressful commutes, which Navaco and Gonzalez (2011) note has been shown to be associated with "negative mood on arrival at work, negative mood at home in the evening, lowered frustration tolerance, cognitive performance impairments, illness, work absences, job instability, lowered residential satisfaction, and lowered overall life satisfaction." Thus, elevated stress from worsening commuting conditions may put downward pressure on workplace productivity as well as overall worker sentiment. Moreover, increased time spent commuting implies that less time can be spent on health-related activities such as sleep and exercise. As Christian (2012) notes, longer commutes are linked to "behavioral patterns which over time may contribute to obesity and other poor health outcomes."

BENEFITS OF INVESTING IN INFRASTRUCTURE

This section discusses the role of infrastructure in the economy, highlighting the channels through which infrastructure investment can spur overall economic activity in both the short and long run. In the near term, this boost occurs through the demand-side of the economy. Because investing in infrastructure requires raw materials, manufactured goods, and extensive labor, it stimulates economic activity among firms in the supply chain and in households with members searching for employment. In the

Box 6-1: Clean Energy and Transportation Infrastructure

Infrastructure investments can have wide-ranging impacts on patterns of development in a city, the number of cars accessing certain areas, and ultimately environmental outcomes. A sound infrastructure plan takes into account environmental impacts and can help achieve both development and climate improvement goals. Such a plan can accommodate economic growth, encourage new, greener fuels in transportation networks, support public transit, encourage more thoughtful land-use planning, and reduce congestion and pollution from idling. When deciding on a new infrastructure proposal, it is important for Federal, State, and local governments to consider the overall social impact that the proposal will have. This includes not just the financial costs incurred and potential revenues raised, but also indirect benefits such as improved environmental conditions, better health from reduced air pollution, and decreased city congestion—all of which can be more difficult to monetize.

Public transit can often provide an effective way to achieve transportation goals while safeguarding the environment, and recent innovations in green transit have served to amplify these benefits. Finishing a process that began in 1995, Los Angeles County Metropolitan Transportation Authority became the first major U.S. transit agency to replace all diesel buses in its extensive Metro fleet with newer versions that operate instead on clean, alternative energy (Weikel 2011). The transition is estimated to have reduced the emission of greenhouse gases by roughly 300,000 pounds a day, and cancer-causing particulates from the city's buses by 80 percent. Also in California, an 800-mile high-speed rail system—the Nation's first—is in the process of being built and expected to begin operation in 2029 (California High-Speed Rail Authority 2015). By 2040, the new rail system is predicted to decrease the total distance vehicles travel each day by almost 10 million miles and reduce the number of daily flights by roughly 100 or more. This immense project will be funded partly by a state voter-approved $9.95 billion bond measure, and partly by funds made available through the Federal Government.

The push toward clean automobile fuel is also well underway. The American Recovery and Reinvestment Act of 2009 dedicated $17.7 billion to energy-efficient transportation: implementing tax credits for businesses that installed alternative fuel pumps, funding the development of advanced vehicle batteries, and subsidizing the reduction of diesel emissions (National Resources Defense Council 2009). These investments helped to catalyze and accelerate the development of clean energy technologies that have begun to have broad impacts on energy industries. Higher fuel efficiency standards have also pushed auto manu-

facturers toward cleaner low-emissions vehicles. In 2015, through the
Biofuel Infrastructure Partnership, the Federal Government agreed to
match funds provided by states and private partners for pumps that supply renewable fuels to motorists (U.S. Department of Agriculture 2015).
More than 20 states have enrolled in the program, applying for over $130
million of funding—$30 million more than anticipated.

Transportation infrastructure investment can help address congestion and the subsequent pollution it produces. For example, the
Congestion Mitigation and Air Quality Improvement Program provides
funding to State and local governments for projects that will help meet
requirements set by the Clean Air Act. Projects eligible for financing
through this program include ones aimed toward expanding accessibility to public transit, reducing harmful emissions, and ameliorating
traffic congestion. Included in the President's fiscal year 2017 budget
is an initiative to increase Federal funding toward clean transportation
infrastructure, a proposal that is discussed in detail in Box 6-4.

medium and long term, benefits materialize primarily on the supply-side.
Higher-capacity and better-performing infrastructure supports faster, more
reliable transport flows. As a result, households can increase their consumption through reduced travel costs and firms can exploit economies of scale
in their production processes and distribution networks. Investing in new
infrastructure also increases the flow of capital services that households
and firms can utilize to produce valuable commodities and services. These
longer-term supply improvements enable the economy to use private capital, labor, energy, and other inputs more productively, thereby augmenting
the economy's future potential growth.

Short-Term, Demand-Side Benefits

Slack in the economy refers to the underutilization of resources like
labor and capital. When slack exists in the economy, fiscal spending can help
alleviate that slack by augmenting its contribution to public works projects.
In the near term, public investment can reduce unemployment, provide
workers with disposable income, and spur economic activity through the
purchasing of inputs needed for implementing these projects (see Table 6-3).
Government spending has a multiplier effect, which is defined as the dollar
change in output caused by a $1 change in public spending. The multiplier
measures the effects of government spending on overall economic activity
rather than simply the impacts on businesses or households that directly
receive the spending.

Table 6-3

Input-Output Effects of Infrastructure Investment

Industry	Direct Multiplier	Indirect Multiplier on Manufacturing Industries	Indirect Multiplier on Non-Manufacturing Industries	Total Multiplier
Government Investment				
Federal nondefense	1.00	0.10	0.43	1.54
State and local	1.00	0.21	0.44	1.65
Passenger transit	1.00	0.88	1.30	3.19
Electric utilities	1.00	0.12	0.69	1.81
Nonresidential Investment				
Structures (excluding commercial and farm)	1.00	0.39	0.37	1.76
Maintenance and repair	1.01	0.42	0.47	1.89
Core Infrastructure Investment				
Highways and streets	1.00	0.48	0.52	2.00
Electric power generation, transmission, and distribution	1.01	0.18	0.61	1.80
Water, sewage, and other systems	1.00	0.12	0.48	1.60

Note: Multipliers represent the dollar value of output that is generated from investing $1 of input into the industry listed.
Source: Bureau of Economic Analysis, Benchmark Input-Output Accounts 2007; CEA calculations.

The short-run public investment multiplier for economic output has been well-documented. The International Monetary Fund (2014) finds, during times of low growth, a public spending multiplier of 1.5 in the same year as the investment and a slightly higher multiplier of 3 over the next four years. When a government has clearly identified infrastructure needs, an efficient investment process for identifying and directing funding toward those needs, and economic slack, then there is a strong case for increasing public investment in infrastructure. With nominal interest rates at or close to zero percent, the effects of increased government spending can be larger than they would be during normal circumstances when interest rates are higher. When the Central Bank's policy rate is set at zero—which it was from 2009 through 2015—Christiano, Eichenbaum, and Rebelo (2011) and Eggerston (2011) find stronger effects of increased public investment, producing short-run multipliers that range between 2 and 2.5. Because of its labor-intensive nature, spending on transportation is associated with even larger boosts to economic output than other government spending, with a short-run multiplier of about 2.7 (Leduc and Wilson 2014). In addition, to the degree that sustained losses in economic output lead discouraged workers to drop out of the labor force for prolonged periods and make them reluctant to return, alleviating these output losses in the short run can help to increase long-run output. When there is less slack in the economy, or when the Central Bank might tighten monetary policy in response to fiscal spending, fiscal multipliers are much lower (Auerbach and Gorodnichenko 2012).

As shown in Table 6-3, these short-run multipliers are in line with those calculated using the Benchmark Input-Output Accounts from 2007 released by the BEA.[3] The input-output calculations highlight the indirect effects that increased spending in a given industry can have on the rest of the economy. Each additional dollar spent toward infrastructure—whether it is through the Federal or State and local governments; used for highways and streets, electricity, or water and sewage; or devoted to the formation of new capital or the maintenance of current infrastructure—has a multiplier notably larger than 1. The largest multiplier stems from State and local government spending on passenger transit at 3.19, indicating that such an investment leads to more than triple its value in economic output. The indirect multipliers from investing in infrastructure can be especially large for the manufacturing sector (for example, 0.88 for State and local government investment in passenger transit and 0.48 for highways and streets more generally). Positive impacts on the manufacturing sector likely result because constructing, operating, and maintaining public infrastructure relies heavily on manufactured goods. There are also substantial spillovers to non-manufacturing industries, which, being the largest part of the economy, are affected by a general increase in economic activity.

Even as labor markets normalize, increased infrastructure investment would provide, at the very least, short-run boosts to output and jobs. CEA (2014) finds that 68 percent of the jobs created from infrastructure investment would stem from construction. According to the Quarterly Census of Employment and Wages, the average weekly wage for private construction employment in 2014 was $1,058, 7-percent higher than the private-sector average. Thus, most of the employment generated from investing in infrastructure would be well-paying, middle-class jobs. Although the boosts to output and employment are larger when the increase in public spending occurs during a period of greater economic slack, there is still a benefit to increasing government spending on infrastructure today. Beyond the short-term boosts to demand for labor and other resources, however,

---

[3] Data from 2007—as opposed to data from a more recent year—are used because 2007 is the latest year for which the BEA released a more comprehensive breakdown of the industry-by-industry input-output data, providing the cross-section between 389 industries and allowing for the analysis of more disaggregated investment categories such as those displayed in Table 6-3.

infrastructure investment is crucial for supporting long-term growth by providing the necessary supply-side inputs.

Long-Term, Supply-Side Benefits

Well-targeted infrastructure investments increase the economy's long-run growth potential. Macroeconomists have closely examined the link between infrastructure investment and economic development, finding that infrastructure boosts productivity and offers large socioeconomic gains. Public investment in infrastructure propels future productivity growth through several channels: enabling firms to take advantage of economies of scale and increase production through reduced input costs; lowering transport, storage and vehicle maintenance costs for households and firms by easing congestion and improving the quality of roads and highways; increasing the productivity of private capital through improved resource utilization; and increasing workers' access to labor market opportunities, thus facilitating more efficient hiring matches. These effects are especially relevant today as the United States continues to experience lagging productivity growth (see discussion in Chapter 2 and Figure 2-30).

Increasing public infrastructure investment supports growth in labor productivity by augmenting growth in total factor productivity and by increasing the capital intensity of production throughout the economy. Boosting the capital intensity of production occurs both directly, by increasing the accumulated stock of public capital, and indirectly because a larger stock of public infrastructure fosters increased private capital investment. By increasing private-sector output and improving the productivity of private capital, infrastructure spending can induce greater private spending by increasing the returns to investment on private capital.[4] Larger stocks of public capital, and the flow of services they generate, raise the marginal productivity of other inputs to production, including private capital and labor. Because more efficient input use leads to lower costs of production, businesses will expand their production capacity to take advantage of these cost reductions. Through this mechanism, increasing the stock of public capital investment can effectively augment the level of private investment.

Some research found that increasing aggregate public investment by $1 can increase long-term private investment by $0.64 (Pereira 2001). However, this effect was found to vary noticeably among different types of infrastructure: Pereira (2001) estimated that publicly investing $1 in electric and gas facilities, transit systems, and airfields induces a $2.38 rise in long-term private investment, whereas an additional $1 of public investment in

---

[4] See Nadiri and Mamuneas (1996) for an analysis of this mechanism through the highway capital stock.

highways and streets increases private capital investment by only $0.11. Although the effects are more muted for some types of infrastructure, public investment in each amplifies private investment in the long-term. By enticing greater long-run private capital investment, increased public spending spurs capital deepening and, in turn, raises future productivity and thus long-run potential economic growth.

Many studies have assessed the productivity effects of public capital investment for the United States, Organization for Economic Co-operation and Development member nations, and developing countries. The variability and potential biases associated with these estimates are discussed in Box 6-2. A literature review of economic analyses from 1983 to 2008 suggests that on average, a 1-percent increase in public capital leads to a 0.11-percent rise in output (Bom and Ligthart 2014). In 2014, the stock of physical public capital relative to GDP was about 76 percent. Given this elasticity estimate and the size of the public capital stock, the marginal product of public capital is about 14 percent. Thus, given the deficiency in infrastructure described above, a $1 increase in the total value of the public capital stock would raise annual economic output by about $0.14.

Infrastructure's Direct Boost to Productivity

Beyond the ways in which infrastructure boosts economic activity and productivity through spillovers, it also raises productivity directly by increasing capital services used by industry. For example, publically funded highways and airports provide capital services through the transportation of goods that are sold in the private sector. Real capital services from the public capital stock are a flow that is calculated as the sum of the real interest payments on and the depreciation of the capital stock. This definition roughly parallels that used in the calculation of the contribution of private capital to labor productivity growth. A business or government purchases a structure or piece of equipment when the expected present value of the future flow of services from that structure or equipment meets or exceeds the original price. As the capital stock is used and ages, it loses its value (depreciation) in rough proportion to the services that it renders. Interest payments on the funds borrowed to finance the purchase should be added to this flow.

The growth rate of public capital services per private-sector employee-hour and its contribution to nonfarm productivity growth are shown in Table 6-4. Growth of capital services per hour fell from an annual rate of growth of 2.6 percent during the 1947-to-1973 period to only 0.7 percent a year during the 1973-to-1995 period. To derive the direct contribution to nonfarm productivity growth, the growth of public capital services is

Box 6-2: Elasticity of Output to Public Capital

Attempts to gauge the contribution of the public capital stock to economic output have focused on calculating the *output elasticity of public capital,* or the percent change in output that results from a 1-percent increase in public capital.[1] Aschauer (1989) was among the first to estimate the magnitude of this effect for the United States, finding an output elasticity of public capital of 0.39—implying that U.S. public capital investment has been an important factor in influencing historical growth in U.S. economic output. Since that time, an abundance of research has been devoted to gauging the elasticity of a nation's output to its public capital stock, though no consensus has surfaced, as shown in Figure 6-i. While most of the estimates summarized in the Figure cluster near 0.1, they have ranged from as low as -0.14 to as high as 1.14. The following discussion explores the reasons for the wide disparity in the estimates summarized in Figure 6-i.

One reason for the wide variation is that empirical estimates may vary depending upon the time horizon over which the output elasticity is calculated. Looking over the near term is likely to produce lower output

Figure 6-i
Distribution of the Output Elasticity of Public Capital

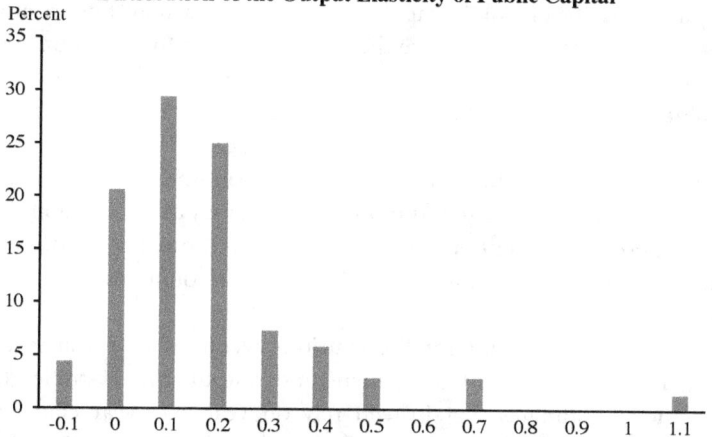

Note: Values on the horizontal axis represent medians of 0.1 percentage point bins. The mean output elasticity of public capital is used from 68 unique papers. Each analysis included incorporates a production function approach that results in a single output elasticity and assesses the capital stock using some measure of public output.
Source: Bom and Ligthart (2014); CEA calculations.

[1] This calculation is different than the spending multipliers mentioned earlier. These measures look at annual changes in economic activity, including the infrastructure spending itself, relative to spending in a given year. The output elasticity of public capital considers the impact from the public capital stock on other economic activity.

elasticities since short-run analyses ignore the long-term nature of public capital's effects on private investment, productivity, and economic growth. New infrastructure may not only take years to complete, but may require years before its productivity boost to society is realized. When evaluated over the long run, the output elasticity of public capital has been found to be on average nearly 0.04 percentage point higher than those calculated over the near term (Melo, Graham, and Brage-Ardao 2013; Bom and Ligthart 2014).

Second, the level of aggregation at which the analysis is conducted can heavily influence the output elasticity calculated. Given its far-reaching nature, the formation of new public capital can augment production capacity, not only in the areas in which structures are built, but in neighboring economies as well. Consequently, analyses that focus on regional data will inherently overlook spillover effects into nearby areas, whereas those that use national data will naturally internalize these effects in their empirical estimates. Not accounting for these spillover impacts can put sizable downward pressure on output elasticity estimates, resulting in values that are more than 0.15 percentage point less than their national-data counterparts (Bom and Ligthart 2014).

Third, analyses that use a production function estimated from historical data on investment and output may spuriously overstate the output elasticity of public capital. Some exercises may find relatively large output elasticities because they fail to account for common trends in the data. Given that time series for output and public capital tend to exhibit common stochastic trends, estimates produced from econometric analyses of their historical levels may produce artificially high results. Time-series analyses that fail to test for common time trends among the variables they employ often find output elasticities of public capital that are 0.1 percentage point on average higher than those that conduct such tests and employ estimation procedures that account for these trends (Bom and Ligthart 2014).

Fourth, to account for the spurious results that can arise from using historical levels of investment and output, many studies have constructed estimates that instead rely on year-over-year changes in these variables. Although this avoids the potential aforementioned bias from using the historical levels of data series, this approach is likely to understate the actual output elasticity, and can produce estimates that appear to be zero, though the true effect may be positive (Hurlin and Minea 2012). One problem with this method is that it assumes that the impact of public capital investment on output occurs instantaneously, rather than requiring a prolonged period for the effects to be felt. Because analyses that rely exclusively on year-over-year changes in investment and output ignore potential inter-temporal long-run relationships that may exist among these variables, their results may underestimate the impact that investments in public capital have on output.

Last, studies that try to measure an output elasticity of public capital may suffer from reverse causality (or endogeneity issues), meaning that changes in economic output influence infrastructure investment and the stock of public capital, rather than the reverse. For example, higher levels of output may increase the demand for public capital or support more favorable fiscal conditions for elevating government investment. In this case, the elasticity of output to public capital may be overstated since favorable business-cycle conditions are artificially strengthening this estimated relationship. Similarly, increasing public investment may be used as a countercyclical measure to spur economic activity when output is depressed. As a result, though the size of the public capital stock may increase, economic output may remain temporarily suppressed, leading to underestimates of the relevant output elasticities. Using econometric techniques that account for potential reverse causality typically lowers the estimated elasticity of output to public capital by about 0.05 percentage point (Bom and Ligthart 2014).

When incorporating the output elasticity of public capital in an economic analysis, it is important to note the time-horizon and the geographic scope of government that is being used. Although Bom and Ligthart (2014) find an average elasticity of output to public capital of about 0.11 percentage point—notably below that reported by Aschauer (1989)—they note that the elasticity of output is heterogeneous across these dimensions. As one illustration, they find that the long-run output elasticity for State and local government spending on core infrastructure is more than twice as large as the short-run output elasticity for Federal spending on total infrastructure.

weighted by its "share" in output.[5] The slowdown in capital services per hour played a small role in causing the post-1973 slowdown in labor productivity growth, with its contribution dropping 0.08 percentage point between the two periods (from 0.18 percentage point a year to 0.10 percentage point a year). Of course, the indirect effects of lower public investment could also have played an important role.

The growth rate of public capital services per employee-hour remained low at only 1.1 percent a year during the 1995-to-2007 period. The growth rate picked up to 2.1 percent a year during the 2007-to-2014 period, a

---

[5] Although public capital services are not included in the official definition of nonfarm output, the definition of nonfarm output has been rescaled so as to include the implicit contribution of public capital.

Table 6-4

Direct Contribution of the Public Capital Stock to Productivity Growth

Time Period	Annual Growth Rate of Capital Services[1]	Annual Growth Rate of Employee-hours	Annual Growth Rate of Public Capital Services per Employee-hour	Average Share of Output at Implicit User Cost[2]	Contribution to Productivity Growth (percentage points)	Annual Labor Productivity Growth in Nonfarm Business Sector
1947–1973	4.0%	1.4%	2.6%	6.0%	0.18	2.8%
1973–1995	2.3%	1.6%	0.7%	7.6%	0.10	1.4%
1995–2007	2.0%	1.0%	1.1%	5.8%	0.07	2.7%
2007–2014	1.9%	–0.2%	2.1%	7.3%	0.18	1.3%

[1] Public capital services equals the sum of real depreciation plus real interest payments on the value of the net real public capital stock.

[2] Public capital services as a share of nonfarm business output, where nonfarm business output has been elevated by the inclusion of public capital services in that output.

Source: Bureau of Economic Analysis; Bureau of Labor Statistics; Haver Analytics; CEA calculations.

pickup that is fully accounted for by a dramatic slowing of employee-hours growth (from 1.0 percent a year to –0.2 percent a year) rather than a pickup in capital services growth (which was about 2.0 percent a year in both the 1995-to-2007 and the 2007-to-2014 periods). Public capital services per employee-hour (which accelerated in the 2007-to-2014 period) does not account for the recent slowdown in productivity growth as it did during the slowdown from the 1947-to-1973 period to the 1973-to-1995 period. That said, faster growth of public capital might have boosted recent productivity growth if suitable capital projects could have been found. Additional public capital investment might also have supported aggregate demand if it was appropriately timed.

Infrastructure Investment and Agglomeration

As workers and firms gather in the same location, the costs of transporting goods and hiring employees decline, leading to lower production costs for firms. An advantageous location or access to natural resources initially attracts businesses and households to a site, and as the surrounding region develops, the costs of doing business there decline and the existence of a thriving business community attracts other firms and consumers. These cost advantages stem from the spatial concentration of firms and workers, and are called agglomeration economies. Investing in high-capacity transportation facilities (such as mass transit) often fosters such agglomeration effects by enabling less-dense areas to urbanize, improving access throughout an urbanized area and reducing the costs associated with transportation.

Thus, ideas are exchanged, workers with specific skills are available, and supply systems can flourish. The benefits of reduced travel costs and more free-flowing, universal access redouble throughout the region. Workers can find jobs that take full advantage of their specialized skills, enabling firms to operate more efficiently and thus spurring other firms and workers in the economy to produce more efficiently. As a result, agglomeration effects can accentuate the impact that infrastructure investment normally has on productivity growth.

Spillover Effects

While investing in infrastructure generates direct benefits in the form of increased employment and higher productivity—benefits that may be magnified through agglomeration effects—it can also offer spillover benefits for neighboring economies. Road and highway infrastructure in particular has led to marked spillover effects (see Box 6-3, which highlights the spill-over effects that stemmed from the formation of the Interstate Highway System). Output in the agricultural sector in particular has benefited through spatial spillovers from road investments. One study finds that a 1-percent increase in outlays on roads in a state is associated with a roughly 0.03-percent expansion in agricultural output in that state, and an average increase of 0.24 percent in adjacent states and their neighbors (Tong et al. 2013). The magnitude and structure of the spillover effects vary based on the location of the state and the paths available for the spillover effect. These effects are especially pronounced in the agriculturally concentrated central United States relative to less agriculturally intensive regions.

Improvements in airport infrastructure offer both direct and spillover gains, which can be geographically extensive because of the network nature of air service; that is, improving an airport in one location results in faster and more reliable connections with many other areas. Investments in air transportation can effectively reduce travel time and promote more reliable flights, enhancing worker productivity and shipping efficiency. Directly, a 10-percent increase in passenger enplanements in a metro area has been found to raise employment in service industries—which account for almost 84 percent of total private employment—by about 1 percent (Brueckner 2003). Indirectly, the expansion of airport infrastructure has been associated with cost savings in manufacturing production not only in states in which the airports are located, but in other states as well. A 1-percent increase in state airport infrastructure stock—defined as airport capital expenditures for construction, land, structure, and equipment—has been found to cor-respond to a decrease in manufacturing costs of about 0.1 percent within that state and between 0.1 and 0.2 percent within other states, with higher

Box 6-3: The Interstate Highway System

What has been called the "greatest public works project in history," the Interstate Highway System remains one of the largest investments in infrastructure by the U.S. Government (DOT 2015e). President Dwight D. Eisenhower recognized the social and economic importance of constructing a highway system in his 1956 State of the Union Address, highlighting that it was needed for "the personal safety, the general prosperity, the national security of the American people" (Public Broadcasting Service 1956). The 47,000-mile highway system, spanning all 48 contiguous states, was a project commissioned by the Federal Aid Highway Act of 1956.

The project pushed public spending on highways to historic highs in the late-1950s and throughout the 1960s. From 1956 to 1970, public spending on highways averaged about 1.7 percent of GDP and accounted for roughly 60 percent of public spending on water and transportation infrastructure (Congressional Budget Office 2015). Highways remain a major part of infrastructure investment. From 2000 to 2014, public spending on highways averaged just above 1 percent of GDP and represented about 41 percent of public spending on water and transportation infrastructure. From increased trade and job growth to more free-flowing and accessible transportation, the construction of the Interstate Highway System demonstrates the potential gains that large-scale infrastructure projects can offer and remains a powerful example of our past investment in infrastructure development.

When drivers switch from a traditional road to a wider, straighter interstate highway, travel costs are substantially reduced. Savings are estimated at $0.19 a mile for automobiles and $0.38 a mile for trucks, stemming from reduced travel time, accidents, and vehicle operating costs (Thompson and Chandra 1998). This effect, combined with decreased travel distance between cities, has been shown to have a positive impact on trade by, for example, allowing for the transportation of heavier goods (Duranton, Morrow, and Turner 2014). Rural counties that became connected by the Interstate Highway System experienced as much as a 10-percentage point increase in trade-related activities per capita (Michaels 2008). Moreover, a 1-percent increase in the highway capital stock per capita in a given northeast metropolitan area—measured using Federal, State, and local government expenditures on highways—was found to be associated with a 0.05-percent rise in annual economic output per capita both in that region and in its nearest neighbor (Chen and Haynes 2015). Beyond the gains from trade, investing in highways has been found to have boosted employment as well: a 10-percent increase in a metropolitan statistical area's stock of interstate highways (measured as kilometers of road) in 1983 resulted in 1.5 percent more employment for that area 20 years later (Duranton and Turner 2012).

From decreased travel costs and increased trade to higher employment and output, the economic effects of a national highway system are clear. The Interstate Highway System provides an interconnectedness that was not there before, a means by which individuals and goods could travel more fluidly throughout the contiguous United States. The effects from the Interstate Highway System were drastic at its implementation, and continue to be substantial today.

spillover effects stemming from states without large hubs (Cohen and Morrison Paul 2003).[6]

Both investment in new public capital and improved maintenance of existing infrastructure can produce spillover effects, again presumably due to the network nature of most transportation infrastructure, where expanding a single facility can improve connections among many origins and destinations. In fact, there is some evidence that the effects from State and local government investment in public capital can be larger for neighboring states than for the ones in which the investments are made. Evaluating annual state-level output and constructing weighted spillover indexes based on the commodity flows across states and the relative magnitudes of neighboring economies, Kalyvitis and Vella (2015) find that outlays for new capital as well as those for operation and maintenance have large positive effects on neighboring economies, calculating average spillover elasticities of output from new public capital and maintenance of 0.09 and 0.34, respectively. The relatively large spillover effects from public spending on operation and maintenance may result because states and localities primarily fund operation and maintenance; as such, only the states and localities that make the investments incur the associated costs, allowing other states to enjoy the benefits without paying for the investment. Yet these authors' estimates for direct output elasticities of public capital for states in which the investments are made are noticeably smaller at near-zero values. This divergence in magnitude between direct and spillover effects from public infrastructure spending on output is one reason why Federal support and trans-state organizations such as the Port Authority of New York and New Jersey are important.

A failure to recognize these spillover effects from the construction and improvement of transportation networks by State and local government

---

[6] A large hub refers to an airport that accounts for at least 1 percent of the country's enplanements of passengers.

agencies responsible for funding public infrastructure may cause those agencies to undervalue the true social gains that such projects offer.

Household Effects

New investments in public transportation infrastructure, especially in expanded transit service, also support more robust and mobile labor markets by reducing geographic mismatches between the skill demands of jobs and workers who can offer specialized skills, and by providing potentially faster and less-costly transportation options to connect workers with jobs. Public infrastructure can directly influence where people choose to live and work since access to public transit can play a crucial role in this decision-making process, especially for households who cannot afford or choose not to own cars. New public transit services can improve labor market efficiency by connecting individuals with jobs to which they may not previously have had access. Kawabata (2003) found that improved access to jobs through public transit noticeably increased the probability that low-skilled workers without automobiles in San Francisco and Los Angeles would be employed, and also increased the likelihood that such employment would be full-time. Another study found that more extensive metropolitan-area public transit infrastructure increases the employment density of central cities by 19 percent, and that a 10-percent rise in bus or rail service per capita increases metropolitan-area wages by, on average, $45 million annually (Chatman and Noland 2014).

Improving public infrastructure can also foster higher city and suburban property values. Possible channels through which this effect can occur include: positive urban employment and spending spillovers from suburban inflows; the positive impact that high-quality infrastructure has on the perception of a metropolitan area; and the spillover of productivity gains from city centers to their surrounding suburbs. Haughwout (1999) found that a $1 billion increase in spending on city infrastructure would raise city property values by $590 million and related suburban property values by $540 million. This result provides a rationale for potential Federal or State involvement in the provision of urban public infrastructure, particularly where large urban regions cross state borders, and where sharing of common administrative overhead across a multi-jurisdictional project leads to more cost-efficient project delivery than undertaking multiple separate projects.

PROSPECTS FOR INCREASED
INFRASTRUCTURE INVESTMENT

Low Interest Rates

Investment in America's infrastructure is arguably as important today as it has been at any point in recent history given its current state of deterioration. The financial environment faced by all levels of government provides even further justification. Yields on 20-year U.S. Treasury bonds as well as on State and local bonds are at near-historic lows, meaning that government agencies can borrow funds to finance long-term projects at costs as low as they have been over the past half-century, as shown in Figure 6-5. This is true even taking into account expected inflation rates. Long term real interest rates have moved decidedly lower in past decades (CEA 2015).

Given historically low borrowing costs and the potential upside boosts to short-run demand and long-run supply, investing in infrastructure would offer benefits that, according to Federal Reserve Vice Chairman Stanley Fischer (2015), "under current circumstances would outweigh the costs of its financing." Infrastructure investments promote current economic activity, augment the value of public capital stocks in the long run, and alleviate the burden on future generations of making needed infrastructure upgrades. During a period of low growth for an advanced economy, the large boost to

Figure 6-5
Government Bond Yields, 1965–2015

Note: The 20-year Treasury was discontinued on December 31, 1986 and restored on October 1, 1993. Data for the interim period are calculated as averages of the 10-year Treasury and 30-year Treasury constant maturity yields.
Source: Federal Reserve Board; Haver Analytics.

output in the near term from high-efficiency public investment can reduce the public-debt-to-GDP ratio (IMF 2014).

Maintenance and Repair

Infrastructure maintenance and repair can generate high returns on investment. Infrastructure depreciates over time, and does so more rapidly when it is used more intensively. Operation and maintenance expenditures allow infrastructure to function properly, deliver its promised benefits, and enable repair of structurally deficient assets. Neglecting proper maintenance and system preservation leads to deficient infrastructure conditions such as roads filled with potholes, traffic delays, power outages, and so on—which can impose sizable short-run costs on its users.

Investing in maintenance is a cost-effective technique for avoiding more expensive repairs in the future. One estimate is that every $1 spent on preventive pavement maintenance reduces future repair costs by $4 to $10 (Baladi et al. 2002). Transportation engineers have developed economic methods that determine the optimal timing for applying preventive maintenance treatments to flexible and rigid pavements by assessing the benefits and costs for each year the treatment could be applied (Peshkin, Hoerner, and Zimmerman 2004). Allowing the condition of transportation infrastructure to deteriorate exacerbates wear and tear on vehicles. Cars and trucks that drive more frequently on substandard roads will require tire changes or other repairs more often—estimated to cost each driver, on average, an additional $516 annually in vehicle maintenance (TRIP 2015). Delaying maintenance can also induce more accidents on transit systems. Not repaving a road, replacing a rail, reinforcing a bridge, or restoring a runway can result in increased vehicle crashes that can disrupt transportation flows and create substantial safety hazards.

The conceptual relationship between spending on maintenance versus new infrastructure and its impact on economic growth is depicted in Figure 6-6. The two are not perfect substitutes, as the latter adds directly to the stock of public capital while the former offsets depreciation on existing infrastructure (Kalaitzidakis and Kalyvitis 2005). Assuming that infrastructure investments are implemented efficiently, effectively, and optimally, then if spending on maintenance is too low relative to new capital investment or vice versa, economic output will grow at a rate below its potential.

To maximize economic growth from increased public investment in infrastructure, governments must properly balance the needs for new infrastructure with those for maintaining the infrastructure that is currently in place. The ratio of public spending on operation and maintenance to new capital for water and transportation infrastructure in the United States

Figure 6-6

**Relationship between Output Growth and the Ratio of Maintenance
Investment to New Infrastructure Investment**

Output Growth Rate

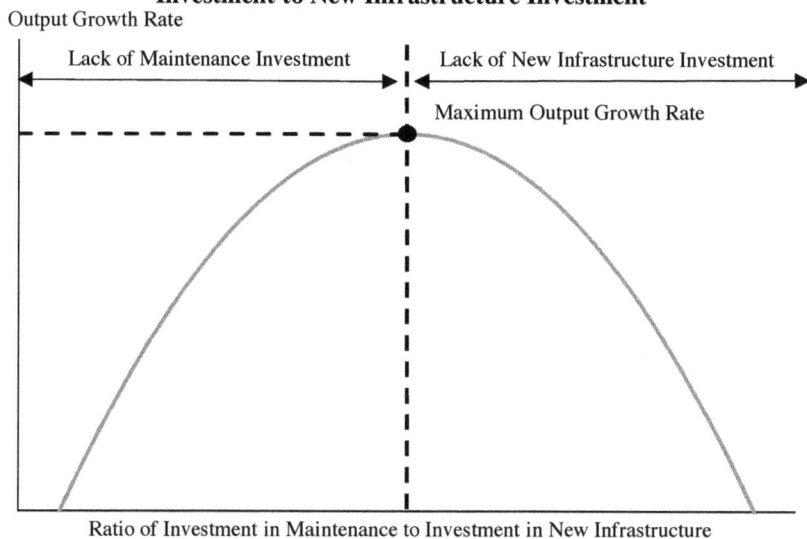

Ratio of Investment in Maintenance to Investment in New Infrastructure

Source: Kalaitzidakis and Kalyvitis (2005).

since 1956 is shown in Figure 6-7. From 1956 to 1970, the ratio of public spending on operation and maintenance to public spending on new capital for water and transportation infrastructure averaged 0.61—meaning that for every $1 spent toward new capital, $0.61 was spent on operation and maintenance. This relatively low public spending ratio largely reflected increased spending toward the continued construction of the Interstate Highway System. Over the 35 years that followed, the public spending ratio for operation and maintenance to new capital averaged 1.00—indicating a balanced approach between funding needs for new capital with those for operation and maintenance. Since then, public spending on water and transportation infrastructure has shifted toward supporting the operation and maintenance of current infrastructure relative to the formation of new capital more heavily than it did in the five decades prior, averaging a public spending ratio of 1.20. Although it is unclear what the optimal ratio is, what is clear is that maximizing growth requires spending on new infrastructure and maintaining in-place assets, not focusing solely on one and entirely ignoring the other.

Figure 6-7

**Ratio of Public Spending on Operation and Maintenance
to Public Spending on New Capital, 1956–2014**

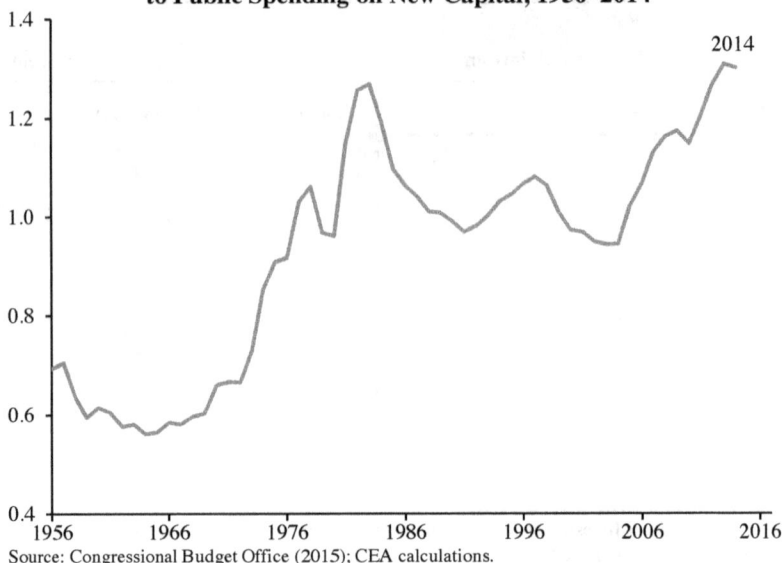

Source: Congressional Budget Office (2015); CEA calculations.

MANAGING AND FUNDING INFRASTRUCTURE PROJECTS

Beyond the need for infrastructure and the economic gains that can result from a well-designed investment, a crucial decision in the infrastructure investment process is how to manage and fund such investments.

User Fees

If infrastructure is funded through conventional methods that rely on general government revenues, all taxpayers bear the costs of new projects. But through a user-fee system, only those who actually use the services that the new infrastructure provides are required to pay for it, which could present a more equitable and viable funding mechanism as long as a project does not generate extensive externalities or spillovers. If there are substantial spillovers, charging for use may dissuade users and lead to a socially inefficient outcome. One potential downfall of the user-fee approach is that revenues are dependent on demand. If the demand for a new transportation asset was over-estimated, then the revenue generated from user fees would be below expectations, causing the entity financially responsible for it to bear the shortfall—though this could lead governments and private entities to be more prudent when selecting which projects to undertake.[7] However, if

[7] One noteworthy example is the Virginia Dulles Greenway project, which defaulted on its bonds in its first few years because predicted demand for the new road system was too rosy.

there is a clear demand for an infrastructure project—which could be gauged by surveying households and firms, noting that there are heavily congested transportation structures nearby, or recognizing the need for maintenance on popular commuter routes—user fees can be an effective approach for funding its development. Although they may be cost effective, user fees are inherently exclusionary because consumers must pay to utilize the structure, which can limit access for low- and moderate-income households.

Public-Private Partnerships

Public-private partnerships (PPPs)—where governments contract with a private firm for provision of some or all aspects of an infrastructure project—have received increasing consideration and use in recent decades in the United States (Buckberg, Kearney, and Stolleman 2015), though they are relied on more heavily in other advanced economies, including Australia, Canada, and the United Kingdom. In July 2014, President Barack Obama launched the Build America Investment Initiative, a government-wide initiative to boost infrastructure investment that includes expanding the market for public-private partnerships. The adoption of PPP financing for infrastructure projects in the United States has been gradual (likely due to the availability of inexpensive financing in the U.S. municipal debt market). Through 2007, less than 15 transportation PPPs had reached financial close in the United States (Engel, Fischer, and Galetovic 2011). As of 2015, PPPs were a feature of approximately 60 infrastructure projects for new facilities in various stages of completion across the United States, with mixed degrees of private-sector involvement (DOT 2015b); more than 15 reached financial close in the three-year period ended April 2015.[8,9]

PPPs can provide a means for avoiding two of the major pitfalls that typically affect an infrastructure project designed and delivered using conventional methods of public funding. First, under the more standard approach to infrastructure provision, each of a number of firms or government entities may be called on to complete individual stand-alone elements of the project. As a result, these firms face incentives to minimize their own costs in providing their single element of the project, without regard for the quality or costliness of the project as a whole. More concretely, the segmented nature of the infrastructure provision process means that private

---

[8] Financial close occurs when all of the project and financing agreements have been signed and project implementation can start.

[9] These PPPs are not uniform as to the project phases that are assigned to the private sector; different project characteristics necessitate different risk sharing arrangements. Roughly 25 of the projects assigned only the responsibilities of designing and building to the private sector, while more than 20 stipulated that the private sector design, build, finance, operate, and maintain the structure.

firms that are not ultimately responsible for operating or maintaining a structure have less incentive to adopt designs or construction methods that minimize total costs over the project's complete life cycle, which includes its construction, operation, and maintenance. By contrast, and depending on how the contract is structured, PPPs can "bundle" the responsibilities of different project phases, so that, for example, a single private firm is responsible for the design, construction, financing, operation, and maintenance of the infrastructure asset. This arrangement provides strong incentives for on-time project delivery and cost minimization over the entire life cycle of the structure (Hart 2003), though PPPs can also be organized so that the private sector is responsible for just some of the phases of the project.

Second, given that the public sector would still be responsible for funding the project under conventional provision, the government would incur most or all of the risk associated with its underutilization or inadequate performance. In other words, should actual use of a project fall short of its expected level, or prove substandard in terms of its engineering or design, the responsible government agency—and ultimately, the taxpayers—would bear much or all of the resulting financial strain. On the other hand, the bundled nature of PPPs allows at least some of the demand and performance risks associated with the project to be transferred from the government agency sponsoring the project to the contracting firm (Buckberg, Kearney, and Stolleman 2015). This arrangement also serves to promote more effective project design and efficient construction. It may even ensure that more reliable and cost-effective materials are used, thus ensuring longevity and reducing the frequency of required maintenance.[10]

Nevertheless, because PPPs have potential drawbacks, it is critical to design them carefully and use them only when appropriate. PPPs in which a government compensates the private entity directly through availability payments do not reduce the demand risk borne by the government, because the private partner must be paid as long as the infrastructure service meets contracted quality standards, even if actual utilization of the service is far below expectations. This drawback, however, can be overcome. Partnerships between government agencies and private firms can be structured to mitigate the demand risks faced by the government in developing a new infrastructure asset. For example, a PPP contract could stipulate that the private firm finance the project and receive compensation through the collection of

---

[10] This incentive is especially relevant if the builder is also responsible for the maintenance of the structure.

user fees or shadow tolls.[11] Through this mechanism, the government could mitigate downside risks such as project cost overruns or revenue shortfalls, thereby insulating the government from budgetary risks associated with unexpected developments. However, private investors may require a higher rate of return on their investment in exchange for being exposed to these uncertainties.[12]

Another risk associated with PPPs is that by outsourcing some or all elements of a project to private businesses, the government relinquishes some of its control over planning, constructing, and potentially even operating and maintaining the structure. Although this feature is often seen as beneficial in that the private sector is perceived as being able to manage the project more efficiently, there still exists the risk that the private firm will fail to meet its obligations or that its efforts will lead to excessively high user fees. Moreover, because of their large scale of operation, infrastructure assets often have characteristics of natural monopolies: they can be unique in the role they play for given transportation markets, which in turn may eliminate the need or potential for competing options, which raises the possibility of excessively high prices or profit. Finally, many of the same principal-agent problems that arise in standard public finance, where officials may not make the best decisions on behalf of the public, can arise in PPPs. For example, if local authorities are myopic—with a horizon of the next election or next budget cycle primarily on their minds—they could strike a sub-optimal deal that casts them in a positive light in the short run, but is inefficient in the long term.

While infrastructure assets procured through PPPs are usually returned to public sector control after a contractually stipulated period, many of the perceived risks mentioned above can be mitigated through effective contract design. The government can retain a certain level of control—regulatory or otherwise—over the private entity or entities. A contract can stipulate quality levels that structures must satisfy, restrict the prices that can be charged for using assets, and require sharing of excess revenues or profit as well as shortfalls in order to achieve a balanced and mutually acceptable

---

[11] Shadow tolls involve periodic payments from the government to the private firm based on how many users the asset attracts per time period. Like user fees, shadow tolls provide an incentive for the private party to construct and manage the asset efficiently, thus transferring demand risk from the government to the private party. Shadow tolls differ though in that they require that the government funds the private entity.

[12] Importantly, paying a higher return to the private partner to bear the demand risk need not result in the project realizing efficiency gains. In contrast to bundled design and construction risk, for example, the transfer of demand risk to the private partner in and of itself will not induce it to take actions that lower the overall cost of the project. This is due to the fact that the private partner can do little to affect utilization, unlike the way in which its actions can substantially affect overall design and construction costs.

allocation of risks (Buckberg, Kearney, and Stollman 2015). Governments can also institute requirements for competitive bidding processes that are transparent and objective. In contracting the responsibility of financing an infrastructure project to the private sector, State and local governments can also initiate the development of new assets without having the budgetary resources necessary for financing.

THE ROLE OF THE FEDERAL GOVERNMENT

With the exception of freight railroads, the Federal Government plays a key role in funding and developing transportation infrastructure. A Federal presence is particularly valuable when these transportation projects offer multi-state or nationwide benefits. One reason for Federal involvement is that State and local governments may undervalue the benefits of new infrastructure projects by not accounting fully for their positive spillover effects on nearby areas. States and localities may not have financial capacity to build new infrastructure assets or to provide maintenance for structures in need of extensive repair. Without Federal assistance, such initiatives may be repeatedly postponed or bypassed entirely because of budgetary restrictions, causing their potential benefits to be delayed or foregone completely. Additionally, the private sector may lack the incentives or resources needed to adequately complete or operate new transportation infrastructure projects, which are often large and complex.

The Federal Government has an essential role in helping transportation planners and project managers collaborate on transportation infrastructure investments across jurisdictional and geographic boundaries. These efforts can enhance the economic competitiveness of metropolitan and non-metropolitan areas along major corridors that are critical for supporting current and future freight and passenger flows. Federal expertise and resources are used to promote comprehensive multimodal planning that better integrates safety into surface transportation projects. For example, Federal law requires that the State and metropolitan transportation planning processes be consistent with Strategic Highway Safety Plans.

The Federal Government has the capacity to stimulate improvements in infrastructure that maintain the resilience of the national economy, coordinate multi-state planning for emergencies, and protect and repair interconnected transportation systems. Recent extreme weather events such as hurricanes Katrina, Rita, and Sandy, the 2012 national drought, the recent California drought, and other natural disasters have demonstrated the disruptions and other costs that can result from inadequate investment in infrastructure supporting multiple transportation modes. In 2005, the damage to transportation facilities caused by hurricanes Katrina and Rita totaled more than $1.1 billion, in addition to the costs to repair the I-10 Twin Span Bridge as well as repair and replace rail lines, pipelines, ports, waterways, and airports (Transportation Research Board 2008). In 2012, Hurricane Sandy flooded roads, subways, airport runways, marine terminals, and railroad tracks in New York and New Jersey, illustrating the widespread and cascading effects of disasters and justifying a Federal response for assistance and coordination. The costs associated with these extreme events include prolonged disruption of transportation systems, substantial capital damage, suppressed economic activity, and even loss of life.

The Federal Government contributes to infrastructure investment through direct expenditures and with incentives indirectly provided through the tax system, sometimes referred to as tax expenditures. The direct expenditures are spending on infrastructure (such as funding of dams and water resources) and grants and loan subsidies to states for transportation projects. States and localities have operational control over how the money is spent, though they must comply with certain conditions to receive Federal funding. The Federal Government subsidizes the issuance of municipal bonds by offering tax preferences that lower the cost of debt for transportation projects. State and local governments typically finance infrastructure projects with tax-preferred bonds, which are repaid with general tax receipts or from revenues collected from users of the infrastructure project. Public infrastructure investments by the private sector may also be eligible for tax-preferred financing through Private Activity Bonds if 95 percent or more of the bond proceeds are used for surface transportation or other qualified projects. State and local governments typically determine whether to provide private financing for public infrastructure investments in their jurisdictions. Federal funding and financing programs for transportation infrastructure are discussed below.

Federal Grants

One avenue through which the Federal Government has funded infrastructure investment is the Transportation Investment Generating Economic Recovery (TIGER) discretionary grant program, which was initially created as part of the 2009 American Recovery and Reinvestment Act to fund highway, transit, rail, port, and other surface transportation projects subsequently funded through annual appropriations. The TIGER program developed a merit-based competitive approach for local project sponsors to obtain Federal funds, where projects are evaluated based on the extent to which they promote the strategic goals of maintaining the Nation's economic competitiveness, ensuring environmental sustainability, improving the livability of communities, making transportation safer, and maintaining infrastructure in a state of good repair. A Government Accountability Office (2014) review of 20 projects from 2009 to 2012 showed that about half of the total construction costs for TIGER projects were funded by non-Federal sources with sizable contributions from counties, cities, and other local agencies. Notably, every dollar invested through the TIGER program generated an estimated co-investment of 3.5 dollars, highlighting the effectiveness of the program.

The TIGER grants promote a merit-based competitive approach to directing Federal investment in transportation infrastructure. The TIGER eligibility requirements allow funding for multi-modal, multi-jurisdictional projects along with port and freight rail projects, all of which may have limited access to Federal funds. TIGER can provide capital funding directly to any public entity, including municipalities, counties, port authorities, and tribal governments, in contrast to traditional Federal transportation programs that provide funding primarily to State departments of transportation and public transit agencies. A survey of state experiences with the TIGER grant program showed that the opportunity to utilize long-standing Federal expertise in planning transportation investments allowed many states to find new and innovative ways to speed up project delivery. The TIGER program has been heavily oversubscribed with a 20:1 ratio of requests to available funding, reflecting a large demand for high-quality infrastructure projects across the country.

Federal Lending and Loan Guarantees

The Transportation Infrastructure Finance and Innovation Act (TIFIA) lending program assists State and local governments in financing infrastructure projects, such as toll roads, that are supported by user fees. Created in 1998 as part of the Transportation Equity Act for the 21st Century, the program has authorized approximately $3 billion of Federal funds to cover $22 billion of loans. The program's fundamental goal is to leverage Federal funds by attracting private and non-federal co-investment in surface transportation infrastructure projects, such as highways, bridges, intercity passenger rails, certain types of freight rail, and public transit. TIFIA requires that two-thirds of project costs come from State, local, or private sources. Borrowers benefit from improved access to capital markets and can potentially achieve earlier completion of large-scale, capital intensive projects. The program has become increasingly popular since its inception and was relied on widely during the financial crisis (Altman, Klein, and Krueger 2015). The FAST Act (discussed below) reduced TIFIA's annual authority from $1 billion to an average of $287 million a year.

Tax-Exempt Bonds

Transportation infrastructure projects provide a long-term stream of benefits and, with appropriate fee structures, can generate revenues for repayment over time from users of the projects. Construction of these projects is often financed through borrowing by State and local governments. Municipal bonds are issued by States and localities to finance a broad spectrum of public infrastructure, including roads, bridges, airports, utility systems, schools, and a limited number of private sector activities. The Federal government subsidizes the issuance of municipal bonds by offering tax exemptions and other preferences that lower the cost of issuing debt for these projects.

Tax-exempt bonds, which pay interest to bondholders that is not subject to Federal income taxes, are the dominant and most well-established type of tax-preferred debt, dating from the beginning of the Federal income tax in 1913 (CBO 2009). Purchasers of this debt are willing to accept a lower interest rate compared to rates offered on taxable debt of comparable risk and maturity. Infrastructure project development is stimulated when States and localities can readily access low-cost financing, and tax-exempt bonds reduce the borrowing costs they incur, thus encouraging infrastructure development. When State and local governments issue bonds, they retain control over capital projects, so priorities for infrastructure projects and decisions on the value and timing of tax-exempt debt issues are made by State and local governments. These entities repay all principal and interest on such debt, while the Federal government effectively contributes a smaller portion by foregoing tax revenue it would otherwise collect.

From 2004 through 2013, the amount of tax-preferred debt issued to finance new infrastructure projects initiated by the public and private sectors totaled $2.02 trillion.[13] About 73 percent, or approximately $1.5 trillion, was used by States and localities. Private capital investments to fund projects with a public purpose such as hospitals or housing accounted for the remainder (about $542 billion).

After falling substantially during the Great Recession, the amount of new tax-exempt debt issued each year has rebounded considerably. Since 2010, long-term government bond issues have grown at a rate of 15.2 percent, driven primarily by two factors. First, the demand for debt financing reflects expanded investment in public infrastructure projects. Second, the steady decline in interest rates charged to municipal borrowers has provided cheaper options for borrowers to finance capital spending by issuing debt.

---

[13] CEA calculations drawn from Tax-Exempt Bond Statistics data through the Internal Revenue Service. The bond issuance data cover long-term maturity debt (13 months or more), which is generally used to finance construction or other capital improvement projects.

Transportation bonds accounted for a major share—nearly 18 percent—of governmental obligations issued to finance new investment in infrastructure from 2010 to 2013. Excluding housing—which accounts for less than 1 percent of tax-exempt government bonds—transportation has been the fastest-growing use of tax-exempt government bonds, rising on average just over 28 percent a year since 2010.

Build America Bonds

Another way the Federal government has provided resources for infrastructure recently is through the Build America Bonds (BABs) program. BABs, introduced as part of the American Recovery and Reinvestment Act, were designed to encourage State and local governments to invest in economically critical infrastructure projects. State and local governments were authorized to issue special taxable bonds that received either a 35-percent direct federal subsidy to the borrower (Direct Payment BABs) or a Federal tax credit worth 35 percent of the interest owed to investors (Tax Credit BABs). BABs broadened the pool of investors and eased the supply pressure in the municipal bond market while bringing down borrowing costs.

Through the BABs program, the U.S. Department of the Treasury was able to harness the efficiencies of the taxable debt market, resulting in lower average borrowing costs for States and localities. State and local governments were able to obtain cheaper financing (averaging about 54 basis points) than through the regular municipal bond market (Ang, Bhansali, and Xing 2010). On a present value basis, BAB issuers saved an estimated $20 billion in borrowing costs compared to traditional tax-exempt municipal debt (U.S. Department of the Treasury 2011). This savings was considerably greater than the net cost to the Federal Government from the BABs program. The program lasted roughly 20 months, and 2,275 separate BABs amounting to $181 billion were issued by State and local governments across all 50 states, the District of Columbia, and two territories. Unlike other infrastructure programs, BABs were not divided equally across states but were distributed on the basis of the demand for new infrastructure by states and localities. The result was that the 100 largest metropolitan areas accounted for nearly half of all funding for BABs issuances.

The BABs program was successful in spurring investment in economically critical infrastructure projects across the country and stimulated job-intensive projects. From 2009 through the program's expiration in 2010, BABs financed a third of all new State and local government long-term debt issuances.

Recent Legislation

In December 2015, President Barack Obama signed into law the Fixing America's Surface Transportation (FAST) Act, which authorized roughly $306 billion in spending for highways, transit, rail, and safety over the next five years. While the FAST Act offered important benefits by increasing transportation funding and providing greater certainty on funding over the coming years, it fell short of the level of investment needed to fully modernize U.S. infrastructure and the $478 billion that the Administration proposed as part of its GROW AMERICA proposal. Of that approved spending, approximately $226 billion has been designated for highways and approximately $61 billion for transit projects. Based on CEA assumptions about the future rates of inflation, these dollar amounts translate to increases in investment of about 4 percent for highways and 7 percent for transit in real terms. The law also reauthorized the collection of Federal taxes on gasoline and other fuels, which are frequently used to fund transportation projects and raise approximately $35 billion in revenues annually—with most of the tax revenue stemming from gasoline (18.4 cents per gallon) and diesel fuels (24.4 cents per gallon).

The FAST Act established new Federal grant programs, expanded current programs, and furthered initiatives to improve safety and innovation. The Act established the Nationally Significant Freight and Highway Projects competitive grant program aimed to support economically beneficial projects that will facilitate improved freight movement. This $4.5 billion discretionary grant program will be complemented by $6.3 billion in Federal-aid formula funding for states to invest directly into projects that contribute to the efficient movement of goods. The FAST Act also established the Federal-State Partnership for State of Good Repair grant program to improve critical passenger rail assets for which maintenance had been deferred as well as the Consolidated Rail Infrastructure and Safety Improvements program to support rail projects more generally.

The Act expanded State eligibility for Federal lending through TIFIA and the Railroad Rehabilitation Improvement and Financing programs. The application processes for these programs will be consolidated into the Surface Transportation Innovative Finance Bureau within the Office of the Secretary of Transportation, another FAST Act creation, which will strengthen the programs through streamlined review and transparent approval processes. The Innovative Finance Bureau will also help to promote public-private partnership procurements of large-scale infrastructure projects through expanded technical assistance. The Act established a formula freight program, to be administered by the Federal Highway Administration, which will fund critical transportation projects that would

Box 6-4: 21st Century Clean Transportation Plan

The President's fiscal year 2017 budget proposes a 21st Century Clean Transportation Plan that expands investments in clean transportation infrastructure by 50 percent above current levels in nominal terms. The 21st Century Clean Transportation Plan consists of four components designed to put America on a long-term course to reduce reliance on oil, cut carbon pollution, and strengthen resilience to the adverse impacts of climate change. The initiative aims to transform our transportation system using targeted Federal investments, to stimulate State and local innovations in smarter, cleaner, and regional transportation systems, to accelerate the adoption of low-carbon technologies, autonomous vehicles, and intelligent transportation systems, and to provide funding to maintain and increase the safety of our transportation systems as they evolve.

Innovative methods to reduce congestion, manage sprawl, and improve air quality while providing affordable access to jobs are essential as the United States experiences continued population growth in mid-sized and large urban areas. The program will distribute capital funds to expand transit systems in cities, suburbs, and rural areas, and make high-speed rail a viable alternative to flying in major regional corridors. Other targeted investments include funding to invest in new rail technologies, modernize the Nation's freight system, and expand support for the TIGER competitive grant program for innovative local road, rail, transit, and port projects.

A second component of the initiative will assist State and local governments to develop smarter and cleaner regional transportation systems. The plan provides incentives for State and local governments to maximize the returns on public investments and deliver more efficient results by reforming existing transportation formula funding. The initiative creates a Climate Smart Fund to reward states that leverage Federal funding to cut carbon pollution and improve efficiency in the transportation sector.

The plan advances specific proposals to promote the adoption of low-carbon, cost-competitive intelligent transportation systems. Working with State and local governments and leveraging public-private partnerships, the initiative sets the goal that all Americans have access to at least one alternative transportation fuel by 2020, including electric vehicle charging, advanced biofuel fuel pumps, and others low-carbon options.

benefit freight movements. The Act also provided funds to improve transportation safety by supporting projects that will alleviate highway congestion, reduce accidents, and improve rail safety.

Included in the President's fiscal year 2017 budget is a proposal, discussed in Box 6-4, to expand the development of clean transportation infrastructure.

CONCLUSION

As discussed throughout this chapter, infrastructure investment is important for the economy. At its core, strengthening our Nation's transportation infrastructure improves economic opportunities for both households and businesses, and supports the interconnectivity of individuals, firms, and regions. In the long run, investing in infrastructure boosts the economy's productivity and thus spurs output growth. Reliable infrastructure facilitates the efficient exchange of goods, labor, and innovative ideas. From the Erie Canal in the early 1800s to the Transcontinental Railroad in the 1860s, to the Interstate Highway System in the 1950s and 1960s, previous generations of Americans have made these investments, and they were instrumental in putting the country on a path for sustained economic growth.

By 2040, our population is expected to increase by more than 60 million people, and continued investment in infrastructure is essential to increasing productivity and spurring continued economic growth. Improvements in infrastructure provide more capital to the economy, thereby increasing labor productivity, reducing congestion and time lost in traffic, and enhancing market efficiency. Workers benefit from reduced commuting times, making it easier for them to move between jobs and expanding labor force opportunities. Businesses are able to manage their inventories more efficiently and transport goods faster and more cheaply, helping them to access new suppliers and markets. Concentrated investment in infrastructure may even draw market participants together and build new cooperative efficiencies, magnifying the resulting productivity gains. By making these investments in a smart way, we can make our transportation system both more efficient and more climate friendly.

Investing in U.S. infrastructure boosts both short-run demand and long-run supply. The former generates new economic activity by increasing employment and workers' earnings. The longer-run effect stems from increased productivity in the use of labor, private capital, and other resources, thus allowing opportunities for both consumers and businesses to flourish. Sufficient infrastructure, especially that supporting transportation, is a fundamental underpinning of continued economic prosperity. Whether it is flying across the country, shipping goods across state borders, or simply commuting to work each day, households and firms alike depend on adequate infrastructure. As our economy strives to increase investment and productivity, public spending on infrastructure can play an important role.

CHAPTER 7

THE 70TH ANNIVERSARY OF THE COUNCIL OF ECONOMIC ADVISERS

A lmost exactly 70 years ago, on February 20, 1946, President Harry Truman signed the Employment Act of 1946 into law. Born out of America's experience during the Great Depression, this law reflected Congress's desire to prevent an economic calamity of that scale from ever recurring. Yet the immediate practical consequences of the Employment Act were modest: it created two institutions, the Joint Economic Committee on the Economic Report—subsequently renamed the Joint Economic Committee (JEC)—and the Council of Economic Advisers (CEA). Together with the JEC, it was hoped that CEA would help to "defend the ramparts against depression" (Flash 1965).

CEA is in many ways a distinctive institution, both within the administration and in the international context. The CEA chair reports directly to the President on economic issues, but CEA has no regulatory authority and few prescribed operational responsibilities. For most of its history, CEA has had a small staff drawn mostly from the academic economics community and hired on the basis of professional expertise. The views it expresses are grounded in economic analysis, and are based on applying economic theory and empirical research to the often-novel situations in which policymakers find themselves.

However, CEA is also a part of the Executive Office of the President, working collaboratively with other departments within the Executive Office of the President and the administration more broadly to advance the President's agenda. CEA plays a distinctive role in the administration, but like other components of the administration, it also communicates and operates as part of a team on behalf of the President.

While the Council has made useful contributions to economic policymaking throughout its history, its role and influence have varied depending on the needs of the President, the economic issues facing the country, and the personnel of CEA itself. Because CEA has no fixed statutory responsibilities except for assisting in the preparation of the annual *Economic Report of the President*, its role and influence depend on the degree to which it can be useful and relevant to the President and other senior decision makers.

On the 70th Anniversary of the Employment Act of 1946, this chapter explores the origins of the Council of Economic Advisers, describes its core functions, and examines several key moments from its history. The chapter first examines the legislative origins of CEA and provides an overview of its institutional structure and policy priorities. It then focuses on four interrelated functions of CEA: helping to develop and evaluate economic policies for consideration by the President and the administration; helping to advance the President's economic agenda; gathering, analyzing, and interpreting information on economic trends and developments, and informing the President about the state of the economy; and engaging the economics community. The chapter draws on historical examples and former CEA chairs' and members' accounts—including boxes from six former chairs about their experiences at CEA—to illustrate each of these functions and their inherent challenges, and identifies several institutional lessons for ensuring CEA's continued effectiveness.

GOALS AND DUTIES

Origins of CEA—Legislative History of the Employment Act of 1946

The Employment Act ultimately signed into law in February 1946 was markedly different from the original bill that Senator James E. Murray introduced in the Senate in January 1945. The original Senate bill (S.380), which was called the Full Employment Act, aimed to "set postwar economic policy in a simple Keynesian mold" (Stein 1988), through "solidly entrench[ing] a strong bias toward active countercyclical fiscal policy in the core of the American executive branch" (DeLong 1996). S.380 provided that the government first define full employment, and then "establish and maintain programs to ensure an inflation-free, fully employed economy" (Mills 1988). The operational plan included the following key points:

> *(1) [I]t would be the responsibility of the federal government to ensure that anyone wishing to work would be able to locate a job;*
> *(2) the [P]resident was to prepare each year a National Production and Employment Budget which would include estimates of the size*

and composition of the labor force, investment plans for all levels of government, plus those of the private sector; (3) if insufficient investment existed to provide full employment, then the [P]resident would develop programs to achieve this level of employment. He was to have similar responsibility for, and powers over, the control of inflation; (4) this budget was to be prepared in the Executive Office of the President; and (5) this bill would establish a Joint Congressional Committee on the National Budget to study the [P]resident's document and either recommend or change any legislation implied in it" (Mills 1988).

By contrast, the House substitute bill, called the Employment and Production Act of 1946, "rejected the fundamental principles of the Senate bill" (Bailey 1950). It removed the declaration of the Federal Government's responsibility for maintaining full employment, the accompanying commitment of government resources, the affirmation of the right to employment opportunity, and the National Production and Employment Budget program. It also provided for a Council of Economic Advisers to be "composed of three members at $15,000 a year, whose duties were to submit recommendations to the President whenever inflation or unemployment threatened, to consult with economic groups, and to submit annual and quarterly reports on economic trends" (Bailey 1950).

The Employment Act that emerged from the Joint Conference Committee and was signed into law reflects an attempt to reconcile the profoundly different economic views contained in the House and Senate bills. In the final law, the words "full employment" were ultimately replaced with "maximum employment, production and purchasing power." The law also included language specifying that part of the Federal Government's purpose is "to foster and promote free competitive enterprise." Instead of the National Production and Employment Budget, the law called for an annual *Economic Report of the President*, "setting forth . . . current and foreseeable trends in the levels of employment, production, and purchasing power . . . and a program for carrying out the policy [to promote] conditions under which there will be afforded useful employment for those able, willing, and seeking to work" (Employment Act 1946; DeLong 1996). Meanwhile, the language from the House bill establishing the Council of Economic Advisers was kept mostly intact.[1]

---

[1] The law also established what is now known as the Joint Economic Committee, a standing joint committee of Congress, whose original functions were to coordinate economic policymaking, to monitor the subjects in the *Economic Report*, and to produce its own yearly report in response to the President's *Economic Report* (Tollestrup 2015).

The balance struck in the final Employment Act meant that CEA's role could be interpreted differently depending on whether one emphasizes the language from the House bill or from the Senate bill. Because of this dichotomy, from the beginning, the Council faced "a divergence of expectations regarding its brand of economic analysis, its policy recommendations, and its mode of operations" (Flash 1965). Consistent with that initial diversity of views, CEA has focused on different policies over the course of its history, as discussed in this chapter.

Institutional Structure

CEA has an unusual—and perhaps unique—institutional structure. Partially due to concerns about Executive Branch overreach during the Roosevelt Administration, Congress intentionally provided CEA with limited resources and specified a Council of three rather than one single adviser. CEA is currently headed by a chair and two members, each of whom is required to be "exceptionally qualified" to analyze economic developments and recommend economic policy (Employment Act 1946).[2] Today, CEA's staff is composed of academic economists and economics graduate students who are on leave from their university positions, career government economists on temporary assignment from other agencies, some recent college graduates who have studied economics, and a small statistical, forecasting, and administrative staff.

Unlike in many other governments, where the top professional economist reports to the finance minister or another cabinet minister, the CEA chair is expected to participate at the Cabinet level in discussions about economic policy. Although in some other countries, such as Germany, the government has a separate set of economic advisers who are expected to make independent recommendations, they are not integrated into day-to-day government decision-making in the same way as CEA.

CEA's institutional structure has shaped the role that it plays in economic policymaking. For example, CEA's lack of regulatory authority and its few operational responsibilities mean that its influence depends largely on its relationship with the President and the rest of the Executive Branch. As such, CEA's influence has waxed and waned at various points in its history, depending on the strength of these relationships as well as the soundness and persuasiveness of its analysis. However, CEA's position in the Executive Office of the President also allows it to take a broader perspective on economic policy and place less weight on the day-to-day exigencies of running the Federal Government. As former CEA Chairman Martin Feldstein put

---

[2] As a result of the Presidential Appointment Efficiency and Streamlining Act of 2011, the two non-chair CEA members no longer require Senate confirmation.

it, "[t]he CEA and its chairman have the luxury of trying to discern what is in the best interest of the country and of providing that analysis and advice directly to the [P]resident and to the cabinet as a whole" (1992).

Similarly, CEA's small size has also had a strong influence on how it functions. Being a small organization has enabled CEA to be more flexible, efficient, less rigid and hierarchical, and less formal than would be possible otherwise. However, it also means that CEA plays a limited role in more expansive and resource-intensive matters, consistent with its lack of formal regulatory and operational responsibilities.

Both Roger Porter, a scholar of the American Presidency and former White House economic adviser, and former CEA Chairman R. Glenn Hubbard argue that CEA's small size, its professional reputation, and its limited operational responsibilities have contributed to its longevity (Porter 1997; Hubbard 2002). Porter notes that "of the nearly 50 entities that have been located in the Executive Office of the President since it was created in 1939, the CEA is one of only 11 that remain" (1997).

Policy Focus

CEA's policy focus has evolved over the years. While countercyclical fiscal policy was the focus of the Employment Act of 1946, CEA has long since worked on a variety of other microeconomic and macroeconomic issues. For example, CEA works on macroeconomic subjects such as long-term growth, financial markets, and international macroeconomics. CEA helps to frame public discussions on macroeconomic policy, and it chairs the "Troika" forecasting process—an interagency system first formed during the Kennedy Administration, in which the Council of Economic Advisers, the Department of the Treasury, and the Office of Management and Budget jointly produce regular macroeconomic forecasts used for planning the President's Budget (see Box 7-1 for former CEA Chair Laura D'Andrea Tyson's discussion of the difficulty of economic forecasting and the role of fiscal policy in the Clinton Administration).

While macroeconomic issues continue to be an important part of CEA's portfolio, in recent decades CEA has devoted an increasing amount of attention to microeconomic issues that arise in the context of legislation, regulatory processes, and other administrative actions. Former CEA Chairman Charles Schultze reports that the proportion of CEA's annual *Economic Report* focused on microeconomic subjects grew dramatically from 1947 through 1995 (1996).

This evolution is due to a number of factors. In part, it reflects a reduced emphasis by the economics profession on fiscal policy as a macroeconomic tool and an increased recognition of the importance of monetary

Box 7-1: Former CEA Chair Laura D'Andrea Tyson (1993 – 1995)

A primary responsibility of CEA along with OMB and the Treasury is the development of economic forecasts on which the administration's annual and long-term budget projections depend. The budget deficit, widely used as an indicator of fiscal policy stance and central to political debates, is highly sensitive to the economy's performance. Yet forecasting that performance is an exercise fraught with uncertainty and subject to significant errors that get larger as the forecasting period lengthens.

In January 1993, at the beginning of the Clinton Presidency, the economy was underperforming relative to forecasts, and much weaker than expected macroeconomic conditions were producing much higher than expected budget deficits. Confronting a deteriorating budgetary outlook, the new Clinton CEA worked with the rest of the Clinton economic team to develop a budget plan to cut the deficit by $500 billion over 5 years while honoring the President's top fiscal priorities to increase public investment and expand the earned income tax credit. The administration's economic forecasts underpinning this plan reflected the prevailing consensus among economists that the growth rate of potential output was around 2.5%, resting on a labor productivity growth rate in the 1.2% range, and a NAIRU of about 5.5%. Yet this prevailing consensus proved to be wrong—during the next five years, the economy outperformed the administration's forecasts by a considerable margin.

But in January 1995, despite passage of Clinton's budget plan in August 1993 and the stronger than expected economic conditions it fostered, projected budget deficits were still increasing, albeit at a slower pace, and the new Republican controlled Congress was demanding an administration plan to balance the budget within 7 years. As the underlying economic forecasts improved, CEA helped craft a new administration plan to achieve balance within 10 years without economically indefensible cuts in spending in priority areas including health care, education, infrastructure and research. The administration's plan was rejected by Congress, which used government shutdowns and threats of default on the federal debt to force the administration's hand. These tactics failed and in 1996, the administration and Congress agreed instead on a modest budget package that funded the government at current-law levels.

The economy continued to outperform forecasts, and CEA worked with President Clinton to develop a plan to balance the budget in 5 years. He announced the plan in February 1997 shortly after his re-election. Critics accused the President of "flip flopping" on the budget, but what had changed was not his fiscal policy stance, but the surprisingly strong economic conditions that resulted in larger than expected projected reductions in the deficit. Indeed, as the President and Congress worked toward a 5-year balanced budget deal in the spring of 1997, the Congressional Budget Office (CBO) announced that it was reducing its 5-year deficit projection by another $225 billion. Over the entire period between 1994 and 2000, actual budget outcomes were about $2.6 trillion better than those projected by the CBO in 1993, with CBO's estimates showing that stronger than expected economic conditions accounted for about 38 percent of this improvement with policy changes accounting for another 25 percent. Since CBO's estimates did not include the effects of these policy changes on aggregate economic performance, its estimate of their contribution to the improving budgetary outlook should be interpreted as a lower bound estimate of their actual effects.[1]

An economic boom that far exceeded forecasts was a major factor behind the remarkable budgetary improvement. But what explains the economy's extraordinary performance—a growth rate in excess of 3.8%, a labor productivity growth rate at 3%, nearly double the 1975-1995 rate, and an unemployment rate falling to 4% with low inflation at 2.6%—a combination of macroeconomic outcomes unfathomable when President Clinton took office? And what was the role of his policies in fostering this performance?

The most important economic variable underlying budget outcomes is the rate of growth, and a key volatile and unpredictable driver of economic growth is the productivity growth rate. In standard economic models, there are two main sources of labor productivity growth—capital deepening and technological progress. Both were in overdrive in the late 1990s.

As the 1995 *Economic Report* pointed out, there is a strong correlation between investment rates and labor productivity growth across industrial countries, and business investment soared in the US during the 1995-2000 period. President Clinton's fiscal policies were premised on an untested theory that a credible sustained reduction in the budget deficit would increase national savings, resulting in a significant decline in long-term interest rates that in turn would boost investment spending. The economy's performance during the second half of the 1990s was consistent with the theory's predictions: as the projected borrowing needs of the Federal Government declined, national savings increased, and long-term interest rates continued their gradual decline. Lower borrowing costs in turn fuelled stronger investment spending.

---

[1] Douglas Elmendorf, Jeffrey Liebman and David Wilcox. 2002. "Fiscal Policy and Social Security Policy during the 1990s." In Jeffrey Frankel and Peter Orszag, eds. *American Economic Policy in the 1990s*. Cambridge: MIT Press. 61-119.

But this was only part of the story. The boom in information technology along with the resulting lower cost of computers and IT capital also fed the surge in business investment as did the soaring stock market.[2] As the anticipated productivity benefits of the 50-year old computer revolution began to intensify and spread throughout the economy, businesses were motivated to invest to reap these benefits.

The economy also benefitted from other unpredicted and unpredictable positive supply shocks, including a deceleration in health care costs in 1994-1995, moderate wage settlements, falling oil prices, and a soaring dollar. All of these beneficial developments ameliorated the predicted tradeoff between strong growth and low unemployment on the one hand and low inflation on the other.

As a result, the Federal Reserve—whose independence was staunchly defended by the Clinton economic team—was able to pursue a monetary policy that focused on the growth side of its dual mandate. Indeed, Federal Reserve Chairman Greenspan often mentioned positive productivity surprises in his explanation of Fed policy during the second half of the 1990s. And consistent with economic theory, the combination of tighter fiscal policy and relatively easy monetary policy held down real interest rates and created a macroeconomic climate that supported a growth-enhancing investment boom.

I have met former President Clinton many times since 2001 when his term of office ended. With a touch of humor, he often reminds me that as CEA Chair I provided forecasts that significantly underestimated the economy's macro performance. I humbly respond that I was simply providing unbiased forecasts based on the prevailing consensus among economists, a consensus that was proven wrong. I also remind him that as an economic forecaster and policy-maker it is wise to err on the side of caution.

[2] Alan Blinder and Janet Yellen. 2001. *The Fabulous Decade: Macroeconomic Lessons from the 1990s*, New York: The Century Foundation Press.

policy. By the early 1980s, the focus on macroeconomic stabilization policy had shifted to the Federal Reserve, and the economics profession had come to see a smaller role for discretionary countercyclical fiscal policy. However, this has changed again in recent years, as the length and severity of the Great Recession and its aftermath have precipitated a resurgence of interest in discretionary fiscal policy.

In addition, the Federal Government now plays a larger regulatory role in areas including health care, the environment, and labor markets than it did when CEA was first formed—a time before the establishment of, for example, the Environmental Protection Agency, the Department of Health and Human Services, the Department of Transportation, the Department of Education, and the Occupational Safety and Health Administration. At the same time, the field of economics has broadened to include not only traditional areas like macroeconomics and finance, but also subjects such as health care and the environment. As a result, a considerably larger fraction of CEA's work today is devoted to analyzing regulatory issues in areas like health, labor, and the environment than during its early years.

Despite the evolution in CEA's institutional structure and policy priorities over the years, CEA has continued to fulfill its functions under the Employment Act, which—as outlined above—can be understood as being organized around four interconnected functions: (1) helping to develop economic policy; (2) helping to advance the President's economic agenda; (3) gathering, analyzing, and interpreting information on economic trends and developments; and (4) engaging with the economics community. Of course, these functions overlap to some extent—for example, monitoring economic trends and engaging the economics community help to inform the formulation of economic policies. Yet examining how CEA has fulfilled these four functions over the course of its history is useful both for understanding how its work supports the President, and for illustrating certain characteristics which have helped to render it a more effective and durable institution.

Help to Develop Economic Policy

The Employment Act provides that CEA shall "develop and recommend to the President national economic policies to foster and promote free competitive enterprise, to avoid economic fluctuations or to diminish the effects thereof, and to maintain employment, production, and purchasing power." CEA performs many different tasks to fulfill this function, including working collaboratively with other offices and agencies to develop legislative proposals (such as the President's Budget and State of the Union initiatives), providing analysis to support regulatory processes, and supporting other administrative initiatives.

Although the Employment Act signaled that the Federal Government would be held responsible for how the economy functioned, its language reflected a careful balance between supporting macroeconomic management as well as a less active approach to the business cycle. As a result, CEA is not tied to one macroeconomic philosophy, but instead has "march[ed] alternately under these two banners" over the course of its history (Hargrove and Morley 1984).

The perspective of CEA has varied depending on the ideology of different administrations, the particular people chosen as chair, members and staff of the Council, the understanding of the economics profession more broadly, and the specific economic circumstances facing the country. However, CEA has consistently advanced a perspective that emphasizes the importance of decentralized decisions to the effective functioning of our market economy, but which also recognizes that the Federal Government has an important role in macroeconomic stabilization, in correcting market failures, and in ensuring that everyone participates sufficiently in the economy's benefits. Indeed, the Council's very first *Report* rejected both complete laissez-faire and overreliance on fiscal and monetary remedies as approaches to macroeconomic policy, denoting these two positions, respectively, as the "Spartan Doctrine of Laissez Faire" and the "Roman Doctrine of an External Remedy" (CEA 1946).

Keyserling and "Full-Employment Economics"

Perhaps the closest CEA has ever come to endorsing the "Roman" view was during the Truman Administration, when CEA was chaired by Leon Keyserling, the second person to hold that position. Before becoming CEA chairman, Keyserling had served as vice chairman of CEA and had previously worked as a legislative assistant on Capitol Hill, where he helped author, among other things, the Employment Act of 1946. Keyserling was influenced by proto-Keynesian theories, and became a major advocate of "full-employment economics—harnessing government spending to foster employment by creating demand and promoting consumer spending" (Wehrle 2004). Keyserling believed, "despite the grim experience of the 1930s, that the potential of the American economy was unlimited, and that with the proper combination of countercyclical and long-term economic policy, economic growth could produce and maintain abundance for all" (Brazelton 1997).

Unable to find political support for dramatically expanding domestic social programs, an increasingly frustrated Keyserling turned to defense spending as a means to advance his full-employment agenda. After Russia detonated an atomic bomb in August 1949, President Truman ordered that the State and Defense departments conduct a review of the national security situation and develop a planning document, which eventually became known as NSC 68. When war broke out in Korea, the Truman Administration definitively committed to the rapid mobilization of military resources called for in NSC 68.

While Keyserling was not a central figure in directing the mobilization effort, he actively promoted it and defended its economic viability.

Keyserling and the Council participated in the National Security Council's so-called "costing exercise" to estimate the cost of the military mobilization. CEA also helped to draft the economics chapter of NSC 68, and CEA defended the economic feasibility of a massive defense expansion against the view—held by the Secretary of Defense and the Budget Director—that it would precipitate "ruinous inflation, intolerable economic dislocation, or both" (Flash 1965). Keyserling also helped to forestall the implementation of direct price controls, believing they would dampen expanded production. In doing all of this, the Council helped to persuade policymakers that the Truman Administration's national security objectives were compatible with its economic ones.

For a few years, Keyserling successfully used the Korean War mobilization to promote his expansionist agenda. During the war, unemployment fell below 4 percent, and labor leaders appointed by Truman to various planning agencies helped to redirect some military spending to economically depressed regions and industries in the United States (Wehrle 2004).

By the end of the Korean War, however, Keyserling's influence, and support for his policies, had diminished. As inflation began to mount, the Council found itself torn between competing objectives: Keyserling warned the President about inflationary pressure, yet he also worried that excessive focus on inflation would be used as a pretext to dampen spending. This ambivalence served to exacerbate confusion within the administration about the proper course of action, and in turn, undercut the Council's influence toward the end of the Truman Presidency (Flash 1965).

The Heller Council and the 1964 Tax Cut

Another particularly notable instance where CEA played a large role in advocating for countercyclical policy occurred during the Kennedy and Johnson Administrations. In the early months of Kennedy's Presidency, unemployment had reached almost 7 percent and economic growth had been lackluster. Two schools of thought developed on the source of the problem: the first group, which included CEA Chairman Walter Heller, argued that the problem was insufficient aggregate demand, and that public spending or tax reductions were necessary to boost demand for goods and services; by contrast, the second group argued that there were structural deficiencies in the economy, and that increasing spending would only aggravate the problem (Norton 1977).

Drawing on relatively new macroeconomic concepts such as the fiscal multiplier and the full employment surplus, CEA made the case that the economy suffered from insufficient demand, emphasizing "the gap between progress and potential, the resistance to improvement of unemployment, and the drag of the wartime tax structure" (Flash 1965). The Council presented its argument publicly on several occasions: before the Joint Economic Committee in 1961, and in the 1962 and 1963 *Economic Report of the President*. In the 1963 *Economic Report*, the Council strongly advocated for a tax cut to boost demand:

> *[F]or all its advances, the Nation is still falling substantially short of its economic potential ... Private initiative and public policy must join hands to break the barriers built up by the years of slack since 1957 and bring the Nation into a new period of sustained full employment and rapid economic growth ... The main block to full employment is an unrealistically heavy burden of taxation. The time has come to remove it.*

Through these efforts, CEA helped solidify support for the tax reduction. President John F. Kennedy pushed for it in his 1963 State of the Union address, and it was ultimately signed into law by President Lyndon B. Johnson in 1964. CEA did not design the specific details of the tax reduction, but it helped to make the supporting economic case.

Edward Flash, a scholar of public administration, argues that this moment constituted a turning point in the Council's history by helping to align economic policymaking with economic thinking at that time:

> *As demonstrated by the Administration's tax program, the primary significance of the Heller Council is that it was the most important single creative force in the development of a new approach to economic policy. As the Employment Act of 1946 ratified the government's responsibility for the nation's economic welfare (and hence its acceptance of Keynesian principles), the tax proposals of 1963 signaled the policy-maker's recognition that expenditure-revenue combinations leading to deficits can be a constructive force in economic growth. Policy thinking became more consistent with economic thinking. A new tradition was established. The Council analyzed, advocated, articulated, and gained acceptance for new economic values, new techniques of economic analysis, and new concepts of fiscal policy as a positive contributor to national economic well-being (1965).*

Moreover, Flash notes that winning President Kennedy's approval for implementing countercyclical policy at a time of existing budget deficits was a notable achievement, especially considering that the President had previously committed himself to balancing the Federal budget.

Countercyclical Policy in Other Administrations

CEA has engaged in deliberations about countercyclical fiscal policy at some point during most administrations in the post-World War II era. As discussed later, CEA Chairman Arthur F. Burns helped to convince President Dwight D. Eisenhower to support counter-recessionary tax cuts, "the first time massive tax cuts were made at a time of Federal budgetary deficit to counter a recession" (Norton 1977). The Gardner Ackley CEA tried but failed to convince President Johnson to raise taxes in 1965 to avoid inflation. The Alan Greenspan CEA advocated for, and the Ford Administration proposed, a fiscal stimulus in 1975 that was considerably more moderate than what was ultimately enacted by Congress, and called for "greater fiscal restraint" in the 1976 *Economic Report* (CEA 1976). The Schultze CEA advocated for an additional stimulus in 1977 during the Carter Administration (Schultze 1996), while the Michael J. Boskin CEA advocated for set of tax measures to stimulate the economy during the George H.W. Bush Administration (Frankel 2003). The Laura D. Tyson CEA advocated for a small one-time expenditure stimulus as part of a larger deficit reduction program during the Clinton Administration. The R. Glenn Hubbard, N. Gregory Mankiw, and Harvey S. Rosen CEAs promoted tax cuts enacted in 2001 and 2003 as a means of stimulating the economy during a period of sluggish economic activity (CEA 2002; CEA 2004; Rosen and Forbes 2005).

Most recently, under the leadership of CEA Chairs Edward Lazear, Christina Romer, and Austan Goolsbee, CEA played a role in designing countercyclical measures that were passed in response to the 2008-09 global financial crisis and its aftermath. The Council conducted the overall macroeconomic analysis that helped identify the need for, and design of, countercyclical fiscal measures, most notably the American Recovery and Reinvestment Act of 2009 (see Box 7-2 for former CEA Chair Christina Romer's account of the role that CEA played in the Obama Administration's response to the financial crisis).

CEA has also pushed to defend existing automatic stabilizers—features of the tax and transfer system that automatically offset fluctuations in economic activity—against policy changes, such as balanced-budget proposals, that would interfere with them. Charles Schultze observes that "[w]hile most Republican CEAs throughout the period continued to be more cautious than their Democratic counterparts about the advice they gave on the use of fiscal policy for stabilization purposes, the difference was one of degree, not of kind" (1996).

Box 7-2: Former CEA Chair Christina Romer (2009 – 2010)

President Obama was elected in the middle of the severe financial crisis in November 2008. Even with incomplete data and rapidly changing conditions, it was clear at the time that the crisis was having a rapid and disastrous impact on the rest of the economy. Firms unable to get loans were laying off workers, consumers were deserting stores, and unemployed families were struggling to keep their homes.

Because of the crisis, the incoming economics team had to start designing many of the policy responses during the transition—before we had the resources or the skills of the professional staffs at our agencies. That was certainly true of the fiscal stimulus package that the President worked closely with Congress to craft, and which was signed into law as the American Recovery and Reinvestment Act less than a month after his inauguration. From late November on, the economics team debated and planned a package of tax cuts, infrastructure spending, and aid to those directly affected by the crisis to try to help stabilize the economy and make it stronger in the future.

Though we were a skeletal team—just the member nominees and two graduate students who would eventually become staff economists—the transition Council of Economic Advisers attempted to do what CEA always does: bring the best evidence and economic analysis to bear on the problem. We gathered economic projections from a wide range of public- and private-sector forecasters. In the spirit of bipartisan professionalism that has always characterized CEA, the outgoing chair, Edward Lazear, and his staff shared the evidence they had about the economy and where it was heading. We also collected the best estimates available of the likely effects of different types of fiscal actions from the economics literature, professional agencies such as the Federal Reserve, and private forecasters.

As we put the forecasts and the estimates of the effects of fiscal stimulus together, it quickly became apparent that the fiscal packages being considered by most analysts and Congress were too small. This was a once-in-a-century problem that required a once-in-a-century response. The analysis we presented to the President-Elect in mid-December 2008 helped persuade him to work with Congress for a larger, more effective package. Though the final legislation was still not has large as the President would have desired given the terrible recession, at $787 billion, the American Recovery and Reinvestment Act was by far the largest discretionary fiscal stimulus in American history. And a burgeoning literature on its effects confirms that the Act was essential in helping to halt the decline and turn the economy around.

In designing the Recovery Act, one component around which there was substantial uncertainty was aid to State and local governments. Rising unemployment was devastating state tax revenues, and economists feared that state balanced-budget requirements would force State and local governments to cut spending and employment just as their economies and citizens needed those funds and jobs the most. For this reason, the incoming economics team urged Congress to include in the Recovery Act transfers from the Federal Government to the States to stabilize their coffers. As a practical matter, this was accomplished primarily by temporarily increasing the fraction of Medicaid spending (always a joint Federal/State program) covered by the Federal Government. The final Recovery Act included roughly $140 billion of state fiscal relief of this and other sorts.

Though the logic of the action was sound, because such fiscal transfers are rare there was only limited empirical evidence on their likely effects. CEA helped fill that knowledge gap by doing a careful study of the state fiscal relief done through the Recovery Act. The study, conducted by four CEA staff economists, was included in CEA's first quarterly report to Congress on the effects of the Recovery Act. CEA economists used the fact that some of the variation in the fiscal relief across States was due to pre-existing differences in the generosity of their Medicaid programs, rather than to state economic conditions, to accurately identify the employment effects of these transfers. The estimates indicated that the effects were substantial. Indeed, the estimated job effects were sufficiently large that the state fiscal relief appeared to be one of the most cost-effective components of the legislation. The four economists ultimately expanded their study into a paper, which was published in the *American Economic Journal: Economic Policy* (where it won the best paper prize in 2013).[1]

This CEA analysis of state fiscal relief was influential in subsequent policy discussions and recommendations. Though the American economy started growing again in the summer of 2009, job losses continued throughout the year and unemployment remained painfully high. The economics team debated at length the relative merits of many measures to spur job growth. Interestingly, about the only thing we *didn't* debate was the desirability of additional state fiscal relief. What had been a logical but untested action in the Recovery Act was now understood to have been an effective job-creation tool—thanks in part to CEA's analysis. There was easy agreement that it belonged in any second comprehensive

---

[1] Gabriel Chodorow-Reich, Laura Feiveson, Zachary Liscow, and William Gui Woolston. 2012. "Does State Fiscal Relief During Recessions Increase Employment? Evidence from the American Recovery and Reinvestment Act." *American Economic Journal: Economic Policy* 4(3): 118–145.

jobs package. And in early December 2009, President Obama proposed additional action, which included further funds for State and local governments as a significant part.

Sadly, Congress did not accept all of the President's recommendations, and fewer additional job creation measures were taken that winter than were needed. But additional state fiscal relief resurfaced in a more limited form in a bill the President signed on August 10, 2010. As part of a multi-faceted act, Congress appropriated $10 billion in aid to State and local governments to help maintain teacher jobs. A treasured memento of my time at CEA is one of the pens the President used to sign that bill. It is a reminder that rigorous empirical analysis by one of the smallest agencies in Washington can sometimes spur legislation that creates jobs and helps heal a troubled economy.

Microeconomic Policy

In recent decades, CEA has increasingly spent its time applying core microeconomic lessons: that individuals and organizations' behavior is shaped by the incentives they face; that markets are generally an efficient way of organizing economic activity; that public policy can sometimes improve the functioning of markets, such as in the presence of externalities (when the market does not fully take social costs and benefits into account) or informational problems; and that policy choices can affect whether the benefits of markets are narrowly or broadly shared. Schultze writes that "the injection of basic microeconomic principles, well back from the frontiers of research, can significantly raise the quality of the debate" (1996).

Although CEA's views on some particular microeconomic issues have evolved over time and with administrations, this shared commitment to a basic microeconomic canon has ensured a substantial amount of continuity. Under both Republican and Democratic administrations, the Council has argued that reshaping incentives is often a better way of addressing market failures than imposing command-and-control regulation. It has also pushed for policies that promote overall economic efficiency, rather than the well-being of specific sectors, industries, or firms. Charles Schultze notes that "despite some areas of disagreement, a succession of CEAs under both parties has given similar advice on a wide range of microeconomic matters" (1996).

CEA has also frequently provided more detailed technical or empirical expertise, such as analyzing the effect of policies on incentives or performing cost-benefit analyses. Former CEA Chairman Joseph Stiglitz enumerates a number of specific "narrow microeconomic initiatives" in which CEA has played an important role, such as designing tradable permits in pollutants, incorporating risk and discounting into cost-benefit analysis, and introducing auction mechanisms (1997). During negotiations over the Clean Air Act Amendments of 1990, CEA was viewed as the "repository of neutral competence" and was called on to produce unbiased cost estimates of a range of different provisions (Porter 1997). In recent years, empirical research has become an especially important part of CEA's portfolio, reflecting the proliferation of available data and the economics profession's shift toward empirical work. This trend has benefited the field of microeconomics in particular (Stevenson 2014).

CEA has also helped to advocate for, or contribute to, the generation of new policy proposals. For example, the Burns Council supported the Federal Aid Highway Act of 1954, which began the present Interstate Highway System. The Heller Council under Presidents Kennedy and Johnson was especially prolific, "helping to shape transportation and trade bills, aiding in the development of the monetary 'twist' policy, helping to keep mortgage rates down, [and] developing the rationale of the wage-price guideposts" (Flash 1965). It also helped to develop the idea of the War on Poverty.[3] Other CEAs have helped to initiate or push for (sometimes successfully; sometimes not) various other reforms, such spectrum auctions, pension simplification and indexed bonds, reforms of the air-traffic control system, housing sector reform, and a comprehensive approach to natural-disaster policy (Stiglitz 1997). During the negotiations over the Kyoto Protocol on Climate Change, former CEA Chair Janet Yellen testified on a number of occasions regarding the cost savings that could be achieved through emissions trading and participation by developing countries (Hahn and Stavins 2002). (See Box 7-3 for former CEA Chairman N. Gregory Mankiw's description of CEA's role in trying to reform Fannie Mae and Freddie Mac during the George W. Bush Administration.)

---

[3] Walter Heller gives the following account of the impetus for the War on Poverty: "Then around Christmas of 1962, [President Kennedy] read Dwight MacDonald's poverty articles in the New Yorker that helped get him started. Then he asked to see some other things that had been written… He asked to see these things, read them and was obviously deeply affected … So first of all I had Bob [Lampman] put together the things he had done—the best work on the subject in the United States—namely measuring what had happened to poverty, what the sources of poverty were, what groups were impacted, why people were mired in poverty. We gave Kennedy this factual account about in March of 1963. Then something triggered my political interest in it: in June it was said that some Republican group—I've forgotten which Republican policy committee—was going to zero in on the poverty problem. At that point I wrote my basic memo to Kennedy saying in effect, 'You really should have in your 1964 program an attack—(I didn't call it a war on poverty, but an attack)—on poverty, and here are the kinds of things that it might include. Unless you tell us not to, we're going to go ahead and work on them.' We worked on them through the summer and—this, I think is well known— the very last thing I talked to him about—three days before the assassination—was the poverty program, and he said, 'It's going to be part of my program.' We didn't know how big it was to be" (Hargrove and Morley 1984).

Box 7-3: Former CEA Chairman N. Gregory Mankiw (2003 – 2005)

Looking back at my experience as CEA chair, I am struck by the broad range of questions the Council had to confront. Should corporate dividends be taxed at the same rate as ordinary income? What effect does Chinese exchange-rate policy have on the American economy? How should accountants treat executive stock options when computing a company's earnings? Why aren't U.S. utilities building new nuclear power plants? How should "means" be defined when means-testing a Medicare entitlement? What is the best way for policymakers to help speed the nascent recovery from the dot-com collapse?

For a professional economist, working at CEA is both demanding and exhilarating. Confronting such a large range of issues is inevitably a learning experience—and one done in short order and with high stakes. It is a great honor to play a small part in trying to steer public policy in a better direction and thereby improve the lives of our fellow citizens.

With the benefit of hindsight, one issue from my time at CEA is particularly notable: the oversight of Fannie Mae and Freddie Mac. CEA was part of a White House team that tried to reform these government-sponsored enterprises (GSEs). We recognized that the GSEs were problematic. Their private goal of profit maximization did not mesh well with the implicit government guarantee of their debts.

In a speech I gave in November 2003 to a conference of bank supervisors, I described the situation as follows: "The enormous size of the mortgage-backed securities market means that any problems at the GSEs matter for the financial system as a whole. This risk is a systemic issue also because the debt obligations of the housing GSEs are widely held by other financial institutions. The importance of GSE debt in the portfolios of other financial entities means that even a small mistake in GSE risk management could have ripple effects throughout the financial system."

The administration sought legislation that would create and empower a more effective regulator. The regulator would have the authority to set both risk-based and minimum capital standards for GSEs; to review and, if appropriate, reject new GSE activities; and to wind down the affairs of a troubled GSE through receivership. We also wanted to make the GSEs less political. We recommended removing presidentially appointed directors from their boards and giving the regulator a permanent funding mechanism by allowing it to assess the GSEs rather than relying on the congressional appropriations process.

In the end, the administration failed in this effort, at least while I was there. Legislation to improve the oversight of Fannie and Freddie was enacted only in July 2008, well after the imbalances that led to the 2007-08 financial crisis had built up, making the problems apparent to everyone. In 2003 and 2004, with financial markets still placid, Fannie and Freddie had lots of friends in Congress (on both sides of the aisle) who blocked the White House's reform efforts. But we fought the good fight. And subsequent history shows, I believe, that we were on the right side of the issue.

Did CEA at the time foresee the housing boom and bust that unfolded over the next six years? No, of course not. But we did recognize the vulnerabilities of the GSEs, which were major players in the huge market for mortgage-backed securities. Would the proposed reforms have prevented the financial crisis? No, probably not. But they might have made it less severe and more manageable.

People often ask me whether it is frustrating to work in Washington, noting how hard it is to get anything done. Yes, in some ways, it is. This episode is only one example where our good policy (as my White House colleagues and I saw it) was subverted by an uncooperative legislature.

Yet, over time, I have come to appreciate that frustration for those in policy jobs is not a bug in the system but rather a feature. The founding fathers, in their great wisdom, built this tension into the system. In high school civics classes, it goes by the name "checks and balances."

A common lament is that there is too much gridlock in Washington, and maybe there is. But imagine that your least favorite candidate wins the next presidential election. Might you be grateful when the new President and his or her CEA chair become frustrated while trying to implement their new ideas for economic policy?

Ensuring that Policies are in the Public Interest

CEA also plays an important role in providing analyses to demonstrate that some policies, while superficially appealing or offering substantial benefits to particular sectors or firms, are not cost-effective or in the national interest. Joseph Stiglitz claims that "the money saved from just one of the many bad projects the CEA had helped stop ... would have been enough to provide us with a permanent endowment" (1997). Former CEA Chairman Ben Bernanke also emphasized this function when describing economists' role in policymaking more generally, while at the same time emphasizing the limitations of economics:

> Economics is a highly sophisticated field of thought that is superb at explaining to policymakers precisely why the choices they made in the past were wrong. About the future, not so much. However, careful economic analysis does have one important benefit, which is that it can help kill ideas that are completely logically inconsistent or wildly at variance with the data. This insight covers at least 90 percent of proposed economic policies (2013).

Box 7-4: Former CEA Chairman Joseph Stiglitz (1995 – 1997)

My four years at the Council (two as a member and two as chairman) were perhaps the most memorable in my life. There were many battles—some which we won, some which we lost, some in which we achieved a temporary victory, and some which we lost in the short run only to see our positions vindicated with time. We came into government at an exciting time. The fall of the Iron Curtain had redefined the economic agenda. Our challenge was to find the right balance between the market and the state. The Council saw its role as helping to clarify the principles, and then applying these principles to the major issues of the day.

The Council of Economic Advisers had an important *positive* agenda, as we pushed to reshape trade, welfare, and environmental policies. To name one example, we successfully pushed for inflation indexed bonds, arguing that they could provide retirees with insurance against inflation—which they could not obtain in other ways—and that the risk premium that the market would likely pay for these bonds would generate revenues, important then as now in the context of budgetary constraints. Some opposed inflation indexed bonds, ostensibly because there would be little demand for them but perhaps grounded in the fact that the low turnover on such bonds meant they would generate few fees for Wall Street. Our view that there would be demand was vindicated and Treasury Inflation Protected Securities (TIPS) have proven to be a durable, useful, and informative part of the financial landscape.

Some of the most intense battles we fought now seem dated, and that may have been partly because of our success. Today, there is a broad consensus against "corporate welfare"—and especially tax expenditures that both distort the economy and increase inequality, even if they have shown enormous resilience. At the time, the topic was politically sensitive, but we drew up a list of them for the President, and that list has only gotten longer with time.

But we also did a lot to stop bad ideas and in collaboration with many allies across government, we succeeded in many arenas. We forged an alliance with the Antitrust Division of the Department of Justice to block a proposal to sustain the price of aluminum through the creation of a global aluminum cartel. We helped overcome legislative attempts to change the mandate of the Federal Reserve to focus only on inflation and not on unemployment, and helped defeat a constitutional amendment to require a balanced budget.

One temporary victory contains important lessons for CEA's commitment to understanding incentives. For years, we succeeded in blocking the privatization of the United States Enrichment Corporation

(USEC). USEC was responsible for producing and marketing enriched uranium, the key ingredient in nuclear power plants and in atomic bombs. CEA argued that private incentives to create markets for USEC's product conflicted with national and global interests in non-proliferation. Even worse, USEC was entrusted with bringing into the United States the enriched uranium from deactivated Russian warheads. We worried that USEC's profit-making incentives would induce them to do what they could to avoid bringing the uranium into the United States. CEA's concerns proved justified, as we uncovered that USEC had refused an offer to buy substantial amounts of uranium from Russia. This discovery halted the privatization, albeit only temporarily. But USEC's continued travails—leading even to proposals for renationalization—vindicated CEA's position.

The Council was also engaged in other international issues. We opposed the policy of Chinese containment that was pursued in the earliest days of the Clinton Administration, and when the administration changed course toward re-engagement, we became active participants in that process. Our expertise in the transition from Communism to a market economy, especially in Russia, gave us a seat at the table in discussions over policies in that part of the world.

The Council was actively engaged in trade policy, not just pushing back against protectionist measures but defining the *principles* that should guide market access initiatives. We questioned unfettered capital flows across borders, a view that has become "officially" vindicated by the IMF's endorsement of it.

As I think back over the years at the Council, one of the things that is striking is how many of the issues we focused on then have since risen to the top of the agenda. One was climate change. The Council was actively engaged in thinking about economic strategies that would reduce our emissions and those of the rest of the world. I served on the Intergovernmental Panel on Climate Change (which shared the 2007 Nobel Peace Prize with former Vice President Al Gore).

Another was inequality. We debated the causes and what could be done about it, and included a full chapter on the topic in the 1997 *Economic Report of the President*. Our analysis highlighted how reducing capital gains tax rates would enhance the country's already worsening inequality and further distort the economy.

As we engaged in these discussions and many more, CEA developed an enormously strong sense of comradery. It was these bonds as much as the ideas themselves that I think about when I reflect upon my four years at the Council.

There were many lessons that I draw from these and a multitude of other examples during my four years in the Council. The Council can stop bad ideas and initiate goods ones. Given its small—but highly dedicated—staff, it must be focused and use leverage. It is most effective when it works closely with other agencies, at multiple levels—interacting both with staff and top political appointees. This is even truer today, with an increasingly large number of departments having a chief economist. Not to sound too imperial, but economics and economic analysis enter into every aspect of public decision-making. Incentives matter. And this is true not just in the arena of domestic policy, but also foreign policy. Finally, most of the important issues are long run—whatever we do today, we will be dealing with them for years to come. The Council can play an important role in shaping, and elevating, the public debate.

As I wrote 20 years ago in celebration of the Council's 50th anniversary,[1] CEA is an important institutional innovation that has served the country well. Like other agencies in government, it has a "special interest," one that often gets short shrift in day-to-day political life: the national interest.

---

[1] Joseph Stiglitz. 1997. "Looking Out for the National Interest: The Principles of the Council of Economic Advisers." *American Economic Review* 87 (2): 109-113.

Some examples of this function are especially noteworthy (see Box 7 -4 for former CEA Chairman Joseph Stiglitz's account of CEA's role in evaluating and generating policy proposals during the Clinton Administration). For instance, the Heller Council argued against a proposal during the Kennedy Administration to use nuclear explosives to widen the Panama Canal. In the Nixon Administration, CEA played a leading role in the analysis that led to the conclusion that the government should not subsidize the development of a supersonic transport or SST plane, dubbed the "sure-to-be-subsidized transport" (Schultze 1996). Under President Ronald Reagan, CEA participated in a Gold Commission, which investigated the feasibility of returning to the gold standard, and ultimately advised against doing so.

Of course, the President makes policy decisions based on a wide range of other advice and perspectives, and economic considerations often are not paramount. Furthermore, as former CEA Chairman Herbert Stein points out, not all policy proposals lend themselves to such definitive economic conclusions:

> *The range of uncertainty [in economics] has been very great and the range of disagreements among respected people is very great. The political figure making a decision has this great range from which to choose, and he has to make a choice on some basis other than what*

can be reported to him as the perceived wisdom of the economics profession because that perceived wisdom gives pretty wide range (Hargrove and Morley 1984).

Finally, economic advice is only useful to policymakers if it is communicated well. Former CEA Chairman Martin Baily emphasizes that when CEA is assessing proposals from Congress or other parts of the administration, it is important for it "to frame those issues in a way that can help foster useful discussion among policymakers" (2006).

HELP TO ADVANCE THE PRESIDENT'S ECONOMIC AGENDA

Another primary function of CEA is to help advance the President's economic agenda. As outlined in CEA's 1961 statement before the Joint Economic Committee, "[t]he Council has a responsibility to explain to the Congress and to the public the general economic strategy of the President's program, especially as it relates to the objectives of the Employment Act." CEA accomplishes this through several different means: writing the annual *Economic Report of the President* and testifying before the Joint Economic Committee, producing reports on specific policy proposals or issues, delivering speeches, writing op-eds, speaking with reporters, and in more recent years, writing blog posts and engaging the public on social media outlets.

Despite the fact that CEA draws heavily from academia and performs economic research, it is not an academic institution or an independent body. Instead, CEA is part of the team that helps to develop the President's agenda—and its public communications are intended to complement that role, while reflecting rigorous economic research. Like communications from any other component of the Executive Office of the President or the administration more generally, statements from CEA are intended to be consistent with the President's agenda and economic policy.

As many commentators and former CEA chairs have observed, there can be a tension between CEA's duty to advance the President's agenda and its responsibility to provide expert economic advice. For most of its history, CEA has managed to strike a successful balance between these roles. As Edward Flash notes, CEA's reports are "not ... partisan tracts but rather documents oriented to the economic policies and values of the Administration" (1965). However, there are inherent challenges entailed by fulfilling these dual responsibilities. This section uses the conflict between CEA's first chairman, Edwin G. Nourse, and its second, Leon H. Keyserling, to explore these challenges. It also draws some institutional lessons to ensure the Council's continued effectiveness.

Nourse and Keyserling

The three years (1946-49) during which Nourse and Keyserling served on the Council together were difficult ones. Nourse opposed Keyserling's "full-employment economics" and expansionist agenda, and held different views than Keyserling on inflation and countercyclical policy. Their disagreements on economic policy were exacerbated by ambiguity surrounding the Council's organizational structure. Although Nourse was the official chairman, he and the two members had functionally equivalent roles and responsibilities, and each of them got one vote when making decisions. Consequently, it was not always clear who was speaking on behalf of the Council, and Edward Flash reports that by 1948, "the Council could no longer report to the President in a single voice, as memoranda and reports began to incorporate differing individual viewpoints" (1965).

Nourse and Keyserling also held fundamentally different views about how the Council should operate. Nourse, who had enjoyed a distinguished career as an agricultural economist, viewed the Council as a "scientific agency" that should be objective and scrupulously avoid politics. Nourse summarized his view of the Council in a letter to President Truman accepting the offer of chairmanship:

> The Council of Economic Advisers is conceived as a scientific agency of the Federal Government. Its prime function is to bring the best available methods of social science to the service of the Chief Executive and of the Congress in formulating national policy from year to year and from month to month. There is no occasion for the Council to become involved in any way in the advocacy of particular measures or in the rival beliefs and struggles of the different economic and political interest groups. It should give a clearer and more comprehensive picture than we have ever had as to the economic state of the nation, as to factors which are tending to retard prosperity, and as to the probable effect of various remedial measures which may be under consideration by the Executive or the Congress (Flash 1965).

Nourse believed that the Council's function should be limited to providing advice, and did not view himself as "being an active participant in, or advocate of, the President's program, involved in day-to-day affairs, or in the promotion of his program" (Norton 1977). Indeed, he took this notion so seriously that he argued that members of the Council should not testify before any Congressional committees other than appropriation committees.

By contrast, Keyserling had actively engaged in public policy before arriving at CEA: he had served as a legislative assistant to Senator Robert Wagner and as a staff member of the Senate Committee on Banking and Currency, worked in different capacities at various public housing agencies, and participated in numerous Democratic election campaigns. He—and to a lesser extent, CEA's other member, John D. Clark—believed that the Council should not only provide advice, but also should participate in the policy process and advocate for the President's policies. As discussed above, for example, he did not hesitate to involve himself in the Korean War mobilization, since it aligned with his views of the necessity of economic expansion. In addition, he felt that the Council's advice should not be limited to economics, and should include "social and political aspects" as well (Norton 1977). Keyserling and Clark also thought it was entirely appropriate for them to testify before Congressional committees. Ultimately, it became necessary for President Truman to resolve the disagreement, siding with Keyserling and Clark.

After three years of service as chairman of CEA, Nourse tendered his resignation to President Truman. Nourse had become increasingly frustrated that he was "unable to develop satisfactory relations or channels of communication with the President and the White House," while Keyserling, who was more "operationally and promotionally included than Nourse," had an easier time operating within a political environment (Flash 1965). Keyserling was named chairman about six months after Nourse's departure.

Although Keyserling outlasted Nourse, the acrimony between the two men, along with the perception of Keyserling as being overly political, contributed to questions about the Council's future. Criticism began to intensify toward the later part of the Truman Administration, and in 1949, the Hoover Commission on Government Reorganization recommended that CEA be replaced with an Office of the Economic Adviser that would have a single head, but a similar staff (Nourse 1953).

Once Republicans won the White House and both houses of Congress in 1952, the future status of the Council was unclear. Toward the end of the Truman Administration, Congress cut the Council's budget for fiscal year 1953 by 25 percent, but a group of Senators who supported the Council managed to have its funds distributed so as to fully fund it for the first nine months of the fiscal year (Flash 1965). Funds ran out on March 1, 1953, around six weeks after President Dwight D. Eisenhower took office, by which time most of CEA's staff had dispersed. The new Congress refused President Eisenhower's request to extend funds for the end of the fiscal year, instead providing funding for a single economic assistant to the President (Porter 1991). It was "widely believed at the time that the Council's shut-down towards the end of the Truman Administration was a result of excess politicking under Keyserling's chairmanship" (Naveh 1981), though Keyserling himself disputed this perception.

Eventually, Arthur F. Burns, who had been appointed as President Eisenhower's sole economic adviser, convinced the President and Congress to keep CEA, arguing that "the President definitely needed economic advice on a continual basis and on a professional level … [and] that a deliberative body would serve the President better than a single economic adviser" (Hargrove and Morley 1984). Congress restored CEA's appropriation and Burns was sworn in as chairman in March 1953.

Burns also helped to persuade President Eisenhower to reorganize CEA. Together with staff from the Budget Bureau (the precursor to the Office of Management and Budget), he worked to develop Reorganization Plan No. 9, which formally established the chair as the leader of CEA, and gave her or him responsibility for representing the Council to the President. However, Hugh Norton writes that perhaps Burns's greatest "contribution was his success, at least in appearance, in removing the Council from the area of partisanship into which it had fallen in the late Truman-Keyserling period … To what degree this was merely an illusion is debatable, but at least he created the image" (1977).

Institutional Lessons

The discord between Nourse and Keyserling and its political fall-out illustrates that CEA chairs and members need to be able to operate effectively within a political environment without it affecting the integrity of their economic advice. Put more succinctly, Charles Schultze advises that "CEA members should see themselves as partisan advocates of the efficient solution" (1996). Former CEA Chairman Murray Weidenbaum writes that subsequent CEA chairs and members have "tried to avoid the two extremes of the Truman Administration so as not to be pegged as either advocate or oracle" (1996).

Political values and judgments intersect with CEA's role in a number of ways. As Schultze notes, CEA must have some political sensibilities to be effective: "[t]he CEA chairman and members cannot be effective if they are seen as political eunuchs, with little understanding of the political stakes involved" (1996). Arthur Okun concurs, "[i]t is far more important for society and for the profession to have economists who maintain rapport with the President and thus have the greatest influence on the inside" (Naveh 1981). Similarly, former CEA Member William A. Niskanen recommends that "[m]embers of the CEA, and other senior policy advisers, should be selected on the basis of three criteria: professionalism, loyalty to the fundamental goals of the government in their area of responsibility, and an ability to operate in a political environment" (1986).

Moreover, although CEA's strength is providing unvarnished economic advice, it is impossible to divorce this advice from the broader context of the Administration's goals and objectives. While economists can help policymakers to weigh tradeoffs among different policy options or to design policies so that they are more likely to achieve their stated objective, how those tradeoffs are weighed and goals are set often depends on values. In addition, policy recommendations themselves are more relevant if they can be implemented, which in turn depends on a range of political factors like legislative feasibility and how the policy is described and contextualized. Finally, CEA chairs are selected and agree to serve because they at least broadly share the goals and values of the President and the administration. Beyond the chair, however, there is no guarantee that CEA members, or especially staff economists and researchers, share a political or philosophical agreement with the President.

As dictated in the Employment Act of 1946, CEA's advice must ultimately be guided by its own analysis of which economic policies will foster and promote free competitive enterprise, avoid economic fluctuations, and maintain employment, production, and purchasing power. Former CEA chairs, members, and staff offer several specific pieces of advice as to how to successfully strike this balance: they advise that CEA should not publicly advocate for policies that are not supported by economic analysis, and that CEA should stick to giving economic advice, not political advice. CEA's comparative advantage is economics, and as illustrated by Keyserling's tenure and its aftermath, straying outside this function risks damaging the institution's credibility.

Others advise that the Council should not get too involved in policy coordination. CEA's limited staff and resources, combined with the academic background of most of its staff, render it poorly equipped to serve as a policy coordinating body. One episode that illustrates this lesson occurred during the Johnson Administration, when CEA was responsible for the day-to-day administration of wage-price guideposts to combat inflation. Reflecting on the experience, Walter Heller remarked that there was no other appropriate agency to handle the wage-price guideposts, but that it was "diversionary" and that "the Council has to stay away from that kind of operational responsibility" (Hargrove and Morley 1984).

Excessive involvement in policy coordination can also have the effect of undermining CEA's institutional credibility, due to the types of compromises that are necessary. Hugh Norton writes that CEA's efforts to administer the wage-price guidelines "had the effect of weakening the general moral authority of the Council" (1977). Charles Schultze refused to move his office from the Eisenhower Executive Office Building to the West Wing and serve as an economic policy coordinator because "[h]e felt it would compromise his objectivity and burden him with administrative duties inconsistent with his role as the head of the President's in-house economic think tank" (Eizenstat 1992). Stuart Eizenstat, President Carter's domestic policy adviser, argues that "[t]he CEA cannot provide both detached, Olympian economic advice and become enmeshed in the daily, inter-agency compromises and political log-rolling" (1992).

This is not to say that CEA should not contribute to operational matters at all. To the contrary, it is quite common for CEA to participate in interagency committees, and CEA occasionally even chairs some committees. Yet the academic background of most of CEA's staff and its mission to provide expert economic advice, render it unsuited to serve as a policy or strategic coordinator.

Recognizing this, most recent Presidents have relied on some other institutional body or senior White House aides to coordinate economic policy.[4] Since 1993, the National Economic Council has been responsible for coordinating economic policymaking. These arrangements have largely served to augment CEA's effectiveness by permitting it to focus on providing economic advice and analysis and giving the Council greater exposure to the President. Roger Porter writes:

> *What might appear on the surface as a competitive arrangement has rarely been viewed by the participants as a zero-sum game. To the contrary, both the CEA chairman and the White House economic-policy assistant have usually viewed the other as an ally and often as a trusted confidant (1997).*

Former CEA Chairman Alan Krueger writes that the development of the National Economic Council "elevated the Council of Economic Advisers, freeing it to advocate efficient economic programs and ensuring that the [P]resident had its input" (2000).

---

[4] For example, President Eisenhower established the Advisory Board on Economic Growth and Stability and the Council on Foreign Economic Policy; President Nixon created the Cabinet Committee on Economic Policy, the Council on International Economic Policy, and the Council on Economic Policy; President Ford established the Economic Policy Board; President Carter created the Economic Policy Group; and President Reagan established the Economic Policy Council. Most of these committees or councils have not continued in the same form from one administration to the next (Orszag et al. 2002; Porter 1983).

GATHER, ANALYZE, AND INTERPRET INFORMATION ON ECONOMIC TRENDS AND DEVELOPMENTS

Another one of CEA's functions under the Employment Act of 1946 is to "to gather timely and authoritative information concerning economic developments and economic trends." This includes staying up to date on major trends in the macroeconomy, financial markets, and labor markets, as well as in sectors such as health care, energy, and housing. This role is important not only because developments in these sectors can be the bases for motivating future policies, but also because the President, senior White House staff, and the public need to understand these issues.

CEA fulfills this role through a variety of different means, including: sending regular memos to the President on the evening before key data releases; providing daily, weekly, or monthly updates on developments in the economy; writing more detailed one-off memos to the President and the senior White House team on specific issues; producing public reports on relevant economic topics or trends; and publishing the annual *Economic Report of the President*. Sometimes, the President will call for CEA to explicate a particular issue. For example, Murray Weidenbaum reports having a "pleasant—but spirited and extended—difference of views [with President Ronald Reagan] on the matter of seasonally adjusted versus unadjusted reports on employment and unemployment" (1988). In many cases, this work does not immediately motivate or advance a particular policy, but the ongoing monitoring and communicating information about the economy ultimately helps to inform the development, prioritization, and public reception of economic policies (see Box 7-5 for former CEA Chairman Alan Greenspan's history of the weekly Gross National Product measurement that CEA developed and used to assess the need for expansionary fiscal measures during the Ford Administration).

The Burns Council and the 1953-54 Recession

The 1953-54 recession represented an early test of this information-gathering function. By the time President Eisenhower took office in 1953, the economy had fully recovered from a mild recession that had occurred a few years earlier, and the unemployment rate was at its lowest point since World War II. However, in July 1953, the United States signed the Korean armistice, and the public anticipated that a substantial decline in military expenditures would soon follow, sparking concern about an impending recession (Engelbourg 1980).

During the summer of 1953, the newly reconstituted Council grew increasingly worried about the possibility of a recession, and spent the next

Box 7-5: Former CEA Chairman Alan Greenspan (1974 – 1977)

In the autumn of 1974, industrial production began to fall rapidly, and unemployment started to increase rapidly. That the economy was heading into a recession (if it were not in fact already in one) didn't require much debate. By Christmas, the key question for the Ford Administration's economic policy was whether we were experiencing an inventory recession, which would mean a sharp but temporary erosion in production and employment as businesses worked off excess inventories, or a far more dangerous softening in the economy engendered by a persistent weakness in final demand. This was the burning issue for the President. For a short-term inventory correction, the optimum policy, as we saw it, was to do as little as politically possible.

The political advice being offered to the administration was unequivocal. It was typified by the March 1975 testimony of AFL-CIO president George Meany to Congress that "America is in the worst economic emergency since the Great Depression … The situation is frightening now and it is growing more ominous by the day. This is not just another recession, for it has no parallel in the five recessions in the post-World War II period. America is far beyond the point where the situation can correct itself. Massive government action is needed."

The Council of Economic Advisers had no real time measure of the state of demand and inventories. Official estimates of gross national product (GNP) and its components would answer the vexing question. But the data required to make the key policy choices would become available weeks, perhaps months, in the future. In December 1974, however, CEA developed what amounted to a weekly GNP. It would not have passed the exacting statistical publication standards of the Bureau of Economic Analysis of the Department of Commerce, but it was more than adequate—in fact, quite instrumental—in answering the question of whether we were experiencing an inventory recession, a final demand recession, or both.

While the Department of Commerce has since abandoned its weekly retail sales series, it nonetheless did yeoman service during that period in indicating that personal consumption expenditures were not undergoing a downward plunge. This was confirmed by the timely 10-day data of full coverage of motor vehicle sales. The other sectors of the economy had to be estimated more indirectly. Industry trade sources, coupled with the latest data on building permits (which leads residential construction) outlined the residential sector for us. Survey forecasts of plant and equipment, monthly new orders and shipments for machinery, data on nonresidential construction, and, with a delay, imports of capital equipment constructed a crude proxy for capital investment. From the unemployment insurance system we were able to develop a rough indicator of aggregate hours worked, which, combined with an estimate of output per work hour (which were little more than educated guesses), yielded a rough preliminary estimate of total real GNP, which was then adjusted to reconcile with its component parts.

These data indicated, with some degree of robustness, something that we knew for a fact only much later: that the rate of inventory liquidation—the gap between GNP and final demand—was exceptionally large by historic standards. That gap reflected the fact that production had been cut well below the level of final demand in order to work off the excess inventories that had accumulated. Therefore, if final demand continued to stabilize, as apparently it was doing in the early weeks of 1975, the recession's low point was close at hand and a marked rebound from the downturn was highly likely. Inventory liquidation cannot go on indefinitely. The rate must eventually slow, and that process closes the gap between final demand and production, sometimes quite rapidly.

It soon became clear from the weekly insured unemployment data and several qualitative indicators that the worst was over.[1] At that point we could conclude that further expansionary fiscal measures beyond the modest initiatives of the Ford Administration would be unnecessary and in the long run could turn out to be counterproductive. Short-term emergency GNP monitoring was no longer necessary and the short, but admirable, history of the weekly GNP came to a close.

---

[1] Real GDP rose 6.2 percent from Q1:1975 to Q1:1976.

few months documenting economic data showing worsening conditions. CEA's new chairman, Arthur Burns, was an expert on business cycles, and was considered to be "a champion of empirical, or inductive, economics, preferring to draw conclusions and base policy upon observable facts rather than deductively from theoretical relationships and models" (Flash 1965). Thus, over the next several months, the Council monitored various economic indicators, such as unemployment, stock prices, commercial construction, new housing starts, farm income, business inventory accumulation, and business sales, and submitted regular updates to the President and other agencies.

In addition to monitoring economic developments, the Council also began actively helping to develop a counter-recessionary strategy. First, the Council attempted to convince the Federal Reserve to ease the money supply and credit, and Burns "lost no opportunity to seek its cooperation" (Norton 1977). (Note that the Federal Reserve has long-established independence, and Executive Branch policy in recent administrations has been to not comment on or in any way attempt to influence its actions.) Second, CEA advocated for reducing Federal taxes to stimulate demand, contrary to the views of then-Treasury Secretary George Humphrey, who was concerned about tax cuts adding to the deficit.[5] Finally, CEA advocated for increased public works spending, developing various proposals and publicly calling for it in the 1954 *Economic Report of the President*. However, Burns recognized that public works projects would take a long time to implement and take effect, and the Council ultimately advised that extra public works funds should only be requested if unemployment reached six million in 1954, which never came close to occurring (Engelbourg 1980). Thus, although the Council and others within the administration devoted much deliberation to planning public works activities, in the end, their practical effects were fairly minimal.

In the end, the economy experienced a relatively short and mild recession, an outcome that helped CEA reach "a high-water mark of prestige and acceptance" (Flash 1965).[6] Moreover, as noted previously, this was the first time that a major tax cut had been implemented at the time of a budgetary shortfall to counter a recession. According to the 1966 *Economic Report of the President*, the administration's actions in 1954 established "the bipartisan character of expansionary fiscal policies ... for the first time" (CEA 1966).

That being said, some have argued that the Council's work in monitoring and informing the administration and the public about economic developments was ultimately more influential than its direct efforts to promote specific countercyclical policies. Edward Flash writes:

> *Burns' inductive economics reinforced policy objectives and provided an excellent analysis of unfolding developments ... Except for underestimating the reductions in government expenditures for fiscal 1954 and allegedly overestimating administrative budget flexibility, the Council correctly assessed the mildness of the recession and provided*

---

[5] Only a couple years later, their roles in the debate were reversed. In 1956, Burns and Humphrey took opposite sides in another dispute, with Humphrey arguing for a tax reduction and Burns arguing against it, because inflation was beginning to pick up. Humphrey scheduled a meeting to make his case to President Eisenhower. Burns's account of the meeting is as follows: "Eisenhower greeted us with his customary enthusiasm: 'My two friends, just the two men I wanted to see. I just had a damn fool businessman in here saying that we ought to lower taxes now, this at a time when inflation is beginning to heat up—to lower taxes! Can you imagine any idiocy like that?' I took out a handkerchief and covered my face ... It was all I could do to control myself from bursting out laughing. Well, there was talk about all kinds of things for about an hour and a quarter. I did not say one word. I was waiting for Humphrey; but he never got around to the subject of the meeting" (Hargrove and Morley 1984).
[6] Chairman Burns's efforts also won praise from President Eisenhower, with the President remarking to him one day, "Arthur, my boy, you would have made a fine chief of staff overseas during the war" (Norton 1977).

an informational basis for appropriate Administration policies.
Through Burns, the Council kept the President and the Cabinet
informed; through ABEGS [the Advisory Board on Economic Growth
and Stability], chaired by Burns, the Council accomplished the same
thing with departments and agencies. To the President, Burns pro-
vided constant and expert counsel; to the departments he conveyed
an overview of recession developments and governmental counter-
moves that transcended particular operational operations and out-
look (1965).

By contrast, Flash argues that "it appears reasonable to conclude that
… one, the Council's influence on the [F]ederal [G]overnment's actions of
tax reduction and monetary easing which most significantly contributed to
recovery was minor and two, those instances where its influence was significant involved actions that did not bulk large in recovery impact" (1965).
For instance, he notes that much of the tax reduction that was enacted had
already been scheduled to go into effect: the personal income tax reduction
was implemented as a result of legislation enacted during the Korean War
mobilization, and the excess profits tax was scheduled to expire automatically. CEA did persuade the President to pass an additional tax reduction of
$1.4 billion, but by the time it was implemented, the recovery was already
underway.

The 1970s and Stagflation

Of course, there have also been moments in CEA's history where its
interpretation of economic trends and its understanding of the appropriate
policy response have proved deficient. Herbert Stein notes that the 1970s
were a particularly difficult time for CEA:

The later Nixon years, the Ford years and the Carter years were
a period in which the CEA struggled with problems for which the
economics profession was unprepared. High unemployment and high
inflation persisted. Fiscal policy was dominated by concern with ris-
ing expenditures and deficits. The growth rate of potential output
seemed to be slowing down for reasons that were not understood
(1996).

Stein writes that CEA's "most serious error" during the Nixon
Administration was thinking that the natural rate of unemployment was 4
percent. This led the Council to think that it only had to let unemployment
rise slightly above that before inflation would start to dissipate. Yet CEA was
proven wrong, and when unemployment rose to 6 percent with no sign of

progress, "confidence in the policy of 'gradualism' evaporated … [which] helped to set the stage for the radical move to price and wage controls, which the CEA had not foreseen and did not want" (1996).

More generally, Stein comments that two institutional deficiencies of CEA are that "it does not look far enough ahead, but gets too engrossed in immediate problems … [and that] like the government as a whole, is deficient in contingency planning." To remedy the first problem, Stein advises that "[i]t might be useful to segregate a portion of the staff, under the guidance of one of the members, to think only of what the economy and its problems might look like in, say, 25 years" (1996).

ENGAGE THE ECONOMICS COMMUNITY

The final function of CEA is to engage with the economics community, by staying abreast of the latest academic research and by sharing new insights with policymakers, and in turn, by communicating the administration's actions and plans to the economics community. This function helps to support the administration's efforts to develop economic policies and to articulate and advance the President's agenda. While the academic character of CEA may not have been originally intended by Congress when it created CEA, this engagement has arguably made the Council a more effective and durable institution.

The Origins of Economists in the White House

Although CEA is now closely identified with the economics profession, this was not originally the case. J. Bradford DeLong writes that "[e]stablishing in the White House staff a group of short-term employees with a primary allegiance to economists' sense of the public interest may have been the furthest thing from the minds of those who wrote Section 4 of the 1946 Employment Act" (1996). Rather, during the lead-up to the passage of the Employment Act, "[t]here were some people in Congress who envisioned the Council as a representative body … [and that] each one of the three basic sectors of the American economy; agriculture, industry and labor, should be represented on the Council" (Naveh 1981). Some supporters of the Employment Act wanted CEA to be staffed by people who had experience working in government or business, while others wanted to appoint academic economists.

In the end, the first CEA under President Truman included representation from all of these backgrounds. Nourse was an agricultural economist who had spent much of his career at the Brookings Institution; Keyserling was a lawyer who had completed graduate coursework in economics, and had experience working in government and ties to organized labor; and Clark was a former oil industry executive and a business school dean. By comparison, the staff recruited to serve on the first Council was comprised of "[e]conomists who integrated government experience and academic training" ... almost all of whom "could be called government careerists" (Naveh 1981).

The shift toward hiring more academic economists commenced under the Burns Council, and intensified during the Heller Council. In part, Burns started hiring academic economists due to a scarcity of available labor: "Burns had a hard time finding qualified economists who at the same time, were not too closely identified with the previous administrations, would agree to work for President Eisenhower, [and] would stay in Washington at the time [of] Senator McCarthy's investigations." Meanwhile, academic institutions were a "convenient supplier of temporary personnel" (Naveh 1981). Burns also saw hiring academics as a means of depoliticizing CEA and establishing its credibility, which was especially important since CEA had come to be viewed as excessively political during Keyserling's tenure.

Institutional Advantages and Challenges

CEA's economic perspective and academic character have, as Burns intended, helped to insulate it against politics to some extent. As discussed above, the Council has held a number of the same positions under both Democratic and Republican administrations. In large part, this is because CEA tends to reflect the policy views of the economics profession, and on many (but not all) issues, "there is a distinct consensus among economists" (Schultze 1996). Murray Weidenbaum notes that when Congress in 1995 was debating whether to continue to fund CEA, "every active Republican ex-chairman came to the defense of the CEA as well as the Democratic economists who served on the [C]ouncil" (1996). When the administration changes, the leadership of CEA changes too, but there is a tradition of its staff continuing to serve through the first summer of the subsequent administration.

Some former CEA chairs have claimed that the institutional structure of CEA can help to reinforce its economic perspective. For example, Joseph Stiglitz argues that the fact that CEA is composed of "citizen-bureaucrats" who know they will be returning to their academic perches shortly means that they "have a long-term incentive to maintain [their] professional reputations" (1997), and that this creates an incentive for CEA staff to ensure that its recommendations are economically defensible. This point is echoed by former CEA Chairman Martin Feldstein (1992) and former CEA Member Jeffrey Frankel (2003). Of course, CEA's perspective is not unique,

Box 7-6: Former CEA Chairman Martin Feldstein (1982 – 1984)

I became Chairman of President Ronald Reagan's Council of Economic Advisers in the summer of 1982. I served for two years, the maximum time allowed by Harvard's policy of leave for government service. Acting as CEA chairman provided a crash course in a wide range of economic issues, including exchange rates, financial regulation and emerging market deficits, as well as an education in how the political process works inside the administration and with Congress.

Ronald Reagan made his economic goals very clear: lowering the rate of inflation, reducing the government's share of gross domestic product (GDP) while increasing defense spending, lowering tax rates, and reducing government regulation. Although he left it to others to work out the details, he made these things happen because of his skills in speaking to the American public and his ability to compromise in working with the Congress. He succeeded in achieving his goals, although never to the extent that he wanted. Government spending fell from 21.6 percent of GDP in 1981 to 20.5 percent in 1989, while the defense share rose from 5.0 percent to 5.5 percent, taxes fell from 19.1 percent of GDP to 17.8 percent, and the fiscal deficit excluding interest on the national debt (the primary balance) fell from 0.3 percent to minus 0.3 percent.

Although the Democrats had an overwhelming majority in the House of Representatives for the entire eight years of the Reagan presidency, the President achieved major tax reform (a revenue-neutral reduction of the top personal tax rate from 50 percent to 28 percent), a major reform of Social Security (raising the future age for full benefits from 65 to 67), and a free trade agreement with Canada.

The Federal Reserve under Chairman Paul Volcker (who had been appointed by President Jimmy Carter and later reappointed by President Reagan) achieved a rapid fall in inflation from 12.5 percent in 1980 to 3.8 percent in 1982 and 1983. This disinflation involved double-digit interest rates and a sharp economic downturn. One of my challenges as CEA chairman was to defend the Federal Reserve's actions against critics both inside and outside the administration.

The overall budget deficit increased sharply from 2.5 percent of GDP in 1981 to 5.9 percent of GDP in 1983. The 25-percent cut in personal tax rates that was enacted in 1981 was not expected to result in such a large deficit increase because, with tax brackets not indexed to inflation before 1986, it was projected that the high inflation that prevailed before the tax cuts would raise taxable incomes to offset the cut in tax rates. The unexpectedly rapid fall in inflation reduced the offsetting tax revenue. Although some of the rise in the fiscal deficit was also due to the recession that began in 1981, a net increase in the structural deficit remained. I joined forces with Budget Director David Stockman to argue that revenue increases as well as spending cuts were needed to shrink that structural deficit. Although the political side of the White House criticized me for this position, President Reagan made no objections and did support annual revenue-raising changes in corporate taxation while sticking with his promise not to raise taxes on "hard-working families struggling to make ends meet."

Although there were very good economists in several different cabinet departments, I realized that they each had two roles. In addition to advising the cabinet member who was the head of their department, they had to represent their department's position at interdepartmental meetings. I therefore found myself debating with these economists at meetings while suspecting that they were presenting their department's positions rather than their professional judgments. Perhaps they didn't mind losing some of those debates.

In my meetings with economic officials of other countries, I came to appreciate the unique role of the Council. As CEA chairman, I reported directly to the President and presented my own views in testimony to Congress. In contrast, the senior economic officials in other countries were often political figures rather than professional economists, or were economists who reported only privately to a minister of finance.

The team at the CEA is also unusual in being academics serving for only one or two years (except for the very valuable long-term statistical staff). This meant having very high quality people who brought up-to-date professional thinking, but who had to learn quickly the details of policy issues. William Poole and William Niskanen were already members of the CEA when I arrived and continued to work with me during my two years. The people I recruited as members of the staff included Democrats as well as Republicans, chosen for their analytic abilities, including Larry Summers, Paul Krugman, John Cochrane and Jeff Frankel, as well as younger economists Ken Froot, Larry Lindsey, Greg Mankiw and Katherine Utgoff, and others whose political affiliations I did not know. Although the White House personnel office was surprised when they eventually discovered some of their political affiliations, there was no attempt to change these appointments or limit what I did in my second-year appointments.

One of the many pleasures in working with President Reagan was his positive and optimistic attitude. It no doubt made it possible for him to work successfully with both Republicans and Democrats in Congress. But it sometimes made it difficult for me to convince him of the need to adopt certain policy changes. I recall one occasion after I had just had one of my Oval Office meetings with the President in which I said that it would be very risky not to make a particular policy change. The President asked whether continuing with the current policy was sure to create a problem. I said that I couldn't be certain of that but that the current policy would have a very low probability of success. I thought that my argument would have persuaded a typical prudent corporate CEO to make the change that I was suggesting. But the President decided not to do so.

As I left the Oval Office I realized that the President's optimism and his willingness to take a long shot on policy was not an accident but was based on his own life history. He started as a radio sports announcer but was soon a major movie star in Hollywood. When his movie career came to an end, he eventually went on to become a popular California governor. He later ran for the nomination as Republican candidate for the presidency but was defeated. But the next time around he won the nomination, was elected overwhelmingly, and was reelected four years later with an even larger margin. And there I was, after his long string of improbable successes, trying to persuade him not to do something because it was unlikely to happen.

and policy analysts throughout the Federal Government often hold similar views as CEA, but CEA is unusual in that providing an economic perspective is essentially its sole institutional purpose (see Box 7-6 for former CEA Chairman Martin Feldstein's discussion of CEA's unusual institutional structure and CEA's role in informing fiscal policy during the Reagan Administration).

CEA's academic character also helps to bring fresh perspectives on policy into the government, both by bringing in new people who have new ideas, and through keeping open the channels of communication with academia. It also means that CEA's views about policy tend to reflect economists' current understanding of how best to promote the public interest. For example, Charles Schultze notes that CEA regularly supported antitrust policies under the Eisenhower, Kennedy, Ford, and Nixon Administrations, but that its support for such policies waned during the 1980s as the economics profession's views shifted (1996). In recent years, growing evidence of "economic rents" has led CEA, along with many in the economics profession, to increasingly emphasize the importance of fostering more competitive markets as a means to address inequality and raise real incomes (see discussion in Chapter 1). In this way, Edwin Nourse's view of CEA as a "doorway through which the best thinking of systematic economics … may be brought into clear and effective focus at the point of executive decision as to national economic policy and action" has been vindicated (Norton 1977).

Of course, relying on short-term academic economists also presents some notable challenges: CEA's staff have little institutional memory and often do not enter government with much knowledge about policy decision-making processes or much understanding of the details of how Federal programs function. In addition, as discussed above, though it is critical to provide unvarnished economic advice, such advice is likely to be more useful if it is at least presented with an awareness of the broader political context. These constraints result in a substantial learning curve for many incoming CEA staff, and if they are not surmounted, can present barriers to engaging effectively in the policy process. Some CEAs have attempted to attenuate these obstacles by including a few government economists on staff and by relying on several career staff members for institutional memory.

Conclusion

Many of CEA's contributions are due to its unique institutional structure: that it is a small organization with no regulatory authority of its own, few direct operational responsibilities, and populated by academic economists. Yet its contributions are also dependent on the ability of its staff to balance operating effectively in a necessarily political environment without being overly influenced by politics, and to be effective in advocating for their positions while providing objective economic advice. All in all, given the divergent objectives reflected in the Employment Act of 1946, CEA's turbulent early years, and its unusual institutional structure, CEA has proven to be a durable and effective advocate for the public interest.

REFERENCES

CHAPTER 1

American Civil Liberties Union. 2013. "The War on Marijuana in Black and White." Accessed January 31, 2016.

Aizer, Anna, Shari Eli, Joseph P. Ferrie, and Adriana Lleras-Muney. 2014. "The Long Term Impact of Cash Transfers to Poor Families." NBER Working Paper 20103.

Autor, David. 2010. "The Polarization of Job Opportunities in the U.S. Labor Market." Center for American Progress, the Hamilton Project.

Bakija, Jon, Adam Cole and Bradley T. Heim. 2010. "Jobs and Income Growth of Top Earners and the Causes of Changing Income Inequality: Evidence from U.S. Tax Return Data." Department of Economics Working Paper 2010–24. Williams College.

Boskin, Michael J. 1972. "Unions and Relative Real Wages." *The American Economic Review* 62(3): 466-472.

Bricker, Jesse, Lisa J. Dettling, Alice Henriques, Joanne W. Hsu, Kevin B. Moore, John Sabelhaus, Jeffrey Thompson, and Richard A. Windle. 2014. "Changes in U.S. Family Finances from 2010 to 2013: Evidence from the Survey of Consumer Finances." *Federal Reserve Bulletin*, Vol. 100, No. 4.

Brown, David W., Amanda E. Kowalski, and Ithai Z. Lurie. 2015. "Medicaid as an Investment in Children: What is the Long-term Impact on Tax Receipts?" National Bureau of Economic Research Working Paper No. 20835.

Card, David, Thomas Lemieux, and W. Craig Riddell. 2004. "Unions and Wage Inequality." *Journal of Labor Research*, 25(4): 519-559.

Carson, Ann. 2015. "Prisoners in 2014." Bureau of Justice Statistics, Department of Justice.

Chetty, Raj, Nathaniel Hendren, Patrick Kline, Emmanuel Saez, and Nicholas Turner. 2014. "Is the United States Still a Land of Opportunity? Recent Trends in Intergenerational Mobility." NBER Working Paper 19844.

Chetty, Raj, Nathaniel Hendren, Patrick Kline, and Emmanuel Saez. 2014. "Where is the Land of Opportunity? The Geography of Intergenerational Mobility in the United States." *Quarterly Journal of Economics*, 129 (4):1553-1623.

Chetty, Raj, John N. Friedman, and Jonah Rockoff. 2011. "New Evidence on the Long-Term Impacts of Tax Credits." Internal Revenue Service Statistics of Income Working Paper.

Cingano, Federico. (2014), "Trends in Income Inequality and its Impact on Economic Growth." OECD Social, Employment and Migration Working Papers, No. 163. OECD Publishing.

Congressional Budget Office. 2013. "The Distribution of Household Income and Federal Taxes, 2010." Publication No. 4613.

Corak, Miles. 2011. "Inequality from Generation to Generation: the United States in Comparison." University of Ottawa. Accessed January 31, 2016.

Council of Economic Advisers. 2014. "Eleven Facts about American Families and Work."

_____. 2015a. "Fines, Fees, and Bail." Issue Brief.

_____. 2015b. "Long-Term Benefits of the Supplemental Nutrition Assistance Program," Issue Brief.

_____. 2015c. "Worker Voice in a Time of Rising Inequality." Issue Brief.

Duesenberry, James. 1949. *Income, Saving and the Theory of Consumer Behavior*. Harvard University Press, Cambridge, MA.

Duncan and Murnane (2011); Putnam, Robert. 2015. *Our Kids: The American Dream in Crisis*. New York, New York: Simon & Schuster.

Furman, Jason. 2015a. "Barriers to Shared Growth: The Case of Land Use Regulation and Economic Rents." Remarks at the Urban Institute.

_____. 2015b. "Occupational Licensing and Economic Rents." Remarks at the Brookings Institution.

Furman, Jason and Peter Orszag. 2015. "A Firm-Level Perspective on the Role of Rents in the Rise in Inequality." Presentation at "A Just Society" Centennial Event in Honor of Joseph Stiglitz Columbia University, October 16, 2015.

Glaeser, Edward L., and Joseph Gyourko. 2003. "The Impact of Building Restrictions on Housing Affordability." *Economic Policy Review*, 9 (2): 21-39.

Glaeser, Edward L., Joseph Gyourko, and Raven E. Saks. 2005. "Why Have Housing Prices Gone Up?" *American Economic Review*, 95(2): 329-333.

Goldin, Claudia and Lawrence F. Katz. 2009. "The Race between Education and Technology:The Evolution of U.S. Educational Wage Differentials, 1890 to 2005." NBER Working Paper No. 12984.

Greene, Karen. 1969. "Occupational Licensing and the Supply of Nonprofessional Manpower." Washington, DC: Manpower Administration, U.S. Department of Labor.

Gyourko, Joseph, and Raven Molloy. 2015. "Regulation and Housing Supply." in Duranton,Gilles, J. Vernon Henderson, and William C. Strange eds., *Handbook of Regional and Urban Economics*, Volume 5B. Handbook of Regional and Urban Economics. Amsterdam; San Diego and Oxford: Elsevier Science.

Hoynes, Hilary W., Diane Whitmore Schanzenbach, and Douglas Almond. 2012. "Long Run Impacts of Childhood Access to the Safety Net." National Bureau of Economic Research Working Paper No. 18535.

Johnson, Janna E., and Morris M. Kleiner. 2014. "Is Occupational Licensing a Barrier to Interstate Migration?" Working Paper, University of Minnesota.

Kleiner, Morris M. 1990. "Are There Economic Rents for More Restrictive Occupational Licensing Practices?" 42nd Annual Proceedings. United States: Industrial Relations Research Association 177-185.

_____. 2006. "Licensing Occupations: Ensuring Quality or Restriction Competition?" W.E. Upjohn Institute for Employment Research 1-15. Kalamazoo, MI: Upjohn Institute Press.

_____. 2015. "Reforming Occupational Licensing Policies." Discussion Paper 2015-01. The Hamilton Project.

Kleiner, Morris M. and Alan B. Krueger. 2010. "The Prevalence and Effects of Occupational Licensing." *British Journal of Industrial Relations,* Vol. 48, No. 4: 676-687.

_____. 2013. "Analyzing the Extent and Influence of Occupational Licensing on the Labor Market." *Journal of Labor Economics,* Vol. 31, No. 2: S173-S202.

Liebman, Jeffrey B. 1998. "The Impact of the Earned Income Tax Credit on Incentives and Income Distribution." *Tax Policy and the Economy,* Vol. 12. MIT Press.

Milanovic, Branko. 2012. "Global Income Inequality by the Numbers: in History and Now." Policy Research Working Paper 6259. The World Bank Development Research Group.

Minor -Harper, Stephanie. 1986. "State and Federal Prisoners, 1925-85." Bureau of Justice Statistics, Department of Justice.

Mishel, Lawrence, Josh Bivens, Elise Gould, and Heidi Shierholz. 2012. *The State of Working America,* 12th ed. Economic Policy Institute. Cornell University Press.

Okun, Arthur. 1975. *Equality and Efficiency: The Big Trade-Off.* Washington DC: Brookings Institution.

Ostry, Jonathan D., Andrew Berg, and Charalambos G. Tsangarides. 2014. "Redistribution, Inequality, and Growth." IMF Staff Discussion Note. IMF Research Department.

Piketty, Thomas. 2014. *Capital in the Twenty-First Century.* Harvard University Press.

Pikkety, Thomas and Emmanuel Saez. 2015 (updating 2003 text). "Income Inequality in the United States, 1913-1998." *Quarterly Journal of Economics,* Vol. 118 (1).

RealtyTrac. 2015. "Home Price Appreciation Outpaces Wage Growth in 76 Percent of U.S. Markets During Housing Recovery."

Saez, Emmanuel and Gabriel Zucman. 2014. "Wealth Inequality in the United States Since 1913: Evidence from Capitalized Income Tax Data." NBER Working Paper 20625.

The Leadership Conference on Civil and Human Rights. "Chapter Three: Race, Sentencing and the "Tough Crime" Movement." Accessed January 31, 2016.

Troy, Leo and Neil Sheflin. 1985. *Union Sourcebook: Membership Structure, Finance, Directory*. West Orange, NJ: Industrial Relations Data Information Services.

Weil, David. 1992. "Building Safety: The Role of Construction Unions in Enforcement of OSHA." *Journal of Labor Research*, 13(1): 121-132.

Western, Bruce and Jake Rosenfeld. 2011. "Unions, Norms, and the Rise in U.S. Wage Inequality." *American Sociological Review*, 76(4): 513-537.

World Top Income Database (WTID). "The World Top Incomes Database." Alvaredo, Facundo, Tony Atkinson, Thomas Piketty, Emmanuel Saez, and Gabriel Zucman. Accessed January 30, 2016.

CHAPTER 2

Ball, Laurence and Sandeep Mazumder. 2011. "Inflation Dynamics and the Great Recession." International Monetary Fund Working Paper WP/11/121.

Been, Vicki, Ingrid Gould Ellen, Michael Gedal, Edward Glaeser, and Brian J. McCabe. 2014. "Preserving History or Hindering Growth? The Heterogeneous Effects of Historic Districts on Local Housing Markets in New York City." National Bureau of Economics Working Paper No. 20446.

Board of Governors of the Federal Reserve System. 2015. "Federal Reserve Issues FOMC Statement." December 16.

Bricker, Jesse, Lisa Dettling, Alice Henriques, Joanne Hsu, Kevin Moore, John Sabelhaus, Jeffrey Thompson, Richard Windle, Sebastian Devlin-Foltz, and Jacob Krimmel. 2014. "Changes in U.S. Family Finances from 2010 to 2013: Evidence from the Survey of Consumer Finances." *Federal Reserve Bulletin* 100 (4).

Brynjolfsson, Erik and JooHee Oh. 2012. "The Attention Economy: Measuring the Value of Free Digital Services on the Internet." Proceedings of the 33rd International Conference on Information Systems, Economics and Value of IS. Orlando. December 14.

Chetty, Raj, Nathaniel Hendren, Patrick Kline, and Emmanuel Saez. 2014. "Where is the Land of Opportunity? The Geography of Intergenerational Mobility in the United States." *The Quarterly Journal of Economics* 129 (4): 1553–1623.

Congressional Budget Office (CBO). 2013a. "Macroeconomic Effects of Alternative Budgetary Paths."

_____. 2013b. "The Economic Impact of S. 744, the Border Security, Economic Opportunity, and Immigration Modernization Act."

_____. 2015. "A Macroeconomic Analysis of the President's 2016 Budget."

Council of Economic Advisers (CEA). 1997. "Economic Report of the President."

_____. 2014. "The All-of-the-Above Energy Strategy as a Path to Sustainable Economic Growth."

_____. 2015a. "A Better Measure of Economic Growth: Gross Domestic Output (GDO)."

_____. 2015b. "Economic Report of the President."

_____. 2015c. "Explaining the U.S. Petroleum Consumption Surprise."

_____. 2015d. "Long-Term Interest Rates: A Survey."

Decker, Ryan, John Haltiwanger, Ron Jarmin, and Javier Miranda. 2014. "The Role of Entrepreneurship in US Job Creation and Economic Dynamism." *Journal of Economic Perspectives* 28 (3): 3–24.

_____. Forthcoming. "Changing Business Dynamism: Volatility of vs. Responsiveness to Shocks?" *American Economic Review.*

Engen, Eric, Thomas Laubach, and Dave Reifschneider. 2015. "The Macroeconomic Effects of the Federal Reserve's Unconventional Monetary Policies." Finance and Economics Discussion Series 2015–05. Board of Governors of the Federal Reserve System.

European Commission. 2013. "Transatlantic Trade and Investment Partnership: The Economic Analysis Explained."

Fieller, E.C. 1954. "Some Problems in Interval Estimation." *Journal of the Royal Statistical Society* 16 (2): 175–85.

Gudell, Svenja. 2015. "Q3 Negative Equity: Still Coming Down, Still Messing Things Up." Zillow Briefs – Negative Equity. December 2.

Glaeser, Edward L. and Bryce A. Ward. 2008. "The Causes and Consequences of Land Use Regulation: Evidence from Greater Boston." *Journal of Urban Economics* 65 (3): 265–78.

Glaeser, Edward L., Joseph Gyourko, and Raven Saks. 2005. "Why Have Housing Prices Gone Up?" *American Economic Review* 95 (2): 329–333.

Goodman, Laurie, Rolf Pendall, and Jun Zhu. 2015. "Headship and Homeownership: What Does the Future Hold?" Washington: Urban Institute.

Gyourko, Joseph, Albert Saiz, and Anita Summers. 2008. "A New Measure of the Local Regulatory Environment for Housing Markets: The Wharton Residential Land Use Regulatory Index." *Urban Studies* 45 (3): 693–729.

Gyourko, Joseph and Raven Molloy. 2015. "Regulation and Housing Supply." In Gilles Duranton, J. Vernon Henderson, and William C. Strange, eds., *Handbook of Regional and Urban Economics: Volume 5B.* Amsterdam, San Diego and Oxford: Elsevier Science. 1289–1337.

Hamilton, James D. 2003. "What is an Oil Shock?" *Journal of Econometrics* 113 (2): 363–98.

Hatzius, Jan and Kris Dawsey. 2015. "Doing the Sums on Productivity Paradox v2.0." US Economics Research Issue 15/30. New York: Goldman Sachs.

Hsieh, Chang-Tai and Enrico Moretti. 2015. "Why Do Cities Matter? Local Growth and Aggregate Growth." National Bureau of Economics Working Paper No. 21154.

Ihrig, Jane, Elizabeth Klee, Canlin Li, Brett Schulte, and Min Wei. 2015. "Expectations about the Federal Reserve's Balance Sheet and the Term Structure of Interest Rates." Finance and Economics Discussion Affairs Series 2015–047. Board of Governors of the Federal Reserve System.

International Monetary Fund (IMF). 2014. "World Economic Outlook, October 2014: Legacies, Clouds, Uncertainties." Washington.

———. 2015. "World Economic Outlook, October 2015: Adjusting to Lower Commodity Prices." Washington.

Joint Center for Housing Studies. 2015. "The State of the Nation's Housing." Cambridge, MA: Joint Center for Housing Studies of Harvard University.

Kilian, Lutz. 2014. "Oil Price Shocks: Causes and Consequences." *Annual Review of Resource Economics* 6 (1): 133–54.

Kocin, Paul J. and Louis Uccellini. 2004. "A Snowfall Impact Scale Derived from Northeast Storm Snowfall Distributions." *Bulletin of the American Meteorological Society* 85 (2): 177–94.

McCulla, Stephanie H., and Shelly Smith. 2015. "The 2015 Annual Revision of the National Income and Product Accounts." *Survey of Current Business* 95 (8): 1–31.

Molloy, Raven, Christopher L. Smith, and Abigail Wozniak. 2011. "Internal Migration in the United States." *Journal of Economic Perspectives* 25 (3): 173–96.

Moulton, Brent. 2015. "Harmonizing BEA's Measures of GDP, GDI, and Value Added: Update Session." Presentation at the Bureau of Economic Analysis Advisory Committee. May 8.

Nakamura, Leonard I. and Rachel H. Soloveichik. 2015. "Valuing 'Free' Media across Countries in GDP." Federal Reserve Bank of Philadelphia Working Paper 15–25.

NIPA Handbook. "Concepts and Methods of the U.S. National Income and Product Accounts." 2014. Methodology Papers, National Accounts (February). Bureau of Economic Analysis.

Nordhaus, William D. 2006. "Principles of National Accounting for Non-Market Accounts." In Dale Jorgenson, J. Steven Landefeld, and William Nordhaus, eds., *Architecture for the National Accounts*. Chicago: University of Chicago Press. 141–59.

Petri, Peter A. and Michael G. Plummer. 2016. "The Economic Effects of the Trans-Pacific Partnership: New Estimates." Working Paper Series WP 16–2. Washington: Peterson Institute for International Economics.

Polivka, Anne E., Stephen M. Miller. 1998. "The CPS after the Redesign: Refocusing the Economic Lens." In John Haltiwanger, Marilyn E. Manser, and Robert Topel, eds., *Labor Statistics Measurement Issues*. Chicago: University of Chicago Press. 249–89.

Sahm, Claudia. 2013. "Why Have Americans' Income Expectations Declined So Sharply?" Finance and Economics Discussion Series Notes September 26. Board of Governors of the Federal Reserve System.

Staiger, Douglas, James H. Stock, and Mark W. Watson. 1997. "How Precise are Estimates of the Natural Rate of Unemployment?" In Christina

Romer and David Romer, eds., *Reducing Inflation: Motivation and Strategy*. Chicago: University of Chicago Press. 195–246.

Summers, Lawrence H. 2015. "Reflections on Secular Stagnation." Keynote Address at Julius-Rabinowitz Center, Princeton University. Princeton, NJ. February 19.

Varian, Hal. 2011. "Economic Value of Google to US Advertisers and Customers." Keynote Address at the Web 2.0 Expo 2011 Conference. San Francisco. March 28–31.

Vidangos, Ivan. 2015. "Deleveraging and Recent Trends in Household Debt." Finance and Economics Discussion Series Notes April 6. Board of Governors of the Federal Reserve System.

Yellen, Janet. 2011. "The Federal Reserve's Asset Purchase Program." Speech at the Allied Social Science Associations Annual Meeting, Brimmer Policy Forum. Denver. January 8.

CHAPTER 3

Bacchetta, Philippe and Eric van Wincoop. 2013. "Explaining Sudden Spikes in Global Risk." *Journal of International Economics* 89 (2): 511–521.

Bénétrix, Agustín, Philip Lane, and Jay Shambaugh. 2015. "International Currency Exposures, Valuation Effects and the Global Financial Crisis." *Journal of International Economics* 96 (S1): S98–S109.

Borio, Claudio. 2014. "The Financial Cycle and Macroeconomics: What have we learnt?" *Journal of Banking & Finance* (45): 182–98.

Brunnermeier, Markus. 2001. *Asset Pricing Under Asymmetric Information: Bubbles, Crashes, Technical Analysis, and Herding*. Oxford, UK: Oxford University Press.

Conference Board Total Economy Database. 2015. "Productivity Brief Summary Tables: 1999–2015."

Council of Economic Advisers (CEA). 2015a. "Economic Report of the President."

———. 2015b. "The Economic Benefits of U.S. Trade."

Eichengreen, Barry, Donghyun Park, and Kwanho Shin. 2015. "The Global Productivity Slump: Common and Country-Specific Factors." National Bureau of Economics Working Paper No. 21556.

Fajgelbaum, Pablo and Amit Khandelwal. 2014. "Measuring the Unequal Gains from Trade." National Bureau of Economics Working Paper No. 20331.

International Monetary Fund (IMF). 2004. "World Economic Outlook, September 2004: The Global Demographic Transition." Washington.

_____. 2011. "World Economic Outlook, September 2011: Slowing Growth, Rising Risks." Washington.

_____. 2012. "World Economic Outlook, October 2012: Coping with High Debt and Sluggish Growth." Washington.

_____. 2013. "World Economic Outlook, October 2013: Transitions and Tensions." Washington.

_____. 2014. "World Economic Outlook, October 2014: Legacies, Clouds, Uncertainties." Washington.

_____. 2015a. "Global Financial Stability Report – Vulnerabilities, Legacies, and Policy Challenges: Risks Rotating to Emerging Markets." Washington.

_____. 2015b. "Macroeconomic Developments and Prospects in Low-Income Developing Countries: 2015." International Monetary Fund Policy Papers Series. Washington.

_____. 2015c. "Regional Economic Outlook – Sub-Saharan Africa: Navigating Headwinds." Washington.

_____. 2015d. "World Economic Outlook, October 2015: Adjusting to Lower Commodity Prices." Washington.

_____. 2016. "World Economic Outlook Update, January 2016: Subdued Demand, Diminished Prospects." Washington.

Jordà, Òscar, Moritz Schularick, and Taylor Alan. 2011. "Financial Crises, Credit Booms, and External Imbalances: 140 Years of Lessons." *International Monetary Fund Economic Review* 59 (2): 340–378.

_____. 2013. "When Credit Bites Back." *Journal of Money, Credit and Banking* 45 (S2): 3-28.

Kalwij, Adriaan. 2010. "The Impact of Family Policy Expenditure on Fertility in Western Europe." *Demography* 47 (2): 503-519.

Karam, Philippe, Dirk Muir, Joana Pereira, and Anita Tuladhar. 2011 "Beyond Retirees." *Finance and Development* 48 (2): 12–15.

Kohsaka, Akira. 2013. *Aging and Economic Growth in the Pacific Region*. Abingdon, Oxon: Routledge.

Mühleisen, Martin and Hamid Faruqee. 2001 "Japan: Population Aging and the Fiscal Challenge." *Finance and Development* 38 (1).

Organisation for Economic Co-operation and Development. 2014. "OECD Economic Outlook." *OECD Economic Outlook* 2014 (2). Paris: OECD Publishing.

————. 2015. "OECD Economic Outlook." *OECD Economic Outlook* 2015 (2). Paris: OECD Publishing.

Petri, Peter A. and Michael G. Plummer. 2016. "The Economic Effects of the Trans-Pacific Partnership: New Estimates." Working Paper No. 16–2. Washington: Peterson Institute for International Economics.

Riker, David. 2010. "Do Jobs In Export Industries Still Pay More? And Why?" Manufacturing and Services Economics Brief No. 2. U.S. Department of Commerce, International Trade Association.

————. 2015. "Export-Intensive Industries Pay More on Average: An Update." *Journal of International Commerce and Economics* 6 (4).

Riker, David and Brandon Thurner. 2011. "Weekly Earnings in Export-Intensive U.S. Services Industries." Manufacturing and Services Economics Brief No. 4. U.S. Department of Commerce, International Trade Association.

Scharfstein, David and Jeremy Stein. 1990. "Herd Behavior and Investment." *The American Economic Review* 80 (3): 465–479.

U.S. Census Bureau. 2012. "Ownership Characteristics of Classifiable U.S. Exporting Firms: 2007." *Survey of Business Owners Special Report* Issue June.

Veldkamp, Laura. 2006. "Information Markets and the Comovement of Asset Price." *The Review of Economic Studies* 73 (3): 823–845.

————. 2011. *Information Choice in Macroeconomics and Finance*. Princeton, NJ: Princeton University Press.

Wong, Chack-Kie, Kwong-Leung Tang, and Shengquan Ye. 2011. "The Perceived Importance of Family-Friendly Policies to Childbirth Decision among Hong Kong Women." *International Journal of Social Welfare* 20 (4): 381–392.

World Bank. 2016. "Global Economic Prospects: Spillovers amid Weak Growth." Washington.

Chapter 4

Acevedo-Garcia, Dolores and Kimberly A. Lochner. 2003. "Residential Segregation and Health." In Ichiro Kawachi and Lisa F. Berkman, eds., *Neighborhoods and Health*. New York: Oxford University Press.

Adhvaryu, Achyuta, James Fenske, and Anant Nyshadham. 2014. "Early Life Circumstance and Adult Mental Health." University of Oxford Department of Economics Discuss Paper Series ISSN 1471-0498.

Administration for Children and Families. 2015. "Home Visiting Program Model Effects." U.S. Department of Health and Human Services.

Aizer, Anna and Janet Currie. 2014. "The Intergenerational Transmission of Inequality: Maternal Disadvantage and Health at Birth." *Science* 344: 856-861.

Aizer, Anna, Laura Stroud, and Stephen Buka. Forthcoming. "Maternal Stress and Child Outcomes: Evidence from Siblings." *Journal of Human Resources*.

Aizer, Anna, Shari Eli, Joseph Ferrie, and Adriana Lleras-Muney. Forthcoming. "The Long Term Impact of Cash Transfers to Poor Families." *American Economic Review*.

Almond, Douglas and Bhashkar Mazumder. 2011. "Health Capital and the Prenatal Environment: The Effect of Ramadan Observance during Pregnancy." *American Economic Journal: Applied Economics* 3 (4): 56–85.

Almond, Douglas and Janet Currie. 2011. "Killing Me Softly: The Fetal Origins Hypothesis." *Journal of Economic Perspectives* 25 (3): 153-72.

Almond, Douglas, Hilary Hoynes, and Diane Whitmore Schanzenbach. 2011. "Inside the War on Poverty: The Impact of Food Stamps on Birth Outcomes." *The Review of Economics and Statistics* 93 (2): 387-403.

Almond, Douglas, Kenneth Y. Chay, and Michael Greenstone. 2006. "Civil Rights, the War on Poverty, and Black-White Convergence in

Infant Mortality in the Rural South and Mississippi." MIT Department of Economics Working Paper 07-04.

American Correctional Association. 2012. *Directory of Adult and Juvenile Correctional Facilities*. 32.

Anderson, Michael L. 2008. "Multiple Inference and Gender Differences in the Effects of Early Intervention: A Reevaluation of the Abecedarian, Perry Preschool, and Early Training Projects." *Journal of the American Statistical Association* 103 (484): 1481-1495.

Autor, David, David Figlio, Krzysztof Karbownik, Jeffrey Roth, and Melanie Wasserman. 2015. "Family Disadvantage and the Gender Gap in Behavioral and Educational Outcomes." Institute for Policy Research at Northwestern University Working Paper 15-16.

_____. 2016. "School Quality and the Gender Gap in Educational Achievement." National Bureau of Economic Research Working Paper No. 21908.

Baker, Michael, Jonathan Gruber, and Kevin Milligan. 2008. "Universal Child Care, Maternal Labor Supply, and Family Well-Being." *Journal of Political Economy* 116 (4): 709-745.

_____. 2015. "Non-Cognitive Deficits and Young Adult Outcomes: The Long-Run Impacts of a Universal Child Care Program." National Bureau of Economic Research Working Paper No. 21571.

Barnett, W. Steven. 1996. *Lives in the Balance: Age-27 Benefit-Cost Analysis of the High/Scope Perry Preschool Program*. Ypsilanti: High/Scope Press.

Barnett, W. Steven and Leonard N. Masse. 2007. "Comparative Benefit-Cost Analysis of the Abecedarian Program and its Policy Implications." *Economics of Education Review* 26 (1): 113-125.

Bartik, Timothy J., William Gormley, and Shirley Adelstein. 2012. "Earnings Benefits of Tulsa's Pre-K Program for Different Income Groups." *Economics of Education Review* 31 (6): 1143-1161.

Bartik, Timothy J. 2014. From Preschool to Prosperity: The Economic Payoff to Early Childhood Education. Kalamazoo: W.E. Upjohn Institute for Employment Research.

Becker, Gary S. 1962. "Investment in Human Capital: A Theoretical Analysis." *Journal of Political Economy* 70 (5): 9-49.

Belfield, Clive R., Milagros Nores, Steve Barnett, and Lawrence Schweinhart. 2006. "The High/Scope Perry Preschool Program Cost–Benefit Analysis Using Data from the Age-40 Follow-Up." *Journal of Human Resources* 41 (1): 162-190.

Ben-Porath, Yoram. 1967. "The Production of Human Capital and the Life Cycle of Earnings." *Journal of Political Economy* 75 (4): 352-365.

Bernal, Raquel and Michael P. Keane. 2011. "Child Care Choices and Children's Cognitive Achievement: The Case of Single Mothers." *Journal of Labor Economics* 29 (3): 459-512.

Berquin, P. C., J. N. Giedd, L. K. Jacobsen, S. D. Hamburger, A. L. Krain, J. L. Rapoport, and F. X. Castellanos. 1998. "Cerebellum in Attention-Deficit Hyperactivity Disorder: A Morphometric MRI Study." *Neurology* 50 (4): 1087–1093.

Bertrand, Marianne and Jessica Pan. 2013. "The Trouble with Boys: Social Influences and the Gender Gap in Disruptive Behavior." *American Economic Journal: Applied Economics* 5 (1): 32-64.

Billings, Stephen B., David J. Deming, and Jonah Rockoff. 2014. "School Segregation, Educational Attainment, and Crime: Evidence from the End of Busing in Charlotte-Mecklenburg." *The Quarterly Journal of Economics* 129 (1): 435-476.

Bitler, Marianne P., Hilary W. Hoynes, and Thurston Domina. 2014. "Experimental Evidence on Distributional Effects of Head Start." National Bureau of Economic Research Working Paper No. 20434.

Bitler, Marianne P. and Janet Currie. 2005. "Does WIC Work? The Effects of WIC on Pregnancy and Birth Outcomes." *Journal of Policy Analysis and Management* 24 (1): 73-91.

Black, Sandra E. 1999. "Do Better Schools Matter? Parental Valuation of Elementary Education." *The Quarterly Journal of Economics* 114 (2): 577-599.

Black, Sandra E., Paul J. Devereux, and Kjell G. Salvanes. 2007. "From the Cradle to the Labor Market? The Effect of Birth Weight on Adult Outcomes." *The Quarterly Journal of Economics* 122 (1): 409–439.

_____. 2016. "Does Grief Transfer across Generations? Bereavements during Pregnancy and Child Outcomes." *American Economic Journal: Applied Economics* 8 (1): 193-223.

Black, Sandra E., Paul J. Devereux, Katrine V. Løken, and Kjell G. Salvanes. 2012. "Care or Cash? The Effect of Child Care Subsidies on Student Performance." National Bureau of Economic Research Working Paper No. 18086.

Black, Sandra E., Paul J. Devereux, Petter Lundborg, and Kaveh Majlesi. 2015 "Poor Little Rich Kids? The Determinants of the Intergenerational Transmission of Wealth." National Bureau of Economic Research Working Paper No. 21409.

Brooks-Gunn, Jeanne, C.M. McCarton, P.H. Casey, M.C. McCormick, C.R. Bauer, J.C. Bernbaum, J. Tyson, M. Swanson, F.C. Bennett, D.T. Scott, J.T. Tonascia, and C.L. Meinert. 1994. "Early Intervention in Low-Birth-Weight Premature Infants: Results through Age 5 Years from the Infant Health and Development Program." *Journal of the American Medical Association* 272 (16): 1257-1262.

Brown, David W., Amanda E. Kowalski, and Ithai Z. Lurie. 2015. "Medicaid as an Investment in Children: What is the Long-term Impact on Tax Receipts?" National Bureau of Economic Research Working Paper No. 20835.

Campbell, Frances A. and Craig T. Ramey. 1995. "Cognitive and School Outcomes for High-Risk African-American Students at Middle Adolescence: Positive Effects of Early Intervention." *American Educational Research Journal* 32 (4): 743-772.

Campbell, Frances A., Elizabeth P. Pungello, Shari Miller-Johnson, Margaret Burchinal, and Craig T. Ramey. 2001. "The Development of Cognitive and Academic Abilities: Growth Curves From an Early Childhood Educational Experiment." *Developmental Psychology* 37 (2): 231-242.

Campbell, Frances A., Elizabeth P. Pungello, Kirsten Kainz, Margaret Burchinal, Yi Pan, Barbara H. Wasik, Oscar Barbarin, Joseph J. Sparling, and Craig T. Ramey. 2012. "Adult Outcomes as a Function of an Early Childhood Educational Program: An Abecedarian Project Follow-Up." *Developmental Psychology* 48 (4): 1033-1043.

Campbell, Frances A., Gabriella Conti, James J. Heckman, Seong Hyeok Moon, Rodrigo Pinto, Elizabeth Pungello, and Yi Pan. 2014. "Early Childhood Investments Substantially Boost Adult Health." *Science* 343 (6178): 1478-1485.

Campbell, Jennifer A., Rebekah J. Walker, and Leonard E. Egede. 2015. "Associations between Adverse Childhood Experiences, High-Risk Behaviors, and Morbidity in Adulthood." *American Journal of Preventive Medicine.*

Card, David and Jesse Rothstein. 2007. "Racial Segregation and the Black-White Test Score Gap." *Journal of Public Economics* 91 (11-12): 2158-2184.

Carneiro, Pedro, Claire Crawford, and Alissa Goodman. 2007. "The Impact of Early Cognitive and Non-Cognitive Skills on Later Outcomes." London School of Economics Centre for the Economics of Education.

Carneiro, Pedro and Rita Ginja. 2014. "Long-Term Impacts of Compensatory Preschool on Health and Behavior: Evidence from Head Start." *American Economic Journal: Economic Policy* 6 (4): 135-173.

Cascio, Elizabeth U. and Diane Schanzenbach. 2013. "The Impacts of Expanding Access to High-Quality Preschool Education." *Brookings Papers on Economic Activity* Fall 2013: 127-192.

Centers for Disease Control and Prevention. 2015. "Number of Children Tested and Confirmed BLL's >=10 ug/dL by State, Year, and BLL Group, Children <72 Months Old."

Centers for Medicare and Medicaid Services. "Children." Accessed 29 January 2016. https://www.medicaid.gov/medicaid-chip-program-information/by-population/children/children.html.

Chay, Kenneth Y., Jonathan Guryan, and Bhashkar Mazumder. 2009. "Birth Cohort and the Black-White Achievement Gap: The Roles of Access and Health Soon After Birth." National Bureau of Economic Research Working Paper No. 15078.

Chen, Alice, Emily Oster, and Heidi Williams. 2015. "Why is Infant Mortality Higher in the US than in Europe?" Working Paper.

Chetty, Raj, John N. Friedman, and Jonah Rockoff. 2011. "New Evidence on the Long-Term Impacts of Tax Credits." Internal Revenue Service Statistics of Income Working Paper.

———. 2014. "Measuring the Impacts of Teachers II: Teacher Value-Added and Student Outcomes in Adulthood." *American Economic Review* 104 (9): 2633-2679.

Chetty, Raj, Nathaniel Hendren, Frina Lin, Jeremy Majerovitz, and Benjamin Scuderi. 2016. "Childhood Environment and Gender Gaps in Adulthood." National Bureau of Economic Research Working Paper No. 21936.

Chetty, Raj, Nathaniel Hendren, Patrick Kline, and Emmanuel Saez. 2014. "Where is the Land of Opportunity? The Geography of Intergenerational Mobility in the United States." *The Quarterly Journal of Economics 129* (4): 1553-1623.

Chetty, Raj and Nathaniel Hendren. 2015. "The Impacts of Neighborhoods on Intergenerational Mobility: Childhood Exposure Effects and County-Level Estimates." Harvard University and National Bureau of Economic Research Working Paper.

Chetty, Raj, Nathaniel Hendren, and Lawrence F. Katz. Forthcoming. "The Effects of Exposure to Better Neighborhoods on Children: New Evidence from the Moving to Opportunity Experiment." *American Economic Review.*

Cohen, Sheldon, Joseph Schwartz, Elissa Epel, Clemens Kirschbaum, Steve Sidney, and Teresa Seeman. 2006. "Socioeconomic Status, Race and Diurnal Cortisol Decline in the Coronary Artery Risk Development in Young Adults (CARDIA) Study." *Psychosomatic Medicine* 68: 41–50.

Cohodes, Sarah, Daniel Grossman, Samuel Kleiner, and Michael F. Lovenheim. 2014. "The Effect of Child Health Insurance Access on Schooling: Evidence from Public Insurance Expansions." National Bureau of Economic Research Working Paper No. 20178.

Coleman-Jensen, Alisha, Matthew P. Rabbit, Christian Gregory, and Anita Singh. 2015. "Household Food Security in the United States in 2014." USDA Economic Research Report No. 194.

Coleman, John and Leo Hendry. 1999. *The Nature of Adolescence* 3. Routledge.

College Board. 2015. "Average Published Undergraduate Charges by Sector, 2015-16."

Conti, Gabriella, James J. Heckman, and Rodrigo Pinto. 2015. "The Effects of Two Influential Early Childhood Interventions on Health and Healthy Behaviors." National Bureau of Economic Research Working Paper No. 21454.

Council of Economic Advisers. 2014. "The President's Proposal to Expand the Earned Income Tax Credit."

_____. 2015a. "The Economics of Early Childhood Investments."

_____. 2015b. "The Economics of Family-Friendly Workplace Policies." In *Economic Report of the President*.

_____. 2015c. "Long-Term Benefits of the Supplemental Nutrition Assistance Program."

Cunha, Flavio and James Heckman. 2007. "The Technology of Skill Formation." *American Economic Review* 97 (2): 31-47.

Cunha, Flavio, James J. Heckman, Lance Lochner, and Dimitriy V. Masterov. 2006. "Interpreting the Evidence on Life Cycle Skill Formation." In *Handbook of the Economics of Education*. 26th ed. Vol. 1. Elsevier B.V. 698-747.

Currie, Janet and Duncan Thomas. 2000. "School Quality and the Longer-Term Effects of Head Start." *Journal of Human Resources* 35 (4): 755-774.

Currie, Janet. 2001. "Early Childhood Education Programs." *Journal of Economic Perspectives* 15 (2): 213-238.

Currie, Janet and Enrico Moretti. 2003. "Mother's Education and the Intergenerational Transmission of Human Capital: Evidence from College Openings." *The Quarterly Journal of Economics* 118 (4): 1495-1532.

Currie, Janet and Ishita Rajani. 2015. "Within-Mother Estimates of the Effects of the WIC on Birth Outcomes in New York City." *Economic Inquiry* 53 (4): 1691-1701.

Currie, Janet and Maya Rossin-Slater. 2015. "Early-Life Origins of Lifecycle Wellbeing: Research and Policy Implications." *Journal of Policy Analysis and Management* 34 (10): 208-42.

Cutler, David M. and Edward L. Glaeser. 1997. "Are Ghettos Good or Bad?" *The Quarterly Journal of Economics* 112 (3): 827- 872.

Dahl, Gordon B. and Lance Lochner. 2012. "The Impact of Family Income on Child Achievement: Evidence from the Earned Income Tax Credit." *American Economic Review* 102 (5): 1927–56.

Deming, David. 2009. "Early Childhood Intervention and Life-Cycle Skill Development: Evidence from Head Start." *American Economic Journal: Applied Economics* 1 (3): 111-134.

Dickerson, Niki T. 2007. "Black Employment, Segregation, and the Social Organization of Metropolitan Labor Markets." *Economic Geography* 83 (3): 283-307.

Dobbie, Will and Roland G. Fryer, Jr. 2011. "Are High-Quality Schools Enough to Increase Achievement Among the Poor? Evidence from the Harlem Children's Zone." *American Economic Journal: Applied Economics* 3 (3): 158-187.

Dodge, Kenneth A, Benjamin Goodman, Robert A. Murphy, Karen O'Donnell, and Jeannine Sato. 2013. "Randomized Controlled Trial of Universal Postnatal Nurse Home Visiting: Impact on Emergency Care." *Pediatrics* 132 (2): S140-S146.

Duncan, Greg J. and Aaron J. Sojourner. 2014. "Can Intensive Early Childhood Intervention Programs Eliminate Income-Based Cognitive and Achievement Gaps?" Presented for Legislative Leadership Institute.

Duncan, Greg J., Ariel Kalil, and Kathleen M. Ziol-Guest. 2015. "Parent Income-Based Gaps in Schooling, Earnings and Family Income: Cross-Cohort Trends in the NLSYs and the PSID." Working Paper.

Duncan, Greg J., Kathleen M. Ziol-Guest, and Ariel Kalil. 2010. "Early-Childhood Poverty and Adult Attainment, Behavior, and Health." *Child Development* 81 (1): 306-325.

Duncan, Greg J. and Katherine Magnuson. 2011. "Introduction: The American Dream, Then and Now." In Duncan, Greg J. and Richard H. Murnane, eds., *Whither Opportunity? Rising Inequality, Schools, and Children's Life Chances*. New York: Russell Sage Foundation. 47-69.

_____. 2013. "Investing in Preschool Programs." *Journal of Economic Perspectives* 27 (2): 109-132.

Duncan, Greg J., Katherine Magnuson, and Elizabeth Votruba-Drzal. 2014. "Boosting Family Income to Promote Child Development." *Future of Children* 24 (1): 99-120.

Duncan, Greg J. and Richard J. Murnane. 2011. *Whither Opportunity? Rising Inequality, Schools, and Children's Life Chances*. New York: Russell Sage Foundation.

Eissa, Nada and Jeffrey B. Liebman. 1996. "Labor Supply Response to the Earned Income Tax Credit." *The Quarterly Journal of Economics* 111 (2): 605-637.

Eissa, Nada and Hilary Hoynes. 2011. "Redistribution and Tax Expenditures: The Earned Income Tax Credit." *National Tax Journal* 64 (2): 689-729.

Evans, Gary W. and Michelle A. Schamberg. 2009. "Childhood poverty, chronic stress, and adult working memory." *Proceedings of the National Academy of Science of the United States of America* 106 (16): 6545-6549.

Falk, Gene and Margot L. Crandall-Hollick. 2014. "The Earned Income Tax Credit (EITC): An Overview." Congressional Research Service.

Falk, Gene. 2015. "The Temporary Assistance for Needy Families (TANF) Block Grant: Responses to Frequently Asked Questions." Congressional Research Service.

Felitti, Vincent J., Robert F. Anda, Dale Nordenberg, David F. Williamson, Alison M. Spitz, Valerie Edwards, Mary P. Koss, and James S. Marks. 1998. "Relationship of Childhood Abuse and Household Dysfunction to Many of the Leading Causes of Death in Adults: The Adverse Childhood Experiences (ACE) Study." *American Journal of Preventive Medicine* 14 (4): 245-258.

Figlio, David, Jonathan Guryan, Krzysztof Karbownik, and Jeffrey Roth. 2014. "The Effects of Poor Neonatal Health on Children's Cognitive Development." *American Economic Review* 104 (12): 3921-3955.

Fitzpatrick, Maria D. 2008. "Starting School at Four: The Effect of Universal Pre-Kindergarten on Children's Academic Achievement." *The B.E. Journal of Economic Analysis and Policy* 8 (1).

Flaherty, E.G., R. Thompson, H. Dubowitz, E.M. Harvey, D.J. English, M.D. Everson, L.J. Proctor, and D.K. Runyan. 2013. "Adverse Childhood Experiences and Child Health in Early Adolescence." *Journal of the American Medical Association Pediatrics* 167 (7): 622-629.

Fryer, Roland G., Jr. 2014. "Injecting Charter School Best Practices into Traditional Public Schools: Evidence from Field Experiments." *The Quarterly Journal of Economics* 129 (3): 1335-1407.

Fryer, Ronald G., Jr. and Steven D. Levitt. 2013. "Testing for Racial Differences in the Mental Ability of Young Children." *American Economic Review* 103 (2): 981-1005.

Gassman-Pines, Anna and Laura E. Bellows. 2015. "The Timing of SNAP Benefit Receipt and Children's Academic Achievement." Association of Public Policy Analysis and Management Fall Conference, Miami, FL.

Gennetian, Lisa, Roopa Seshadri, Nathan Hess, Aaron Winn, and Robert George. 2015. "Food Stamp Benefit Cycles and Student Disciplinary Infractions." Working Paper.

Georgieff, Michael K. 2007. "Nutrition and the Developing Brain: Nutrient Priorities and Measurement." *American Journal of Clinical Nutrition* 85 (2): 6145-6205.

Gormley, William T. Jr., and Ted Gayer. 2005. "Promoting School Readiness in Oklahoma: An Evaluation of Tulsa's Pre-K Program." *Journal of Human Resources* 40 (3): 533-558.

Gormley, William T., Jr., Ted Gayer, Deborah Phillips, and Brittany Dawson. 2005. "The Effects of Universal Pre-K on Cognitive Development." *Developmental Psychology* 41 (6): 872-884.

Gothro, Andrew and Carole Trippe. 2010. "Multiple Benefit Receipt among Individuals Receiving Food Assistance and Other Government Assistance." Mathematica Policy Research.

Green, B. L., C. Ayoub, J. Dym-Bartlett, A. VonEnde, C. J. Furrer, R. Chazan-Cohen, C. Vallotton, and J. Klevens. 2014. "The effect of Early Head Start on child welfare system involvement: A first look at longitudinal child maltreatment outcomes." *Children and Youth Services Review* 42: 127-135.

Gross, Ruth T., Donna Spiker, and Christine W. Haynes. 1997. *Helping Low Birth Weight, Premature Babies: The Infant Health and Development Program.* Stanford University Press.

Halle, Tamara, Nicole Forry, Elizabeth Hair, Kate Perper, Laura Wandner, Julia Wessel, and Jessica Vick. 2009. "Disparities in Early Learning and Development: Lessons from the Early Childhood Longitudinal Study – Birth Cohort (ECLS-B)." Publication No. 2009-52. Washington, DC: Child Trends.

Hastings, Justine S. and Ebonya Washington. 2010. "The First of the Month Effect: Consumer Behavior and Store Responses." *American Economic Journal: Economic Policy* 2 (2): 142-162.

Havnes, Tarjei and Magne Mogstad. 2011. "No Child Left Behind: Subsidized Child Care and Children's Long-Run Outcomes." *American Economic Journal: Economic Policy* 3 (2): 97-129.

Health Resources and Services Administration. 2013. "Prenatal Care Utilization." Child Health USA 2013. U.S. Department of Health and Human Services.

Heckman, James J. 2006. "Skill Formation and the Economics of Investing in Disadvantaged Children." *Science* 312 (5782): 1900-1902.

Heckman, James J., David Olds, Rodrigo Pinto, and Maria Rosales. 2014. "A Reanalysis of the Nurse Family Partnership Program: The Memphis Randomized Control Trial." University of Chicago Center for the Economics of Human Development.

Heckman, James J., Jora Stixrud, and Sergio Urzua. 2006. "The Effects of Cognitive and Noncognitive Abilities on Labor Market Outcomes and Social Behavior." *Journal of Labor Economics* 24 (3): 411-482.

Heckman, James J., Seong Hyeok Moon, Rodrigo Pinto, Peter A. Savelyev, and Adam Yavitz. 2010. "The Rate of Return to the High/Scope Perry Preschool Program." *Journal of Public Economics* 94 (1): 114-128.

Herbst, Chris M. 2010. "The Labor Supply Effects of Child Care Costs and Wages in the Presence of Subsidies and the Earned Income Tax Credit." *Review of Economics of the Household* 8 (2): 199-230.

_____. 2014. "Universal Child Care, Maternal Employment, and Children's Long-Run Outcomes: Evidence from the U.S. Lanham Act of 1940." IZA Discussion Paper No. 7846.

Herbst, Chris M. and Erdal Tekin. 2010. "The Impact of Child Care Subsidies on Child Well-being: Evidence from Geographic Variation in the Distance to Social Service Agencies." National Bureau of Economic Research Working Paper No. 16250.

_____. 2014. "Child Care Subsidies, Maternal Health, and Child-Parent Interactions: Evidence from Three Nationally Representative Datasets." *Health Economics* 23 (8): 894-916.

Hill, Carolyn, William Gormley, and Shirley Adelstein. 2015. "Do the Short-Term Effects of a High-Quality Preschool Program Persist?" *Early Childhood Research Quarterly* 32: 60-79.

Hillis, Susan D., Robert F. Anda, Shanta R. Dube, Vincent J. Felitti, Polly A. Marchbanks, and James S. Marks. 2004. "The Association Between Adverse Childhood Experiences and Adolescent Pregnancy, Long-Term Psychosocial Consequences, and Fetal Death." *Pediatrics* 113 (2): 320-327.

Hoynes, Hilary W., Diane Whitmore Schanzenbach, and Douglas Almond. Forthcoming. "Long Run Impacts of Childhood Access to the Safety Net." *American Economic Review.*

Hoynes, Hilary W., Doug Miller, and David Simon. 2015. "Income, the Earned Income Tax Credit, and Infant Health." *American Economic Journal: Economic Policy* 7 (1): 172-211.

Hoynes, Hilary W., Marianne Page, and Ann Huff Stevens. 2011. "Can Targeted Transfers Improve Birth Outcomes? Evidence from the Introduction of the WIC Program." *Journal of Public Economics* 95 (7-8): 813-827.

Internal Revenue Service. 2015. "Individual Income Tax Returns 2013." *Statistics of Income—2013.* Publication 1304 (Rev. 08-2015).

Isaacs, Julia B. 2012. "Starting School at a Disadvantage: The School Readiness of Poor Children." *Brookings Social Genome Project Research* (3) 5: 1-22.

Isen, Adam, Maya Rossin-Slater, and W. Reed Walker. Forthcoming. "Every Breath You Take—Every Dollar You'll Make: The Long-Term Consequences of the Clean Air Act of 1970." *Journal of Political Economy.*

Jensen, Arthur R. 1980. *Bias in Mental Testing.* New York: Free Press.

Joyce, Ted, Diane Gibson, and Silvie Colman. 2005. "The Changing Association between Prenatal Participation in WIC and Birth Outcomes in New York City." *Journal of Policy Analysis and Management* 24 (4): 661-685.

Kalil, Ariel. 2014. "Proposal 2: Addressing the Parenting Divide to Promote Early Childhood Development for Disadvantaged Children." Hamilton Project, Policies to Address Poverty in America.

Kalil, Ariel, Rebecca Ryan, and Michael Corey. 2012. "Diverging Destinies: Maternal Education and the Developmental Gradient in Time with Children." *Demography* 49: 1361–83.

Karoly, Lynn A., Peter W. Greenwood, Susan S. Everingham, Jill Houbé, M. Rebecca Kilburn, C. Peter Rydell, Matthew Sanders, and James Chiesa. 1998. *Investing in Our Children: What We Know and Don't Know About the Costs and Benefits of Early Childhood Interventions.* Santa Monica: RAND.

Kearney, Melissa S. and Philip B. Levine. 2015. "Early Childhood Education by MOOC: Lessons from Sesame Street." National Bureau of Economic Research Working Paper No. 21229.

Kilburn, M. Rebecca. 2014. "Evidence on Home Visiting and Suggestions for Implementing Evidence-Based Home Visiting Through MIECHV." RAND Corporation Testimony presented before the House Ways and Means Committee, Subcommittee on Human Resources on April 2, 2014.

Kline, Patrick and Christopher Walters. 2015. "Evaluating Public Programs with Close Substitutes: The Case of Head Start." National Bureau of Economic Research Working Paper No. 21658.

Knudsen, Eric I., James J. Heckman, Judy L. Cameron, and Jack P. Shonkoff. 2006. "Economic, Neurobiological, and Behavior Perspectives on Building America's Future Workforce." *Proceedings of the National Academy of Science* 103 (27): 10155-10162.

Krueger, Alan B. 2003. "Economic Considerations and Class Size." *The Economic Journal* 113 (485): F34-36.

Kunz-Ebrecht, Sabine R., Clemens Kirschbaum, and Andrew Steptoe. 2004. "Work Stress, Socioeconomic Status and Neuroendocrine Activation over the Working Day." *Social Science and Medicine* 58: 1523–1530.

Laughlin, Lynda. 2013. "Who's Minding the Kids? Child Care Arrangements: Spring 2011." Census Bureau Household Economic Studies.

Lavy, Victor, Analia Schlosser, and Adi Shany. 2016. "Out of Africa: Human Capital Consequences of In Utero Conditions." National Bureau of Economic Research Working Paper No. 21894.

Lefebvre, Pierre and Philip Merrigan. 2008. "Child-Care Policy and the Labor Supply of Mothers with Young Children: A Natural Experiment from Canada." *Journal of Labor Economics* 26 (3): 519-548.

Lefebvre, Pierre, Philip Merrigan, and Matthieu Verstraete. 2006. "Impact of Early Childhood Care and Education on Children's Preschool Cognitive Development: Canadian Results from a Large Quasi-experiment." CIRPEE Working Paper No. 06-36.

Leventhal, Tama and Jeanne Brooks-Gunn. 2000. "The Neighborhoods They Live In: The Effects of Neighborhood Residence on Child and Adolescent Outcomes." *Psychological Bulletin* 162 (2): 309-337.

Lipsey, M.W., D.C. Farran, and K.G. Hofer. 2015. "A Randomized Control Trial of the Effects of a Statewide Voluntary Prekindergarten Program on Children's Skills and Behaviors through Third Grade." Peabody Research Institute Research Report.

Liu, Li, Ling-Li Zeng, Yaming Li, Qiongmin Ma, Baojuan Li, Hui Shen, and Dewen Hu. 2012. "Altered Cerebellar Functional Connectivity with Intrinsic Connectivity Networks in Adults with Major Depressive Disorder." *PLoS ONE* 7.

Love, John M., Ellen E. Kisker, Christine Ross, Jill Constantine, Kimberly Boller, Rachel Chazan-Cohen, Christy Brady-Smith, Allison S. Fuligni, Helen Raikes, Jeanne Brooks-Gunn, Louisa B. Tarullo, Peter Z. Shochet, Diane Paulsell, and Cheri Vogel. 2005. "The Effectiveness of Early Head Start for 3-Year-Old Children and Their Parents: Lessons for Policy and Programs." *Developmental Psychology* 41 (6): 885-901.

Love, John M., Ellen E. Kisker, Christine M. Ross, Peter Z. Schochet, Jeanne Brooks-Gunn, Diane Paulsell, Kimberly Boller, Jill Constantine, Cheri Vogel, Allison Sidle Fuligni, and Christy Brady-Smith. 2002. "Making a Difference in the Lives of Infants and Toddlers and Their Families: The Impacts of Early Head Start. Volume I: Final Technical Report." Prepared for the U.S. Department of Health and Human Services.

Ludwig, Jens and Douglas Miller. 2007. "Does Head Start Improve Children's Life Chances? Evidence from a Regression Discontinuity Design." *The Quarterly Journal of Economics* 122 (1): 159-208.

Mani, Anandi, Sendhil Mullainathan, Eldar Shafir, and Jiaying Zhao. 2013. "Poverty Impedes Cognitive Function." *Science* 341 (6149): 976-908.

Maxfield, Michelle. 2013. "The Effects of the Earned Income Tax Credit on Child Achievement and Long-Term Educational Achievement." Michigan State University Job Market Paper.

McCarton, C.M., J. Brooks-Gunn, I.F. Wallace, C.R. Bauer, F.C. Bennett, J.C. Bernbaum, R.S. Broyles, P.H. Casey, M.C. McCormick, D.T. Scott, J. Tyson, J. Tonascia, and C.L. Meinert. 1997. "Results at Age 8 Years of Early Intervention for Low-Birthweight Premature Infants: The Infant Health and Development Program." *Journal of the American Medical Association* 277 (2): 126-132.

McClellan, Jack M., Ezra Susser, and Mary-Claire King. 2006. "Maternal Famine, De Novo Mutations, and Schizophrenia." *Journal of the American Medical Association* 296 (5): 582–584.

McCormick, M.C., J. Brooks-Gunn, S.L. Buka, J. Goldman, J. Yu, M. Salganik, D.T. Scott, F.C. Bennett, L.L. Kay, J.C. Bernbaum, C.R. Bauer, C. Martin, E.R. Woods, MA. Martin, and P.H. Casey. 2006. "Early Intervention in Low Birth Weight Premature Infants: Results at 18 Years of Age for the Infant Health and Development Program." *Pediatrics* 117 (3): 771-780.

Meyer, Bruce D. and Dan T. Rosenbaum. 2001. "Welfare, the Earned Income Tax Credit and the Labor Supply of Single Mothers." *The Quarterly Journal of Economics* 116 (3): 1063-1114.

Meyer, Bruce D. and Laura R. Wherry. 2012. "Saving Teens: Using a Policy Discontinuity to Estimate the Effects of Medicaid Eligibility." National Bureau of Economic Research Working Paper No. 18309.

Michelmore, Katherine. 2013. "The Effect of Income on Educational Attainment: Evidence from State Earned Income Tax Credit Expansions." Working Paper.

Miller, Sarah and Laura R. Wherry. 2015. "The Long-Term Effects of Early Life Medicaid Coverage." University of Michigan Working Paper.

Milligan, Kevin and Mark Stabile. 2011. "Do Child Tax Benefits Affect the Well-Being of Children? Evidence from Canadian Child Benefit Expansions." *American Economic Journal Economic Policy* 3 (3): 175–205.

Mogreet. 2013. "2013 Guide to Text Messaging Regulations & Best Practices."

National Center for Education Statistics. 2015. "Public School Revenue Sources." *The Condition of Education*. U.S. Department of

Education. Accessed 3 February 2016. http://nces.ed.gov/programs/coe/indicator_cma.asp.

National Research Council and Institute of Medicine. 2000. *From Neurons to Neighborhoods: The Science of Early Childhood Development. Committee on Integrating the Science of Early Childhood Development.* Jack P. Shonkoff and Deborah A. Phillips, eds. Commission on Behavioral and Social Sciences and Education. Washington, DC: National Academy Press.

National Scientific Council on the Developing Child. 2007. "The Timing and Quality of Early Experiences Combine to Shape Brain Architecture." Harvard Center on the Developing Child Working Paper No. 5.

Neidell, Matthew J. 2004. "Air Pollution, Health, and Socio-economic Status: The Effect of Outdoor Air Quality on Childhood Asthma." *Journal of Health Economics* 23 (6): 1209-1236.

Neugebauer, Richard, Hans Wijbrand Hoek, and Ezra Susser. 1999. "Prenatal Exposure to Wartime Famine and Development of Antisocial Personality Disorder in Early Adulthood." *Journal of the American Medical Association* 282 (5): 455–462.

Nichols, Austin and Jesse Rothstein. 2015. "The Earned Income Tax Credit (EITC)." National Bureau of Economic Research Working Paper No. 21211.

Nielsen, Eric. 2015. "The Income-Achievement Gap and Adult Outcome Inequality." Finance and Economics Discussion Series No. 2015-041. Washington, DC: Board of Governors of the Federal Reserve System.

Oden, Sherri, Lawrence Schweinhart, David Weikart, Sue Marcus, and Yu Xie. 2000. *Into Adulthood: A Study of the Effects of Head Start.* Ypsilanti: High/Scope Press.

Office of Head Start. 2015. "Early Head Start Program Facts for Fiscal Year 2012." U.S. Department of Health and Human Services. Accessed 29 January 2016. http://eclkc.ohs.acf.hhs.gov/hslc/tta-system/ehsnrc/about-ehs#fact.

Office for Civil Rights. 2014. "Civil Rights Data Collection: Data Snapshot: School Discipline." U.S. Department of Education.

Olds, David, John Eckenrode, Charles R. Henderson, Harriet Kitzman, Jane Powers, Robert Cole, Kimberly Sidora, Pamela Morris, Lisa M. Pettit, and Dennis Luckey. 1997. "Long-term Effects of Home Visitation on Maternal Life Course and Child Abuse and Neglect: Fifteen-Year Follow-up of a Randomized Trial." *Journal of the American Medical Association* 278 (8): 637-643.

Olds, David, Charles R. Henderson Jr., Robert Cole, John Eckenrode, Harriet Kitzman, Dennis Luckey, Lisa Pettitt, Kimberly Sidora, Pamela Morris, and Jane Powers. 1998. "Long-term Effects of Nurse Home Visitation on Children's Criminal and Antisocial Behavior: 15-Year Follow-up of a Randomized Controlled Trial." *Journal of the American Medical Association* 280 (14): 1238-1244.

Persson, Petra and Maya Rossin-Slater. 2015. "Family Ruptures, Stress, and the Mental Health of the Next Generation." Working Paper.

Puma, Michael, Stephen Bell, Ronna Cook, Camilla Heid, Pam Broene, Frank Jenkins, Andrew Mashburn, and Jason Downer. 2012. "Third Grade Follow-Up to the Head Start Impact Study: Final Report." Office of Planning, Research, and Evaluation Report No. 2012-45. Washington, DC: U.S. Department of Health and Human Services.

Ramey, Craig T. and Frances A. Campbell. 1984. "Preventive Education for High-Risk Children: Cognitive Consequences of the Carolina Abecedarian Project." *American Journal of Mental Deficiency* 88: 515-523.

Ramey, Garey and Valerie A. Ramey. 2010. "The Rug Rat Race." *Brookings Papers on Economic Activity* Spring 2010: 129-199.

Rawlings, Lynette. 2015. "Understanding the Environmental Contexts of Boys and Young Men of Color." Urban Institute.

Reardon, Sean F. 2011. "The Widening Academic Achievement Gap between the Rich and the Poor: New Evidence and Possible Explanations." In Duncan, Greg J. and Richard H. Murnane, eds., *Whither Opportunity? Rising Inequality, Schools, and Children's Life Chances.* New York: Russell Sage Foundation. 91-116.

Reyes, Jessica W. 2015a. "Lead Exposure and Behavior: Effects on Antisocial and Risky Behavior among Children and Adolescents." *Economic Inquiry* 53 (3): 1580-1605.

_____. 2015b. "Lead Policy and Academic Performance: Insights from Massachusetts." *Harvard Educational Review* 85 (1): 75-107.

Reynolds, Arthur J., Majida Mehana, and Judy A. Temple. 1995. "Does Preschool Intervention Affect Children's Perceived Competence?" *Journal of Applied Developmental Psychology* 16 (2): 211-230.

Reynolds, Arthur J., Judy A. Temple, Dylan L. Robertson, and Emily A. Mann. 2001. "Long-term Effects of an Early Childhood Intervention on Educational Achievement and Juvenile Arrest: A 15-Year Follow-up of Low-Income Children in Public Schools." *Journal of the American Medical Association* 285 (18): 2339-2346.

———. 2002. "Age 21 Cost-Benefit Analysis of the Title I Chicago Child-Parent Centers." *Educational Evaluation and Policy Analysis* 24 (4): 267-303.

Reynolds, Arthur J., Judy A. Temple, Suh-Ruu Ou, Irma A. Arteaga, and Barry A.B. White. 2011. "School-Based Early Childhood Education and Age-28 Well-Being: Effects by Timing, Dosage, and Subgroups." *Science* 333 (6040): 360-364.

Rosales, Francisco J., J. Steven Reznick, and Steven H. Zeisel. 2009. "Understanding the Role of Nutrition in the Brain & Behavioral Development of Toddlers and Preschool Children: Identifying and Overcoming Methodological Barriers." *Nutritional Neuroscience* 12 (5): 190-202.

Rossin-Slater, Maya. 2013. "WIC in Your Neighborhood: New Evidence on the Impacts of Geographic Access to Clinics." *Journal of Public Economics* 102: 51-69.

Schweinhart, Lawrence J. 2003. "Benefits, Costs, and Explanation of the High/Scope Perry Preschool Program." Presentation at the Meeting of the Society for Research in Child Development, Tampa, Florida.

Schweinhart, Lawrence J. and David P. Weikart. 1981. "Effects of the Perry Preschool Program on Youths through Age 15." *Journal of Early Intervention* 4 (1): 29-39.

Schweinhart, Lawrence J., Jeanne Montie, Zongping Xiang, William S. Barnett, Clive R. Belfield, and Milagros Nores. 2005. *Lifetime Effects: The High/Scope Perry Preschool Study Through Age 40.* Ypsilanti: High/Scope Press.

Shapiro, Jesse M. 2005. "Is There a Daily Discount Rate? Evidence from the Food Stamp Nutrition Cycle." *Journal of Public Economics* 89 (2-3): 303-325.

Solon, Gary. 1992. "Intergenerational Income Mobility in the United States." *American Economic Review* 82 (3): 393-408.

Spaulding, Shayne, Robert Lerman, Harry Holzer, and Lauren Eyster. 2015. "Expanding Economic Opportunity for Young Men and Boys of Color through Employment and Training." Urban Institute Research Report.

Smith, Alex. 2015. "The Long-Run Effects of Universal Pre-K on Criminal Activity." Working Paper.

Stoner, Rich, Maggie L. Chow, Maureen P. Boyle, Susan M. Sunkin, Peter R. Mouton, Subhojit Roy, Anthony Wynshaw-Boris, Sophia A. Colamarino, Ed S. Lein, and Eric Courchesne. 2014. "Patches of Disorganization in the Neocortex of Children with Autism." *New England Journal of Medicine* 370 (13): 1209–1219.

Subramanian, S. V., Dolores Acevedo-Garcia, and Theresa L. Osypuk. 2005. "Racial Residential Segregation and Geographic Heterogeneity in Black/White Disparity in Poor Self-Rated Health in the US: A Multilevel Statistical Analysis." *Social Science and Medicine* 60 (8): 1667-1679.

Susser, Ezra, Richard Neugebauer, Hans W Hoek, Alan S Brown, Shang Lin, Daniel Labovitz, and Jack M Gorman. 1996. "Schizophrenia after Prenatal Famine: Further Evidence." *Archives of General Psychiatry* 53 (1): 25.

Susser, Ezra S. and Shang P. Lin. 1992. "Schizophrenia after prenatal exposure to the Dutch Hunger Winter of 1944-1945." *Archives of General Psychiatry* 49 (12): 983.

Sweet, Monica A. and Mark I. Appelbaum. 2004. "Is Home Visiting an Effective Strategy? A Meta-Analytic Review of Home Visiting Programs for Families with Young Children." *Child Development* 75 (5): 1435-1456.

Tamis-LeMonda, Catherine, Jacqueline Shannon, Natasha Cabrera, and Michael Lamb. 2004. "Father and Mothers at Play with Their 2- and 3- Year-Olds: Contributions to Language and Cognitive Development." *Child Development* 75 (6): 1806-1820.

Tax Policy Center. 2013. "Taxation and the Family: What is the Child Tax Credit?" *The Tax Policy Briefing Book.*

Temple, Judy A. and Arthur J. Reynolds. 2007. "Benefits and Costs of Investments in Preschool Education: Evidence from the Child–Parent Centers and Related Programs." *Economics of Education Review* 26 (1): 126-144.

Thompson, Ross. 2014. "Stress and Child Development." *Future of Children* 24 (1): 41–59.

Todd, Jessica E. 2014. "Revisiting the Supplemental Nutrition Assistance Program cycle of food intake: Investigating heterogeneity, diet quality, and a large boost in benefit amounts." *Applied Economic Perspectives and Policy* 37 (3): 437-458.

U.S. Census Bureau. 2015. "School Enrollment: CPS October 2014." Table 3.

U.S. Department of Agriculture. 2015. "Supplemental Nutrition Assistance Program (SNAP) Eligibility." Accessed 29 January 2016. http://www.fns.usda.gov/snap/eligibility.

U.S. Department of Education. 2015. "It's Time for Equitable Spending of State and Local Dollars."

———. "Public School Expenditures." National Center for Education Statistics.

———. "IDEA Part B Child Count and Educational Environments Collection." EDFacts Data Warehouse.

Vallotton, C.D., T. Harewood, C.A. Ayoub, B. Pan, A.M. Mastergeorge, and H. Brophy-Herb. 2012. "Buffering Boys and Boosting Girls: The Protectice and Promotive Effects of Early Head Start for Children's Expressive Language in the Context of Parenting Stress." *Early Childhood Research Quarterly* 27 (4): 695-707.

Vernon-Feagans, Lynne, Margaret Burchinal, and Irina Mokrova. 2015. "Diverging Destinies in Rural America." In P.R. Amato, ed., *Families in an Era of Increasing Inequality: Diverging Destinies* 5. Switzerland: Springer International.

Vogel, Cheri, Jeanne Brooks-Gunn, Anne Martin, and Mary M. Klute. 2013. "Impacts of Early Head Start Participation on Child and Parent Outcomes at Ages 2, 3, and 5." *Monographs of the Society for Research in Child Development* 78 (1): 36-63.

Walters, Christopher R. 2015. "Inputs in the Production of Early Childhood Human Capital: Evidence from Head Start." *American Economic Journal: Applied Economics* 7 (4): 76-102.

Wherry, Laura R., Sarah Miller, Robert Kaestner, and Bruce D. Meyer. 2015. "Childhood Medicaid Coverage and Later Life Health Care Utilization." National Bureau of Economic Research Working Paper No. 20929.

Wong, Vivian C., Thomas D. Cook, W. Steven Barnett, and Kwanghee Jung. 2008. "An Effectiveness-Based Evaluation of Five State Pre-Kindergarten Programs." *Journal of Policy Analysis and Management* 27 (1): 122-154.

York, Benjamin N. and Susanna Loeb. 2014. "One Step at a Time: the Effects of an Early Literacy Text Messaging Program for Parents of Preschoolers." Center for Education Policy Analysis Working Paper.

Zickuhr, Kathryn and Aaron Smith. 2012. "Digital Differences." Pew Research Center Report.

CHAPTER 5

Acemoglu, Daron, Simon Johnson, and James A. Robinson. 2005. "The Rise of Europe: Atlantic Trade, Institutional Change, and Economic Growth." *American Economic Review* 95(3): 546–579.

Aghion, Philippe, Nick Bloom, Richard Blundell, Rachel Griffith, and Peter Howitt. 2005. "Competition and Innovation: An Inverted-U Relationship." *Quarterly Journal of Economics* 120(2): 701-728.

Aghion, Philippe, Richard Blundell, Rachel Griffith, Peter Howitt, and Susanne Prantl. 2004. "Entry and Productivity Growth: Evidence from Microlevel Panel Data." *Journal of the European Economic Association* 2(2-3): 265-276.

Akcigit, U., D. Hanley, and N. Serrano-Velarde. 2012. "Back to Basics: Basic Research Spillovers, Innovation Policy, and Growth." University of Pennsylvania mimeo.

Amiti, Mary, and Shang-Jin Wei. 2009. "Service offshoring and productivity: Evidence from the US." *The World Economy* 32(2): 203–220.

Arrow, Kenneth J. 1962. "Economic Welfare and the Allocation of Resources for Inventions." In *The Rate and Direction of Inventive Activity: Economic and Social Factors*, edited by R.R. Nelson, 609-626. Princeton, NJ: Princeton University Press.

Atkin, David, Azam Chaudhry, Shamyla Chaudry, Amit K. Khandelwal, and Eric Verhoogen. 2015. "Organizational Barriers to Technology Adoption: Evidence from Soccer-Ball Producers in Pakistan." NBER Working Paper 21417.

Autor, David H. 2015. "Why Are There Still So Many Jobs? The History and Future of Workplace Automation" *Journal of Economic Perspectives* 29(3): 3–30.

Autor, David H. and David Dorn. 2013. "The Growth of Low-Skill Service Jobs and the Polarization of the US Labor Market." *American Economic Review* 103(5): 1553–1597.

Autor, David H., Frank Levy, and Richard J. Murnane. 2003. "The Skill Content of Recent Technological Change: An Empirical Exploration." *The Quarterly Journal of Economics* (November): 1279–1333.

Aw, Bee Yan, Mark J. Roberts, and Daniel Yi Xu. 2008. "R&D Investments, Exporting, and the Evolution of Firm Productivity." *American Economic Review* 98(2): 451–56.

Balasubramanian, Natarajan, and Jagadeesh Sivadasan. 2011. "What Happens When Firms Patent? New Evidence from U.S. Economic Census Data." *Review of Economics and Statistics* 93(1): 126–146.

Bartel, Ann, Casey Ichniowski, and Kathryn Shaw. 2007. "How Does Information Technology Affect Productivity? Plant-Level Comparisons of Product Innovation, Process Improvement, and Worker Skills." *The Quarterly Journal of Economics* 122(4): 1721–1758.

Beede, David N. 2014. "Competition Among U.S. Broadband Service Providers." U.S. Department of Commerce, Economics and Statistics Administration. http://www.esa.doc.gov/sites/default/files/competition-among-us-broadband-service-providers.pdf

Black, Sandra E. and Lisa M. Lynch. 2004. "What's the Driving the New Economy?: The Benefits of Workplace Innovation." *The Economic Journal* 114(493): 97–116.

Bloom, Nicholas, Benn Eifert, Aprajit Mahajan, David McKenzie, and John Roberts. 2013. "Does Management Matter? Evidence From India." *The Quarterly Journal of Economics* 128(1): 1-51.

Bloom, Nicholas, Raffaella Sadun, and John Van Reenen. 2012. "Americans do I.T. Better: US Multinationals and the Productivity Miracle." *American Economic Review* 102(1): 167–201.

Bloom, Nicholas, Mark Schankerman, and John Van Reenen. 2013. "Identifying Technology Spillovers and Product Market Rivalry." July. *Econometrica* 81(4): 1347-1393.

Boler, Esther Ann, Andreas Moxnes, and Karen Helene Ulltveit-Moe. 2015. "R&D, International Sourcing and the Joint Impact on Firm Performance." *American Economic Review*, forthcoming.

Chien, Colleen V. 2015. "Startups and Patent Trolls," *Stanford Technology Law Review*, Forthcoming.

The Conference Board. 2015. "Total Economy Database." https://www.conference-board.org/data/economydatabase/

Council of Economic Advisers. 2010. *Economic Report of the President.* February.

_____. 2014. *Economic Report of the President.* February.

_____. 2015a. *Economic Report of the President.* February.

_____. 2015b. "Mapping the Digital Divide." http://www.whitehouse.gov/sites/default/files/wh_digital_divide_issue_brief.pdf

Council of Economic Advisers (CEA), Department of Labor, and the Department of the Treasury. 2015. "Occupational Licensing: A Framework for Policymakers."

Crafts, N.F.R. 2004. "Steam as a General Purpose Technology: A Growth Accounting Perspective." *The Economic Journal* 114 (495), 338–351.

Czernich, Nina, Oliver Falck, Tobias Kretschmer, and Ludger Woessmann. 2011. "Broadband Infrastructure and Economic Growth." *The Economic Journal* 121(552): 505–532.

De Loecker, Jan and Pinelopi Koujianou Goldberg. 2014. "Firm Performance in a Global Market." *Annual Review of Economics* 6(1): 201–227.

Decker, Ryan, John Haltiwanger, Ron S. Jarmin, and Javier Miranda. 2014. "The Secular Decline in Business Dynamism in the U.S." University of Maryland working paper.

Education Superhighway. 2015. "2015 State of the States. A Report on the State of Broadband Connectivity in America's Public Schools." November. http://cdn.educationsuperhighway.org/assets/sos/full_report-c2e60c6937930e8ca5cdbf49d45d45c8.pdf

Fairlie, Robert. 2014. "Race and the Digital Divide." Contributions to Economic Analysis and Policy, B.E. Journals. UC Santa Cruz:

Department of Economics, UCSC. Retrieved from: http://escholar-ship.org/uc/item/48h8h99w

Feldman, Robin and Mark A. Lemley. 2015. "Do Patent Licensing Demands Mean Innovation?" *Iowa Law Review*, 101.

Feuer, Alan. 2012. "On The Waterfront, Rise of the Machines." *The New York Times*. September 28.

Field, Anne. 2015. "Enter the Smart Warehouse." June 13. http://newsroom.cisco.com/feature-content?articleId=1635631

Frey, Carl Benedikt and Michael A. Osborne. 2013. "The Future of Employment: How Susceptible Are Jobs to Computerisation?" Oxford Martin Programme on the Impacts of Future Technology.

Furman, Jason. 2015. "Productivity Growth in the Advanced Economies: The Past, the Present, and Lessons for the Future." July 9. Remarks given at the Peterson Institute for International Economics.

Furman, Jason, and Peter Orszag. 2015. "A Firm-Level Perspective on the Role of Rents in the Rise in Inequality." Paper presented at Columbia University's "A Just Society" Centennial Event in Honor of Joseph Stiglitz, New York, NY.

Galasso, Alberto and Schankerman, Mark. 2015. "Patent Rights and Innovation by Small and Large Firms," NBER Working Paper 21769.

Garcia-Macia, Daniel, Chang-Tai Hsieh, and Peter J. Klenow. 2015. "How Destructive is Innovation?" Stanford University working paper.

Garfield, Leanna. 2016. "These Four-foot-tall Robots Could Change the Way Warehouse Workers Do Their Jobs." *TechInsider*. February 2.

Gilson, Ronald J. 1999. "The Legal Infrastructure of High Technology Industrial Districts: Silicon Valley, Route 128, and Covenants Not to Compete." *New York University Law Review* 74: 575–629.

Goos, Maarten, Alan Manning, and Anna Salomons. 2014. "Explaining Job Polarization: Routine-Biased Technological Change and Offshoring." *American Economic Review* 104(8): 2509–26.

Gordon, Robert J. 2012. "Is US economic Growth Over? Faltering Innovation Confronts the Six Headwinds." September. Centre for Economic Policy Research, Policy Insight No. 63.

Graetz, Georg and Guy Michaels. 2015. "Robots at Work." Centre for Economic Performance Discussion Paper No. 1335.

Graham, Stuart JH, Cheryl Grim, Tariqul Islam, Alan C. Marco, and Javier Miranda. 2015. "Business Dynamics of Innovating Firms: Linking US Patents with Administrative Data on Workers and Firms." US Census Bureau Center for Economic Studies Paper No. CES-WP-15-19.

Greene, Karen. 1969. "Occupational Licensing and the Supply of Nonprofessional Manpower." Washington, DC: Manpower Administration, U.S. Department of Labor.

Griliches, Zvi. 1986. "Productivity, R&D, and the Basic Research at the Firm Level in the 1970s." *American Economic Review* 76(1): 141–154.

_____. 1989. "Patents: Recent Trends and Puzzles." *Brookings Papers on Economic Activity: Microeconomics*, 291-330.

_____. 1992. "The Search for R&D Spillovers." *Scandinavian Journal of Economics* 94(0): S29–47.

Grueber, Martin, and Tim Studt. 2013. "2014 Global R&D Funding Forecast." December. Battelle Memorial Institute and R&D Magazine.

Halpern, Laszlo, Miklos Koren, and Adam Szeidl. 2015. "Imported Inputs and Productivity." *American Economic Review*, forthcoming.

Hourihan, Matt, and David Parkes. 2015. "Omnibus Sets Up Major Boosts for Several Science Agencies." AAAS. December 17. http://www.aaas.org/news/omnibus-sets-major-boosts-several-science-agencies

International Federation of Robotics. 2014. "World Robotics 2014." IFR Statistical Department.

_____. 2015. "World Robotics 2015." IFR Statistical Department.

Jones, Charles I. 2002. "Sources of U.S. Economic Growth in a World of Ideas." *American Economic Review* 92(1): 220–239.

Jones, Charles I. and John C. Williams. 1998. "Measuring the Social Return to R&D." *Quarterly Journal of Economics* 113(4): 1119–1135.

Jorgenson, Dale W. and Kevin J. Stiroh. 2000. "Raising the Speed Limit: U.S. Economic Growth in the Information Age." *Brookings Papers on Economic Activity* 2000(1): 125-235.

Keynes, John Maynard. 1930. "Economic Possibilities for our Grandchildren." In *Essays in Persuasion*. London: Macmillan and Co., Ltd.

Kiebzak, Stephen, Rafert, Greg and Tucker, Catherine. 2016. "The Effect of Patent Litigation and Patent Assertion Entities on Entrepreneurial Activity." *Research Policy* 45(1): 218–231.

King, Robert G., and Ross Levine. 1993. "Finance, Entrepreneurship and Growth." *Journal of Monetary Economics* 32(3): 513–542.

Kleiner, Morris M. 1990. "Are There Economic Rents for More Restrictive Occupational Licensing Practices?" 42nd Annual Proceedings. United States: Industrial Relations Research Association, 177-185.

———. 2006. "Licensing Occupations: Ensuring Quality or Restriction Competition?" W.E. Upjohn Institute for Employment Research, 1-15. Kalamazoo, MI: Upjohn Institute Press. http://dx.doi.org/10.17848/9781429454865.

Kleiner, Morris M. and Alan B. Krueger. 2013. "Analyzing the Extent and Influence of Occupational Licensing on the Labor Market." *Journal of Labor Economics* 31(2): S173-S202.

Kolko, Jed. 2012. "Broadband and Local Growth." *Journal of Urban Economics* 71(1): 100–113.

Kuhn, Peter and Hani Mansour. 2014. "Is Internet Job Search Still Ineffective?" *The Economic Journal* 124: 1213–1233.

Lemley, Mark A. and A. Douglas Melamed. 2013. "Missing the Forest for the Trolls." *Columbia Law Review* 8(113): 2117–2189.

Manyika, James, Susan Lund, Kelsey Robinson, John Valentino, and Richard Dobbs. 2015. "A Labor Market That Works: Connecting Talent With Opportunity In the Digital Age." June. McKinsey Global Institute. http://www.mckinsey.com/~/media/McKinsey/dotcom/Insights/Employment%20and%20growth/Connecting%20talent%20with%20opportunity%20in%20the%20digital%20age/MGI_Online_talent_A_labor_market_that_works_Full_report_June_2015.ashx

Marx, Matt, Jasjit Singh, and Lee Fleming. 2015. "Regional Disadvantage? Employee Non-compete Agreements and Brain Drain." *Research Policy* 44(2): 394–404

McKinsey Global Institute. 2015. "Four Fundamentals of Workplace Automation." McKinsey Quarterly, November 2015. Available:http://www.mckinsey.com/insights/business_technology/four_fundamentals_of_workplace_automation

Melitz, Marc J. 2003. "The Impact of Trade on Intra-Industry Realloca-tions and Aggregate Industry Productivity." *Econometrica* 71(6): 1695–1725.

Najarzadeh, Reza, Farzad Rahimzadeh, and Michael Reed. 2014. "Does the Internet Increase Labor Productivity? Evidence From a Cross-Country Dynamic Panel." *Journal of Policy Modeling* 36(6): 986–993.

National Science Foundation. 2014. "Table 4-3. U.S. R&D Expenditures, by Performing Sector, Source of Funds, and Character of Work: 2011." *Science and Engineering Indicators 2014*.

National Telecommunications and Information Administration and Economics and Statistics Administration in the U.S. Department of Commerce. 2013. "Exploring the Digital Nation. America's Emerging Online Experience." June. https://www.ntia.doc.gov/files/ntia/publications/exploring_the_digital_nation_-_americas_emerging_online_experience.pdf

Nelson, Richard R. 1959. "The Simple Economics of Basic Scientific Research." *Journal of Political Economy* 67(3): 297–306.

North, Douglass C. and Weingast, Barry R. 1989. "Constitutions and Commitment: The Evolution of Institutions Governing Public Choice in Seventeenth-Century England." *Journal of Economic History* 49(4): 803–32.

OECD. 2013. "OECD Communications Outlook 2013," OECD Publishing. http://dx.doi.org/10.1787/comms_outlook-2013-en

———. 2015. Main Science and Technology Indicators. Vol. 2015/1. OECD Publishing. Paris. DOI: http://dx.doi.org/10.1787/msti-v2015-1-en

Oliner, Stephen D., and Daniel E. Sichel. 2002. "Information Technology and Productivity: Where Are We Now and Where Are We Going?" *Federal Reserve Bank of Atlanta Economic Review* 87 (Third Quarter): 15-44.

Peri, Giovanni, Kevin Shih, and Chad Sparber. 2014. "Foreign Stem Workers and Native Wages and Employment in U.S. Cities." NBER Working Paper No. 20093.

Png, Ivan PL. 2015. "Law and Innovation: Evidence from State Trade Secrets Laws." *Review of Economics and Statistics*, forthcoming.

PricewaterhouseCoopers and National Venture Capital Association. 2016. "Moneytree Report. Q4/2015/full year 2015 summary."

January. https://www.pwcmoneytree.com/Reports/FullArchive/National_2015-4.pdf

PWC. 2013. "2013 Patent Litigation Study: Big Cases Make Headlines, While Patent Cases Proliferate," available at http://www.pwc.com/en_US/us/forensic-services/publications/assets/2013-patent-litigation-study.pdf.

———. 2015. "The Sharing Economy. Consumer Intelligence Series," available at https://www.pwc.com/us/en/technology/publications/assets/pwc-consumer-intelligence-series-the-sharing-economy.pdf.

Rawley, Evan. 2010. "Diversification, Coordination Costs, and Organizational Rigidity: Evidence from Microdata." *Strategic Management Journal* 31(8): 873–891.

Rayle, Lisa, Susan Shaheen, Nelson Chan, Danielle Dai, and Robert Cervero. 2014. "App-Based, On-Demand Ride Services: Comparing Taxi and Ridesourcing Trips and User Characteristics in San Francisco." University of California Transportation Center. http://www.uctc.net/research/papers/UCTC-FR-2014-08.pdf

Robb, Alicia M. and David T. Robinson. 2012. "The Capital Structure Decisions of New Firms." *Review of Financial Studies* 27(1): 153-179.

Romer, Paul. 1994. "New Goods, Old Theory, and the Welfare Costs of Trade Restrictions." *Journal of Development Economics* 43(1): 5–38.

RPX. 2014. "2013 NPE Litigation Report," available at http://www.rpxcorp.com/wp-content/uploads/2014/01/RPX-2013-NPE-Litigation-Report.pdf.

———. 2015. "2014 NPE Litigation Report," available at http://www.rpxcorp.com/wp-content/uploads/sites/2/2015/03/RPX_Litigation-Report-2014_FNL_040615.pdf

Sander, Alison, and Meldon Wolfgang. 2014. "The Rise of Robotics." BCG Perspectives. https://www.bcgperspectives.com/content/articles/business_unit_strategy_innovation_rise_of_robotics/

Schmitt, John, Heidi Schierholz, and Lawrence Mishel. 2013. "Don't Blame the Robots. Assessing the Job Polarization Explanation of Growing Wage Inequality." Economic Policy Institute. http://www.epi.org/publication/technology-inequality-dont-blame-the-robots/

Scott Morton, Fiona and Carl Shapiro. 2014. "Strategic Patent Acquisitions." *Antitrust Law Journal* 79 (2): 463–499.

_____. 2015. "Patent Assertions: Are We Any Closer to Aligning Rewards to Contribution?" *Innovation Policy and the Economy*, forthcoming.

Seamans, Robert C. 2012. "Fighting City Hall: Entry Deterrence and Technology Upgrades in Cable TV Markets." *Management Science* 58(3): 461–475.

Solow, Robert M. 2007. "On Macroeconomic Models of Free-Market Innovation and Growth." In *Entrepreneurship, Innovation, and the Growth Mechanism of the Free-Enterprise Economies*, edited by Eytan Sheshinski, Robert J. Strom, and William Baumol. Princeton, NJ: Princeton University Press.

Sperling, Gene. 2013. "The Case for a Manufacturing Renaissance." July 25. Remarks given at the Brookings Institution.

Stevenson, Betsey. 2008. "The Internet and Job Search." NBER Working Paper 13886.

Sutton, John. 2012. *Competing in Capabilities: The Globalization Process.* Oxford, UK: Oxford University Press.

Wadhwa, Vivek, AnnaLee Saxenian, Ben A. Rissing, and G. Gereffi. 2007. "America's New Immigrant Entrepreneurs: Part I." Duke Science, Technology & Innovation Paper No. 23.

Zervas, Georgios, Davide Proserpio, and John Byers. 2015. "The Rise of the Sharing Economy: Estimating the Impact of Airbnb on the Hotel Industry." Proceedings of the Sixteenth ACM Conference on Economics and Computation, Pages 637–637.

CHAPTER 6

Altman, Roger C., Aaron Klein, and Alan B. Krueger. 2015. "Financing U.S. Transportation Infrastructure in the 21st Century." *The Hamilton Project Discussion Paper* 2015-04, The Hamilton Project, May.

Ang, Andrew, Vineer Bhansali, and Yuhang Xing. 2010. "Build America Bonds." *Journal of Fixed Income* 20(1): 67–73.

Aschauer, David A. 1989. "Is public expenditure productive?" *Journal of Monetary Economics* 23(2): 177–200.

Auerbach, Alan J. and Yuriy Gorodnichenko. 2012. "Measuring the Output Responses to Fiscal Policy." *American Economic Journal: Economic Policy* 4(2): 1–27.

Baladi, Gilbert, Tunwin Svasdisant, Thomas Van, Neeraj Buch, and Karim Chatti. 2002. "Cost-Effective Preventive Maintenance: Case Studies." *Transportation Research Record* 1795(02-3026):17–26.

Barth, Matthew and Kanok Boriboonsomsin. 2008. "Real-World Carbon Dioxide Impacts of Traffic Congestion." *Transportation Research Record: Journal of the Transportation Research Board* 2058: 163–171.

Bom, Pedro R. D. and Jenny E. Ligthart. 2014. "What Have We Learned From Three Decades of Research on the Productivity of Public Capital." *Journal of Economic Surveys* 28(5): 889-916.

Brueckner, Jan K. 2003. "Airline Traffic and Urban Economic Development." *Urban Studies* 40(8): 1455–1469.

Buckberg, Elaine, Owen Kearney, and Neal Stolleman. 2015. "Expanding the Market for Infrastructure Public-Private Partnerships: Alternative Risk and Profit Sharing Approaches to Align Sponsor and Investor Interests." U.S. Department of the Treasury Office of Economic Policy White Paper, April.

California High-Speed Rail Authority. 2015. "High-Speed Rail Program Fact Sheets."

Chatman, Daniel G. and Robert B. Noland. 2014. "Transit Service, Physical Agglomeration and Productivity in US Metropolitan Areas." *Urban Studies* 51(5): 917–937.

Chen, Zhenhua and Kingsley E. Haynes. 2015. "Regional Impact of Public Transportation Infrastructure: A Spatial Panel Assessment of the U.S. Northeast Megaregion." *Economic Development Quarterly* 29(3): 275–291.

Christian, Thomas J. 2012. "Trade-Offs Between Commuting Time and Health-Related Activities." *Journal of Urban Health: Bulletin of the New York Academy of Medicine* 89(5): 746–757.

Christiano, Lawrence, Martin Eichenbaum, and Sergio Rebelo. 2011. "When Is the Government Spending Multiplier Large?" *Journal of Political Economy* 119(1): 78–121.

Cohen, Jeffery P. and Catherine J. Morrison Paul. 2003. "Airport infrastructure spillovers in a network system." *Journal of Urban Economics* 54(3): 459–473.

Congressional Budget Office. 2009. "Subsidizing Infrastructure Investment with Tax-Preferred Bonds." with the Joint Committee on Taxation, October.

______. 2015. "Public Spending on Transportation and Water Infrastructure, 1956 to 2014." March.

Council of Economic Advisers. 2014. "An Economic Analysis of Transportation Infrastructure Investment." July.

______. 2015. "Long-term Interest Rates: A Survey." July.

Duranton, Gilles and Matthew A. Turner. 2012. "Urban Growth and Transportation." *Review of Economic Studies* 1: 1–36.

Duranton, Gilles, Peter M. Morrow, and Matthew A. Turner. 2014. "Roads and Trade: Evidence from the US." *Review of Economic Studies* 81(2): 681–724.

Engel, Eduardo, Ronald Fischer, and Alexander Galetovic. 2011. "Public-Private Partnerships to Revamp U.S. Infrastructure." The Hamilton Project, Discussion Paper 2011-02.

Eggertsson, Gauti B. 2011. "What Fiscal Policy is Effective at Zero Interest Rates?" ed. Daron Acemoglu and Michael Woodford. *NBER Macroeconomics Annual 2010* 25: 59–112.

Fischer, Stanley. 2015. "What have we learned from the crises of the last 20 years?" *Remarks at the International Monetary Conference*, Toronto, Ontario, June 1.

Hart, Oliver. 2003. "Incomplete Contracts and Public Ownership: Remarks, and an Application to Public-Private Partnerships." *The Economic Journal* 113(486): C69–C76.

Haughwout, Andrew F. 1999. "Regional Fiscal Cooperation in Metropolitan Areas: An Exploration." *Journal of Policy Analysis and Management* 18(4): 579–600.

Hurlin, Christophe and Alexandru Minea. 2013. "Is public capital really productive? A methodological reappraisal." *European Journal of Operational Research* 228(1): 122–130.

Hymel, Kent. 2009. "Does traffic congestion reduce employment growth?" *Journal of Urban Economics* 65: 127–135.

International Monetary Fund. 2014. "Is it Time for an Infrastructure Push? The Macroeconomic Effects of Public Investment." *World Economic Outlook*, Chapter 3, October.

Kalaitzidakis, Pantelis and Sarantis Kalyvitis. 2005. "Financing 'New' Public Investment and/or Maintenance in Public Capital for Growth? The Canadian Experience." *Economic Inquiry* 43: 586–600.

Kalyvitis, Sarantis and Eugenia Vella. 2015. "Productivity Effects of Public Capital Maintenance: Evidence from U.S. States." *Economic Inquiry* 53(1): 72-90.

Kawabata, Mizuki. 2003. "Job Access and Employment among Low-Skilled Autoless Workers in US Metropolitan Areas." *Environment and Planning A* 35(9): 1651–1668.

Leduc, Sylvain and Daniel Wilson. 2012. "Roads to Prosperity or Bridges to Nowhere? Theory and Evidence on the Impact of Public Infrastructure Investment." *NBER Macroeconomics Annual* 27(1): 89–142.

Melo, Patricia C., Daniel J. Graham, and Ruben Brage-Ardao. 2013. "The productivity of transport infrastructure investment: A meta-analysis of empirical evidence." *Regional Science and Urban Economics* 43: 695–706.

Michaels, Guy. 2008. "The Effect of Trade on the Demand for Skill: Evidence from the Interstate Highway System." *Review of Economics and Statistics* 90(4): 683–701.

Nadiri, M. Ishaq and Theofanis P. Mamuneas. 1996. "Contribution of Highway Capital to Industry and National Productivity Growth." Report prepared for Federal Highway Administration, Office of Policy Development, September.

Natural Resources Defense Council. 2009. "Summary of Energy and Transportation Provisions in the Economic Recovery Bill." NRDC Legislative Facts, December.

Novaco, Raymond W. and Oscar I. Gonzalez. 2011. "Commuting and well-being." in *Technology and Psychology Well-being* (Ed. Yair Amichai-Hamburger): 174–205.

Pereira, Alfredo M. 2001. "On the Effects of Public Investment on Private Investment: What Crowds in What?" *Public Finance Review* 29(1): 3–25.

Peshkin, David G., Todd E. Hoerner, and Kathryn A. Zimmerman. 2004. "Optimal Timing of Pavement Preventive Maintenance Treatment Applications." National Cooperative Highway Research Program, National Transportation Board, Report 523.

Public Broadcasting Service. 1956. "State of the Union Address, 1956."

Schrank, David, Bill Eisele, Tim Lomax, and Jim Bak. 2015. "2015 Urban Mobility Scorecard." Texas A&M Transportation Institute and INRIX, August.

Thompson, Eric C. and Amitabh Chandra. 1998. "Economic Impact of Interstate Highways in Kentucky." In Berger, Mark C., Glenn C. Blomquist, Richward W. Furst, and Steven N. Allen (Eds.), Kentucky Annual Economic Report 1998: 55–62.

Tong, Tingting, Tun-Hsiang Edward Yu, Seong-Hoon Cho, Kimberly Jensen, and Daniel De La Torre Ugarte. 2013. "Evaluating the spatial spillover effects of transportation infrastructure on agricultural output across the United States." *Journal of Transport Geography* 30: 47–55.

TRIP. 2015. "Bumpy Roads Ahead: America's Roughest Rides and Strategies to Make our Roads Smoother." July.

Urban Land Institute. 2011. "Infrastructure 2011: A Strategic Priority." With Ernst & Young, Washington, DC.

U.S. Government Accountability Office. 2014. "Surface Transportation: Department of Transportation Should Measure the Overall Performance and Outcomes of the TIGER Discretionary Grant Program." *Report to the Ranking Member, Committee on Environment and Public Works, U.S. Senate*, GAO-14-766, September.

U.S. Department of Agriculture. 2015. "USDA Announces $210 Million to be Invested in Renewable Energy Infrastructure through the Biofuel Infrastructure Partnership." October 28.

U.S. Department of Transportation. 2013. "2013 Status of the Nation's Highways, Bridges, and Transit: Conditions & Performance." U.S. Federal Highway Administration, Report to Congress.

_____. 2015a. "Freight Facts and Figures 2015." Bureau of Transportation Statistics, January.

_____. 2015b. "Public-Private Partnerships: Project Profiles." U.S. Federal Highway Administration. http://www.fhwa.dot.gov/ipd/p3/default.aspx.

_____. 2015c. "Table 1-27: Condition of U.S. Roadways by Functional System." Bureau of Transportation Statistics.

_____. 2015d. "Table 1-28: Condition of U.S. Bridges." Bureau of Transportation Statistics.

_____. 2015e. "The Interstate System." U.S. Federal Highway Administration. https://www.fhwa.dot.gov/highwayhistory/interstate.cfm.

U.S. Department of the Treasury. 2011. "Treasury Analysis of Build America Bonds Issuance and Savings." Washington, DC: U.S. Department of the Treasury.

Transportation Research Board. 2008. "Potential Impacts of Climate Change on U.S. Transportation." Transportation Research Board Special Report 290, National Research Council, Washington, DC.

Weikel, Dan. 2011. "Diesel Era Ends for MTA Buses." *Los Angeles Times*. January 13.

Chapter 7

Arrow, Kenneth. 2015. Discussion at CEA. Washington. September 18.

Bailey, Stephen K. 1950. Congress Makes a Law: *The Story Behind the Employment Act of 1946*. New York: Columbia University Press.

Baily, Martin. 2006. Interview with the Federal Reserve Bank of Richmond. Washington. August 8.

Bernanke, Ben S. 2013. "The Ten Suggestions." Baccalaureate Ceremony, Princeton University. Princeton, New Jersey. June 2.

Blinder, Alan S., and Janet L. Yellen. 2001. *The Fabulous Decade: Macroeconomic Lessons from the 1990s*. New York: The Century Foundation.

Blinder, Alan S., and Mark Zandi. 2010. "How the Great Recession Was Brought to an End." Princeton University and Moody's Analytics.

Bonafede, Dom. 1982. "Reagan's Economic Advisers Share Task of Shaping and Explaining Reaganomics." *National Journal*. February 6.

Brazelton, W. Robert. 1997. "Retrospectives: The Economics of Leon Hirsch Keyserling." *Journal of Economic Perspectives* 11 (4): 189-197.

_____. 2001. *Designing U.S. Economic Policy: An Analytical Biography of Leon   H. Keyserling*. New York: Palgrave.

Chodorow-Reich, Gabriel, Laura Feiveson, Zachary Liscow, and William Gui Woolston. 2012. "Does State Fiscal Relief During Recessions Increase Employment? Evidence from the American Recovery and Reinvestment Act." *American Economic Journal: Economic Policy* 4 (3): 118–145.

Council of Economic Advisers (CEA). 1946. *First Annual Report to the President*.

_____. 1961. *The Economic Report of the President*.

_____. 1963. *The Economic Report of the President*.

_____. 1966. *The Economic Report of the President*.

_____. 1976. *The Economic Report of the President*.

_____. 1995. *The Economic Report of the President*.

_____. 2002. *The Economic Report of the President*.

_____. 2004. *The Economic Report of the President*.

_____. 2014. *The Economic Report of the President*.

DeLong, J. Bradford. 1996. "Keynesianism, Pennsylvania Avenue Style: Some Economic Consequences of the Employment Act of 1946." *Journal of Economic Perspectives* 10 (3): 41-53.

Eizenstat, Stuart E. 1992. "Economists and White House Decisions." *Journal of Economic Perspectives* 6 (3): 65-71.

Elmendorf, Douglas W., Jeffery B. Liebman, and David W. Wilcox. 2002. "Fiscal Policy and Social Security Policy during the 1990s." In Jeffrey Frankel and Peter R. Orszag, eds., *American Economic Policy in the 1990s*. Cambridge: MIT Press. 61-119.

Employment Act of 1946. 1946. Pub. L. 79-304, ch. 33, Sec. 2, 60 Stat. 23.

Engelbourg, Saul. 1980. "The Council of Economic Advisers and the Recession of 1953-1954." *Business History Review* 54 (2): 192–214.

Feldstein, Martin, ed. 1989. "How the CEA Advises Presidents." *Challenge* 32 (6): 51-55.

_____. 1992. "The Council of Economic Advisers and Economic Advising in the United States." *The Economic Journal* 102 (414): 1223-1234.

_____. 1994. *American Economic Policy in the 1980s*. Chicago: The University of Chicago Press.

Flash, Edward S., Jr. 1965. *Economic Advice and Presidential Leadership: The Council of Economic Advisers*. New York: Columbia University Press.

Frankel, Jeffrey. 2003. "What an Economic Adviser Can Do When He Disagrees with the President." *Challenge* 46 (3): 29-52.

Frankel, Jeffrey, and Peter R. Orszag, eds. 2002. *American Economic Policy in the 1990s*. Cambridge: MIT Press.

Furman, Jason. 2015. "It Could Have Happened Here: The Policy Response That Helped Prevent a Second Great Depression." Speech at Macroeconomic Advisers' 25th Annual Washington Policy Seminar. Washington. September 9.

_____. 2015. "Productivity Growth in the Advanced Economies: The Past, the Present, and Lessons for the Future." Speech at Peterson Institute for International Economics. Washington. July 9.

Galbraith, James K. 1994. "The 1994 Council of Economic Advisers Report: A Review." *Challenge* 37 (3): 12-16.

_____. 1995. "Economic Report of the President: A Review." *Challenge* 38 (3): 5-9.

Genovese, Michael A. 1987. "The Presidency and Styles of Economic Management." *Congress & The Presidency* 14 (3): 151-167.

Gross, Betram M., and John P. Lewis. 1954. "The President's Economic Staff During the Truman Administration." *The American Political Science Review* 48 (1): 114-130.

Hahn, Robert W., and Robert N. Stavins. 2002. "National Environmental Policy During the Clinton Years." In Jeffrey Frankel and Peter R. Orszag, eds., *American Economic Policy in the 1990s*. Cambridge: MIT Press. 983-1025.

Hargrove, Erwin C., and Samuel A. Morley, eds. 1984. *The President and the Council of Economic Advisers: Interviews with CEA Chairmen*. Boulder, CO: Westview Press.

Hubbard, R. Glenn. 2002. "Comments." In Jeffrey Frankel and Peter R. Orszag, eds., *American Economic Policy in the 1990s*. Cambridge: MIT Press. 983-1025.

Krueger, Alan B. 2000. "Honest Brokers Separate Policy from Sausage for the White House." *The New York Times*. November 9.

Mankiw, NG. 2003. "Remarks at the Conference of State Bank Supervisors: State Banking Summit and Leadership Conference." Washington. November 6.

Mills, Geofrey T. 1988. "Introduction." In Robert Sobel and Bernard S. Katz, eds., *Biographical Directory of the Council of Economic Advisers*. Westport, CT: Greenwood Press.

Naveh, David. 1981. "The Political Role of Academic Advisers: The Case of the U.S. President's Council of Economic Advisers, 1946-1976." *Presidential Studies Quarterly* 11 (4): 492-510.

Niskanen, William A. 1986. "Out of the Trenches: Economists and Politicians." *Journal of Policy Analysis and Management* 5 (2): 234-244.

Norton, Hugh S. 1977. *The Employment Act and the Council of Economic Advisers, 1946-1976*. Columbia: University of South Carolina Press.

Nourse, Edwin G. 1953. *Economics in the Public Service: Administrative Aspects of the Employment Act*. New York: Harcourt, Brace and Company.

Orszag, Jonathan M., Peter R. Orszag, and Laura D. Tyson. 2002. "The Process of Economic Policy-Making During the Clinton Administration." In Jeffrey Frankel and Peter R. Orszag, eds., *American Economic Policy in the 1990s*. Cambridge: MIT Press. 983-1025.

Porter, Roger B. 1980. *Presidential Decision Making: The Economic Policy Board*. Cambridge: Cambridge University Press.

———. 1983. "Economic Advice to the President: From Eisenhower to Reagan." *Political Science Quarterly* 98 (3): 403-426.

———. 1991. "The Council of Economic Advisers." In Colin Campbell and Margaret Jane Wyszomirski, eds., *Executive Leadership in Anglo-American Systems*. Pittsburgh: University of Pittsburgh Press.

———. 1997. "Presidents and Economists: The Council of Economic Advisers." *American Economic Review* 87 (2): 103-106.

Romer, Christina D. 2011. "Back from the Brink." In Asli Demirgüç-Kunt, Douglas D. Evanoff, and George G. Kaufman, eds., *The International Financial Crisis: Have the Rules of Finance Changed?* Singapore: World Scientific Publishing Company. 15-31.

Rosen, Harvey S., and Kristin J. Forbes. 2005. "The Economic Outlook." Testimony before the Joint Economic Committee. Washington. April 14.

Schultze, Charles L. 1996. "The CEA: An Inside Voice for Mainstream Economics." *Journal of Economic Perspectives* 10 (3): 23-29.

Stein, Herbert. 1988. *Presidential Economics: The Making of Economic Policy from Roosevelt to Reagan and Beyond.* Washington: American Enterprise Institute.

_____. 1991. "The Washington Economist: What Economic Advisers Do." American Enterprise Institute.

_____. 1996. "A Successful Accident: Recollections and Speculations about the CEA." *Journal of Economic Perspectives* 10 (3): 3-21.

_____. 1996. *The Fiscal Revolution in America: Policy in Pursuit of Reality.* Washington: American Enterprise Institute.

Stevenson, Betsey. 2014. "The Role of the Council of Economic Advisers in Bringing Economic Research to Policy Making." Speech at the Federal Reserve. Washington. May 30.

Stiglitz, Joseph. 1997. "Looking Out for the National Interest: The Principles of the Council of Economic Advisers." *American Economic Review* 87 (2): 109-113.

The Economist. 2010. "Ranking CEAs: The best since the 1960s?" *Free Exchange.* February 25.

Tobin, James, and Murray Weidenbaum, eds. 1988. *Two Revolutions in Economic Policy: The First Economic Reports of Presidents Kennedy and Reagan.* Cambridge: MIT Press.

Tollestrup, Jessica. 2015. "History and Authority of the Joint Economic Committee." *Congressional Research Service.*

Tyson, Laura D'Andrea. 1994. "From Stagnation to Renewed Growth." *Challenge* 37 (3): 17-22.

Wallich, Henry C. 1984. "The German Council of Economic Advisers in an American Perspective." *Journal of Institutional and Theoretical Economics* 140 (2): 355-363.

Wehrle, Edmund F. 2004. "Guns, Butter, Leon Keyserling, the AFL-CIO, and the Fate of Full-Employment Economics." *Historian* 66 (4): 730–748.

Weidenbaum, Murray L. 1983. "An Economist in Government: Views of a Presidential Adviser." *Contemporary Issues Series* 5. Center for the Study of American Business.

_____. 1986. "The Role of the President's Council of Economic Advisers: Theory and Reality." *Presidential Studies Quarterly* 16 (3): 460-466.

_____. 1988. "The Role of the Council of Economic Advisers." *The Journal of Economic Education* 19 (3): 237-243.

_____. 1996. "The Employment Act of 1946: A Half Century of Presidential Policymaking." *Presidential Studies Quarterly* 26 (3): 880-886.

White, Lawrence J. 1981. *Reforming Regulation: Processes and Problems.* Englewood Cliffs, N.J: Prentice-Hall, Inc.

A P P E N D I X   A

REPORT TO THE PRESIDENT ON THE ACTIVITIES OF THE COUNCIL OF ECONOMIC ADVISERS DURING 2015

LETTER OF TRANSMITTAL

COUNCIL OF ECONOMIC ADVISERS
Washington, D.C., December 31, 2015

MR. PRESIDENT:

The Council of Economic Advisers submits this report on its activities during calendar year 2015 in accordance with the requirements of the Congress, as set forth in section 10(d) of the Employment Act of 1946 as amended by the Full Employment and Balanced Growth Act of 1978.

Sincerely yours,

Jason Furman, *Chairman*
Sandra E. Black, *Member*
Jay C. Shambaugh, *Member*

COUNCIL MEMBERS AND THEIR DATES OF SERVICE

Name	Position	Oath of office date	Separation date
Edwin G. Nourse	Chairman	August 9, 1946	November 1, 1949
Leon H. Keyserling	Vice Chairman	August 9, 1946	
	Acting Chairman	November 2, 1949	
	Chairman	May 10, 1950	January 20, 1953
John D. Clark	Member	August 9, 1946	
	Vice Chairman	May 10, 1950	February 11, 1953
Roy Blough	Member	June 29, 1950	August 20, 1952
Robert C. Turner	Member	September 8, 1952	January 20, 1953
Arthur F. Burns	Chairman	March 19, 1953	December 1, 1956
Neil H. Jacoby	Member	September 15, 1953	February 9, 1955
Walter W. Stewart	Member	December 2, 1953	April 29, 1955
Raymond J. Saulnier	Member	April 4, 1955	
	Chairman	December 3, 1956	January 20, 1961
Joseph S. Davis	Member	May 2, 1955	October 31, 1958
Paul W. McCracken	Member	December 3, 1956	January 31, 1959
Karl Brandt	Member	November 1, 1958	January 20, 1961
Henry C. Wallich	Member	May 7, 1959	January 20, 1961
Walter W. Heller	Chairman	January 29, 1961	November 15, 1964
James Tobin	Member	January 29, 1961	July 31, 1962
Kermit Gordon	Member	January 29, 1961	December 27, 1962
Gardner Ackley	Member	August 3, 1962	
	Chairman	November 16, 1964	February 15, 1968
John P. Lewis	Member	May 17, 1963	August 31, 1964
Otto Eckstein	Member	September 2, 1964	February 1, 1966
Arthur M. Okun	Member	November 16, 1964	
	Chairman	February 15, 1968	January 20, 1969
James S. Duesenberry	Member	February 2, 1966	June 30, 1968
Merton J. Peck	Member	February 15, 1968	January 20, 1969
Warren L. Smith	Member	July 1, 1968	January 20, 1969
Paul W. McCracken	Chairman	February 4, 1969	December 31, 1971
Hendrik S. Houthakker	Member	February 4, 1969	July 15, 1971
Herbert Stein	Member	February 4, 1969	
	Chairman	January 1, 1972	August 31, 1974
Ezra Solomon	Member	September 9, 1971	March 26, 1973
Marina v.N. Whitman	Member	March 13, 1972	August 15, 1973
Gary L. Seevers	Member	July 23, 1973	April 15, 1975
William J. Fellner	Member	October 31, 1973	February 25, 1975
Alan Greenspan	Chairman	September 4, 1974	January 20, 1977
Paul W. MacAvoy	Member	June 13, 1975	November 15, 1976
Burton G. Malkiel	Member	July 22, 1975	January 20, 1977
Charles L. Schultze	Chairman	January 22, 1977	January 20, 1981
William D. Nordhaus	Member	March 18, 1977	February 4, 1979
Lyle E. Gramley	Member	March 18, 1977	May 27, 1980
George C. Eads	Member	June 6, 1979	January 20, 1981
Stephen M. Goldfeld	Member	August 20, 1980	January 20, 1981
Murray L. Weidenbaum	Chairman	February 27, 1981	August 25, 1982
William A. Niskanen	Member	June 12, 1981	March 30, 1985
Jerry L. Jordan	Member	July 14, 1981	July 31, 1982

COUNCIL MEMBERS AND THEIR DATES OF SERVICE

Name	Position	Oath of office date	Separation date
Martin Feldstein	Chairman	October 14, 1982	July 10, 1984
William Poole	Member	December 10, 1982	January 20, 1985
Beryl W. Sprinkel	Chairman	April 18, 1985	January 20, 1989
Thomas Gale Moore	Member	July 1, 1985	May 1, 1989
Michael L. Mussa	Member	August 18, 1986	September 19, 1988
Michael J. Boskin	Chairman	February 2, 1989	January 12, 1993
John B. Taylor	Member	June 9, 1989	August 2, 1991
Richard L. Schmalensee	Member	October 3, 1989	June 21, 1991
David F. Bradford	Member	November 13, 1991	January 20, 1993
Paul Wonnacott	Member	November 13, 1991	January 20, 1993
Laura D'Andrea Tyson	Chair	February 5, 1993	April 22, 1995
Alan S. Blinder	Member	July 27, 1993	June 26, 1994
Joseph E. Stiglitz	Member	July 27, 1993	
	Chairman	June 28, 1995	February 10, 1997
Martin N. Baily	Member	June 30, 1995	August 30, 1996
Alicia H. Munnell	Member	January 29, 1996	August 1, 1997
Janet L. Yellen	Chair	February 18, 1997	August 3, 1999
Jeffrey A. Frankel	Member	April 23, 1997	March 2, 1999
Rebecca M. Blank	Member	October 22, 1998	July 9, 1999
Martin N. Baily	Chairman	August 12, 1999	January 19, 2001
Robert Z. Lawrence	Member	August 12, 1999	January 12, 2001
Kathryn L. Shaw	Member	May 31, 2000	January 19, 2001
R. Glenn Hubbard	Chairman	May 11, 2001	February 28, 2003
Mark B. McClellan	Member	July 25, 2001	November 13, 2002
Randall S. Kroszner	Member	November 30, 2001	July 1, 2003
N. Gregory Mankiw	Chairman	May 29, 2003	February 18, 2005
Kristin J. Forbes	Member	November 21, 2003	June 3, 2005
Harvey S. Rosen	Member	November 21, 2003	
	Chairman	February 23, 2005	June 10, 2005
Ben S. Bernanke	Chairman	June 21, 2005	January 31, 2006
Katherine Baicker	Member	November 18, 2005	July 11, 2007
Matthew J. Slaughter	Member	November 18, 2005	March 1, 2007
Edward P. Lazear	Chairman	February 27, 2006	January 20, 2009
Donald B. Marron	Member	July 17, 2008	January 20, 2009
Christina D. Romer	Chair	January 29, 2009	September 3, 2010
Austan D. Goolsbee	Member	March 11, 2009	
	Chairman	September 10, 2010	August 5, 2011
Cecilia Elena Rouse	Member	March 11, 2009	February 28, 2011
Katharine G. Abraham	Member	April 19, 2011	April 19, 2013
Carl Shapiro	Member	April 19, 2011	May 4, 2012
Alan B. Krueger	Chairman	November 7, 2011	August 2, 2013
James H. Stock	Member	February 7, 2013	May 19, 2014
Jason Furman	Chairman	August 4, 2013	
Betsey Stevenson	Member	August 6, 2013	August 7, 2015
Maurice Obstfeld	Member	July 21, 2014	August 28, 2015
Sandra E. Black	Member	August 10, 2015	
Jay C. Shambaugh	Member	August 31, 2015	

REPORT TO THE PRESIDENT
ON THE ACTIVITIES OF THE
COUNCIL OF ECONOMIC ADVISERS
DURING 2015

The Council of Economic Advisers was established by the Employment Act of 1946 to provide the President with objective economic analysis and advice on the development and implementation of a wide range of domestic and international economic policy issues. The Council is governed by a Chairman and two Members. The Chairman is appointed by the President and confirmed by the United States Senate. The Members are appointed by the President.

THE CHAIRMAN OF THE COUNCIL

Jason Furman was confirmed by the Senate on August 1, 2013 as the 28th Chairman of the Council of Economic Advisers. Furman has served the President since the beginning of the Administration, previously holding the position of Principal Deputy Director of the National Economic Council and Assistant to the President. Immediately prior to the Administration, Furman was Economic Policy Director for the President's campaign in 2008 and a member of the Presidential Transition Team.

Furman held a variety of posts in public policy and research before his work with President Obama. In public policy, Furman worked at both the Council of Economic Advisers and National Economic Council during the Clinton administration and also at the World Bank. In research, Furman was a Senior Fellow at the Brookings Institution and the Center on Budget and Policy Priorities and also has served in visiting positions at various universities, including NYU's Wagner Graduate School of Public Policy. Furman has conducted research in a wide range of areas, such as fiscal policy, tax policy, health economics, Social Security, and domestic and international macroeconomics. In addition to numerous articles in scholarly journals and periodicals, Furman is the editor of two books on economic policy. Furman holds a Ph.D. in economics from Harvard University.

The Members of the Council

Sandra E. Black was appointed by the President on August 10, 2015. She is on leave from the University of Texas, Austin where she holds the Audre and Bernard Rapoport Centennial Chair in Economics and Public Affairs and is a Professor of Economics. She received her B.A. from the University of California, Berkeley and her Ph.D. in economics from Harvard University.

Jay C. Shambaugh was appointed by the President on August 31, 2015. He is on leave from George Washington University where he is a Professor of Economics and International Affairs. Dr. Shambaugh received a B.A. from Yale, an M.A.L.D. from The Fletcher School at Tufts University, and a Ph.D. in Economics from the University of California, Berkeley.

Betsey Stevenson resigned as Member of the Council on August 7, 2015 to return to the University of Michigan, where she is Associate Professor of Public Policy and Economics.

Maurice Obstfeld resigned as Member of the Council on August 28, 2015 to join the International Monetary Fund as Economic Counsellor and Director of Research while on leave from the University of California, Berkeley where he is Professor of Economics.

Areas of Activities

A central function of the Council is to advise the President on all economic issues and developments. In the past year, as in previous years, advising the President on policies to spur economic growth and job creation, and evaluating the effects of these policies on the economy, have been priorities.

The Council works closely with various government agencies, including the National Economic Council, the Office of Management and Budget, White House senior staff, and other officials and engages in discussions on numerous policy matters. In the area of international economic policy, the Council coordinates with other units of the White House, the Treasury Department, the State Department, the Commerce Department, and the Federal Reserve on matters related to the global financial system.

Among the specific economic policy areas that received attention in 2015 were: college affordability and quality; health care cost growth and the Affordable Care Act; infrastructure investment; regulatory measures; trade policies; poverty and income inequality; unemployment insurance and the minimum wage; labor force participation; job training; corporate taxation; regional development; the economic cost of carbon pollution; renewable fuel standards; energy policy; intellectual property and innovation; and foreign direct investment. The Council also worked on several issues related to the quality of the data available for assessing economic conditions.

The Council prepares for the President, the Vice President, and the White House senior staff a daily economic briefing memo analyzing current economic developments and almost-daily memos on key economic data releases. Chairman Furman also presents a monthly briefing on the state of the economy and the Council's energy analysis to senior White House officials.

The Council, the Department of Treasury, and the Office of Management and Budget—the Administration's economic "troika"— are responsible for producing the economic forecasts that underlie the Administration's budget proposals. The Council initiates the forecasting process twice each year, consulting with a wide variety of outside sources, including leading private sector forecasters and other government agencies.

The Council was an active participant in the trade policy process, participating in the Trade Policy Staff Committee and the Trade Policy Review Group. The Council provided analysis and opinions on a range of trade-related issues involving the enforcement of existing trade agreements, reviews of current U.S. trade policies, and consideration of future policies. The Council also participated on the Trade Promotion Coordinating Committee, helping to examine the ways in which exports may support economic growth in the years to come. In the area of investment and security, the Council participated on the Committee on Foreign Investment in the United States (CFIUS), reviewing individual cases before the committee.

The Council is a leading participant in the Organisation for Economic Co-operation and Development (OECD), an important forum for economic cooperation among high-income industrial economies. Chairman Furman is chairman of the OECD's Economic Policy Committee, and Council Members and staff participate actively in working-party meetings on macroeconomic policy and coordination, and contribute to the OECD's research agenda.

The Council issued a wide range of reports in 2015. In February, the Council released a report on the use of big data and its effects on differential pricing. That same month, CEA analyzed the effects of conflicted investment advice on retirement savings and its role in lower investment returns for American families. In March, the Council celebrated the Affordable Care Act's (ACA) fifth anniversary with a report analyzing progress on coverage, cost and quality. The Council, in recognition of Equal Pay Day, released an issue brief on the gender pay gap, recent trends, and explanations for these developments.

In May, the Council issued a report on the economic benefits of U.S. trade, focusing on the positive gains from trade integration. Also in May, in tandem with the Domestic Policy Council and the Office of Management and Budget, the Council released a report on rural child poverty. There, the Council analyzed poverty measurement tools, and policy levers targeted at rural poverty. In June, the Council reported on U.S. petroleum consumption, and the decrease in domestic petroleum consumption in recent years. In July, the Council continued analysis of the ACA, and released a report on the consequences of State decisions to not expand Medicaid, finding that millions of Americans are denied health care coverage as a result of these choices.

The Council focused in 2015 on investments in children and youth, releasing a July report on the economic costs of youth disadvantage and gaps in opportunity for young men of color. The Council also focused on macroeconomic monitoring, issuing a report on long-term interest rates and an issue brief on improving the measurement of economic growth by examining Gross Domestic Output, which combines measurement of income and production. The Council produced a July issue brief on the digital divide, and the unevenly distributed benefits of access to the Internet. A framework for policymakers was released that same month in partnership with the Departments of Labor and Treasury on occupational licensing, and the inefficiencies and inequities incurred by current licensing regimes.

In August, the Council expanded its work on gender equality, releasing an issue brief on opportunities for women in business, the strides made by women in the labor market, and barriers that remain for women in business careers. In the fall, the Council focused on institutions of higher education in the United States, releasing a report on using federal data to measure and improve their performance. In support of broader efforts around worker voice, the Council issued an October issue brief on worker voice in a time of rising inequality, focusing on increasing wage and income inequality and the role of unions in wage distribution. In December, the Council released an issue brief on fines, fees and bails, and the system of payments in the criminal justice system that disproportionately impact low-income Americans. Finally, in December, the Council released a report on food insecurity, focusing on the long-term benefits of the Supplemental Nutrition Assistance Program in reducing poverty in the United States. All of the aforementioned reports can be found on the Council's website and some of them are incorporated into this annual report as well. (http://www.whitehouse.gov/administration/eop/cea/factsheets-reports.)

The Council continued its efforts to improve the public's understanding of economic developments and of the Administration's economic policies through briefings with the economic and financial press, speeches, discussions with outside economists, and regular updates on major data releases and postings of CEA's Reports on the White House and CEA blogs. The Chairman and Members also regularly met to exchange views on the economy with the Chairman and Members of the Board of Governors of the Federal Reserve System.

Public Information

The Council's annual Economic Report of the President is an important vehicle for presenting the Administration's domestic and international economic policies. It is available for purchase through the Government Printing Office, and is viewable on the Internet at www.gpo.gov/erp.

The Council frequently prepared reports and blog posts in 2015, and the Chairman and Members gave numerous public speeches. The reports, posts and texts of speeches are available at the Council's website, www. whitehouse.gov/cea. Finally, the Council published the monthly Economic Indicators, which is available online at www.gpo.gov/economicindicators.

The Staff of the Council of Economic Advisers

The staff of the Council consists of the senior staff, senior economists, staff economists, research economists, research assistants, and the administrative and support staff. The staff at the end of 2015 was:

Senior Staff

Andrea Taverna	Chief of Staff
Matthew Fiedler	Chief Economist
Steven N. Braun	Director of Macroeconomic Forecasting
Anna Y. Lee	Director of Finance and Administration
Adrienne Pilot	Director of Statistical Office

Senior Economists

Kenneth Gillingham	Energy, Environment
Laura Giuliano	Labor, Education
Gregory Leiserson	Tax, Retirement, Budget
Timothy A. Park	Agriculture, Infrastructure, Evaluation

Nirupama S. Rao .... Labor, Education
Katheryn N. Russ .... International Trade, Finance
Claudia Sahm .... Macroeconomics, Housing
Robert C. Seamans. .... Innovation, Technology, Industrial
                                   Organization

Staff Economists

Amy Filipek. .... Macroeconomics, Housing
Martha Gimbel .... Labor
E. Mallick Hossain .... Macroeconomics, Retirement
Rahul Rekhi. .... Health, Budget
Gabriel Scheffler. .... Health, Labor
Emily Weisburst .... Labor, Criminal Justice

Research Economists

Lydia Cox. .... Energy, International Trade
Harris R. Eppsteiner. .... Labor, Immigration
Samuel Himel .... Housing, Infrastructure, Industrial
                                   Organization
Emma Rackstraw .... Labor, Education
Jason Sockin .... Macroeconomics, Infrastructure

Research Assistants

Ayushi Narayan .... Education, Agriculture
William Weber .... Macroeconomics, International Trade
Samuel Young .... Heath, Tax

Statistical Office

The Statistical Office gathers, administers, and produces statistical information for the Council. Duties include preparing the statistical appendix to the Economic Report of the President and the monthly publication Economic Indicators. The staff also creates background materials for economic analysis and verifies statistical content in Presidential memoranda. The Office serves as the Council's liaison to the statistical community.

Brian A. Amorosi .... Statistical Analyst
Jonathan Sheppard. .... Economic Statistician

Office of the Chairman and Members

Jeff Goldstein . . . . Special Assistant to the Chairman

Eric Van Nostrand . . . . Special Assistant to the Chairman and Staff Economist

Jamie Keene. . . . . Special Assistant to the Members

Administrative Office

The Administrative Office provides general support for the Council's activities. This includes financial management, human resource management, travel, operations of facilities, security, information technology, and telecommunications management support.

Doris T. Searles. . . . . Administrative and Information Management Specialist

Interns

Student interns provide invaluable help with research projects, day-to-day operations, and fact-checking. Interns during the year were: Gisel Acquatella, Jonathan Adelman, Joshua Allyn, Hunter Baehren, Shantanu Banerjee, Olga Baranoff, Jeffrey Bryant, Cherie Chung, Jasper Clarkberg, Neha Dalal, Yasmine Di Giulio, Jelicia Diggs, Tyler Finn, John Hassett, Apsara Iyer, Madeleine Jones, Samantha Kagan, Sylvia Klosin, Jessica Kong, Maxwell Liebeskind, Jonathan Mallek, Siddharth Mandava, Noah Mathews, Julienne Pasichow, Jana Parsons, Kavi J. Patel, Matthew Schneider, Annemarie Schweinert, Hershil Shah, Andrew Smith, and Brian Wolfe.

DEPARTURES IN 2015

The senior economists who resigned in 2015 (with the institutions to which they returned after leaving the Council in parentheses) were: Jane Dokko (Brookings Institution), Joshua Linn (Resources for the Future), Cynthia Nickerson (USDA), Jennifer Poole (American University), Timothy Simcoe (Boston University), Linda Tesar (University of Michigan), and Abigail Wozniak (University of Notre Dame).

The staff economist who departed in 2015 was Timothy Hyde.

The research economists who departed in 2015 were Krista Ruffini, Brian Moore, and Susannah Scanlan.

Jessica Schumer resigned from her position as Chief of Staff and General Counsel. Jordan Matsudaira resigned from his position as Chief Economist. Matthew Aks resigned from his position as Special Assistant to the Chairman and Research Economist. Wenfan Chen resigned from her position as Economic Statistician. Noah Mann resigned from his position as Policy Analyst. Katherine Rodihan resigned from her position as Special Assistant to the Members.

APPENDIX B

STATISTICAL TABLES RELATING TO INCOME, EMPLOYMENT, AND PRODUCTION

C O N T E N T S

Page

GOVERNMENT FINANCE, INTEREST RATES, AND MONEY STOCK
—*Continued*

General Notes

Detail in these tables may not add to totals due to rounding.

Because of the formula used for calculating real gross domestic product (GDP), the chained (2009) dollar estimates for the detailed components do not add to the chained-dollar value of GDP or to any intermediate aggregate. The Department of Commerce (Bureau of Economic Analysis) no longer publishes chained-dollar estimates prior to 1999, except for selected series.

Because of the method used for seasonal adjustment, the sum or average of seasonally adjusted monthly values generally will not equal annual totals based on unadjusted values.

Unless otherwise noted, all dollar figures are in current dollars.

Symbols used:
p Preliminary.
... Not available (also, not applicable).

Data in these tables reflect revisions made by source agencies through February 5, 2016, unless otherwise noted.

Excel versions of these tables are available at *www.gpo.gov/erp*.

GDP, Income, Prices, and Selected Indicators

Table B–1. Percent changes in real gross domestic product, 1965–2015

[Percent change from preceding period; quarterly data at seasonally adjusted annual rates]

Year or quarter	Gross domestic product	Personal consumption expenditures			Gross private domestic investment							Change in private inventories
		Total	Goods	Services	Total	Fixed investment					Residential	
						Total	Nonresidential					
							Total	Structures	Equipment	Intellectual property products		
1965	6.5	6.3	7.1	5.5	13.8	10.4	16.7	15.9	18.2	12.7	-2.6	
1966	6.6	5.7	6.3	4.9	9.0	6.2	12.3	6.8	15.5	13.2	-8.4	
1967	2.7	3.0	2.0	4.1	-3.5	-.9	-.3	-2.5	-1.0	7.8	-2.6	
1968	4.9	5.7	6.2	5.3	6.0	7.0	4.8	1.4	6.1	7.5	13.5	
1969	3.1	3.7	3.1	4.4	5.6	5.9	7.0	5.4	8.3	5.4	3.1	
1970	.2	2.4	.8	3.9	-6.1	-2.1	-.9	.3	-1.8	-.1	-5.2	
1971	3.3	3.8	4.2	3.5	10.3	6.9	.0	-1.6	.8	.4	26.6	
1972	5.2	6.1	6.5	5.8	11.3	11.4	8.7	3.1	12.7	7.0	17.4	
1973	5.6	5.0	5.2	4.7	10.9	8.6	13.2	8.2	18.5	5.0	-.6	
1974	-.5	-.8	-3.6	1.9	-6.6	-5.6	.8	-2.2	2.1	2.9	-19.6	
1975	-.2	2.3	.7	3.8	-16.2	-9.8	-9.0	-10.5	-10.5	.9	-12.1	
1976	5.4	5.6	7.0	4.3	19.1	9.8	5.7	2.4	6.1	10.9	22.1	
1977	4.6	4.2	4.3	4.1	14.3	13.6	10.8	4.1	15.5	6.6	20.5	
1978	5.6	4.4	4.1	4.6	11.6	11.6	13.8	14.4	15.1	7.1	6.7	
1979	3.2	2.4	1.6	3.1	3.5	5.8	10.0	12.7	8.2	11.7	-3.7	
1980	-.2	-.3	-2.5	1.6	-10.1	-5.9	.0	5.9	-4.4	5.0	-20.9	
1981	2.6	1.5	1.2	1.7	8.8	2.7	6.1	8.0	3.7	10.9	-8.2	
1982	-1.9	1.4	.7	2.0	-13.0	-6.7	-3.6	-1.6	-7.6	6.2	-18.1	
1983	4.6	5.7	6.4	5.2	9.3	7.5	-.4	-10.8	4.6	7.9	42.0	
1984	7.3	5.3	7.2	3.9	27.3	16.2	16.7	13.9	19.4	13.7	14.8	
1985	4.2	5.3	5.3	5.3	-.1	5.5	6.6	7.1	5.5	9.0	2.3	
1986	3.5	4.2	5.6	3.2	.2	1.8	-1.7	-11.0	1.1	7.0	12.4	
1987	3.5	3.4	1.8	4.5	2.8	.6	.1	-2.9	.4	3.9	2.0	
1988	4.2	4.2	3.7	4.5	2.5	3.3	5.0	.7	6.6	7.1	-.9	
1989	3.7	2.9	2.5	3.2	4.0	3.2	5.7	2.0	5.3	11.7	-3.2	
1990	1.9	2.1	.6	3.0	-2.6	-1.4	1.1	1.5	-2.1	8.4	-8.5	
1991	-.1	.2	-2.0	1.6	-6.6	-5.1	-3.9	-11.1	-4.6	6.4	-8.9	
1992	3.6	3.7	3.2	4.0	7.3	5.5	2.9	-6.0	5.9	6.0	13.8	
1993	2.7	3.5	4.2	3.1	8.0	7.7	7.5	-.3	12.7	4.2	8.2	
1994	4.0	3.9	5.3	3.1	11.9	8.2	7.9	1.8	12.3	4.0	9.0	
1995	2.7	3.0	3.0	3.0	3.2	6.1	9.7	6.4	12.1	7.3	-3.4	
1996	3.8	3.5	4.5	2.9	8.8	8.9	9.1	5.7	9.5	11.3	8.2	
1997	4.5	3.8	4.8	3.2	11.4	8.6	10.8	7.3	11.1	13.0	2.4	
1998	4.5	5.3	6.7	4.6	9.5	10.2	10.8	5.1	13.1	10.8	8.6	
1999	4.7	5.3	7.9	3.9	8.4	8.8	9.7	.1	12.5	12.4	6.3	
2000	4.1	5.1	5.2	5.0	6.5	6.9	9.1	7.8	9.7	8.9	.7	
2001	1.0	2.6	3.0	2.4	-6.1	-1.6	-2.4	-1.5	-4.3	.5	.9	
2002	1.8	2.6	3.9	1.9	-.6	-3.5	-6.9	-17.7	-5.4	-.5	6.1	
2003	2.8	3.1	4.8	2.2	4.1	4.0	1.9	-3.9	3.2	3.8	9.1	
2004	3.8	3.8	5.1	3.2	8.8	6.7	5.2	-.4	7.7	5.1	10.0	
2005	3.3	3.5	4.1	3.2	6.4	6.8	7.0	1.7	9.6	6.5	6.6	
2006	2.7	3.0	3.6	2.7	2.1	2.0	7.1	7.2	8.6	4.5	-7.6	
2007	1.8	2.2	2.7	2.0	-3.1	-2.0	5.9	12.7	3.2	4.8	-18.8	
2008	-.3	-.3	-2.5	.8	-9.4	-6.8	-.7	6.1	-6.9	3.0	-24.0	
2009	-2.8	-1.6	-3.0	-.9	-21.6	-16.7	-15.6	-18.9	-22.9	-1.4	-21.2	
2010	2.5	1.9	3.4	1.2	12.9	1.5	2.5	-16.4	15.9	1.9	-2.5	
2011	1.6	2.3	3.1	1.8	5.2	6.3	7.7	2.3	13.6	3.6	.5	
2012	2.2	1.5	2.7	.8	10.6	9.8	9.0	12.9	10.8	3.9	13.5	
2013	1.5	1.7	3.1	1.0	4.5	4.2	3.0	1.6	3.2	3.8	9.5	
2014	2.4	2.7	3.3	2.4	5.4	5.3	6.2	8.1	5.8	5.2	1.8	
2015 p	2.4	3.1	3.8	2.8	4.8	4.0	2.9	-1.5	3.1	5.8	8.7	
2012: I	2.7	2.4	4.9	1.2	9.7	14.7	12.2	19.9	16.0	1.9	27.5	
II	1.9	.7	1.1	.5	10.2	6.9	7.5	10.3	8.8	3.8	3.7	
III	.5	1.1	2.7	.2	-1.1	.1	-2.1	-4.0	-3.3	1.4	10.7	
IV	.1	1.1	2.3	.5	-3.2	6.9	3.7	-7.3	7.3	6.8	22.3	
2013: I	1.9	2.5	6.1	.7	7.1	4.9	4.0	-6.0	6.3	7.8	9.1	
II	1.1	1.4	1.2	1.5	5.2	2.6	1.0	11.7	-.8	-3.2	9.1	
III	3.0	1.7	2.6	1.2	13.7	3.8	3.5	17.9	-3.8	5.2	4.9	
IV	3.8	3.5	3.1	3.7	4.2	5.1	8.7	4.0	14.7	3.5	-8.1	
2014: I	-.9	1.3	1.1	1.4	-2.5	6.0	8.3	19.1	3.5	7.8	-2.8	
II	4.6	3.8	6.7	2.4	12.6	5.6	4.4	-.2	6.5	4.8	10.4	
III	4.3	3.5	4.1	3.1	7.4	7.9	9.0	-1.9	16.4	6.6	3.4	
IV	2.1	4.3	4.1	4.3	2.1	2.5	.7	4.3	-4.9	6.9	10.0	
2015: I	.6	1.8	1.1	2.1	8.6	3.3	1.6	-7.4	2.3	7.4	10.1	
II	3.9	3.6	5.5	2.7	5.0	5.2	4.1	6.2	.3	8.3	9.3	
III	2.0	3.0	5.0	2.1	-.7	3.7	2.6	-7.2	9.9	-.8	8.2	
IV p	.7	2.2	2.4	2.0	-2.5	.2	-1.8	-5.3	-2.5	1.6	8.1	

See next page for continuation of table.

[Percent change from preceding period; quarterly data at seasonally adjusted annual rates]

Year or quarter	Net exports of goods and services			Government consumption expenditures and gross investment					Final sales of domestic product	Gross domestic purchases[1]	Final sales to private domestic purchasers[2]	Gross domestic income (GDI)[3]	Average of GDP and GDI
	Net exports	Exports	Imports	Total	Federal			State and local					
					Total	National defense	Non-defense						
1965		2.8	10.6	3.2	0.8	-1.3	7.9	6.6	5.9	6.9	7.2	6.4	6.4
1966		6.9	14.9	8.7	10.7	12.9	3.6	6.2	6.1	6.9	5.8	6.0	6.3
1967		2.3	7.3	7.9	10.1	12.5	1.9	5.0	3.3	3.0	2.1	3.0	2.9
1968		7.9	14.9	3.4	1.5	1.6	1.3	6.0	5.1	5.2	6.0	5.0	4.9
1969		4.9	5.7	.2	-2.4	-4.1	3.9	3.5	3.2	3.2	4.2	3.3	3.2
1970		10.7	4.3	-2.0	-6.1	-8.2	1.0	2.9	.9	-.1	1.4	-.1	.0
1971		1.7	5.3	-1.8	-6.4	-10.2	5.6	3.1	2.7	3.5	4.4	3.0	3.1
1972		7.8	11.3	-.5	-3.1	-6.9	7.2	2.2	5.2	5.4	7.3	5.5	5.4
1973		18.8	4.6	-.3	-3.6	-5.1	.2	2.8	5.2	4.8	5.8	5.8	5.7
1974		7.9	-2.3	2.3	.7	-1.0	4.6	3.7	-.3	-1.2	-1.9	-.6	-.5
1975		-.6	-11.1	2.2	.5	-1.0	3.9	3.6	1.0	-1.1	-.4	-.5	-.4
1976		4.4	19.5	.5	.2	-.5	1.6	.8	4.0	6.5	6.4	5.1	5.2
1977		2.4	10.9	1.2	2.2	1.0	4.7	.4	4.4	5.3	6.2	4.8	4.7
1978		10.5	8.7	2.9	2.5	.8	6.0	3.3	5.5	5.5	6.0	5.5	5.5
1979		9.9	1.7	1.9	2.3	2.7	1.7	1.5	3.6	2.5	3.2	2.4	2.8
1980		10.8	-6.6	1.9	4.4	3.9	5.4	-.2	.6	-1.9	-1.7	-.1	-.2
1981		1.2	2.6	1.0	4.5	6.2	1.0	-2.0	1.5	2.7	1.8	3.0	2.8
1982		-7.6	-1.3	1.8	3.7	7.2	-3.6	.1	-.6	-1.3	-.5	-1.0	-1.4
1983		-2.6	12.6	3.8	6.5	7.3	4.7	1.3	4.3	5.9	6.1	3.3	4.0
1984		8.2	24.3	3.6	3.3	5.2	-1.4	3.8	5.4	8.7	7.6	7.8	7.5
1985		3.3	6.5	6.8	7.9	8.8	5.7	5.7	5.4	4.5	5.3	4.0	4.1
1986		7.7	8.5	5.4	5.9	6.9	3.1	5.0	3.8	3.7	3.7	3.0	3.3
1987		10.9	5.9	3.0	3.8	5.1	.2	2.2	3.1	3.2	2.8	4.3	3.9
1988		16.2	3.9	1.3	-1.3	-.2	-4.3	3.9	4.4	3.3	4.0	5.1	4.6
1989		11.6	4.4	2.9	1.7	-.2	7.2	4.0	3.5	3.1	3.0	2.5	3.1
1990		8.8	3.6	3.2	2.1	.3	7.3	4.1	2.1	1.5	1.3	1.5	1.7
1991		6.6	-.1	1.2	.0	-1.0	2.4	2.2	.2	-.7	-.9	.0	.0
1992		6.9	7.0	.5	-1.5	-4.5	5.9	2.1	3.3	3.6	4.0	3.3	3.4
1993		3.3	8.6	-.8	-3.5	-5.1	.0	1.2	2.7	3.3	4.3	2.2	2.5
1994		8.8	11.9	.1	-3.5	-4.9	-.8	2.8	3.4	4.4	4.7	4.4	4.2
1995		10.3	8.0	.5	-2.6	-4.0	.0	2.7	3.2	2.6	3.6	3.4	3.1
1996		8.2	8.7	1.0	-1.2	-1.6	-.5	2.4	3.8	3.9	4.6	4.3	4.0
1997		11.9	13.5	1.9	-.8	-2.7	2.8	3.6	4.0	4.7	4.8	5.1	4.8
1998		2.3	11.7	2.1	-.9	-2.1	1.3	3.8	4.5	5.5	6.4	5.3	4.9
1999		2.6	10.1	3.4	2.0	1.5	2.7	4.2	4.7	5.5	6.1	4.4	4.5
2000		8.6	13.0	1.9	.3	-.9	2.3	2.8	4.2	4.8	5.5	4.7	4.4
2001		-5.8	-2.8	3.8	3.9	3.5	4.7	3.7	1.9	1.2	1.7	1.1	1.0
2002		-1.7	3.7	4.4	7.2	7.0	7.4	2.9	1.3	2.3	1.3	1.4	1.6
2003		1.8	4.5	2.2	6.8	8.5	4.1	-.4	2.8	3.1	3.3	2.3	2.5
2004		9.8	11.4	1.6	4.5	6.0	2.0	-.1	3.4	4.3	4.4	3.7	3.8
2005		6.3	6.3	.6	1.7	2.0	1.3	.0	3.4	3.5	4.2	3.6	3.4
2006		9.0	6.3	1.5	2.5	2.0	3.5	.9	2.6	2.6	2.8	4.0	3.3
2007		9.3	2.5	1.6	1.7	2.5	.3	1.5	2.0	1.1	1.3	.1	.9
2008		5.7	-2.6	2.8	6.8	7.5	5.5	.3	.2	-1.3	-1.7	-.8	-.6
2009		-8.8	-13.7	3.2	5.7	5.4	6.2	1.6	-2.0	-3.8	-4.6	-2.6	-2.7
2010		11.9	12.7	.1	4.4	3.2	6.4	-2.7	1.1	2.9	1.9	2.7	2.6
2011		6.9	5.5	-3.0	-2.7	-2.3	-3.4	-3.3	1.7	1.6	2.9	2.2	1.9
2012		3.4	2.2	-1.9	-1.9	-3.4	.9	-1.9	2.1	2.1	2.9	3.3	2.7
2013		2.8	1.1	-2.9	-5.7	-6.7	-4.0	-1.0	1.4	1.2	2.2	1.3	1.4
2014		3.4	3.8	-.6	-2.4	-3.8	-.1	.6	2.4	2.5	3.2	2.6	2.5
2015 *p*		1.1	5.0	.8	-.3	-1.2	1.2	1.4	2.2	3.0	3.3	....	....
2012: I		2.7	2.4	-1.9	-.4	-3.7	5.6	-3.0	3.3	2.6	4.5	7.7	5.2
II		4.6	2.0	-1.9	-2.9	-4.4	-.4	-1.2	1.4	1.5	1.8	.6	1.2
III		2.0	.6	-1.2	.5	.8	-.1	-2.3	.7	.3	.9	-.1	.2
IV		-.5	-3.8	-3.8	-5.5	-8.1	-1.1	-2.6	1.6	-.5	2.2	3.5	1.8
2013: I		1.0	.8	-4.5	-9.3	-10.3	-7.6	-1.1	1.6	1.8	3.0	-.5	.7
II		4.9	5.5	-2.0	-5.6	-5.8	-5.4	.4	.7	1.3	1.6	2.9	2.0
III		4.2	2.4	-2.2	-5.8	-7.6	-2.6	.2	1.5	2.7	2.1	.4	1.7
IV		10.9	1.0	-2.7	-6.6	-5.8	-7.9	-.1	4.0	2.5	3.8	2.7	3.2
2014: I		-6.7	2.8	.0	.3	-4.6	8.9	-.2	.4	.5	2.2	.6	-.2
II		9.8	9.6	1.2	-1.2	-.5	-2.2	2.6	3.5	4.7	4.2	4.8	4.7
III		1.8	-.8	3.7	3.7	4.5	2.5	.6	4.3	3.8	4.3	5.1	4.7
IV		5.4	10.3	-1.4	-5.7	-10.3	2.1	1.3	2.1	2.9	3.9	2.9	2.5
2015: I		-6.0	7.1	-.1	1.1	1.0	1.2	-.8	-.2	2.5	2.0	.4	.5
II		5.1	3.0	2.6	.0	.3	-.5	4.3	3.9	3.6	3.9	2.2	3.0
III		.7	2.3	1.8	.2	-1.4	2.8	2.8	2.7	2.2	3.2	2.7	2.3
IV *p*		-2.5	1.1	.7	2.7	3.6	1.4	-.6	1.2	1.1	1.8	....	....

[1] Gross domestic product (GDP) less exports of goods and services plus imports of goods and services.
[2] Personal consumption expenditures plus gross private fixed investment.
[3] Gross domestic income is deflated by the implicit price deflator for GDP.

Note: Percent changes based on unrounded GDP quantity indexes.

Source: Department of Commerce (Bureau of Economic Analysis).

TABLE B–2. Gross domestic product, 2000–2015

[Quarterly data at seasonally adjusted annual rates]

Year or quarter	Gross domestic product	Personal consumption expenditures			Gross private domestic investment							
						Fixed investment						Change in private inventories
							Nonresidential				Residential	
		Total	Goods	Services	Total	Total	Total	Structures	Equipment	Intellectual property products		

						Billions of dollars						
2000	10,284.8	6,792.4	2,452.9	4,339.5	2,033.8	1,979.2	1,493.8	318.1	766.1	409.5	485.4	54.5
2001	10,621.8	7,103.1	2,525.2	4,577.9	1,928.6	1,966.9	1,453.9	329.7	711.5	412.6	513.0	–38.3
2002	10,977.5	7,384.1	2,598.6	4,785.5	1,925.0	1,906.5	1,348.9	282.9	659.6	406.4	557.6	18.5
2003	11,510.7	7,765.5	2,721.6	5,044.0	2,027.9	2,008.7	1,371.7	281.8	669.0	420.9	636.9	19.3
2004	12,274.9	8,260.0	2,900.3	5,359.8	2,276.7	2,212.8	1,463.1	301.8	719.2	442.1	749.7	63.9
2005	13,093.7	8,794.1	3,080.3	5,713.8	2,527.1	2,467.5	1,611.5	345.6	790.7	475.1	856.1	59.6
2006	13,855.9	9,304.0	3,235.8	6,068.2	2,680.6	2,613.7	1,776.3	415.6	856.1	504.6	837.4	67.0
2007	14,477.6	9,750.5	3,361.6	6,388.9	2,643.7	2,609.3	1,920.6	496.9	885.8	537.9	688.7	34.5
2008	14,718.6	10,013.6	3,375.7	6,637.9	2,424.8	2,456.8	1,941.0	552.4	825.1	563.4	515.9	–32.0
2009	14,418.7	9,847.0	3,198.4	6,648.5	1,878.1	2,025.7	1,633.4	438.2	644.3	550.9	392.2	–147.6
2010	14,964.4	10,202.2	3,362.8	6,839.4	2,100.8	2,039.3	1,658.2	362.0	731.8	564.3	381.1	61.5
2011	15,517.9	10,689.3	3,596.5	7,092.8	2,239.9	2,198.1	1,812.1	381.6	838.2	592.2	386.0	41.8
2012	16,155.3	11,050.6	3,739.1	7,311.5	2,511.7	2,449.9	2,007.7	448.0	937.9	621.7	442.2	61.8
2013	16,663.2	11,392.3	3,836.8	7,555.5	2,665.0	2,593.2	2,084.3	462.1	972.3	649.9	508.9	71.8
2014	17,348.1	11,865.9	3,948.4	7,917.5	2,860.0	2,782.9	2,233.7	507.0	1,036.7	690.0	549.2	77.1
2015 ᵖ	17,937.8	12,267.9	3,978.6	8,289.3	3,017.8	2,911.3	2,302.4	497.0	1,075.7	729.6	608.9	106.5
2012: I	15,973.9	10,956.2	3,714.4	7,241.8	2,460.8	2,395.3	1,971.5	439.7	920.4	611.4	423.8	65.4
II	16,121.9	11,008.3	3,717.2	7,291.1	2,534.8	2,445.5	2,016.2	455.7	940.7	619.7	429.4	89.3
III	16,227.9	11,073.6	3,744.7	7,328.9	2,529.9	2,455.9	2,011.7	452.8	935.4	623.6	444.1	74.1
IV	16,297.3	11,164.3	3,780.0	7,384.3	2,521.3	2,502.9	2,031.2	443.8	955.2	632.3	471.7	18.4
2013: I	16,440.7	11,271.8	3,827.7	7,444.1	2,578.3	2,541.8	2,052.1	438.2	969.1	644.8	489.6	36.5
II	16,526.8	11,322.8	3,810.5	7,512.3	2,620.4	2,571.7	2,064.6	453.9	968.0	642.7	507.1	48.7
III	16,727.5	11,417.7	3,844.0	7,573.7	2,711.5	2,606.0	2,085.9	474.4	959.3	652.2	520.0	105.6
IV	16,957.6	11,556.9	3,864.8	7,692.1	2,749.9	2,653.5	2,134.5	481.8	992.8	660.0	519.0	96.4
2014: I	16,984.3	11,640.3	3,874.7	7,765.6	2,751.1	2,708.4	2,181.9	504.9	1,003.5	673.6	526.4	42.7
II	17,270.0	11,813.0	3,951.5	7,861.5	2,841.6	2,752.7	2,211.7	505.7	1,023.2	682.8	540.9	88.9
III	17,522.1	11,949.1	3,987.4	7,961.7	2,910.2	2,821.8	2,267.0	505.4	1,065.3	696.3	554.8	88.3
IV	17,615.9	12,061.4	3,980.1	8,081.3	2,937.2	2,848.7	2,274.1	512.0	1,055.0	707.2	574.6	88.5
2015: I	17,649.3	12,055.5	3,901.5	8,153.9	2,995.9	2,868.6	2,280.7	499.3	1,063.5	717.8	588.0	127.3
II	17,913.7	12,228.4	3,978.1	8,250.2	3,025.5	2,897.9	2,297.9	503.8	1,064.6	729.6	600.0	127.5
III	18,060.2	12,359.0	4,024.1	8,334.9	3,030.6	2,935.3	2,319.4	496.0	1,090.9	732.4	615.9	95.3
IV ᵖ	18,128.2	12,429.0	4,010.9	8,418.1	3,019.2	2,943.4	2,311.6	489.1	1,083.9	738.6	631.8	75.8

						Billions of chained (2009) dollars						
2000	12,559.7	8,170.7	2,588.3	5,599.3	2,375.5	2,316.2	1,647.7	533.5	726.9	426.1	637.9	66.2
2001	12,682.2	8,382.6	2,666.6	5,731.0	2,231.4	2,280.0	1,608.4	525.4	695.7	428.0	643.7	–46.2
2002	12,908.8	8,598.8	2,770.2	5,838.2	2,218.2	2,201.1	1,498.0	432.5	658.0	425.9	682.7	22.5
2003	13,271.1	8,867.6	2,904.5	5,966.9	2,308.7	2,289.5	1,526.1	415.8	679.0	442.2	744.5	22.6
2004	13,773.5	9,208.2	3,051.9	6,156.6	2,511.3	2,443.9	1,605.4	414.1	731.2	464.9	818.9	71.4
2005	14,234.2	9,531.8	3,177.2	6,353.4	2,672.6	2,611.0	1,717.4	421.2	801.6	495.0	872.6	64.3
2006	14,613.8	9,821.7	3,292.5	6,526.6	2,730.0	2,662.5	1,839.6	451.5	870.8	517.5	806.6	71.6
2007	14,873.7	10,041.6	3,381.8	6,656.4	2,644.1	2,609.6	1,948.4	509.0	898.3	542.4	654.8	35.5
2008	14,830.4	10,007.2	3,297.8	6,708.6	2,396.0	2,432.6	1,934.4	540.2	836.1	558.8	497.7	–33.7
2009	14,418.7	9,847.0	3,198.4	6,648.5	1,878.1	2,025.7	1,633.4	438.2	644.3	550.9	392.2	–147.6
2010	14,783.8	10,036.3	3,308.7	6,727.6	2,120.4	2,056.2	1,673.8	366.3	746.7	561.3	382.4	58.2
2011	15,020.6	10,263.5	3,411.8	6,851.4	2,230.4	2,186.7	1,802.3	374.7	847.9	581.3	384.5	37.6
2012	15,354.6	10,413.2	3,504.3	6,908.1	2,465.7	2,400.4	1,964.1	423.1	939.2	603.8	436.5	54.7
2013	15,583.3	10,590.4	3,612.8	6,977.0	2,577.3	2,501.9	2,023.7	429.7	969.5	626.9	478.0	61.4
2014	15,961.7	10,875.7	3,731.2	7,144.6	2,717.7	2,633.8	2,148.3	464.6	1,026.2	659.5	486.4	68.0
2015 ᵖ	16,341.8	11,211.3	3,871.5	7,341.6	2,849.2	2,739.9	2,209.7	457.6	1,057.5	697.5	528.9	95.1
2012: I	15,291.0	10,379.0	3,480.1	6,898.0	2,429.6	2,360.4	1,938.1	419.5	924.4	596.1	422.5	56.0
II	15,362.4	10,396.6	3,489.8	6,906.0	2,489.1	2,399.8	1,973.7	429.9	944.0	601.7	426.3	76.6
III	15,380.8	10,424.1	3,513.5	6,909.7	2,482.0	2,400.4	1,963.4	425.5	936.0	603.7	437.3	70.6
IV	15,384.3	10,453.2	3,533.6	6,918.8	2,462.2	2,441.0	1,981.4	417.5	952.7	613.8	459.8	15.5
2013: I	15,457.2	10,518.2	3,586.0	6,931.4	2,505.1	2,470.6	2,000.7	411.0	967.4	625.3	469.9	25.2
II	15,500.2	10,554.3	3,596.8	6,956.8	2,537.2	2,486.3	2,005.7	422.6	965.3	620.3	480.3	39.6
III	15,614.4	10,598.9	3,620.2	6,978.1	2,619.7	2,509.5	2,023.1	440.4	956.0	628.3	486.0	93.6
IV	15,761.5	10,690.4	3,648.1	7,041.7	2,647.1	2,541.0	2,065.5	444.7	989.3	633.7	475.9	87.2
2014: I	15,724.9	10,724.7	3,658.3	7,065.7	2,630.5	2,578.3	2,106.9	464.6	997.9	645.7	472.6	36.9
II	15,901.5	10,826.3	3,718.0	7,108.5	2,709.5	2,613.4	2,129.8	464.4	1,013.7	653.4	484.4	77.1
III	16,068.8	10,918.6	3,755.2	7,163.8	2,758.1	2,663.5	2,176.3	462.3	1,053.1	663.8	488.5	79.9
IV	16,151.4	11,033.3	3,793.2	7,240.4	2,772.5	2,679.7	2,180.0	467.1	1,040.0	675.0	500.2	78.2
2015: I	16,177.3	11,081.2	3,803.7	7,277.4	2,830.2	2,701.4	2,188.6	458.2	1,046.0	687.1	512.4	112.8
II	16,333.6	11,178.9	3,855.0	7,325.3	2,864.8	2,735.5	2,210.6	465.2	1,046.9	701.0	524.0	113.5
III	16,414.0	11,262.4	3,902.0	7,363.4	2,859.7	2,760.7	2,224.9	456.6	1,072.0	699.6	534.4	85.5
IV ᵖ	16,442.3	11,322.5	3,925.4	7,400.3	2,842.0	2,762.2	2,214.7	450.5	1,065.1	702.4	545.0	68.6

See next page for continuation of table.

[Quarterly data at seasonally adjusted annual rates]

| Year or quarter | Net exports of goods and services | | | Government consumption expenditures and gross investment | | | | | Final sales of domestic product | Gross domestic purchases [1] | Final sales to private domestic purchasers [2] | Gross domestic income (GDI) [3] | Average of GDP and GDI |
| | Net exports | Exports | Imports | Total | Federal | | | State and local | | | | | |
					Total	National defense	Non-defense						
									Billions of dollars				
2000	−375.8	1,096.8	1,472.6	1,834.4	632.4	391.7	240.7	1,202.0	10,230.2	10,660.6	8,771.6	10,384.3	10,334.5
2001	−368.7	1,026.7	1,395.4	1,958.8	669.2	412.7	256.5	1,289.5	10,660.1	10,990.5	9,070.0	10,736.8	10,679.3
2002	−426.5	1,002.5	1,429.0	2,094.9	740.6	456.8	283.8	1,354.3	10,959.0	11,404.0	9,290.5	11,050.3	11,013.9
2003	−503.7	1,040.3	1,543.9	2,220.8	824.8	519.9	304.9	1,396.0	11,491.4	12,014.3	9,774.2	11,524.3	11,517.5
2004	−619.2	1,181.5	1,800.7	2,357.4	892.4	570.2	322.1	1,465.0	12,211.1	12,894.1	10,472.8	12,283.5	12,279.2
2005	−721.2	1,308.9	2,030.1	2,493.7	946.3	608.3	338.1	1,547.4	13,034.1	13,814.9	11,261.6	13,129.2	13,111.5
2006	−770.9	1,476.3	2,247.3	2,642.2	1,002.0	642.4	359.6	1,640.2	13,788.9	14,626.8	11,917.7	14,073.2	13,964.5
2007	−718.5	1,664.6	2,383.2	2,801.9	1,049.8	678.7	371.0	1,752.2	14,443.2	15,196.2	12,359.8	14,460.1	14,468.9
2008	−723.1	1,841.9	2,565.0	3,003.2	1,155.6	754.1	401.5	1,847.6	14,750.6	15,441.6	12,470.5	14,619.2	14,668.9
2009	−395.4	1,587.7	1,983.2	3,089.1	1,217.7	788.3	429.4	1,871.4	14,566.3	14,814.2	11,872.7	14,343.4	14,381.1
2010	−512.7	1,852.3	2,365.0	3,174.0	1,303.9	832.8	471.1	1,870.2	14,902.8	15,477.0	12,241.5	14,915.2	14,939.8
2011	−580.0	2,106.4	2,686.4	3,168.7	1,303.5	836.9	466.5	1,865.3	15,476.2	16,097.9	12,887.4	15,556.3	15,537.1
2012	−565.7	2,198.2	2,763.8	3,158.6	1,292.5	817.8	474.7	1,866.1	16,093.5	16,720.8	13,500.5	16,358.5	16,256.9
2013	−508.4	2,263.3	2,771.7	3,114.2	1,230.6	767.7	463.0	1,883.6	16,591.4	17,171.6	13,985.5	16,840.8	16,752.0
2014	−530.0	2,341.9	2,871.9	3,152.1	1,219.9	748.2	471.6	1,932.3	17,270.9	17,878.1	14,648.8	17,560.1	17,454.1
2015 *p*	−531.9	2,253.0	2,784.9	3,184.0	1,224.7	740.9	483.9	1,959.3	17,831.4	18,469.8	15,179.2	....	....
2012: I	−614.7	2,169.6	2,784.3	3,171.6	1,300.5	826.4	474.1	1,871.0	15,908.4	16,588.6	13,351.6	16,192.6	16,083.2
II	−580.9	2,199.8	2,780.7	3,159.6	1,293.7	818.8	474.9	1,865.9	16,032.6	16,702.8	13,453.9	16,290.2	16,206.0
III	−535.2	2,209.4	2,744.5	3,159.6	1,297.0	821.5	475.5	1,862.6	16,153.9	16,763.1	13,529.5	16,371.8	16,299.8
IV	−531.8	2,214.0	2,745.8	3,143.5	1,278.9	804.6	474.3	1,864.6	16,278.9	16,829.2	13,667.3	16,579.5	16,438.4
2013: I	−529.2	2,226.6	2,755.8	3,119.8	1,250.4	783.8	466.6	1,869.4	16,404.2	16,969.9	13,813.6	16,626.2	16,533.4
II	−527.8	2,237.6	2,765.4	3,111.4	1,234.2	772.3	461.9	1,877.2	16,478.1	17,054.6	13,894.5	16,787.2	16,657.0
III	−512.4	2,264.3	2,776.7	3,110.7	1,220.4	759.2	461.1	1,890.3	16,621.9	17,239.9	14,023.6	16,882.6	16,805.0
IV	−464.3	2,324.5	2,788.8	3,115.1	1,217.6	755.4	462.2	1,897.5	16,861.2	17,421.9	14,210.4	17,067.2	17,012.4
2014: I	−529.4	2,301.5	2,830.8	3,122.3	1,214.8	746.8	468.0	1,907.5	16,941.6	17,513.7	14,348.7	17,159.6	17,072.0
II	−530.9	2,356.2	2,887.0	3,146.3	1,216.9	748.4	468.4	1,929.4	17,181.0	17,800.9	14,565.7	17,457.0	17,363.5
III	−514.6	2,360.6	2,875.2	3,177.4	1,233.1	759.5	473.6	1,944.3	17,433.8	18,036.6	14,770.9	17,746.1	17,634.1
IV	−545.2	2,349.5	2,894.6	3,162.5	1,214.7	738.2	476.5	1,947.8	17,527.4	18,161.1	14,910.1	17,877.8	17,746.8
2015: I	−551.6	2,257.3	2,808.9	3,149.5	1,218.2	739.0	479.2	1,931.3	17,522.0	18,200.9	14,924.1	17,901.6	17,775.4
II	−519.3	2,280.0	2,799.3	3,179.2	1,220.7	740.1	480.6	1,958.4	17,786.2	18,433.0	15,126.3	18,094.0	18,003.9
III	−530.4	2,259.8	2,790.2	3,201.0	1,224.3	738.2	486.1	1,976.6	17,964.9	18,590.6	15,294.3	18,272.1	18,136.1
IV *p*	−526.4	2,214.7	2,741.1	3,206.5	1,235.6	746.1	489.5	1,970.9	18,052.4	18,654.7	15,372.3	....	....
									Billions of chained (2009) dollars				
2000	−477.8	1,258.4	1,736.2	2,498.2	817.7	512.3	305.4	1,689.1	12,494.9	13,057.9	10,494.9	12,681.2	12,620.4
2001	−502.1	1,184.9	1,687.0	2,592.4	849.8	530.0	319.7	1,751.5	12,729.6	13,208.5	10,669.0	12,819.5	12,750.9
2002	−584.3	1,164.5	1,748.8	2,705.8	910.8	567.3	343.3	1,802.4	12,888.9	13,518.4	10,805.0	12,994.4	12,951.5
2003	−641.9	1,185.0	1,826.9	2,764.3	973.0	615.4	357.5	1,795.3	13,249.0	13,938.5	11,162.3	13,286.8	13,278.9
2004	−734.8	1,300.6	2,035.3	2,808.2	1,017.1	652.7	364.5	1,792.8	13,702.2	14,531.7	11,657.9	13,783.1	13,778.3
2005	−782.3	1,381.9	2,164.2	2,826.2	1,034.8	665.5	369.4	1,792.3	14,168.8	15,040.3	12,149.9	14,272.7	14,253.5
2006	−794.3	1,506.8	2,301.0	2,869.3	1,060.9	678.8	382.1	1,808.8	14,542.3	15,431.6	12,490.8	14,842.9	14,728.4
2007	−712.6	1,646.4	2,359.0	2,914.4	1,078.7	695.6	383.1	1,836.1	14,836.2	15,606.8	12,655.0	14,855.8	14,864.8
2008	−557.8	1,740.8	2,298.6	2,994.8	1,152.3	748.1	404.2	1,842.4	14,865.7	15,399.9	12,441.1	14,730.2	14,780.3
2009	−395.4	1,587.7	1,983.2	3,089.1	1,217.7	788.3	429.4	1,871.4	14,566.3	14,814.2	11,872.7	14,343.4	14,381.1
2010	−458.8	1,776.6	2,235.4	3,091.4	1,270.7	813.5	457.1	1,820.8	14,722.2	15,244.9	12,092.5	14,735.2	14,759.5
2011	−459.4	1,898.3	2,357.7	2,997.4	1,236.4	795.0	441.4	1,761.0	14,979.0	15,483.9	12,448.1	15,057.7	15,039.1
2012	−447.1	1,963.2	2,410.2	2,941.6	1,213.5	768.2	445.3	1,728.1	15,292.3	15,804.3	12,806.0	15,547.8	15,451.2
2013	−417.5	2,018.1	2,435.6	2,854.9	1,144.1	716.6	427.5	1,710.2	15,511.4	16,001.4	13,082.6	15,749.5	15,666.4
2014	−442.5	2,086.4	2,528.9	2,828.4	1,116.3	689.1	427.0	1,720.8	15,881.7	16,428.5	13,497.7	16,156.8	16,059.2
2015 *p*	−547.1	2,109.5	2,656.5	2,859.9	1,113.5	681.0	432.2	1,745.0	16,237.2	16,891.1	13,938.4	....	....
2012: I	−462.7	1,942.6	2,405.3	2,963.7	1,223.9	777.9	446.0	1,739.8	15,225.0	15,757.6	12,732.9	15,500.4	15,395.7
II	−452.7	1,964.4	2,417.0	2,949.4	1,214.8	769.2	445.6	1,734.5	15,276.9	15,818.1	12,788.7	15,522.8	15,442.6
III	−446.8	1,974.1	2,420.9	2,940.9	1,216.2	770.8	445.4	1,724.7	15,302.7	15,830.2	12,816.9	15,517.1	15,449.0
IV	−426.0	1,971.7	2,397.8	2,912.3	1,199.0	754.7	444.2	1,713.3	15,364.6	15,811.3	12,885.5	15,650.6	15,517.4
2013: I	−425.9	1,976.6	2,402.6	2,878.8	1,170.1	734.4	435.6	1,708.5	15,424.7	15,883.9	12,979.6	15,631.6	15,544.4
II	−434.2	2,000.5	2,434.7	2,864.1	1,153.2	723.6	429.5	1,710.4	15,451.9	15,935.9	13,031.1	15,744.4	15,622.3
III	−428.3	2,021.1	2,449.4	2,848.1	1,136.3	709.4	426.7	1,711.1	15,508.9	16,043.9	13,098.5	15,759.2	15,686.8
IV	−381.5	2,074.2	2,455.7	2,828.5	1,116.9	698.8	418.0	1,710.6	15,660.0	16,141.9	13,221.2	15,863.4	15,812.5
2014: I	−434.0	2,038.7	2,472.7	2,828.4	1,117.8	690.6	427.0	1,709.6	15,675.7	16,160.3	13,292.0	15,887.3	15,806.1
II	−443.3	2,086.8	2,530.1	2,836.5	1,114.5	689.8	424.6	1,720.8	15,809.7	16,346.6	13,428.3	16,073.6	15,987.5
III	−429.1	2,096.0	2,525.1	2,849.2	1,124.7	697.3	427.1	1,723.5	15,978.6	16,498.9	13,569.8	16,274.3	16,171.6
IV	−463.6	2,123.9	2,587.5	2,839.0	1,108.3	678.6	429.4	1,729.3	16,062.9	16,617.2	13,700.8	16,391.5	16,271.5
2015: I	−541.2	2,091.4	2,632.5	2,838.5	1,111.3	680.3	430.7	1,725.9	16,053.8	16,720.8	13,770.1	16,408.6	16,293.0
II	−534.6	2,117.5	2,652.1	2,856.9	1,111.3	680.8	430.2	1,744.1	16,209.7	16,870.7	13,901.6	16,498.0	16,415.8
III	−546.1	2,121.1	2,667.2	2,869.7	1,112.0	678.4	433.2	1,756.2	16,319.3	16,962.4	14,010.1	16,606.6	16,510.3
IV *p*	−566.5	2,107.8	2,674.3	2,874.5	1,119.4	684.4	434.7	1,753.6	16,366.0	17,010.4	14,071.9	....	....

[1] Gross domestic product (GDP) less exports of goods and services plus imports of goods and services.
[2] Personal consumption expenditures plus gross private fixed investment.
[3] For chained dollar measures, gross domestic income is deflated by the implicit price deflator for GDP.

Source: Department of Commerce (Bureau of Economic Analysis).

Table B–3. Quantity and price indexes for gross domestic product, and percent changes, 1965–2015

[Quarterly data are seasonally adjusted]

| Year or quarter | Index numbers, 2009=100 | | | | | | Percent change from preceding period[1] | | | | | |
| | Gross domestic product (GDP) | | | Personal consumption expenditures (PCE) | | Gross domestic purchases price index | Gross domestic product (GDP) | | | Personal consumption expenditures (PCE) | | Gross domestic purchases price index |
	Real GDP (chain-type quantity index)	GDP chain-type price index	GDP implicit price deflator	PCE chain-type price index	PCE less food and energy price index		Real GDP (chain-type quantity index)	GDP chain-type price index	GDP implicit price deflator	PCE chain-type price index	PCE less food and energy price index	
1965	27.580	18.744	18.702	18.681	19.325	18.321	6.5	1.8	1.8	1.4	1.3	1.7
1966	29.399	19.271	19.227	19.155	19.762	18.830	6.6	2.8	2.8	2.5	2.3	2.8
1967	30.205	19.831	19.786	19.637	20.367	19.346	2.7	2.9	2.9	2.5	3.1	2.7
1968	31.688	20.674	20.627	20.402	21.240	20.164	4.9	4.3	4.3	3.9	4.3	4.2
1969	32.683	21.691	21.642	21.326	22.238	21.149	3.1	4.9	4.9	4.5	4.7	4.9
1970	32.749	22.836	22.784	22.325	23.281	22.287	.2	5.3	5.3	4.7	4.7	5.4
1971	33.833	23.996	23.941	23.274	24.377	23.450	3.3	5.1	5.1	4.3	4.7	5.2
1972	35.609	25.035	24.978	24.070	25.165	24.498	5.2	4.3	4.3	3.4	3.2	4.5
1973	37.618	26.396	26.337	25.368	26.126	25.888	5.6	5.4	5.4	5.4	3.8	5.7
1974	37.424	28.760	28.703	28.009	28.196	28.511	–.5	9.0	9.0	10.4	7.9	10.1
1975	37.350	31.431	31.361	30.348	30.558	31.116	–.2	9.3	9.3	8.4	8.4	9.1
1976	39.361	33.157	33.083	32.013	32.415	32.821	5.4	5.5	5.5	5.5	6.1	5.5
1977	41.175	35.209	35.135	34.091	34.495	34.977	4.6	6.2	6.2	6.5	6.4	6.6
1978	43.466	37.680	37.602	36.479	36.802	37.459	5.6	7.0	7.0	7.0	6.7	7.1
1979	44.846	40.790	40.706	39.714	39.479	40.730	3.2	8.3	8.3	8.9	7.3	8.7
1980	44.736	44.480	44.377	43.978	43.093	44.963	–.2	9.0	9.0	10.7	9.2	10.4
1981	45.897	48.658	48.520	47.908	46.857	49.088	2.6	9.4	9.3	8.9	8.7	9.2
1982	45.020	51.624	51.530	50.553	49.881	51.876	–1.9	6.1	6.2	5.5	6.5	5.7
1983	47.105	53.658	53.565	52.729	52.466	53.697	4.6	3.9	3.9	4.3	5.2	3.5
1984	50.525	55.564	55.466	54.724	54.645	55.483	7.3	3.6	3.5	3.8	4.2	3.3
1985	52.666	57.341	57.240	56.661	56.898	57.151	4.2	3.2	3.2	3.5	4.1	3.0
1986	54.516	58.504	58.395	57.887	58.850	58.345	3.5	2.0	2.0	2.2	3.4	2.1
1987	56.403	59.935	59.885	59.650	60.719	59.985	3.5	2.4	2.6	3.0	3.2	2.8
1988	58.774	62.036	61.982	61.974	63.290	62.092	4.2	3.5	3.5	3.9	4.2	3.5
1989	60.937	64.448	64.392	64.641	65.869	64.516	3.7	3.9	3.9	4.3	4.1	3.9
1990	62.107	66.841	66.773	67.440	68.492	67.040	1.9	3.7	3.7	4.3	4.0	3.9
1991	62.061	69.057	68.996	69.652	70.886	69.112	–.1	3.3	3.3	3.3	3.5	3.1
1992	64.267	70.632	70.569	71.494	73.021	70.720	3.6	2.3	2.3	2.6	3.0	2.3
1993	66.032	72.315	72.248	73.279	75.008	72.324	2.7	2.4	2.4	2.5	2.7	2.3
1994	68.698	73.851	73.785	74.803	76.680	73.835	4.0	2.1	2.1	2.1	2.2	2.1
1995	70.566	75.393	75.324	76.356	78.324	75.421	2.7	2.1	2.1	2.1	2.1	2.1
1996	73.245	76.767	76.699	77.981	79.801	76.729	3.8	1.8	1.8	2.1	1.9	1.7
1997	76.531	78.088	78.012	79.327	81.196	77.852	4.5	1.7	1.7	1.7	1.7	1.5
1998	79.937	78.935	78.859	79.936	82.200	78.359	4.5	1.1	1.1	.8	1.2	.7
1999	83.682	80.065	80.065	81.110	83.291	79.579	4.7	1.4	1.5	1.5	1.3	1.6
2000	87.107	81.890	81.887	83.131	84.747	81.644	4.1	2.3	2.3	2.5	1.7	2.6
2001	87.957	83.755	83.754	84.736	86.281	83.209	1.0	2.3	2.3	1.9	1.8	1.9
2002	89.528	85.040	85.039	85.873	87.750	84.360	1.8	1.5	1.5	1.3	1.7	1.4
2003	92.041	86.735	86.735	87.572	89.047	86.196	2.8	2.0	2.0	2.0	1.5	2.2
2004	95.525	89.118	89.120	89.703	90.751	88.729	3.8	2.7	2.7	2.4	1.9	2.9
2005	98.720	91.985	91.988	92.261	92.711	91.851	3.3	3.2	3.2	2.9	2.2	3.5
2006	101.353	94.812	94.814	94.729	94.786	94.783	2.7	3.1	3.1	2.7	2.2	3.2
2007	103.156	97.340	97.337	97.102	96.832	97.372	1.8	2.7	2.7	2.5	2.2	2.7
2008	102.855	99.219	99.246	100.065	98.827	100.244	–.3	1.9	2.0	3.1	2.1	2.9
2009	100.000	100.000	100.000	100.000	100.000	100.000	–2.8	.8	.8	–.1	1.2	–.2
2010	102.532	101.226	101.221	101.653	101.286	101.527	2.5	1.2	1.2	1.7	1.3	1.5
2011	104.174	103.315	103.311	104.149	102.800	103.970	1.6	2.1	2.1	2.5	1.5	2.4
2012	106.491	105.220	105.214	106.121	104.741	105.805	2.2	1.8	1.8	1.9	1.9	1.8
2013	108.077	106.935	106.929	107.572	106.355	107.319	1.5	1.6	1.6	1.4	1.5	1.4
2014	110.701	108.694	108.686	109.105	107.981	108.982	2.4	1.6	1.6	1.4	1.5	1.5
2015 p	113.337	109.775	109.767	109.425	109.409	109.355	2.4	1.0	1.0	.3	1.3	.3
2012: I	106.050	104.466	104.466	105.563	104.101	105.274	2.7	2.1	2.1	2.3	2.3	2.4
II	106.545	104.930	104.943	105.885	104.589	105.579	1.9	1.8	1.8	1.2	1.9	1.2
III	106.672	105.547	105.508	106.232	104.912	105.930	.5	2.4	2.2	1.3	1.2	1.3
IV	106.696	105.937	105.935	106.804	105.363	106.439	.1	1.5	1.6	2.2	1.7	1.9
2013: I	107.202	106.333	106.363	107.166	105.819	106.807	1.9	1.5	1.6	1.4	1.7	1.4
II	107.501	106.625	106.623	107.284	106.140	107.020	1.1	1.1	1.0	.4	1.2	.8
III	108.293	107.154	107.128	107.728	106.508	107.479	3.0	2.0	1.9	1.7	1.4	1.7
IV	109.313	107.630	107.589	108.108	106.954	107.969	3.8	1.8	1.7	1.4	1.7	1.8
2014: I	109.059	108.025	108.009	108.540	107.334	108.390	–.9	1.5	1.6	1.6	1.4	1.6
II	110.283	108.621	108.611	109.117	107.860	108.910	4.6	2.2	2.2	2.1	2.0	1.9
III	111.444	109.049	109.044	109.441	108.232	109.325	4.3	1.6	1.6	1.2	1.4	1.5
IV	112.017	109.067	109.067	109.322	108.498	109.304	2.1	.1	.1	–.4	1.0	–.1
2015: I	112.196	109.112	109.099	108.795	108.758	108.864	.6	.1	.1	–1.9	1.0	–1.6
II	113.280	109.685	109.674	109.391	109.264	109.271	3.9	2.1	2.1	2.2	1.9	1.5
III	113.838	110.045	110.029	109.740	109.636	109.614	2.0	1.3	1.3	1.3	1.4	1.3
IV p	114.034	110.260	110.254	109.775	109.976	109.672	.7	.8	.8	.1	1.2	.2

[1] Quarterly percent changes are at annual rates.

Source: Department of Commerce (Bureau of Economic Analysis).

Table B-4. Growth rates in real gross domestic product by area and country, 1997–2016

[Percent change]

Area and country	1997–2006 annual average	2007	2008	2009	2010	2011	2012	2013	2014	2015[1]	2016[1]
World	4.0	5.7	3.1	.0	5.4	4.2	3.4	3.3	3.4	3.1	3.4
Advanced economies	2.8	2.8	.2	-3.4	3.1	1.7	1.2	1.1	1.8	1.9	2.1
Of which:											
United States	3.3	1.8	-.3	-2.8	2.5	1.6	2.2	1.5	2.4	2.5	2.6
Euro area[2]	2.3	3.0	.5	-4.6	2.0	1.6	-.8	-.3	.9	1.5	1.7
Germany	1.5	3.4	.8	-5.6	3.9	3.7	.6	.4	1.6	1.5	1.7
France	2.4	2.4	.2	-2.9	2.0	2.1	.2	.7	.2	1.1	1.3
Italy	1.5	1.5	-1.0	-5.5	1.7	.6	-2.8	-1.7	-.4	.8	1.3
Spain	3.9	3.8	1.1	-3.6	.0	-.6	-2.1	-1.2	1.4	3.2	2.7
Japan	0.9	2.2	-1.0	-5.5	4.7	-.5	1.7	1.6	.0	.6	1.0
United Kingdom	3.1	2.6	-.3	-4.3	1.9	1.6	.7	1.7	2.9	2.2	2.2
Canada	3.4	2.0	1.2	-2.7	3.4	3.0	1.9	2.0	2.5	1.2	1.7
Other advanced economies	4.0	5.1	1.8	-1.0	5.9	3.3	2.0	2.2	2.8	2.1	2.4
Emerging market and developing economies	5.4	8.7	5.8	3.1	7.5	6.3	5.2	5.0	4.6	4.0	4.3
Regional groups:											
Commonwealth of Independent States[3]	5.5	9.0	5.3	-6.3	4.6	4.8	3.4	2.2	1.0	-2.8	.0
Russia	5.0	8.5	5.2	-7.8	4.5	4.3	3.4	1.3	.6	-3.7	-1.0
Excluding Russia	6.6	10.4	5.6	-2.5	5.0	6.2	3.6	4.2	1.9	-.7	2.3
Emerging and Developing Asia	7.1	11.2	7.3	7.5	9.6	7.9	6.8	7.0	6.8	6.6	6.3
China	9.4	14.2	9.6	9.2	10.6	9.5	7.7	7.7	7.3	6.9	6.3
India[4]	6.6	9.8	3.9	8.5	10.3	6.6	5.1	6.9	7.3	7.3	7.5
ASEAN-5[5]	3.5	6.2	5.4	2.4	6.9	4.7	6.2	5.1	4.6	4.7	4.8
Emerging and Developing Europe	4.1	5.5	3.1	-3.0	4.8	5.4	1.3	2.9	2.8	3.4	3.1
Latin America and the Caribbean	3.1	5.7	3.9	-1.3	6.1	4.9	3.1	2.9	1.3	-.3	-.3
Brazil	2.7	6.0	5.0	-.2	7.6	3.9	1.8	2.7	.1	-3.8	-3.5
Mexico	3.3	3.1	1.4	-4.7	5.1	4.0	4.0	1.4	2.3	2.5	2.6
Middle East, North Africa, Afghanistan, and Pakistan ..	4.8	6.3	5.2	2.2	4.9	4.5	5.0	2.3	2.8	2.5	3.6
Saudi Arabia	3.9	6.0	8.4	1.8	4.8	10.0	5.4	2.7	3.6	3.4	1.2
Sub-Saharan Africa	5.0	7.6	6.0	4.1	6.6	5.0	4.3	5.2	5.0	3.5	4.0
Nigeria	7.2	9.1	8.0	9.0	10.0	4.9	4.3	5.4	6.3	3.0	4.1
South Africa	3.4	5.4	3.2	-1.5	3.0	3.2	2.2	2.2	1.5	1.3	.7

[1] All figures are forecasts as published by the International Monetary Fund. For the United States, advance estimates by the Department of Commerce show that real GDP rose 2.4 percent in 2015.

[2] For 2016, includes data for: Austria, Belgium, Cyprus, Estonia, Finland, France, Germany, Greece, Ireland, Italy, Latvia, Lithuania, Luxembourg, Malta, Netherlands, Portugal, Slovak Republic, Slovenia, and Spain.

[3] Includes Georgia,Turkmenistan, and Ukraine, which are not members of the Commonwealth of Independent States but are included for reasons of geography and similarity in economic structure.

[4] Data and forecasts are presented on a fiscal year basis and output growth is based on GDP at market prices.

[5] Consists of Indonesia, Malaysia, Philippines, Thailand, and Vietnam.

Note: For details on data shown in this table, see *World Economic Outlook*, October 2015, and *World Economic Outlook Update*, January 2016, published by the International Monetary Fund.

Sources: International Monetary Fund and Department of Commerce (Bureau of Economic Analysis).

TABLE B–5. Real exports and imports of goods and services, 1999–2015

[Billions of chained (2009) dollars; quarterly data at seasonally adjusted annual rates]

Year or quarter	Exports of goods and services					Imports of goods and services				
	Total	Goods [1]			Services [1]	Total	Goods [1]			Services [1]
		Total	Durable goods	Nondurable goods			Total	Durable goods	Nondurable goods	
1999	1,159.1	819.4	533.8	288.0	338.6	1,536.2	1,286.9	724.4	572.8	245.4
2000	1,258.4	902.2	599.3	301.9	354.3	1,736.2	1,455.4	834.4	624.4	276.4
2001	1,184.9	846.7	549.5	300.1	336.6	1,687.0	1,408.4	782.2	641.1	274.6
2002	1,164.5	817.8	518.7	305.7	345.7	1,748.8	1,461.1	815.3	659.3	283.6
2003	1,185.0	833.1	528.0	312.0	350.8	1,826.9	1,533.0	850.4	698.9	289.6
2004	1,300.6	904.5	586.0	323.4	395.4	2,035.3	1,704.1	969.3	745.7	326.4
2005	1,381.9	970.6	641.0	333.2	410.3	2,164.2	1,817.9	1,051.6	774.8	341.1
2006	1,506.8	1,062.0	710.1	355.2	443.5	2,301.0	1,925.4	1,145.2	787.7	370.5
2007	1,646.4	1,141.5	770.8	373.9	504.1	2,359.0	1,960.9	1,174.5	794.2	393.5
2008	1,740.8	1,211.5	810.2	404.2	528.3	2,298.6	1,887.9	1,129.0	766.1	408.2
2009	1,587.7	1,065.1	671.6	393.5	522.6	1,983.2	1,590.3	893.8	696.5	392.9
2010	1,776.6	1,218.3	784.8	434.0	558.0	2,235.4	1,826.7	1,095.2	735.8	407.8
2011	1,898.3	1,297.6	852.0	448.2	600.6	2,357.7	1,932.1	1,197.9	745.9	424.2
2012	1,963.2	1,344.2	890.8	457.5	618.7	2,410.2	1,972.2	1,283.3	715.1	437.1
2013	2,018.1	1,382.3	908.6	476.7	635.5	2,435.6	1,991.3	1,327.2	698.2	443.5
2014	2,086.4	1,443.0	943.6	501.8	642.9	2,528.9	2,076.5	1,421.4	699.7	450.8
2015 ᵖ	2,109.5	1,439.7	918.4	522.0	668.1	2,656.5	2,178.8	1,496.8	730.7	476.1
2012: I	1,942.6	1,332.2	895.0	443.4	610.1	2,405.3	1,969.9	1,281.0	715.3	434.1
II	1,964.4	1,347.6	890.3	461.1	616.4	2,417.0	1,978.1	1,286.1	718.2	437.9
III	1,974.1	1,355.0	890.8	467.2	618.6	2,420.9	1,981.2	1,283.2	722.9	438.6
IV	1,971.7	1,341.9	887.2	458.5	629.9	2,397.8	1,959.4	1,283.2	704.1	437.7
2013: I	1,976.6	1,343.3	889.4	457.9	633.3	2,402.6	1,964.7	1,297.5	697.9	437.1
II	2,000.5	1,367.8	913.5	459.8	632.4	2,434.7	1,990.4	1,319.8	703.1	443.5
III	2,021.1	1,384.6	907.9	479.3	636.1	2,449.4	2,003.3	1,339.5	699.2	445.2
IV	2,074.2	1,433.4	923.6	509.7	640.2	2,455.7	2,006.8	1,352.0	692.7	448.1
2014: I	2,038.7	1,398.4	918.2	483.1	639.8	2,472.7	2,029.9	1,364.9	702.6	441.3
II	2,086.8	1,439.1	940.3	501.0	647.3	2,530.1	2,078.4	1,422.1	700.8	450.1
III	2,096.0	1,460.1	956.9	505.9	635.4	2,525.1	2,074.1	1,429.1	691.8	449.4
IV	2,123.9	1,474.3	958.8	517.2	649.1	2,587.5	2,123.8	1,469.5	703.6	462.2
2015: I	2,091.4	1,429.3	918.4	511.8	660.6	2,632.5	2,161.1	1,483.6	725.8	469.8
II	2,117.5	1,452.0	925.9	526.8	664.4	2,652.1	2,178.4	1,490.7	735.9	472.1
III	2,121.1	1,448.8	921.6	527.8	670.7	2,667.2	2,186.0	1,504.0	731.2	479.5
IV ᵖ	2,107.8	1,428.7	907.9	521.5	676.7	2,674.3	2,189.5	1,509.0	729.9	483.1

[1] Certain goods, primarily military equipment purchased and sold by the Federal Government, are included in services. Repairs and alterations of equipment are also included in services.

Source: Department of Commerce (Bureau of Economic Analysis).

TABLE B-6. Corporate profits by industry, 1965–2015

[Billions of dollars; quarterly data at seasonally adjusted annual rates]

Year or quarter	Total	Corporate profits with inventory valuation adjustment and without capital consumption adjustment												Rest of the world
		Domestic industries												
		Total	Financial			Nonfinancial								
			Total	Federal Reserve banks	Other	Total	Manu-facturing	Trans-porta-tion[1]	Utilities	Whole-sale trade	Retail trade	Infor-mation	Other	
SIC:[2]														
1965	81.9	77.2	9.3	1.3	8.0	67.9	42.1	11.4		3.8	4.9		5.7	4.7
1966	88.3	83.7	10.7	1.7	9.1	73.0	45.3	12.6		4.0	4.9		6.3	4.5
1967	86.1	81.3	11.2	2.0	9.2	70.1	42.4	11.4		4.1	5.7		6.6	4.8
1968	94.3	88.6	12.9	2.5	10.4	75.7	45.8	11.4		4.7	6.4		7.4	5.6
1969	90.8	84.2	13.6	3.1	10.6	70.6	41.6	11.1		4.9	6.4		6.5	6.6
1970	79.7	72.6	15.5	3.5	12.0	57.1	32.0	8.8		4.6	6.1		5.8	7.1
1971	94.7	86.8	17.9	3.3	14.6	69.0	40.0	9.6		5.4	7.3		6.7	7.9
1972	109.3	99.7	19.5	3.3	16.1	80.3	47.6	10.4		7.2	7.5		7.6	9.5
1973	126.6	111.7	21.1	4.5	16.6	90.6	55.0	10.2		8.8	7.0		9.6	14.9
1974	123.3	105.8	20.8	5.7	15.1	85.1	51.0	9.1		12.2	2.8		10.0	17.5
1975	144.2	129.6	20.4	5.6	14.8	109.2	63.0	11.7		14.3	8.4		11.8	14.6
1976	182.1	165.6	25.6	5.9	19.7	140.0	82.5	17.5		13.7	10.9		15.3	16.5
1977	212.8	193.7	32.6	6.1	26.5	161.1	91.5	21.2		16.4	12.8		19.2	19.1
1978	246.7	223.8	40.8	7.6	33.1	183.1	105.8	25.5		16.7	13.1		22.0	22.9
1979	261.0	226.4	41.8	9.4	32.3	184.6	107.1	21.6		20.0	10.7		25.2	34.6
1980	240.6	205.2	35.2	11.8	23.5	169.9	97.6	22.2		18.5	7.0		24.6	35.5
1981	252.0	222.3	30.3	14.4	15.9	192.0	112.5	25.1		23.7	10.7		20.1	29.7
1982	224.8	192.2	27.2	15.2	12.0	165.0	89.6	28.1		20.7	14.3		12.3	32.6
1983	256.4	221.4	36.2	14.6	21.6	185.2	97.3	34.3		21.9	19.3		12.3	35.1
1984	294.3	257.7	34.7	16.4	18.3	223.0	114.2	44.7		30.4	21.5		12.1	36.6
1985	289.7	251.6	46.5	16.3	30.2	205.1	107.1	39.1		24.6	22.8		11.4	38.1
1986	273.3	233.8	56.4	15.5	40.8	177.4	75.6	39.3		24.4	23.4		14.7	39.5
1987	314.6	266.5	60.3	16.2	44.1	206.2	101.8	42.0		18.9	23.3		20.3	48.0
1988	366.2	309.2	66.9	18.1	48.8	242.3	132.8	46.8		20.4	19.8		22.5	57.0
1989	373.1	305.9	78.3	20.6	57.6	227.6	122.3	41.9		22.0	20.9		20.5	67.1
1990	391.2	315.1	89.6	21.8	67.8	225.5	120.9	43.5		19.4	20.3		21.3	76.1
1991	434.2	357.8	120.4	20.7	99.7	237.3	109.3	54.5		22.3	26.9		24.3	76.5
1992	459.7	386.6	132.4	18.3	114.1	254.2	109.8	57.7		25.3	28.1		33.4	73.1
1993	501.9	425.0	119.9	16.7	103.2	305.1	122.9	70.1		26.5	39.7		45.8	76.9
1994	589.3	511.3	125.9	18.5	107.4	385.4	162.6	83.9		31.4	46.3		61.2	78.0
1995	667.0	574.0	140.3	22.9	117.3	433.7	199.8	89.0		28.0	43.9		73.1	92.9
1996	741.8	639.8	147.9	22.5	125.3	492.0	220.4	91.2		39.9	52.0		88.5	102.0
1997	811.0	703.4	162.2	24.3	137.9	541.2	248.5	81.0		48.1	63.4		100.3	107.6
1998	743.8	641.1	138.9	25.6	113.3	502.1	220.4	72.6		50.6	72.3		86.3	102.8
1999	762.2	640.2	154.6	26.7	127.9	485.6	219.4	49.3		46.8	72.5		97.6	122.0
2000	730.3	584.1	149.7	31.2	118.5	434.4	205.9	33.8		50.4	68.9		75.4	146.2
NAICS:[2]														
1998	743.8	641.1	138.9	25.6	113.3	502.1	193.5	12.8	33.3	57.3	62.5	33.1	109.7	102.8
1999	762.2	640.2	154.6	26.7	127.9	485.6	184.5	7.2	34.4	55.6	59.5	20.8	123.5	122.0
2000	730.3	584.1	149.7	31.2	118.5	434.4	175.6	9.5	24.3	59.5	51.3	−11.9	126.1	146.2
2001	698.7	528.3	195.0	28.9	166.1	333.3	75.1	−.7	22.5	51.1	71.3	−26.4	140.2	170.4
2002	795.1	636.3	270.7	23.5	247.2	365.6	75.1	−6.0	11.1	55.8	83.7	−3.1	149.0	158.8
2003	959.9	793.3	306.5	20.1	286.5	486.7	125.3	4.8	13.5	59.3	90.5	16.3	177.1	166.6
2004	1,215.2	1,010.1	349.4	20.0	329.4	660.7	182.7	12.0	20.5	74.7	93.2	52.7	224.9	205.0
2005	1,621.2	1,382.1	409.7	26.6	383.1	972.4	277.7	27.7	30.8	96.2	121.7	91.3	327.2	239.1
2006	1,815.7	1,559.6	415.1	33.8	381.3	1,144.4	349.7	41.2	55.1	105.9	132.5	107.0	353.1	256.2
2007	1,708.9	1,355.5	301.5	36.0	265.5	1,054.0	321.9	23.9	49.5	103.2	119.0	108.4	328.2	353.4
2008	1,345.5	938.8	95.4	35.1	60.4	843.4	240.6	28.8	30.1	90.6	80.3	92.2	280.8	406.7
2009	1,479.2	1,122.0	362.9	47.3	315.5	759.2	171.4	22.4	23.8	89.3	108.7	81.2	262.3	357.2
2010	1,799.7	1,404.5	406.3	71.6	334.8	998.2	287.6	44.7	30.3	102.4	118.6	95.1	319.5	395.2
2011	1,738.5	1,316.6	375.9	75.9	300.0	940.7	298.1	30.4	9.8	94.4	114.3	83.8	309.9	421.9
2012	2,116.6	1,706.3	479.0	71.7	407.3	1,227.2	395.7	53.8	12.5	135.3	154.1	100.6	375.2	410.3
2013	2,164.9	1,750.1	423.6	79.6	344.1	1,326.4	426.4	53.0	26.4	145.5	159.4	129.4	386.3	414.8
2014	2,204.9	1,786.6	423.4	103.4	320.0	1,363.2	439.8	65.3	27.7	147.7	158.4	126.5	397.7	418.2
2013: I	2,127.5	1,736.0	428.6	70.2	358.4	1,307.4	407.6	53.8	19.0	151.2	158.3	121.4	396.0	391.5
II	2,172.5	1,761.1	416.5	73.5	342.9	1,344.6	418.7	51.4	33.1	147.7	167.5	131.1	395.2	411.4
III	2,167.5	1,741.0	419.8	82.0	337.9	1,321.2	420.2	51.3	30.5	144.6	163.8	125.4	385.5	426.5
IV	2,192.0	1,762.2	429.6	92.6	337.0	1,332.5	459.0	55.6	23.1	138.6	148.0	139.8	368.4	429.9
2014: I	2,054.4	1,639.9	379.8	97.3	282.5	1,260.1	380.4	58.5	38.9	125.7	142.5	131.0	383.3	414.5
II	2,203.7	1,795.0	441.7	104.8	337.0	1,353.3	454.7	70.0	32.0	134.5	154.7	131.1	376.4	408.6
III	2,295.0	1,867.9	447.3	106.8	340.5	1,420.7	458.0	72.2	23.1	170.1	157.7	123.2	416.3	427.1
IV	2,266.3	1,843.6	424.9	104.8	320.1	1,418.7	466.1	60.6	16.9	160.5	178.8	120.9	414.9	422.7
2015: I	2,351.5	1,957.8	421.9	100.5	321.4	1,536.0	534.6	83.3	24.9	169.1	189.4	142.9	391.8	393.6
II	2,414.2	2,009.1	456.2	103.2	352.9	1,553.0	537.0	86.3	28.4	163.5	175.1	150.6	412.0	405.1
III	2,382.5	2,000.4	458.6	106.4	352.2	1,541.8	532.9	97.4	13.2	168.2	180.6	146.7	402.9	382.0

[1] Data on Standard Industrial Classification (SIC) basis include transportation and public utilities. Those on North American Industry Classification System (NAICS) basis include transporation and warehousing. Utilities classified separately in NAICS (as shown beginning 1998).
[2] SIC-based industry data use the 1987 SIC for data beginning in 1987 and the 1972 SIC for prior data. NAICS-based data use 2002 NAICS.

Note: Industry data on SIC basis and NAICS basis are not necessarily the same and are not strictly comparable.

Source: Department of Commerce (Bureau of Economic Analysis).

[Billions of chained (2009) dollars]

Year	Income of farm operators from farming [1]							
	Gross farm income						Production expenses	Net farm income
	Total	Value of agricultural sector production				Direct Federal Government payments		
		Total	Crops [2,3]	Animals and animal products [3]	Farm-related income [4]			
1950	240.8	238.8	96.0	132.0	10.8	2.1	141.5	99.3
1951	260.9	258.9	95.6	152.1	11.2	1.9	152.3	108.6
1952	251.7	249.9	102.2	135.7	12.0	1.8	152.0	99.8
1953	226.8	225.4	93.1	120.1	12.2	1.4	141.3	85.4
1954	222.7	221.1	94.0	115.3	11.8	1.7	142.1	80.6
1955	215.1	213.6	91.6	110.0	12.0	1.5	142.4	72.6
1956	210.9	207.5	89.7	106.2	11.6	3.4	141.0	69.9
1957	208.8	202.7	81.9	109.0	11.7	6.1	142.2	66.5
1958	228.5	222.1	88.0	121.9	12.2	6.4	151.3	77.2
1959	219.3	215.4	85.5	116.8	13.1	3.9	157.3	62.0
1960	220.3	216.3	89.5	113.5	13.4	4.0	156.3	64.0
1961	229.0	220.5	89.3	117.4	13.8	8.4	161.4	67.5
1962	236.2	226.5	92.9	119.5	14.0	9.7	168.9	67.3
1963	239.2	229.9	98.9	116.4	14.6	9.4	174.3	64.9
1964	229.8	218.0	91.7	111.2	15.1	11.8	172.8	57.0
1965	248.3	235.2	101.5	118.4	15.3	13.1	179.5	68.8
1966	261.9	244.9	95.0	134.2	15.6	17.0	189.4	72.4
1967	254.8	239.2	96.9	126.0	16.3	15.5	192.5	62.2
1968	250.8	234.0	91.5	126.3	16.2	16.7	191.2	59.6
1969	260.1	242.6	90.7	135.2	16.6	17.5	194.2	65.9
1970	257.6	241.3	89.9	134.7	16.7	16.3	194.7	62.9
1971	258.9	245.8	97.6	131.1	17.0	13.1	196.3	62.6
1972	284.2	268.4	103.7	147.4	17.3	15.8	206.5	77.7
1973	374.7	364.8	163.1	183.2	18.5	9.9	244.6	130.2
1974	341.6	339.8	170.9	148.9	20.0	1.8	246.8	94.8
1975	319.9	317.4	160.4	136.8	20.2	2.6	238.8	81.2
1976	310.4	308.2	145.9	140.6	21.7	2.2	249.5	60.8
1977	308.9	303.7	145.3	134.4	24.1	5.2	252.4	56.5
1978	340.9	332.8	150.2	156.2	26.4	8.0	274.0	66.9
1979	369.5	366.1	163.4	174.5	28.2	3.4	302.3	67.2
1980	335.6	332.7	144.7	158.1	29.9	2.9	299.3	36.3
1981	341.8	337.8	162.2	144.7	31.0	4.0	286.6	55.2
1982	318.0	311.2	139.1	136.6	35.5	6.8	271.8	46.2
1983	286.7	269.4	106.0	130.5	32.9	17.3	260.2	26.6
1984	302.3	287.1	139.9	129.6	17.6	15.2	255.6	46.7
1985	280.9	267.5	128.5	120.3	18.7	13.4	231.2	49.7
1986	266.9	246.7	108.2	120.9	17.5	20.2	213.7	53.2
1987	281.0	253.0	107.6	126.4	19.1	27.9	217.6	63.4
1988	286.8	263.5	111.7	126.8	25.0	23.3	222.9	63.9
1989	297.3	280.4	126.4	129.5	24.5	16.9	225.2	72.1
1990	295.9	282.0	124.5	134.7	22.8	13.9	226.7	69.2
1991	278.1	266.2	117.6	126.3	22.3	11.9	219.8	58.3
1992	283.9	271.0	126.1	123.4	21.5	13.0	212.9	71.0
1993	283.5	265.0	114.3	127.2	23.5	18.5	218.9	64.6
1994	292.6	282.0	136.1	121.5	24.4	10.7	221.4	71.2
1995	279.6	270.0	127.2	116.4	26.4	9.7	226.9	52.8
1996	307.2	297.6	150.7	119.9	27.0	9.6	230.4	76.8
1997	304.8	295.2	144.1	123.3	27.8	9.6	239.1	65.7
1998	294.7	279.0	129.4	119.3	30.3	15.7	235.0	59.7
1999	293.4	266.6	115.9	118.9	31.8	26.9	233.9	59.6
2000	295.1	266.8	116.0	121.0	29.8	28.4	233.2	61.9
2001	298.4	271.6	113.5	127.0	31.1	26.8	232.8	65.5
2002	271.1	256.5	115.1	109.9	31.5	14.6	225.1	46.0
2003	298.3	279.2	125.2	121.1	33.0	19.1	228.0	70.3
2004	330.9	316.3	140.4	139.4	36.5	14.6	232.8	98.1
2005	324.5	298.0	124.3	137.5	36.1	26.5	238.9	85.6
2006	306.0	289.4	125.2	125.9	38.3	16.7	245.5	60.6
2007	348.8	336.6	155.2	142.2	39.2	12.2	276.9	71.9
2008	367.4	355.1	175.2	140.5	39.4	12.3	288.6	78.8
2009	336.5	324.3	164.6	119.5	40.2	12.2	274.3	62.3
2010	352.2	339.9	166.1	138.5	35.3	12.2	276.0	76.1
2011	406.9	396.8	192.9	158.4	45.4	10.1	296.6	110.3
2012	424.7	414.6	202.3	160.7	51.5	10.1	335.8	89.0
2013	452.0	441.7	218.1	169.2	54.4	10.3	336.7	115.3
2014	442.2	433.3	188.1	197.6	47.6	9.0	359.1	83.1
2015 ᵖ	399.3	389.5	169.3	174.2	46.0	9.8	348.4	50.9

[1] The GDP chain-type price index is used to convert the current-dollar statistics to 2009=100 equivalents.
[2] Crop receipts include proceeds received from commodities placed under Commodity Credit Corporation loans.
[3] The value of production equates to the sum of cash receipts, home consumption, and the value of the change in inventories.
[4] Includes income from forest products sold, the gross imputed rental value of farm dwellings, machine hire and custom work, and other sources of farm income such as commodity insurance indemnities.

Note: Data for 2015 are forecasts.

Source: Department of Agriculture (Economic Research Service).

TABLE B-8. New private housing units started, authorized, and completed and houses sold, 1972–2015

[Thousands; monthly data at seasonally adjusted annual rates]

Year or month	New housing units started				New housing units authorized [1]				New housing units completed	New houses sold
	Total	1 unit	2 to 4 units [2]	5 units or more	Total	1 unit	2 to 4 units	5 units or more		
1972	2,356.6	1,309.2	141.2	906.2	2,218.9	1,033.1	148.6	1,037.2	2,003.9	718
1973	2,045.3	1,132.0	118.2	795.0	1,819.5	882.1	117.0	820.5	2,100.5	634
1974	1,337.7	888.1	68.0	381.6	1,074.4	643.8	64.4	366.2	1,728.5	519
1975	1,160.4	892.2	64.0	204.3	939.2	675.5	63.8	199.8	1,317.2	549
1976	1,537.5	1,162.4	85.8	289.2	1,296.2	893.6	93.1	309.5	1,377.2	646
1977	1,987.1	1,450.9	121.7	414.4	1,690.0	1,126.1	121.3	442.7	1,657.1	819
1978	2,020.3	1,433.3	125.1	462.0	1,800.5	1,182.6	130.6	487.3	1,867.5	817
1979	1,745.1	1,194.1	122.0	429.0	1,551.8	981.5	125.4	444.8	1,870.8	709
1980	1,292.2	852.2	109.5	330.5	1,190.6	710.4	114.5	365.7	1,501.6	545
1981	1,084.2	705.4	91.2	287.7	985.5	564.3	101.8	319.4	1,265.7	436
1982	1,062.2	662.6	80.1	319.6	1,000.5	546.4	88.3	365.8	1,005.5	412
1983	1,703.0	1,067.6	113.5	522.0	1,605.2	901.5	133.7	570.1	1,390.3	623
1984	1,749.5	1,084.2	121.4	543.9	1,681.8	922.4	142.6	616.8	1,652.2	639
1985	1,741.8	1,072.4	93.5	576.0	1,733.3	956.6	120.1	656.6	1,703.3	688
1986	1,805.4	1,179.4	84.0	542.0	1,769.4	1,077.6	108.4	583.5	1,756.4	750
1987	1,620.5	1,146.4	65.1	408.7	1,534.8	1,024.4	89.3	421.1	1,668.8	671
1988	1,488.1	1,081.3	58.7	348.0	1,455.6	993.8	75.7	386.1	1,529.8	676
1989	1,376.1	1,003.3	55.3	317.6	1,338.4	931.7	66.9	339.8	1,422.8	650
1990	1,192.7	894.8	37.6	260.4	1,110.8	793.9	54.3	262.6	1,308.0	534
1991	1,013.9	840.4	35.6	137.9	948.8	753.5	43.1	152.1	1,090.8	509
1992	1,199.7	1,029.9	30.9	139.0	1,094.9	910.7	45.8	138.4	1,157.5	610
1993	1,287.6	1,125.7	29.4	132.6	1,199.1	986.5	52.4	160.2	1,192.7	666
1994	1,457.0	1,198.4	35.2	223.5	1,371.6	1,068.5	62.2	241.0	1,346.9	670
1995	1,354.1	1,076.2	33.8	244.1	1,332.5	997.3	63.8	271.5	1,312.6	667
1996	1,476.8	1,160.9	45.3	270.8	1,425.6	1,069.5	65.8	290.3	1,412.9	757
1997	1,474.0	1,133.7	44.5	295.8	1,441.1	1,062.4	68.4	310.3	1,400.5	804
1998	1,616.9	1,271.4	42.6	302.9	1,612.3	1,187.6	69.2	355.5	1,474.2	886
1999	1,640.9	1,302.4	31.9	306.6	1,663.5	1,246.7	65.8	351.1	1,604.9	880
2000	1,568.7	1,230.9	38.7	299.1	1,592.3	1,198.1	64.9	329.3	1,573.7	877
2001	1,602.7	1,273.3	36.6	292.8	1,636.7	1,235.6	66.0	335.2	1,570.8	908
2002	1,704.9	1,358.6	38.5	307.9	1,747.7	1,332.6	73.7	341.4	1,648.4	973
2003	1,847.7	1,499.0	33.5	315.2	1,889.2	1,460.9	82.5	345.8	1,678.7	1,086
2004	1,955.8	1,610.5	42.3	303.0	2,070.1	1,613.4	90.4	366.2	1,841.9	1,203
2005	2,068.3	1,715.8	41.1	311.4	2,155.3	1,682.0	84.0	389.3	1,931.4	1,283
2006	1,800.9	1,465.4	42.7	292.8	1,838.9	1,378.2	76.6	384.1	1,979.4	1,051
2007	1,355.0	1,046.0	31.7	277.3	1,398.4	979.9	59.6	359.0	1,502.8	776
2008	905.5	622.0	17.5	266.0	905.4	575.6	34.4	295.4	1,119.7	485
2009	554.0	445.1	11.6	97.3	583.0	441.1	20.7	121.1	794.4	375
2010	586.9	471.2	11.4	104.3	604.6	447.3	22.0	135.3	651.7	323
2011	608.8	430.6	10.9	167.3	624.1	418.5	21.6	184.0	584.9	306
2012	780.6	535.3	11.4	233.9	829.7	518.7	25.9	285.1	649.2	368
2013	924.9	617.6	13.6	293.7	990.8	620.8	29.0	341.1	764.4	429
2014	1,003.3	647.9	13.7	341.7	1,052.1	640.3	29.9	382.0	883.8	437
2015 *p*	1,111.2	715.3	11.5	384.4	1,178.1	690.1	32.4	455.6	965.7	501
2014: Jan	888	577	....	303	1,002	621	30	351	847	446
Feb	951	604	....	336	1,030	613	24	393	872	417
Mar	963	649	....	300	1,061	622	29	410	911	410
Apr	1,039	639	....	391	1,074	622	27	425	826	410
May	986	637	....	340	1,017	626	29	362	903	457
June	927	597	....	307	1,033	648	38	347	797	408
July	1,095	657	....	422	1,041	640	30	371	861	403
Aug	966	643	....	306	1,040	643	35	362	905	454
Sept	1,026	661	....	353	1,053	653	26	374	948	459
Oct	1,079	705	....	357	1,120	652	32	436	917	472
Nov	1,007	670	....	328	1,079	663	28	388	867	449
Dec	1,080	724	....	336	1,077	685	24	368	939	495
2015: Jan	1,080	706	....	368	1,059	657	27	375	975	521
Feb	900	600	....	292	1,098	626	28	444	865	545
Mar	954	623	....	311	1,038	642	26	370	806	485
Apr	1,190	735	....	436	1,140	666	32	442	999	508
May	1,072	697	....	366	1,250	681	34	535	1,010	513
June	1,211	687	....	510	1,337	692	34	611	959	469
July	1,152	759	....	382	1,130	680	28	422	995	500
Aug	1,116	734	....	376	1,161	699	30	432	959	507
Sept	1,207	741	....	455	1,105	694	37	374	1,019	457
Oct	1,071	715	....	344	1,161	715	34	412	983	482
Nov *p*	1,179	794	....	378	1,282	727	29	526	959	491
Dec *p*	1,149	768	....	365	1,204	732	35	437	1,013	544

[1] Authorized by issuance of local building permits in permit-issuing places: 20,100 places beginning with 2014; 19,300 for 2004–2013; 19,000 for 1994–2003; 17,000 for 1984–93; 16,000 for 1978–83; and 14,000 for 1972–77.
[2] Monthly data do not meet publication standards because tests for identifiable and stable seasonality do not meet reliability standards.

Note: One-unit estimates prior to 1999, for new housing units started and completed and for new houses sold, include an upward adjustment of 3.3 percent to account for structures in permit-issuing areas that did not have permit authorization.

Source: Department of Commerce (Bureau of the Census).

TABLE B–9. Median money income (in 2014 dollars) and poverty status of families and people, by race, 2006-2014

Race, Hispanic origin, and year	Families[1]						People below poverty level		Median money income (in 2014 dollars) of people 15 years old and over with income[2]			
	Number (millions)	Median money income (in 2014 dollars)[2]	Below poverty level				Number (millions)	Percent	Males		Females	
			Total		Female householder, no husband present				All people	Year-round full-time workers	All people	Year-round full-time workers
			Number (millions)	Percent	Number (millions)	Percent						
TOTAL (all races)[3]												
2006	78.5	$68,582	7.7	9.8	4.1	28.3	36.5	12.3	$37,886	$52,790	$23,501	$41,084
2007	77.9	70,057	7.6	9.8	4.1	28.3	37.3	12.5	37,904	52,780	23,889	41,296
2008	78.9	67,648	8.1	10.3	4.2	28.7	39.8	13.2	36,463	52,537	22,945	40,342
2009[4]	78.9	66,303	8.8	11.1	4.4	29.9	43.6	14.3	35,513	54,249	23,125	41,085
2010[5]	79.6	65,408	9.4	11.8	4.8	31.7	46.3	15.1	34,970	54,457	22,559	41,739
2011	80.5	64,185	9.5	11.8	4.9	31.2	46.2	15.0	34,723	52,966	22,213	40,722
2012	80.9	64,179	9.5	11.8	4.8	30.9	46.5	15.0	34,959	52,261	22,190	41,265
2013[6]	81.2	64,859	9.1	11.2	4.6	30.6	45.3	14.5	35,804	51,777	22,424	41,261
2013[7]	82.3	66,542	9.6	11.7	5.2	32.2	46.3	14.8	36,213	52,259	22,488	41,365
2014	81.7	66,632	9.5	11.6	4.8	30.6	46.7	14.8	36,302	51,456	22,240	40,797
WHITE, non-Hispanic[8]												
2006	54.7	77,340	3.4	6.2	1.6	22.0	16.0	8.2	42,934	59,232	24,338	43,312
2007	53.9	79,856	3.2	5.9	1.5	20.7	16.0	8.2	42,673	58,764	24,763	44,164
2008	54.5	77,048	3.4	6.2	1.5	20.7	17.0	8.6	41,135	57,559	23,915	43,401
2009[4]	54.5	74,306	3.8	7.0	1.7	23.3	18.5	9.4	40,590	57,896	24,208	44,429
2010[5]	53.8	74,819	3.9	7.2	1.7	24.1	19.3	9.9	40,344	59,345	23,579	44,881
2011	54.2	73,506	4.0	7.3	1.8	23.4	19.2	9.8	40,157	58,700	23,396	43,552
2012	54.0	73,703	3.8	7.1	1.7	23.4	18.9	9.7	39,957	57,998	23,615	43,484
2013[6]	53.8	73,812	3.7	6.9	1.6	22.6	18.8	9.6	40,779	57,380	24,169	43,484
2013[7]	54.7	75,853	4.0	7.3	1.9	25.8	19.6	10.0	41,525	59,838	24,121	43,782
2014	53.8	76,658	3.9	7.3	1.7	23.7	19.7	10.1	41,072	58,712	24,005	44,236
BLACK[8]												
2006	9.3	44,936	2.0	21.6	1.5	36.6	9.0	24.3	29,430	41,657	22,431	36,325
2007	9.3	45,836	2.0	22.1	1.5	37.3	9.2	24.5	29,484	41,946	22,553	36,071
2008	9.4	43,851	2.1	22.0	1.5	37.2	9.4	24.7	27,769	42,457	22,208	35,391
2009[4]	9.4	42,382	2.1	22.7	1.5	36.7	9.9	25.8	26,193	43,433	21,484	35,828
2010[5]	9.6	41,908	2.3	24.1	1.7	38.7	10.7	27.4	25,296	40,963	21,333	36,966
2011	9.7	42,628	2.3	24.2	1.7	39.0	10.9	27.6	24,711	42,394	20,795	36,997
2012	9.8	41,778	2.3	23.7	1.6	37.8	10.9	27.2	25,699	41,055	20,644	36,182
2013[6]	9.9	42,269	2.3	22.8	1.6	38.5	11.0	27.2	25,262	42,311	20,372	35,960
2013[7]	9.9	42,576	2.2	22.4	1.7	36.7	10.2	25.2	25,531	41,099	21,413	35,208
2014	9.9	43,151	2.3	22.9	1.6	37.2	10.8	26.2	26,569	41,292	20,966	35,329
ASIAN[8]												
2006	3.3	87,610	.3	7.8	.1	15.4	1.4	10.3	43,935	61,177	26,069	47,259
2007	3.3	88,072	.3	7.9	.1	16.1	1.3	10.2	42,468	58,476	27,809	47,175
2008	3.5	80,906	.3	9.8	.1	16.7	1.6	11.8	40,253	56,942	25,410	48,611
2009[4]	3.6	82,787	.3	9.4	.1	16.9	1.7	12.5	41,191	58,954	26,861	49,243
2010[5]	3.9	81,675	.4	9.3	.1	21.1	1.9	12.2	38,899	57,013	25,586	45,519
2011	4.2	76,840	.4	9.7	.1	19.1	2.0	12.3	38,247	59,247	23,200	43,592
2012	4.1	80,288	.4	9.4	.1	19.2	1.9	11.7	41,479	62,129	24,061	47,815
2013[6]	4.4	77,652	.4	8.7	.1	14.9	1.8	10.5	40,810	61,138	25,246	45,814
2013[7]	4.4	84,148	.4	10.2	.1	25.7	2.3	12.0	43,489	62,220	26,266	47,992
2014	4.5	82,732	.4	8.9	.1	18.9	2.1	12.0	40,901	60,299	25,391	48,546
HISPANIC (any race)[8]												
2006	10.2	46,968	1.9	18.9	.9	36.0	9.2	20.6	27,537	34,722	18,503	30,170
2007	10.4	46,319	2.0	19.7	1.0	38.4	9.9	21.5	27,919	34,773	19,123	31,005
2008	10.5	44,496	2.2	21.3	1.0	39.2	11.0	23.2	26,393	34,328	18,052	30,174
2009[4]	10.4	43,839	2.4	22.7	1.1	38.8	12.4	25.3	24,558	34,910	17,887	30,767
2010[5]	11.3	42,674	2.7	24.3	1.3	42.6	13.5	26.5	24,345	34,577	17,691	31,594
2011	11.6	42,171	2.7	22.9	1.3	41.2	13.2	25.3	24,981	33,778	17,715	31,687
2012	12.0	42,033	2.8	23.5	1.3	40.7	13.6	25.6	25,358	33,528	17,246	30,427
2013[6]	12.1	42,961	2.6	21.6	1.3	40.4	12.7	23.5	25,827	33,488	18,053	31,303
2013[7]	12.4	41,609	2.9	23.1	1.4	40.5	13.4	24.7	24,597	32,896	17,229	31,680
2014	12.5	45,114	2.7	21.5	1.3	37.9	13.1	23.6	26,675	35,114	17,585	30,829

[1] The term "family" refers to a group of two or more persons related by birth, marriage, or adoption and residing together. Every family must include a reference person.

[2] Adjusted by consumer price index research series (CPI-U-RS).

[3] Data for American Indians and Alaska natives, native Hawaiians and other Pacific Islanders, and those reporting two or more races are included in the total but not shown separately.

[4] Beginning with data for 2009, the upper income interval used to calculate median incomes was expanded to $250,000 or more.

[5] Reflects implementation of Census 2010-based population controls comparable to succeeding years.

[6] The 2014 Current Population Survey (CPS) Annual Social and Economic Supplement (ASEC) included redesigned income questions, which were implemented to a subsample of the 98,000 addresses using a probability split panel design. These 2013 data are based on the 2014 ASEC sample of 68,000 addresses that received income questions similar to those used in the 2013 ASEC and are consistent with data in earlier years.

[7] These 2013 data are based on the 2014 ASEC sample of 30,000 addresses that received redesigned income questions and are consistent with data in later years.

[8] The CPS allows respondents to choose more than one race. Data shown are for "white alone, non-Hispanic," "black alone," and "Asian alone" race categories. ("Black" is also "black or African American.") Family income and Hispanic origin are based on the reference person.

Note: Poverty thresholds are updated each year to reflect changes in the consumer price index (CPI-U).
For details see publication Series P-60 on the Current Population Survey and Annual Social and Economic Supplements.

Source: Department of Commerce (Bureau of the Census).

TABLE B–10. Changes in consumer price indexes, 1947–2015

[For all urban consumers; percent change]

December to December	All items	All items less food and energy					Food			Energy [4]		C-CPI-U [5]
		Total [1]	Shelter [2]	Medical care [3]	Apparel	New vehicles	Total [1]	At home	Away from home	Total [1,3]	Gasoline	
1947	8.8	....	....	6.9	8.2		11.3	....	....	....	16.4	
1948	3.0	....	....	5.8	5.1	11.5	-.8	-1.1	....	....	6.2	
1949	-2.1	....	....	1.4	-7.4	4.0	-3.9	-3.7	....	....	1.6	
1950	5.9	....	....	3.4	5.3	.2	9.8	9.5	....	....	1.6	
1951	6.0	....	....	5.8	5.7	9.7	7.1	7.6	....	....	2.1	
1952	.8	....	....	4.3	-2.9	4.4	-1.0	-1.3	....	....	.5	
1953	.7	....	3.2	3.5	.7	-1.7	-1.1	-1.6	....	....	10.1	
1954	-.7	....	1.8	2.3	-.7	1.3	-1.8	-2.3	0.9	....	-1.4	
1955	.4	....	.9	3.3	.5	-2.3	-.7	-1.0	1.4	....	4.2	
1956	3.0	....	2.6	3.2	2.5	7.8	2.9	2.7	2.7	....	3.1	
1957	2.9	....	3.4	4.7	.9	2.0	2.8	3.0	3.9	....	2.2	
1958	1.8	1.7	.8	4.5	.2	6.1	2.4	1.9	2.1	-0.9	-3.8	
1959	1.7	2.0	2.0	3.8	1.3	-.2	-1.0	-1.3	3.3	4.7	7.0	
1960	1.4	1.0	1.6	3.2	1.5	-3.0	3.1	3.2	2.4	1.3	1.2	
1961	.7	1.3	.8	3.1	.4	.2	-.7	-1.6	2.3	-1.3	-3.2	
1962	1.3	1.3	.8	2.2	.6	-1.0	1.3	1.3	3.0	2.2	3.8	
1963	1.6	1.6	1.9	2.5	1.7	-.4	2.0	1.6	1.8	-.9	-2.4	
1964	1.0	1.2	1.5	2.1	.4	-.6	1.3	1.5	1.4	.0	.0	
1965	1.9	1.5	2.2	2.8	1.3	-2.9	3.5	3.6	3.2	1.8	4.1	
1966	3.5	3.3	4.0	6.7	3.9	.0	4.0	3.2	5.5	1.7	3.2	
1967	3.0	3.8	2.8	6.3	4.2	2.8	1.2	.3	4.6	1.7	1.5	
1968	4.7	5.1	6.5	6.2	6.3	1.4	4.4	4.0	5.6	1.7	1.5	
1969	6.2	6.2	8.7	6.2	5.2	2.1	7.0	7.1	7.4	2.9	3.4	
1970	5.6	6.6	8.9	7.4	3.9	6.6	2.3	1.3	6.1	4.8	2.5	
1971	3.3	3.1	2.7	4.6	2.1	-3.2	4.3	4.3	4.4	3.1	-.4	
1972	3.4	3.0	4.0	3.3	2.6	.2	4.6	5.1	4.2	2.6	2.8	
1973	8.7	4.7	7.1	5.3	4.4	1.3	20.3	22.0	12.7	17.0	19.6	
1974	12.3	11.1	11.4	12.6	8.7	11.4	12.0	12.4	11.3	21.6	20.7	
1975	6.9	6.7	7.2	9.8	2.4	7.3	6.6	6.2	7.4	11.4	11.0	
1976	4.9	6.1	4.2	10.0	4.6	4.8	.5	-.8	6.0	7.1	2.8	
1977	6.7	6.5	8.8	8.9	4.3	7.2	8.1	7.9	7.9	7.2	4.8	
1978	9.0	8.5	11.4	8.8	3.1	6.2	11.8	12.5	10.4	7.9	8.6	
1979	13.3	11.3	17.5	10.1	5.5	7.4	10.2	9.7	11.4	37.5	52.1	
1980	12.5	12.2	15.0	9.9	6.8	7.4	10.2	10.5	9.6	18.0	18.9	
1981	8.9	9.5	9.9	12.5	3.5	6.8	4.3	2.9	7.1	11.9	9.4	
1982	3.8	4.5	2.4	11.0	1.6	1.4	3.1	2.3	5.1	1.3	-6.7	
1983	3.8	4.8	4.7	6.4	2.9	3.3	2.7	1.8	4.1	-.5	-1.6	
1984	3.9	4.7	5.2	6.1	2.0	2.5	3.8	3.6	4.2	.2	-2.5	
1985	3.8	4.3	6.0	6.8	2.8	3.6	2.6	2.0	3.8	1.8	3.0	
1986	1.1	3.8	4.6	7.7	.9	5.6	3.8	3.7	4.3	-19.7	-30.7	
1987	4.4	4.2	4.8	5.8	4.8	1.8	3.5	3.5	3.7	8.2	18.6	
1988	4.4	4.7	4.5	6.9	4.7	2.2	5.2	5.6	4.4	.5	-1.8	
1989	4.6	4.4	4.9	8.5	1.0	2.4	5.6	6.2	4.6	5.1	6.5	
1990	6.1	5.2	5.2	9.6	5.1	2.0	5.3	5.8	4.5	18.1	36.8	
1991	3.1	4.4	3.9	7.9	3.4	3.2	1.9	1.3	2.9	-7.4	-16.2	
1992	2.9	3.3	2.9	6.6	1.4	2.3	1.5	1.5	1.4	2.0	2.0	
1993	2.7	3.2	3.0	5.4	.9	3.3	2.9	3.5	1.9	-1.4	-5.9	
1994	2.7	2.6	3.0	4.9	-1.6	3.3	2.9	3.5	1.9	2.2	6.4	
1995	2.5	3.0	3.5	3.9	.1	1.9	2.1	2.0	2.2	-1.3	-4.2	
1996	3.3	2.6	2.9	3.0	-.2	1.8	4.3	4.9	3.1	8.6	12.4	
1997	1.7	2.2	3.4	2.8	1.0	-.9	1.5	1.0	2.6	-3.4	-6.1	
1998	1.6	2.4	3.3	3.4	-.7	.0	2.3	2.1	2.5	-8.8	-15.4	
1999	2.7	1.9	2.5	3.7	-.5	-.3	1.9	1.7	2.3	13.4	30.1	
2000	3.4	2.6	3.4	4.2	-1.8	.0	2.8	2.9	2.4	14.2	13.9	2.6
2001	1.6	2.7	4.2	4.7	-3.2	-.1	2.8	2.6	3.0	-13.0	-24.9	1.3
2002	2.4	1.9	3.1	5.0	-1.8	-2.0	1.5	.8	2.3	10.7	24.8	2.0
2003	1.9	1.1	2.2	3.7	-2.1	-1.8	3.6	4.5	2.3	6.9	6.8	1.7
2004	3.3	2.2	2.7	4.2	-.2	.6	2.7	2.4	3.0	16.6	26.1	3.2
2005	3.4	2.2	2.6	4.3	-1.1	-.4	2.3	1.7	3.2	17.1	16.1	2.9
2006	2.5	2.6	4.2	3.6	.9	-.9	2.1	1.4	3.2	2.9	6.4	2.3
2007	4.1	2.4	3.1	5.2	-.3	-.3	4.9	5.6	4.0	17.4	29.6	3.7
2008	.1	1.8	1.9	2.6	-1.0	-3.2	5.9	6.6	5.0	-21.3	-43.1	.2
2009	2.7	1.8	.3	3.4	1.9	4.9	-.5	-2.4	1.9	18.2	53.5	2.5
2010	1.5	.8	.4	3.3	-1.1	-.2	1.5	1.7	1.3	7.7	13.8	1.3
2011	3.0	2.2	1.9	3.5	4.6	3.2	4.7	6.0	2.9	6.6	9.9	2.9
2012	1.7	1.9	2.2	3.2	1.8	1.6	1.8	1.3	2.5	.5	1.7	1.5
2013	1.5	1.7	2.5	2.0	.6	.4	1.1	.4	2.1	.5	-1.0	1.3
2014	.8	1.6	2.9	3.0	-2.0	.5	3.4	3.7	3.0	-10.6	-21.0	.5
2015	.7	2.1	3.2	2.6	-.9	.2	.8	-.4	2.6	-12.6	-19.7	.3

[1] Includes other items not shown separately.
[2] Data beginning with 1983 incorporate a rental equivalence measure for homeowners' costs.
[3] Commodities and services.
[4] Household energy--electricity, utility (piped) gas service, fuel oil, etc.--and motor fuel.
[5] Chained consumer price index (C-CPI-U) introduced in 2002. Reflects the effect of substitution that consumers make across item categories in response to changes in relative prices. Data for 2015 are subject to revision.

Note: Changes from December to December are based on unadjusted indexes.
Series reflect changes in composition and renaming beginning in 1998, and formula and methodology changes in 1999.

Source: Department of Labor (Bureau of Labor Statistics).

Table B–11. Civilian labor force, 1929–2015

[Monthly data seasonally adjusted, except as noted]

Year or month	Civilian noninstitutional population [1]	Civilian labor force					Not in labor force	Civilian labor force participation rate [2]	Civilian employment/ population ratio [3]	Unemployment rate, civilian workers [4]
		Total	Employment			Unemployment				
			Total	Agricultural	Nonagricultural					
		Thousands of persons 14 years of age and over							Percent	
1929	....	49,180	47,630	10,450	37,180	1,550	....	....	....	3.2
1930	....	49,820	45,480	10,340	35,140	4,340	....	....	....	8.7
1931	....	50,420	42,400	10,290	32,110	8,020	....	....	....	15.9
1932	....	51,000	38,940	10,170	28,770	12,060	....	....	....	23.6
1933	....	51,590	38,760	10,090	28,670	12,830	....	....	....	24.9
1934	....	52,230	40,890	9,900	30,990	11,340	....	....	....	21.7
1935	....	52,870	42,260	10,110	32,150	10,610	....	....	....	20.1
1936	....	53,440	44,410	10,000	34,410	9,030	....	....	....	16.9
1937	....	54,000	46,300	9,820	36,480	7,700	....	....	....	14.3
1938	....	54,610	44,220	9,690	34,530	10,390	....	....	....	19.0
1939	....	55,230	45,750	9,610	36,140	9,480	....	....	....	17.2
1940	99,840	55,640	47,520	9,540	37,980	8,120	44,200	55.7	47.6	14.6
1941	99,900	55,910	50,350	9,100	41,250	5,560	43,990	56.0	50.4	9.9
1942	98,640	56,410	53,750	9,250	44,500	2,660	42,230	57.2	54.5	4.7
1943	94,640	55,540	54,470	9,080	45,390	1,070	39,100	58.7	57.6	1.9
1944	93,220	54,630	53,960	8,950	45,010	670	38,590	58.6	57.9	1.2
1945	94,090	53,860	52,820	8,580	44,240	1,040	40,230	57.2	56.1	1.9
1946	103,070	57,520	55,250	8,320	46,930	2,270	45,550	55.8	53.6	3.9
1947	106,018	60,168	57,812	8,256	49,557	2,356	45,850	56.8	54.5	3.9
		Thousands of persons 16 years of age and over								
1947	101,827	59,350	57,038	7,890	49,148	2,311	42,477	58.3	56.0	3.9
1948	103,068	60,621	58,343	7,629	50,714	2,276	42,447	58.8	56.6	3.8
1949	103,994	61,286	57,651	7,658	49,993	3,637	42,708	58.9	55.4	5.9
1950	104,995	62,208	58,918	7,160	51,758	3,288	42,787	59.2	56.1	5.3
1951	104,621	62,017	59,961	6,726	53,235	2,055	42,604	59.2	57.3	3.3
1952	105,231	62,138	60,250	6,500	53,749	1,883	43,093	59.0	57.3	3.0
1953	107,056	63,015	61,179	6,260	54,919	1,834	44,041	58.9	57.1	2.9
1954	108,321	63,643	60,109	6,205	53,904	3,532	44,678	58.8	55.5	5.5
1955	109,683	65,023	62,170	6,450	55,722	2,852	44,660	59.3	56.7	4.4
1956	110,954	66,552	63,799	6,283	57,514	2,750	44,402	60.0	57.5	4.1
1957	112,265	66,929	64,071	5,947	58,123	2,859	45,336	59.6	57.1	4.3
1958	113,727	67,639	63,036	5,586	57,450	4,602	46,088	59.5	55.4	6.8
1959	115,329	68,369	64,630	5,565	59,065	3,740	46,960	59.3	56.0	5.5
1960	117,245	69,628	65,778	5,458	60,318	3,852	47,617	59.4	56.1	5.5
1961	118,771	70,459	65,746	5,200	60,546	4,714	48,312	59.3	55.4	6.7
1962	120,153	70,614	66,702	4,944	61,759	3,911	49,539	58.8	55.5	5.5
1963	122,416	71,833	67,762	4,687	63,076	4,070	50,583	58.7	55.4	5.7
1964	124,485	73,091	69,305	4,523	64,782	3,786	51,394	58.7	55.7	5.2
1965	126,513	74,455	71,088	4,361	66,726	3,366	52,058	58.9	56.2	4.5
1966	128,058	75,770	72,895	3,979	68,915	2,875	52,288	59.2	56.9	3.8
1967	129,874	77,347	74,372	3,844	70,527	2,975	52,527	59.6	57.3	3.8
1968	132,028	78,737	75,920	3,817	72,103	2,817	53,291	59.6	57.5	3.6
1969	134,335	80,734	77,902	3,606	74,296	2,832	53,602	60.1	58.0	3.5
1970	137,085	82,771	78,678	3,463	75,215	4,093	54,315	60.4	57.4	4.9
1971	140,216	84,382	79,367	3,394	75,972	5,016	55,834	60.2	56.6	5.9
1972	144,126	87,034	82,153	3,484	78,669	4,882	57,091	60.4	57.0	5.6
1973	147,096	89,429	85,064	3,470	81,594	4,365	57,667	60.8	57.8	4.9
1974	150,120	91,949	86,794	3,515	83,279	5,156	58,171	61.3	57.8	5.6
1975	153,153	93,775	85,846	3,408	82,438	7,929	59,377	61.2	56.1	8.5
1976	156,150	96,158	88,752	3,331	85,421	7,406	59,991	61.6	56.8	7.7
1977	159,033	99,009	92,017	3,283	88,734	6,991	60,025	62.3	57.9	7.1
1978	161,910	102,251	96,048	3,387	92,661	6,202	59,659	63.2	59.3	6.1
1979	164,863	104,962	98,824	3,347	95,477	6,137	59,900	63.7	59.9	5.8
1980	167,745	106,940	99,303	3,364	95,938	7,637	60,806	63.8	59.2	7.1
1981	170,130	108,670	100,397	3,368	97,030	8,273	61,460	63.9	59.0	7.6
1982	172,271	110,204	99,526	3,401	96,125	10,678	62,067	64.0	57.8	9.7
1983	174,215	111,550	100,834	3,383	97,450	10,717	62,665	64.0	57.9	9.6
1984	176,383	113,544	105,005	3,321	101,685	8,539	62,839	64.4	59.5	7.5
1985	178,206	115,461	107,150	3,179	103,971	8,312	62,744	64.8	60.1	7.2
1986	180,587	117,834	109,597	3,163	106,434	8,237	62,752	65.3	60.7	7.0
1987	182,753	119,865	112,440	3,208	109,232	7,425	62,888	65.6	61.5	6.2
1988	184,613	121,669	114,968	3,169	111,800	6,701	62,944	65.9	62.3	5.5
1989	186,393	123,869	117,342	3,199	114,142	6,528	62,523	66.5	63.0	5.3

[1] Not seasonally adjusted.
[2] Civilian labor force as percent of civilian noninstitutional population.
[3] Civilian employment as percent of civilian noninstitutional population.
[4] Unemployed as percent of civilian labor force.

See next page for continuation of table.

[Monthly data seasonally adjusted, except as noted]

Year or month	Civilian noninstitutional population [1]	Civilian labor force					Not in labor force	Civilian labor force participation rate [2]	Civilian employment/population ratio [3]	Unemployment rate, civilian workers [4]
		Total	Employment			Unemployment				
			Total	Agricultural	Non-agricultural					
	Thousands of persons 16 years of age and over								Percent	
1990	189,164	125,840	118,793	3,223	115,570	7,047	63,324	66.5	62.8	5.6
1991	190,925	126,346	117,718	3,269	114,449	8,628	64,578	66.2	61.7	6.8
1992	192,805	128,105	118,492	3,247	115,245	9,613	64,700	66.4	61.5	7.5
1993	194,838	129,200	120,259	3,115	117,144	8,940	65,638	66.3	61.7	6.9
1994	196,814	131,056	123,060	3,409	119,651	7,996	65,758	66.6	62.5	6.1
1995	198,584	132,304	124,900	3,440	121,460	7,404	66,280	66.6	62.9	5.6
1996	200,591	133,943	126,708	3,443	123,264	7,236	66,647	66.8	63.2	5.4
1997	203,133	136,297	129,558	3,399	126,159	6,739	66,837	67.1	63.8	4.9
1998	205,220	137,673	131,463	3,378	128,085	6,210	67,547	67.1	64.1	4.5
1999	207,753	139,368	133,488	3,281	130,207	5,880	68,385	67.1	64.3	4.2
2000 [5]	212,577	142,583	136,891	2,464	134,427	5,692	69,994	67.1	64.4	4.0
2001	215,092	143,734	136,933	2,299	134,635	6,801	71,359	66.8	63.7	4.7
2002	217,570	144,863	136,485	2,311	134,174	8,378	72,707	66.6	62.7	5.8
2003	221,168	146,510	137,736	2,275	135,461	8,774	74,658	66.2	62.3	6.0
2004	223,357	147,401	139,252	2,232	137,020	8,149	75,956	66.0	62.3	5.5
2005	226,082	149,320	141,730	2,197	139,532	7,591	76,762	66.0	62.7	5.1
2006	228,815	151,428	144,427	2,206	142,221	7,001	77,387	66.2	63.1	4.6
2007	231,867	153,124	146,047	2,095	143,952	7,078	78,743	66.0	63.0	4.6
2008	233,788	154,287	145,362	2,168	143,194	8,924	79,501	66.0	62.2	5.8
2009	235,801	154,142	139,877	2,103	137,775	14,265	81,659	65.4	59.3	9.3
2010	237,830	153,889	139,064	2,206	136,858	14,825	83,941	64.7	58.5	9.6
2011	239,618	153,617	139,869	2,254	137,615	13,747	86,001	64.1	58.4	8.9
2012	243,284	154,975	142,469	2,186	140,283	12,506	88,310	63.7	58.6	8.1
2013	245,679	155,389	143,929	2,130	141,799	11,460	90,290	63.2	58.6	7.4
2014	247,947	155,922	146,305	2,237	144,068	9,617	92,025	62.9	59.0	6.2
2015	250,801	157,130	148,834	2,422	146,411	8,296	93,671	62.7	59.3	5.3
2013: Jan	244,663	155,666	143,249	2,046	141,156	12,417	88,997	63.6	58.5	8.0
Feb	244,828	155,313	143,359	2,069	141,315	11,954	89,514	63.4	58.6	7.7
Mar	244,995	155,034	143,352	2,017	141,276	11,681	89,961	63.3	58.5	7.5
Apr	245,175	155,365	143,622	2,055	141,571	11,743	89,810	63.4	58.6	7.6
May	245,363	155,483	143,842	2,110	141,746	11,641	89,880	63.4	58.6	7.5
June	245,552	155,753	144,003	2,107	141,900	11,750	89,799	63.4	58.6	7.5
July	245,756	155,662	144,300	2,201	142,051	11,362	90,094	63.3	58.7	7.3
Aug	245,959	155,568	144,284	2,222	142,010	11,284	90,391	63.2	58.7	7.3
Sept	246,168	155,749	144,447	2,189	142,254	11,302	90,419	63.3	58.7	7.3
Oct	246,381	154,694	143,537	2,171	141,491	11,158	91,686	62.8	58.3	7.2
Nov	246,567	155,352	144,555	2,112	142,435	10,796	91,215	63.0	58.6	6.9
Dec	246,745	155,083	144,684	2,208	142,501	10,399	91,663	62.9	58.6	6.7
2014: Jan	246,915	155,285	145,092	2,161	142,922	10,192	91,630	62.9	58.8	6.6
Feb	247,085	155,560	145,185	2,137	143,098	10,375	91,526	63.0	58.8	6.7
Mar	247,258	156,187	145,772	2,133	143,544	10,415	91,071	63.2	59.0	6.7
Apr	247,439	155,376	145,677	2,162	143,504	9,699	92,063	62.8	58.9	6.2
May	247,622	155,511	145,792	2,057	143,737	9,719	92,111	62.8	58.9	6.2
June	247,814	155,684	146,214	2,158	144,090	9,470	92,130	62.8	59.0	6.1
July	248,023	156,090	146,438	2,180	144,213	9,651	91,934	62.9	59.0	6.2
Aug	248,229	156,080	146,464	2,288	144,128	9,617	92,149	62.9	59.0	6.2
Sept	248,446	156,129	146,834	2,384	144,420	9,296	92,317	62.8	59.1	6.0
Oct	248,657	156,363	147,374	2,402	145,057	8,989	92,294	62.9	59.3	5.7
Nov	248,844	156,442	147,389	2,399	145,042	9,053	92,402	62.9	59.2	5.8
Dec	249,027	156,142	147,439	2,355	145,132	8,704	92,885	62.7	59.2	5.6
2015: Jan	249,723	157,025	148,104	2,417	145,683	8,920	92,699	62.9	59.3	5.7
Feb	249,899	156,878	148,231	2,424	145,801	8,646	93,022	62.8	59.3	5.5
Mar	250,080	156,890	148,333	2,556	145,681	8,557	93,190	62.7	59.3	5.5
Apr	250,266	157,032	148,509	2,419	146,065	8,523	93,234	62.7	59.3	5.4
May	250,455	157,367	148,748	2,395	146,336	8,619	93,089	62.8	59.4	5.5
June	250,663	156,984	148,722	2,548	146,198	8,262	93,679	62.6	59.3	5.3
July	250,876	157,115	148,866	2,369	146,444	8,249	93,761	62.6	59.3	5.3
Aug	251,096	157,061	149,043	2,350	146,666	8,018	94,035	62.6	59.4	5.1
Sept	251,325	156,867	148,942	2,368	146,535	7,925	94,458	62.4	59.3	5.1
Oct	251,541	157,096	149,197	2,394	146,864	7,899	94,446	62.5	59.3	5.0
Nov	251,747	157,367	149,444	2,424	147,110	7,924	94,380	62.5	59.4	5.0
Dec	251,936	157,833	149,929	2,411	147,587	7,904	94,103	62.6	59.5	5.0

[5] Beginning in 2000, data for agricultural employment are for agricultural and related industries; data for this series and for nonagricultural employment are not strictly comparable with data for earlier years. Because of independent seasonal adjustment for these two series, monthly data will not add to total civilian employment.

Note: Labor force data in Tables B–11 through B–13 are based on household interviews and usually relate to the calendar week that includes the 12th of the month. Historical comparability is affected by revisions to population controls, changes in occupational and industry classification, and other changes to the survey. In recent years, updated population controls are introduced annually with the release of January data, so data are not strictly comparable with earlier periods. Particularly notable changes were introduced for data in the years 1953, 1960, 1962, 1972, 1973, 1978, 1980, 1990, 1994, 1997, 1998, 2000, 2003, 2008 and 2012. For definitions of terms, area samples used, historical comparability of the data, comparability with other series, etc., see *Employment and Earnings* or concepts and methodology of the CPS at http://www.bls.gov/cps/documentation.htm#concepts.

Source: Department of Labor (Bureau of Labor Statistics).

TABLE B–12. Civilian unemployment rate, 1972–2015

[Percent [1]; monthly data seasonally adjusted, except as noted]

Year or month	All civilian workers	Males Total	Males 16–19 years	Males 20 years and over	Females Total	Females 16–19 years	Females 20 years and over	Both sexes 16–19 years	By race White[2]	By race Black or African American[2]	By race Asian[2]	Hispanic or Latino ethnicity[3]	Married men, spouse present	Women who maintain families[4]
1972	5.6	5.0	15.9	4.0	6.6	16.7	5.4	16.2	5.1	10.4	....	....	2.8	7.2
1973	4.9	4.2	13.9	3.3	6.0	15.3	4.9	14.5	4.3	9.4	....	7.5	2.3	7.1
1974	5.6	4.9	15.6	3.8	6.7	16.6	5.5	16.0	5.0	10.5	....	8.1	2.7	7.0
1975	8.5	7.9	20.1	6.8	9.3	19.7	8.0	19.9	7.8	14.8	....	12.2	5.1	10.0
1976	7.7	7.1	19.2	5.9	8.6	18.7	7.4	19.0	7.0	14.0	....	11.5	4.2	10.1
1977	7.1	6.3	17.3	5.2	8.2	18.3	7.0	17.8	6.2	14.0	....	10.1	3.6	9.4
1978	6.1	5.3	15.8	4.3	7.2	17.1	6.0	16.4	5.2	12.8	....	9.1	2.8	8.5
1979	5.8	5.1	15.9	4.2	6.8	16.4	5.7	16.1	5.1	12.3	....	8.3	2.8	8.3
1980	7.1	6.9	18.3	5.9	7.4	17.2	6.4	17.8	6.3	14.3	....	10.1	4.2	9.2
1981	7.6	7.4	20.1	6.3	7.9	19.0	6.8	19.6	6.7	15.6	....	10.4	4.3	10.4
1982	9.7	9.9	24.4	8.8	9.4	21.9	8.3	23.2	8.6	18.9	....	13.8	6.5	11.7
1983	9.6	9.9	23.3	8.9	9.2	21.3	8.1	22.4	8.4	19.5	....	13.7	6.5	12.2
1984	7.5	7.4	19.6	6.6	7.6	18.0	6.8	18.9	6.5	15.9	....	10.7	4.6	10.3
1985	7.2	7.0	19.5	6.2	7.4	17.6	6.6	18.6	6.2	15.1	....	10.5	4.3	10.4
1986	7.0	6.9	19.0	6.1	7.1	17.6	6.2	18.3	6.0	14.5	....	10.6	4.4	9.8
1987	6.2	6.2	17.8	5.4	6.2	15.9	5.4	16.9	5.3	13.0	....	8.8	3.9	9.2
1988	5.5	5.5	16.0	4.8	5.6	14.4	4.9	15.3	4.7	11.7	....	8.2	3.3	8.1
1989	5.3	5.2	15.9	4.5	5.4	14.0	4.7	15.0	4.5	11.4	....	8.0	3.0	8.1
1990	5.6	5.7	16.3	5.0	5.5	14.7	4.9	15.5	4.8	11.4	....	8.2	3.4	8.3
1991	6.8	7.2	19.8	6.4	6.4	17.5	5.7	18.7	6.1	12.5	....	10.0	4.4	9.3
1992	7.5	7.9	21.5	7.1	7.0	18.6	6.3	20.1	6.6	14.2	....	11.6	5.1	10.0
1993	6.9	7.2	20.4	6.4	6.6	17.5	5.9	19.0	6.1	13.0	....	10.8	4.4	9.7
1994	6.1	6.2	19.0	5.4	6.0	16.2	5.4	17.6	5.3	11.5	....	9.9	3.7	8.9
1995	5.6	5.6	18.4	4.8	5.6	16.1	4.9	17.3	4.9	10.4	....	9.3	3.3	8.0
1996	5.4	5.4	18.1	4.6	5.4	15.2	4.8	16.7	4.7	10.5	....	8.9	3.0	8.2
1997	4.9	4.9	16.9	4.2	5.0	15.0	4.4	16.0	4.2	10.0	....	7.7	2.7	8.1
1998	4.5	4.4	16.2	3.7	4.6	12.9	4.1	14.6	3.9	8.9	....	7.2	2.4	7.2
1999	4.2	4.1	14.7	3.5	4.3	13.2	3.8	13.9	3.7	8.0	....	6.4	2.2	6.4
2000	4.0	3.9	14.0	3.3	4.1	12.1	3.6	13.1	3.5	7.6	3.6	5.7	2.0	5.9
2001	4.7	4.8	16.0	4.2	4.7	13.4	4.1	14.7	4.2	8.6	4.5	6.6	2.7	6.6
2002	5.8	5.9	18.1	5.3	5.6	14.9	5.1	16.5	5.1	10.2	5.9	7.5	3.6	8.0
2003	6.0	6.3	19.3	5.6	5.7	15.6	5.1	17.5	5.2	10.8	6.0	7.7	3.8	8.5
2004	5.5	5.6	18.4	5.0	5.4	15.5	4.9	17.0	4.8	10.4	4.4	7.0	3.1	8.0
2005	5.1	5.1	18.6	4.4	5.1	14.5	4.6	16.6	4.4	10.0	4.0	6.0	2.8	7.8
2006	4.6	4.6	16.9	4.0	4.6	13.8	4.1	15.4	4.0	8.9	3.0	5.2	2.4	7.1
2007	4.6	4.7	17.6	4.1	4.5	13.8	4.0	15.7	4.1	8.3	3.2	5.6	2.5	6.5
2008	5.8	6.1	21.2	5.4	5.4	16.2	4.9	18.7	5.2	10.1	4.0	7.6	3.4	8.0
2009	9.3	10.3	27.8	9.6	8.1	20.7	7.5	24.3	8.5	14.8	7.3	12.1	6.6	11.5
2010	9.6	10.5	28.8	9.8	8.6	22.8	8.0	25.9	8.7	16.0	7.5	12.5	6.8	12.3
2011	8.9	9.4	27.2	8.7	8.5	21.7	7.9	24.4	7.9	15.8	7.0	11.5	5.8	12.4
2012	8.1	8.2	26.8	7.5	7.9	21.1	7.3	24.0	7.2	13.8	5.9	10.3	4.9	11.4
2013	7.4	7.6	25.5	7.0	7.1	20.3	6.5	22.9	6.5	13.1	5.2	9.1	4.3	10.2
2014	6.2	6.3	21.4	5.7	6.1	17.7	5.6	19.6	5.3	11.3	5.0	7.4	3.4	8.6
2015	5.3	5.4	18.4	4.9	5.2	15.5	4.8	16.9	4.6	9.6	3.8	6.6	2.8	7.4
2014: Jan	6.6	6.7	22.7	6.2	6.4	18.6	5.9	20.7	5.7	12.1	4.8	8.3	3.8	9.1
Feb	6.7	6.9	24.5	6.3	6.4	18.4	5.9	21.4	5.8	11.9	5.9	8.1	3.8	9.1
Mar	6.7	6.7	23.6	6.1	6.7	18.1	6.2	20.9	5.7	12.2	5.5	7.9	3.7	9.0
Apr	6.2	6.4	21.5	5.9	6.1	17.1	5.6	19.3	5.3	11.5	5.8	7.4	3.5	8.5
May	6.2	6.3	20.6	5.8	6.2	18.0	5.7	19.3	5.4	11.4	5.6	7.7	3.3	8.4
June	6.1	6.3	22.2	5.7	5.9	18.5	5.4	20.3	5.3	10.8	4.8	7.6	3.4	8.1
July	6.2	6.2	21.9	5.7	6.1	18.4	5.6	20.2	5.3	11.6	4.2	7.6	3.3	9.1
Aug	6.2	6.2	21.2	5.7	6.1	17.4	5.6	19.3	5.3	11.5	4.6	7.4	3.3	9.3
Sept	6.0	5.9	22.2	5.4	6.0	17.7	5.5	19.9	5.1	11.0	4.5	7.0	2.9	8.3
Oct	5.7	5.6	19.9	5.1	5.9	17.7	5.4	18.8	4.9	10.8	5.0	6.8	3.0	8.7
Nov	5.8	5.9	17.6	5.4	5.7	17.4	5.2	17.5	5.0	10.9	4.7	6.6	3.2	8.2
Dec	5.6	5.8	19.4	5.3	5.4	14.0	5.0	16.8	4.8	10.4	4.2	6.5	3.0	7.8
2015: Jan	5.7	5.8	20.0	5.3	5.5	17.8	5.0	18.9	4.9	10.3	4.0	6.7	2.9	8.1
Feb	5.5	5.8	17.7	5.2	5.4	16.3	4.9	17.0	4.7	10.3	4.0	6.7	3.0	7.7
Mar	5.5	5.6	19.8	5.1	5.3	15.3	4.9	17.6	4.7	10.0	3.2	6.8	2.8	8.1
Apr	5.4	5.5	17.8	5.0	5.4	16.3	4.9	17.1	4.7	9.6	4.4	6.9	3.0	7.0
May	5.5	5.5	20.4	5.0	5.4	15.2	5.0	17.8	4.7	10.2	4.1	6.7	2.9	6.8
June	5.3	5.3	20.1	4.8	5.2	15.8	4.7	17.9	4.6	9.5	3.8	6.6	2.8	7.8
July	5.3	5.2	17.6	4.8	5.3	14.9	4.9	16.3	4.6	9.1	4.0	6.8	2.8	8.0
Aug	5.1	5.1	17.6	4.7	5.1	15.9	4.7	16.8	4.4	9.4	3.5	6.6	2.8	8.1
Sept	5.1	5.1	16.8	4.7	5.0	15.6	4.5	16.2	4.4	9.2	3.7	6.4	2.8	7.1
Oct	5.0	5.1	16.7	4.7	4.9	14.9	4.5	15.8	4.4	9.2	3.5	6.4	2.8	7.5
Nov	5.0	5.2	18.1	4.7	4.9	13.0	4.6	15.6	4.4	9.4	3.9	6.4	2.7	6.9
Dec	5.0	5.2	17.7	4.7	4.8	14.4	4.4	16.1	4.5	8.3	4.0	6.3	2.7	5.8

[1] Unemployed as percent of civilian labor force in group specified.
[2] Beginning in 2003, persons who selected this race group only. Prior to 2003, persons who selected more than one race were included in the group they identified as the main race. Data for "black or African American" were for "black" prior to 2003. See *Employment and Earnings* or concepts and methodology of the CPS at http://www.bls.gov/cps/documentation.htm#concepts for details.
[3] Persons whose ethnicity is identified as Hispanic or Latino may be of any race.
[4] Not seasonally adjusted.

Note: Data relate to persons 16 years of age and over.
See Note, Table B–11.

Source: Department of Labor (Bureau of Labor Statistics).

TABLE B–13. Unemployment by duration and reason, 1972–2015

[Thousands of persons, except as noted; monthly data seasonally adjusted [1]]

Year or month	Un-employ-ment	Duration of unemployment						Reason for unemployment					
		Less than 5 weeks	5–14 weeks	15–26 weeks	27 weeks and over	Average (mean) duration (weeks)[2]	Median duration (weeks)	Job losers[3]			Job leavers	Re-entrants	New entrants
								Total	On layoff	Other			
1972	4,882	2,242	1,472	601	566	12.0	6.2	2,108	582	1,526	641	1,456	677
1973	4,365	2,224	1,314	483	343	10.0	5.2	1,694	472	1,221	683	1,340	649
1974	5,156	2,604	1,597	574	381	9.8	5.2	2,242	746	1,495	768	1,463	681
1975	7,929	2,940	2,484	1,303	1,203	14.2	8.4	4,386	1,671	2,714	827	1,892	823
1976	7,406	2,844	2,196	1,018	1,348	15.8	8.2	3,679	1,050	2,628	903	1,928	895
1977	6,991	2,919	2,132	913	1,028	14.3	7.0	3,166	865	2,300	909	1,963	953
1978	6,202	2,865	1,923	766	648	11.9	5.9	2,585	712	1,873	874	1,857	885
1979	6,137	2,950	1,946	706	535	10.8	5.4	2,635	851	1,784	880	1,806	817
1980	7,637	3,295	2,470	1,052	820	11.9	6.5	3,947	1,488	2,459	891	1,927	872
1981	8,273	3,449	2,539	1,122	1,162	13.7	6.9	4,267	1,430	2,837	923	2,102	981
1982	10,678	3,883	3,311	1,708	1,776	15.6	8.7	6,268	2,127	4,141	840	2,384	1,185
1983	10,717	3,570	2,937	1,652	2,559	20.0	10.1	6,258	1,780	4,478	830	2,412	1,216
1984	8,539	3,350	2,451	1,104	1,634	18.2	7.9	4,421	1,171	3,250	823	2,184	1,110
1985	8,312	3,498	2,509	1,025	1,280	15.6	6.8	4,139	1,157	2,982	877	2,256	1,039
1986	8,237	3,448	2,557	1,045	1,187	15.0	6.9	4,033	1,090	2,943	1,015	2,160	1,029
1987	7,425	3,246	2,196	943	1,040	14.5	6.5	3,566	943	2,623	965	1,974	920
1988	6,701	3,084	2,007	801	809	13.5	5.9	3,092	851	2,241	983	1,809	816
1989	6,528	3,174	1,978	730	646	11.9	4.8	2,983	850	2,133	1,024	1,843	677
1990	7,047	3,265	2,257	822	703	12.0	5.3	3,387	1,028	2,359	1,041	1,930	688
1991	8,628	3,480	2,791	1,246	1,111	13.7	6.8	4,694	1,292	3,402	1,004	2,139	792
1992	9,613	3,376	2,830	1,453	1,954	17.7	8.7	5,389	1,260	4,129	1,002	2,285	937
1993	8,940	3,262	2,584	1,297	1,798	18.0	8.3	4,848	1,115	3,733	976	2,198	919
1994	7,996	2,728	2,408	1,237	1,623	18.8	9.2	3,815	977	2,838	791	2,786	604
1995	7,404	2,700	2,342	1,085	1,278	16.6	8.3	3,476	1,030	2,446	824	2,525	579
1996	7,236	2,633	2,287	1,053	1,262	16.7	8.3	3,370	1,021	2,349	774	2,512	580
1997	6,739	2,538	2,138	995	1,067	15.8	8.0	3,037	931	2,106	795	2,338	569
1998	6,210	2,622	1,950	763	875	14.5	6.7	2,822	866	1,957	734	2,132	520
1999	5,880	2,568	1,832	755	725	13.4	6.4	2,622	848	1,774	783	2,005	469
2000	5,692	2,558	1,815	669	649	12.6	5.9	2,517	852	1,664	780	1,961	434
2001	6,801	2,853	2,196	951	801	13.1	6.8	3,476	1,067	2,409	835	2,031	459
2002	8,378	2,893	2,580	1,369	1,535	16.6	9.1	4,607	1,124	3,483	866	2,368	536
2003	8,774	2,785	2,612	1,442	1,936	19.2	10.1	4,838	1,121	3,717	818	2,477	641
2004	8,149	2,696	2,382	1,293	1,779	19.6	9.8	4,197	998	3,199	858	2,408	686
2005	7,591	2,667	2,304	1,130	1,490	18.4	8.9	3,667	933	2,734	872	2,386	666
2006	7,001	2,614	2,121	1,031	1,235	16.8	8.3	3,321	921	2,400	827	2,237	616
2007	7,078	2,542	2,232	1,061	1,243	16.8	8.5	3,515	976	2,539	793	2,142	627
2008	8,924	2,932	2,804	1,427	1,761	17.9	9.4	4,789	1,176	3,614	896	2,472	766
2009	14,265	3,165	3,828	2,775	4,496	24.4	15.1	9,160	1,630	7,530	882	3,187	1,035
2010	14,825	2,771	3,267	2,371	6,415	33.0	21.4	9,250	1,431	7,819	889	3,466	1,220
2011	13,747	2,677	2,993	2,061	6,016	39.3	21.4	8,106	1,230	6,876	956	3,401	1,284
2012	12,506	2,644	2,866	1,859	5,136	39.4	19.3	6,877	1,183	5,694	967	3,345	1,316
2013	11,460	2,584	2,759	1,807	4,310	36.5	17.0	6,073	1,136	4,937	932	3,207	1,247
2014	9,617	2,471	2,432	1,497	3,218	33.7	14.0	4,878	1,007	3,871	824	2,829	1,086
2015	8,296	2,399	2,302	1,267	2,328	29.2	11.6	4,063	974	3,089	819	2,535	879
2014: Jan	10,192	2,467	2,442	1,679	3,597	35.2	15.6	5,372	1,022	4,350	809	2,882	1,171
Feb	10,375	2,386	2,602	1,575	3,773	36.7	16.0	5,407	1,026	4,381	806	2,972	1,222
Mar	10,415	2,453	2,575	1,684	3,675	35.2	15.9	5,450	1,043	4,407	799	3,018	1,162
Apr	9,699	2,427	2,360	1,559	3,400	34.6	15.9	5,164	1,026	4,138	790	2,600	1,076
May	9,719	2,548	2,365	1,443	3,352	34.2	14.5	4,915	982	3,933	871	2,852	1,060
June	9,470	2,434	2,402	1,508	3,113	33.6	13.5	4,803	1,004	3,800	853	2,744	1,059
July	9,651	2,540	2,434	1,421	3,193	32.8	13.5	4,815	983	3,831	856	2,882	1,089
Aug	9,617	2,656	2,413	1,496	2,978	32.1	13.2	4,770	1,086	3,683	856	2,877	1,053
Sept	9,296	2,377	2,515	1,441	2,969	32.1	13.3	4,555	947	3,608	819	2,813	1,095
Oct	8,989	2,481	2,304	1,428	2,894	32.7	13.4	4,337	862	3,475	790	2,858	1,062
Nov	9,053	2,494	2,374	1,399	2,829	32.8	12.8	4,474	1,076	3,398	839	2,756	1,037
Dec	8,704	2,371	2,309	1,261	2,772	32.5	12.6	4,330	963	3,367	796	2,679	966
2015: Jan	8,920	2,390	2,332	1,371	2,776	32.0	13.4	4,246	919	3,327	851	2,836	1,026
Feb	8,646	2,432	2,251	1,317	2,677	31.4	13.0	4,177	1,027	3,150	880	2,632	949
Mar	8,557	2,488	2,330	1,255	2,547	30.4	12.1	4,194	1,004	3,190	870	2,666	812
Apr	8,523	2,707	2,339	1,162	2,503	30.5	11.6	4,130	959	3,171	824	2,649	867
May	8,619	2,397	2,507	1,286	2,491	30.5	11.6	4,263	1,041	3,222	823	2,584	963
June	8,262	2,347	2,350	1,385	2,128	28.1	11.4	4,060	1,040	3,019	767	2,488	931
July	8,249	2,471	2,249	1,182	2,190	28.3	11.4	4,116	989	3,127	844	2,441	827
Aug	8,018	2,106	2,354	1,254	2,189	28.3	12.1	4,014	968	3,046	787	2,344	846
Sept	7,925	2,373	2,211	1,228	2,109	26.3	11.3	3,883	901	2,982	778	2,443	832
Oct	7,899	2,339	2,295	1,227	2,132	28.0	11.1	3,944	936	3,007	790	2,435	812
Nov	7,924	2,412	2,253	1,270	2,054	27.9	10.7	3,873	939	2,934	800	2,449	847
Dec	7,904	2,405	2,192	1,235	2,085	27.6	10.5	3,796	937	2,859	821	2,476	858

[1] Because of independent seasonal adjustment of the various series, detail will not sum to totals.
[2] Beginning with 2011, includes unemployment durations of up to 5 years; prior data are for up to 2 years.
[3] Beginning with 1994, job losers and persons who completed temporary jobs.

Note: Data relate to persons 16 years of age and over.
See Note, Table B–11.

Source: Department of Labor (Bureau of Labor Statistics).

TABLE B–14. Employees on nonagricultural payrolls, by major industry, 1972–2015

[Thousands of jobs; monthly data seasonally adjusted]

Year or month	Total non-agricultural employment	Total private	Goods-producing industries Total	Mining and logging	Construction	Manufacturing Total	Manufacturing Durable goods	Manufacturing Non-durable goods	Private service-providing industries Total	Trade, transportation, and utilities [1] Total	Trade, transportation, and utilities [1] Retail trade
1972	73,798	60,333	22,299	672	3,957	17,669	10,630	7,039	38,034	14,788	8,038
1973	76,912	63,050	23,450	693	4,167	18,589	11,414	7,176	39,600	15,349	8,371
1974	78,389	64,086	23,364	755	4,095	18,514	11,432	7,082	40,721	15,693	8,536
1975	77,069	62,250	21,318	802	3,608	16,909	10,266	6,643	40,932	15,606	8,600
1976	79,502	64,501	22,025	832	3,662	17,531	10,640	6,891	42,476	16,128	8,966
1977	82,593	67,334	22,972	865	3,940	18,167	11,132	7,035	44,362	16,765	9,359
1978	86,826	71,014	24,156	902	4,322	18,932	11,770	7,162	46,858	17,658	9,879
1979	89,933	73,865	24,997	1,008	4,562	19,426	12,220	7,206	48,869	18,303	10,180
1980	90,533	74,158	24,263	1,077	4,454	18,733	11,679	7,054	49,895	18,413	10,244
1981	91,297	75,117	24,118	1,180	4,304	18,634	11,611	7,023	50,999	18,604	10,364
1982	89,689	73,706	22,550	1,163	4,024	17,363	10,610	6,753	51,156	18,457	10,372
1983	90,295	74,284	22,110	997	4,065	17,048	10,326	6,722	52,174	18,668	10,635
1984	94,548	78,389	23,435	1,014	4,501	17,920	11,050	6,870	54,954	19,653	11,223
1985	97,532	81,000	23,585	974	4,793	17,819	11,034	6,784	57,415	20,379	11,733
1986	99,500	82,661	23,318	829	4,937	17,552	10,795	6,757	59,343	20,795	12,078
1987	102,116	84,960	23,470	771	5,090	17,609	10,767	6,842	61,490	21,302	12,419
1988	105,378	87,838	23,909	770	5,233	17,906	10,969	6,938	63,929	21,974	12,808
1989	108,051	90,124	24,045	750	5,309	17,985	11,004	6,981	66,079	22,510	13,108
1990	109,527	91,112	23,723	765	5,263	17,695	10,737	6,958	67,389	22,666	13,182
1991	108,427	89,881	22,588	739	4,780	17,068	10,220	6,848	67,293	22,281	12,896
1992	108,802	90,015	22,095	689	4,608	16,799	9,946	6,853	67,921	22,125	12,828
1993	110,935	91,946	22,219	666	4,779	16,774	9,901	6,872	69,727	22,378	13,021
1994	114,398	95,124	22,774	659	5,095	17,020	10,132	6,889	72,350	23,128	13,491
1995	117,407	97,975	23,156	641	5,274	17,241	10,373	6,868	74,819	23,834	13,897
1996	119,836	100,297	23,409	637	5,536	17,237	10,486	6,751	76,888	24,239	14,143
1997	122,951	103,287	23,886	654	5,813	17,419	10,705	6,714	79,401	24,700	14,389
1998	126,157	106,248	24,354	645	6,149	17,560	10,911	6,649	81,894	25,186	14,609
1999	129,240	108,933	24,465	598	6,545	17,322	10,831	6,491	84,468	25,771	14,970
2000	132,024	111,235	24,649	599	6,787	17,263	10,877	6,386	86,585	26,225	15,280
2001	132,087	110,969	23,873	606	6,826	16,441	10,336	6,105	87,096	25,983	15,239
2002	130,649	109,136	22,557	583	6,716	15,259	9,485	5,774	86,579	25,497	15,025
2003	130,347	108,764	21,816	572	6,735	14,509	8,964	5,546	86,948	25,287	14,917
2004	131,787	110,166	21,882	591	6,976	14,315	8,925	5,390	88,284	25,533	15,058
2005	134,051	112,247	22,190	628	7,336	14,227	8,956	5,271	90,057	25,959	15,280
2006	136,453	114,479	22,530	684	7,691	14,155	8,981	5,174	91,949	26,276	15,353
2007	137,999	115,781	22,233	724	7,630	13,879	8,808	5,071	93,548	26,630	15,520
2008	137,242	114,732	21,335	767	7,162	13,406	8,463	4,943	93,398	26,293	15,283
2009	131,313	108,758	18,558	694	6,016	11,847	7,284	4,564	90,201	24,906	14,522
2010	130,361	107,871	17,751	705	5,518	11,528	7,064	4,464	90,120	24,636	14,440
2011	131,932	109,845	18,047	788	5,533	11,726	7,273	4,453	91,798	25,065	14,668
2012	134,175	112,255	18,420	848	5,646	11,927	7,470	4,457	93,834	25,476	14,841
2013	136,381	114,529	18,738	863	5,856	12,020	7,548	4,472	95,791	25,862	15,079
2014	138,958	117,076	19,226	891	6,151	12,185	7,674	4,512	97,850	26,383	15,357
2015 p	141,865	119,858	19,583	820	6,446	12,317	7,755	4,562	100,275	26,920	15,641
2014: Jan	137,574	115,767	18,966	873	5,999	12,094	7,591	4,503	96,801	26,147	15,259
Feb	137,742	115,925	19,010	875	6,020	12,115	7,610	4,505	96,915	26,142	15,241
Mar	138,014	116,186	19,066	879	6,062	12,125	7,624	4,501	97,120	26,182	15,262
Apr	138,324	116,468	19,127	885	6,103	12,139	7,634	4,505	97,341	26,253	15,301
May	138,537	116,683	19,146	885	6,115	12,146	7,647	4,499	97,537	26,293	15,310
June	138,843	116,950	19,189	890	6,128	12,171	7,667	4,504	97,761	26,361	15,347
July	139,075	117,194	19,254	896	6,169	12,189	7,684	4,505	97,940	26,410	15,369
Aug	139,293	117,425	19,297	898	6,194	12,205	7,696	4,509	98,128	26,434	15,377
Sept	139,579	117,662	19,340	904	6,219	12,217	7,704	4,513	98,322	26,484	15,406
Oct	139,779	117,852	19,378	902	6,233	12,243	7,723	4,520	98,474	26,529	15,420
Nov	140,110	118,176	19,428	900	6,256	12,272	7,740	4,532	98,748	26,615	15,478
Dec	140,402	118,455	19,492	897	6,301	12,294	7,754	4,540	98,963	26,656	15,477
2015: Jan	140,623	118,669	19,552	890	6,351	12,311	7,764	4,547	99,117	26,698	15,510
Feb	140,888	118,921	19,568	875	6,378	12,315	7,769	4,546	99,353	26,750	15,539
Mar	140,972	119,011	19,548	859	6,371	12,318	7,769	4,549	99,463	26,788	15,564
Apr	141,223	119,252	19,569	844	6,409	12,316	7,765	4,551	99,683	26,815	15,578
May	141,496	119,508	19,574	824	6,426	12,324	7,767	4,557	99,934	26,861	15,605
June	141,724	119,734	19,571	820	6,426	12,325	7,765	4,560	100,163	26,909	15,640
July	142,001	119,979	19,585	812	6,437	12,336	7,762	4,574	100,394	26,963	15,671
Aug	142,151	120,102	19,562	803	6,441	12,318	7,756	4,562	100,540	26,978	15,675
Sept	142,300	120,264	19,550	790	6,451	12,309	7,749	4,560	100,714	26,987	15,681
Oct	142,595	120,568	19,581	786	6,484	12,311	7,745	4,566	100,987	27,011	15,702
Nov	142,875	120,847	19,634	771	6,549	12,314	7,733	4,581	101,213	27,087	15,754
Dec p	143,137	121,098	19,688	764	6,597	12,327	7,734	4,593	101,410	27,109	15,753

[1] Includes wholesale trade, transportation and warehousing, and utilities, not shown separately.

Note: Data in Tables B–14 and B–15 are based on reports from employing establishments and relate to full- and part-time wage and salary workers in nonagricultural establishments who received pay for any part of the pay period that includes the 12th of the month. Not comparable with labor force data (Tables B–11 through B–13), which include proprietors, self-employed persons, unpaid family workers, and private household workers; which count persons as

See next page for continuation of table.

TABLE B–14. Employees on nonagricultural payrolls, by major industry, 1972–2015—*Continued*

[Thousands of jobs; monthly data seasonally adjusted]

Year or month	Private industries—Continued						Government			
	Private service-providing industries—Continued									
	Information	Financial activities	Professional and business services	Education and health services	Leisure and hospitality	Other services	Total	Federal	State	Local
1972	2,056	3,784	5,523	4,863	5,121	1,900	13,465	2,815	2,859	7,790
1973	2,135	3,920	5,774	5,092	5,341	1,990	13,862	2,794	2,923	8,146
1974	2,160	4,023	5,974	5,322	5,471	2,078	14,303	2,858	3,039	8,407
1975	2,061	4,047	6,034	5,497	5,544	2,144	14,820	2,882	3,179	8,758
1976	2,111	4,155	6,287	5,756	5,794	2,244	15,001	2,863	3,273	8,865
1977	2,185	4,348	6,587	6,052	6,065	2,359	15,258	2,859	3,377	9,023
1978	2,287	4,599	6,972	6,427	6,411	2,505	15,812	2,893	3,474	9,446
1979	2,375	4,843	7,312	6,768	6,631	2,637	16,068	2,894	3,541	9,633
1980	2,361	5,025	7,544	7,077	6,721	2,755	16,375	3,000	3,610	9,765
1981	2,382	5,163	7,782	7,364	6,840	2,865	16,180	2,922	3,640	9,619
1982	2,317	5,209	7,848	7,526	6,874	2,924	15,982	2,884	3,640	9,458
1983	2,253	5,334	8,039	7,781	7,078	3,021	16,011	2,915	3,662	9,434
1984	2,398	5,553	8,464	8,211	7,489	3,186	16,159	2,943	3,734	9,482
1985	2,437	5,815	8,871	8,679	7,869	3,366	16,533	3,014	3,832	9,687
1986	2,445	6,128	9,211	9,086	8,156	3,523	16,838	3,044	3,893	9,901
1987	2,507	6,385	9,608	9,543	8,446	3,699	17,156	3,089	3,967	10,100
1988	2,585	6,500	10,090	10,096	8,778	3,907	17,540	3,124	4,076	10,339
1989	2,622	6,562	10,555	10,652	9,062	4,116	17,927	3,136	4,182	10,609
1990	2,688	6,614	10,848	11,024	9,288	4,261	18,415	3,196	4,305	10,914
1991	2,677	6,561	10,714	11,556	9,256	4,249	18,545	3,110	4,355	11,081
1992	2,641	6,559	10,970	11,948	9,437	4,240	18,787	3,111	4,408	11,267
1993	2,668	6,742	11,495	12,362	9,732	4,350	18,989	3,063	4,488	11,438
1994	2,738	6,910	12,174	12,872	10,100	4,428	19,275	3,018	4,576	11,682
1995	2,843	6,866	12,844	13,360	10,501	4,572	19,432	2,949	4,635	11,849
1996	2,940	7,018	13,462	13,761	10,777	4,690	19,539	2,877	4,606	12,056
1997	3,084	7,255	14,335	14,185	11,018	4,825	19,664	2,806	4,582	12,276
1998	3,218	7,565	15,147	14,570	11,232	4,976	19,909	2,772	4,612	12,525
1999	3,419	7,753	15,957	14,939	11,543	5,087	20,307	2,769	4,709	12,829
2000	3,630	7,783	16,666	15,252	11,862	5,168	20,790	2,865	4,786	13,139
2001	3,629	7,900	16,476	15,814	12,036	5,258	21,118	2,764	4,905	13,449
2002	3,395	7,956	15,976	16,398	11,986	5,372	21,513	2,766	5,029	13,718
2003	3,188	8,078	15,987	16,835	12,173	5,401	21,583	2,761	5,002	13,820
2004	3,118	8,105	16,394	17,230	12,493	5,409	21,621	2,730	4,982	13,909
2005	3,061	8,197	16,954	17,676	12,816	5,395	21,804	2,732	5,032	14,041
2006	3,038	8,367	17,566	18,154	13,110	5,438	21,974	2,732	5,075	14,167
2007	3,032	8,348	17,942	18,676	13,427	5,494	22,218	2,734	5,122	14,362
2008	2,984	8,206	17,735	19,228	13,436	5,515	22,509	2,762	5,177	14,571
2009	2,804	7,838	16,579	19,630	13,077	5,367	22,555	2,832	5,169	14,554
2010	2,707	7,695	16,728	19,975	13,049	5,331	22,490	2,977	5,137	14,376
2011	2,674	7,697	17,332	20,318	13,353	5,360	22,086	2,859	5,078	14,150
2012	2,676	7,784	17,932	20,769	13,768	5,430	21,920	2,820	5,055	14,045
2013	2,706	7,886	18,515	21,086	14,254	5,483	21,853	2,769	5,046	14,037
2014	2,726	7,977	19,062	21,439	14,696	5,567	21,882	2,733	5,064	14,084
2015 *p*	2,750	8,124	19,672	22,055	15,128	5,625	22,007	2,754	5,103	14,150
2014: Jan	2,721	7,915	18,770	21,220	14,494	5,534	21,807	2,733	5,048	14,026
Feb	2,716	7,931	18,831	21,248	14,512	5,535	21,817	2,730	5,055	14,032
Mar	2,724	7,933	18,878	21,290	14,561	5,552	21,828	2,728	5,054	14,046
Apr	2,723	7,942	18,942	21,312	14,605	5,564	21,856	2,726	5,058	14,072
May	2,717	7,951	18,981	21,367	14,662	5,566	21,854	2,726	5,058	14,070
June	2,723	7,967	19,047	21,408	14,693	5,562	21,893	2,729	5,063	14,101
July	2,728	7,981	19,093	21,449	14,714	5,565	21,881	2,730	5,061	14,090
Aug	2,737	7,994	19,148	21,501	14,735	5,579	21,868	2,733	5,048	14,087
Sept	2,735	8,008	19,199	21,551	14,771	5,574	21,917	2,735	5,069	14,113
Oct	2,729	8,014	19,227	21,578	14,818	5,579	21,927	2,735	5,079	14,113
Nov	2,732	8,033	19,292	21,628	14,856	5,592	21,934	2,742	5,080	14,112
Dec	2,733	8,041	19,360	21,677	14,901	5,595	21,947	2,746	5,088	14,113
2015: Jan	2,734	8,061	19,370	21,731	14,924	5,599	21,954	2,743	5,092	14,119
Feb	2,738	8,070	19,409	21,790	14,989	5,607	21,967	2,747	5,096	14,124
Mar	2,735	8,082	19,436	21,828	14,989	5,605	21,961	2,747	5,094	14,120
Apr	2,745	8,089	19,505	21,905	15,010	5,614	21,971	2,750	5,096	14,125
May	2,747	8,098	19,585	21,962	15,059	5,622	21,988	2,752	5,096	14,140
June	2,751	8,117	19,661	22,017	15,089	5,619	21,990	2,752	5,099	14,139
July	2,756	8,137	19,707	22,075	15,125	5,631	22,022	2,751	5,098	14,173
Aug	2,753	8,150	19,742	22,137	15,158	5,622	22,049	2,753	5,106	14,190
Sept	2,766	8,153	19,782	22,192	15,208	5,626	22,036	2,754	5,113	14,169
Oct	2,771	8,164	19,873	22,251	15,261	5,637	22,027	2,752	5,114	14,161
Nov	2,753	8,182	19,921	22,315	15,307	5,648	22,028	2,758	5,110	14,160
Dec *p*	2,761	8,192	19,981	22,369	15,338	5,660	22,039	2,766	5,109	14,164

Note (cont'd): employed when they are not at work because of industrial disputes, bad weather, etc., even if they are not paid for the time off; which are based on a sample of the working-age population; and which count persons only once—as employed, unemployed, or not in the labor force. In the data shown here, persons who work at more than one job are counted each time they appear on a payroll.

Establishment data for employment, hours, and earnings are classified based on the 2012 North American Industry Classification System (NAICS). For further description and details see *Employment and Earnings.*

Source: Department of Labor (Bureau of Labor Statistics).

Table B-15. Hours and earnings in private nonagricultural industries, 1972–2015

[Monthly data seasonally adjusted]

Year or month	All employees							Production and nonsupervisory employees [1]						
	Average weekly hours	Average hourly earnings		Average weekly earnings				Average weekly hours	Average hourly earnings		Average weekly earnings			
				Level		Percent change from year earlier					Level		Percent change from year earlier	
		Current dollars	1982–84 dollars[2]	Current dollars	1982–84 dollars[2]	Current dollars	1982–84 dollars[2]		Current dollars	1982–84 dollars[3]	Current dollars	1982–84 dollars[3]	Current dollars	1982–84 dollars[3]
1972								36.9	$3.90	$9.26	$143.87	$341.73	8.0	4.4
1973								36.9	4.14	9.26	152.59	341.36	6.1	−.1
1974								36.4	4.43	8.93	161.61	325.83	5.9	−4.5
1975								36.0	4.73	8.74	170.29	314.77	5.4	−3.4
1976								36.1	5.06	8.85	182.65	319.32	7.3	1.4
1977								35.9	5.44	8.93	195.58	321.15	7.1	.6
1978								35.8	5.88	8.96	210.29	320.56	7.5	−.2
1979								35.6	6.34	8.67	225.69	308.74	7.3	−3.7
1980								35.2	6.85	8.26	241.07	290.80	6.8	−5.8
1981								35.2	7.44	8.14	261.53	286.14	8.5	−1.6
1982								34.7	7.87	8.12	273.10	281.84	4.4	−1.5
1983								34.9	8.20	8.22	286.43	287.00	4.9	1.8
1984								35.1	8.49	8.22	298.26	288.73	4.1	.6
1985								34.9	8.74	8.18	304.62	284.96	2.1	−1.3
1986								34.7	8.93	8.22	309.78	285.25	1.7	.1
1987								34.7	9.14	8.12	317.39	282.12	2.5	−1.1
1988								34.6	9.44	8.07	326.48	279.04	2.9	−1.1
1989								34.5	9.80	7.99	338.34	275.97	3.6	−1.1
1990								34.3	10.20	7.91	349.63	271.03	3.3	−1.8
1991								34.1	10.51	7.83	358.46	266.91	2.5	−1.5
1992								34.2	10.77	7.79	368.20	266.43	2.7	−.2
1993								34.3	11.05	7.78	378.89	266.64	2.9	.1
1994								34.5	11.34	7.79	391.17	268.66	3.2	.8
1995								34.3	11.65	7.78	400.04	267.05	2.3	−.6
1996								34.3	12.04	7.81	413.25	268.17	3.3	.4
1997								34.5	12.51	7.94	431.86	274.02	4.5	2.2
1998								34.5	13.01	8.15	448.59	280.90	3.9	2.5
1999								34.3	13.49	8.27	463.15	283.79	3.2	1.0
2000								34.3	14.02	8.30	480.99	284.78	3.9	.3
2001								34.0	14.54	8.38	493.74	284.58	2.7	−.1
2002								33.9	14.96	8.50	506.54	287.97	2.6	1.2
2003								33.7	15.37	8.55	517.76	287.96	2.2	.0
2004								33.7	15.68	8.50	528.81	286.62	2.1	−.5
2005								33.8	16.12	8.44	544.00	284.82	2.9	−.6
2006								33.9	16.75	8.50	567.06	287.70	4.2	1.0
2007	34.4	$20.92	$10.09	$719.88	$347.19			33.8	17.42	8.59	589.18	290.57	3.9	1.0
2008	34.3	21.56	10.01	739.05	343.26	2.7	−1.1	33.6	18.06	8.56	607.42	287.80	3.1	−1.0
2009	33.8	22.18	10.34	750.09	349.63	1.5	1.9	33.1	18.61	8.88	615.96	293.83	1.4	2.1
2010	34.1	22.56	10.35	769.66	352.96	2.6	1.0	33.4	19.05	8.90	636.19	297.33	3.3	1.2
2011	34.3	23.03	10.24	791.07	351.68	2.8	−.4	33.6	19.44	8.77	652.89	294.66	2.6	−.9
2012	34.5	23.50	10.24	809.83	352.72	2.4	.3	33.7	19.74	8.73	665.65	294.24	2.0	−.1
2013	34.4	23.96	10.29	825.37	354.30	1.9	.4	33.7	20.13	8.78	677.73	295.53	1.8	.4
2014	34.5	24.47	10.34	845.00	356.94	2.4	.7	33.7	20.61	8.85	694.91	298.54	2.5	1.0
2015 ᵖ	34.5	25.03	10.56	864.59	364.78	2.3	2.2	33.7	21.04	9.08	709.13	305.91	2.0	2.5
2014: Jan	34.4	24.23	10.31	833.51	354.49	2.0	.4	33.5	20.40	8.81	683.40	295.28	2.0	.4
Feb	34.3	24.33	10.34	834.52	354.58	1.7	.6	33.4	20.50	8.85	684.70	295.68	1.3	.4
Mar	34.6	24.33	10.32	841.82	357.02	2.5	.9	33.7	20.49	8.83	690.51	297.65	2.3	.9
Apr	34.5	24.34	10.30	839.73	355.46	2.3	.3	33.7	20.52	8.83	691.52	297.47	2.4	.4
May	34.5	24.40	10.30	841.80	355.26	2.1	.0	33.7	20.55	8.81	692.54	297.06	2.4	.3
June	34.5	24.47	10.31	844.22	355.69	2.0	.0	33.7	20.59	8.82	693.88	297.10	2.3	.3
July	34.5	24.48	10.30	844.56	355.46	2.4	.4	33.7	20.63	8.83	695.23	297.45	2.7	.8
Aug	34.5	24.55	10.34	846.98	356.76	2.2	.4	33.8	20.67	8.85	698.65	299.24	2.7	1.1
Sept	34.5	24.56	10.34	847.32	356.68	2.3	.7	33.7	20.68	8.85	696.92	298.22	2.3	.7
Oct	34.5	24.58	10.34	848.01	356.68	2.3	.6	33.7	20.71	8.86	697.93	298.70	2.5	1.0
Nov	34.6	24.68	10.41	853.93	360.21	2.4	1.1	33.8	20.76	8.92	701.69	301.64	2.5	1.5
Dec	34.6	24.61	10.42	851.51	360.38	2.6	1.9	33.8	20.73	8.95	700.67	302.62	2.8	2.5
2015: Jan	34.6	24.76	10.55	856.70	365.05	2.8	3.0	33.8	20.81	9.07	703.38	306.65	2.9	3.9
Feb	34.6	24.80	10.54	858.08	364.85	2.8	2.9	33.8	20.83	9.06	704.05	306.14	2.8	3.5
Mar	34.5	24.87	10.58	858.02	363.97	1.9	1.9	33.7	20.89	9.06	703.99	305.22	2.0	2.5
Apr	34.5	24.91	10.56	859.40	364.18	2.3	2.5	33.7	20.93	9.07	705.34	305.58	2.0	2.7
May	34.5	24.97	10.53	861.47	363.44	2.3	2.3	33.6	20.99	9.05	705.26	303.93	1.8	2.3
June	34.5	24.96	10.50	861.12	362.14	2.0	1.8	33.6	21.00	9.02	705.60	303.05	1.7	2.0
July	34.6	25.03	10.51	866.04	363.73	2.5	2.3	33.7	21.05	9.03	709.39	304.28	2.0	2.3
Aug	34.6	25.12	10.58	869.15	365.29	2.6	2.4	33.7	21.11	9.06	711.41	305.47	1.8	2.1
Sept	34.5	25.14	10.58	867.33	365.09	2.4	2.4	33.7	21.12	9.09	711.74	306.50	2.1	2.8
Oct	34.5	25.21	10.59	869.75	365.38	2.6	2.4	33.7	21.21	9.12	714.78	307.23	2.4	2.9
Nov	34.5	25.27	10.61	871.82	366.14	2.1	1.6	33.7	21.23	9.13	715.45	307.57	2.0	2.0
Dec ᵖ	34.5	25.27	10.62	871.82	366.55	2.4	1.7	33.7	21.27	9.16	718.93	309.59	2.6	2.3

[1] Production employees in goods-producing industries and nonsupervisory employees in service-providing industries. These groups account for four-fifths of the total employment on private nonfarm payrolls.

[2] Current dollars divided by the consumer price index for all urban consumers (CPI-U) on a 1982–84=100 base.

[3] Current dollars divided by the consumer price index for urban wage earners and clerical workers (CPI-W) on a 1982–84=100 base.

Note: See Note, Table B–14.

Source: Department of Labor (Bureau of Labor Statistics).

[Index numbers, 2009=100; quarterly data seasonally adjusted]

Year or quarter	Labor productivity (output per hour)		Output[1]		Hours of all persons[2]		Compensation per hour[3]		Real compensation per hour[4]		Unit labor costs		Implicit price deflator[5]	
	Business sector	Nonfarm business sector	Business sector	Nonfarm business sector	Business sector	Nonfarm business sector	Business sector	Nonfarm business sector	Business sector	Nonfarm business sector	Business sector	Nonfarm business sector	Business sector	Nonfarm business sector
1967	42.0	43.8	27.3	27.3	64.9	62.4	10.4	10.6	60.9	62.1	24.7	24.2	23.0	22.5
1968	43.5	45.3	28.7	28.8	65.9	63.5	11.2	11.4	63.0	64.1	25.7	25.1	23.9	23.4
1969	43.7	45.4	29.6	29.7	67.6	65.3	12.0	12.2	63.9	65.0	27.4	26.8	25.0	24.4
1970	44.6	46.1	29.5	29.6	66.3	64.3	12.9	13.0	65.0	65.7	28.9	28.3	26.1	25.5
1971	46.4	47.9	30.7	30.7	66.1	64.1	13.7	13.8	66.0	66.8	29.4	28.9	27.2	26.6
1972	47.9	49.5	32.7	32.8	68.1	66.2	14.5	14.7	68.0	68.9	30.3	29.7	28.1	27.4
1973	49.3	51.0	34.9	35.2	70.7	68.9	15.7	15.8	69.1	69.8	31.7	31.0	29.6	28.4
1974	48.5	50.2	34.4	34.6	70.9	69.0	17.1	17.3	68.0	68.8	35.3	34.5	32.5	31.4
1975	50.2	51.6	34.0	34.1	67.8	66.0	19.0	19.2	69.0	69.7	37.8	37.2	35.6	34.7
1976	51.9	53.3	36.3	36.5	70.1	68.4	20.5	20.6	70.4	71.0	39.5	38.7	37.5	36.6
1977	52.8	54.2	38.4	38.6	72.8	71.1	22.1	22.3	71.4	72.2	41.9	41.2	39.7	38.9
1978	53.4	55.0	40.8	41.1	76.5	74.8	24.0	24.2	72.4	73.2	44.9	44.1	42.5	41.5
1979	53.4	54.8	42.3	42.5	79.1	77.5	26.3	26.6	72.5	73.3	49.2	48.5	46.1	45.0
1980	53.4	54.8	41.9	42.1	78.4	76.8	29.1	29.4	72.2	73.0	54.5	53.7	50.2	49.3
1981	54.6	55.7	43.1	43.1	78.9	77.4	31.9	32.3	72.2	73.1	58.4	58.0	54.8	54.0
1982	54.2	55.1	41.8	41.7	77.1	75.7	34.2	34.6	73.1	73.9	63.1	62.8	58.0	57.4
1983	56.2	57.5	44.1	44.4	78.5	77.2	35.8	36.2	73.3	74.1	63.6	62.9	60.0	59.2
1984	57.7	58.8	48.0	48.1	83.1	81.9	37.3	37.7	73.5	74.2	64.7	64.2	61.7	60.9
1985	59.0	59.7	50.2	50.2	85.0	84.0	39.2	39.6	74.6	75.3	66.5	66.3	63.5	62.9
1986	60.7	61.5	52.0	52.1	85.7	84.7	41.4	41.8	77.4	78.2	68.3	68.0	64.3	63.8
1987	61.0	61.8	53.9	54.0	88.2	87.2	43.0	43.4	77.7	78.5	70.5	70.2	65.6	65.1
1988	62.0	62.8	56.2	56.4	90.7	89.8	45.3	45.7	79.0	79.6	73.1	72.6	67.7	67.1
1989	62.7	63.4	58.3	58.5	93.1	92.2	46.7	47.0	78.0	78.5	74.5	74.1	70.2	69.5
1990	64.1	64.7	59.3	59.4	92.5	91.8	49.7	49.9	79.1	79.5	77.6	77.2	72.5	71.8
1991	65.2	65.9	58.9	59.0	90.3	89.6	52.1	52.4	80.1	80.5	79.9	79.6	74.5	74.1
1992	68.1	68.7	61.4	61.4	90.1	89.4	55.2	55.6	82.7	83.3	81.0	80.9	75.7	75.3
1993	68.2	68.8	63.2	63.3	92.6	92.1	56.0	56.2	81.9	82.3	82.1	81.8	77.5	77.0
1994	68.8	69.4	66.2	66.3	96.3	95.4	56.6	56.9	81.0	81.6	82.2	82.0	78.9	78.5
1995	69.0	69.9	68.3	68.6	99.0	98.1	57.7	58.1	80.7	81.2	83.5	83.0	80.2	79.8
1996	71.1	71.8	71.5	71.7	100.6	99.8	60.1	60.4	81.8	82.3	84.5	84.2	81.5	80.9
1997	72.4	73.0	75.3	75.4	103.9	103.3	62.3	62.5	83.0	83.4	85.9	85.7	82.7	82.3
1998	74.7	75.2	79.2	79.4	106.0	105.6	65.9	66.2	86.7	87.0	88.3	88.0	83.1	82.8
1999	77.3	77.7	83.6	83.8	108.1	107.9	68.8	68.9	88.7	88.8	89.1	88.8	83.7	83.6
2000	79.9	80.2	87.3	87.5	109.3	109.0	73.9	74.0	92.0	92.3	92.4	92.3	85.3	85.2
2001	82.1	82.4	87.9	88.1	107.0	106.9	77.3	77.3	93.6	93.6	94.1	93.8	86.8	86.6
2002	85.6	86.0	89.5	89.7	104.5	104.3	79.0	79.0	94.2	94.3	92.2	91.9	87.4	87.3
2003	88.9	89.1	92.3	92.5	103.8	103.7	82.0	82.0	95.6	95.7	92.1	92.0	88.6	88.5
2004	91.8	91.9	96.5	96.6	105.1	105.1	85.8	85.7	97.4	97.4	93.4	93.3	90.7	90.3
2005	93.7	93.8	100.1	100.2	106.8	106.9	88.8	88.8	97.6	97.6	94.8	94.7	93.5	93.4
2006	94.6	94.7	103.3	103.4	109.1	109.3	92.3	92.3	98.3	98.3	97.6	97.5	96.0	96.0
2007	96.0	96.2	105.5	105.8	109.8	110.0	96.4	96.3	99.8	99.7	100.4	100.1	98.2	97.9
2008	96.8	96.9	104.2	104.4	107.7	107.8	99.0	98.9	98.6	98.6	102.2	102.1	99.8	99.4
2009	100.0	100.0	100.0	100.0	100.0	100.0	100.0	100.0	100.0	100.0	100.0	100.0	100.0	100.0
2010	103.3	103.3	103.2	103.2	99.9	99.9	101.9	102.0	100.2	100.3	98.6	98.7	101.1	101.0
2011	103.4	103.5	105.3	105.5	101.9	101.9	104.1	104.2	99.3	99.4	100.7	100.7	103.3	102.8
2012	104.1	104.4	108.4	108.8	104.1	104.1	107.0	107.0	100.0	100.0	102.7	102.5	105.3	104.7
2013	104.6	104.4	110.6	110.6	105.7	105.9	108.3	108.2	99.7	99.6	103.6	103.6	106.9	106.3
2014	105.2	105.2	113.9	114.0	108.3	108.4	111.1	111.1	100.7	100.7	105.6	105.7	108.4	107.9
2015 p	105.8	105.8	117.2	117.1	110.8	110.7	114.3	114.4	103.4	103.6	108.0	108.2	109.1	109.0
2012: I	103.9	104.2	107.8	108.1	103.7	103.7	105.7	105.8	99.3	99.4	101.7	101.5	104.5	104.0
II	104.5	104.9	108.5	108.8	103.8	103.7	106.4	106.5	99.7	99.8	101.7	101.5	105.0	104.5
III	104.3	104.6	108.6	109.1	104.2	104.2	106.5	106.5	99.4	99.4	102.1	101.8	105.7	105.1
IV	103.8	104.1	108.7	109.1	104.8	104.9	109.3	109.3	101.4	101.3	105.3	105.0	106.0	105.3
2013: I	104.1	104.0	109.4	109.6	105.1	105.3	106.6	106.6	98.7	98.6	102.7	102.5	106.4	105.7
II	104.2	104.0	109.8	109.9	105.4	105.6	108.5	108.3	100.3	100.1	104.1	104.1	106.6	106.0
III	104.6	104.4	110.9	110.8	106.0	106.2	108.6	108.5	99.9	99.8	103.9	104.0	107.1	106.5
IV	105.4	105.3	112.2	112.2	106.5	106.6	109.2	109.1	100.0	100.0	103.6	103.7	107.4	107.0
2014: I	104.5	104.4	111.8	111.9	107.0	107.2	110.7	110.6	100.9	100.8	106.0	106.0	107.8	107.4
II	105.2	105.1	113.3	113.4	107.7	107.9	110.5	110.4	100.1	100.0	105.0	105.0	108.4	107.8
III	105.9	105.9	114.8	114.9	108.5	108.5	111.2	111.3	100.4	100.5	105.0	105.1	108.7	108.3
IV	105.2	105.3	115.6	115.6	109.9	109.8	112.0	112.2	101.4	101.6	106.5	106.5	108.5	108.2
2015: I	104.9	105.0	115.8	115.8	110.4	110.2	112.4	112.6	102.5	102.7	107.1	107.2	108.5	108.3
II	105.8	105.9	117.2	117.2	110.7	110.7	114.0	114.1	103.2	103.3	107.7	107.8	109.1	109.0
III	106.5	106.5	117.8	117.7	110.6	110.6	115.2	115.3	103.9	104.0	108.1	108.3	109.4	109.2
IV p	105.8	105.7	118.0	117.8	111.5	111.5	115.5	115.7	104.1	104.3	109.2	109.5	109.4	109.4

[1] Output refers to real gross domestic product in the sector.
[2] Hours at work of all persons engaged in sector, including hours of employees, proprietors, and unpaid family workers. Estimates based primarily on establishment data.
[3] Wages and salaries of employees plus employers' contributions for social insurance and private benefit plans. Also includes an estimate of wages, salaries, and supplemental payments for the self-employed.
[4] Hourly compensation divided by consumer price series. The trend for 1978-2014 is based on the consumer price index research series (CPI-U-RS). The change for prior years, 2015, and recent quarters is based on the consumer price index for all urban consumers (CPI-U).
[5] Current dollar output divided by the output index.

Source: Department of Labor (Bureau of Labor Statistics).

Table B–17. Federal receipts, outlays, surplus or deficit, and debt, fiscal years 1950–2017

[Billions of dollars; fiscal years]

Fiscal year or period	Total			On-budget			Off-budget			Federal debt (end of period)		Addendum: Gross domestic product
	Receipts	Outlays	Surplus or deficit (−)	Receipts	Outlays	Surplus or deficit (−)	Receipts	Outlays	Surplus or deficit (−)	Gross Federal	Held by the public	
1950	39.4	42.6	−3.1	37.3	42.0	−4.7	2.1	0.5	1.6	256.9	219.0	279.0
1951	51.6	45.5	6.1	48.5	44.2	4.3	3.1	1.3	1.8	255.3	214.3	327.4
1952	66.2	67.7	−1.5	62.6	66.0	−3.4	3.6	1.7	1.9	259.1	214.8	357.5
1953	69.6	76.1	−6.5	65.5	73.8	−8.3	4.1	2.3	1.8	266.0	218.4	382.5
1954	69.7	70.9	−1.2	65.1	67.9	−2.8	4.6	2.9	1.7	270.8	224.5	387.7
1955	65.5	68.4	−3.0	60.4	64.5	−4.1	5.1	4.0	1.1	274.4	226.6	407.0
1956	74.6	70.6	3.9	68.2	65.7	2.5	6.4	5.0	1.5	272.7	222.2	439.0
1957	80.0	76.6	3.4	73.2	70.6	2.6	6.8	6.0	.8	272.3	219.3	464.2
1958	79.6	82.4	−2.8	71.6	74.9	−3.3	8.0	7.5	.5	279.7	226.3	474.3
1959	79.2	92.1	−12.8	71.0	83.1	−12.1	8.3	9.0	−.7	287.5	234.7	505.6
1960	92.5	92.2	.3	81.9	81.3	.5	10.6	10.9	−.2	290.5	236.8	535.1
1961	94.4	97.7	−3.3	82.3	86.0	−3.8	12.1	11.7	.4	292.6	238.4	547.6
1962	99.7	106.8	−7.1	87.4	93.3	−5.9	12.3	13.5	−1.3	302.9	248.0	586.9
1963	106.6	111.3	−4.8	92.4	96.4	−4.0	14.2	15.0	−.8	310.3	254.0	619.3
1964	112.6	118.5	−5.9	96.2	102.8	−6.5	16.4	15.7	.6	316.1	256.8	662.9
1965	116.8	118.2	−1.4	100.1	101.7	−1.6	16.7	16.5	.2	322.3	260.8	710.7
1966	130.8	134.5	−3.7	111.7	114.8	−3.1	19.1	19.7	−.6	328.5	263.7	781.9
1967	148.8	157.5	−8.6	124.4	137.0	−12.6	24.4	20.4	4.0	340.4	266.6	838.2
1968	153.0	178.1	−25.2	128.1	155.8	−27.7	24.9	22.3	2.6	368.7	289.5	899.3
1969	186.9	183.6	3.2	157.9	158.4	−.5	29.0	25.2	3.7	365.8	278.1	982.3
1970	192.8	195.6	−2.8	159.3	168.0	−8.7	33.5	27.6	5.9	380.9	283.2	1,049.1
1971	187.1	210.2	−23.0	151.3	177.3	−26.1	35.8	32.8	3.0	408.2	303.0	1,119.3
1972	207.3	230.7	−23.4	167.4	193.5	−26.1	39.9	37.2	2.7	435.9	322.4	1,219.5
1973	230.8	245.7	−14.9	184.7	200.0	−15.2	46.1	45.7	.3	466.3	340.9	1,356.0
1974	263.2	269.4	−6.1	209.3	216.5	−7.2	53.9	52.9	1.1	483.9	343.7	1,486.2
1975	279.1	332.3	−53.2	216.6	270.8	−54.1	62.5	61.6	.9	541.9	394.7	1,610.6
1976	298.1	371.8	−73.7	231.7	301.1	−69.4	66.4	70.7	−4.3	629.0	477.4	1,790.3
Transition quarter	81.2	96.0	−14.7	63.2	77.3	−14.1	18.0	18.7	−.7	643.6	495.5	472.6
1977	355.6	409.2	−53.7	278.7	328.7	−49.9	76.8	80.5	−3.7	706.4	549.1	2,028.4
1978	399.6	458.7	−59.2	314.2	369.6	−55.4	85.4	89.2	−3.8	776.6	607.1	2,278.2
1979	463.3	504.0	−40.7	365.3	404.9	−39.6	98.0	99.1	−1.1	829.5	640.3	2,570.0
1980	517.1	590.9	−73.8	403.9	477.0	−73.1	113.2	113.9	−.7	909.0	711.9	2,796.8
1981	599.3	678.2	−79.0	469.1	543.0	−73.9	130.2	135.3	−5.1	994.8	789.4	3,138.4
1982	617.8	745.7	−128.0	474.3	594.9	−120.6	143.5	150.9	−7.4	1,137.3	924.6	3,313.9
1983	600.6	808.4	−207.8	453.2	660.9	−207.7	147.3	147.4	−.1	1,371.7	1,137.3	3,541.1
1984	666.4	851.8	−185.4	500.4	685.6	−185.3	166.1	166.2	−.1	1,564.6	1,307.0	3,952.8
1985	734.0	946.3	−212.3	547.9	769.4	−221.5	186.2	176.9	9.2	1,817.4	1,507.3	4,270.4
1986	769.2	990.4	−221.2	568.9	806.8	−237.9	200.2	183.5	16.7	2,120.5	1,740.6	4,536.1
1987	854.3	1,004.0	−149.7	640.9	809.2	−168.4	213.4	194.8	18.6	2,346.0	1,889.8	4,781.9
1988	909.2	1,064.4	−155.2	667.7	860.0	−192.3	241.5	204.4	37.1	2,601.1	2,051.6	5,155.1
1989	991.1	1,143.7	−152.6	727.4	932.8	−205.4	263.7	210.9	52.8	2,867.8	2,190.7	5,570.0
1990	1,032.0	1,253.0	−221.0	750.3	1,027.9	−277.6	281.7	225.1	56.6	3,206.3	2,411.6	5,914.6
1991	1,055.0	1,324.2	−269.2	761.1	1,082.5	−321.4	293.9	241.7	52.2	3,598.2	2,689.0	6,110.1
1992	1,091.2	1,381.5	−290.3	788.8	1,129.2	−340.4	302.4	252.3	50.1	4,001.8	2,999.7	6,434.7
1993	1,154.3	1,409.4	−255.1	842.4	1,142.8	−300.4	311.9	266.6	45.3	4,351.0	3,248.4	6,794.9
1994	1,258.6	1,461.8	−203.2	923.5	1,182.4	−258.8	335.0	279.4	55.7	4,643.3	3,433.1	7,197.8
1995	1,351.8	1,515.7	−164.0	1,000.7	1,227.1	−226.4	351.1	288.7	62.4	4,920.6	3,604.4	7,583.4
1996	1,453.1	1,560.5	−107.4	1,085.6	1,259.6	−174.0	367.5	300.9	66.6	5,181.5	3,734.1	7,978.3
1997	1,579.2	1,601.1	−21.9	1,187.2	1,290.5	−103.2	392.0	310.6	81.4	5,369.2	3,772.3	8,483.2
1998	1,721.7	1,652.5	69.3	1,305.9	1,335.9	−29.9	415.8	316.6	99.2	5,478.2	3,721.1	8,954.8
1999	1,827.5	1,701.8	125.6	1,383.0	1,381.1	1.9	444.5	320.8	123.7	5,605.5	3,632.4	9,510.5
2000	2,025.2	1,789.0	236.2	1,544.6	1,458.2	86.4	480.6	330.8	149.8	5,628.7	3,409.8	10,148.2
2001	1,991.1	1,862.8	128.2	1,483.6	1,516.0	−32.4	507.5	346.8	160.7	5,769.9	3,319.6	10,564.6
2002	1,853.1	2,010.9	−157.8	1,337.8	1,655.2	−317.4	515.3	355.7	159.7	6,198.4	3,540.4	10,876.9
2003	1,782.3	2,159.9	−377.6	1,258.5	1,796.9	−538.4	523.8	363.0	160.8	6,760.0	3,913.4	11,332.4
2004	1,880.1	2,292.8	−412.7	1,345.4	1,913.3	−568.0	534.7	379.5	155.2	7,354.7	4,295.5	12,088.6
2005	2,153.6	2,472.0	−318.3	1,576.1	2,069.7	−493.6	577.5	402.2	175.3	7,905.3	4,592.2	12,888.9
2006	2,406.9	2,655.1	−248.2	1,798.5	2,233.0	−434.5	608.4	422.1	186.3	8,451.4	4,829.0	13,684.7
2007	2,568.0	2,728.7	−160.7	1,932.9	2,275.0	−342.2	635.1	453.6	181.5	8,950.7	5,035.1	14,322.9
2008	2,524.0	2,982.5	−458.6	1,865.9	2,507.8	−641.8	658.0	474.8	183.3	9,986.1	5,803.1	14,752.4
2009	2,105.0	3,517.7	−1,412.7	1,451.0	3,000.7	−1,549.7	654.0	517.0	137.0	11,875.9	7,544.7	14,414.6
2010	2,162.7	3,457.1	−1,294.4	1,531.0	2,902.4	−1,371.4	631.7	554.7	77.0	13,528.8	9,018.9	14,798.5
2011	2,303.5	3,603.1	−1,299.6	1,737.7	3,104.5	−1,366.8	565.8	498.6	67.2	14,764.2	10,128.2	15,379.2
2012	2,450.0	3,537.0	−1,087.0	1,880.5	3,029.4	−1,148.9	569.5	507.6	61.9	16,050.9	11,281.1	16,027.2
2013	2,775.1	3,454.6	−679.5	2,101.8	2,820.8	−719.0	673.3	633.8	39.5	16,719.4	11,982.7	16,498.1
2014	3,021.5	3,506.1	−484.6	2,285.9	2,800.1	−514.1	735.6	706.1	29.5	17,794.5	12,779.9	17,183.5
2015	3,249.9	3,688.3	−438.4	2,479.5	2,945.2	−465.7	770.4	743.1	27.3	18,120.1	13,116.7	17,803.4
2016 (estimates)	3,335.5	3,951.0	−615.8	2,537.8	3,161.6	−623.8	797.7	789.7	8.0	19,433.3	14,128.7	18,472.0
2017 (estimates)	3,643.7	4,147.2	−503.5	2,816.9	3,318.6	−501.8	826.9	828.6	−1.7	20,149.4	14,763.2	19,302.8

Note: Fiscal years through 1976 were on a July 1–June 30 basis; beginning with October 1976 (fiscal year 1977), the fiscal year is on an October 1–September 30 basis. The transition quarter is the three-month period from July 1, 1976 through September 30, 1976.

See Budget of the United States Government, Fiscal Year 2017, for additional information.

Sources: Department of Commerce (Bureau of Economic Analysis), Department of the Treasury, and Office of Management and Budget.

TABLE B–18. Federal receipts, outlays, surplus or deficit, and debt, as percent of gross
domestic product, fiscal years 1945–2017

[Percent; fiscal years]

Fiscal year or period	Receipts	Outlays		Surplus or deficit (−)	Federal debt (end of period)	
		Total	National defense		Gross Federal	Held by public
1945	19.9	41.0	36.6	−21.0	114.9	103.9
1946	17.2	24.2	18.7	−7.0	118.9	106.1
1947	16.1	14.4	5.4	1.7	107.6	93.9
1948	15.8	11.3	3.5	4.5	96.0	82.4
1949	14.2	14.0	4.8	.2	91.3	77.4
1950	14.1	15.3	4.9	−1.1	92.1	78.5
1951	15.8	13.9	7.2	1.9	78.0	65.5
1952	18.5	18.9	12.9	−.4	72.5	60.1
1953	18.2	19.9	13.8	−1.7	69.5	57.1
1954	18.0	18.3	12.7	−.3	69.9	57.9
1955	16.1	16.8	10.5	−.7	67.4	55.7
1956	17.0	16.1	9.7	.9	62.1	50.6
1957	17.2	16.5	9.8	.7	58.6	47.2
1958	16.8	17.4	9.9	−.6	59.0	47.7
1959	15.7	18.2	9.7	−2.5	56.9	46.4
1960	17.3	17.2	9.0	.1	54.3	44.3
1961	17.2	17.8	9.1	−.6	53.4	43.5
1962	17.0	18.2	8.9	−1.2	51.6	42.3
1963	17.2	18.0	8.6	−.8	50.1	41.0
1964	17.0	17.9	8.3	−.9	47.7	38.7
1965	16.4	16.6	7.1	−.2	45.4	36.7
1966	16.7	17.2	7.4	−.5	42.0	33.7
1967	17.8	18.8	8.5	−1.0	40.6	31.8
1968	17.0	19.8	9.1	−2.8	41.0	32.2
1969	19.0	18.7	8.4	.3	37.2	28.3
1970	18.4	18.6	7.8	−.3	36.3	27.0
1971	16.7	18.8	7.0	−2.1	36.5	27.1
1972	17.0	18.9	6.5	−1.9	35.7	26.4
1973	17.0	18.1	5.7	−1.1	34.4	25.1
1974	17.7	18.1	5.3	−.4	32.6	23.1
1975	17.3	20.6	5.4	−3.3	33.6	24.5
1976	16.6	20.8	5.0	−4.1	35.1	26.7
Transition quarter	17.2	20.3	4.7	−3.1	34.0	26.2
1977	17.5	20.2	4.8	−2.6	34.8	27.1
1978	17.5	20.1	4.6	−2.6	34.1	26.6
1979	18.0	19.6	4.5	−1.6	32.3	24.9
1980	18.5	21.1	4.8	−2.6	32.5	25.5
1981	19.1	21.6	5.0	−2.5	31.7	25.2
1982	18.6	22.5	5.6	−3.9	34.3	27.9
1983	17.0	22.8	5.9	−5.9	38.7	32.1
1984	16.9	21.5	5.8	−4.7	39.6	33.1
1985	17.2	22.2	5.9	−5.0	42.6	35.3
1986	17.0	21.8	6.0	−4.9	46.7	38.4
1987	17.9	21.0	5.9	−3.1	49.1	39.5
1988	17.6	20.6	5.6	−3.0	50.5	39.8
1989	17.8	20.5	5.4	−2.7	51.5	39.3
1990	17.4	21.2	5.1	−3.7	54.2	40.8
1991	17.3	21.7	4.5	−4.4	58.9	44.0
1992	17.0	21.5	4.6	−4.5	62.2	46.6
1993	17.0	20.7	4.3	−3.8	64.0	47.8
1994	17.5	20.3	3.9	−2.8	64.5	47.7
1995	17.8	20.0	3.6	−2.2	64.9	47.5
1996	18.2	19.6	3.3	−1.3	64.9	46.8
1997	18.6	18.9	3.2	−.3	63.3	44.5
1998	19.2	18.5	3.0	.8	61.2	41.6
1999	19.2	17.9	2.9	1.3	58.9	38.2
2000	20.0	17.6	2.9	2.3	55.5	33.6
2001	18.8	17.6	2.9	1.2	54.6	31.4
2002	17.0	18.5	3.2	−1.5	57.0	32.5
2003	15.7	19.1	3.6	−3.3	59.7	34.5
2004	15.6	19.0	3.8	−3.4	60.8	35.5
2005	16.7	19.2	3.8	−2.5	61.3	35.6
2006	17.6	19.4	3.8	−1.8	61.8	35.3
2007	17.9	19.1	3.8	−1.1	62.5	35.2
2008	17.1	20.2	4.2	−3.1	67.7	39.3
2009	14.6	24.4	4.6	−9.8	82.4	52.3
2010	14.6	23.4	4.7	−8.7	91.4	60.9
2011	15.0	23.4	4.6	−8.5	96.0	65.9
2012	15.3	22.1	4.2	−6.8	100.1	70.4
2013	16.8	20.9	3.8	−4.1	101.3	72.6
2014	17.6	20.4	3.5	−2.8	103.6	74.4
2015	18.3	20.7	3.3	−2.5	101.8	73.7
2016 (estimates)	18.1	21.4	3.3	−3.3	105.2	76.5
2017 (estimates)	18.9	21.5	3.2	−2.6	104.4	76.5

Note: See Note, Table B–17.

Sources: Department of the Treasury and Office of Management and Budget.

TABLE B–19. Federal receipts and outlays, by major category, and surplus or deficit, fiscal years 1950–2017

[Billions of dollars; fiscal years]

Fiscal year or period	Receipts (on-budget and off-budget)					Outlays (on-budget and off-budget)										Surplus or deficit (−) (on-budget and off-budget)
	Total	Individual income taxes	Corporation income taxes	Social insurance and retirement receipts	Other	Total	National defense Total	Department of Defense, military	International affairs	Health	Medicare	Income security	Social security	Net interest	Other	
1950	39.4	15.8	10.4	4.3	8.9	42.6	13.7	....	4.7	0.3	....	4.1	0.8	4.8	14.2	−3.1
1951	51.6	21.6	14.1	5.7	10.2	45.5	23.6	....	3.6	.3	....	3.4	1.6	4.7	8.4	6.1
1952	66.2	27.9	21.2	6.4	10.6	67.7	46.1	....	2.7	.3	....	3.7	2.1	4.7	8.1	−1.5
1953	69.6	29.8	21.2	6.8	11.7	76.1	52.8	....	2.1	.3	....	3.8	2.7	5.2	9.1	−6.5
1954	69.7	29.5	21.1	7.2	11.9	70.9	49.3	....	1.6	.3	....	4.4	3.4	4.8	7.1	−1.2
1955	65.5	28.7	17.9	7.9	11.0	68.4	42.7	....	2.2	.3	....	5.1	4.4	4.9	8.9	−3.0
1956	74.6	32.2	20.9	9.3	12.2	70.6	42.5	....	2.4	.4	....	4.7	5.5	5.1	10.1	3.9
1957	80.0	35.6	21.2	10.0	13.2	76.6	45.4	....	3.1	.5	....	5.4	6.7	5.4	10.1	3.4
1958	79.6	34.7	20.1	11.2	13.6	82.4	46.8	....	3.4	.5	....	7.5	8.2	5.6	10.3	−2.8
1959	79.2	36.7	17.3	11.7	13.5	92.1	49.0	....	3.1	.7	....	8.2	9.7	5.8	15.5	−12.8
1960	92.5	40.7	21.5	14.7	15.6	92.2	48.1	....	3.0	.8	....	7.4	11.6	6.9	14.4	.3
1961	94.4	41.3	21.0	16.4	15.7	97.7	49.6	....	3.2	.9	....	9.7	12.5	6.7	15.2	−3.3
1962	99.7	45.6	20.5	17.0	16.5	106.8	52.3	50.1	5.6	1.2	....	9.2	14.4	6.9	17.2	−7.1
1963	106.6	47.6	21.6	19.8	17.6	111.3	53.4	51.1	5.3	1.5	....	9.3	15.8	7.7	18.3	−4.8
1964	112.6	48.7	23.5	22.0	18.5	118.5	54.8	52.6	4.9	1.8	....	9.7	16.6	8.2	22.6	−5.9
1965	116.8	48.8	25.5	22.2	20.3	118.2	50.6	48.8	5.3	1.8	....	9.5	17.5	8.6	25.0	−1.4
1966	130.8	55.4	30.1	25.5	19.8	134.5	58.1	56.6	5.6	2.5	0.1	9.7	20.7	9.4	28.5	−3.7
1967	148.8	61.5	34.0	32.6	20.7	157.5	71.4	70.1	5.6	3.4	2.7	10.3	21.7	10.3	32.1	−8.6
1968	153.0	68.7	28.7	33.9	21.7	178.1	81.9	80.4	5.3	4.4	4.6	11.8	23.9	11.1	35.1	−25.2
1969	186.9	87.2	36.7	39.0	23.9	183.6	82.5	80.8	4.6	5.2	5.7	13.1	27.3	12.7	32.6	3.2
1970	192.8	90.4	32.8	44.4	25.2	195.6	81.7	80.1	4.3	5.9	6.2	15.7	30.3	14.4	37.2	−2.8
1971	187.1	86.2	26.8	47.3	26.8	210.2	78.9	77.5	4.2	6.8	6.6	22.9	35.9	14.8	40.0	−23.0
1972	207.3	94.7	32.2	52.6	27.8	230.7	79.2	77.6	4.8	8.7	7.5	27.7	40.2	15.5	47.3	−23.4
1973	230.8	103.2	36.2	63.1	28.3	245.7	76.7	75.0	4.1	9.4	8.1	28.3	49.1	17.3	52.8	−14.9
1974	263.2	119.0	38.6	75.1	30.6	269.4	79.3	77.9	5.7	10.7	9.6	33.7	55.9	21.4	52.9	−6.1
1975	279.1	122.4	40.6	84.5	31.5	332.3	86.5	84.9	7.1	12.9	12.9	50.2	64.7	23.2	74.8	−53.2
1976	298.1	131.6	41.4	90.8	34.3	371.8	89.6	87.9	6.4	15.7	15.8	60.8	73.9	26.7	82.7	−73.7
Transition quarter	81.2	38.8	8.5	25.2	8.8	96.0	22.3	21.8	2.5	3.9	4.3	15.0	19.8	6.9	21.4	−14.7
1977	355.6	157.6	54.9	106.5	36.6	409.2	97.2	95.1	6.4	17.3	19.3	61.1	85.1	29.9	93.0	−53.7
1978	399.6	181.0	60.0	121.0	37.7	458.7	104.5	102.3	7.5	18.5	22.8	61.5	93.9	35.5	114.6	−59.2
1979	463.3	217.8	65.7	138.9	40.8	504.0	116.3	113.6	7.5	20.5	26.5	66.4	104.1	42.6	120.2	−40.7
1980	517.1	244.1	64.6	157.8	50.6	590.9	134.0	130.9	12.7	23.2	32.1	86.6	118.5	52.5	131.3	−73.8
1981	599.3	285.9	61.1	182.7	69.5	678.2	157.5	153.9	13.1	26.9	39.1	100.3	139.6	68.8	133.0	−79.0
1982	617.8	297.7	49.2	201.5	69.3	745.7	185.3	180.7	12.3	27.4	46.6	108.2	156.0	85.0	125.0	−128.0
1983	600.6	288.9	37.0	209.0	65.6	808.4	209.9	204.4	11.8	28.6	52.6	123.0	170.7	89.8	121.8	−207.8
1984	666.4	298.4	56.9	239.4	71.8	851.8	227.4	220.9	15.9	30.4	57.5	113.4	178.2	111.1	117.8	−185.4
1985	734.0	334.5	61.3	265.2	73.0	946.3	252.7	245.1	16.2	33.5	65.8	129.0	188.6	129.5	130.9	−212.3
1986	769.2	349.0	63.1	283.9	73.2	990.4	273.4	265.4	14.1	35.9	70.2	120.7	198.8	136.0	141.3	−221.2
1987	854.3	392.6	83.9	303.3	74.5	1,004.0	282.0	273.9	11.6	40.0	75.1	124.1	207.4	138.6	125.2	−149.7
1988	909.2	401.2	94.5	334.3	79.2	1,064.4	290.4	281.9	10.5	44.5	78.9	130.4	219.3	151.8	138.7	−155.2
1989	991.1	445.7	103.3	359.4	82.7	1,143.7	303.6	294.8	9.6	48.4	85.0	137.6	232.5	169.0	158.1	−152.6
1990	1,032.0	466.9	93.5	380.0	91.5	1,253.0	299.3	289.7	13.8	57.7	98.1	148.8	248.6	184.3	202.3	−221.0
1991	1,055.0	467.8	98.1	396.0	93.1	1,324.2	273.3	262.3	15.8	71.2	104.5	172.6	269.0	194.4	223.3	−269.2
1992	1,091.2	476.0	100.3	413.7	101.3	1,381.5	298.3	286.8	16.1	89.5	119.0	199.7	287.6	199.3	171.9	−290.3
1993	1,154.3	509.7	117.5	428.3	98.8	1,409.4	291.1	278.5	17.2	99.4	130.6	210.1	304.6	198.7	157.7	−255.1
1994	1,258.6	543.1	140.4	461.5	113.7	1,461.8	281.6	268.6	17.1	107.1	144.7	217.3	319.6	202.9	171.4	−203.2
1995	1,351.8	590.2	157.0	484.5	120.1	1,515.7	272.1	259.4	16.4	115.4	159.9	223.8	335.8	232.1	160.2	−164.0
1996	1,453.1	656.4	171.8	509.4	115.4	1,560.5	265.7	253.1	13.5	119.4	174.2	229.7	349.7	241.1	167.2	−107.4
1997	1,579.2	737.5	182.3	539.4	120.1	1,601.1	270.5	258.3	15.2	123.8	190.0	235.0	365.3	244.0	157.3	−21.9
1998	1,721.7	828.6	188.7	571.8	132.6	1,652.5	268.2	255.8	13.1	131.4	192.8	237.8	379.2	241.1	188.9	69.3
1999	1,827.5	879.5	184.7	611.8	151.5	1,701.8	274.8	261.2	15.2	141.0	190.4	242.5	390.0	229.8	218.1	125.6
2000	2,025.2	1,004.5	207.3	652.9	160.6	1,789.0	294.4	281.0	17.2	154.5	197.1	253.7	409.4	222.9	239.7	236.2
2001	1,991.1	994.3	151.1	694.0	151.7	1,862.8	304.7	290.2	16.5	172.2	217.4	269.8	433.0	206.2	243.1	128.2
2002	1,853.1	858.3	148.0	700.8	146.0	2,010.9	348.5	331.8	22.3	196.5	230.9	312.7	456.0	170.9	273.1	−157.8
2003	1,782.3	793.7	131.8	713.0	143.9	2,159.9	404.7	387.1	21.2	219.5	249.4	334.6	474.7	153.1	302.6	−377.6
2004	1,880.1	809.0	189.4	733.4	148.4	2,292.8	455.8	436.4	26.9	240.1	269.4	333.1	495.5	160.2	311.8	−412.7
2005	2,153.6	927.2	278.3	794.1	154.0	2,472.0	495.3	474.1	34.6	250.5	298.6	345.8	523.3	184.0	339.8	−318.3
2006	2,406.9	1,043.9	353.9	837.8	171.2	2,655.1	521.8	499.3	29.5	252.7	329.9	352.5	548.5	226.6	393.5	−248.2
2007	2,568.0	1,163.5	370.2	869.6	164.7	2,728.7	551.3	528.5	28.5	266.4	375.4	366.0	586.2	237.1	317.9	−160.7
2008	2,524.0	1,145.7	304.3	900.2	173.7	2,982.5	616.1	594.6	28.9	280.6	390.8	431.3	617.0	252.8	365.2	−458.6
2009	2,105.0	915.3	138.2	890.9	160.5	3,517.7	661.0	636.7	37.5	334.3	430.1	533.2	683.0	186.9	651.6	−1,412.7
2010	2,162.7	898.5	191.4	864.8	207.9	3,457.1	693.5	666.7	45.2	369.1	451.6	622.2	706.7	196.2	372.6	−1,294.4
2011	2,303.5	1,091.5	181.1	818.8	212.1	3,603.1	705.6	678.1	45.7	372.5	485.7	597.3	730.8	230.0	435.5	−1,299.6
2012	2,450.0	1,132.2	242.3	845.3	230.2	3,537.0	677.9	650.9	47.2	346.7	471.8	541.3	773.3	220.4	458.3	−1,087.0
2013	2,775.1	1,316.4	273.5	947.8	237.4	3,454.6	633.4	607.8	46.2	358.3	497.8	536.5	813.6	220.9	347.9	−679.5
2014	3,021.5	1,394.6	320.7	1,023.5	282.7	3,506.1	603.5	577.9	46.7	409.4	511.7	513.6	850.5	229.0	341.7	−484.6
2015	3,249.9	1,540.8	343.8	1,065.3	300.0	3,688.3	589.6	562.5	48.6	482.2	546.2	508.8	887.8	223.2	402.0	−438.4
2016 (estimates)	3,335.5	1,627.8	292.6	1,100.8	314.3	3,951.3	604.5	576.3	46.4	525.9	595.3	528.2	929.4	240.0	481.6	−615.8
2017 (estimates)	3,643.7	1,788.0	418.7	1,141.2	295.8	4,147.2	617.0	586.8	55.8	567.6	605.0	535.9	972.6	302.7	490.7	−503.5

Note: See Note, Table B–17.

Sources: Department of the Treasury and Office of Management and Budget.

TABLE B–20. Federal receipts, outlays, surplus or deficit, and debt, fiscal years 2012–2017

[Millions of dollars; fiscal years]

Description	Actual				Estimates	
	2012	2013	2014	2015	2016	2017
RECEIPTS, OUTLAYS, AND SURPLUS OR DEFICIT						
Total:						
Receipts	2,449,988	2,775,103	3,021,487	3,249,886	3,335,502	3,643,742
Outlays	3,536,951	3,454,647	3,506,114	3,688,292	3,951,307	4,147,224
Surplus or deficit (–)	–1,086,963	–679,544	–484,627	–438,406	–615,805	–503,482
On-budget:						
Receipts	1,880,487	2,101,829	2,285,922	2,479,514	2,537,845	2,816,874
Outlays	3,029,363	2,820,836	2,800,061	2,945,215	3,161,649	3,318,636
Surplus or deficit (–)	–1,148,876	–719,007	–514,139	–465,701	–623,804	–501,762
Off-budget:						
Receipts	569,501	673,274	735,565	770,372	797,657	826,868
Outlays	507,588	633,811	706,053	743,077	789,658	828,588
Surplus or deficit (–)	61,913	39,463	29,512	27,295	7,999	–1,720
OUTSTANDING DEBT, END OF PERIOD						
Gross Federal debt	16,050,921	16,719,434	17,794,483	18,120,106	19,433,320	20,149,416
Held by Federal Government accounts	4,769,790	4,736,721	5,014,584	5,003,414	5,304,581	5,386,220
Held by the public	11,281,131	11,982,713	12,779,899	13,116,692	14,128,738	14,763,197
Federal Reserve System	1,645,285	2,072,283	2,451,743	2,461,947	....	....
Other	9,635,846	9,910,430	10,328,156	10,654,745	....	....
RECEIPTS BY SOURCE						
Total: On-budget and off-budget	2,449,988	2,775,103	3,021,487	3,249,886	3,335,502	3,643,742
Individual income taxes	1,132,206	1,316,405	1,394,568	1,540,802	1,627,834	1,787,973
Corporation income taxes	242,289	273,506	320,731	343,797	292,561	418,734
Social insurance and retirement receipts	845,314	947,820	1,023,458	1,065,257	1,100,796	1,141,206
On-budget	275,813	274,546	287,893	294,885	303,139	314,338
Off-budget	569,501	673,274	735,565	770,372	797,657	826,868
Excise taxes	79,061	84,007	93,368	98,279	96,821	110,060
Estate and gift taxes	13,973	18,912	19,300	19,232	21,094	22,399
Customs duties and fees	30,307	31,815	33,926	35,041	36,721	39,537
Miscellaneous receipts	106,838	102,638	136,136	147,478	159,675	122,833
Deposits of earnings by Federal Reserve System	81,957	75,767	99,235	96,468	116,445	64,818
All other	24,881	26,871	36,901	51,010	43,230	58,015
Legislative proposals [1]	....	....	....	....	....	1,000
OUTLAYS BY FUNCTION						
Total: On-budget and off-budget	3,536,951	3,454,647	3,506,114	3,688,292	3,951,307	4,147,224
National defense	677,852	633,446	603,457	589,564	604,452	616,981
International affairs	47,184	46,231	46,686	48,576	46,443	55,814
General science, space, and technology	29,060	28,908	28,570	29,412	30,803	31,500
Energy	14,858	11,042	5,270	6,838	7,458	7,166
Natural resources and environment	41,631	38,145	36,171	36,034	42,580	43,530
Agriculture	17,791	29,678	24,386	18,500	25,574	26,164
Commerce and housing credit	40,647	–83,199	–94,861	–37,905	–26,723	–22,485
On-budget	37,977	–81,286	–92,330	–36,195	–27,275	–23,665
Off-budget	2,670	–1,913	–2,531	–1,710	552	1,180
Transportation	93,019	91,673	91,938	89,533	92,361	100,230
Community and regional development	25,132	32,336	20,670	20,670	27,852	21,118
Education, training, employment, and social services	90,823	72,808	90,615	122,061	113,932	107,556
Health	346,742	358,315	409,449	482,223	525,860	567,567
Medicare	471,793	497,826	511,688	546,202	595,317	604,967
Income security	541,344	536,511	513,644	508,843	528,181	535,856
Social security	773,290	813,551	850,533	887,753	929,444	972,596
On-budget	140,387	56,009	25,946	30,990	32,779	39,514
Off-budget	632,903	757,542	824,587	856,763	896,665	933,082
Veterans benefits and services	124,595	138,938	149,616	159,738	178,173	180,770
Administration of justice	56,277	52,601	50,457	51,903	64,415	63,906
General government	28,041	27,737	26,913	20,969	24,463	29,279
Net interest	220,408	220,885	228,956	223,181	240,003	302,697
On-budget	332,801	326,535	329,222	319,149	330,657	391,026
Off-budget	–112,393	–105,650	–100,266	–95,968	–90,654	–88,329
Allowances	....	....	....	....	1,875	10,500
Undistributed offsetting receipts	–103,536	–92,785	–88,044	–115,803	–101,156	–108,488
On-budget	–87,944	–76,617	–72,307	–99,795	–84,251	–91,143
Off-budget	–15,592	–16,168	–15,737	–16,008	–16,905	–17,345

[1] Includes Undistributed Allowance for Immigration Reform.

Note: See Note, Table B–17.

Sources: Department of the Treasury and Office of Management and Budget.

Table B-21. Federal and State and local government current receipts and expenditures, national income and product accounts (NIPA) basis, 1965–2015

[Billions of dollars; quarterly data at seasonally adjusted annual rates]

Year or quarter	Total government			Federal Government			State and local government			Addendum: Grants-in-aid to State and local governments
	Current receipts	Current expenditures	Net government saving (NIPA)	Current receipts	Current expenditures	Net Federal Government saving (NIPA)	Current receipts	Current expenditures	Net State and local government saving (NIPA)	
1965	179.7	181.0	−1.4	120.4	125.9	−5.5	65.8	61.7	4.1	6.6
1966	202.1	203.9	−1.8	137.4	144.3	−7.0	74.1	68.9	5.2	9.4
1967	216.9	231.7	−14.8	146.3	165.7	−19.5	81.6	76.9	4.7	10.9
1968	251.2	260.7	−9.5	170.6	184.3	−13.7	92.5	88.2	4.3	11.8
1969	282.5	283.5	−1.0	191.8	196.9	−5.1	104.3	100.2	4.1	13.7
1970	285.7	317.5	−31.8	185.1	219.9	−34.8	118.9	115.9	3.0	18.3
1971	302.1	352.4	−50.2	190.7	241.5	−50.8	133.6	133.0	.6	22.1
1972	345.4	385.9	−40.5	219.0	267.9	−48.9	156.9	148.5	8.4	30.5
1973	388.5	416.6	−28.0	249.2	286.9	−37.7	172.8	163.1	9.6	33.5
1974	430.0	468.3	−38.3	278.5	319.1	−40.6	186.4	184.1	2.3	34.9
1975	440.9	543.5	−102.5	276.8	373.8	−97.0	207.7	213.3	−5.6	43.6
1976	505.4	582.4	−77.1	322.6	402.4	−79.9	231.9	229.1	2.8	49.1
1977	567.0	630.5	−63.5	363.9	435.8	−71.9	257.9	249.5	8.4	54.8
1978	645.7	692.0	−46.4	423.8	483.7	−59.8	285.3	271.9	13.4	63.5
1979	728.8	765.1	−36.3	487.0	531.5	−44.5	305.8	297.6	8.2	64.0
1980	799.3	880.2	−80.9	533.7	619.9	−86.3	335.3	329.9	5.4	69.7
1981	918.7	1,000.3	−81.7	621.1	706.9	−85.8	367.0	362.9	4.1	69.4
1982	940.5	1,110.3	−169.7	618.7	783.3	−164.6	388.1	393.2	−5.1	66.3
1983	1,001.7	1,205.4	−203.7	644.8	849.8	−205.0	424.8	423.6	1.3	67.9
1984	1,114.4	1,285.9	−171.4	711.2	903.5	−192.3	475.6	454.7	20.9	72.3
1985	1,216.5	1,391.8	−175.4	775.7	971.3	−195.6	516.9	496.7	20.3	76.2
1986	1,292.3	1,484.5	−192.2	817.9	1,030.6	−212.7	556.8	536.4	20.4	82.4
1987	1,406.1	1,557.2	−151.1	899.5	1,062.7	−163.2	585.0	572.9	12.1	78.4
1988	1,506.5	1,646.9	−140.4	962.4	1,119.8	−157.3	629.9	612.9	17.0	85.7
1989	1,631.4	1,780.6	−149.2	1,042.5	1,199.1	−156.6	680.8	673.4	7.4	91.8
1990	1,712.9	1,920.2	−207.4	1,087.6	1,288.5	−200.9	729.6	736.0	−6.5	104.4
1991	1,763.3	2,034.6	−271.3	1,107.8	1,354.0	−246.2	779.5	804.6	−25.1	124.0
1992	1,848.2	2,218.4	−370.2	1,154.4	1,487.0	−332.7	835.6	873.1	−37.5	141.7
1993	1,952.3	2,301.4	−349.0	1,231.0	1,542.8	−311.8	877.1	914.3	−37.2	155.7
1994	2,096.5	2,377.2	−280.7	1,329.3	1,583.0	−253.7	934.1	961.0	−27.0	166.8
1995	2,222.8	2,495.1	−272.4	1,417.4	1,658.2	−240.8	979.8	1,011.4	−31.5	174.5
1996	2,387.4	2,578.3	−191.0	1,536.3	1,714.8	−178.5	1,032.6	1,045.0	−12.5	181.5
1997	2,565.0	2,654.5	−89.5	1,667.3	1,758.5	−91.2	1,085.8	1,084.1	1.7	188.1
1998	2,737.7	2,719.6	18.1	1,789.8	1,787.0	2.7	1,148.7	1,133.3	15.4	200.8
1999	2,908.1	2,832.2	75.9	1,905.4	1,838.8	66.6	1,221.8	1,212.6	9.2	219.2
2000	3,138.2	2,971.8	166.4	2,068.2	1,911.7	156.5	1,303.1	1,293.2	9.9	233.1
2001	3,123.2	3,174.0	−50.8	2,031.8	2,017.4	14.5	1,352.6	1,417.9	−65.3	261.3
2002	2,971.9	3,363.3	−391.4	1,870.6	2,141.1	−270.5	1,388.4	1,509.4	−120.9	287.2
2003	3,048.0	3,572.2	−524.3	1,895.1	2,297.9	−402.9	1,474.6	1,596.0	−121.4	321.7
2004	3,270.3	3,777.9	−507.6	2,027.4	2,426.6	−399.2	1,575.1	1,683.4	−108.4	332.2
2005	3,669.0	4,040.3	−371.3	2,303.5	2,608.2	−304.7	1,708.8	1,775.4	−66.6	343.4
2006	4,007.9	4,274.3	−266.4	2,537.7	2,764.8	−227.0	1,810.9	1,850.3	−39.4	340.8
2007	4,208.8	4,547.2	−338.4	2,667.2	2,932.8	−265.7	1,900.6	1,973.3	−72.7	359.0
2008	4,117.5	4,916.6	−799.0	2,579.5	3,213.5	−634.0	1,909.1	2,074.1	−165.1	371.0
2009	3,699.5	5,220.3	−1,520.8	2,238.4	3,487.2	−1,248.8	1,919.2	2,191.2	−271.9	458.1
2010	3,936.5	5,502.5	−1,566.0	2,443.3	3,772.0	−1,328.7	1,998.5	2,235.8	−237.3	505.3
2011	4,132.2	5,592.2	−1,460.1	2,574.1	3,818.3	−1,244.1	2,030.5	2,246.4	−215.9	472.5
2012	4,312.3	5,623.1	−1,310.8	2,699.1	3,789.1	−1,090.1	2,057.2	2,277.9	−220.8	444.0
2013	4,827.6	5,655.7	−828.0	3,141.3	3,782.2	−640.9	2,136.5	2,323.6	−187.1	450.1
2014	4,995.4	5,794.6	−799.2	3,265.2	3,896.7	−631.5	2,225.0	2,392.7	−167.7	494.8
2015 ᵖ	....	5,953.0	....	....	4,023.2	....	....	2,461.4	....	531.5
2012: I	4,258.1	5,589.9	−1,331.8	2,664.2	3,771.2	−1,107.1	2,033.6	2,258.3	−224.7	439.7
II	4,284.3	5,616.7	−1,332.4	2,678.6	3,780.6	−1,102.0	2,044.7	2,275.2	−230.4	439.1
III	4,300.9	5,602.7	−1,301.9	2,687.7	3,767.3	−1,079.5	2,056.1	2,278.4	−222.3	443.0
IV	4,405.8	5,683.1	−1,277.3	2,765.8	3,837.4	−1,071.6	2,094.2	2,299.8	−205.6	454.1
2013: I	4,659.3	5,630.4	−971.1	2,976.7	3,767.3	−790.6	2,123.1	2,303.5	−180.4	440.5
II	4,947.6	5,645.5	−697.9	3,253.8	3,779.8	−525.9	2,144.3	2,316.3	−172.0	450.5
III	4,766.1	5,671.8	−905.7	3,086.4	3,794.1	−707.7	2,138.0	2,336.1	−198.0	458.4
IV	4,937.6	5,675.1	−737.5	3,248.2	3,787.7	−539.6	2,140.5	2,338.5	−197.9	451.1
2014: I	4,914.6	5,723.1	−808.5	3,215.5	3,834.7	−619.2	2,167.7	2,357.0	−189.3	468.6
II	4,987.1	5,777.3	−790.2	3,256.3	3,886.3	−630.0	2,214.9	2,375.2	−160.3	484.2
III	5,031.7	5,847.8	−816.1	3,293.4	3,943.5	−650.1	2,252.3	2,418.4	−166.0	514.1
IV	5,048.3	5,830.3	−781.9	3,295.7	3,922.4	−626.7	2,265.1	2,420.3	−155.2	512.5
2015: I	5,113.0	5,842.7	−729.7	3,356.5	3,935.8	−579.3	2,282.0	2,432.4	−150.4	525.5
II	5,216.0	5,944.7	−728.7	3,440.4	4,014.6	−574.2	2,295.8	2,450.3	−154.5	520.2
III	5,256.4	6,015.5	−759.1	3,475.2	4,079.8	−604.5	2,320.3	2,475.0	−154.6	539.2
IV ᵖ	....	6,009.1	....	....	4,062.5	....	....	2,487.8	....	541.2

Note: Federal grants-in-aid to State and local governments are reflected in Federal current expenditures and State and local current receipts. Total government current receipts and expenditures have been adjusted to eliminate this duplication.

Source: Department of Commerce (Bureau of Economic Analysis).

TABLE B–22. State and local government revenues and expenditures, fiscal years 1954–2013

[Millions of dollars]

Fiscal year [1]	General revenues by source [2]							General expenditures by function [2]				
	Total	Property taxes	Sales and gross receipts taxes	Individual income taxes	Corporation net income taxes	Revenue from Federal Government	All other [3]	Total [4]	Education	Highways	Public welfare [4]	All other [4,5]
1954	29,012	9,967	7,276	1,127	778	2,966	6,898	30,701	10,557	5,527	3,060	11,557
1955	31,073	10,735	7,643	1,237	744	3,131	7,583	33,724	11,907	6,452	3,168	12,197
1956	34,670	11,749	8,691	1,538	890	3,335	8,467	36,715	13,224	6,953	3,139	13,399
1957	38,164	12,864	9,467	1,754	984	3,843	9,252	40,375	14,134	7,816	3,485	14,940
1958	41,219	14,047	9,829	1,759	1,018	4,865	9,701	44,851	15,919	8,567	3,818	16,547
1959	45,306	14,983	10,437	1,994	1,001	6,377	10,514	48,887	17,283	9,592	4,136	17,876
1960	50,505	16,405	11,849	2,463	1,180	6,974	11,634	51,876	18,719	9,428	4,404	19,325
1961	54,037	18,002	12,463	2,613	1,266	7,131	12,562	56,201	20,574	9,844	4,720	21,063
1962	58,252	19,054	13,494	3,037	1,308	7,871	13,488	60,206	22,216	10,357	5,084	22,549
1963	62,891	20,089	14,456	3,269	1,505	8,722	14,850	64,815	23,776	11,135	5,481	24,423
1963–64	68,443	21,241	15,762	3,791	1,695	10,002	15,952	69,302	26,286	11,664	5,766	25,586
1964–65	74,000	22,583	17,118	4,090	1,929	11,029	17,251	74,678	28,563	12,221	6,315	27,579
1965–66	83,036	24,670	19,085	4,760	2,038	13,214	19,269	82,843	33,287	12,770	6,757	30,029
1966–67	91,197	26,047	20,530	5,825	2,227	15,370	21,198	93,350	37,919	13,932	8,218	33,281
1967–68	101,264	27,747	22,911	7,308	2,518	17,181	23,599	102,411	41,158	14,481	9,857	36,915
1968–69	114,550	30,673	26,519	8,908	3,180	19,153	26,117	116,728	47,238	15,417	12,110	41,963
1969–70	130,756	34,054	30,322	10,812	3,738	21,857	29,973	131,332	52,718	16,427	14,679	47,508
1970–71	144,927	37,852	33,233	11,900	3,424	26,146	32,372	150,674	59,413	18,095	18,226	54,940
1971–72	167,535	42,877	37,518	15,227	4,416	31,342	36,156	168,549	65,813	19,021	21,117	62,598
1972–73	190,222	45,283	42,047	17,994	5,425	39,264	40,210	181,357	69,713	18,615	23,582	69,447
1973–74	207,670	47,705	46,098	19,491	6,015	41,820	46,542	199,222	75,833	19,946	25,085	78,358
1974–75	228,171	51,491	49,815	21,454	6,642	47,034	51,735	230,722	87,858	22,528	28,156	92,180
1975–76	256,176	57,001	54,547	24,575	7,273	55,589	57,191	256,731	97,216	23,907	32,604	103,004
1976–77	285,157	62,527	60,641	29,246	9,174	62,444	61,125	274,215	102,780	23,058	35,906	112,472
1977–78	315,960	66,422	67,596	33,176	10,738	69,592	68,435	296,984	110,758	24,609	39,140	122,478
1978–79	343,236	64,944	74,247	36,932	12,128	75,164	79,822	327,517	119,448	28,440	41,898	137,731
1979–80	382,322	68,499	79,927	42,080	13,321	83,029	95,467	369,086	133,211	33,311	47,288	155,276
1980–81	423,404	74,969	85,971	46,426	14,143	90,294	111,599	407,449	145,784	34,603	54,105	172,957
1981–82	457,654	82,067	93,613	50,738	15,028	87,282	128,925	436,733	154,282	34,520	57,996	189,935
1982–83	486,753	89,105	100,247	55,129	14,258	90,007	138,008	466,516	163,876	36,655	60,906	205,080
1983–84	542,730	96,457	114,097	64,871	16,798	96,935	153,571	505,008	176,108	39,419	66,414	223,068
1984–85	598,121	103,757	126,376	70,361	19,152	106,158	172,317	553,899	192,686	44,989	71,479	244,745
1985–86	641,486	111,709	135,005	74,365	19,994	113,099	187,314	605,623	210,819	49,368	75,868	269,568
1986–87	686,860	121,203	144,091	83,935	22,425	114,857	200,350	657,134	226,619	52,355	82,650	295,510
1987–88	726,762	132,212	156,452	88,350	23,663	117,602	208,482	704,921	242,683	55,621	89,090	317,527
1988–89	786,129	142,400	166,336	97,806	25,926	125,824	227,838	762,360	263,898	58,105	97,879	342,479
1989–90	849,502	155,613	177,885	105,640	23,566	136,802	249,996	834,818	288,148	61,057	110,518	375,094
1990–91	902,207	167,999	185,570	109,341	22,242	154,099	262,955	908,108	309,302	64,937	130,402	403,467
1991–92	979,137	180,337	197,731	115,638	23,880	179,174	282,376	981,253	324,652	67,351	158,723	430,526
1992–93	1,041,643	189,744	209,649	123,235	26,417	198,663	293,935	1,030,434	342,287	68,370	170,705	449,072
1993–94	1,100,490	197,141	223,628	128,810	28,320	215,492	307,099	1,077,665	353,287	72,067	183,394	468,916
1994–95	1,169,505	203,451	237,268	137,931	31,406	228,771	330,677	1,149,863	378,273	77,109	196,703	497,779
1995–96	1,222,821	209,440	248,993	146,844	32,009	234,891	350,645	1,193,276	398,859	79,092	197,354	517,971
1996–97	1,289,237	218,877	261,418	159,042	33,820	244,847	371,233	1,249,984	418,416	82,062	203,779	545,727
1997–98	1,365,762	230,150	274,883	175,630	34,412	255,048	395,639	1,318,042	450,365	87,214	208,120	572,343
1998–99	1,434,029	239,672	290,993	189,309	33,922	270,624	409,505	1,402,369	483,259	93,018	218,957	607,134
1999–2000	1,541,322	249,178	309,290	211,661	36,059	291,950	443,186	1,506,797	521,612	101,336	237,336	646,512
2000–01	1,647,161	263,689	320,217	226,334	35,296	324,033	477,592	1,626,063	563,572	107,235	261,622	693,634
2001–02	1,684,879	279,191	324,123	202,832	28,152	360,546	490,035	1,736,866	594,694	115,295	285,464	741,413
2002–03	1,763,212	296,683	337,787	199,407	31,369	389,264	508,702	1,821,917	621,335	117,696	310,783	772,102
2003–04	1,887,397	317,941	361,027	215,215	33,716	423,112	536,386	1,908,543	655,182	117,215	340,523	795,622
2004–05	2,026,034	335,779	384,266	242,273	43,256	438,558	581,902	2,012,110	688,314	126,350	365,295	832,151
2005–06	2,197,475	364,559	417,735	268,667	53,081	452,975	640,458	2,123,663	728,917	136,502	373,846	884,398
2006–07	2,330,611	388,905	440,470	290,278	60,955	464,914	685,089	2,264,035	774,170	145,011	389,259	955,595
2007–08	2,421,977	409,540	449,945	304,902	57,231	477,441	722,919	2,406,183	826,061	153,831	408,920	1,017,372
2008–09	2,429,672	434,818	434,128	270,942	46,280	537,949	705,555	2,500,796	851,689	154,338	437,184	1,057,586
2009–10	2,510,846	443,947	435,571	261,510	44,108	623,801	701,909	2,542,231	860,118	155,912	460,230	1,065,971
2010–11	2,618,037	445,771	463,979	285,293	48,422	647,606	726,966	2,583,805	862,271	153,895	494,682	1,072,957
2011–12	2,598,906	447,120	476,544	307,256	48,934	585,128	733,924	2,593,180	869,223	160,327	489,430	1,074,200
2012–13	2,690,427	455,442	496,439	338,471	53,039	584,652	762,383	2,643,122	876,566	158,745	516,389	1,091,421

[1] Fiscal years not the same for all governments. See Note.
[2] Excludes revenues or expenditures of publicly owned utilities and liquor stores and of insurance-trust activities. Intergovernmental receipts and payments between State and local governments are also excluded.
[3] Includes motor vehicle license taxes, other taxes, and charges and miscellaneous revenues.
[4] Includes intergovernmental payments to the Federal Government.
[5] Includes expenditures for libraries, hospitals, health, employment security administration, veterans' services, air transportation, sea and inland port facilities, parking facilities, police protection, fire protection, correction, protective inspection and regulation, sewerage, natural resources, parks and recreation, housing and community development, solid waste management, financial administration, judicial and legal, general public buildings, other government administration, interest on general debt, and other general expenditures, not elsewhere classified.

Note: Except for States listed, data for fiscal years listed from 1963–64 to 2012–13 are the aggregation of data for government fiscal years that ended in the 12-month period from July 1 to June 30 of those years; Texas used August and Alabama and Michigan used September as end dates. Data for 1963 and earlier years include data for government fiscal years ending during that particular calendar year.

Source: Department of Commerce (Bureau of the Census).

TABLE B–23. U.S. Treasury securities outstanding by kind of obligation, 1977–2015

[Billions of dollars]

End of fiscal year or month	Total Treasury securities outstanding [1]	Marketable							Nonmarketable				
		Total [2]	Treasury bills	Treasury notes	Treasury bonds	Treasury inflation-protected securities			Total	U.S. savings securities [3]	Foreign series [4]	Government account series	Other [5]
						Total	Notes	Bonds					
1977	697.8	443.5	156.1	241.7	45.7	....	....	....	254.3	75.6	21.8	140.1	16.8
1978	767.2	485.2	160.9	267.9	56.4				282.0	79.9	21.7	153.3	27.1
1979	819.1	506.7	161.4	274.2	71.1				312.4	80.6	28.1	176.4	27.4
1980	906.8	594.5	199.8	310.9	83.8				312.3	73.0	25.2	189.8	24.2
1981	996.8	683.2	223.4	363.6	96.2				313.6	68.3	20.5	201.1	23.7
1982	1,141.2	824.4	277.9	442.9	103.6				316.8	67.6	14.6	210.5	24.1
1983	1,376.3	1,024.0	340.7	557.5	125.7				352.3	70.6	11.5	234.7	35.6
1984	1,560.4	1,176.6	356.8	661.7	158.1				383.8	73.7	8.8	259.5	41.8
1985	1,822.3	1,360.2	384.2	776.4	199.5				462.1	78.2	6.6	313.9	63.3
1986	2,124.9	1,564.3	410.7	896.9	241.7				560.5	87.8	4.1	365.9	102.8
1987	2,349.4	1,676.0	378.3	1,005.1	277.6				673.4	98.5	4.4	440.7	129.8
1988	2,601.4	1,802.9	398.5	1,089.6	299.9				798.5	107.8	6.3	536.5	148.0
1989	2,837.9	1,892.8	406.6	1,133.2	338.0				945.2	115.7	6.8	663.7	159.0
1990	3,212.7	2,092.8	482.5	1,218.1	377.2				1,119.9	123.9	36.0	779.4	180.6
1991	3,664.5	2,390.7	564.6	1,387.7	423.4				1,273.9	135.4	41.6	908.4	188.5
1992	4,063.8	2,677.5	634.3	1,566.3	461.8				1,386.3	150.3	37.0	1,011.0	188.0
1993	4,410.7	2,904.9	658.4	1,734.2	497.4				1,505.8	169.1	42.5	1,114.3	179.9
1994	4,691.7	3,091.6	697.3	1,867.5	511.8				1,600.1	178.6	42.0	1,211.7	167.8
1995	4,953.0	3,260.4	742.5	1,980.3	522.6				1,692.6	183.5	41.0	1,324.3	143.8
1996	5,220.8	3,418.4	761.2	2,098.7	543.5				1,802.4	184.1	37.5	1,454.7	126.1
1997	5,407.6	3,439.6	701.9	2,122.2	576.2	24.4	24.4		1,968.0	182.7	34.9	1,608.5	141.9
1998	5,518.7	3,331.0	637.6	2,009.1	610.4	58.8	41.9	17.0	2,187.6	180.8	35.1	1,777.3	194.4
1999	5,647.3	3,233.0	653.2	1,828.8	643.7	92.4	67.6	24.8	2,414.3	180.0	31.0	2,005.2	198.1
2000	5,622.1	2,992.8	616.2	1,611.3	635.3	115.0	81.6	33.4	2,629.4	177.7	25.4	2,242.9	183.3
2001 [1]	5,807.5	2,930.7	734.9	1,433.0	613.0	134.9	95.1	39.7	2,876.7	186.5	18.3	2,492.1	179.9
2002	6,228.2	3,136.7	868.3	1,521.6	593.0	138.9	93.7	45.1	3,091.5	193.3	12.5	2,707.3	178.4
2003	6,783.2	3,460.7	918.2	1,799.5	576.9	166.1	120.0	46.1	3,322.5	201.6	11.0	2,912.2	197.7
2004	7,379.1	3,846.1	961.5	2,109.6	552.0	223.0	164.5	58.5	3,533.0	204.2	5.9	3,130.0	192.9
2005	7,932.7	4,084.9	914.3	2,328.8	520.7	307.1	229.1	78.0	3,847.8	203.6	3.1	3,380.6	260.5
2006	8,507.0	4,303.0	911.5	2,447.2	534.7	395.6	293.9	101.7	4,203.9	203.7	3.0	3,722.7	274.5
2007	9,007.7	4,448.1	958.1	2,458.0	561.1	456.9	335.7	121.2	4,559.5	197.1	3.0	4,026.8	332.6
2008	10,024.7	5,236.0	1,489.8	2,624.8	582.9	524.5	380.2	144.3	4,788.7	194.3	3.0	4,297.7	293.8
2009	11,909.8	7,009.7	1,992.5	3,773.8	679.8	551.7	396.2	155.5	4,900.1	192.5	4.3	4,454.3	248.4
2010	13,561.6	8,498.3	1,788.5	5,255.9	849.9	593.8	421.1	172.7	5,063.3	188.7	4.2	4,645.3	225.1
2011	14,790.3	9,624.5	1,477.5	6,412.5	1,020.4	705.7	509.4	196.3	5,165.8	185.1	3.0	4,793.9	183.8
2012	16,066.2	10,749.7	1,616.0	7,120.7	1,198.2	807.7	584.7	223.0	5,316.5	183.8	3.0	4,939.3	190.4
2013	16,738.2	11,596.2	1,530.0	7,758.0	1,366.2	936.4	685.5	250.8	5,142.0	180.0	3.0	4,803.1	156.0
2014	17,824.1	12,294.2	1,411.0	8,167.8	1,534.1	1,044.7	765.2	279.5	5,529.9	176.7	3.0	5,212.5	137.7
2015	18,150.6	12,853.8	1,358.0	8,372.7	1,688.3	1,135.4	832.1	303.3	5,296.9	172.8	.3	5,013.5	110.3
2014: Jan	17,293.0	11,825.3	1,486.0	7,929.1	1,421.2	959.1	701.7	257.4	5,467.7	178.8	3.0	5,143.6	142.3
Feb	17,463.2	12,011.4	1,614.0	7,949.3	1,437.2	968.0	701.6	266.4	5,451.8	178.6	3.0	5,131.1	139.1
Mar	17,601.2	12,135.5	1,652.0	7,992.9	1,450.2	984.5	717.1	267.3	5,465.7	178.3	3.0	5,144.0	140.4
Apr	17,508.4	12,016.5	1,459.0	8,034.2	1,463.2	989.2	720.9	268.3	5,491.9	178.1	3.0	5,166.5	144.3
May	17,517.2	12,048.6	1,449.0	8,027.9	1,479.1	1,008.6	738.6	270.0	5,468.5	178.0	3.0	5,143.4	144.2
June	17,632.6	12,084.2	1,388.0	8,093.3	1,492.1	1,019.2	741.1	278.1	5,548.3	177.6	3.0	5,223.9	143.8
July	17,687.1	12,162.9	1,410.0	8,123.3	1,505.1	1,013.8	734.8	279.0	5,524.3	177.3	3.0	5,203.1	140.8
Aug	17,749.2	12,245.3	1,452.0	8,116.6	1,521.1	1,031.9	752.4	279.6	5,503.9	177.0	3.0	5,186.5	137.4
Sept	17,824.1	12,294.2	1,411.0	8,167.8	1,534.1	1,044.7	765.2	279.5	5,529.9	176.7	3.0	5,212.5	137.7
Oct	17,937.2	12,362.6	1,413.9	8,199.7	1,547.1	1,050.2	764.0	286.2	5,574.6	176.6	.3	5,258.7	139.0
Nov	18,005.6	12,421.4	1,439.9	8,189.9	1,563.2	1,063.9	777.5	286.4	5,584.1	176.4	.3	5,263.1	144.4
Dec	18,141.4	12,518.4	1,457.9	8,229.2	1,576.2	1,077.6	791.9	285.7	5,623.0	175.9	.3	5,298.2	148.6
2015: Jan	18,082.3	12,483.3	1,412.9	8,239.9	1,589.2	1,063.7	779.5	284.2	5,599.0	175.6	.3	5,277.4	145.8
Feb	18,155.9	12,570.3	1,472.9	8,230.1	1,594.6	1,067.1	775.5	291.6	5,585.5	175.3	.3	5,265.2	144.8
Mar	18,152.1	12,643.8	1,477.9	8,264.4	1,607.6	1,075.2	785.0	290.2	5,508.3	174.9	.3	5,183.1	150.0
Apr	18,152.6	12,645.5	1,432.9	8,284.0	1,620.6	1,074.2	782.9	291.3	5,507.1	174.6	.3	5,182.7	149.5
May	18,153.3	12,688.4	1,447.0	8,264.6	1,637.0	1,093.2	800.1	293.0	5,464.8	174.3	.3	5,147.5	142.7
June	18,152.0	12,711.1	1,395.0	8,305.4	1,650.0	1,102.4	801.7	300.7	5,440.9	173.9	.3	5,134.9	131.8
July	18,151.3	12,813.4	1,440.0	8,335.1	1,663.0	1,101.9	799.7	302.2	5,337.9	173.6	.3	5,043.0	121.1
Aug	18,151.2	12,846.5	1,424.0	8,338.8	1,675.3	1,122.1	818.9	303.3	5,304.6	173.2	.3	5,017.9	113.2
Sept	18,150.6	12,853.8	1,358.0	8,372.7	1,688.3	1,135.4	832.1	303.3	5,296.9	172.8	.3	5,013.5	110.3
Oct	18,153.0	12,803.0	1,273.0	8,385.7	1,701.3	1,141.0	831.0	310.0	5,350.0	172.5	.3	5,070.5	106.7
Nov	18,827.3	13,122.6	1,506.0	8,422.6	1,711.8	1,152.2	842.7	309.5	5,704.7	172.1	.3	5,426.3	106.0
Dec	18,922.2	13,206.6	1,514.0	8,456.8	1,724.8	1,167.9	858.6	309.4	5,715.6	171.6	.3	5,436.8	107.0

[1] Data beginning with January 2001 are interest-bearing and non-interest-bearing securities; prior data are interest-bearing securities only.

[2] Data from 1986 to 2002 and 2005 to 2015 include Federal Financing Bank securities, not shown separately. Beginning with data for January 2014, includes Floating Rate Notes, not shown separately.

[3] Through 1996, series is U.S. savings bonds. Beginning 1997, includes U.S. retirement plan bonds, U.S. individual retirement bonds, and U.S. savings notes previously included in "other" nonmarketable securities.

[4] Nonmarketable certificates of indebtedness, notes, bonds, and bills in the Treasury foreign series of dollar-denominated and foreign-currency-denominated issues.

[5] Includes depository bonds; retirement plan bonds through 1996; Rural Electrification Administration bonds; State and local bonds; special issues held only by U.S. Government agencies and trust funds and the Federal home loan banks; for the period July 2003 through February 2004, depositary compensation securities; and beginning August 2008, Hope bonds for the HOPE For Homeowners Program.

Note: The fiscal year is on an October 1–September 30 basis.

Source: Department of the Treasury.

TABLE B–24. Estimated ownership of U.S. Treasury securities, 2002–2015

[Billions of dollars]

End of month	Total public debt [1]	Federal Reserve and Intra-govern-mental hold-ings [2]	Held by private investors									
			Total privately held	De-pository institu-tions [3]	U.S. savings bonds [4]	Pension funds		Insurance compa-nies	Mutual funds [6]	State and local govern-ments	Foreign and inter-national [7]	Other inves-tors [8]
						Private [5]	State and local govern-ments					
2002: Mar	6,006.0	3,156.8	2,849.2	201.7	192.0	152.7	163.3	125.6	261.0	327.6	1,057.2	368.3
June	6,126.5	3,276.7	2,849.8	217.4	192.8	152.1	153.9	136.0	245.8	333.6	1,123.1	295.0
Sept	6,228.2	3,303.5	2,924.7	219.6	193.3	154.5	156.3	149.4	248.3	338.6	1,188.6	276.1
Dec	6,405.7	3,387.2	3,018.5	231.8	194.9	154.0	158.9	161.3	272.1	354.7	1,235.6	255.3
2003: Mar	6,460.8	3,390.8	3,070.0	162.6	196.9	166.0	162.1	163.5	282.7	350.0	1,275.2	310.9
June	6,670.1	3,505.4	3,164.7	155.0	199.2	170.5	161.3	166.0	285.4	347.9	1,371.9	307.7
Sept	6,783.2	3,515.3	3,267.9	158.0	201.6	168.2	155.5	168.5	271.0	356.2	1,443.3	345.8
Dec	6,998.0	3,620.1	3,377.9	165.3	203.9	172.4	148.6	166.4	271.2	361.8	1,523.1	365.2
2004: Mar	7,131.1	3,628.3	3,502.8	172.7	204.5	169.8	143.6	172.4	275.2	372.8	1,670.0	321.8
June	7,274.3	3,742.8	3,531.5	167.8	204.6	173.1	134.9	174.6	252.3	390.1	1,735.4	298.7
Sept	7,379.1	3,772.0	3,607.1	146.3	204.2	173.7	140.1	182.9	249.4	393.0	1,794.5	322.9
Dec	7,596.1	3,905.6	3,690.5	133.4	204.5	173.3	149.4	188.5	256.1	404.9	1,849.3	331.3
2005: Mar	7,776.9	3,921.6	3,855.3	149.4	204.2	176.8	157.2	193.3	264.3	429.3	1,952.2	328.7
June	7,836.5	4,033.5	3,803.0	135.9	204.2	180.4	165.9	195.0	248.6	461.1	1,877.5	334.4
Sept	7,932.7	4,067.8	3,864.9	134.0	203.6	183.6	161.1	200.7	246.6	493.6	1,929.6	312.0
Dec	8,170.4	4,199.8	3,970.6	129.4	205.2	184.4	154.2	202.3	254.1	512.2	2,033.9	294.8
2006: Mar	8,371.2	4,257.2	4,114.0	113.0	206.0	186.2	152.9	200.3	254.2	515.7	2,082.1	403.6
June	8,420.0	4,389.2	4,030.8	119.5	205.2	191.6	149.6	196.1	243.4	531.6	1,977.8	416.1
Sept	8,507.0	4,432.8	4,074.2	113.6	203.7	201.7	149.3	196.8	234.2	542.3	2,025.3	407.3
Dec	8,680.2	4,558.1	4,122.1	114.8	202.4	216.1	153.4	197.9	248.2	570.5	2,103.1	315.6
2007: Mar	8,849.7	4,576.6	4,273.1	119.8	200.3	219.6	156.3	185.4	263.2	608.3	2,194.8	325.3
June	8,867.7	4,715.1	4,152.6	110.4	198.6	220.6	162.3	168.9	257.6	637.8	2,192.0	204.4
Sept	9,007.7	4,738.0	4,269.7	119.7	197.1	225.4	153.2	155.1	292.7	643.1	2,235.3	248.0
Dec	9,229.2	4,833.5	4,395.7	128.8	196.5	228.7	144.2	141.9	343.5	647.8	2,353.2	210.1
2008: Mar	9,437.6	4,694.7	4,742.9	125.0	195.4	240.1	135.4	152.1	466.7	646.4	2,506.3	275.6
June	9,492.0	4,685.8	4,806.2	112.7	195.0	243.8	135.5	159.4	440.3	635.1	2,587.4	297.1
Sept	10,024.7	4,692.7	5,332.0	130.0	194.3	252.7	136.7	163.4	631.4	614.0	2,802.4	407.2
Dec	10,699.8	4,806.4	5,893.4	105.0	194.1	259.7	129.9	171.4	758.2	601.4	3,077.2	596.5
2009: Mar	11,126.9	4,785.2	6,341.7	125.7	194.0	272.5	137.0	191.0	721.1	588.2	3,265.7	846.6
June	11,545.3	5,026.8	6,518.5	140.8	193.6	281.6	144.6	200.0	711.8	588.5	3,460.8	796.7
Sept	11,909.8	5,127.1	6,782.7	198.2	192.5	285.5	145.6	210.2	668.5	583.6	3,570.6	928.0
Dec	12,311.3	5,276.9	7,034.4	202.5	191.3	295.6	151.4	222.0	668.8	585.6	3,685.1	1,032.2
2010: Mar	12,773.1	5,259.8	7,513.3	269.3	190.2	304.4	153.6	225.7	678.5	585.0	3,877.9	1,228.7
June	13,201.8	5,345.1	7,856.7	266.1	189.6	316.1	150.1	231.8	676.8	584.4	4,070.0	1,371.8
Sept	13,561.6	5,350.5	8,211.1	322.8	188.7	327.4	145.2	240.6	671.0	586.0	4,324.2	1,405.1
Dec	14,025.2	5,656.2	8,368.9	319.3	187.9	336.9	153.7	248.4	721.7	595.7	4,435.6	1,369.8
2011: Mar	14,270.0	5,958.9	8,311.1	321.0	186.7	349.7	157.9	253.5	749.4	585.3	4,481.4	1,226.2
June	14,343.1	6,220.4	8,122.7	279.4	186.0	258.6	158.0	254.8	767.3	572.4	4,690.6	955.5
Sept	14,790.3	6,328.0	8,462.4	293.8	185.1	381.7	155.7	259.6	814.1	557.8	4,912.1	902.4
Dec	15,222.8	6,439.6	8,783.3	279.7	185.2	401.0	160.7	271.8	895.5	561.3	5,006.9	1,021.2
2012: Mar	15,582.3	6,397.2	9,185.1	317.0	184.8	416.5	169.4	271.5	970.6	567.1	5,145.1	1,143.1
June	15,855.5	6,475.8	9,379.7	303.2	184.7	437.1	171.2	268.6	964.6	585.2	5,310.9	1,154.3
Sept	16,066.2	6,446.8	9,619.4	338.2	183.8	457.8	171.4	269.5	985.4	592.7	5,476.1	1,144.5
Dec	16,432.7	6,523.7	9,909.1	347.7	182.5	477.5	172.8	270.6	1,034.5	604.2	5,573.8	1,245.6
2013: Mar	16,771.6	6,656.8	10,114.8	338.9	181.7	474.6	173.7	266.6	1,104.0	610.0	5,725.0	1,240.3
June	16,738.2	6,773.3	9,964.9	300.2	180.9	463.6	178.5	262.6	1,081.0	609.1	5,595.0	1,293.9
Sept	16,738.2	6,834.2	9,904.0	293.2	180.0	367.7	182.6	262.3	1,091.6	583.9	5,652.8	1,290.0
Dec	17,352.0	7,205.3	10,146.6	321.1	179.2	486.5	188.2	264.7	1,121.9	586.3	5,792.6	1,206.2
2014: Mar	17,601.2	7,301.5	10,299.7	368.3	178.3	493.0	188.9	266.7	1,127.9	586.0	5,948.3	1,142.1
June	17,632.6	7,461.0	10,171.6	407.2	177.6	498.0	189.4	273.6	984.3	606.4	6,018.7	1,016.5
Sept	17,824.1	7,490.8	10,333.2	470.9	176.7	507.1	185.2	280.0	1,032.7	602.3	6,069.2	1,009.0
Dec	18,141.4	7,578.9	10,562.6	513.7	175.9	516.8	176.8	284.9	1,060.6	622.3	6,156.0	1,055.5
2015: Mar	18,152.1	7,521.3	10,630.8	511.7	174.9	462.4	172.7	294.9	1,142.3	639.2	6,172.5	1,060.2
June	18,152.0	7,536.5	10,615.5	515.4	173.9	402.4	169.1	292.6	1,099.3	626.8	6,177.6	1,158.4
Sept	18,150.6	7,488.7	10,661.9	513.4	172.8	337.7	167.9	297.4	1,091.6	634.3	6,106.2	1,340.6
Dec	18,922.2	7,711.2	11,211.0	....	171.6	....	....	....	....	....	....	....

[1] Face value.
[2] Federal Reserve holdings exclude Treasury securities held under repurchase agreements.
[3] Includes U.S. chartered depository institutions, foreign banking offices in U.S., banks in U.S. affiliated areas, credit unions, and bank holding companies.
[4] Current accrual value includes myRA.
[5] Includes Treasury securities held by the Federal Employees Retirement System Thrift Savings Plan "G Fund."
[6] Includes money market mutual funds, mutual funds, and closed-end investment companies.
[7] Includes nonmarketable foreign series, Treasury securities, and Treasury deposit funds. Excludes Treasury securities held under repurchase agreements in custody accounts at the Federal Reserve Bank of New York. Estimates reflect benchmarks to this series at differing intervals; for further detail, see *Treasury Bulletin* and http://www.treasury.gov/resource-center/data-chart-center/tic/pages/index.aspx.
[8] Includes individuals, Government-sponsored enterprises, brokers and dealers, bank personal trusts and estates, corporate and noncorporate businesses, and other investors.

Note: Data shown in this table are as of January 27, 2016.

Source: Department of the Treasury.

[Percent per annum]

Year and month	U.S. Treasury securities					Corporate bonds (Moody's)		High-grade municipal bonds (Standard & Poor's)[3]	New-home mortgage yields[4]	Prime rate charged by banks[5]	Discount window (Federal Reserve Bank of New York)[5,6]		Federal funds rate[7]
	Bills (at auction)[1]		Constant maturities[2]			Aaa[3]	Baa				Primary credit	Adjustment credit	
	3-month	6-month	3-year	10-year	30-year								
1947	0.594					2.61	3.24	2.01		1.50–1.75		1.00	
1948	1.040					2.82	3.47	2.40		1.75–2.00		1.34	
1949	1.102					2.66	3.42	2.21		2.00		1.50	
1950	1.218					2.62	3.24	1.98		2.07		1.59	
1951	1.552					2.86	3.41	2.00		2.56		1.75	
1952	1.766					2.96	3.52	2.19		3.00		1.75	
1953	1.931		2.47	2.85		3.20	3.74	2.72		3.17		1.99	
1954	.953		1.63	2.40		2.90	3.51	2.37		3.05		1.60	
1955	1.753		2.47	2.82		3.06	3.53	2.53		3.16		1.89	1.79
1956	2.658		3.19	3.18		3.36	3.88	2.93		3.77		2.77	2.73
1957	3.267		3.98	3.65		3.89	4.71	3.60		4.20		3.12	3.11
1958	1.839		2.84	3.32		3.79	4.73	3.56		3.83		2.15	1.57
1959	3.405	3.832	4.46	4.33		4.38	5.05	3.95		4.48		3.36	3.31
1960	2.93	3.25	3.98	4.12		4.41	5.19	3.73		4.82		3.53	3.21
1961	2.38	2.61	3.54	3.88		4.35	5.08	3.46		4.50		3.00	1.95
1962	2.78	2.91	3.47	3.95		4.33	5.02	3.18		4.50		3.00	2.71
1963	3.16	3.25	3.67	4.00		4.26	4.86	3.23	5.89	4.50		3.23	3.18
1964	3.56	3.69	4.03	4.19		4.40	4.83	3.22	5.83	4.50		3.55	3.50
1965	3.95	4.05	4.22	4.28		4.49	4.87	3.27	5.81	4.54		4.04	4.07
1966	4.88	5.08	5.23	4.93		5.13	5.67	3.82	6.25	5.63		4.50	5.11
1967	4.32	4.63	5.03	5.07		5.51	6.23	3.98	6.46	5.63		4.19	4.22
1968	5.34	5.47	5.68	5.64		6.18	6.94	4.51	6.97	6.31		5.17	5.66
1969	6.68	6.85	7.02	6.67		7.03	7.81	5.81	7.81	7.96		5.87	8.21
1970	6.43	6.53	7.29	7.35		8.04	9.11	6.51	8.45	7.91		5.95	7.17
1971	4.35	4.51	5.66	6.16		7.39	8.56	5.70	7.74	5.73		4.88	4.67
1972	4.07	4.47	5.72	6.21		7.21	8.16	5.27	7.60	5.25		4.50	4.44
1973	7.04	7.18	6.96	6.85		7.44	8.24	5.18	7.96	8.03		6.45	8.74
1974	7.89	7.93	7.84	7.56		8.57	9.50	6.09	8.92	10.81		7.83	10.51
1975	5.84	6.12	7.50	7.99		8.83	10.61	6.89	9.00	7.86		6.25	5.82
1976	4.99	5.27	6.77	7.61		8.43	9.75	6.49	9.00	6.84		5.50	5.05
1977	5.27	5.52	6.68	7.42	7.75	8.02	8.97	5.56	9.02	6.83		5.46	5.54
1978	7.22	7.58	8.29	8.41	8.49	8.73	9.49	5.90	9.56	9.06		7.46	7.94
1979	10.05	10.02	9.70	9.43	9.28	9.63	10.69	6.39	10.78	12.67		10.29	11.20
1980	11.51	11.37	11.51	11.43	11.27	11.94	13.67	8.51	12.66	15.26		11.77	13.35
1981	14.03	13.78	14.46	13.92	13.45	14.17	16.04	11.23	14.70	18.87		13.42	16.39
1982	10.69	11.08	12.93	13.01	12.76	13.79	16.11	11.57	15.14	14.85		11.01	12.24
1983	8.63	8.75	10.45	11.10	11.18	12.04	13.55	9.47	12.57	10.79		8.50	9.09
1984	9.53	9.77	11.92	12.46	12.41	12.71	14.19	10.15	12.38	12.04		8.80	10.23
1985	7.47	7.64	9.64	10.62	10.79	11.37	12.72	9.18	11.55	9.93		7.69	8.10
1986	5.98	6.03	7.06	7.67	7.78	9.02	10.39	7.38	10.17	8.33		6.32	6.80
1987	5.82	6.05	7.68	8.39	8.59	9.38	10.58	7.73	9.31	8.21		5.66	6.66
1988	6.69	6.92	8.26	8.85	8.96	9.71	10.83	7.76	9.19	9.32		6.20	7.57
1989	8.12	8.04	8.55	8.49	8.45	9.26	10.18	7.24	10.13	10.87		6.93	9.21
1990	7.51	7.47	8.26	8.55	8.61	9.32	10.36	7.25	10.05	10.01		6.98	8.10
1991	5.42	5.49	6.82	7.86	8.14	8.77	9.80	6.89	9.32	8.46		5.45	5.69
1992	3.45	3.57	5.30	7.01	7.67	8.14	8.98	6.41	8.24	6.25		3.25	3.52
1993	3.02	3.14	4.44	5.87	6.59	7.22	7.93	5.63	7.20	6.00		3.00	3.02
1994	4.29	4.66	6.27	7.09	7.37	7.96	8.62	6.19	7.49	7.15		3.60	4.21
1995	5.51	5.59	6.25	6.57	6.88	7.59	8.20	5.95	7.87	8.83		5.21	5.83
1996	5.02	5.09	5.99	6.44	6.71	7.37	8.05	5.75	7.80	8.27		5.02	5.30
1997	5.07	5.18	6.10	6.35	6.61	7.26	7.86	5.55	7.71	8.44		5.00	5.46
1998	4.81	4.85	5.14	5.26	5.58	6.53	7.22	5.12	7.07	8.35		4.92	5.35
1999	4.66	4.76	5.49	5.65	5.87	7.04	7.87	5.43	7.04	8.00		4.62	4.97
2000	5.85	5.92	6.22	6.03	5.94	7.62	8.36	5.77	7.52	9.23		5.73	6.24
2001	3.44	3.39	4.09	5.02	5.49	7.08	7.95	5.19	7.00	6.91		3.40	3.88
2002	1.62	1.69	3.10	4.61	5.43	6.49	7.80	5.05	6.43	4.67		1.17	1.67
2003	1.01	1.06	2.10	4.01		5.67	6.77	4.73	5.80	4.12	2.12		1.13
2004	1.38	1.57	2.78	4.27		5.63	6.39	4.63	5.77	4.34	2.34		1.35
2005	3.16	3.40	3.93	4.29		5.24	6.06	4.29	5.94	6.19	4.19		3.22
2006	4.73	4.80	4.77	4.80	4.91	5.59	6.48	4.42	6.63	7.96	5.96		4.97
2007	4.41	4.48	4.35	4.63	4.84	5.56	6.48	4.42	6.41	8.05	5.86		5.02
2008	1.48	1.71	2.24	3.66	4.28	5.63	7.45	4.80	6.05	5.09	2.39		1.92
2009	.16	.29	1.43	3.26	4.08	5.31	7.30	4.64	5.14	3.25	.50		.16
2010	.14	.20	1.11	3.22	4.25	4.94	6.04	4.16	4.80	3.25	.72		.18
2011	.06	.10	.75	2.78	3.91	4.64	5.66	4.29	4.56	3.25	.75		.10
2012	.09	.13	.38	1.80	2.92	3.67	4.94	3.14	3.69	3.25	.75		.14
2013	.06	.09	.54	2.35	3.45	4.24	5.10	3.96	4.00	3.25	.75		.11
2014	.03	.06	.90	2.54	3.34	4.16	4.85	3.78	4.22	3.25	.75		.09
2015	.06	.17	1.02	2.14	2.84	3.89	5.00	3.48	4.01	3.26	.76		.13

[1] High bill rate at auction, issue date within period, bank-discount basis. On or after October 28, 1998, data are stop yields from uniform-price auctions. Before that date, they are weighted average yields from multiple-price auctions.

See next page for continuation of table.

TABLE B–25. Bond yields and interest rates, 1947–2015—*Continued*

[Percent per annum]

Year and month	U.S. Treasury securities					Corporate bonds (Moody's)		High-grade municipal bonds (Standard & Poor's)	New-home mortgage yields [4]	Prime rate charged by banks [5]	Discount window (Federal Reserve Bank of New York) [5, 6]		Federal funds rate [7]
	Bills (at auction) [1]		Constant maturities [2]										
	3-month	6-month	3-year	10-year	30-year	Aaa [3]	Baa				Primary credit	Adjustment credit	
											High-low	High-low	High-low
2011: Jan	0.15	0.18	1.03	3.39	4.52	5.04	6.09	5.02	4.75	3.25–3.25	0.75–0.75	....	0.17
Feb	.14	.17	1.28	3.58	4.65	5.22	6.15	4.92	4.94	3.25–3.25	0.75–0.75	....	.16
Mar	.11	.16	1.17	3.41	4.51	5.13	6.03	4.70	4.98	3.25–3.25	0.75–0.75	....	.14
Apr	.06	.12	1.21	3.46	4.50	5.16	6.02	4.71	4.91	3.25–3.25	0.75–0.75	....	.10
May	.04	.08	.94	3.17	4.29	4.96	5.78	4.34	4.86	3.25–3.25	0.75–0.75	....	.09
June	.04	.10	.71	3.00	4.23	4.99	5.75	4.22	4.61	3.25–3.25	0.75–0.75	....	.09
July	.03	.08	.68	3.00	4.27	4.93	5.76	4.24	4.55	3.25–3.25	0.75–0.75	....	.07
Aug	.05	.09	.38	2.30	3.65	4.37	5.36	3.92	4.29	3.25–3.25	0.75–0.75	....	.10
Sept	.02	.05	.35	1.98	3.18	4.09	5.27	3.79	4.36	3.25–3.25	0.75–0.75	....	.08
Oct	.02	.06	.47	2.15	3.13	3.98	5.37	3.94	4.19	3.25–3.25	0.75–0.75	....	.07
Nov	.01	.05	.39	2.01	3.02	3.87	5.14	3.95	4.26	3.25–3.25	0.75–0.75	....	.08
Dec	.02	.05	.39	1.98	2.98	3.93	5.25	3.76	4.18	3.25–3.25	0.75–0.75	....	.07
2012: Jan	.02	.06	.36	1.97	3.03	3.85	5.23	3.43	4.09	3.25–3.25	0.75–0.75	....	.08
Feb	.08	.11	.38	1.97	3.11	3.85	5.14	3.25	4.01	3.25–3.25	0.75–0.75	....	.10
Mar	.09	.14	.51	2.17	3.28	3.99	5.23	3.51	3.72	3.25–3.25	0.75–0.75	....	.13
Apr	.08	.14	.43	2.05	3.18	3.96	5.19	3.47	3.93	3.25–3.25	0.75–0.75	....	.14
May	.09	.14	.39	1.80	2.93	3.80	5.07	3.21	3.88	3.25–3.25	0.75–0.75	....	.16
June	.09	.14	.39	1.62	2.70	3.64	5.02	3.30	3.80	3.25–3.25	0.75–0.75	....	.16
July	.10	.14	.33	1.53	2.59	3.40	4.87	3.14	3.76	3.25–3.25	0.75–0.75	....	.16
Aug	.11	.14	.37	1.68	2.77	3.48	4.91	3.07	3.67	3.25–3.25	0.75–0.75	....	.13
Sept	.10	.13	.34	1.72	2.88	3.49	4.84	3.02	3.62	3.25–3.25	0.75–0.75	....	.14
Oct	.10	.15	.37	1.75	2.90	3.47	4.58	2.89	3.58	3.25–3.25	0.75–0.75	....	.16
Nov	.11	.15	.36	1.65	2.80	3.50	4.51	2.68	3.46	3.25–3.25	0.75–0.75	....	.16
Dec	.08	.12	.35	1.72	2.88	3.65	4.63	2.73	3.40	3.25–3.25	0.75–0.75	....	.16
2013: Jan	.07	.11	.39	1.91	3.08	3.80	4.73	2.93	3.41	3.25–3.25	0.75–0.75	....	.14
Feb	.10	.12	.40	1.98	3.17	3.90	4.85	3.09	3.49	3.25–3.25	0.75–0.75	....	.15
Mar	.09	.11	.39	1.96	3.16	3.93	4.85	3.27	3.61	3.25–3.25	0.75–0.75	....	.14
Apr	.06	.09	.34	1.76	2.93	3.73	4.59	3.22	3.66	3.25–3.25	0.75–0.75	....	.15
May	.05	.08	.40	1.93	3.11	3.89	4.73	3.39	3.55	3.25–3.25	0.75–0.75	....	.11
June	.05	.09	.58	2.30	3.40	4.27	5.19	4.02	3.64	3.25–3.25	0.75–0.75	....	.09
July	.04	.08	.64	2.58	3.61	4.34	5.32	4.51	4.07	3.25–3.25	0.75–0.75	....	.09
Aug	.04	.07	.70	2.74	3.76	4.54	5.42	4.77	4.33	3.25–3.25	0.75–0.75	....	.08
Sept	.02	.04	.78	2.81	3.79	4.64	5.47	4.74	4.44	3.25–3.25	0.75–0.75	....	.08
Oct	.05	.08	.63	2.62	3.68	4.53	5.31	4.50	4.47	3.25–3.25	0.75–0.75	....	.09
Nov	.07	.10	.58	2.72	3.80	4.63	5.38	4.51	4.39	3.25–3.25	0.75–0.75	....	.08
Dec	.07	.09	.69	2.90	3.89	4.62	5.38	4.55	4.37	3.25–3.25	0.75–0.75	....	.09
2014: Jan	.05	.07	.78	2.86	3.77	4.49	5.19	4.38	4.45	3.25–3.25	0.75–0.75	....	.07
Feb	.06	.08	.69	2.71	3.66	4.45	5.10	4.25	4.04	3.25–3.25	0.75–0.75	....	.07
Mar	.05	.08	.82	2.72	3.62	4.38	5.06	4.16	4.35	3.25–3.25	0.75–0.75	....	.08
Apr	.04	.05	.88	2.71	3.52	4.24	4.90	4.02	4.33	3.25–3.25	0.75–0.75	....	.09
May	.03	.05	.83	2.56	3.39	4.16	4.76	3.80	4.01	3.25–3.25	0.75–0.75	....	.09
June	.03	.06	.90	2.60	3.42	4.25	4.80	3.72	4.27	3.25–3.25	0.75–0.75	....	.10
July	.03	.06	.97	2.54	3.33	4.16	4.73	3.75	4.25	3.25–3.25	0.75–0.75	....	.09
Aug	.03	.05	.93	2.42	3.20	4.08	4.69	3.53	4.25	3.25–3.25	0.75–0.75	....	.09
Sept	.02	.05	1.05	2.53	3.26	4.11	4.80	3.55	4.23	3.25–3.25	0.75–0.75	....	.09
Oct	.02	.05	.88	2.30	3.04	3.92	4.69	3.35	4.23	3.25–3.25	0.75–0.75	....	.09
Nov	.02	.07	.96	2.33	3.04	3.92	4.79	3.49	4.16	3.25–3.25	0.75–0.75	....	.09
Dec	.04	.11	1.06	2.21	2.83	3.79	4.74	3.39	4.14	3.25–3.25	0.75–0.75	....	.12
2015: Jan	.03	.10	.90	1.88	2.46	3.46	4.45	3.16	4.05	3.25–3.25	0.75–0.75	....	.11
Feb	.02	.07	.99	1.98	2.57	3.61	4.51	3.26	3.91	3.25–3.25	0.75–0.75	....	.11
Mar	.02	.11	1.02	2.04	2.63	3.64	4.54	3.29	3.93	3.25–3.25	0.75–0.75	....	.11
Apr	.03	.10	.87	1.94	2.59	3.52	4.48	3.40	3.92	3.25–3.25	0.75–0.75	....	.12
May	.02	.08	.98	2.20	2.96	3.98	4.89	3.77	3.89	3.25–3.25	0.75–0.75	....	.12
June	.01	.08	1.07	2.36	3.11	4.19	5.13	3.76	3.98	3.25–3.25	0.75–0.75	....	.13
July	.03	.12	1.03	2.32	3.07	4.15	5.20	3.73	4.10	3.25–3.25	0.75–0.75	....	.13
Aug	.09	.21	1.03	2.17	2.86	4.04	5.19	3.57	4.12	3.25–3.25	0.75–0.75	....	.14
Sept	.06	.23	1.01	2.17	2.95	4.07	5.34	3.56	4.09	3.25–3.25	0.75–0.75	....	.14
Oct	.01	.10	.93	2.07	2.89	3.95	5.34	3.48	4.02	3.25–3.25	0.75–0.75	....	.12
Nov	.13	.33	1.20	2.26	3.03	4.06	5.46	3.50	4.00	3.25–3.25	0.75–0.75	....	.12
Dec	.26	.52	1.28	2.24	2.97	3.97	5.46	3.23	4.03	3.50–3.25	1.00–0.75	....	.24

[2] Yields on the more actively traded issues adjusted to constant maturities by the Department of the Treasury. The 30-year Treasury constant maturity series was discontinued on February 18, 2002, and reintroduced on February 9, 2006.
[3] Beginning with December 7, 2001, data for corporate Aaa series are industrial bonds only.
[4] Effective rate (in the primary market) on conventional mortgages, reflecting fees and charges as well as contract rate and assuming, on the average, repayment at end of 10 years. Rates beginning with January 1973 not strictly comparable with prior rates.
[5] For monthly data, high and low for the period. Prime rate for 1947–1948 are ranges of the rate in effect during the period.
[6] Primary credit replaced adjustment credit as the Federal Reserve's principal discount window lending program effective January 9, 2003.
[7] Since July 19, 1975, the daily effective rate is an average of the rates on a given day weighted by the volume of transactions at these rates. Prior to that date, the daily effective rate was the rate considered most representative of the day's transactions, usually the one at which most transactions occurred.

Sources: Department of the Treasury, Board of Governors of the Federal Reserve System, Federal Housing Finance Agency, Moody's Investors Service, and Standard & Poor's.

TABLE B–26. Money stock and debt measures, 1975–2015

[Averages of daily figures, except debt end-of-period basis; billions of dollars, seasonally adjusted]

Year and month	M1 Sum of currency, demand deposits, travelers checks, and other checkable deposits	M2 M1 plus savings deposits, retail MMMF balances, and small time deposits [1]	Debt Debt of domestic nonfinancial sectors [2]	Percent change From year or 6 months earlier [3] M1	M2	From previous period [4] Debt
December:						
1975	287.1	1,016.2	2,311.0	4.7	12.6	9.3
1976	306.2	1,152.0	2,562.9	6.7	13.4	11.0
1977	330.9	1,270.3	2,892.8	8.1	10.3	12.9
1978	357.3	1,366.0	3,286.7	8.0	7.5	13.8
1979	381.8	1,473.7	3,682.2	6.9	7.9	12.0
1980	408.5	1,599.8	4,045.1	7.0	8.6	9.6
1981	436.7	1,755.5	4,459.4	6.9	9.7	10.2
1982	474.8	1,906.4	4,895.6	8.7	8.6	10.5
1983	521.4	2,123.8	5,492.1	9.8	11.4	12.1
1984	551.6	2,306.8	6,302.3	5.8	8.6	14.8
1985	619.8	2,492.6	7,334.6	12.4	8.1	16.1
1986	724.7	2,729.2	8,212.6	16.9	9.5	12.0
1987	750.2	2,828.8	8,930.6	3.5	3.6	9.0
1988	786.7	2,990.6	9,747.9	4.9	5.7	9.2
1989	792.9	3,154.4	10,482.9	.8	5.5	7.4
1990	824.7	3,272.7	11,198.6	4.0	3.8	6.6
1991	897.0	3,371.6	11,722.5	8.8	3.0	4.7
1992	1,024.9	3,423.1	12,278.2	14.3	1.5	4.7
1993	1,129.6	3,472.4	13,020.0	10.2	1.4	5.9
1994	1,150.7	3,482.7	13,701.9	1.9	.3	5.2
1995	1,127.5	3,624.4	14,382.8	−2.0	4.1	4.9
1996	1,081.3	3,802.4	15,135.2	−4.1	4.9	5.2
1997	1,072.3	4,015.1	15,972.1	−.8	5.6	5.5
1998	1,095.0	4,354.4	17,019.5	2.1	8.5	6.6
1999	1,122.2	4,614.9	18,177.4	2.5	6.0	6.6
2000	1,088.5	4,899.5	19,061.7	−3.0	6.2	4.8
2001	1,183.1	5,400.6	20,173.4	8.7	10.2	5.9
2002	1,219.9	5,736.2	21,518.7	3.1	6.2	6.7
2003	1,305.8	6,031.5	23,220.4	7.0	5.1	7.7
2004	1,375.8	6,384.2	26,065.5	5.4	5.8	9.1
2005	1,374.9	6,649.0	28,294.6	−.1	4.1	8.6
2006	1,368.2	7,039.1	30,723.5	−.5	5.9	8.4
2007	1,376.5	7,441.7	33,179.8	.6	5.7	8.1
2008	1,606.9	8,163.6	34,934.3	16.7	9.7	5.7
2009	1,698.7	8,468.5	35,749.7	5.7	3.7	3.4
2010	1,842.6	8,772.2	37,039.1	8.5	3.6	4.3
2011	2,170.0	9,629.8	38,203.5	17.8	9.8	3.5
2012	2,461.5	10,420.3	39,963.8	13.4	8.2	5.0
2013	2,660.5	10,985.4	41,453.0	8.1	5.4	4.0
2014	2,927.3	11,636.4	43,248.7	10.0	5.9	4.4
2015	3,082.0	12,299.4	....	5.3	5.7	....
2014: Jan	2,688.4	11,033.8	....	11.6	6.3	....
Feb	2,712.9	11,098.9	....	12.7	6.3	....
Mar	2,746.1	11,153.5	41,858.2	12.3	6.3	4.1
Apr	2,770.9	11,212.3	....	11.1	5.3	....
May	2,790.5	11,281.8	....	12.6	6.5	....
June	2,820.8	11,335.3	42,288.0	12.1	6.4	4.2
July	2,836.8	11,402.0	....	11.0	6.7	....
Aug	2,807.4	11,438.7	....	7.0	6.1	....
Sept	2,869.6	11,476.6	42,747.6	9.0	5.8	4.5
Oct	2,874.0	11,528.6	....	7.4	5.6	....
Nov	2,884.7	11,566.7	....	6.8	5.1	....
Dec	2,927.3	11,636.4	43,248.7	7.6	5.3	4.7
2015: Jan	2,937.9	11,703.5	....	7.1	5.3	....
Feb	2,985.1	11,800.1	....	12.7	6.3	....
Mar	2,990.2	11,835.1	43,502.7	8.4	6.2	2.5
Apr	2,995.6	11,888.0	....	8.5	6.2	....
May	2,989.8	11,923.9	....	7.3	6.2	....
June	3,015.3	11,970.6	43,988.9	6.0	5.7	4.6
July	3,034.6	12,032.5	....	6.6	5.6	....
Aug	3,042.0	12,097.8	....	3.8	5.0	....
Sept	3,057.2	12,157.5	44,197.3	4.5	5.4	2.0
Oct	3,038.1	12,178.0	....	2.8	4.9	....
Nov	3,087.2	12,257.3	....	6.5	5.6	....
Dec	3,082.0	12,299.4	....	4.4	5.5	....

[1] Money market mutual fund (MMMF). Savings deposits include money market deposit accounts.
[2] Consists of outstanding debt securities and loans of the U.S. Government, State and local governments, and private nonfinancial sectors. Quarterly data shown in last month of quarter. End-of-year data are for fourth quarter.
[3] Annual changes are from December to December; monthly changes are from six months earlier at a simple annual rate.
[4] Annual changes are from fourth quarter to fourth quarter. Quarterly changes are from previous quarter at annual rate.

Note: For further information on the composition of M1 and M2, see the H.6 release of the Federal Reserve Board.

Source: Board of Governors of the Federal Reserve System.

www.ingramcontent.com/pod-product-compliance
Lightning Source LLC
Chambersburg PA
CBHW060130280326
41932CB00012B/1473